The Competence Approach To Parenting

Joseph M. Strayhorn, Jr., M.D.

Psychological Skills Press
Wexford, Pennsylvania

Psychological Skills Press
263 Seasons Drive
Wexford, PA 15090
www.psyskills.com

Author's email: joestrayhorn@juno.com

ISBN 1-931773-02-5

Contents

Chapter 1: What Is the Competence Approach?

Chapter Overview:

The time you invest in learning to do the best possible job of parenting can provide a greater payoff than almost any other activity. Parenting well greatly increases the quality of life, not only for your children, but also for yourself.

Which ways of improving children's behavior do not work well? Some people try to get children to "get their hostility out" by beating on something or yelling or doing some other angry thing. When children follow this advice, they're usually practicing being hostile, not getting anything "out." Another couple of ways of making things worse while trying to make them better seem to be opposites of one another: the "tough and strict" strategy of yelling when the child misbehaves, and the "nice and lenient" strategy of giving the child whatever he wants when he's upset. Both of these can interrupt misbehavior in the short run, but reinforce it in the long run. They buy temporary relief at the cost of future trouble. Another way to fail is to give the child good influences for too little time. The child soaks up influence every waking moment. The higher the fraction of the child's waking moments you can arrange to have the positive influences I will describe, the better off your child will be. The earlier in the child's life you can start, the better. Something else that doesn't work is to expect the child to learn to cope with a very bad situation when you should really change the situation or get the child out of it. Examples include an abusive teacher, a curriculum that's over the child's head, or a bad babysitter.

What is the competence approach? Almost everything I suggest in this book can be organized by using two lists. The first is a list of competences or skills that help people be happy and productive. The second is a list of ways to influence another person to get better in any of those skills. Your job as a parent is to use those influences to promote those skills. I'll tell you lots of specific activities you can use in doing this. It's liberating to realize that you can foster goals so complex as psychological health and harmony among people by activities that promote these skills. The catch is that promoting and learning these skills take lots of time. But nurturing psychologically competent children is more valuable than anything else people do. In fact, you might enjoy holding in mind a vision: the image of a culture where the time and energy most people presently waste on vain pursuits is spent on activities that help children learn to handle life well. Every hour you spend on this goal works to change human culture.

****

This book is written for those parents who take seriously the job of helping their children to develop their full potentials to be healthy, happy, productive human beings.

This book is to help parents help their children become productive, joyous, honest, kind, and resilient people. It's to solve and prevent behavior problems: problems of aggression, shyness, fear of failure, oppositionalism, short attention span, low frustration tolerance, tantrums, hostility, and others. It's to help children learn not only to avoid these problems, but also to live well.

Although learning good parenting is one of the most altruistic, loving and giving things one can do, it is also one of the activities that is most in your self-interest! Families have an "emotional climate." If you live in a family where there is a great deal of negative emotion going on between children or between children and parents, it takes a toll on you. There are few things more in your own self-interest than to make your family one where people support each other and have fun with each other.

This book is also for people who are "parenting" other people's children. A wise person said, "All children are 'our' children." Teachers, child care workers, uncles, grandmothers, babysitters, tutors, coaches, and people who encounter children anywhere can use expertise in fostering the positive development of children. Ideally, someday everyone in the culture will take into account the principles of child-nurturing in almost all decisions, since almost everything we do has effects upon our younger generation.

There's a dividend to learning these principles that even goes beyond the task of work with children. Many of the principles of dealing with children are simply good human relationship principles. They are also applicable to relationships with spouse, coworkers, and friends.

Is your child's personality influenced by genetics, by "nature" as well as influences after birth? Without a doubt, genetics plays a large role in personality. But if your child is already born, the genetics are an accomplished fate (at least at the time of this writing). For that reason we'll concentrate here on nurture.

What Doesn't Work Well

This book will tell in great detail what I've seen people do to get better relationships with their children and help their children become more positive people. But first I want to warn you about some of the "blind alleys" on which people waste precious time, in the quest for psychological health. These are all approaches I've tried or seen people try in my career as a child psychiatrist. We could talk for a long time about the evidence that these don't work well. But perhaps a word to the wise will be sufficient: don't count on these!

Getting Hostility Out

One of the most frequent complaints of parents and teachers is that a child is hostile or disobedient or rebellious or mean. OK, if the child is acting that way, he must have some anger inside him, right? And if the problem is anger inside him, if he can just get it out, in a harmless way, he'll be pleasant and nice after that, right? Sounds reasonable. So the angry person, according to this theory, needs to express anger, and have a "catharsis," just as a constipated person needs a laxative or "cathartic." According to this hypothesis, it makes good sense to get the child to beat a pillow or scream or break something cheap to let the angry feelings out in a harmless way, or to talk about the angry feelings so that they will not build up to the point that there is an "explosion." It all sounds logical and reasonable from the armchair.

There's one main problem: it doesn't work. Expressing anger usually does not get rid of it. Recently I heard about a child who punched another child in the face at school. Someone said to him, "Why did you do that?" The child replied, "Because my pillow was at home." The child had been told to get his anger out by beating on a pillow; the child bought into the notion that you have to get anger out somehow or another; the other child's body happened to be the most convenient place to express the anger.

After someone punches someone else, or screams in anger, or beats on something, does his anger usually disappear? Unfortunately not. Should that be surprising, when we think about emotions other than anger? Suppose we have some "joyousness inside us," that for some strange reason we wanted to get rid of. In an effort to rid ourselves of this emotion, we get together with friends, joke, sing, dance, hug each other, and generally celebrate. When we express this joyousness, do we "release" it, and render it all gone from us, and then feel sad and depressed? Of course not. We have practiced feeling good and have probably stimulated ourselves to feel even better. Why should it be different with anger?

We need another theory. Here's one, with diametrically opposite implications. It also sounds logical and reasonable from the armchair. We can call this the rehearsal hypothesis. This says that when we practice any behavior, such as expressing anger or beating on pillows, we usually strengthen that behavior, making it more likely to occur again, and also we make more likely other behaviors in the same "response class." Thus practicing hitting other people in a "socially acceptable" way in a boxing match by this theory would make hitting people in other situations more likely, not less likely.

When scientists have two reasonable-sounding hypotheses, how can they tell which one to go by? The answer comes from doing experiments.

Many experiments have been done, pitting the rehearsal hypothesis against the catharsis hypothesis. We give children violent toys, and see whether in real life they hit other children more (as the rehearsal hypothesis would predict) or less (as the catharsis hypothesis would predict). We look at families, and examine how much they yell in anger at one another, and how much they hit each other. We see whether the people who express verbal hostility more often hit each other more often (as the rehearsal hypothesis would predict) or less often (as catharsis would predict). We interview people who have experienced something unwanted, and encourage some of them to talk about their feelings of anger and others to talk about other topics. We see whether those who talk about their anger become less angry (as the catharsis hypothesis would predict) or more angry (as the rehearsal hypothesis would predict). We show people violent movies and see if afterwards they are less prone to hostile actions (as the catharsis hypothesis would predict) or more prone to hostile actions (as the rehearsal hypothesis would predict).

When we look at the research, what do we find? To make a long story short, and to oversimplify only a bit—rehearsal wins and catharsis loses. In study after study it appears that the more practice you give people at being hostile and imagining hostile interactions, the more hostile they are.

So if you want to help children by getting negative emotions out, consider a "paradigm shift." Start thinking in terms of getting the positive patterns in. Consider "unasking" the question of "How do we help children get their anger out," and ask the alternative question, "How do we help children deal with frustrating or provocative situations in the most intelligent and effective manner possible?"

Caution: this doesn't mean that talking about anger and fearfulness and other unpleasant emotions is always, or even usually, bad or nonproductive! Sometimes talking about anger is a child's first step in formulating a problem that needs to be solved. Sometimes it's the child's first step in learning to trust someone enough to tell them about what's on her mind. Sometimes it is the first step in learning to forgive. Sometimes it mobilizes the child to use appropriate assertion or even aggression to get out of a situation where she is being victimized.

I want you to avoid thinking that expressing a negative emotion gets it out and gets rid of it, or even that that notion of "getting rid of it" is a meaningful idea. Emotions are something we do, not something we have. When we do anger a lot, we might in the short run get tired of doing it, but for the long run we have practiced doing it. When we do a lot of loving and caring and enjoying, and feeling proud about our accomplishments, we practice doing those emotions too. To a certain extent, most people can do the emotions they choose, and if one develops the knowhow, exercising conscious control over emotions as well as thoughts and behaviors becomes more and more feasible.

Now let's talk about another strategy that very frequently gets tried when a child has a behavior problem. Often it gets tried over and over hundreds of times. It's responsible for lots of bad feeling and bad behavior. It keeps getting tried over and over because in the short run, it often seems to "work."

Yelling at the Misbehavior

Consider the following scenario.

Act 1: Little Johnny is pulling Susie's hair, laughing at her cries of distress.

Act 2: The adult sees him and yells, "Hey, cut that out! What do you think you're doing: stop that!"

Act 3: Johnny stops and wanders off, and the adult diverts attention somewhere else.

From the adult's short run point of view, the intervention of yelling at the misbehavior has "worked." The adult told the child to stop, and the child did stop. That's pretty simple, isn't it?

But let's stop and ask the most important question. What has happened to Johnny's long run tendency to do hurtful behaviors? After this scenario, is his tendency stronger or weaker? Is a future episode of hurting more probable than before, or less probable?

To answer this question, we have to look at Johnny's behavior over days and weeks, and not just at the time of his being yelled at. And what I find over and over for many children is that yelling at them for misbehavior tends to increase the misbehavior in the long run, even though it may stop it in the short run.

Why should this be? What could possibly make a child 'want,' on some level, to get yelled at by an adult, so that the yelling would make the misbehavior more frequent? I have a theory about this. My guess is that throughout centuries of evolution, children who have elicited any sort of emotion from adults, even negative emotion, have tended to survive more than children who elicited indifference from adults. The children whom everyone forgot about may have been eaten by saber-toothed tigers, while those who irritated adults enough to be noticed frequently may have gotten saved. The young child can survive with lots of angry commands being barked at him, better than he can survive being totally neglected. Thus it would make sense that our brains would become hard-wired to do the things that elicit adult emotion and interest in us when we are young.

When someone does something irritating or unkind, it is natural for most people to yell out angry reprimands, especially if the offender is not very powerful. For this reason some schools are hotbeds of hostility, with teachers doing lots of yelling at students. For this reason some parents describe themselves as yelling in response to children's negative behavior many times a day. And as if to compound ineffective strategies upon one another, sometimes a student has problems at school and not at home; when the teacher's yelling at the child doesn't work, the teacher calls the parents up and the parents start yelling at the child at home as well. The result is that the negative relationship and hostility at school gets imported into the home setting.

We'll talk again later on about how important are the tones of voice in which you speak to children. There are just two points left to be made here, in addition to the major idea that many children find their misbehavior reinforced by adults' yelling. First, children tend to speak to other people, including both peers and adults, in the tone of voice in which they are spoken to. That means that if you often yell at your children in an angry or irritated or commanding tone, I'll bet you'll sooner or later hear your child yelling either at you or someone else (a sibling or a peer) in the same tone. Second, children gradually come to talk to themselves in the tone of voice in which they are spoken to. In childhood, we plant in our memory banks ways of talking to ourselves. If we hear a lot of "What do you think you're doing!s" and "How many times have I told you not to do that!s" then we tend to speak to ourselves in the same way—sometimes for the remainder of a lifetime.

If parents and teachers can stop yelling at misbehavior, and start yelling with pleasure about the child's positive behaviors, and speak in a very subdued and disappointed but calm voice about the child's misbehavior (if it is mentioned at all), often that change in itself is enough to bring about a great change in children's behavior. If you've been a yeller at misbehavior, and if you close this book and do nothing more than stop yelling at the misbehavior and start yelling with joy at the positive behavior, I think you will see effects of this change alone that will gratify you tremendously.

Giving the Child Whatever She Wants

The strategy of trying to meet a child's every wish and tolerating any unpleasant behavior is the other side of the coin from yelling at the child's misbehavior. Like yelling at a misbehavior, giving the child whatever she wants can in the short run make negative behavior go away, and thus reinforce the parent for doing it. Is the child screaming angrily because she wants a popsicle? Then giving the child the popsicle will probably in the short run make the angry screaming stop. But it will even more surely reinforce that angry screaming so as to make it more likely to occur the next time. Is the child screaming angrily because she wants more attention from the parent at that moment? Then giving the attention will probably have the same effect as the popsicle.

Giving the child whatever she wants is the ineffective strategy that very "nice" people tend to overuse; yelling at misbehavior is the strategy that "tough" people tend to overuse. And since most of our personalities contain a blend of niceness and toughness, often the same parent will use first one, then the other ineffective strategy. A parent will try giving the child whatever she wants, gradually building up resentment and irritation at being the child's slave, and then when a certain threshold of irritation is reached, the same parent will switch to yelling at the misbehavior. Or sometimes two parents will polarize themselves into roles where one is "strict" and the other is "lenient." The strict one yells at misbehavior and the lenient one gives the child whatever she wants.

If you're into the pattern of giving the child whatever she wants, you can greatly help the child by trying to meet the child's wishes much more frequently after the child has done something positive (such as asking politely) than when the child has done something negative (such as bossing you and slapping you). What complicates this strategy, however, is the fact that you have to take into account the reasonableness of the child's wants. If the child wants three popsicles after a full meal, you're in a different situation than if the child wants a meal after a long time without food.

When the child's wish is very reasonable but the request for it is very impolite, you want to avoid reinforcing the politeness but you also want to meet the child's reasonable need. One way to do this is to take advantage of the "time gradient of reinforcement," by granting the wish, but with a delay occurring after the impolite request. For example, the young child commands, "I need something to eat; get me something now!" The adult ignores this, but supplies something for the child to eat ten minutes later when the reinforcement does not immediately follow the bratty request.

Another complicating factor is the child's developmental level. If the child is an infant, then giving the child whatever she wants is usually exactly the strategy to use. In fact, one of the difficult things about parenting is that the strategy and mind-set of meeting the child's every need, which results in a happy, cheerful infant, will usually result in a spoiled and entitled preschooler.

An Hour a Week with an Expert, With Nothing In Between

Here's a way that many people have thought about children's problems. "Is it normal? If it is, we'll hope he grows out of it. If it isn't, we'll want to take the child to an expert, e.g. a child psychotherapist, to get it fixed. So tell us, which is it?"

Sometimes this way of thinking is useful. For example, it is "normal" for three year olds to wet the bed, and it would be a waste of time and energy for anyone to get too bothered about this symptom. It is "normal" for a two year old to suck the thumb.

However, for the most common problems such as hostility, aggression, sadness, fearfulness, and defiance, the best answer to this question is often a suggestion to "Unask the question." A much better question usually is, "How desirable is this pattern that the child exhibits?" If it is very undesirable, then do something about it, whether it's normal or not.

But what should the "something" be? The answer is usually to make the sum total of all the influences the child receives during every moment of his life as favorable as possible. This is a very important concept that runs throughout this book: there is no waking moment where the child is not experiencing some sort of influence upon what he is becoming. At any given moment, a child is practicing acting in some way or another. He is experiencing either positive, negative, or neutral stimuli (either internal or external), which tend to reinforce, punish, or extinguish, respectively, the behavior that came just before it. He is often seeing models of other people's behavior. Fortunately or unfortunately, you can't put him in suspended animation where he is not being affected for better or worse by what is going on around him.

When we think of things in this way, no one should expect an hour of psychotherapy for a child each week to have much effect, unless it sets off a chain of causal events that also affect the other hours. If the child is old enough, the child can perhaps do formal "homework" in between sessions, or can informally think about and rehearse things that will achieve a "multipier effect" and make the one hour that is spent worth much more than an hour. If the child is young, the persons that usually must do the homework are the parents. When a parent comes to me with a problem the child was having, one of the main things I try to do is to get the parent to start using the techniques described in this book, for as many of the child's waking hours per week as possible. If there are other people who spend lots of time with the child, I try to get them to use the same approaches, or to help the parent work select people or train people to do so. The higher the fraction of the 168 hours we cover with positive influences, the better a chance we have for success.

Some colleagues and I did a study in which during one year we worked with preschool children in individual sessions, whether or not the parents were interested in joining us; the second year we concentrated almost all our effort on teaching parents to work with children the same way we had the previous year. The results were hugely superior the second year. The experience taught me an important lesson. You have to take into account to what goes on with a child every minute of his life, and the more favorable influences those minutes contain, the better. And that's true, whether the child has severe problems, mild problems, or is the next thing to perfection itself.

Starting Too Late

We might call the next ineffective strategy "fiddling while Rome is burning," or "starting too late." Children are very susceptible to adult influence when they are young. The older the child gets, the more the child has the power to say, "Who needs you? Get out of my life." As the child gets older, the child does not find the adult's attention such a powerful reward. As the child gets older, any aggressive misbehavior is much more difficult for the adult to overcome by physical guidance, i.e. nonviolent physical force. So for antisocial behavior, aggression, dishonesty, laziness, and disruptive behavior, an early start seems critical. For problems with anxiety, perfectionism, guilt, and inhibitions, there is an immediate pain that motivates anyone people to solve these problems at any age. An early start may not be as critical as it is with antisocial behavior.

Is there a cutoff age, after which all is lost, for any pattern of human behavior? The evidence definitely does not support this. There is always hope. Anyone who truly wants to improve his or her way of living can do so, at any age. But if you still have the chance, influence with the greatest of care the uncritically absorbent minds that characterize most infants, toddlers, preschoolers, and early grade school children. And if your child has problems with disobedience, verbal hostility, or physical aggression, start without delay to solve these problems.

Failing to Rescue the Child from Victimization

Learning psychological skills does not solve all of children's problems. There are some situations that a child should not have to learn to handle, especially at a young age. Example: At school, a child is regularly being hit and verbally abused by a couple of older children. The child experiences bad dreams, fear of going to school, and trouble concentrating on schoolwork. Is the treatment of choice to take the child to a nightmare expert or a concentration coach? No, our first priority is to make sure there is adequate supervision at school, that the "rule of law" prevails, that the child is protected and need not be afraid. Speaking to the teachers, principal, parents of the other children, and if necessary instituting legal action or withdrawing the child from the school—whatever it takes to end the victimization—is the first priority intervention. Helping the child deal with the lingering harmful effects of being victimized is the second priority.

Of course, coping with a little verbal hostility from peers is a normal and expected part of growing up. But if hostility and rejection are regular and repeated, even if the child is not being physically harmed, something should be done to protect the child.

Here are other examples. A child is in a class where for one reason or another (perhaps some difficulty with learning) the work he is being asked to do is too difficult for him, and he regularly experiences the humiliation and frustration of repeated failure. Or a child is receiving day care with another family where an older teen exposes the child to pornographically violent videos. Or two parents are getting a divorce and the child becomes a pawn in the conflict between them. The rule still holds: first priority is to improve or help the child escape the bad situation, and second priority is to try to help him cope with the negative influences he's received.

Sometimes the child is being victimized by a biological insult. Examples: a young child is getting dust in the mouth from a house where the lead content of the house dust is poisonous. Or the child is drinking from a water source contaminated by lead. Or the child is exposed to a heater that gives off carbon monoxide.

This book will primarily concern itself with learning-based interventions. But always keep in mind that if your child is in a situation he should not have to cope with, the first priority is to get him out of it.

The Competence Approach: The Skills and Methods

The Competence Approach is simply the idea that psychological health consists of several skills that you can foster in several ways. You can learn these skills just as you learn dancing or typing or mathematics or any other skill. We will spend lots of time thinking about two sets of concepts. The first is the skills someone needs for psychological health. The second is a list of the ways that one person can help another person, or himself, to learn these skills; these are the methods of influence. Each combination of a psychological skill and a method of influence is a way of helping a child. Modeling frustration tolerance, reinforcing good conflict resolution, instructing in carefulness, and providing practice in social initiations are all ways of promoting psychological health.

If we were talking about becoming a competent tennis player rather than becoming competent in life, we would talk in terms of the skill of stroking with the forehand, the skill of serving, the skill of getting into position before the stroke and judging where to get to, and so forth. We would talk about methods of influence such as showing the student how to do a stroke (or modeling it for him or her), letting the student practice it (or providing practice opportunity), and giving feedback, particularly when the student did it right—saying, "Yes! That's it!" (The statement "That's it" also constitutes *positive reinforcement*. Positive reinforcement is defined as something that happens after you do something, that makes it more likely that you'll do the same thing again.)

You can teach psychological skills just as you teach tennis skills. We will talk about skills such as the art of feeling good about one's own acts of kindness to another person, sustaining attention to tasks, resolving conflicts with other people, handling frustration, feeling good about accomplishments, having conversations with people, and many others. We'll talk about various methods of influence: modeling, providing practice opportunities, reinforcement, and six other basic strategies to influence the child to gain these crucial skills.

So what are we aiming for, in promoting psychological competence in the child? We're aiming to pick out the psychological skills that are of most importance, of highest priority for the child at any given time, and to supply the influences that are most powerful in fostering those skills.

What Does Work: Logging In Learning Hours

All skills require practice, and psychological skills are no different.

It has been estimated that it would take 50 practice hours for the average person to get reasonably skilled—not expert— at playing the harmonica, 150 hours for the guitar, and 450 hours for the piano. Yet over and over, in my practice of child psychiatry, I see children with obvious skill deficiencies in certain psychological skills, who have received zero hours of systematic training in those skills. For example, a child goes into tantrums or rages over minor frustrations, but has received no systematic training in fortitude. Or a child's quality of life is decreased by his being disorganized, but neither he nor his parents have received any training on how to increase organization skills. Or a parent and child are having trouble communicating with each other, and get into painful conflicts with each other. How many hours has each logged in to the process of learning listening skills, and conflict-resolution conversation skills? Often none. Or someone with tension headaches or anxiety symptoms has been getting treatment off and on, and has had the symptoms for many years. How much time has that person spent practicing the specific skills of relaxing the muscles and calming the mind? Often none. Or sometimes the person has spent one hour getting instruction and a couple of 15-minute sessions trying to practice, and when that doesn't solve the problem, the person has concluded that "it doesn't work." If people applied the same thinking to learning to play the harmonica, guitar, or piano, they would universally conclude that instruction and practice in these skills "don't work." If the same thinking were applied to basketball-playing skills, the team that thought that way would lose every game.

Why do people expect psychological skills to come with such less work than other skills? Perhaps part of the problem is that we live in a society where people constantly hear, via advertising, that simply buying something is the solution to any problem, and not repetitive, steady work at it. Perhaps part of the problem is the "medical model" in which you go and get a diagnosis and take the particular pill that controls your illness. Although this model is sometimes very helpful, there is hardly a physical ailment that can't be at least partially prevented or alleviated by some "life style" project involving sustained effort. Perhaps part of the problem is that the wonderful advances in psychopharmacology that have occurred in recent years, that allow some people to experience improvement in happiness and productivity simply by taking a pill, lead people to expect that it should always be that easy.

Sometimes psychological skills seem to come with no conscious work. With a favorable enough genetic disposition, and/or favorable enough models and reinforcers in the environment, people can get started practicing positive patterns early, and continue to "practice psychological skills" simply in living life. But the optimistic message is this: even when things seem to be getting off track, conscious targeted effort can bolster psychological skills. Like the tortoise who beat the hare, sometimes people initially handicapped in certain psychological skills can surpass those who are initially more gifted, by sustained, steady effort.

Our World Needs These Skills More Than Anything Else

If we think globally, there's a broader purpose to the undertaking. In an earlier draft of this chapter, I wrote the sentence, "None of us can change the world." Upon further reflection, I realized that the opposite is true: None of us can keep from changing the world. Maybe the change will not be tremendous, but everything we do makes it a little different. I understand that students of "chaos theory" and meteorology have determined that the wind generated by the beating of the wings of a butterfly on one side of the world can set off a chain of events that can make the difference as to whether a hurricane occurs on the other side of the world. The interpersonal world and the storms of unkindness known as war and riots and murders and assaults may indeed be influenced by the actions you take with your children. Each foray that anyone makes into kindness, rationality, productivity, and psychological health sets a model and provides an inspiration for everyone who observes that person.

We live in a world where the biggest problem is people's inhumanity to one another. I believe that a tremendous investment of time into the activities prescribed in this book could go a long way toward eliminating this problem. This book envisions a world where people spend lots of time talking with each other, doing "mutually gratifying activities" with each other, noticing and memorializing in writing and in other media their positive and imitation-worthy behaviors, reading "modeling stories" of psychological skills, making dramas with one another, learning competences, playing games that practice psychological skills, singing songs that model psychological skills. This is a world where adults spend time playing with children and tutoring them, and where great importance is placed upon older children's learning to do these activities proficiently with younger children.

In our society people often say, "The time just isn't there. The time spent in making a living just doesn't leave much time left over for such things." Yet with all this shortage of time, we as a culture have billions of dollars to allocate to professional athletics, billions of hours to sit and watch them play, but not much time to play games with children. We have billions of dollars to produce inane or violent television shows and billions of hours to sit and watch them, but little time to do dramatic play with children. We have billions of dollars to make popular musicians rich, and we spend billions of hours listening to popular music, but little time to spend singing and dancing around with children. We spend billions of dollars trying to get lawyers to resolve our conflicts, but we don't have much time to teach conflict-resolution to children. We spend huge amounts of labor, creativity, and money on advertising every possible product to each other, yet we don't have the resources to "advertise" to children the value of gaining the crucial psychological skills.

I once did the math to find that with the revenues taken in by a blockbuster violent action-and-adventure movie in its first year, we would have had enough resources to tutor individually every first grade child in ten medium sized cities, for an hour every week day for a year.

Our news media speak almost daily about economic growth as a highly desirable goal; we would better think in terms of the way human efforts are distributed. Violent movies contribute to the gross national product just as much as the tutoring that could have been done instead, but the effects on society are vastly different. Thus this book is partly about what we as a culture could be doing more of, if we could somehow do less of the wasteful, nonproductive, and counterproductive activities that in such a large degree make up the gross national product. As you read this book, see if you agree that this imagined world would be far superior to that of our present culture. If you do, your own efforts will certainly change the world at least a little bit.

Chapter 2: Psychological Skills

Chapter Overview:

What exactly does a child need to learn to get good at, if you want her to be psychologically healthy, or to have character, or to be equipped to handle life well? The more your family thinks about those competences, the better the chance to get good at them. It's worth a lot of work to get these concepts into everyone's working vocabulary. I define here 62 competences, divided into sixteen groups: productivity, joyousness, kindness, honesty, fortitude, good decisions (including individual decision-making and joint decision making), nonviolence, respectful talk, relationship-building, self-discipline, loyalty, conservation, self-care, compliance, positive fantasy rehearsal, and courage.

Here's a quick way to get started using the skills axis. Pick the three skills or skill groups that are highest priority for your child now. For each skill, think of some concrete, specific behaviors that would be positive examples. Watch for your child to do positive examples like these, and rejoice openly if you see them. Watch for opportunities to provide models of these skills to your child. Watch for chances to let your child practice these skills. If you see your child doing more and more concrete examples, you are seeing growth in the skill.

****

As a parent, a large part of your job is to try to help your child achieve psychological health. But what is psychological health? What should a psychologically healthy individual be able to do? It will be worth your while to think for a long time about what things a psychologically healthy individual can do well, and what some examples would be of doing those things well. The clearer the picture you have of what healthy psychological functioning is, the easier it will be to help your child achieve it.

For some parents enlarging your job description in this way may be somewhat daunting. For example: a couple was having behavior problems with their boy. At first they had the attitude, "We're not really interested in psychological skills. All we want to know is what to do when he hits, or when he has tantrums, or when he yells hostile things at people, or refuses to go to bed. When he's not doing these things, he does OK." The attitude was, "If it's not broken, don't fix it. I'm just interested in fixing this one type of problem behavior." My answer to these parents was that in a half hour I could give advice about what to do immediately after those behaviors occur. But if that's all they do, they are much more likely to come back to me and complain that "I did what you said, and it didn't work." Or that "it worked for a few weeks, but now there are problems again." This is the reason why I ask parents to change their thinking: to start thinking about building psychological skills, and not just about stamping out problems.

We began thinking about the boy's problems in the following terms: If he hits and is hostile to other children, the solution is not just that he stops hitting and being hostile; it's also that he starts getting more pleasure from being kind and making others feel good. If he has a tantrum whenever he doesn't get his way, we want him not just to stop having tantrums; we want him to start showing more examples of fortitude, and feeling proud about those examples. If he is scared of going to bed, we want him not just to stop thinking scary thoughts; we want to help him start thinking comforting thoughts that give him security. Children, like adults, are always doing or thinking something. Nature abhors a vacuum. Children can stop doing problematic things much easier if there is some adaptive, desirable pattern to fill up the vacuum.

His parents found that there's another very important reason for thinking about what skills you want to see more of rather than just thinking about what you want less of. When you are trying to increase the frequency of something the child does, you do it by congratulations, positive attention, celebration, setting and presenting positive models, providing opportunities for positive practice, and other pleasant interactions. Working with the boy when he was not exhibiting problematic behavior, by immediately celebrating the positive patterns he exhibited, recalling and re-enacting those patterns later on, putting on plays that model desirable patterns, reading stories that illustrate kindness, and other such activities proved to be much fun for all of them. These activities tend to strengthen the relationship: make deposits in the emotional bank account rather than withdrawals. Also, the parents found that the sorts of celebrating sentences that they said when they saw him doing a positive example of one of his top-priority skills were just the sorts of sentences that they wanted to hear him saying to other people more often, and to himself. And sure enough, they gradually began to hear lots more utterances of "Congratulations" and "Wow! Hey! That's interesting!" coming from him over time.

It was very useful for his parents also to use reprimands and punishment to decrease his negative behavior, and we will spend time on these techniques later on. I'm not advocating a total abandonment of punishment. But the more you can emphasize the positive, the more successful you're likely to be. Sometimes you can bring out the good behavior so much that it just crowds out the bad behavior, without your having to do anything specific about bad behavior other than ignore it.

So if you want to proceed systematically, here's how I recommend you start out.

1. Get very familiar with all the psychological skills listed in this chapter. Think and read about how the positive examples of these skills look and sound.
2. Decide on the three or four psychological skills that are of highest priority for your child to develop at this time. If you're trying to solve problems, pick the skills that you think are most likely to help your child get over them. If you are acting preventively, pick some skills to focus on for now, and rotate to a different group later on.
3. Get in your mind a very concrete list of positive examples of each of those skills, that you can watch carefully for. That way when you see the skills developing, you can give them a boost by paying attention to them and celebrating them.

In the table that follows there is a list of 62 psychological skills, in 16 groups. (I call this an "axis" rather than a plain old "list" because the American Psychiatric Association's Diagnostic and Statistical Manuals have looked at psychiatric problems in terms of several "axes"; I propose the skills axis as one more.)Your time will be well spent in reviewing this list and pondering how your child is doing in each of these.

The psychological skills axis is just as useful for adults as for children. Psychological skills are the patterns that help us deal with life, from its beginning to its end.

Goals are very important: if you don't know what you want to accomplish, you're much less likely to accomplish it. The skills on the axis are the goals for psychological development to pursue as long as you have an influence on your child.

You may be thinking, "I want more than just skill in my child. I want character, personality, psychological adjustment, morality, and motivation." As you study the skills axis, you'll find that it covers all of these. I use the word *skill* much more broadly than most people do. The concepts on the skills axis were taken from a variety of sources—all that I could get my hands on—and they represent an attempt to combine all these ideas into a common language. We can talk, for example, about the "character trait" of honesty, or we can talk about the "skill" of being honest when it is difficult to be so. We can talk about the "psychic structure" of having a conscience that is not too harsh and punitive, or we can consider feeling an appropriate degree of misgivings or guilt about wrong actions as a skill. We can talk about the "motivation" to do kind acts, or we can talk about the skill of feeling good when one helps others—delivering to oneself the pleasure that provides the driving force for the motivation. The skills axis is the result of translating different types of language into the language of skills. It's good to do this, because all these skills can be learned, can become habitual, and involve patterns of thinking, feeling, or acting.

Here's another advantage of using the skills axis concepts to think about life: they are specific enough to lead you to clear action steps. Imagine that Dr. Alexander observes her daughter Grace, who is having problems in preschool. Dr. Alexander concludes, "She just isn't having a good time. She somehow isn't making it, there. She's miserable. But other kids seem to be having a good time. She's different somehow." These concepts do indicate that there's a problem to solve, but they're too general to give much indication of how to solve it.

After a thorough education in skills axis concepts, Dr. Alexander observes and reflects upon Grace's behavior again. Now she comes away with the following conclusions: "She's not very good at starting up interactions with other children; for that reason I think she's very lonesome. Once she gets started, however, she can usually play pretty nicely. She's also not very good at handling failure in a performance, and gets humiliated too easily to be able to enjoy singing and dancing with the other children. But she's good at complying with the teacher and at sustaining attention to things. I want to try to help her with skills of starting interactions and handling failure, and see if that makes her more happy."

After the skills axis education, Dr. Alexander is much more equipped to help her child than she was before. She is now ready to help the child learn the skills that are responsible for the child's unhappiness. If she also becomes well versed in using modeling, monitoring, reinforcement, attribution, and the other methods of influence to be outlined later, and has access to ancillary materials we will talk about to aid in these things, then she can form a very concrete plan to help her daughter.

What words we use to conceptualize the world really affect how we handle it. The parent, or the child, who has the skills concepts in his or her vocabulary has tools that will be helpful in promoting psychological growth.

Children can and should get these concepts into their vocabularies. Even preschool children have learned to think in terms of the skills. I will speak later about systematic ways to teach these concepts. I would recommend that any adult seriously interested in promoting children's psychological growth go through them and get very familiar with them. One major way to get these concepts into the child's vocabulary is to comment favorably on examples that the child did, or that the parent or someone else did. The child shares a toy with someone, and the adult says, "That was a kind act that you did!" The child asks for something and gets told "No," and handles this with equanimity. The adult says, "That was a good example of fortitude!" In each of these cases the child is not only getting recognition and approval, but is getting some instruction in the meaning of the concepts of kindness and fortitude.

There is a song, a jingle, that I have used to help people remember the sixteen psychological skill groups. (This is on a collection of songs I recorded, entitled *Spirit of Nonviolence*.) The words are as follows:

What are the qualities that make life better?
What makes people good?
What lets people live in happiness and peace
And brother- and sisterhood?

Productivity, joyousness, kindness
Honesty, fortitude
Good decisions made every day
Nonviolence and not being rude.

Friendship-building, self-discipline, loyalty
Conservation and self-care
Compliance and positive fantasy rehearsal
And courage, if you dare.

The table that follows presents the full list of psychological skills.

The Psychological Skills Axis

Group 1: Productivity

1. Purposefulness. Having a sense of purpose that drives activity
2. Persistence. Sustaining attention, concentrating, focusing, staying on task
3. Competence-development. Working toward competence in job, academics, recreation, life skills
4. Organization. Organizing goals, priorities, time, money, and physical objects; planfulness

Group 2. Joyousness

5. Enjoying aloneness. Having a good time by oneself, tolerating not getting someone's attention
6. Pleasure from approval. Enjoying approval, compliments, and positive attention from others
7. Pleasure from accomplishments. Self-reinforcement for successes.
8. Pleasure from my own kindness. Feeling pleasure from doing kind, loving acts for others
9. Pleasure from discovery. Enjoying exploration and satisfaction of curiosity
10. Pleasure from others' kindness. Feeling gratitude for what others have done
11. Pleasure from blessings. Feeling joy from the blessings of luck or fate
12. Pleasure from affection. Enjoying physical affection without various fears interfering
13. Favorable attractions. Having feelings of attraction aroused in ways consonant with happiness
14. Gleefulness. Playing, becoming childlike, experiencing glee, being spontaneous
15. Humor. Enjoying funny things, finding and producing comedy in life

Group 3: Kindness

16. Kindness. Nurturing someone, being kind and helpful
17. Empathy. Recognizing other people's feelings, seeing things from another's point of view
18. Conscience. Feeling appropriate guilt, avoiding harming others

Group 4: Honesty

19. Honesty. Being honest and dependable, especially when it is difficult to be so
20. Awareness of my abilities. Being honest and brave in assessing my strengths and weaknesses.

Group 5: Fortitude

21. Frustration-tolerance. Handling frustration, tolerating adverse circumstances, fortitude
22. Handling separation. Tolerating separation from close others, or loss of a relationship

23. Handling rejection. Tolerating it when people don't like or accept you or want to be with you
24. Handling criticism. Dealing with disapproval and criticism and lack of respect from others
25. Handling mistakes and failures. Regretting mistakes without being overly self-punitive
26. Magnanimity, non-jealousy. Handling it when someone else gets what you want
27. Painful emotion-tolerance. Tolerating painful emotions; avoiding the vicious cycle of "feeling bad about feeling bad"
28. Fantasy-tolerance. Tolerating unwanted mental images, confident that they will not be enacted

Group 6: Good decisions
6a: Individual decision-making
29. Positive aim. Aiming toward making things better. Seeking reward and not punishment
30. Reflectiveness. Thinking before acting, letting thoughts mediate between situation and action
31. Fluency. Using words to conceptualize the world: verbal skills
32. Awareness of your emotions. Recognizing and being able to verbalize your own feelings
33. Awareness of control. Accurately assessing the degree of control you have over specific events
34. Decision-making. Defining a problem, gathering information, generating options, predicting and evaluating consequences, making a choice

6b: Joint decision-making, including conflict resolution
35. Toleration. Non-bossiness. Tolerating a wide range of other people's behavior
36. Rational approach to joint decisions. Deciding rationally on stance and strategies
37. Option-generating. Generating creative options for solutions to problems
38. Option-evaluating. Justice skills: Recognizing just solutions to interpersonal problems
39. Assertion. Dominance, sticking up for yourself, taking charge, enjoying winning.
40. Submission: Conciliation, giving in, conceding, admitting you were wrong, being led
41. Differential reinforcement. Reinforcing positive behavior and avoiding reinforcing the negative

Group 7: Nonviolence
42. Forgiveness and anger control. Forgiving, handling an insult or injury by another
43. Nonviolence. Being committed to the principle of nonviolence and working to foster it

Group 8: Respectful talk, not being rude
44. Respectful talk, not being rude. Being sensitive to words, vocal tones and facial expressions that are accusing,

punishing or demeaning, and avoiding them unless there is a very good reason

Group 9: Friendship-Building, Relationship-Building
45. Discernment and Trusting. Accurately appraising others. Not distorting with prejudice, overgeneralization, wish-fulfilling fantasies. Deciding what someone can be trusted for and trusting when appropriate.
46. Self-disclosure. Disclosing and revealing oneself to another when it is safe
47. Gratitude. Expressing gratitude, admiration, and other positive feelings toward others
48. Social initiations. Starting social interaction; getting social contact going.
49. Socializing. Engaging well in social conversation or play
50. Listening. Empathizing, encouraging another to talk about his own experience

Group 10: Self-discipline
51. Self-discipline. Delay of gratification, self-control. Denying oneself pleasure for future gain

Group 11: Loyalty
52. Loyalty. Tolerating and enjoying sustained closeness, attachment, and commitment to another

Group 12: Conservation
53. Conservation and Thrift. Preserving resources for ourselves and future generations. Foregoing consumption on luxuries, but using resources more wisely. Financial delay of gratification skills.

Group 13: Self-care
54. Carefulness. Feeling appropriate fear and avoiding unwise risks
55. Habits of self-care. Healthy habits regarding drinking, smoking, drug use, exercise, and diet
56. Relaxation. Calming yourself, letting your mind drift pleasantly, letting your body be at ease
57. Self-nurture. Delivering assuring or care-taking thoughts to yourself, and feeling comforted from these thoughts

Group 14: Compliance
58. Compliance. Obeying, submitting to legitimate and reasonable authority

Group 15: Positive fantasy rehearsal
59. Imagination and positive fantasy rehearsal. Using fantasy as a tool in rehearsing or evaluating a plan, or adjusting to an event or situation

Group 16: Courage
60. Courage. Estimating danger, overcoming fear of nondangerous situations, handling danger rationally
61. Depending. Accepting help, being dependent without shame, asking for help appropriately
62. Independent thinking. Making decisions independently, carrying out actions independently

About the Order of the Skills

I have regrouped the skills since the time of their original publication. At that time I tried to group them in a rough developmental sequence, using the ideas of Erik Erickson about how psychological development takes place. Since that time, I've become convinced that all of these skills begin developing very early, and all of them can continue developing late in life. For example, I originally listed trusting (including deciding who is trustworthy in what ways) at the beginning of the list, to correspond with Erickson's stage of "basic trust versus mistrust." But decisions on whom to trust for what are very complex and people continue to develop this skill throughout adult life. Conversely, many other skills such as productivity, joyousness, and kindness probably get their start very early in life. I finally gave up on making the order of skills correspond to stages of life development.

As the skills are now grouped, the sixteen group headings in themselves cover psychological health fairly well, even for those people who do not go into the depth required to get familiar with all sixty-two individual skills. The sixteen skill groups also seem to cover principles of ethics fairly well also; they permit a merging of psychological skills and ethical principles.

The names of the first few skill groups, even without the rest, form a rough approximation to defining psychological health. When someone asked Sigmund Freud what the psychologically healthy person should be able to do, he replied, "To love and to work" – I translate that as kindness and productivity. Since it's difficult to sustain working or being kind without deriving pleasure from these activities, we should add joyousness to the very short list. Productivity, joyousness, and kindness in themselves form a pretty good image of a psychologically healthy person, and a good person.

A Trek Through the Skills Axis

It's good to spend time thinking about what the psychologically healthy person can do. The paragraphs that follow are only an introduction. The other way of learning about psychological skills is to reflect on particular concrete examples of each one of them. As we'll talk about later, there are lots of stories, plays, and vignettes I've written that help to do this. But let's start by simply describing them.

Group 1: Productivity

The productivity group has to do with using effort to accomplish something. It is linked to the concept of "work capacity" – how much effort is someone capable of expending before saying to himself, "I've had enough!" The infant who learns to roll or crawl to get closer to some object of curiosity is practicing productivity. The toddler who tries various techniques to engage an adult's attention is also expending effort to accomplish a goal, even though the toddler usually can't express this goal in words. Academic and career work are only the most obvious manifestations of productivity. Work toward improvement of psychological skills is an extremely important portion of this skill. I put the productivity group first because people can improve in all other skills, if they can work at them enough.

1. Purposefulness: Having a sense of purpose that drives activity

The essence of productivity is striving toward goals. The skill of purposefulness includes having goals, and having worthy goals. What are goals that are worthy of directing life's effort? Unless we give children a different answer, I fear that the answer they get from today's media-oriented society is that we live in order to consume goods, get famous, be beautiful, and triumph over our foes through violent competition. It should worry us to read polls asking young people whom they admire the most, and to see actors who portray violent "heroes" regularly showing up, while the names of Nobel Peace Prize winners are forgotten if ever noticed. The rampant violence in today's U.S. culture is probably partly due to lack of messages to young people that there is a higher purpose in existence than to beat the enemy. For females, the goal of being beautiful is constantly presented in the media. Among adolescents and young adults with anorexia and bulimia, a very helpful process is to consider whether there is a higher purpose in existence than adjusting how one looks.

In forming worthy goals, a useful orienting notion is the overarching goal of making the world a better place, and of enjoying doing that. The qualifier to such a seemingly grandiose idea is that making even one person happier makes the world a better place.

One of the jobs of parents is to transmit to children your highest and best ideas of the purposes of existence. If you don't do this, the mass culture will transmit other ideas.

2. Persistence. Sustaining attention, concentrating, focusing, staying on task

Having worthy goals is not enough for productivity; you also have to log in enough effort to accomplish them. The inability to keep working long enough is one of the defining features of Attention Deficit Hyperactivity Disorder, the most frequent reason why children receive drug treatment. Our biological makeup has lots to do with how easy it is for us to pay attention. But lots of evidence suggests that sustaining attention to tasks, like any other skill, gets better with practice and reinforcement and the other influences I'll talk about later. For young children, listening when someone reads books, and having conversations, and doing dramatic play with toy people, when done for longer and longer periods of time, constitute what I call practice in attending to verbally encoded information. And the tasks of schoolwork, which later will put great demands upon the child's attention span, also involve attending to verbally encoded material. I had the pleasure of directing a research study that found what you might have expected: when parents spend time reading to, talking with, and playing with preschool aged children, the children develop better attention skills.

3. Competence-development. Working toward competence in job, academics, recreation, life skills

There is a story of two people who sawed wood all day; one worked continuously; the other stopped from time to time. Yet the second sawed much more wood. When the first one asked, "How did you do it," the second answered, "During the time I stopped sawing, I sharpened the saw." The moral is: invest effort in the activities that make other effort more effective. The person who can take pleasure at getting more competent at skills has a real advantage for psychological health.

4. Organization. Organizing goals, priorities, time, money, and physical objects; planfulness

Disorganization is one of the biggest enemies of productivity. The ability to make and follow plans, use to-do lists, use appointment books, make and follow budgets, file papers, and organize physical objects is crucial to those who would be successful in this complex world. Although the literature on these skills is more often classed in business sections than mental health sections of libraries, the skills are central to mental health. Children are often given medication for disorganization that is thought to be a manifestation of attention problems; few of these children are systematically taught organization skills.

The skill of self-discipline is another that is crucial to productivity. This skill is so crucial to so many other areas of life that it is given its own group; we'll come to it later.

Group 2. Joyousness

Our brains constantly signal us to avoid pain and seek enjoyment. Some people's lives seem to be based around a "pain economy": if they do this or that, they will reduce their fear or guilt. Others seem more based on an economy of seeking the positive: if they do this or that, they will feel proud or happy. You can train two rats to run in a maze by different methods. One gets its feet shocked until it finds its way out of the maze. The second gets some tasty food when it finds its way out. Both may be doing the same behavior, but the second is probably enjoying the process more! Similarly, two people can be performing on stage. One may be thinking, "I can't screw up, or I'll look like an idiot!" The second may be thinking, "What a thrill it will be to put on a good performance!" The second point of view is much more conducive to happy performance!

The ability to take pleasure in various aspects of life is not just biologically determined – we program and reprogram ourselves with respect to what to feel good about. As parents, one of our main goals is to help children take pleasure in the sorts of things that will help them the most.

5. Enjoying aloneness. Having a good time by oneself, tolerating not getting someone's attention

It's a cliché to speak of a child acting up "to get attention." But commonsense wisdom is correct that attention-seeking is a frequent motive for children's misbehavior. Children often do unkind or irritating things, not out of malice, but because these behaviors get people to look at them and talk to them. For example, a child at school pokes another, just to get some interaction going. A five-year-old child whines or knocks things over just because people in the family are not noticing her.

One answer to this problem is "differential attention," or giving more attention to positive behavior than negative behavior. We'll talk about this much more, later.

But some children need to learn to exist on a leaner diet of attention. They need to get the ability to be at peace with themselves for longer times. Being with people, but not attended to, is sometimes harder than actually being by oneself.

As parents we wish our children to be able to take pleasure both in solitary activity and in a variety of aspects of social activity, many of which are included in the other joyousness skills.

6. Pleasure from approval. Enjoying approval, compliments, and positive attention from others

People constantly send us signals – sometimes subtle, sometimes otherwise – about whether they approve or disapprove of our behavior. Although people can become overly dependent on others' approval, the ability to take pleasure in approval is one of the major skills that keeps us on the right track, keeps us oriented toward activity that makes others feel good instead of upsetting them.

7. Pleasure from accomplishments. Self-reinforcement for successes

This skill is the ability to say, "Hooray for me, I did something good," when appropriate, and to feel good in response to that thought. The external world usually does not offer us payoffs for our effort on a schedule that maximizes our accomplishments. For example, the child who is doing homework may experience no immediate external reward, and may even experience very little delayed external reward. But if the child can deliver himself his own reward, his own feelings of pleasure from accomplishment, he will enjoy the process of homework more, and will be much more likely to complete it.

8. Pleasure from your own kindness. Feeling pleasure from doing kind, loving acts for others

If all children could somehow be "programmed" to feel great pleasure from making others happy, the world would be transformed in a major way. But even though this utopian fantasy may never occur, the person who can take pleasure from making others feel good has a major advantage for happiness. This person can take great pleasure from the sorts of actions that create stable and happy relationships and useful economic results.

9. Pleasure from discovery. Enjoying exploration and satisfaction of curiosity

Great development of this skill results in a learner who expends effort not just to get grades or to do better than someone else, but who takes direct joy in finding out about the world.

10. Pleasure from others' kindness. Feeling gratitude for what others have done

The person with this skill appreciates what others have done. Not only is this person less likely to be called a spoiled brat; the appreciation feels good and directly makes the person happy.

11. Pleasure from blessings. Celebrating and feeling the blessings of luck or fate

With this skill the person takes pleasure from the blessings that are outside of any human being's control – chief among them being the existence of such a complex universe, the existence of life, and the chance to be alive.

Pleasure from blessings, pleasure from others' kindness, and pleasure from one's own accomplishments and acts of kindness are the antidotes to what Beck has called the depressive triad: a negative view of the self, other people, and the world.

12. Pleasure from affection. Enjoying physical affection without various fears interfering

Physical affection is one of the great pleasures of life. Along with the self-discipline and self-care skills required to avoid inappropriate or harmful physical contact, we want our children to be able to take pleasure in the physical contact that is appropriate and good.

13. Favorable attractions. Having feelings of attraction aroused in ways consonant with happiness

Some people find themselves attracted to people who are not good for them. For example, some women find themselves attracted to "tough guys" who end up being abusive to them, passing up relationships with more kind and rational men who somehow don't have the "chemistry." Some people tend to seek mates who are helpless and in need of a rescue, those who make them a "knight in shining armor." But the job of knighthood and rescuing can get old fast. Some people are attracted to others purely on the basis of their physical appearance, disregarding their psychological skill strengths and weaknesses. The skill of favorable attractions means you're attracted to the sort of people who are good for you.

14. Gleefulness. Playing, becoming childlike, experiencing glee, being spontaneous

The skills of gleefulness, silliness, and humor are directly related to happiness. In our efforts to help children become "mature" and "responsible" we should not forget the importance of these skills. Generating pleasure from silliness and humor is a major anti-depression strategy. It helps greatly in making life worth living.

15. Humor. Enjoying funny things, finding and producing comedy in life

The ability to appreciate and produce humor is useful for social relations and enjoyment of life. One of the purposes of humor is to allow enjoyment to come even from the tribulations of life (as in "We'll look back on this and think it's funny.") Humor is a very complex skill. It's very difficult to teach. One can develop a mean-spirited sense of humor that seeks out the negative aspects of other people in order to laugh at them.

Group 3: Kindness

16. Kindness. Nurturing someone, being kind and helpful

The skill of kindness should go on the priority list for almost every child. It is vital to all of human relations. Perhaps this is why it is central to most of the world's religions and most systems of ethics. If your child learns to take genuine pleasure in doing kind things, he tends to have friends and be accepted by them; he tends to give pleasure to you and get the sense that you enjoy having him around. A child who enjoys his own acts of kindness has an immediate source of pleasure from sensing that he has made someone feel good; he also gets a more delayed pleasure when people are grateful or kind in return.

17. Empathy. Recognizing other people's feelings, seeing things from the other's point of view

The essence of kindness is making other people happier, and empathy allows us to tell whether we are making others happy or not. The skill of empathy involves being able to pick up on the often subtle cues that reveal what other people are feeling—the nuances of tone of voice, facial expression, and behavior that give clues as to how to act with people. Those without this skill often unintentionally lose friends. Do you know anyone who blithely keeps talking forever, and doesn't seem to pick up on the glances at the watch, the fidgeting, and the direction of eye movements that would tell most people, "Shut up and give me my turn to talk?" Or have you known a child who can't infer the subtle point where roughhousing or teasing other children ceases to be fun and the message is, "I'm not kidding! Back off!" Empathy allows people to get accurate feedback from others.

18. Conscience. Feeling appropriate guilt, avoiding harming others

The skill of conscience, of feeling bad about hurting others, is another where balance is required. Total lack of conscience leads to antisocial behavior; too severe a conscience leads to depression and possible suicide. Feeling just bad enough about harming other people is a skill that the psychologically healthy person should have in her habit repertoire.

Group 4: Honesty

19. Honesty. Being honest and dependable, especially when it is difficult to be so

The habit of honesty has probably been studied too little by mental health professionals. But as M. Scott Peck has pointed out, comfortableness with deceit is necessary for almost all forms of evil and antisocial behavior—because one must lie to avoid bearing the consequences of it.

20. Awareness of my abilities. Being honest and brave in assessing your own strengths and weaknesses

Many people go through their lives with very significant skill deficiencies, yet they never get around to working on them, acknowledging them to someone else, or even acknowledging them to themselves. Why? Because it is painful to admit faults. In a sense it's pleasant to convince yourself that you're doing everything right, and that all problems are someone else's fault. But such pleasantness comes at a dear price, because by giving up responsibility for outcomes, we also give up a feeling of ability to control them. We can purchase blamelessness by convincing ourselves of helplessness.

At other times it's somehow more pleasant for people to think, "I am totally unable to do this, I'm worthless in this area." How can overdoing your skill deficiencies be a relatively pleasant thing to do? Because it gets you off the hook, and again avoids responsibility. For example, it's sometimes easier to say, "I am just no good at schoolwork," than "I could be good at schoolwork, but I am making choices that make me not succeed." The first proposition avoids responsibility, at the cost of accepting helplessness.

With respect to your own abilities, "the truth shall set you free," even though that truth may be painful.

Group 5: Fortitude

21. Frustration-tolerance, fortitude. Handling frustration, tolerating adverse circumstances.

One way of looking at life is that you are constantly dealing with either things you don't like, or things you do like. If you can handle both undesirable situations and desirable situations very well, you will do OK. Joyousness has to do with handling desirable situations, and fortitude with undesirable ones.

We put fortitude very high on a child's priority list when the child has tantrums when he can't get candy at the grocery store check-out line; when he yells or hits when he has to turn off the TV and go somewhere; when he cries when another child preempts his playing with what he wanted; when he gets overly upset or mad when a game doesn't go his way, and so on. Fortitude, the ability to handle adversity, is a key skill. Unfortunately, positive examples of its presence usually attract much less attention than negative examples of its absence. When a child yells at a hundred decibels and kicks the parents when he can't get what he wants, that attracts attention. When the child says, "May I have this," and the parent says "No, you'll have to wait," and the child says nothing and goes along cooperatively, that usually doesn't attract so much attention. But since attention reinforces behavior, using "differential attention" in just the opposite way would be better for the child. One of the benefits of thinking in terms of skills is that you can learn not to overlook positive examples of skills like frustration tolerance.

Here's a list of types of thoughts people have in response to frustrations, as well as to favorable situations. Learning to choose consciously how one wants to think is key to almost all psychological skills. Fortitude is only one of the groups that is particularly fostered by getting very familiar with these types of thoughts and learning to choose consciously what patterns you want to dwell upon.

The Twelve Types of Thoughts

1. Awfulizing
2. Getting down on yourself
3. Blaming someone else
4. Not awfulizing
5. Not getting down on yourself
6. Not blaming someone else
7. Goal-setting
8. Listing options and choosing
9. Learning from the experience
10. Celebrating luck
11. Celebrating someone else's choice
12. Celebrating your own choice

We'll study these at greater length later on. But you can probably guess, from the names of these thoughts, how some are more conducive to fortitude than others.

22. Handling separation. Tolerating separation from close others, or loss of a relationship.

Handling the actual moment of "Good-bye" from a parent or other caregiver is the most concrete example of skills of handling separation. Handling it when a friend moves away, a love relationship ends, or when one becomes a widow or widower all involve variations upon the skill of handling separation. Sometimes the difficult part of a separation is being rejected by another—the blow to one's self-concept; at other times it is pure loss of the relationship and the bond. Being skilled at separation does not mean that there is no pain involved. If I felt no pain, ever, when a beloved spouse died, I would be less than human. The good reasons why separations feel bad are the same reasons why people form social bonds in the first place. Part of human nature is to have a hard-wired need for other people. But the skill of tolerating separation is one of degree: not feeling extreme pain over minor separations, not letting major separations produce total paralysis of the ability to enjoy life and contribute to others.

23. Handling rejection. Tolerating it when people don't like or accept you or want to be with you

Rejections are stressful in several ways. There's the pure displeasure of losing a relationship and breaking a bond of attachment. There's also the insult, the message about what you are: you're not worthy of friendship for this person. There's the pain of generalization, of the thought, "Maybe I'm not worthy of the friendship of other people as well." Those who hurt the worst are those who generalize the farthest: "I'm not worthy of any relationship with anybody." It shouldn't be surprising that lots of suicidal people have recently suffered rejections.

The good news is that people can learn to handle rejection better. They can learn to tell themselves, "There are more fish in the sea," rather than "This means I'm a terrible person." Interestingly, those who can handle rejection well may get rejected less often: people find others more desirable when they are so needy or desperate for acceptance.

24. Handling criticism. Dealing with disapproval and criticism and lack of respect from others

Handling criticism is a skill in short supply among us human beings. You move toward diagnosing a shortage in this skill when a child has tantrums whenever she is corrected, or when she gets depressed and sullen for a long time whenever she gets feedback that her work at school is not perfect. You consider this skill deficiency when a peer who calls the child a name gets an instant fight.

The skill of handling criticism begins with the recognition that no one is perfect. Imperfection is not (usually) a crime. When you are criticized, it's good to do some self-appraisal, to ask yourself, how much truth is there in the criticism. If the criticism is false, the tasks are to celebrate internally that the criticism isn't true, and to decide whether and how to deal with the other person's misperception or malice. If the criticism is true, the tasks are to learn from it and to decide how much effort to put into improving. The verbal skills of responding without unnecessary self-effacement or hostility can be studied in great complexity.

25. Handling mistakes and failures. Regretting mistakes without being overly self-punitive

Skill in handling mistakes and failures is one of several skills where a delicate balance is called for. If a child goes into a depression when she gets a B on a test rather than an A, or feels suicidally guilty upon missing a basketball shot in a game, we say with confidence that the child feels overly bad about mistakes and failures. Freud would have said that the child had a "harsh and punitive superego." Eric Berne would have said that the child has an internal "critical parent" that is too hard on the child. On the other hand, the child who cares not a whit whether he passes or fails, and who is unfazed when he makes mistakes that prove expensive or self-destructive, may have an even worse problem. The skillful people feel worse about mistakes and failures than about successes, but not so bad that they paralyze efforts toward improvement.

26. Magnanimity, non-jealousy. Handling it when someone else gets what I want.

A special case of frustration is not only not getting what you want, but also seeing someone else get it. Jealousy, envy, and rage are often the responses in the unskilled individual rather than sheer disappointment. But learning to handle this situation is central to family life, especially in coexisting with siblings. The "Oedipal Conflict" so dramatized by the Freudians, in which a child wants to exclusively possess one parent and is jealous of the attention the other parent gets, is in skills language a challenge to the skill of nonjealousy and magnanimity.

27. Painful emotion-tolerance. Tolerating feeling bad without making that make me feel worse.
28. Fantasy-tolerance. Tolerating unwanted mental images, confident that they will not be enacted.

The skills of painful emotion-tolerance and fantasy-tolerance have to do with being able to feel bad and have unacceptable ideas come into the mind without getting into a vicious cycle about them. For example: someone gets anxious, thinks "This is awful, I'm dying," and those thoughts make the person more anxious, which make the person surer that death is imminent. Or someone notices himself fantasying someone else's death, and gets so scared by it that he can't function. The skillful patterns involve "gutting out" unpleasant feelings and thoughts until things get better and avoiding vicious cycles.

Group 6: Good decisions

This group of skills allows people to come up with good responses to situations. When examining the skills of individual decision-making, we consider the individual as the unit. When thinking about joint decision-making, we think about a decision that will affect more than one person, and the skills that the individual uses to work out agreements with others.

6a: Individual decision-making

29. Positive aim. Aiming toward making things better. Seeking reward and not punishment

Decision-making is the art of making good outcomes happen. In order to do this, you need first to desire good outcomes for yourself and others, rather than bad ones. The skill of positive aim is the opposite of being a masochist and sadist. How does one ever get into the habit of wanting, on some level, to get sick, get hurt, or to fail? Perhaps it's a case of conditioning: when these things happened, someone took care of me, when I was doing well and succeeding, I didn't get what I wanted. How do people develop pleasure in making things turn out badly for others, even people who have not harmed one in any way, such as those whose computers are damaged by viruses? The answer to this question is complex, but the skill of positive aim is an antidote to aiming to harm oneself or others.

30. Thinking before acting. Letting thoughts mediate between situation and action

The skill of thinking before acting is a prerequisite for good decision-making. Many situations we face are too complex to respond to by reflex or by doing what comes naturally. We often need to take the time to send a decision through the more complex pathways of thought and calculation rather than to respond by reflex. People with problems of impulsiveness should put this skill on their priority list.

31. Fluency. Using words to conceptualize the world: verbal skills

Using language fluently enhances psychological health. When I have words to name what is going on, I'm better able to think about it, understand it, and respond to it intelligently. One of the major ways to help children process the interpersonal and intrapsychic world is to teach them the words they can use to think about life most effectively. For example: if the child has no words in his vocabulary for self-discipline, long-term goal, and temptation, then the child is more likely to default to thinking, "This isn't fun, therefore I'm not going to do it." But the child who has these words is more able to think, "This isn't fun, but it will help me achieve my long term goal. I need to use self-discipline and pass up the short-term temptation." Thus vocabulary can empower the person to enact patterns that were otherwise not possible.

32. Awareness of your own emotions. Recognizing, and being able to verbalize your own feelings

An important subset of verbal fluency is being able to recognize and put into words one's own feelings. Some psychiatrists have described a set of patients as "alexithymic," or without words for feelings. Being able to express your feelings is certainly not a solution to all problems, but it is a very important starting point. If all you know is that you feel lousy, you're not very close to a solution. However, if you identify your feeling as guilt, or loneliness, or anger, and if you figure out why you're feeling this way, then you're closer to a solution. You're guided in the direction of making recompense, finding some company, or getting someone to quit doing something irritating.

33. Awareness of control. Accurately assessing the degree of control one has over specific events

The "serenity prayer" refers to more than serenity: the serenity to accept the things I cannot change, the courage to change the things I can, and the wisdom to know the difference. The wisdom to know the difference equals the skill of awareness of control. The child who feels totally responsible for his parent's break-up is usually making the error of feeling more control than is real; the child who disavows to himself any responsibility for vandalism carried out by a group of which he was a part is usually making the error of feeling less control than is real. The person who remembers conflicts with other people as simply arising out of the blue, with the other person's doing something obnoxious, and who can't remember or understand the role that she herself played in the gradually escalating hostility, is making a very common error that denies her own control. It is important to realize that this skill, like all others, can be learned and practiced and improved.

34. Decision-making. Defining a problem, gathering information, generating options, predicting and evaluating consequences, making a choice

The skill of rational decision-making is one which has benefited from burgeoning research in recent decades. The process—defining the problem, gathering information, listing options, evaluating options by predicting consequences and weighing probabilities of consequences—is the analogy, for one person, of the joint-decision process for two people. It is sometimes comforting to realize that all the negative experiences of the past do not necessarily need to be worked through: for a reasonably happy life, all that is usually needed is to make reasonably good decisions a reasonably large fraction of the time. If your child can learn to make decisions that are at least not in obvious contradiction to what she wants, most of the time, she will be ahead of what most people seem to do.

Decision-making should be not only rational, but moral. It's not good enough for a child to be a cunning decision-maker on how to be selfish and materialistic in the most carefully plotted way. Rather, a sense of principle, an idea of what constitutes right and wrong, is extremely important. Students of the development of moral reasoning in children, such as Jean Piaget and Lawrence Kohlberg, have spoken of various stages of moral development. The early stages are hedonistic: you think that what is good is what gives you pleasure. Intermediate stages may be based upon authoritarian reasoning (i.e. actions are good because they follow the law) and bargaining-based reasoning (it is good to do good things to others because it makes it more likely that they'll do good back). The highest stages are principle-based: I choose to adopt certain principles, a belief system, that will guide me whenever I make a specific moral judgment. One such principle is the Golden Rule: Do unto others as you would have them do unto you. A similar principle is the philosopher Emmanuel Kant's "categorical imperative": act so that you can wish that the principle behind your action would become a universal rule for all to follow. The utilitarian philosophers, such as Jeremy Bentham and John Stewart Mill, would use as the central moral principle the goal of maximizing the total happiness in the world.

6b: Joint decision-making, including conflict resolution

What happens when what one person decides affects another person? Particularly, what happens when two people want different things in such situations? What happens when two people can't both get their way in some immediately obvious manner? Too often the result is violence. Civilization means that conflict is handled in some way other than that the most powerful wins.

35. Toleration. Non-bossiness. Tolerating a wide range of other people's behavior.

People can generate unnecessary conflict by being too picky. When other people have to act just in one certain way, many of them are not going to like it. Thus toleration of a wide range of other people's behavior means that a lot of joint decisions are much easier. It's easier to say "OK, that's fine with me," when you have this skill.

36. Rational approach to joint decisions. Deciding rationally on stance and strategies.

Many people approach conflict with strong emotions: anger, or perhaps fear. This skill means fully using the cool, thinking part of the brain, searching for the best outcome rather than being driven to lash out or submit.

37. Option-generating. Generating creative options for solutions to problems.

A very important skill is generating reasonable options. In a research effort I made, I gave children the following situation:

Pat and Lee live together. Pat likes to make a dish with fish and sauerkraut, that gives off a very strong smell. Lee does not like that smell at all, and it bothers Lee whenever Pat makes his dish. What do you think they can do about their problem?

Research on the problem-solving process initiated by Spivack and Shure, among others, has strongly suggested that the children who are able to think of greater numbers of nonaggressive options for the solution of problems like these tend to be better adjusted, as rated by teachers, peers, and parents. In other words: the child who can not think of anything they could do, or the child who can only think of options such as Pat's using a grenade on Lee, Lee's poisoning Pat's sauerkraut, and so forth, tend not to do as well in relations with others. Those who can think of options such as Pat's cooking the dish on an outdoor grill, using a large fan to remove the smell from the house, Pat's cooking the dish only when Lee will be away for a long enough time for the odor to go away, and so forth, tend to do better with people.

Thinking of options in situations like this is a skill that can be improved with practice.

The skill of option-generating is obviously also applicable to individual decisions, notwithstanding the fact that I arbitrarily put it in the joint decisions group.

38. Option-evaluating. Justice skills: Recognizing just solutions to interpersonal problems

Once options are listed, a decision needs to be made as to which options are more just, more likely to work. A child achieves a major development when she realizes that justice should be "blind" to who the persons involved are. That is, if it's only fair you should not interrupt me, then it should also be fair that I should not interrupt you. In other words, "Because it makes me feel good" is not a sufficient reason to explain why a certain option is just.

39. Assertion. Dominance, sticking up for oneself, taking charge, enjoying winning.

40. Submission: Conciliation, giving in, conceding, admitting one was wrong, being led

In the process of joint problem-solving, both assertion and submission skills are necessary. The person who automatically gives in, who is unable to state the case for his own point of view, and whom people use to "mop up the floor" is lacking in assertion skills. On the other hand, the person who feels that he can never give in, that his manhood or personhood is threatened if he ever backs down, is lacking in submission skills, and if he meets another submission-deficient individual, he risks ending up in deadly battle. A healthy mixture of assertion skills and submission skills, with good judgment as to when to invoke each of them, characterizes the psychological healthy person.

41. Differential reinforcement. Reinforcing positive behavior and avoiding reinforcing the negative.

The skill of differential reinforcement, of seeking out the good that others do and focusing on it and recognizing it, and at the same time trying not to reinforce the undesired behaviors, represents a different approach to conflict than the highly language-oriented set of negotiation skills. Sometimes it works better. For example: a child's whining causes conflict with his mother. It may be more useful for the mother to reinforce requests made in a non-whiny voice and to ignore those made in a whiny voice, than to negotiate with the child about whining.

Group 7: Nonviolence

42. Forgiveness and anger control. Forgiving, handling an insult or injury by another

There is no one who does not from time to time get insulted, harmed, injured, or taken advantage of by another person. Anger can be a useful emotion, in mobilizing energy to oppose those who would take advantage of us. On the other hand, when anger is not useful to us, it is good for us to be able to let it go. It can be very destructive to believe that the only way to let anger go is to "let it out." Feeling angry is a behavior that one can cease to do, voluntarily, just as one can voluntarily cease to hit oneself with a fist when it becomes clear that this behavior is only causing pain.

43. Nonviolence. Being committed to the principle of nonviolence and working to foster it.

In a world where the human race has gained the technological power to extinguish itself, and where many children live in environments where gunfire aimed at other human beings is part of everyday life, devoting at least some effort to improving this situation is the mark of a person with a sense of priorities. Enlisting children in efforts to promote nonviolence on a societal level has been found to help them choose nonviolent solutions to problems individually.

Group 8: Respectful talk, not being rude

44. Respectful talk, not being rude. Being sensitive to words, vocal tones and facial expressions that are accusing, punishing or demeaning, and avoiding them unless there is a very good reason.

Disrespectful, hostile talk does not "get out" hostility – it tends to escalate it. This skill is to verbal aggression as the skill of nonviolence is to physical aggression. Yelling, taunting, and profane language directed at others are often the predecessors to physical violence.

Both nonviolence and respectful talk could be subsumable under the skill of kindness. But it is too easy for people to feel that they are very kind people, when they are kind to their friends and rude or violent toward their enemies. For this reason, ethical systems have found it useful to incorporate specific rules against the harmful as well as in favor of the helpful.

Group 9: Friendship-Building, Relationship Building

45. Discernment and Trusting. Accurately appraising others. Not distorting with prejudice, overgeneralization, wish-fulfilling fantasies. Deciding what someone can be trusted for and trusting when appropriate.

Trusting is not just believing that someone is saying the truth. At its most basic level, it is the belief that someone is not out to harm you, and that the person may even wish you well. Without this belief, forming relationships is quite scary. Children who have been raised in very unkind or abusive environments naturally have trouble with this skill. But sometimes other children overgeneralize from the unkindness of one or few people, and conclude that all are unkind. A child who has been jeered by one child needs the skill of discernment to keep from assuming that all other children will act the same.

Studies have shown that children with conduct problems, e.g. aggression, hostility, tend to interpret ambiguous actions of other people as motivated by the intent to harm. For example, if you show a picture of someone with the hand raised, friendly children tend more to guess that the hand is raised in a greeting, whereas aggressive children tend to guess that the hand is raised to hit or slap. The skill of trusting is basic to how we interpret other people's actions. If someone doesn't speak to me, does that mean that person is trying to reject me and make me feel bad, or is it that the person is preoccupied, shy, or doesn't see me? A sense of paranoia about other people's intentions is the opposite of the skill of trusting.

But sometimes people's intentions are not good, and it is possible to err on the side of gullibility as well as paranoia. Suspicion is very appropriate at certain times. Thus the skill of trusting requires discrimination and choosing, trusting at times and mistrusting at other times, rather than having blind faith in others' goodness.

46. Self-disclosure. Disclosing and revealing oneself to another when it is safe

The skill of self-disclosure allows a person to talk with a trusted friend, to disclose whatever is on one's mind, without great fears of humiliation or shame or exploitation. Many people spend a great deal of time in psychotherapy learning this skill. A psychotherapist once wrote, concerning psychological disorders, that "You are only as sick as your secrets." For many people, the biggest hurdle on the way to psychological health is the notion that their problems are so shameful that they must be hidden from everyone.

47. Gratitude. Expressing gratitude, admiration, and other positive feelings toward others

The skill of *feeling* good about other people's kind acts was listed in the joyousness group. The skill of *communicating* appreciation to others is listed under friendship-building. Children who lack this skill sometimes find themselves without friends.

48. Social initiations. Starting social interaction; getting social contact going.

The skill of social initiations is the art of starting talking or playing with adults or other children. Five year old Timmy was a child that other children disliked. Timmy was in a group free play situation, and he wanted to start playing with other children. So he went up to two children playing building a house with Legos, and said to them, "Come here, look what I have!" The children ignored him because they were already wrapped up in what they were doing. In frustration, Timmy then knocked over the house they were building. Now they were really mad at him. But his motive was not malice—he just wanted to get some interaction going, and he didn't know how to do it more skillfully. Rick, on the other hand, was a popular child. Rick happened to be interested also in starting playing Legos with two boys. Rick started by squatting down near the boys and watching what they were doing for several seconds. Then he joined them, unobtrusively. He first said, "Looks like the roof is ready to go on! ... This looks like a good piece for the roof."

For older people, the skill of social initiations entails choosing an appropriate moment to say, "Hello, how are you?" or an appropriate moment to introduce oneself, or an appropriate remark about what is happening, or other ways to get interaction started comfortably.

49. Socializing. Engaging well in social conversation or play.

Once friendly interaction is started, the art of continuing it in a mutually gratifying way is what I call the skill of socializing. For very young children this is primarily oriented around toys and play; for older children there is more of a premium on structured games; for both older children and adults, there is a particular premium on conversation skills.

50. Listening. Empathizing, encouraging another to talk about his own experience.

The art of listening is crucial to friendship-building as well as joint decision and other skills. Here I am not talking about a child's "listening" to parental commands and carrying them out—that's the skill of compliance. I'm talking about the skill of hearing someone say, "Wow, I can't believe how many problems we had to do for homework! Whew, they're all done!" and replying with something like, "Sounds like you're really relieved to have them finished!" rather than something like "I'm taking a field trip tomorrow," or "That wasn't so many you had to do. Quit bellyaching." The art of empathic reflection of the other person's thoughts and feelings was perfected by Carl Rogers and used in client-centered therapy. It soon became apparent that reflective listening was too useful to confine to therapy. Much good has been accomplished when family members, coworkers, and other people learn to listen empathically to one another.

The empathic reflection of the other person's thoughts or feelings can be taught to children as young as first grade. Children who can be empathic to other children have another skill conducive to making and keeping friends, since the world is populated with people who would like other people to show an interest in them and really listen to what they have to say.

Group 10: Self discipline

51. Self discipline. Delay of gratification, self control. Denying oneself pleasure for future gain.

Pleasure and pain evolved in our brains to give us a "first approximation" guide as to what to do. For example, we get pleasure from caloric intake and from sexual activity, partly so we won't forget to eat and starve to death, or forget to procreate and let the species die out. It's pleasurable to rest when we're tired and seek stimulation when we're bored.

But one of the major challenges of existence is that not everything that is most immediately pleasurable is the best choice. It's often better to pass up the pleasurable food, to forego sexual activity, to save money rather than spend it, to prepare one's taxes rather than go and bet on the horse races, to do homework rather than play video games, to hold one's tongue rather than lash out at someone who is acting obnoxiously. In these cases our thinking brain, our decision-making on what is best to do, has to override the part that seeks pleasure and avoids pain. Doing this has been called self-discipline, self-control, delay of gratification, self-regulation, and will power.

One of the crucial maneuvers in exercising self-discipline is to provide yourself internal gratification with each step of work that his done. For example, a student takes a practice test that he has made up; while doing so he imagines himself doing well on the real test that will occur soon. He imagines how good he will feel to be well-prepared. Thus by the miracle of imagination, he brings a portion of the future gratification into the present.

Group 11: Loyalty
52. Loyalty. Tolerating and enjoying sustained closeness, attachment, and commitment to another

The skill of loyalty is what enables a person to stick in a relationship when the going gets tough, not to be a fair-weather friend, not to capriciously drop one person when another becomes more interesting. It's also what enables people to take seriously the commitments they make to others.

Group 12: Conservation
53. Conservation and Thrift. Preserving resources for ourselves and future generations. Foregoing consumption on luxuries, but using resources more wisely. Financial delay of gratification skills.

The skill of saving money and avoiding unnecessary consumption is not a topic I see mentioned frequently in the mental health literature. But money represents another area where striking an ideal balance between present and future, between delay of gratification and consumption of gratification, is crucial to a happy life. Neither spendthriftiness nor miserliness is conducive to happy living. I label this skill so as to emphasize the saving aspect, since in our present day culture those who save too much seem quite rare compared to those who consume too much. A constant barrage of advertising seems to be quite persuasive!

This skill involves foregoing consumption not only in the interest of the self, but of others. It's difficult to argue that huge consumption on luxuries is ethical when there are people who are starving, sick and uncared for, uneducated, and living in violence, and when the fate of the entire human race is threatened by nuclear and other forms of destruction. A dollar spent on entertainment or prestige possessions is a dollar that cannot be spent on more worthy causes.

Group 13: Self-care
54. Carefulness. Feeling appropriate fear and avoiding unwise risks

The skills of courage and carefulness need to be balanced with one another. Between the two, I would rather that my own children err on the side of carefulness! Taking unnecessary risks, while feeling invulnerable to danger, is a good way to get killed, permanently injured, or to receive big setbacks. Fear, like anger and guilt, did not arise for no reason. Assessing when danger is present and either avoiding it or working to protect oneself from it are skills that every human being should have in the repertoire.

55. Habits of self-care. Healthy habits regarding drinking, smoking, drug use, exercise, and diet

Habits of self-care are a set of skills, most of which also involve self-discipline. Avoiding cigarettes, alcohol, and other unnecessary drugs, avoiding speeding in cars, eating healthy foods, and getting adequate sleep and exercise are habits with huge consequences upon physical health. If the entire population could adopt just the healthy habits listed in the last sentence, there is no doubt that vast amounts of illness, disability, and premature death could be avoided.

56. Relaxation. Calming oneself, letting the mind drift pleasantly and the body be at ease

In the first half of the twentieth century Jacobson promoted the technique of progressive muscular relaxation as a remedy for what were then called nervous ailments. Jacobson taught people to relax by learning to sense the tension in muscles and consciously make muscles go limp all over the body. His technique is still extremely useful. Large numbers of research studies attest to the usefulness of learning relaxation, including some studies where relaxation was to be a control group contrasting with something else expected to be more effective. Later in this book I'll go into more detail about other techniques that have arisen after Jacobson. Imagery techniques are a prominent addition to the armamentarium: e.g. imagining oneself in relaxing surroundings, imagining and recalling nurturing and kind interactions between people. Biofeedback procedures also are a useful adjunct. Relaxation skills are useful enough to be part of the routine education of every child.

57. Self-nurture. Delivering assuring or care taking thoughts to oneself, feeling comforted thereby

The skill of kindness to others, when reflected upon oneself, produces the skill of self-nurture. This is the ability to comfort oneself, to "be one's own best friend." Many depressed or suicidal individuals are deficient in the skill of saying friendly things to themselves and refusing to be hostile to themselves.

Group 14: Compliance

58. Compliance. Obeying, submitting to legitimate and reasonable authority

There are better things to do with life than to oppose all authority. In order for organizations, including families, to run smoothly, people commonly put more decision-making power in some people's hands than in others – for example, more power in a thirty-five year old adult than in a 6 year old child! Compliance skill is almost always on the priority list of children who get labels of "oppositional" or "antisocial." But the issue of compliance is important for all children.

Compliance in children is a vital skill for an adult's mental health! I have seen parents who exhibit clinical symptoms of depression that appear to be mainly brought on by the stresses of dealing with a very noncompliant child. When every transition from one place or one activity to the next becomes a power struggle, an adult's quality of life is greatly reduced. The interesting point is that the child's quality of life is correspondingly reduced. The child is much happier when reasonable rules are followed and reasonable commands obeyed without a struggle.

The skill of compliance is a very important predecessor to self-discipline skills. I obey a reasonable and legitimate authority, even when I don't feel like it, because I know the long-run consequences will be more favorable. If I get good at obeying a reasonable parent who tells me to do things that make me better off in the long run, even when they are not immediately pleasurable, I am getting lots of practice that will help me obey the directives that I myself generate – and this is self-discipline.

Compliance is to be balanced by skills of independent thinking. I speak of compliance as obeying *reasonable* authority; there are many out there who would like to be obeyed despite being unreasonable and bad! If I should be ordered by a fascist dictator to execute innocent individuals, I would hope to exercise the skill of independent thinking, not the skill of compliance. Classic studies have found people all too willing to carry out harmful acts toward other people simply because someone who seems to be in authority tells them to do it.

Group 15: Positive fantasy rehearsal

59. Imagination and positive fantasy rehearsal. Using fantasy as a tool in rehearsing or evaluating a plan, or adjusting to an event or situation

The skill of imagination is the ability to deal with situations that are not actually present—to create a mental representation and work with it instead. We can practice skills in imagination. We can desensitize ourselves to scary situations by imagining ourselves handling them well. We can use imagination to anticipate problems in our plans and having solutions handy beforehand. We can use imagination to enhance the quality of our humor and enrich our vision of living. For this reason, daydreaming, fantasy play, and storytelling among children are not simply pleasurable activities—they are exercise of a vital skill.

Group 16: Courage

This group lists a general skill of courage, and two specific types of courage that frequently need to be targeted.

60. Courage. Estimating danger, overcoming fear of nondangerous situations, handling danger rationally

Anxiety is one of the most common complaints of people who come to mental health professionals. Courage skills are the direct antidote to unrealistic fears. A variety of techniques have become known to help people reduce those fears that are not useful to them, and applying these techniques can dramatically change lives for the better.

61. Depending. Accepting help, being dependent without shame, asking for help appropriately

The courage to admit, "I could use some help on this" is often the major hurdle for psychological development. Especially in the mental health arena, "needing help" is stigmatized. "You need help with your problems" can be a jabbing insult. Many people seem to confuse the thought "I can use some help with a psychological skill deficiency," a thought that applies to almost everyone, with "I am crazy and should be locked up permanently," a thought that applies to almost no one.

The courage to ask for help is needed not only in seeking mental health treatment. People have driven around in frustration looking for places, too proud to ask the person standing on the corner who could have given them clear and easy directions. People have gradually gone deaf without having the courage to ask for hearing aids. People have gone through life unable to read, without being able to go to someone for tutoring. People have watched lumps on their bodies gradually grow into fatal cancers without having the courage to ask a doctor to examine them.

The skill of depending is at the bedrock of much further development. A child who can depend well on a parent comes to care about the parent's approval and disapproval. The child learns what things get your approval and disapproval, and gradually starts supplying approval and disapproval to herself, thus acquiring a conscience. But if dependency is disrupted, and the child doesn't see the parent as much as a source of gratification, the child will not care as much about the parent's approval and disapproval. The foundation of the process is not built.

The skill of depending starts to develop as soon as an infant starts to be held, comforted, spoken to, fed, and cleaned. This skill is practiced throughout childhood whenever the child is the recipient of a kind, giving act.

62. Independent thinking. Making decisions independently, carrying out actions independently

Just as dependence can require great courage, so can independence. It is possible to need other people too much, to fear their loss or disapproval so much that one will do anything—use drugs, engage in unwanted sexual encounters—to remain a part of the group. The skills of independent thinking and acting allow one to say to others, "I know you would like for me to do this. But here is my decision, and I'm going to act on it, whether you like it or not." Perhaps a two year old who says "No!" may be practicing this skill in ways that prepare for crucial resistance of peer influence in adolescence. Or at least, that idea may be a consolation to the parent when the child first learns that short and powerful word!

The Skills Axis as Curriculum Outline and Menu of Targets

If you have thoughtfully read through these descriptions of all sixty-two skills, congratulations. Although lengthy, the skills axis is very useful. There are two major ways that you can use it. One is as a "curriculum outline" of what you want to cover in the "course" on psychological health that you give your children. With most people that course will not be a formal one (although one of my main goals has been to create materials that permit just that). But even in the absence of a formal course, it's good to provide influences toward all these skills, or at least all the groups, during some point in childhood.

The second use of the psychological skills axis is as a menu of targets. If the child has a problem – e.g. sadness, lack of friends, low motivation toward schoolwork, etc. – then which skills can we improve in order to solve the problem? Often we can pick three or four skills whose improvement will greatly remedy the situation.

Moving Along the "Abstraction Ladder" in Thinking About Fostering Psychological Growth

In using the skill concepts to solve particular behavior problems, it's best if we can move flexibly up and down what has been called the "abstraction ladder." The abstraction ladder has to do with whether our words refer to something specific and concrete (lower on the abstraction ladder) or something held in common by a large number of concrete and specific examples (higher on the abstraction ladder).

Suppose someone thinks that a child "acts bratty" or "seems maladjusted." Brattiness and maladjustment are concepts that could refer to large numbers of possible concrete behaviors and circumstances; for this reason they are concepts high on the "abstraction ladder." They are also negative descriptions of the child.

A good next step is to answer the question, "What are specific examples of brattiness, or maladjustment?" The answer should take the form of specific incidents. "When he couldn't get candy at the grocery store check-out, he screamed for a minute." "When he had to turn off his television show to go to the doctor, he cried with an angry voice and said to me, 'Why do you always do these things to me!'" "When he was building a tower with some blocks and his toddler sibling knocked them down, he got so upset that he kicked his own toys around." These descriptions bring up concrete mental images. They are therefore lower on the "abstraction ladder." We have moved from abstract negative generalizations to concrete negative examples.

The next step is to move back up the abstraction ladder, to a skills axis concept, a concept of the positive skill the child needs more of, a concept that will be useful than the concept of brattiness or maladjustment. You look at the specific negative examples and see what they have in common. All three of the examples I just cited had something very important in common: they were cases where the child could have used more frustration tolerance, or fortitude. So fortitude gets tentatively put on our list of high priority skills for the child to improve in. We've now moved back up the abstraction ladder; the concept names a positive skill we would like to see developing more thoroughly in the child.

If we see and recall more examples where fortitude would greatly help the child, we become more sure that it is on our priority list. If, on the other hand, we see only a steady stream of positive examples of fortitude, we conclude that our previous examples were a fluke. Thus the more examples we gather, the more sure we are one way or another about the child's skill.

Now that we have moved up the abstraction ladder to the skill concept, we want to move back down the abstraction ladder one more time, to generate a list of positive examples of the skillful pattern. We want to think of all the positive examples of fortitude that we can: the child remains calm when he opens the refrigerator and finds that it doesn't have what he wanted in it; the child quickly finds another goal after asking an older child to pick him up, but the older child isn't interested in that game; the child remains calm when in preschool he is enjoying a puzzle, but has to interrupt his activity so that his group can go outside. We want to generate as big a list of these possible positive examples of the each high-priority skill as we can.

We have thus moved down the abstraction ladder to the specific negative events, back up it to the positive skill concept, and back down it to the specific positive examples of the skillful pattern. When we reach the stage of concrete and specific positive examples, we can do several things. We can give the child models of those positive examples, so as to get the desirable patterns of thought, feeling, and behavior into the child's memory bank. We can watch for specific positive examples the child does in real life and make sure to reinforce them. And with the more abstract skill concept in mind, we can recognize other concrete examples that didn't make it onto our original list, when we see them. And finally, we hope that generalization will occur so that when the child gets lots of attention and approval, for example for certain instances of fortitude, the child will be more likely to come out with other examples of fortitude.

Think about the following exercises.

Exercise. When thinking about the question, "Which of these skills could my child most benefit from growing in, at this time," search through your memory for specific examples of problem behavior or unhappy emotion that you've noticed. Think to yourself, "What could my child have known how to do better, that would have helped him in this situation?" For each problem situation, come up with one or two or three psychological skills. Do this for several problem situations. If the same psychological skills come to mind over and over again, these are the ones you will choose to put on the priority list.

If you are using this book for prevention rather than for cure, simply think of three or four skills that seem would be most useful and productive to focus on at this time.

Exercise. For the three or four psychological skills that you have decided are most important for your child to develop, try to think of as many concrete positive examples of that skill as you can, and write them down. This is the answer to the question, "What could I envision my child doing if she were very accomplished in this skill?" For example, if the skill is fortitude, you might include such examples as not getting too upset when she can't visit a friend, not putting up a fuss after being told she can't have some candy, and saying "That's OK, don't worry about it" when someone forgets to do something she wanted done. Imagine little movies of skillful behavior, and jot down their plots. Compare your list with the sample list of concrete examples that are present in tables 2 and 3.

If you're successful in these two exercises, you will have a large list of positive things to watch for. And this is important. You want to be watching for a wide range of positive behavior from your child. You want to have enough examples in mind that you will see positive examples very often.

When you do the process of generating specific examples, you find that appropriate examples vary depending upon the child's age. The notion of what is skillful or desirable changes as the child gets older. That's why it's nice to see some other children your child's age, and particularly some rather happy and well-behaved ones, so that you can develop reasonable expectations of what the child should be able to do.

One of the most common sorts of target behaviors that parents think of is household chores. This is highly appropriate! Useful work in the house can exercise productivity, joyousness, kindness, fortitude, and other skills. Lots of useful work for the family is one of the best antidotes to the extremely common ailment of spoiled brathood. Useful work also helps children have a sense of their own worth – especially if they experience the genuine gratitude of family members for the help they give. I believe most children in current U.S. culture could stand lots more house work.

Having said this: if the child is acting up because of low skills of social initiations, social conversation, and conflict-resolution, then you shouldn't expect a cure from targeting his raking the leaves, washing the dishes, and taking out the trash. You want to look for opportunities to model, provide practice in, and reinforce the specific skills he needs to learn the most. This often means you've got to become a more subtle and refined observer of interactions. The positive examples may not come out and knock you between the eyes and say "notice me" the way they do when the child has washed the dishes and taken out the trash. The positive examples may consist of a positive, enthusiastic tone of voice where previously there was a grumpy one, or an appropriately disappointed response where previously there was an absolutely miserable one.

Compare the types of positive examples you generate with the examples listed in the following sections. These are appropriate for young children. Some of these same behaviors are appropriate for older children and even adults.

Specific Examples of Skills, in the Home

Kindness: Saying "Thanks for the supper" to his or her parent; picking up something his or her mother drops and giving it to her; saying "Good morning" in a cheerful tone to a family member; speaking gently to his or her pet and petting him nicely; saying "That's OK" in a gentle manner when a parent forgets to do something he wanted him or her to do; saying "That's interesting," when his or her sister mentions some of her thoughts; saying "Don't worry about it" in a gentle way when his or her brother seems to feel bad about a mistake he made in a game; giving his or her brother a piece of his or her dessert; saying "What have you been up to?" and listening nicely to his or her sister when she tells him about her day; offering to help a parent carry something; saying "You're welcome" in a gentle way when someone says "Thank you"; sharing a toy with another child; patting another child on the back, affectionately; offering to push someone in the swing; offering to take turns, and letting someone else take the first turn; going up to another child and socializing in a nice way; smiling at someone.

Compliance: Saying "OK" without arguing when he's told it's bedtime; keeping his voice low when his mother asks; playing inside on a rainy day for an hour and following the "no throwing the football inside" rule; leaving something alone that his or her parent asks him or her not to touch; playing gently with his or her friend after his or her mother tells them to stop wrestling, coming when his or her mother says "Come with me"; getting dressed without problems when asked to do so; brushing teeth when asked to do so; following the rule of staying at the table during a meal; turning the television off, or not turning it back on once it is turned off, as requested.

Fortitude: Saying “OK” in a nice way when he asks for some candy and is told he can’t have any; keeping cheerful when the rain spoils his or her plans to play outside with his friend; handling it without yelling when his or her brother breaks one of the things he owns; looking calmly for something he can’t find, without losing his temper; not yelling when he has to stop watching a television show to come to supper or to go out somewhere with his or her parent; being cool when his or her little brother grabs something out of his or her hand—getting it back, if he wants, but not yelling or hitting; being cheerful when he doesn’t get a present that he has asked for; being cheerful when he has to come inside...

Sustaining attention: Listening while someone reads to him or her, for a little longer than before; having a chat with one of his or her parents without having to run off to get into something else; playing with the same toys for a reasonably long time; paying attention to a play that someone puts on for him or her with toy people; telling a story, and staying on the topic for a reasonable time; working at a task longer than before.

Practicing Using Language: Listening while someone reads him or her a story, having a chat with someone; asking a good question about something he is curious about; telling about things he has seen and done; talking back and forth with someone; using a longer sentence than before; using some new words.

Enjoying Aloneness: Playing by himself when his or her parents pay attention to a sibling; paying attention to something else when a parent is on the phone; letting his or her parents talk to each other for a while without interrupting; watching what some peers are doing with each other, without butting in immediately; letting a sibling play with something, and get the parent’s attention, without taking that thing away; drawing a parent’s attention to a sibling in a favorable way; letting a parent read or write or lie down and rest without interrupting, being able to handle it if some peers do not want him or her participating with them in an activity.

Handling your own mistakes and failures: In a game, failing to make a goal or win a point etc. without getting too upset; losing a game without getting discouraged; failing to do something he tries, and then working harder rather than giving up; being corrected for something, and then making an effort to do better; remembering a previous time he made a mistake, and saying “This time I won’t (or will) do X, because I learned from the last time”; talking out loud to himself when he has made a mistake or failure, and saying "What can I do about this? I could do this, or that...";

Social initiations: Watching some peers do whatever they're doing before joining in with them; paying attention to what peers are paying attention to rather than drawing attention to himself; starting to socialize in any way that does not irritate the peer; saying "Hi" to a peer he knows; introducing himself to a peer he doesn't know; asking if some peers would like another participant in an activity; finding someone who is lonely, and talking or playing with that person; offering to share something he has with a peer, as a way of getting interaction started; asking a question about something a peer is doing, as a way of getting interaction started.

Letting the other do what she wants: In playing, letting the other play with a toy without taking it away from her; responding to the other's suggestion of "Let's do this" by saying "OK!"; responding to the other's question of "May I do this?" by saying "Sure!"; responding to the other's looking over her shoulder at something she is doing by tolerating it, rather than asking the other to go away; responding to a younger sister's tapping lightly on her knee by tolerating it rather than bossing her to quit doing it; in dramatic play, letting the other person direct the course of the plot for a while; in dramatic play, when the other person says something like "Pretend this is a lake" or "Pretend that this is a goat," going along with the suggestion; letting sister show off without telling her not to be such a show-off; letting a friend play with something that she is not particularly interested in playing with, without telling the friend to put it down and play with something else.

Courage: Trying an activity she's never tried before; getting to know people she's never met before; venturing the answer to a question raised in a group, when she's not very sure of the answer; doing something in the dark; doing something that is not dangerous that she was inhibited about doing at some point in the past.

Humor: Saying something funny, appreciating it and laughing when someone else says something funny; doing an imitation of something or someone that is funny but not derisive; imagining a silly situation and having fun with it; surprising someone with a trick that is not harmful.
******

Exercise: Choosing Your Own High Priority Skills

I'm going to be mentioning throughout this book that you will get lots better results if you can model for your child some reasonable and systematic efforts at making yourself a better person, rather than just trying to make him a better person. The skills axis is designed for adults as well as children. So I invite you to go back to it, and think about your own life. What skills are highest on your own priority list?

Having a child can be a great way to motivate yourself to “Be all that you can be.” If you use the techniques mentioned in this book upon yourself, in your child’s presence, your child will more likely learn the crucial skills of self-development, and self-starting.

Chapter 3: The Methods of Influence

Chapter Overview:

The two methods of influence that seem to come most automatically to most human beings are nagging and punishment: If the person isn't doing what you want, keep telling her to do it, with gradually increasing irritation, and finally punish her if she doesn't do it. The trouble is that when people are nagged and punished enough, they nag and punish other people back. Vicious cycles get started: people punish each other for punishing each other for punishing each other. A vast amount of human misery results from this cycle.

What are the other options for influencing someone? In this book I'll often refer to nine methods of influence. Objective-formation, or goal-setting, occurs when you help someone get motivated to achieve something. You help the other person to own the goal, so it's theirs, not just yours. Hierarchy means finding a series of baby steps for them to progress along, so that they don't have to risk failure by trying to change in one great leap. Attribution means talking about what the person is, what traits he has, in ways that can become self-fulfilling prophecy. Modeling is giving the person examples of patterns of thought, feeling, and behavior. Providing practice opportunities is offering situations where the person can rehearse patterns. Reinforcement and punishment are the consequences that come after a person's behavior, that make the behavior more or less likely to happen again. Instruction is providing information to the person—for example, helping the child learn the meaning of the word for a psychological competence. You'll be most effective with it when the person isn't feeling defensive and resistant. Stimulus situation control means you try to arrange the environment to bring out certain behavior. Monitoring is measuring and recording behavior, seeing what happens to it over time. Any of these influences can operate in a favorable or unfavorable direction; they can make skills better or worse.

I think you might benefit from thinking about the whole philosophy of influencing children. On the one hand, I urge parents to take as strong a role as they can, arranging influences—especially the nonpunitive ones—that foster the 62 competences. If you renounce this task, you leave your children's personality development in the hands of a rather toxic culture. On the other hand, you'll do well to leave well enough alone and avoid influencing the child in ways experienced as meddlesome and bossy: i.e. lots of commands to do specific things that should be left to the child to decide. The more you channel your energy into the more pleasant and welcomed methods of influence, the happier your job will be.

****

Once you decide on the skills in which you most want your child to grow, at this time, then how do you start fostering those skills? This is a special case of the more fundamental question, how does one person influence another person?

When frustrated parents come to see me, they have usually tried the two major methods of influence that seem to come naturally when a child is doing something undesirable. First, they give repeated instructions or commands to the child—"Quit doing that! Come over here. Don't do that again. Stop it." To the child these repeated instructions often feel like nagging.

The second method of influence is institutionalized in the connotation of the word "discipline." So many times, parents and teachers think about influencing children to act right as a "discipline" question, and the word discipline brings to mind one major method of influence: punishment.

Both of these automatic influence methods, nagging and punishment, are unpleasant both for the parent and for the child. In addition, the child tends to imitate nagging and punishing behaviors. The child soon starts punishing and nagging at the parent. So these methods can produce a vicious circle. The same vicious cycle, of course, can go on between adults. One person punishes and nags the second; this makes the second feel more like punishing and nagging the first; then the first feels even more like punishing and nagging the second. The same vicious cycles go on in the form of warfare between tribes or nations, where one group punishes the other for punishing them.

I would venture to speculate that the vicious cycles of hostility and punishment just named are responsible for at least seventy-five per cent of all human misery.

What is to be done? Fortunately, nagging and punishment represent only a small fraction of the total influence methods that are available. That's why the next task, before we get into specific programs, is for you to expand your consciousness about influence methods.

Here is a list of the nine methods of influence to keep in mind, otherwise known as the official Methods of Influence Axis:

Methods of Influence Axis

1. Objective formation or Goal-Setting
2. Hierarchy
3. Attribution
4. Modeling
5. Practice Opportunities
6. Reinforcement and Punishment
7. Instruction
8. Stimulus Situation Control
9. Monitoring

If we think of the first letter of each of these, they can be remembered by the mnemonic, "OH AM PRISM."

Let's go over what each of these means.

Objective Formation

Objective formation or goal-setting means setting your sights, or helping someone else set her sights, on achieving something, such as getting better at a skill. If the adult helps the child decide that peace and nonviolence are worthy goals, the child will probably be less likely to hit. If the child frequently hears people speak with admiration toward people who have made accomplishments in peaceful and nonviolent ways, the child will be much more likely to adopt this goal than if the admired characters are boxers and fighters. Sometimes objective formation in a young child can be fostered simply by a parent's repetitively stating his or her earnest hope for the child: "It's my earnest hope for you that throughout your life, you'll be able to make other people happy, and to be happy yourself while doing so." At other times asking the child whether he would like to be able to do something better tends to heighten the consciousness of the goal: "I'm curious: are you interested in learning to be braver when you try things like school work, and not be so afraid of failing?" If the child answers yes, and the adult says, "That's great! If you want to improve at something, you almost always can," then the adult is helping the child set appropriate goals.

Hierarchy

Hierarchy means setting up a series of baby steps that will lead to the goal, rather than trying to reach it in one great big jump. For example, a child who is shy and afraid to interact with people might have as his first baby step being able to play or stand and watch alongside another peer who is also playing, and only later actually interact with the peer. A child learning to read first practices enjoying hearing a book read to him. Later she gets interested in looking at the letters of an alphabet book, hearing the alphabet song, and playing games with guessing words from their separate sounds. These and many other small steps precede the moment when she actually looks at a word and calls it out.

Implicit in the idea of hierarchy is that you don't wait until the final goal is accomplished to celebrate. You find out what the child can presently do, and celebrate the best portion of that. You also celebrate every small movement upward.

Suppose a child experiences a frustration, and he folds his hands and stamps his foot and looks angry for a few seconds, muttering, "Oh, that's stupid!" Then he recovers composure and goes on. Is this an example of fortitude to be celebrated? It depends on where on the hierarchy the child's skills have progressed so far. If the last few times the child was in the same situation, he screamed at a hundred decibels, kicked people, broke things, and cried inconsolably, the sequence of behavior I mentioned is a real step up along the hierarchy of fortitude, and deserves to be celebrated.

Attribution

Attribution means that you talk about the person as though he has the potential to gain the skill, rather than talking about how unskillful he is as a person. If a parent says of a child, "He's getting to be a kinder and kinder person the bigger he gets," that's attributing the trait of kindness to the child; if the adult says, "He is just lazy," that's attributing the trait of laziness to the child. The child tends to believe those attributions and act in ways that make them come true.

When I was a young child, my father remarked to another adult, "He's getting to be such a big boy. He likes the types of vegetables that big people eat." After I heard that, I approached the next serving of turnip greens with real gusto. In retrospect, I realize that my father made his remark, knowing I would overhear, with the conscious purpose of influencing me. But what a pleasant way to be influenced that was. So much better than nagging—"Now eat those turnip greens; come on, one more bite," or threats of punishment—"If you don't eat your turnip greens you'll just have to sit here until you do."

Modeling

Modeling means that you show the child examples of how to do the skillful pattern. Modeling can take place in real life, as for example in the models parents give their children; it can also take place through fiction and fantasy, as in the examples that television characters give children for imitation, or the examples given in stories we read to our children, stories we tell about people we admire or dislike, and so forth.

When we see or hear models of thought, feeling, and behavior, we lay down in our memory banks patterns that we can then access when a decision point faces us. In some way we search through the patterns laid down in our memory bank, seeking one that will be most appropriate in the current situation. The more positive, adaptive, reasonable, psychologically skillful patterns are laid down in a child's memory bank, the more likely the search process will be to land on a response pattern that works well. This image, this idea, implies that a major task, if not THE major task, of adult society is to lay down in the memory banks of younger generations those patterns of thought, feeling, and behavior that will make them happy and productive.

Practice

Practice opportunities give the child the chance to try out and rehearse the skillful patterns. A child who is learning to share needs to play with someone else so that he can practice this skill. A child who is learning to talk needs lots of practice talking. But practice opportunities are helpful only if the child at least some of the time is practicing positive patterns. A person learning conflict resolution benefits from dealing with the conflicts of daily life if she is practicing positive patterns and is harmed if she is practicing only negative patterns. A child learning to socialize with friends benefits if he is practicing socializing well, and does not benefit if he is practicing socializing poorly.

The patterns of thought, feeling, and behavior that are laid down in the memory bank by modeling become more accessible, more likely to be chosen, the more they are practiced.

One of the most important ideas in this book is that fantasy rehearsal tends to make patterns more accessible just as does real life practice. Some early research on this topic involved ski racers. After skiing a course a few times, half the racers were asked to practice going down the hill in their imaginations, planning how they could best make each turn, creating a movie in their minds wherein they ski the hill as well as possible. The other half of the racers did some unrelated activity during the same time. When the race was performed, the racers who had rehearsed in fantasy did better, on the average, than those who had not. After this there have been numerous other studies concluding that rehearsal in fantasy "deepens the groove" for the pattern that is rehearsed.

The important thing to realize about fantasy rehearsals that every time a child makes a mental representation of a concrete pattern of thought, feeling, and behavior, the child is performing a fantasy rehearsal of it. This means that when the child narrates a past event, vividly imagines the event while someone else narrates it, acts out a behavior sequence with toy people, causes videogame characters to enact a behavior, sings a song about a behavior sequence, or simply sits and imagines the pattern, a fantasy rehearsal is taking place.

Thus adult society has a second major task: in addition to laying down as many positive patterns in children's memory banks as possible, we need to cause those patterns to run through the child's neuronal circuitry as often as possible. The more fun ways we can find to activate those positive patterns in the brain and cause them to be rehearsed, the better off children will be.

A special case of fantasy practice is called desensitization. In desensitization, you get over an unrealistic fear by fantasy practice, starting with easier situations and working your way up to the most difficult ones. Suppose someone fears starting to socialize with new people. The person constructs a list of situations and actions, and orders them from least scary to most scary. He then repeatedly imagines himself socializing skillfully in those situations, and he imagines a pleasant, reinforcing consequence. He is practicing socializing in an unfearful way, and the fear tends gradually to diminish. We can undo associations with negative feelings by repeatedly practicing a certain image in a safe and pleasant context. By this means people have gotten over fears of heights, of thunderstorms, of being in public places, and many others.

Sometimes undoing the connections between situations and negative emotions is good, and at other times, it can be very bad. For example, a young child seems to have a built-in empathic response of distress when seeing another person hurt and in distress. But by repeatedly being exposed to cartoons in which people are hurt with funny music in the background and no negative consequences occurring, the child gradually loses the tendency toward empathic distress over another's pain, and can even learn to laugh at other's misfortunes. The child has become desensitized to the image of people's being hurt.

Our society in general tends to act toward children as if the principles of modeling and fantasy practice were nonexistent. We nag at children not to hit one another and punish them (sometimes) when they do so, while at the same time inundating them with thousands of violent models on television and giving them thousands of opportunities for violent fantasy practice in videogames.

Reinforcement

Reinforcement means something similar to reward: reinforcement is something that happens after a behavior, that makes it more likely to happen again. Why did psychologists add the word reinforcement to the language, rather than just talking about rewards? One big reason is that you can intend for something to be a punishment, and a child can find it unpleasant, but it can still turn out to increase the frequency of behavior. For example, yelling at children when they misbehave often actually reinforces the misbehavior, rather than reducing its frequency.

If are all we think of when we hear the word "reinforcement" are prizes and outings purposely designed to be rewarding, we lose most of the power and subtlety of the concept. Any time you do anything that the child wants you to do, or that the child prefers to what was going on before, you are reinforcing the behavior that the child did just beforehand. Furthermore, any time you stop doing something that the child experiences as unwanted, you are reinforcing the behavior the child did just beforehand. This means that as long as you are with the child and your behavior is changing, you are frequently reinforcing the child.

For example, you are reading a book in a two-year-old child's presence, and the child is playing with some toy people. The child has a toy person hug another person, and say "Nice baby." You look up from your book and observe the play. If the child wanted your attention, (and it's a safe bet that he did, for most children) you have just reinforced the episode of prosocial fantasy practice in the child's dramatic play, even though you have not said a word or lifted a finger. Or for another example, you come home and hug your spouse, in the child's presence. The child screams jealously, and you immediately stop hugging your spouse and look at the child. You have just reinforced the screaming: the screaming was followed by the cessation of something the child didn't want (the hugging) and the instigation of something the child did want (the look in his direction).

Attention, interest, enthusiasm, and an adult's display of excitement or emotion are the most important reinforcers for young children.

In this book we will give much attention to another kind of reinforcement, callled internal reinforcement. When I do something smart or good and say to myself, "Hooray, I did a good job," I am delivering a reinforcement to myself. The goal of child-rearing and education is to help children learn to do smart and good things because they have an internal value system that recognizes good acts and feels pleasure in them.

In addition to direct reinforcement, "vicarious" reinforcement also exerts an effect. This means that people are influenced by the reinforcement they see other people getting as well as the reinforcement they get directly themselves. Suppose three preschool children are together, an adult asks them to sit down to eat, and one of them sits down. The adult says to the one who sat down, "Thanks for doing what I asked! That makes it so much more convenient for me!" The other two are probably receiving the information that compliance with the request is reinforceable by appreciation; in other words they get vicarious reinforcement that tends to lead them to comply also.

A behavior rapidly becomes carried out more often when it is reinforced on a "continuous schedule," i.e. every time it occurs. For example, every time a child says "Thank you," the parent looks at the child and says "You're welcome," in a pleasant tone. Habits get more staying power when the behavior is reinforced only intermittently. For example, suppose the first child while doing homework gets occasional approving attention from a parent; the second has a parent sit beside him and approve after every bit of work. If a day comes where the parent can not attend at all, the first child will probably be able to get more work done than the second, because the first has gotten used to a leaner schedule of reinforcement. Reinforcing behavior on a continuous schedule at the beginning and then gradually moving to a more intermittent schedule is often the best way to arrive most quickly at a strong habit.

Punishment is the other side of the coin from reinforcement. It is something that comes after a behavior that makes it less likely to happen again. If yelling at a child for whining really reduces the whining, then yelling is functioning as punishment; if yelling increases the whining, then the yelling is functioning as reinforcement and not punishment. If, on the other hand, looking and speaking to the child with a grave and serious demeanor decreases the behavior, that is functioning as punishment.

To emphasize: we do things that we predict will be reinforcing or punishing; we find out whether those acts are reinforcing or punishing only after observing for some time whether the frequency of the behavior increases or decreases.

We will later spend time talking about time out, reprimands, natural consequences, and other specific methods of punishment. While getting into mind the basic principles, however, there are two very important ones to remember.

The first one is the reason for relying as much as possible on the other influence methods, and as little as possible on punishment: it is difficult to punish without simultaneously modeling the act of doing something aversive to someone. For example, if the adult slaps the child for a misbehavior, the adult may be punishing the misbehavior, but the adult is also modeling for the child how to slap. Thus in using punishment we are usually sending a mixture of punishment and modeling influences, and hoping the punishment effect predominates over the modeling effect.

The second principle in the use of punishment is that the consequence that occurs immediately after the behavior in question is for young children most important. Researchers sometimes speak of the "time gradient of reinforcement and punishment;" they mean that the longer after a behavior a consequence occurs, the less effect it has on the behavior. For example, a child hits, and the parent sends the child to a "time out" room. But suppose that in the couple of minutes after the hitting, the parent is struggling with the child, arguing, having a heated discussion, and pleading with the child, before the child finally goes to time out for two more minutes. The immediate consequence for the hitting was not the time out, but the power struggle. If the child finds that struggle reinforcing, the rate of hitting may actually go up. The time out itself came too long after the hitting to do any good.

However, as children get older, they are more able to be influenced by delayed reinforcement and punishment. It is much better to give a delayed punishment that parents agree upon, than to try to give an immediate punishment that sparks a disagreement between the two parents.

As much as I emphasize the use of influence methods other than punishment, there are some behaviors that parents are obligated to punish in some way, each time they occur. Physical violence is one of them, and direct disobedience of a clear and reasonable command by a parent is another.

Instruction

Instruction means teaching or telling the child in a straightforward way what to do or how to do it. As the child gets older, this method becomes more and more useful. There are lots of teaching tools and teaching games that we will speak of later on. The letter I can also stand for Indoctrination, which is like instruction but more unabashedly purports to teach values to children. I'll speak more later about how I can be so unabashed about this, and how to do it.

What is a central principle about instruction? One is that it's much more effective when the instructed person is not feeling criticized, threatened, or defensive, but interested and receptive to the instruction. Instruction given immediately after the child has done something undesirable is usually less effective than instruction given either at a routine, neutral time, or immediately after a positive behavior of the child.

For example: a grade school aged child has been putting off doing her homework. The parent gives the child a lecture, making the points that working for delayed gratification is something very important in life, that often we have to do what isn't most pleasant at the time, and doing our work first and playing second makes things more pleasant in the long run; that way we can enjoy the playing much more, knowing that the work is done. If the child is feeling defensive, the child's tendency will be to argue back, and to think, if not say, that she will do it eventually, that there were good reasons to put it off, and that the parent should lay off.

On the other hand, suppose that the parent saves the lecture and watches for a day when the child does the homework first thing upon getting home. As soon as the child finishes, the parent comes beaming into the child's room, and gives the same lecture, but this time uses the child's behavior as a positive example of the lesson rather than an example that the lesson is meant to counter. It is much more likely that the child will be receptive to the lesson in this case.

Or, suppose the parent and child have a special time each day for conversation and instruction. The parent brings up a couple of examples from his own life, one in which he put something off, and another in which he worked hard first and rewarded himself with play, and then delivers the same lecture. Again, the child is not likely to feel threatened and defensive, because the child is not being criticized by the instruction.

There's a second reason for timing instruction so as to come in response to positive or neutral behavior rather than negative: the attention the child gets during the instruction may be reinforcing.

Explaining the reasons for rules is a rudimentary form of instruction. When a child is prohibited from doing something, it's important that the child understand why it is in his and other people's best interest not to do that thing, and what ethical issues are involved.

The goal of instruction is that the child will have enough information to become internally motivated, to want to do what is best, and to know how to do it expertly. In today's world I fear that we are doing too much extrinsic rewarding and punishing of children and too little instruction. For example, there is much to know about the art of fortitude, how to do it well: how to relax, how to talk to oneself in a way that's conducive to success. Most of the time, however, children are just punished for frustration intolerance, without being taught how to handle frustration well. For another example, I have seen many children who have been punished for poor academic performance when they needed more patient additional instruction and practice instead.

Stimulus Control

Stimulus control means arranging the things in the environment, the stimuli, so that they elicit desirable behavior. If the child is overeating, it would not be a good use of stimulus situation control to have bowls of potato chips placed on numerous tables in the house. If an adult is trying to stop drinking alcohol, a wise use of stimulus situation control is to stay out of bars. If a child has trouble trusting and depending, the stimulus situation of spending a school day with one trustworthy and dependable teacher is probably much better for the child than the situation of spending it shuttling between 5 equally trustworthy and dependable teachers. If the child has trouble paying attention, a good use of stimulus situation control might be to remove all distracting things from the child's reach except the one thing you want him to pay attention to. If the child is argumentative and defiant, reducing unnecessary commands and directives tends to reduce the stimulus that prompts oppositional behavior.

A special case of stimulus control may be referred to as eliminating the competition for a desirable activity. Suppose that you would like for the child to eat her broccoli and peas. Will the child be likely to eat them if on the same plate beside her broccoli and peas there are ice cream and cookies and brownies? People tend to choose among the available alternatives, and pick the one that is most attractive and pleasurable. Or suppose that you would like the child to drift off to sleep at 8:30, but as a competing stimulus there is an exciting television show that can be watched from the child's bed. Limiting the competition for the child's attention, so that "drifting into dreamland" doesn't have such a fierce competitor is usually necessary if the child is to go to sleep at the desired time. Not permitting a television set in a child's bedroom is a good example of stimulus control. If you want the child to take an interest in mind-exercising games, you may have to eliminate some of the competition from fast action video games, by making them unavailable. If you want the child to have conversations with family members, you may have to eliminate some of the competition from the electronic media. If the child is picky and bossy about wanting to be with one parent and rejecting the other, when both parents are kind and positive with the child, the eliminating the competition strategy consists in providing periods of time when one parent only is available to pay attention to the child and the child can either take it or leave it. If the child is influenced by a peer group to use drugs, an example of this strategy is to change the child's school environment such that drug-using peers are unavailable, or available in greatly reduced numbers. Stimulus control that eliminates the elicitors of the less preferred behaviors is often a very potent strategy.

Monitoring

Monitoring means that you keep up with how well the person is doing over time, measuring the results. Suppose a child is having trouble sleeping in his own bed through the night, and after a certain program is started, he gets out of bed 60 times one night, and 15 times the next night. That represents a big improvement, one worth celebrating. But the parent who experiences the 15 times out of bed may not experience it as an improvement unless he or she is actually counting and keeping track. Monitoring allows us to use reinforcement and recounting of positive examples for fantasy practice; without careful monitoring we would not be able to use these other methods of influence. Perhaps for this reason, and perhaps for others, "That which gets measured tends to get improved," with children as well as in the workplace.

Thus ends our examination of the methods of influence axis. With the concepts in the skills axis and the methods of influence axis, we have nearly all the building blocks we need to help a child become psychologically healthy. Most of the rest of this book will provide specific elaborations of how to use various methods of influence to promote various skills.

Before leaving the methods of influence chapter, however, let's talk some about the whole idea of influencing children. I want to advance two ideas that may seem to be contradictory.

First, I recommend not being afraid to influence your child, and to control the influences upon your child as carefully as possible, especially during the early years when it is more possible to do so. You will do well to preempt the influences widely available in a culture that is in many ways generally toxic to children's development, (that is, that of the United States and many other industrialized countries in the early 21st century) and to find influences that will be positive ones.

Second, I recommend the philosophy that freedom is good for children and for all people, and that it is good to adhere to the rule of not impinging upon another person's freedom without a good reason to do so.

Perhaps you know parents who might say, "I don't want to influence my children. I want them to make their own decisions." On the other hand, you may know other parents, or perhaps even the same ones, who try to make sure that the children eat all their green peas rather than leaving a few on the plate, or that their adolescents go to Princeton rather than Amherst, or that they go into neurology instead of family practice. Let's think some about the whole notion of influencing children.

I want to first make a large pitch for working very hard to influence children, especially when they are very young. It's impossible for a child to grow up without being influenced by someone or something. In the early years the child goes from having a very narrow social repertoire of social interactions, to having a very complex set of habits of dealing with people, thinking about himself or herself, and responding emotionally to what is going on. Those habits don't just come out of nowhere. Many of them are directly incorporated from the models that the child gets. If the parent doesn't consciously select and create those models so as to be as favorable as possible, the child will still get models from somewhere. It's impossible for a child not to get models! It's also impossible for a child not to get some pattern of reinforcers and punishments. At any moment that you interact with a child, you are acting in a way that is pleasant, unpleasant, or neutral. The child is continually being either reinforced, punished, or not reinforced for her actions. This is influence. There's no way of escaping it.

We live in a culture where the media, the peer culture, teachers, and other influences command a substantial fraction of the child's influence-moments, and the parent can never take control of or responsibility for all the influence a child receives. But in the early years, when there is much more opportunity to control those influences, the only ethical choice is to maximize their benefit to the child.

Each person chooses his own values. But all of us can only make choices based on the information we have to apply to that choice. For many children, recommendations about what is valuable and desirable in life come many times more frequently from television commercials than from parents or any other source of a mature value system. In such a case, can it be any surprise when the child decides that wearing the "cool" type of shoes to school is much more important than kindness to children who can't afford the right shoes?

Having made this strong pitch for influencing children with all the energy we can muster, to counter a very bad culture, I want to also make a pitch for giving children freedom to choose their own behaviors unless there is a good reason not to, starting from an early age and increasing as children get older. It is oppressive and rebellion-inducing to live with someone who tries to make choices that should be your own. If you are feeling stuffed and satiated, it feels bad to have someone command you to eat more. If you are still cold and want to wear your coat inside a few minutes while you are warming up, it feels bad to have someone command you to take your coat off. If you are extremely restless and want to jiggle your foot while you are making a valiant effort to keep seated, it feels bad to have someone command you to hold your foot still. When we talk about influencing children, the realm of commanding them to do whatever specific individual behavior we feel like their doing at the time is a totally different realm from forming long-term strategies of increasing their psychological skills as much as possible. If we separate out these two types of influence, we will be able to think more clearly what what sorts of control and influence of children we like and don't like.

So much for philosophy and basic concepts, for the moment. The next chapter is designed to start describing an extremely practical method of fostering your child's growth in high-priority skills.

Chapter 4: Rejoicing Over Positive Examples

Chapter Overview:

If you want to build your child's competences, get into habits of thought that lead you to feel enthusiasm and joy when you see your child doing positive examples of those competences. Watch carefully for those examples. When you see them, give enthustic attention and interest. Giving enthusiastic attention is different from praising. In praising, you evaluate a performance. When you give enthusiastic attention, you join the child in paying attention to whatever she is paying attention to, with an upbeat and approving tone of voice. With enthusiastic attention, you don't interrupt the child's attention to what she is doing. The child can come to resent too much praise; it's hard to resent too much enthusiastic attention. Especially for young children, how your voice sounds and what your face looks like are at least as important as what your words are. If you rehearse communicating your pleasure and enthusiasm, you increase your power to bring out the positive in your child.

Here's another way to help your child repeat and enlarge on the positive examples you see her do. You not only respond to them at the moment; you memorialize them and replay them. If you tell someone else about them in the child's presence, you communicate your interest in them. Also you can start a ritual of a "nightly review" of the positive patterns: you tell the child each night about smart or good things he did that day. In this ritual you run the positive examples through the the child's brain circuitry a few more times; this helps the child make the positive examples habit. For older children, this ritual can be converted into a family nightly review. Here everyone in the family celebrates their own and each other's positive behaviors; they also imagine positive behaviors to replace any mistakes they made. If you can keep a "positive behavior diary" in writing, you're using a powerful way to memorialize positive patterns. People's memories of past positive patterns are their most valuable resource in coming up with good responses to future situations.

It's great if you pull out your joyousness and enthusiastic attention as responses to the child's positive examples. But don't wait for the child to do something good before showing the child how to be enthusiastic. When you generate an upbeat spirit, you model it for the child. You also provide a powerful stimulus to bring out positive talk and behavior from the child. Furthermore, your joyous spirit provides evidence that you know something about how to live well, that your value system is "onto something good." It's healthy for your children to know that they don't control your own joy in living—that you get it from a more permanent source.

****

A previous chapter urged you to decide upon some high priority psychological skills to target with your child; the immediately previous chapter listed ways of influencing your child toward more competence in those skills. This chapter will give some very specific ways of responding to your child's positive examples to bring out more positive behavior from your child.

How It Works: The Notion of an Interpersonal Environment

At one point in time the thinking of the experts about a program such as this was fairly simple-minded. People do more often the things they're reinforced for. Give them reinforcers after they do good behaviors, and you'll get more good behaviors out of them.

That notion is still true, and it is very powerful. But the real world is more complex than that. Giving certain types of reinforcers for certain behaviors feels like bribery to both the giver and the receiver. On the other hand, responding with enthusiastic interest, approval and excitement probably works by more influence methods than just reinforcement. Stimulus control and modeling also operate, and these combined with reinforcement go together to create an intangible but very important something I call the "emotional climate" or "interpersonal environment."

By these phrases I refer to how things feel between people, what the prevailing mood is, what sort of tones people speak to each other with, how they look at each other, whether they are in a mood to be nice or to be hostile.

By the things you say in the presence of your children, you contribute to the interpersonal environment. This very intangible environment is a major cause of very tangible physical events: whether people hit each other, break things, run away from home, get admitted to psychiatric hospitals, kill each other, commit suicide, get divorced, get psychosomatic illnesses, do productive work, succeed in school, sleep well, stay friendly, or succeed economically. Sometimes words are "magic." By saying the magic positive words, in the magic positive tones, and by avoiding the words that cast the negative spell, you can make very tangible actions turn out positive.

In thinking about the interpersonal environment, we avoid the "rat and pigeon" model of reinforcement and punishment in thinking about why people do what they do. We take into account that a "reinforcer" or a "punishment" doesn't just strengthen or weaken a given behavior; it also does something to the quality of the relationship between the people involved; it also creates a memory of an emotional tone that predisposes people to kind or hostile acts.

In the next few chapters I will talk about factors that set the emotional tone of a family. Let's list them here:

Seven Factors That Affect the Emotional Climate

1. Stability of time together.

Frequency of time spent together, quantity of time spent, regularity, dependability of time spent.

2. The degree of challenge of the activity.

Is what people are trying to do together too hard, too easy, or just right? The difficulty can be assessed regarding many skill areas: intellectual abilities, physical stamina or coordination, patience, self-disclosure, handling losing, accepting help, social skills, and others. If the task or activity generates lots of negative affect, or passivity, or avoidance behaviors, a participant may need to drop back on the hierarchy of difficulty.

3. Approval versus disapproval.

Of all the utterances that you make, what fraction are approving, and what fraction are disapproving?

4. Directiveness versus responsiveness.

Of all the utterances that you make, what fraction are directive and what fraction are responsive? (Directive means trying to get the person to do something other than what he or she is already doing, OR get the person to pay attention to something other than what she is already paying attention to. Responsive means making a response to what the person is already attending to, without trying to change the person's behavior or focus of attention.)

Examples of directive utterances are commands, suggestions, criticisms, new topic questions, and new topic statements.

Examples of responsive utterances are facilitations, tracking and describing, reflections, follow-up questions, and follow-up statements.

5. Differential Reinforcement.

5.1 Differential attention: How often do you turn your attention toward positive behavior and away from negative behavior? How often do you turn your attention toward negative behavior and away from positive behavior?

5.2 Differential excitement: How often do you show high excitement in response to positive behavior, and low excitement in response to negative behavior? How often do you show high excitement in response to negative behavior, and low excitement in response to positive behavior?

5.3 Differential request-granting: How often do you grant requests that are reasonable and politely stated, and refuse requests that are unreasonable or impolitely state? How often do you use the opposite pattern?

6. Positive models versus negative models.

How many positive models do you expose the person to, and how positive are they? How few negative models do you expose the person to, and how negative are they?

7. Problem solving techniques.

When two people have a problem to solve, do they state it in non-blaming terms? Does each listen empathically to the other's statement of the problem? Do they generate options, and think rationally about the pros and cons of options? Do they avoid raising their voices, interrupting, and insulting, and do they come to a decision together about something to try?

This chapter will deal mainly with ways of responding with approval, attention, and excitement to positive examples.

Prescription for Immediate Response

Here's a general rule, with some qualifications we'll speak of later. Watch and listen to your child, and often give enthusiastic attention when you see positive examples of psychological skills.

Using this principle often requires much more of a revision in thinking than people realize. It requires, first of all, that they move from a short-term focus to a long-term focus. If I am nagging at the child to do something, or threatening the child, I usually define "success" when the child does what I want immediately after I nag or threaten. But when I see a positive example and give enthusiastic attention, the chances are that I won't see the behavior repeated immediately. I may not even see any sign from the child that he enjoyed my enthusiastic attention. I'll have to be patient, and keep using enthusiastic attention for several days, and see if the rate of the positive examples goes up over several days. In our instant-gratification world, this shift in thinking is often very difficult.

Now let's think of some of the qualifications on the rule of giving enthusiastic attention when you see positive examples.

Enthusiastic Attention Doesn't Necessarily Equal Praise

You'll notice that I said "enthusiastic attention" rather than "praise." There's a difference: enthusiastic attention does not necessarily imply an "evaluation" of a "performance."

Suppose Mary is building something with a construction toy, enacting skills of imagination and sustaining attention and thinking before acting.

Here's a way of responding with praise:

"Mary, what a good job you're doing of building that. It really looks great! You're so imaginative!"

Here's a way of responding with enthusiastic attention without praise:

(Parent kneels down and studies what Mary is doing, with a very interested look. Mary says, "This is the part of the space station that picks up the radar signals.") The parent says, "I see! They face in different directions, so they can get them no matter where they come from, huh?"

Suppose I see my son Johnny enact the skill of expressing appreciation to my daughter Mary. Mary has built her something with a construction toy, and Johnny says, in an approving tone, "Wow, Mary, did you build that whole thing! That must have taken you a long time!"

Here's a way of responding to that with praise to Johnny:

"Hey Johnny! I like your saying nice things like that to your sister!"

Here, on the other hand, is enthusiastic attention without praise:

(Parent kneels down beside Johnny and pats him on the back, looks at what Mary has made, and then looks at Johnny.) "I think you're right, Johnny! I couldn't agree with you more!"

Or suppose Johnny enacts the skill of sustaining attention, by studiously pouring over a book for longer than he has before. Here's a way of responding with praise:

"Wow, Johnny, it's great that you've been studying that book for such a long time—you're getting more skilled in paying attention."

Here, on the other hand, is enthusiastic attention without praise:

Parent looks at the book, smiles at Johnny. When Johnny looks up, parent says, "You've been reading that for a long time! It must be interesting!"

For another example: The parent is lying on the floor with Johnny and Mary and the three of them are doing dramatic play. Mary's character says to Johnny's character, "Have you lost your magic bag? I'll help you look for it."

Here's an example of responding with praise:

"Wow, Mary, your character did something nice by offering to help. I sure like to see that."

Here's an example of enthusiastic attention without praise:

"You're going to look for the magic bag too, huh? Maybe I'll look too, and maybe one of us can help that man!"

Praise often interrupts the sequence of interactions somewhat to make an evaluative statement, and enthusiastic attention does not interrupt things as much. In enthusiastic attention, any evaluation is only given implicitly in the positive tone of voice you use.

Why do I make this distinction? Because it's possible to have too much evaluation going on, even if that evaluation is positive, in the form of praise; but it's almost impossible to have too much enthusiastic attention going on. Some children reject praise, as though they don't want to be evaluated one way or the other. Sometimes you don't want to hear that you did a good performance or a bad performance, you just want to be off the stage altogether. You may reject the attempt of the other person to control your behavior through praise, and you may resent the reminder that someone else older and wiser knows what the standard of good and bad quality is. Evaluative praise also can bring on problems of grade inflation: if some scribbles are the greatest work of art a parent has ever seen, where does the child go from there? None of these problems come from enthusiastic attention that responds simultaneously to the child and to what the child is already interested in.

Having said this, let me backtrack and say that the overuse of praise is a problem I seldom see. Praise is good, not bad. Overtly evaluative comments have a very important place in the life of a child. Comments that evaluate behavior are part of how children learn a value system. But it is possible to overdo praise. You want praise to be special and not something that is done over and over so many times that it loses its thrill. Enthusiastic attention, with an approving tone of voice, on the other hand, is something a parent can deliver literally hundreds of times per hour, thousands of times per year, without any negative effects. It can thus unobtrusively reinforce the tiny, positive-side-of-neutral positive acts that are the real building blocks in the child's growth in psychological skills.

Sometimes curiosity is another good way to give enthusiastic attention. "What you just did was very interesting. How did you figure out how to do that?" or "Where did you learn to do that?" Sometimes another brand of enthusiastic attention is just to classify it, with an approving tone of voice: for example, "Hey, what you just did is an example of fortitude!"

Finding Ways to Take Pleasure in the Child

Imagine that you have just given a speech. One person pays you the following compliment: "You really made good use of gestures! Your delivery was very polished! What you said was well organized!" A second person pays you a different compliment: "I'm really glad I came to hear you! I'm going to be able to use what you said, to help people! I'm excited about trying it!" What is the difference between these two? The first is carrying out the role of an evaluator, a judge, giving you a high rating on a performance. The second is in the role of a human being who was affected by what you did, giving you feedback on how your actions affected his emotions. The second person is saying, "You produced positive emotion in me."

The second type of compliment seems to be more universally welcomed, by children as well as adults. The first type presupposes that the performer wants to be evaluated by the evaluatee. The second type only presupposes that one person has interest in what effect his action had on someone else.

So many "behavioral" programs of reinforcement prescribe giving positive responses for good behavior, but overlook one crucial fact: for the reinforcement of the adult to be really meaningful, the adult must actually feel positive emotion. If a parent says, "Oh, thanks, that really makes me feel good," but looks and sounds depressed and frustrated, the utterance will probably not have much effect on the child. That parent will be likely to say, "Yes, I praise and give attention, but it doesn't have any effect." On the other hand, if the parent really gets a very large kick out of what the child did, the tones and looks of approval and excitement are easy to come by.

If you agree with this, then the task of "reinforcing" positive examples is much more complicated than simply mouthing words of pleasure and interest. It may entail rearranging your own pleasure mechanisms, so that you feel pleasure in things you didn't feel pleasure from before!

How, does an adult "psych up" to take pleasure in a child's positive behavior examples? Here are some of the thought patterns I find myself using to help myself feel this pleasure. I look for any ways that the child's positive behavior actually made me better off, made my life better or more interesting, and consciously celebrate those. I contemplate how many years children have ahead of them to use the skills they are learning, and I think about what an accomplishment it will be if I can impart a skill that the child will use well for the rest of his life. I contemplate the violence and hostility that prevails in the world, and think about how good it will be if the skills of be if the skills of kindness are imparted to even one child. I think about how the emotions of childhood experiences tend to get called back by reminders from events throughout the rest of life, and thus reason that if I can have a child experience some very pleasurable productive time, I am seeding memories that will be resources helping the child to feel good throughout a lifetime. I remember with pleasure some of the adults who were kind to me and had fun with me in my childhood, and I remember the feelings I had then; this makes me more sensitive to feeling good about happy productive things the children do. When I am with groups of children, I try not to assume that the children will want to do what I want them to do, and whenever a child actually helps me by doing a task for me or by cooperating with my directions, I feel a combination of relief and gratitude. I think about some of the times in childhood when I had childishly happy times, and I hope to be able to feel some of that child-level pleasure as well as the parental-level pleasure from being proud of the children's accomplishments. I think, for a particular child, about what the child's previous habit was, and I celebrate in my mind if the child rises above the previous habit to a new level of skill.

All this doesn't mean that the adult has to be at the pinnacle of happiness before encountering a child. However, if the adult is able to let the children lift his or her spirits at least temporarily and is able to have fun with the child, the activities described here will be many times more effective.

To summarize this point: look for the ways of thinking about things that will help you to feel pleasure in things the child does. If the child is behaving badly, it is harder to take pleasure in the child. It becomes much easier as some of the techniques described here start to take hold. If it is hard for you at this particular moment to take pleasure in the child very often, don't get too discouraged. But please keep persisting until you are able to honestly say that you take a great deal of satisfaction from things the child does, very often.

The Key Role of Excitement and Emotion

The key dimension of level of energy and excitement is contained in the word enthusiasm. This dimension does not refer to how you choose your words when you speak to your child. Emotion and excitement mainly get conveyed through tone of voice and movement and facial expression. How do we tell whether someone is excited? Unexcited people

talk more slowly
move more slowly
talk in a deeper voice
have a smaller range of pitches in the utterance
talk quietly

And excited people do just the opposite: they

talk more quickly
move more quickly
talk in a higher voice
have a larger range of pitches in the utterance
talk more loudly

The tones of your voice and the looks on your face are nonverbal communication. When it comes to reinforcing a child's behavior, usually the nonverbal communication is more important than the words you say. If you speak to the child with a tone of real enthusiasm and a facial expression of joy, whatever you say will be much more rewarding.

Tones of voice are especially important with young children. Here's a way of understanding why this may be true. If you are a three year old child, you are only part way into the task of learning what words mean. But almost since your moment of birth, you have been able to respond emotionally to smiles and frowns and angry or happy tones of voice. The response to nonverbal language, the language that is the same over all cultures, is hard-wired, built into your brain, whereas the language of your culture is only learned. Doesn't it seem logical that you might respond more strongly to the nonverbal communication than the actual meanings of the words?

Please continue to imagine yourself as a 3 year old child, and imagine yourself doing something smart or good. Imagine someone saying to you with an expressionless face, in a monotone voice, "What you just did was the best thing I've ever seen." Does that hit your pleasure centers?

Now imagine yourself doing the same something smart or good, and imagine someone smiling, and in a very animated voice saying, "Wow! Hey hey! Look at that!"

The monotone response above had lots of semantic meaning, and the animated response conveyed almost no semantic meaning. But the nonverbal information would make the second response much more reinforcing for almost all children. For some reason, children usually get reinforced by displays of energy from the adults who take care of them.

Rehearsing Giving Enthusiastic Attention to the Examples You Have Generated

Noticing the positive examples of high-priority skills and responding with enthusiastic attention, in a way that feels natural and doesn't interrupt things, may sound easy; you may think you're already doing it. You can get better at it than you are now! I haven't achieved perfection in this difficult art, and I have yet to see anyone else do so either.

One of the problems is that some of the positive examples are quiet and do not attract attention, whereas some of the negative examples are loud and attention-grabbing. A child asks for candy at a grocery store counter and is told no. If the child throws a major tantrum, the parent is likely to notice; if the child says to himself, "I can take it," and does not otherwise respond, the parent is likely not to notice or react in any way. How can the parent prime himself to notice the quieter positive things?

A very important task for the parent is to get clearly into mind the good behaviors that you are wanting to see more often from your child, and mentally to rehearse giving approval and attention to these behaviors. In other words, use fantasy rehearsal to improve your own skill of recognizing the positive examples in the child. To do so, do the following exercise.

Exercise: Rehearsing Giving Enthusiastic Attention

To practice giving enthusiastic attention, look again at the list of "positive examples of skills" that you made for your child, the examples you'd like to see more of. If you haven't made your list yet, you can use the lists in Tables 2 and 3 of Chapter 2. Look at each behavior listed, and imagine that you just saw or heard your child doing this example. Then actually say out loud something that constitutes enthusiastic attention, just as you would say it to the child. Practice saying things like this:

You're sticking on that for a long time! How's it coming?

Thanks, that's a big help to me!

You wanted to keep watching television, and you didn't get to, but you stayed cool. That was fortitude!
When you started talking with that boy, he seemed to feel good. Did you figure out that he wanted someone to talk to?
You're thinking of several options, aren't you?
I surely do like it when you say OK like that.

Exercise: Practicing Approving with Different Degrees of Energy

Keep in mind the following three gradations of emotional tone in the voice:
No excitement
Small excitement
Large excitement

And work with the following list of things one might say:
Good for you.
Look what you've done.
You helped me out.
Thank you for doing that.
That's interesting.
You finished it.
We're getting it done.

The exercise is to practice saying these things with each of the three gradations of tone, until you are sure that your tone of voice has the full range and that you are thoroughly familiar with what all parts of the range sound like.

You can do the second part of the exercise with a partner. Pick one of the three tones to use, and say one of the phrases. Let your partner guess what degree of excitement you were trying to portray, and see whether your partner guesses correctly. Use the list of positive examples in tables 2 and 3 in chapter 2, or the list of positive examples you've made for your child, and imagine responses to these positive examples, in addition to practicing with the above phrases.

Is the idea to put large excitement into all the utterances that you make to the child? No. If you did that, you would sound very strange and phony, and probably overload the child. Is the idea to make a calculation of how good the child's behavior is, and then as an accomplished actor or actress, fake the emotion of excitement and enthusiasm? No again. The idea is to have your tone of voice responsive to the way you feel, so that you can communicate your feelings to the child, and also to rig up your own pleasure centers so that you really feel excited about the good things the child does, in proportion to how good they are. A little acting practice, and trying on the tones of voice of large and small excitement, will only aid you in adjusting your own pleasure mechanisms. You rig up your ways of thinking so that when you come out with tones of approval, you don't feel like a phony!

Let's take stock. So far we've done lots of thinking to define the highest priority skills, and we've generated lots of positive examples of each of them. We've practiced watching like a hawk for the positive examples, and upon seeing them, giving enthusiastic attention. We've practiced making the tone of voice very animated and excited when giving such attention. If you do all these things, you will influence your child very positively by doing so. Now, there are three more elements to the plan we outline in this chapter: telling someone else about the good examples, the nightly review, and the positive behavior diary.

Telling Someone Else About the Good Examples

If there are people other than yourself—your spouse, your parents, your friends—who care about your child's development, they will naturally want to hear about the positive examples of your child's growth in psychological skills. Telling them about these examples purely for their own pleasure is a good idea. But there's another benefit for the child. Have you ever heard people talking about you "behind your back," in a positive way? It almost never happens to me, but I if it ever does, it feels great. Plus, it reminds me of whatever positive thing I did, and probably makes me more likely to do it again. In view of the fact that hearing oneself talked about is often a powerful reinforcer of behavior, it makes sense to take opportunities to celebrate your children's positive behaviors with other people.

Sometimes celebrating is not the natural thing to do. Imagine that you are spending the afternoon with little Johnny, and Johnny has said "Thank you," in a nice tone when you got him something to eat. He has also shared a toy airplane with his brother, very cooperatively. He has also done a good example of fortitude: he was playing another fun game with his brother, and he acted very nice when you had to interrupt the game to take them somewhere. But also, during this day, Johnny had a tantrum when you told him he couldn't watch a TV show, and he flailed around and screamed so loudly that you were afraid the neighbors would call the police.

Now your spouse comes in, and says, "How was the afternoon?" Johnny is toddling around in hearing distance. What do you say? Do the positive things get reported, or forgotten? Most people would probably go right into, "I was afraid the police were going to come today!"

I'm suggesting that you do what is for many people the unnatural thing, and to say, "The afternoon had its ups and downs, but some really good things happened. Some of the ones I liked were that Johnny said 'Thank you' when I got him a sandwich, and he let his brother play with the toy airplane he likes so much..."

Notice that we're talking about specific, concrete positive examples, not abstract descriptions: we want to be low on the abstraction ladder. Here's another example: We prefer statements like, "Johnny's brother accidentally knocked his blocks over, and Johnny said, 'Don't worry about it. I know you didn't do it on purpose.'" We get much less mileage out of statements like "Johnny was very good while playing with his brother."

If you want to recount the negative examples to someone else in great detail, I recommend doing so in private, especially with young children. If you feel that the child's behavior was so bad that it would be misleading simply to recount the positive examples, recount the negative using language high on the abstraction ladder, and recount the positive with language low on the abstraction ladder. For example: "This really wasn't a good day. It was very unpleasant to be with Johnny. Nonetheless, there were a few good things: he did say to me, 'May I help you put these toys away,' and then put a whole bunch of poker chips and dice into the box..."

The Nightly Review

Here's what's meant by the nightly review. Let's start by talking about the simplest technique, namely that for preschool aged children. Just before the child goes to bed, remind the child about the positive examples of the high-priority skills you saw and heard the child do today. Say something like, "Before you go to bed, let's remember some things you did today. I remember one thing, you obeyed me really well when I asked you to put your hat and coat on, and you said, 'OK daddy!' Also I sure liked hearing you say 'thank you' so politely when I got your sandwich for you." If the child remembers other good things he did and tells you about them, so much the better. Or, if the child wants to reciprocate by telling you about smart or good things you did, that's great too. If you want to volunteer a positive example you did, and tell the child about it, that's great too. Don't try to pull memories of positive examples out of the child if they don't flow spontaneously.

What if the child seems to take no interest? You don't let that stop you! Instead, you simply make the nightly review very, very short. As in the following: "Well I guess it's about time for lights out. By the way, I really liked it today when you said to your brother, 'Hey, nice drawing!' Well, good night."

I timed myself, and the nightly review portion of that utterance took a little under 10 seconds. Even if the child takes no interest at all, nothing is lost. But as the nightly review gets to be a regular pattern, the child almost always will come to take an interest in it. The main point is this: the parent does not need the child's permission or cooperation in order to do the nightly review. The parent simply does it, and if the child takes an interest, the parent responds with enthusiasm. If the child does not take an interest, the parent simply moves on.

Now suppose someone sits down by the child and says, "Well, you did put your coat on, but I sure didn't like how you picked over your food at supper. And why didn't you come inside when I called you?" That's not the nightly review. Especially with young children, it's not a good idea to keep reminding your child over and over about the bad things he did. Having him go over the undesirable things in his mind is not good because each time he goes over them, in a sense he's practicing doing it again. You want him to be thinking over and over again about good things to do, not the bad things.

So one purpose of the nightly review is to help the child do a "fantasy rehearsal" of the positive behaviors the child did earlier. The nightly review may exert its influence more by fantasy rehearsal and reinforcement for that rehearsal, than by reinforcing the original behavior. For young children, reinforcement or punishment usually has to come fairly quickly after the behavior to be very effective. The most effective consequences come within a second after the behavior. Those that come ten minutes later are often not nearly as effective. Yet the nightly review seems to help. I think that it works by the child's calling up a visual and auditory image of the positive behavior, and feeling good about it. Thus the fantasy practice of the positive behavior is reinforced.

Variations on the Nightly Review for Older Children

As a child gets farther into the grade school years, and even into the high school years, the nightly review should not cease, but it should be different than what I've described so far for younger children. The preschool child doesn't mind being the "center of attraction" for the nightly review, and doesn't mind having lots of positive evaluation focussed solely on himself. As the child gets older, however, the child realizes that the nightly review is a technique for personality improvement, and can start to resent the implication that people think his personality needs to be improved more than someone else's.

Thus as the child gets older, there needs to be more equality in the nightly review technique, less of a one-sided operation, more something that everyone does together. There needs to be more of a sense that the nightly review is a technique for all family members, especially including adults, that the child is let in on, rather than a technique for children. This is one general principle behind the success of any of the methods in this book when applied with older children and adolescents.

As the child gets older, she can take more responsibility for remembering positive patterns herself rather than having a parent do all the remembering.

And finally, as the child gets older, the child can benefit from recalling mistakes as well as positive patterns, trying to determine a positive pattern that would be a desired substitute for the mistake, and fantasy-practicing the preferred substitute. Caution: in all versions of the nightly review, only the person himself should bring up mistakes, not other people, unless people have achieved such a high degree of "nondefensive openness to the truth" that you aren't risking the whole custom by doing so.

Let's forget about children for a minute, and imagine an adult couple. Each night at a certain time, they spend a few minutes in the following activities, given in no particular order:

Each recalls his or her own positive examples from the day and celebrates them.

Each congratulates or thanks the other for positive examples they saw or heard the other do.

Each rehearses in fantasy any positive pattern that is a particularly desirable one.

Each can mention a mistake he made, and mention what positive pattern would be desirable to replace it with next time, and fantasy rehearse the replacement behavior.

Or each can mention a positive pattern he would like to do more often, and fantasy rehearse it, despite having done neither the pattern nor its opposite today.

People don't criticize each other at all during this ritual. They don't pry into each other's lives during this ritual. They don't whine at the other person if the other person can't think of any positive examples, but instead they try to think of a positive example they saw the other person doing.

If you can do this with good feeling, and if you can make it into a regularly recurring ritual, I predict you will find it to be of great value to yourselves. If your spouse doesn't want to participate, or if there is no spouse, then you can do it yourself, out loud or onto a written journal.

Then, you simply allow the children the privilege of being in on it.

The general theme of what I'm saying here will recur over and over. I suggest that you devise self-improvement methods for yourself, and include your children or your whole family in them, rather than having "behavior programs" for your children only. The difference in atmosphere is very important. You want the child to see individuals in the family as working toward higher and higher functioning, rather than someone more powerful inflicting control techniques upon someone who is the identified patient.

This notion of fantasy practice is very important. As I mentioned in the previous chapter, people have been able to improve their skills in all sorts of athletic endeavors, in public speaking, in interpersonal behavior, and other realms by fantasying themselves doing the patterns of thought, feeling, and action that they want to do. It's an underutilized tool, and a very useful one.

This is why I ask you to utilize this tool, by imagining doing certain things with your child. Let's put this tool into practice in an exercise on the nightly review.

Exercise: The Nightly Review

I want you to fantasy practice doing the nightly review, in a way appropriate for your child's age. Get some positive examples in mind, and make a mental movie of yourself holding a nightly review discussion.

Did you imagine yourself doing it? What did you see in your movie? Did you see your child feeling good about the recognition and attention? Did you see problems coming up? For some people, the biggest challenge is simply withholding negative and critical comments.

So now we have three ways of making the positive examples come out more frequently: give immediate attention and approval and excitement; tell a third person about the positive example; and do the nightly review. I am often asked, what if the child doesn't do any good things?

There are several answers to that question. The first answer to that is to study the skills axis very carefully, and watch the child more closely. Almost always, the parent who says this is missing all sorts of good things that the child is doing, by not noticing them. The second answer is to put the child in situations where the good things are more likely to happen, for example in one-on-one interaction with an adult, with nothing in reach except things you want the child to explore. With the combination of these two methods, which I use when a child comes into my office, I have yet to see a child for as long as 30 minutes without there being at least two or three things to celebrate in the child's behavior; often the total is much higher than that.

The third answer is to define celebration-worthiness relative to the child's own baseline habit. In other words, you take all the things the child does and arrange them in order, from most desirable to least desirable. The most desirable 10% or so of the things that the child does are by definition the ones you want to reinforce, even if those things are not the things you eventually want to settle for.

The fourth answer is that the modeling techniques we will talk about in later chapters will go a long way toward making positive behaviors start coming out much quicker and more frequently. When you put lots of positive examples into the memory bank, you can expect the positive examples to start coming out in the behavioral repertoire. But let's save this large topic until later on.

The Positive Behavior Diary

The positive behavior diary is a record of the good things people have done, with the recording done low on the abstraction ladder. The positive behavior diary is a form of monitoring. It also allows you to have a much longer memory for the positive examples you see. The child learns that doing positive examples gets not only attention today, but enduring commemoration.

One of the most powerful ideas in this book is that every image of positive, skillful thought, feeling, and behavior that you can collect is a resource. Every positive pattern that can be stored in the memory bank or on paper or other media, becomes a pattern useful to refer to when searching for a response to a new situation similar to the old one. Therefore it makes sense to collect images of positive responding, with as much zeal as you can muster. One great place to collect these images is from the best examples of what your family members already have done.

Get a spiral notebook or a blank book, or a file folder for loose pieces of paper, or open a file with your word processor. On the first couple of pages, write down the high priority skills that you are particularly wanting to foster. Example of what you might write on first pages:

Important skills:

Enjoying doing kind things
Complying with adults' requests
Putting up with frustration
Expressing glee
Having a good social chat

Be sure to leave some space for new skills when they move into the high priority zone.

Next, start making diary entries. Watch like a hawk for positive examples of any of these, and jot down in the diary a little story telling what your child did that was good in any of the high priority categories.

It's still important that the entries be very concrete. You want the recounting of the positive example to create a mental movie in the mind of the child, with a specific setting, specific characters, and specific utterances and actions.

How not to do it:

7/7/96 Complying: He complied well after lunch today.

How to do it:

7/7/96 Complying: Today after lunch—I: "Could you please help me out by putting napkins in trash can?" He: "Sure, I'd be glad to do that." And he did it.

Here are some more examples of positive behavior diary entries.

4/7/93 Fortitude. "May I watch Terminator on the TV?" "No, too violent, we're boycotting it." "OK. I guess I can handle it."

4/7/93 Enjoying kind acts. To sister: "Want me to read you a story, Jennifer?" "You can pick any one you want." "I like it when you pay attention like that."

4/8/93 Sustaining attention, handling aloneness. While I was on phone, he looked at Children's Pictorial Encyclopedia for 15 minutes.

4/8/93 Conflict resolution. With Alex from across the street. Doing Carmen game on computer vs. bikes and hike outside. "How about if we do the computer for half an hour, and then I get to show you some things outside?"

After you've made these diary entries, then what? Use the same principles as with telling another person about the positive examples, and doing the nightly review. If at any time the child wants the entries read to her, do so with enthusiasm. If the child gives permission and you think the child would enjoy it, let grandmother, uncle, cousin, and next-door-neighbor see the book in the child's presence and chat with the child about the positive examples. Use the book at the nightly review, and every once in a while recount the highlights of positive behaviors of the last week, the last month, etc. In other words, let this book make the child's positive behaviors lead to everlasting fame. Over time, you can watch and see if there are more and more positive examples to choose from, and if it gets easier and easier to pick an entry for the diary. If these things happen, progress is taking place, and you can celebrate! And when you get more ambitious, and want some fun, there are three other things you can do with these positive examples. You can make illustrated stories out of them, you can make plays from them, and you can make songs about them. We will talk more about these later.

The hardest part about this task, (next to getting yourself to do it at all) is to be concrete and specific.

A second tricky thing about this task is looking for positive examples of all the skills on the high priority list for the child, including the subtle examples of very little things the child does or says. Most parents can recognize the child's helping with a household chore as a positive example of helping, but some become overly focussed on this sort of example and miss the others.

Using Tape Recorders for the Positive Behavior Diary

Keeping a positive behavior diary is not very much work, but with the large amount of paperwork in the world, it often doesn't tend to get done. Here's another way of creating a permanent record of positive behaviors that I find quite helpful.

You get two tape recorders, and keep them in the child's room. One tape recorder is the one where you record the stories of the child's positive examples. Each night at bedtime, after you finish reading some stories to the child, you turn on that tape recorder and tell stories, in as interesting and dramatic fashion as you can, of the positive examples you saw the child carry out. The child listens to them. When you are done, you stop the tape recorder and leave the tape at that point, ready to begin again the next night. Then when you have accumulated a full cassette of these modeling stories, you put a new tape in the first recorder, and continue recording new stories each night. In addition, you play a story or two on the second recorder, from the old tape. Thus each evening the child gets reminded of positive examples that have occurred that day, and in the more distant past. You don't have to do any writing at all to make it happen.

Linking the Positive Examples to the Abstract Skill Concepts

You notice that in the sample diary entries I gave earlier, we didn't just narrate the event; we also noted what skill it was an example of. One of the reasons to do that in the positive behavior diary is to make sure that you look for examples of all the high priority skills, not just one or two. But there's another reason. You want to get in the habit of talking with the child about these positive events as examples of the skill, rather than just as isolated events. Example: the child is playing "Chutes and Ladders," and he has bad luck: his person lands on a square that sets him way back in the game. He snaps his finger with displeasure but goes along and plays by the rules, and continues to enjoy the game. It's fine and perfectly good to say to the child, "I like how you didn't get real upset when you got that setback." But if you say something like the following, you also educate the child in the concept of fortitude, or putting up with not getting what he wants: "That was fortitude! That big setback was a frustration for you, but when you went along with the rules and kept on enjoying the game, you were showing you could tolerate it!"

And why do we want the child to become familiar with these concepts? It's so that the next time something unwanted happens to the child, the child to say to himself not something like, "Aw, this is terrible! That's so dumb. Why do things like this happen to me." We want the child to think something like, "Here's a good chance for me to show how skilled I am at putting up with not getting what I want. If I do a good job with that skill, I'll deserve to celebrate and feel good." Can you see how adopting the second way of thinking, if generalized far enough, would lead to a totally different orientation toward the world? It's a world where challenges are continually being thrown at you for the exercise of psychological skills, but where your skills are constantly getting more and more developed with each challenge you face.

The Positive Pattern Diary with Older People

When using the positive pattern diary with older children and adolescents, adults use the technique in the service of their own self-improvement, and invite the children to be a part. If parents are trying to improve themselves, the child will probably not be so rebellious and resistant to attempts to improve himself.

One way to do this is to conduct a family nightly review session, with one person designated as recording secretary. The secretary's job is to record the positive examples that people have done or fantasied about.

The best way to approach this task is to realize that any person's positive example can be a resource for any other person. For example, the image of a child's helpful act can be a resource that can make the parent better able to enter the spirit of helping. The parent's example of delay of gratification or complaince at work can be a resource for the child to use at school—if the child hears about it, and if it's described concretely enough for the child to get a clear image in mind.

Suppose you can't get a spouse and all the siblings to convene for the nightly review. Even one parent can make it work with one child. The parent reviews his own positive patterns and those of any other people, for his own good. If the child takes an interest in what is written or spoken he is welcome to do so.

Enthusiasm and Positivity Not Contingent on the Child's Positive Examples

Adults' enthusiasm and upbeat tones of voice do far more than just to provide reinforcement for whatever the child did in the seconds preceding it. Parents' tones of voice and animation of behavior model for the child. A parent's upbeat enthusiasm is a stimulus situation that sets the stage for all behavior that follows it. Such positivity is very potent in eliciting positive behavior from the child. Even objective-formation is affected: enthusiasm and joyousness in a parent help the child to share the parent's goals. Why? Because an enthusiastic and upbeat parent, who is enjoying life, seems to be onto something good, something a child will want to get in on. Conversely, with an unhappy and irritable parent, the child may think, "If your values [or these psychological skills] are so great, why aren't you happy?" The child is then likely to imitate the peer or the television hero who seems to be enjoying life more than the parent. For adolescents, we should assume that they are on some level thinking, "Show me, with the happiness of your own life, the evidence that the values and competences you endorse are worthwhile."

The conclusion from this thinking is that "noncontingent" positivity from the parent—that which comes out of the blue rather than in reponse to something positive the child did—may be at least as important and constructive as the "contingent reinforcement" the behaviorists promote. Or in other words, don't wait for the child to do something good before you demonstrate enthusiasm! If you can set the stage from the first moment of your interaction with the child, for a positive, upbeat emotional tone, the child is much more likely to respond in kind. When I was a child, often my first experience upon awakening would be to hear my father jubilantly singing a song whose words started out, "Wake with the singing bird, shout out those lucky words, here comes the sun!" I will always be grateful for this noncontingent positivity, despite the fact that often I did not imitate such jubilance in any immediate way.

Now let's summarize the methods advocated so far. After getting familiar with the skill concepts, you pick some high priority skills, and get very clearly in mind a bunch of concrete positive examples for each of them. Then watch like a hawk for any examples you see your child doing. Give enthusiastic attention immediately when you see those examples. Do this with excitement and emotion in your voice and face, so as to communicate accurately the positive emotion you have generated from within. Tell other people about those good things. Sit down each night and review the positive examples; keep a diary (on paper or on tape) to help you remember them. When you review the positive examples, link them to the skill concepts some of the time. Do this as an ongoing self-improvement project as well as a way of positively influencing your child. And don't wait for the child to do positive things before showing the child how to be upbeat and enthusiatic and positive.

I have seen parents bring about rapid and very positive changes in their children by these steps alone.

Chapter 5: Differential Reinforcement and Shaping

Chapter Overview:

When something the child does leads you to pay attention, get excited, or grant a request, the message the child gets is: "Please do more frequently whatever you did just now." Similarly, when you take away attention and excitement and deny requests, the child gets the message: "Please do less frequently what you did just now." Thus you can powerfully help your child by attending and getting excited and granting requests when the child does good things, and turning away attention and getting more serious and denying requests when the child does irritating things. I'm now talking not about the amount of your attention, but its timing. There are many times when you turn your attention toward your child, and many times when you turn your attention away. If you turn attention toward the child immediately after the child does a positive example, and away after a negative example, you are using "differential attention" in the right direction. If you want to use differential attention well in real life, you may have to do lots of practice in your imagination first. "Differential excitement" means that you get more excited about the child's positive behaviors than the negative ones. This means you don't yell when the child acts up; you speak firmly and seriously in a measured tone, or you don't speak at all. On the other hand, you speak with great animation and energy when the child does good things. Differential response-granting is an important part of not raising a "spoiled" child. The "spoiled" person reasons like this: because I want something, someone else should give it to me. The spoiled person uses the following tactic: I will make my wants known to you in such an aversive way that you'll be motivated to give me what I want, just to get me to leave you alone. You can avoid spoiling by granting your child only those requests that are (1) reasonable, (2) politely made, and (3) not preceded by aversive behavior. You make exceptions to this rule only when vital for the child's health or safety. When you want to use differential reinforcement with children, you have to work as a team with other caretakers. It doesn't do for one person to come and rescue the child when the other is trying to ignore.

If you play a cooperative game called the shaping game with your family, you can all practice the fine art of differential reinforcement.

I've emphasized timing rather than amount of attention in this chapter. However, to use differential attention with your child, first you need to have lots of attention to give. If you schedule one-on-one time between you and each of your children, you make it easiest to get going a pleasant, cooperative interaction. You'll find that arranging time alone is worth the effort it takes.

Many children have problems with finishing work. Sometimes the nagging that parents naturally do to try to keep children from dawdling actually reinforces the dawdling. I recommend a procedure in which the parent uses differential reinforcement to help the child finish work. A key sentence is "Please let me know when you're finished with _____." When the child does finish, the parent gives lots of positive attention. At the beginning of such a program, there can be lots of celebrations for finishing small fractions of the task. As time goes on, the amount of independent work the child is expected to do increases gradually.

****

In the last chapter I mentioned types of behavior that contribute to an interpersonal environment:

1. Stability of time together.
2. The degree of challenge of the activity.
3. Approval versus disapproval.
4. Directiveness versus responsiveness.
5. Differential Reinforcement.
    5.1 Differential attention
    5.2 Differential excitement
    5.3 Differential request-granting
6. Positive models versus negative models.
7. Problem solving techniques.

In this chapter we'll focus a great deal more on the fifth of these, differential reinforcement. Getting control of what you reinforce and do not reinforce is a very powerful way of helping your child.

The most powerful reinforcers for children are not gold stars on a chart, prizes from a grab bag, or other tangible objects. They are positive interactions. Among these are:

1. Getting attention from the other person,
2. Getting excitement from the other person,
3. Getting requests granted by the other person.

If you can make your attention, excitement, and request-granting follow positive behavior and not negative behavior as much of the time as possible, you will help your child tremendously.

Ignoring and Differential Attention

In the last chapter we considered the idea that adult attention and excitement, even when it is irritated or scolding, is often reinforcing to many children.

The converse of this principle is also true, powerful, and the main subject of this chapter. If it helps to turn your attention toward the child when the child does something desirable, it also helps to turn your attention away from the child, toward something else, when the child does something undesirable. Turning attention toward certain behaviors and away from others is called differential attention: you attend differently to the desirable and undesirable behaviors.

Suppose a child has a habit of getting whiny and argumentative about little, irrational things, attention-getting opportunities. The child gets together with an adult who can focus attention on the child, but who also has work to do. Suppose that every time the child gets whiny and argumentative, the adult politely excuses himself to do some work. When the child gets more straightforward and cooperative and pleasant, the adult turns attention back to the child, chatting with the child in an approving tone of voice, playing with the child, and doing things the child wants to do. If the adult does this like clockwork, consistently, it probably won't take long for the whininess and argumentativeness to reduce drastically.

The whining and arguing example is another situation where the natural response might be to pay attention to the negative and ignore the positive. Children usually choose to whine because of an unfavorable "reinforcement history": people have done what the child wants to get the child to stop whining. If they pay attention to the whining and don't pay attention to the more pleasant interactions, then differential attention is used, but in the wrong direction.

One interesting piece of research on differential attention took place in a classroom. The researchers went to a classroom during times when the children were supposed to be in their seats doing independent work. They asked the teachers to act in several different ways, and counted, for each condition, the number of times children got out of their seats. The first condition was baseline—whatever the teachers normally did. In the second condition, the researchers asked the teachers to say, without fail, whenever a child got out of his seat, "Sit down." In the third condition, they asked the teachers to go back to what they had been doing before. Fourth, they asked the teachers again to immediately attend to out-of-seat behavior with a "sit down." Fifth, they asked the teachers to ignore the children who were out of their seats, and pay attention to the ones doing their work as they were supposed to. What do you think happened? (Don't read the following paragraph until you've thought about it and made a guess.)

The second and fourth conditions, (when teachers attended to out-of-seat behavior by saying "Sit down,") had more children getting out of seat than in the first or third conditions (when teachers did what came naturally). In the fifth condition, (when the teachers ignored the children who were up and paid attention only to those who were sitting down) the children kept sitting more than ever before. The moral of the story is: paying attention to the good things and ignoring the bad things really works —sometimes. (Let's ignore for the time being the issue of whether educational systems work harder to produce immobility and silence than real learning and competence-development.)

If you take the principle of ignoring to its illogical extreme, you conclude that all you have to do is to ignore all bad behavior and it will go away. Wouldn't it be nice if that were true? In the above-mentioned classroom, if a student had gotten out of his seat, yelled at another student, punched him, and proceeded to rip up his books and papers, while the rest of the students egged on the victim to punch him back, I wouldn't advise the teacher to silently ignore this behavior and attend to the work of the student who is most on-task with seat work. The obvious problem is that adult attention is not the only reinforcer that is out there in the world. Ignoring can be used with great effectiveness when (1) the behavior is not so dangerous or disruptive that it can't be tolerated for the time being, and (2) when the main reinforcer for the behavior is adult attention. If the child is trying to get something from a peer, and not the adult, you have to get the peer to ignore; you can't count on your own ignoring to do the whole job.

For this reason, ignoring is not the only response to negative behavior we will talk about in this book. But it should be the "first line of defense," because the two conditions I just cited hold surprisingly often, especially with young children, and because ignoring is so much easier and less potentially harmful than many of the other methods of dealing with negative behavior.

What does it mean to ignore negative behavior? Here's what effective ignoring isn't:

Sitting and staring at the child with a glum expression

Sitting and obviously trying not to look at the child, with a glum expression, while the child tries to get you to look at him

Saying "I'm not going to pay attention to you when you do that."

What's wrong with these? When you do them, you are totally focussing on the child's behavior. What's going on is the opposite of ignoring. Ignoring is best done by doing something else, particularly something you'll have to or want to do sooner or later anyway. Doing a household chore is the best way to ignore, most of the time. Turning the attention to some other child who also wants it, but who is doing something neutral or desirable, is another good way to ignore.

Example: Johnny has a problem with argumentativeness and verbal hostility. Mrs. Smith and Johnny are talking. Mrs. Smith says, "I wonder if it will snow. I hope not."

Johnny replies, "That's stupid to hope that. You don't know what you're talking about."

At this moment Mrs. Smith says, "Excuse me a minute," and gathers up some of the pieces of mail that are on the kitchen table and table in the front hall, and takes them up to the desk in the bedroom, and files them. She reappears a while later, and says, "Now, those pieces of paper are where they won't get lost."

Now, if Johnny says something in a pleasant tone, she continues interacting with him pleasantly. For example, suppose he says: "I like it when it snows."

She replies, "There are lots of fun things for you to do when it snows, aren't there?"

Exercise: Differential Attention

The key issue in differential attention is timing. Every parent turns her attention toward the child many times, and away from the child many times. If you can just time it so that you are encouraging the positive patterns and discouraging the negative ones, you will help your child enormously.

As you read the following two vignettes, assume that the "shrieking toddler" has a habit of giving blood-curdling yells, with an angry facial expression, often, in a maneuver to get adult attention.

The Shrieking Toddler, First Episode
6:00:00 to 6:00:05 Toddler shrieks.
6:00:05 to 6:00:07 Parent says, "What's the matter!"
6:00:07 to 6:01:00 Toddler plays with toy people and toy house. Parent puts a book back onto the bookshelf and rearranges a few books.
6:01:00 to 6:01:05 Toddler shrieks.
6:01:05 to 6:01:15 Parent tries "distraction" and says to toddler, "buh buh, buh buh!" while smiling and touching toddler on the belly.
6:01:15 to 6:01:18 Toddler laughs.
6:01:18 to 6:01:30 Parent responds to something that someone else says.

****

I think most people will agree that the adult in this example was being very nice, well meaning, and acting in a way that is difficult to criticize too harshly. However, the adult did turn attention to the child twice in this minute and a half of interaction, immediately after the child shrieked, and turned attention away from the child twice, when the child was playing nicely and laughing pleasantly. Thus the child gets two reinforcers for shrieking and two punishments for pleasant play. If this seemingly reasonable and natural adult behavior is continued over a long period of time, the strength of the child's bad habit can build up very high.

Now let's replay this vignette with differential attention being used more favorably.

The Shrieking Toddler, Second Episode
6:00:00 to 6:00:05 Toddler shrieks.
6:00:05 to 6:00:20 Parent puts a book back on the bookshelf and rearranges a couple of books.
6:00:20 to 6:01:00 Toddler plays with toy people and toy house. Parent comes close and says, "Hey, there they go into the house. He's getting into the bathtub!"
6:01:00 to 6:01:05 Toddler shrieks.

6:01:05 to 6:01:15 Parent responds to something that someone else has said.
6:01:15 to 6:01:18 Toddler laughs at something the toddler himself did.
6:01:18 to 6:01:30 Parent laughs back, says "You did something funny!"; toddler laughs back.
****

The casual observer would not recognize how much better for the child the second episode was than the first. But the effect on the child's habits, if this pattern is continued over a long time, can be major. In this second episode, again the adult turned attention away from the child twice and toward the child twice; this time, however, the attention came just after desirable behavior and the attention went away just after undesirable behavior.

Since this principle is so important, let's look at another pair of episodes.

The Grumpy Preschooler: First Episode
A preschooler and the parent are playing in the family room.
6:30:00 to 6:30:03: Preschooler grabs a ball out of the parent's hands.
6:30:04 to 6:30:30: Parent gets up, gets a couple of cups that are out, goes into kitchen, puts them into kitchen sink, comes back.
6:30:30 to 6:31:00 Preschooler rolls ball up an incline and watches it roll back down. Parent meanwhile responds: Hey, there it goes up, and back down it comes!
6:31:00 to 6:31:03: Preschooler gripes, in very whiney voice: This is so stupid, it's just stupid!
6:31:04 to 6:35:00: Parent goes to rest room, then returns to the room.
6:35:00 to 6:35:08: Preschooler says, in a non-irritating voice, "Why won't the ball stay up there?"
6:35:09 to 6:35:12: Parent says, "You want it to stay at the top of the plank, without rolling down?"

****

How many times did the adult turn the attention toward and away from the child? And were the "attention-towards" after positive and "attention-aways" after negative behavior, or vice versa? Contrast that with episode 2.

The Grumpy Preschooler, Second Episode
A preschooler and the parent are playing in the family room.
6:30:00 to 6:30:03: Preschooler grabs a ball out of the parent's hands.
6:30:04: Parent responds: Hey! You grabbed that right out of my hand! You're not supposed to do that!
6:30:10 to 6:31:00 Preschooler rolls ball up an incline and watches it roll back down. Parent is silent.
6:31:00 to 6:31:03: Preschooler gripes: This is so stupid. It's just stupid!
6:31:04 to 6:31:07: Parent responds: I don't see anything stupid about it; what's wrong with it?
6:31:08 to 6:31:11: Child responds in whiny voice: It's just stupid, it just is!

6:31:11 to 6:31:15: Parent responds: I think you're just griping for no reason!
6:31:15 to 6:31:30: Child says, in a non-irritating voice, why won't the ball stay up there?
6:31:30 to 6:35:00: Adult goes to rest room, then returns to room.

In a minute and a half, a child can get attention turned toward him and away from him over 5 or 6 times, with time to spare. How many times does attention get turned toward and away from the child when the parent and child are together for a couple of hours? Or a couple of years? The cumulative effect of the timing of giving and withdrawing of attention, as subtle as it may seem, over a course of months and years gradually accumulates. The more the "attention towards" follow more positive behavior and the the "attention aways" follow less positive behavior, the more positive is the influence upon the child.

Exercise: Differential Attention

Read this vignette, and stop each time the child does something. If the child has done something you like, I want you to think of some way to give attention and approval to the child. If the child is doing something you don't like, imagine yourself ignoring what the child did, and imagine yourself getting interested in some specific other thing.

For this exercise let's just practice ignoring each time the child does something undesirable. It's usually a good thing to try ignoring first, and if it doesn't work after a while, you can try something else.

This exercise will ask you to ignore some provocative behavior, deliberately designed by the child to get you mad. But that's just the sort that is most easily eliminated by ignoring.

The point of the exercise is not just to decide whether to ignore or to approve: it's to have a fantasy rehearsal of yourself doing one or the other. To review this concept: by a fantasy rehearsal I mean that you see in your mind a movie of yourself giving approving attention or ignoring, in the situation that is described. The more vivid you can make that movie, the better.

The vignette begins before breakfast, in the kitchen.

1. The child says, "When are we going over to Grandma's?!" You, the parent say, "It will be in a couple of hours, when the little hand of the clock gets over to right here. It won't be long." The child says, "No! I want to go right now!" and keeps screaming this out, loudly, having a tantrum. (Sample ignoring response to fantasy-rehearse: you get busy making breakfast, concentrating fully on that task.)
2. The child continues yelling, saying, "You don't love me! You just treat me like dirt!" (Sample response to rehearse: you keep making breakfast, pausing momentarily to take the trash out.)
3. After a while the child stops yelling and screaming, and picks up a crayon

and a piece of paper out of his toy box. He starts drawing a picture of a man and a dog. (Sample response to rehearse: You say, "Hey, look at that!" (in an approving tone))
4. The child says, "It's not his dog, it belongs to someone else—it belongs to this person." And the child starts drawing another person. (Sample response: "Oh, I see, that new person owns the dog.")
5. The child after a while says, "I'm not going to let you see it any more. You can't see my drawing." (Sample response: You get up and get busy in the kitchen again.)
6. The child now runs up and gives the drawing to you and says, "Here, I'll let you see it." (Sample response: Adult looks, and says, "Oh, look at this!")
7. It is getting to be time for breakfast. The child says, "Can I help you get breakfast ready?" (Sample response: Parent hands child some napkins, and says, "Thank you for offering! Yes, you can put these napkins on the table!" As the child does it, the parent says, "That's a good example of a nice thing you're doing. You're a help to me.")
8. The child helps with breakfast by pouring some orange juice into glasses. After he gets through pouring, he says, to no one in particular, "I didn't spill any! Not a drop!" (Sample response: Parent remarks, with tone of small approval, "You're getting to be a really good pourer." [And from here on, you're on your own in making up attentive or ignoring responses.])
9. As the family is eating breakfast, the child says, about the oatmeal, "This is yucky!"
10. A couple of seconds later, the child says, "This tastes like vomit."
11. A while later, the child very carefully spreads a reasonable amount of jelly on some toast.
12. The child says, "I like this toast."
13. As breakfast ends, the child says to you, "That shirt you have on is dumb."
14. After a few seconds the child picks up his plate and bowl and sets it on the counter near the sink.
15. After a while you come and say to the child, "It's time to take your bath now. It's time to put the toys away." The child doesn't say anything, but dumps the toys in the box and heads in the direction of the bathroom.
16. The child gets in the bathtub and gets some soap and a washcloth and washes his face, and his arms and body, and shoulders.
17. After his bath, the child says, "Now I'm going to brush my teeth."
18. The child puts toothpaste on his toothbrush, and starts brushing his teeth.
19. As the child gets dressed, he says, "I'm never going to take a bath or brush my teeth again. No one can ever make me."
20. The child bites his fingernails a little bit.
21. The child goes into another room, where his brother is. The child says to his brother, "Want to see that new little car that I got?"

22. As the two children play, you hear the following dialogue: "No it isn't." "It is too. You don't know what you're talking about." "You're the one who doesn't know what you're talking about."

23. Later when the two are playing, you hear the following dialogue: the child we are talking about says, "Hey, you got it! That's good going!" And his brother says "Thanks. That was the first time I ever did it."

24. A little later the child comes up to you and says, "Is it time to go to Grandma's yet?" and you say, "No, we've still got another couple of hours. It won't be until the little hand of the clock gets over here." The child says, "OK", and walks off.

Did you really imagine yourself doing the ignoring or giving approving attention? If you didn't vividly imagine yourself doing each thing, but instead just read the above exercise, please go back and make a vivid movie in your mind. Please imagine yourself doing specific other things when the child is provocative. If you didn't get specific tasks accomplished immediately after the child was provocative, go back and make that movie again.

Another Exercise on Differential Attention

Differential attention is very, very important. In fact, one of the major jobs of a child psychiatrist or psychologist is to help parents and teachers figure out how to use differential attention in a direction that solves the problem rather than in a way that worsens the problem.

Sometimes parents or teachers naturally use differential attention in a way that turns out to worsen the problem. When the child does something undesirable, sometimes the natural thing to do is to pay attention to the child right away, or to keep paying attention to the child until the problem behavior goes away. But this often is like "paying" the child for acting badly or being unhappy. When the child starts getting more attention for acting good and being happy than he gets for acting bad or being unhappy, often his behavior and happiness rapidly improve.

The following exercise asks you to think about each of the situations, and to figure out whether differential attention is probably working in the right direction or in the wrong direction. Contemplate each situation until you fully understand how differential attention is working. Then, if it is working in the wrong direction, figure out a plan whereby it can work in the right direction.

Situation 1. Bedtime problems. The child is having trouble getting to sleep. On nights when the child can't sleep, and comes and asks for the parents, the parent sits in the child's room and rubs the child's back or sings to the child or lies next to the child until the child can get to sleep. On nights when the child can get to sleep, the adult says a quick good night and goes about his or her business.

Situation 2. Dressing problems. The child is having big troubles with getting dressed in the morning. The child gets dressed just before leaving for school, after eating breakfast and chatting with his or her parent for a while. On mornings when the child gets dressed quickly, off they go to school. On mornings when the child dawdles and refuses to get dressed, the parent spends a lot of time prodding and pleading and arguing with the child to get dressed before the child goes to school.

Situation 3. Arguing. A child is an unpleasant arguer. The child has a very tactless, whiny, and grating tone when arguing. When the child is argumentative, the adult will spend lots of time trying to show the child that the child is mistaken, and they will talk back and forth, sometimes with much excitement. When the child is not argumentative, they tend to have much less conversation, and much less animated conversation.

Situation 4. Sibling hostility. The brother and the sister fight with each other. When they start yelling at each other, the parent will come from the other room and say, "Hey, what's going on here?" and try to intervene. When they are playing quietly together, the parent will leave them alone and take care of his or her own business.

Situation 5. Separation problems. A child has tantrums and acts scared when he has to say good-bye to his mother when school starts. When the child cries, the mother says, "Don't worry, you'll be all right. I'll be back in just a while. OK?" And the mother hugs the child and wipes the child's tears off. The mother plans to leave when the child settles down and quits crying. On days when the child doesn't cry, the mother leaves quickly.

Situation 6. Hitting. A child at a preschool is in the habit of hitting other children. Whenever the child hits, the preschool teacher goes up to the child and says, "Johnny, we don't hit. We must use our words. If you wanted something from Teddy you should tell him about it. What did you want? Can you tell Teddy in words?" When the child is not hitting, the teacher is involved in other activities, sometimes the same sort of routine with other children who have hit.

Situation 7. Screaming when he can't get his way. A child is in the habit of screaming when he can't get his way. When he screams, the adult walks away, gets some ear plugs and puts them in, and then goes on about his or her business. When the child stops screaming and has been doing something else for a minute or two, the adult takes the ear plugs out and starts a conversation with the child as though nothing has happened. But the child still isn't given his way. When the child doesn't get his way, and doesn't scream, the adult says, "Good for you! You put up with not getting your way!"

Situation 8. Soiling the pants. A child has frequently soils his pants with feces. When the child soils his pants, the parent gets very emotional and yells at the child. When the child defecates into the toilet, this goes unnoticed most of the time.

Situation 9. Homework. A child tends to procrastinate on his homework. When the child puts off doing the homework, the parent keeps reminding the child to do it, and finally does it with the child, going over each step in the homework. If the child should do the homework independently, the parent would leave the child alone and go on about his or her business.

Situation 10. Head banging. A child is in the habit of banging his head. When he bangs his head, his parent will run to him and pick him up and hold him and talk to him and see what is wrong, and will often wipe his forehead with a wet cloth. When he plays without banging his head, his parent goes on about his or her business.

Situation 11. Hard to please. The child asks for something, and then when she gets it, she changes her mind. For example, she asks for one type of cereal, and when she gets that cereal, she looks at it and says "No! I want the other type!" The parent says, in an animated tone of voice, "Why didn't you say that in the first place then?" The child just repeats, "I don't want it!" The adult has a few more verbal interchanges with her and then usually gets what she wants. When she likes the cereal that she gets the first time, she just eats it while her parent goes on about his business, preparing for them both to leave.

Sample answers to these situations:

Differential attention is working in the wrong direction for all situations except situation 7. Here are sample plans for making differential attention work in the right direction:

Situation 1. New plan for bedtime problems: The parents work out a routine of doing the nightly review and reading stories each night before bed. Then once it is "Good night and lights out," if the child gets out of bed the only attention the child gets is to be directed or led back to the bedroom and the bed. If the child does not get out of bed after "Good night and lights out," the parents hold a little celebration in the morning for the child.

Situation 2. New plan for dressing problems: The parent invites the child to get dressed first thing in the morning after washing, before breakfast and before chatting with the parent. If the child starts getting dressed, the parent stays and chats with the child in a pleasant way. If the child refuses to get dressed, the parent gets busy with something else. The parent forms a custom that when the child is all dressed and ready to go, the parent will spend twenty minutes in dramatic play with the child. The parent starts the dressing soon enough that there will be time for this play if the child does not dawdle too long over dressing. If all else fails, the parent physically dresses the child with as little conversation and excitement as possible.

Situation 3. New plan for arguing. When the child argues in an unpleasant way about whether somebody did something or not, or what makes night and day, or other issues not having to do with compliance, the parent does not respond. If the child has anything close to a pleasant discussion or conversation with the adult, without arguing, the adult responds in a very animated way. If the child argues about something the child is asked to do, the adult refuses to argue, but either physically makes the child comply or imposes a punishment for noncompliance, doing either with a minimum of interchange between adult and child. If the child complies, the adult is very animatedly grateful.

Situation 4. New plan for sibling hostility. When the two children are playing nicely with each other, the parent goes over and sits down with them and watches, and makes an occasional comment without being too intrusive or interrupting the activity. When they start getting angry at each other, the adult leaves the scene and takes care of some business. If they actually hit one another, the adult uses a "time out" with very little talk about the incident. The parent talks about the nice things they did for each other in the nightly review.

Situation 5. New plan for separation problems. When the child starts whining and crying near separation time, the mother leads him very quickly to the substitute caregiver, says good-bye, gives the child's hand to the caregiver, and walks away without looking back. If the child acts cheerful and confident, then the mother takes her time in leaving. If the child acts cheerful and confident the parent talks about this behavior later during the day and at the nightly review. (This plan assumes that the child has had a chance to already gain confidence in the alternate caregiver, and the parent is sure that the alternate caregiver is trustworthy and kind. See the chapter on separation problems.)

Situation 6. New plan for hitting. When the child hits, the child is immediately taken to a rest room where the child must stay by himself for two minutes. There is minimal talk about the hitting at the time. When the child is nice to other children, the adult comes around and says things such as, "I like how you and Jack are cooperating on building your tower," (i.e. praise) or "Hey, that tower is getting pretty tall," (i.e. enthusiastic attention).

Situation 7. Screaming when he can't get his way. The situation as presented illustrates differential attention used in the right direction. If the parent paid attention to the screaming and said, "OK, you can have it, just quit that screaming," the child would be reinforced for screaming and differential attention would work in the wrong direction.

Situation 8. New plan about soiling of pants. When the child does soil, the parent helps the child through a very routine procedure for cleaning the feces out of his underwear and cleaning himself up and changing clothes; during this procedure there is little emotion at all. When the child has a bowel movement into the toilet, the child is to show the parent, who will show some excited pleasure and congratulate the child. (Parents should know, however, that a large fraction of children who soil with feces after achieving the age of 4 or 5 are actually constipated, and the fact that the rectum stays stretched all the time keeps the child from perceiving the stretching that usually signals to the body the urge to have a bowel movement. So the differential attention may not help until the constipation is treated, with guidance from a doctor. Please see the chapter on fecal soiling in this book.)

Situation 9. New plan for homework. The parent fashions a quiet place for the child to do homework. The parent says, "I have some work of my own to do. I'll leave you alone for a while. When you're ready to do your homework, call me, and I'll come down and sit with you and do some reading and writing while you do your work." If the child has a question, the parent attends to it. Every so often the parent takes a look at the child's work, and celebrates progress. The parent pays particular attention to the problems the child got right, going through the thought processes, and letting the child proudly say what his thought processes were. The parent doesn't spend much time on the incorrect problems. The parent explains any principle that the child isn't understanding. When the child is finished with all his homework and has done it well, the parent and child play a game together.

Situation 10. New plan for head banging. The parents start watching very carefully for any positive examples of using language to communicate, doing nice things, being gleeful, and sustaining attention to an activity. They turn their attention to the child whenever the child is doing these things. If the child bangs a little, they ignore. If the child bangs to the point where he needs physical protection, they get him in a hold where he is facing away from them, with his arms crossed in front of him, and hold him for two minutes without speaking to him in any way. They act as if they are paying attention to something else during that time. If this proves too reinforcing they put a helmet on the child and leave it on for 10 minutes each time he bangs, and they ignore him whenever the helmet is on. If he takes frustration in a positive way without head banging, they respond in a very animated way.

Situation 11. New plan for hard to please. The parent explains to the child, at a time other than mealtime, that the child will get one chance to choose what she wants. If she changes her mind after the parent gets it, her only choice is that she can eat it or she can throw it away. If she takes what she chooses and eats it, the parent sits with her and has a pleasant conversation. If she gripes and complains that she doesn't want it, the parent reminds her once and only once that her choice is to eat it or throw it away, and does not respond to griping and complaining after that, but speaks with someone else or does chores.

Differential Excitement

In the previous chapter we stressed that excitement and energy are reinforcing for children. What about the adult's excited and energetic displays of negative emotion, when the child has done something bad? One of the most important realizations I've come to is that for many, many children, such excitement is reinforcing of negative behavior, in the long run. This can be true even if the adult's utterance is meant to, and does, stop the child's behavior in the short run.

Please do an experiment. Imagine yourself yelling out to a child with great irritation and exasperation, "Hey, I thought I told you not to do that! Cut it out" As you do it, listen to the melody of what you're saying. How does the inflection of your voice go? Can you sing the same melody without words, and say, "DAH, da DAH da da-da-da-da DAH dah! DAH da DAH!" Now imagine that you are extremely pleased with the child, and you say, in a tone of large approval, with great excitement and enthusiasm, "Hey, I didn't think you could do that! Way to go!" Now sing that melody without words. Can you hear how close they are? And can you imagine how a child who is reinforced by the second might also be reinforced by the first? Wouldn't it be very difficult to hard-wire a brain that would be greatly reinforced by the first, and not at all reinforced by the second? Either way, the message that comes to the child is, "For these few seconds at least, you're famous, and you're a very big deal."

Many, perhaps most, children tend to do things more often that get people excited, even if the excitement is negative. If you can't make this principle untrue, why not use it? It is an extremely useful principle! All you have to do is to get excited about the good things, but not get excited about the bad things, and by doing so you can help your child act better.

I use the phrase "All you have to do" with some sense of irony, because doing this is much more easily said than done. There's a natural tendency —isn't there?—for parents to do just the opposite of what I'm suggesting. Isn't it more natural to get excited and yell about the negative things, and speak quietly about the positive things? For this reason I recommend that any adults who work with children monitor exactly what causes them to raise their voices and speak quickly in a high pitch. For many adults it comes naturally to do this when the child does something they don't like. This may be reinforcing the undesirable behavior. It has been extremely helpful for many parents to stop yelling about the bad behavior and start yelling about the good behavior. They have found that their children want to get the adult excited, and if they can do that by doing good things, and if they can't do it by doing bad things, they will start doing good things much more often.

Exercise: Get Excited About the Positive and Give Disapproval Quietly

Here is another exercise. The idea is to practice saying reprimands, or disapproving things to the child, in a very unexcited way, and giving approval to the child in a more excited way. You will see below a list of thing to practice saying. Each will be either a reprimand or something approving. Practice saying each of the reprimands slowly and quietly, in an unexcited way. Practice saying the approving statements more quickly and with higher tones, with more excitement.

Don't just read this exercise silently, but say each sentence aloud, with high excitement if it's approval, and low excitement if it's a reprimand.

"You're too smart a boy to be doing things like that."

"I really like it when you share with other children."

"You listened to a long story."

"I don't like to hear that kind of word from you."

"Thank you, you did what I asked you to."

"You know better than to run away like that."

"That's really an interesting idea."

"You're not allowed to throw food. People don't like to eat with people who make messes."

"I like the way the two of you decided to take turns."

"Good for you, you put up with not getting your way."

We've already said in this chapter that if you can ignore negative behavior altogether, that's often better than using low-excitement disapproval. But if you must turn attention to negative behavior, do so with low excitement.

Differential Request-Granting

This section is a very important one in the art of "how not to raise a spoiled brat." Children as a rule frequently ask adults to do things for them. Which requests get granted have a lot to do with whether the child is "spoiled" or not.

What is the definition of a "spoiled" individual? (Adults can be spoiled also.) A "spoiled" person has a feeling of entitlement, that other people should grant their requests simply because she makes them, that others somehow have a moral responsibility to do what she wants them to do. The thought pattern is along the lines of, "I want this; therefore it follows logically that the other person should do it." This thought pattern ignores or weights as relatively unimportant what the other person's wishes or needs are. Thus the spoiled individual tends to

1. request things that are not reasonable to expect from others,

2. get upset, indignant, and/or pouty when those requests are not granted, until they are granted, and

3. make requests in an obnoxious, tyranical, or irritating way.

The spoiled person is usually deficient in the skills of toleration and nonbossiness, of frustration-tolerance, of negotiation skills, and of recognizing just solutions to conflict. For the spoiled person, it seems very meet and right to boss the other person. Frustration-intolerance in the form of whining, crying, complaining, being angry, pouting, or having a tantrum has been rewarded by the other person's request-granting so much that frustration-tolerance seems a foolish strategy. If I am a spoiled person, a just solution to the problem of my wanting something from someone else is that they give it to me, period. I have not gotten an objective sense of what is just and reasonable to expect from another person in return for whatever I am prepared to give; I confuse the question of what is just with the question of what meets my immediate wishes.

How does someone get to be spoiled? Consider the following vignette.

Child: (In a relatively quiet voice) I want a cookie.
Adult: (Is tired, wants to relax, continues to read the newspaper.)
Child: (In a louder, more strident, demanding, whiny voice) I want a cookie! Get me one!
Adult: It's almost supper time.
Child: (Still louder, crying, demanding) I want it! I want it! Get it for me! Get it!
Adult: (Thinks: "I don't need this. Getting the cookie is a small price for stopping this.) Oh all right. Here, take your cookie and be quiet.
Child: (Eats the cookie and turns off the negative behavior, for now. Next episode soon to follow, however.)

By turning off the negative behavior when the adult grants the request, the child is using what's called negative reinforcement to reward the adult for complying. The main point, however, is that the adult's request-granting is selectively reinforcing the child's demandingness, negative emotion, and loud anger. The child is getting the message loud and clear that "the obnoxious wheel gets the grease." The adult is teaching the child, by differential request-granting, to be demanding and unhappy. Eventually the child may learn to go directly to the whiny, crying, demanding request, without passing through the relatively more pleasant stage.

Once the child has learned to scream and loudly demand things in order to get requests granted, breaking the child of this habit will entail some ignoring of tantrums. You will have to deny requests and stay the course through the ensuing tantrum, sometimes many times, before the child learns that a "new deal" is in place and that the conditions of differential reinforcement have changed. You can speed things up by explaining the new deal to the child, at a time when no conflict is "hot." It's helpful to let the child know that you are interested in being a good parent, and part of what that means is reinforcing pleasant behavior and not reinforcing unpleasant behavior. Thus you're obligated not to give the child what he wants when he practices a bad habit, even if you would otherwise like to. Even with such an explanation, often there is no substitute for the child's directly finding out that obnoxious behavior is no longer reinforced.

A more subtle way to produce a spoiled child is to grant too many unreasonable requests, even when they are made in a pleasant and polite tone of voice. Suppose that the child requests that the adult give her constant attention, doing one thing after another that the child requests. If these requests require a great deal of effort and some discomfort from the adult, and the adult goes along with everything the child wants, the child may come to expect that whatever she wants will be given. If the overly-entitled child asks the adult to do a somersault and the adult does not feel like it, it does the child good for the adult to decline, politely. If the overly-entitled child asks the adult to buy something at the store, and the adult knows that the object will not get much productive use or is too expensive, it will do the child good not to get that object. With so much unkindness and stinginess in the world, it is tragic to see a child being spoiled by the mistiming of and wrong type of kindness and generosity.

Another way of producing a spoiled child is to grant too many requests too soon after the child has acted badly. For example: a child refuses to leave a playground, and the parent has to create a major scene to get the child to go home. On the way home, the child asks to stop at the toy store. If the parent does stop there and buy the child something, the parent is giving the child the message that request-granting has nothing to do with how nice the child has been.

Thus to avoid producing a spoiled child, as a general rule the adult should grant children's requests only when they are politely expressed, reasonable, and not too closely following negative behavior. Of course, you can't be rigid; if the toddler's request is to get her leg unstuck from between the slats of her crib, you grant it no matter what the tone of voice or prior behavior. Here the reasonableness of the request overrides the other considerations.

What about polite requests that immediately follow requests of the "spoiled" variety? Consider the following scenario.

Child: (In bossy tone) Get me a popsicle! I want it now!
Adult: You must ask nicely.
Child: Oh, all right. May I have a popsicle, please?

Adult: That's much better. Here's your popsicle.

What's the problem with this? The problem is that the bossy, spoiled-style request set off a chain of events that resulted in request-granting. Furthermore, the bossy request was reinforced by attention. A popsicle is hardly ever a necessity for life. (We'll ignore the times when you and your child are dying of thirst on the desert and you come across a large package of popsicles.) Thus I would recommend the following response.

Child: (In a bossy tone) Get me a popsicle! I want it now!
Adult: No popsicles now.
Child: Please, may I please have a popsicle?
Adult: I'm going out to get the mail now. Want to walk with me?

In this example, once the spoiled-type request is issued, the adult resolves to deny it, no matter what follows. If a half hour later, when there has been lots of intervening activity, the child makes a pleasant and polite request, the parent's granting it will be helpful to the child.

When the child does politely make reasonable requests that follow positive behavior, the adult's granting them is a wonderful way of reinforcing the positive behavior and modeling the skill of compliance.

Caretakers Need to Be a Team

Consider this vignette.

Little Tricia has in a tyrannical tone of voice ordered her father, "Get me some juice, now!"

Father says, "I don't like that way of asking, Tricia. You know how to ask politely."

Tricia begins to scream very loudly, "I want it! You get it for me!" She cries and stamps her feet and screams louder.

Father ignores this response, and starts taking dishes from the sink and putting them in the dishwasher.

At this moment, grandmother walks in, and says to Tricia, "What's the matter, sweetie pie," and picks her up and hugs her.

Tricia whimpers, "I wanted some juice."

The grandmother says, "Well, is that all it is." Getting juice for Tricia, who has now stopped crying, grandmother says to father, "See daddy, how easy that was, all she needed was a little juice."

The moral is clear, I hope. The adults need to communicate with each other and work out a set of common understandings, so that they won't be working at cross-purposes with one another and risk inciting themselves to violent retribution against one another!

Motivation Systems in Families

Let's make a very brief classification of the ways family members are motivated to do what other family members want them to do.

Level 1: Threats and punishments. At this level, I do something you want out of fear that you will hit me, yell at me, put me in time out, or otherwise do something I find aversive.

Level 2: Bargains, prizes, and tangible goods. At this level, I do something you want in order to get points, a trip to someplace I like, a sticker, a toy, money, or the use of the car.

Level 3: Rational reciprocity. Here I do nice things for you and act pleasant, not for any specific reward. I'm motivated just by knowing that the more pleasant I act toward you, the more likely you are to act pleasant toward me. I reason that if I want the family atmosphere to be pleasant, I'd better do my part.

Level 4: Pleasure from the other's pleasure. Here I do nice things for you and act pleasant because I feel happy when I see you happy. I take direct pleasure from your pleasure.

In the real world, few families and few relationships operate only at levels 3 and 4. For many families, moving up from level 1 to level 2 represents a major positive step. Even the best families occasionally use level 1 motivation. A chapter of this book discusses humane punishments for children. Nonetheless, the more your family members are motivated by levels 3 and 4, the better. The more people can be kind to each other just because it makes them happier to do so, or just because they want to contribute to a positive emotional climate in the family, the more the motivation level of the family will be elevated above threats and tangible rewards.

How do you strengthen level 3 and 4 motivation? One way is by appealing to it, invoking it, calling upon it. Like a magician in a primitive tribe invoking spirits to come out and visit the tribe, you can invoke the spirit of generosity and kindness. Consider this dialogue:

Parent: Would you help me carry the groceries in?

Child: Will you pay me?

Parent: No; but the more we help each other in this family, the more we feel good about each other, and that's much more important than money.

I'm not guaranteeing that the child won't respond to this by saying, "Forget it!" especially if the child is steeped in the models of flippant behavior from television sitcoms. But at least the child had encountered a direct appeal to his level 3 motivation; at least he's gotten the suggestion that sometimes people do things for each other for this reason.

The Shaping Game

The "Shaping Game" is a teaching tool that is designed to give you practice in giving attention when someone does something positive, making that attention mention concretely what you like about the positive example, and withholding attention from behavior that is off the desired track, without being punitive about that behavior. In other words, it gives practice in applying a good number of the principles we've talked about so far. It provides practice in two very important skills: celebrating and reinforcing the positive behavior of others, and celebrating your own positive behavior. These skills are the opposites of many problems in relationships and in mood. To be a little more grandiose, let's say that if everyone on Earth became an expert player of the shaping game and generalized the shaping habits to real life, we would have a much better world.

To further sell the shaping game: this book will suggest many exercises and activities for you and your child to do together. When parents and children try these activities, problems sometimes come up that keep the activities from being positive and productive. If you can become an expert player of the shaping game, and generalize its principles to the activities that are suggested, they have much higher chance of going right.

Before talking about the shaping game, let's talk about shaping. What is shaping? It's helping someone learn to do something by reinforcing "successive approximations" to the goal. In other words, you celebrate the baby steps. You give attention and approval as the person does something just a little better than before, or something just a little closer to the goal. When the person gets out of line, you don't disapprove, but you just withhold comment, watchfully waiting for a move in the right direction so that you can reinforce again.

For example, let's say that a young child is not able to pay attention to books at all, and someone wants to stretch the child's ability to sustain attention to books. Is this person well advised to break out a copy of *War and Peace* and go to it with the child? And then if the child's attention wanders, give the tyke a slap? That's the opposite of shaping. To use shaping, the adult might sit and look at a very simple picture book, and when the child looks at it too, for even one second, the adult pats him on the back, and says, "Here's a book," in an approving way. Then the child goes and looks out the window, and the adult just sits there. Then the child comes back and looks at the book, and the adult looks at the child in a positive way, and says, "The book's called Timmy and Matthew Take Turns." The child this time looks at it for three seconds before he turns away. Perhaps the next time the child returns, the adult even gets to read half a line of text. If the adult continues to be patient and to reinforce attending and to avoid punishing the child for anything, the child will probably eventually enjoy hearing books read.

The shaping game is a simulation, a way of getting concentrated practice at the skill of reinforcing successive approximations to a goal behavior.

Here are the rules of the shaping game:

1. There are two people. The "shaper" thinks of some behavior for

the "shapee" to do, and writes it down, without showing the shapee.

2. The object of the game for the shaper is to give clues so that the shapee can do that behavior.

3. The object of the game for the shapee is to do that behavior. (Thus they both have the same goal, and the game is a cooperative one.)

4. The shapee begins the game by doing things like walking around, touching things, saying things, and so forth.

5. The shaper can give clues only by approving of things that the shapee has already done. For example, the shaper can say things like, "I like it that you turned that direction," or "That's good that you are touching that thing," or "Thank you for lifting your arm like that."

6. Criticism or suggestions or commands are against the rules; positive reinforcement only is permitted.

These are the rules. If you have children that are seven years old or more, they will probably enjoy playing the shaping game. I would recommend it. It's a little too difficult for a preschooler. But if you're an adult with a preschool child, what is really helpful is to do this game with another adult or an older child, to practice the skill of shaping. (Being an adult doesn't mean you can't play games with other adults.) And if you do it with each other in the child's presence, the child will catch on how to do it a lot earlier.

The things that people find hard in this game are just the things that are hard for them in working with children. Sometimes in the game, it's hard for the shaper not to criticize the shapee, just as in real life, it's hard for parents to ignore a child when he does something negative. Some shaping game players stump their shapees by withholding approval, waiting for the goal behavior to be done perfectly. Likewise, in real life, it's often hard to give a child approval for the baby steps toward the goal. Sometimes in the game, the shaper will give praise indiscriminately, without waiting for improvement; in real life, when parents hear that praise is good they often give it for things that aren't praiseworthy enough, so that the child gets more feedback about how the parent is feeling at the moment than about the wisdom of the child's own behavior. Some shapers seem to get pleasure out of the shapee's not knowing what to do, rather than taking responsibility for giving the shapee as good clues as he can give. Some shapers can't let their tone of voice communicate degrees of approval that give the person more clues than the words themselves. Some shapers forget that they can say very specifically what they person did that they liked, and just say "That was good" without saying things like "I like it that you lifted your right leg quickly." Some shapers can't resist the urge to criticize or disapprove, or else waste all their energy resisting this urge.

Do you ever make any of the above-mentioned errors in working with children, or other people? (If not, I want to hire you! Or maybe for you to hire me!) If you're like most of us and occasionally make some of the above errors, you can practice reducing them by playing the shaping game.

In a very common vicious cycle, someone fears failure so much that he doesn't try. Not trying leads to further failure. If a parent can acquire a "shaping attitude" toward the child, and the child can get habits of using this shaping attitude toward himself, this vicious cycle is less likely to start and is fixable once it does start. When you are subject to reward for closer approximations to success and no punishments for failure, there is everything to gain and nothing to lose by trying things.

One-on-one Time, Differential Attention, and Positive Behavior

I spent a year seeing children who had been referred for special education classes in the schools because of behavior problems. I would read teachers' reports of horrendously disruptive behavior that the child had exhibited in the classroom. Then the child would come into my office, talk and play, and sometimes take an individually-administered test. The child most often behaved pleasantly and courteously. I was struck by the difference between the Mr. Hyde reported in the classroom and the Dr. Jekyll who acted so reasonably in my office.

What accounted for the difference? Did I have magical powers? Were the teachers' reports falsified? I concluded that the magic was primarily in one-on-one interaction between an adult and a child. In this situation, gone are the conditions where the child must compete for an adult's attention and where bad behavior reliably gets attention. In their place are conditions where the child has the adult's attention, and the adult can very easily give more or less enthusiasm contingent upon the child's behavior. In addition to this, the adult has the opportunity to sense what types of activity the child might enjoy, get immediate feedback from the child on whether the child is enjoying the activity. The adult can sense when the child is getting bored with one activity and needs a switch to another one.

What if you have more than one child? It seems difficult to spend any time with any of them alone. However, I think that one-on-one time is so good that before giving up on it, I would make a very concerted attempt to engineer the logistics so that you can use it. If you are in a two-parent family, try having one parent go into a room alone with one of the children, while the other parent spends time with the rest of them. Each child knows ahead of time that he or she will eventually get a turn with your individual time.

Another option is to hire a babysitter to come and stay with the rest of the children, while you take one child after the next into a room by yourself.

Or, work out an arrangement with another parent, to get together and let the other parent watch the rest of the children, while you have a series of one-on-ones with each of yours. Then you reciprocate for the other parent. Or if your children are old enough to tolerate some aloneness, you can spend individual time with one of them while the other spends time by herself.

It takes a lot of discipline and planning and motivation to do this. That's why people don't do it very often. But if you can do it, you'll find that having relaxed, gentle, upbeat times with each child, and relieving them of the competition for your attention will have positive effects.

This doesn't mean that all adults will have successful and useful interactions with all children, if you can just get them in a one-on-one situation. That's why I go into such detail in this book about how to interact well with a child.

Using Differential Reinforcement to Help Children Get Work Done

For some parents, the advice in the following section has changed their lives. For some children, it has solved problems that otherwise would have resulted in a prescription of medication for attention problems. If your child has trouble completing tasks, take it seriously!

How much time do all the parents in the world spend in prompting, reminding, urging, and nagging children to get their homework and chores done? My guess is that the total time devoted to this is huge. This would not be so sad if prompting, urging, reminding, and nagging worked very well. It would be time well spent. But much of the time, it turns out that these behaviors only seem to reinforce the child's dawdling. Furthermore, the parent and child get into a sequence of behaviors where the parent gets reinforced for getting into a bad mood. The emotional climate of the family declines as a result. The child's dawdling and the parent's crabbiness get increased according to very familiar and well-known principles of learning.

This section will explain how this takes place, and will outline an alternative. In this alternative – namely using "differential reinforcement of task completion" – the time and effort and energy that the parent puts into helping the child work can actually pay off and bear fruit. In this paradigm, the child is reinforced for getting things finished, and the parent is reinforced for being pleasant and in good spirits.

Remember, if something that you do increases the behavior that comes just before it, what you do is a *reinforcer* for that behavior. If, accidentally or purposely, you reinforce some behavior and do not reinforce other behavior, you are using *differential reinforcement* to increase the first and decrease the second.

As I've emphasized, a parent's attention is very often reinforcing to a child, even when the parent isn't intending to reinforce the behavior that leads to the attention. Sometimes by paying attention to one behavior and ignoring another, parents use differential reinforcement in the wrong direction, without even realizing it.

The Problem: The Dawdling – Nagging Paradigm

Now let's consider dawdling behavior. Suppose a parent asks a child to get dressed, take out the trash, do some homework, or clean up a room. The child gets started doing it, and the parent leaves the child alone to do it. At the moment the child completes it, the parent is involved in something else. There is no immediate reinforcement for working. Let's suppose that a child who finds the parent's attention very reinforcing experiments with dawdling. Instead of getting started, the child gets distracted onto something else. The parent reminds the child again, "Come on, remember you need to get going on this."

When the parent makes this utterance, she is delivering attention to the child – a cherished reinforcer. And what behavior does the attention follow? It follows the dawdling. Now the child has found that when he completes the task without dawdling, he gets no attention, but when he dawdles, he does get the parent's attention.

The child dawdles more and more and more. Finally the parent realizes that if the job is going to get done, the parent has to stand over the child and guide the child every step of the way. The child now has snared a big reinforcer, and again the behavior that the parent's attention follows, and reinforces, is dawdling.

So differential reinforcement is working to make the child keep dawdling. But now let's think about what's going on with the parent's behavior. The parent starts to get a little exasperated. "Come on! I said, get going! Now!" When the parent comes forth with this very attentive negative emotion, the child starts working some. The parent relaxes, and soon the child stops working. "No, it's not time for that! Back to work!" the parent utters, with irritation. The child starts working again, for a little while. The child's working is reinforcement for the parent. And what does this reinforcement follow? It follows the parent's negative emotion – anger, irritation, exasperation. The child's work follows this negative emotion more than it follows the parent's relaxation. So the child is accidentally using differential reinforcement with the parent! The child is differentially reinforcing the parent's negative emotion.

The parent differentially reinforces the child's dawdling, and the child differentially reinforces the parent's crabbiness! This is a sorry state of affairs, yet it is an extremely prevalent one. It can get repeated over literally thousands of trials, until dawdling and crabbiness are so thoroughly ingrained in child and parent that both of them are stuck. I believe that this pattern is responsible for a huge amount of human misery.

How can you get out of this unfortunate paradigm if you find yourself getting into it?

The Solution: Differential Reinforcement for Task Completion

Now let's envision a different paradigm. Suppose the parent says, "I see you have some math homework to do here. Here's the page to work on, and here are your pencil and paper. Your job is to get started now. I'm going to be doing some work, but what I want you to do is to call me when you finish the very first problem. That way I can inspect it."

The parent then goes about her business. If the child dawdles, and the parent ignores the child and does her own thing, joyously. If there is another sibling who is getting some work done, the parent attends to that sibling. But when the child calls out, "I finished the first problem," the parent drops what she is doing and runs to inspect it.

"Hey," says the parent, "you did it! All right! How did you figure out how to do this? Did you learn it in class, or from the book?" The parent's emotion is enthusiastic and positive. It's important that there be some emotion and energy in the parent's response, particularly for children who find the parent's emotion reinforcing.

"How about doing the next two problems, and call me when you've finished them, OK? I'm going to be reading the newspaper some."

Again, the parent happily does her own thing, with no attention to the child, until the child calls out, "I'm done!" Again the parent drops the newspaper immediately and attends to the child in an enthusiastic way.

What is going on now? Now the parent's differential reinforcement is for task completion. If the child does more work immediately after the parent's enthusiastic positive response, the parent is now being reinforced by the child for enthusiastic positive emotion instead of crabbiness.

This is the essence of the new paradigm. There are lots of variations upon it. It's a challenge to pick the variation that fits best with the child's present capacity to work independently.

Variations

Over time, very gradually, the parent increases the amount of work that the child is supposed to do before calling the parent to check. This is called going on an intermittent schedule of reinforcement. If the child is supposed to call the parent after two problems, then three, then four, the child is gradually getting used to a "leaner" schedule of reinforcement. The parent is gradually shaping the child's behavior toward more independent work.

In a very important variation, the parent doesn't actually leave the room and come back in order to carry out differential reinforcement. The parent stays in the room, but just shifts attention. For example, the parent has a book to read. When the parent is not attending, she reads her book, and when she is attending, she looks at the child and speaks to the child. This variation is an important way that you might want to do it at the beginning of the program or with a very young learner, whose independent work skills are not highly developed.

Another very important variation is one in which the parent gives attention not only at the completion of the task, but all through the time that the child is working productively on it. The child starts the math problem, and the parent stands looking over the child's shoulder, saying "Yes. You're getting it. That's good. OK, you did it!" Or, the parent just stands and looks with a hand on the child's shoulder. But as soon as the child gets off task, the parent withdraws attention from the child. This variation is also useful for young learners or those with very much undeveloped independent work skills, or at the beginning of the use of this paradigm.

How does the general paradigm work for chores? Imagine that the parent says, "I'd like for you to take the trash out, please. Please let me know when you've done it, and I'll inspect. The inspection will be that I will walk around and make sure the trash cans inside are empty, and see if the trash is put at the right place outside. Until then, I'll be doing some work on cleaning up my own room. Please give a holler when you're done." If the child does not do the task, the parent spends a long time away from the child, cleaning up her own room. If the child does do the task, the parent drops what she is doing and runs to the child. "Wow, that was quick. Are you sure these indoor trash cans are empty? I'll bet they're full. No! Empty! What do you know! Let's see if that trash is at the right place outside. I'll bet not. Wow! They're at the exact right place! Congratulations!"

At the beginning, you may find that using this paradigm is more work than doing the chore yourself! But the work you spend training your child to do chores is a great cause. Through this means your child can learn to do more and more independent work.

How do you make the schedule of reinforcement more intermittent, with chores? After a time, you make a list of chores. You have the child call you for inspection after each one of them is completed. After some time of operating like this, you ask the child to call you after two of them have been completed, or after three of them have been completed. You gradually work your way to the point where the inspection occurs after the whole list has been finished.

Another variation involves keeping track of the time that it takes to do various tasks. The parent starts a timer going (for example the stopwatch function of an electronic watch) when the child begins a certain task. When the child signals that the task is done, the parent stops the timer. (Or the child starts and stops the timer.) Part of the positive feedback the child gets can be on how little time it took to do the certain task. You can start to get a feeling for what amount of time is top flight efficiency, versus what amount of time is average or below average efficiency, for various tasks. If the child himself starts to get a feeling for these, then the child is getting some fairly accurate feedback on his concentration performance for each task.

Another important variation is for the child for whom your attention is not a powerful enough reinforcer in and of itself. You may wish to then use tangible reinforcers, such as junk food. A little bit of junk food, and some positive attention, reinforce task completion. Or each little task is reinforced by the click of a counter. The attainment of a certain number gets the payoff of a little bit of junk food. You want not to fill the child up on junk food, because then this reinforcer is no longer reinforcing, and the child won't want nutritious food at the next meal. But using tiny bits to reinforce task completion will often work well. If you use this option, it's a good idea to withhold junk food at most other times.

In any variation of this program, you want to try to give more attention to correct, accurate, and high-quality performance than to sloppy, inaccurate, and low-quality performance. Sometimes it is easy to use differential reinforcement in the wrong direction, to reinforce incompetent performance: for example when the child does the math problem right, all the parent says is "That's good," whereas when the child does the math problem wrong, the parent takes five minutes to explain where the error was and how to do it correctly. Or when the child does the chore right, the parent just says a quick word of praise, whereas when the child does not do the chore right, the parent gets involved in correcting it. The antidote to this problem is to dwell loud and long over the correct and accurate performances, and to give explanations and corrections for the inaccurate performances in a more crisp and efficient way. It's always helpful to think about shaping. Shaping means at first reinforcing performances that haven't made it to the final standard, then gradually raising the standard. Sometimes at first you want to reinforce time spent on the task, whether the performance is perfect or not. As the child gets better at logging in time on the task, you gradually start using differential reinforcement for higher and higher quality work.

The key concepts to keep in mind, for any of the variations, are that 1) your attention and excitement are usually reinforcing, 2) you want to think in terms of giving reinforcement AFTER a bit of work rather than after some dawdling, and 3) you want to get into that happy state where the child's work is reinforcing you for giving positive attention rather than reinforcing you for nagging at the child.

Chapter 6: Commands, Suggestions, and Responsiveness

Chapter Overview:

Most people—children or adults—don't like to be bossed around. They'll feel like rebelling if bossed around too much. On the other hand, learning to follow someone else's directives is an important skill. Work for the state where both you and your child can competently carry out both child-directed activity and adult-directed activity. In child-directed activity, you follow the child's lead, and in adult-directed activity, you give directions and the child follows.

We can classify things people say to each other somewhere on a scale of directiveness versus responsiveness. With directive utterances you pull the person's attention and behavior where you want them to go; with responsive utterances, you respond to the person's current direction of attention, without changing it. Your children will be more willing to accept your directives when you have first been responsive to their thoughts. If you give too many directives without enough responsiveness, you can gradually raise your child's level of irritation past the rebellion threshold. One study found that when parents were asked to make their children's behavior worse, they could do so by giving lots of stern commands.

The sheer giving of commands doesn't make a child obedient. Rather, obedience comes from (1) a high likelihood that you'll enforce the command, and (2) a high likelihood that the behavior you command is reasonable and worthwhile to carry out. So if you want to help a child obey better, first you eliminate unnecessary commands. When you give a directive, first get clear in your own head how much choice you intend to give the child; then communicate that to the child by phrasing either a command or a suggestion. To eliminate unnecessary commands for young children, get valuable or dangerous objects out of reach as much as you can. Also, provide attractive playthings that can absorb the child's attention.

Once you have given a command to a young child, don't keep repeating it if the child ignores you. That only gives the child practice in disregarding your commands. You can enforce most necessary commands to young children by "physical guidance": gently and calmly moving the child's body to where it needs to be.

****

In this chapter we'll talk about directiveness versus responsiveness with children. These concepts are similar to the ideas of control versus freedom. Let's first define some terms to help us think about how much how much directiveness versus responsiveness our utterances convey.

Directive and Responsive Styles

An directive maneuver attempts to change the direction of the child's attention. For example, toddler Mary is reaching for a ball, and an older child says, "Mary, tell me what my name is!" The older child is redirecting the toddler's attention away from where it was inclined to go. An responsive maneuver responds to the child's current direction of attention, without changing it. For example, toddler Mary is reaching for a ball, and an older child says, "Mary's getting the ball!"

Let's look at an example of different degrees of directiveness and responsiveness. Suppose an older child says, "These guys at school just keep picking on me. I don't know what to do about it." Here's an example of a directive response: "Oh, don't worry about it. By the way, how have your grades been lately?" This response sends the message, "Quit thinking about what's on your mind, and think about something else." Similarly attention-directive would be, "Oh. Well, I'm kind of excited, myself, because I'm getting to go camping tomorrow night." Why is this utterance directive? Because it says, "Quit thinking about what you were thinking about, and direct your attention elsewhere." Directing someone's attention is more subtle than directing the movements of her body, but it can have a major effect just the same. Two responses that totally say, "Keep thinking about what you're wanting to think about, directing your attention with total freedom," might be a concerned glance and the word "Oh?" or "Sounds like a tough problem." A little more directive might be something like "Oh, tell me more about that please." A little more directive might be "When did this start?" and still more directive would be "Maybe a good thing to do in that case is to work really hard to get some friends to be on your side." And a response that not only directs the attention, but directs behavior, would be "Well, tomorrow morning, first thing, I want you to go straight to your teacher and tell him about this. Do you understand?"

Now let's define terms to classify these types of utterances.

When the younger child is getting the ball, and the older child said to the toddler, "Mary's getting the ball," that is what I call tracking and describing: you watch what the child is paying attention to and put words on it. When the person gave a concerned glance and said, "Oh?" that was a facilitation: a grunt that basically communicates, "I'm tuned in and receiving your transmission; you're free to continue." When the person said, "Sounds like a tough problem," that was a reflection: a restatement of at least part of the message that was received from the other person, that lets the other person know the message was received, but doesn't direct the next message.

Now some mid-range utterances, in the middle between responsive and directive. "Tell me more about that please," and "When did this start," are an open-ended follow-up question and a specific follow-up question, respectively. Both stay on the same topic that the person raised; the second is more directive since it specifies a certain subtopic whereas the first lets the person choose what subtopic to go to.

Now the directive utterances. "Maybe a good thing to do in that case is to work really hard to get some friends to be on your side," we can call a suggestion. "By the way, how have your grades been," we can call a new-topic question: the person's attention is requested to move to a new topic altogether. "Oh. Well, I'm kind of excited, myself, because I'm getting to go camping tomorrow night," is a new-topic statement. And finally, "I want you to go straight to your teacher and tell him about this. Do you understand?" is an example of a command.

Now what is the use of all this language? There are lots of uses. But here's a proposition, for starters. On countless occasions there develops irritability, sullenness, rebelliousness, or hostility between people, because one person is too directive and not responsive enough; neither person realizes or even has in his vocabulary the concepts to realize that this is the reason for the bad feelings. Here's a corollary: moving from the more directive to the more responsive communications can sometimes "tame savage beasts," or make unhappy and uncooperative children more happy and cooperative.

Here's what often goes on. When someone wants to think about a certain topic, and is directed off it, she experiences a little low-level irritation. When this happens over and over in rapid succession, the irritation mounts up and up. There is finally a "straw that breaks the camel's back," and the person comes out with a hostile utterance or gesture, and the attention-directive other person is totally baffled, thinking "What did I do to deserve this?" Or, equally likely: the child does something rebellious or naughty, to get back, and the parent, seeing nothing malicious on his part that instigated the child's rebellion, thinks to himself, "This child has a bad disposition by nature."

Here's another proposition. The psychologically healthy child is able to deal both with direction and responsivity from other people; the child with skill deficiencies in submission and compliance can't tolerate the directive style and the child with skill deficiencies in spontaneity, gleefulness, social initiations, social conversation, and courage often is more comfortable with a more directive interaction with an adult. For most children, the responsive style poses less of a challenge to the child's frustration-tolerance than does the directive style.

A similar proposition will follow. But first some more terms. There are certain activities that lend themselves particularly to one or the other style. For example, when I am giving the child a vocabulary test, I am and I am asking question after question and the child is answering, there is lots of direction going on; we may call this adult-directed activity. The typical school classroom involves a great deal of adult-directed activity. On the other hand, when I am doing dramatic play with a young child, or when I am with a child who is chatting with me, I can afford to let the child take his own lead, and I can do lots of responding: we may call this child-directed activity. Here's the proposition: the most fortunate and healthy situation occurs when the parent and child can do both adult-directed activity and child-directed activity in a comfortable and pleasant way. Their repertoires are broad, rather than constricted.

Another proposition: in being with someone with a responsive style, the child is exposed to models that help the child to become more adept at the responsive style. Thus the overly bossy child, the one with skill deficiency in tolerating a wide range of others' behavior, can learn this skill by being around someone who shows him how to do tracking and describing, facilitations, reflections, and follow-up questions. Or in other words, participating in child-directed activity lays down in the child's memory bank the responsive patterns that will then prepare the child to succeed in adult-directed activity. Thus pleasant child-directed activity lays a foundation for future adult-directed activity.

Now having expounded some of the general theory of the directive and the responsive style, let's talk about the least subtle directive communication: commands.

How Unnecessary Commands Stimulate Bad Behavior

I am not advocating a "permissive" environment where children are allowed to do whatever they please no matter how harmful or irritating. It's very important that the child learn to respect the needs of others, refrain from harmful behavior, and obey you well. A child who is allowed total license becomes very disobedient. But the children who learn to obey the best are those whose parents give them fairly few commands, and only when there's a really good reason. This way, the child comes to expect and trust that there's a good reason even if he doesn't understand it at the time. Secondly, the child comes to expect that the if the parent gives a command, the parent will enforce it.

To put this another way: sometimes parents think that giving lots of commands is being "strict" and giving few commands is being "permissive." But it's not the giving of commands that makes a child obedient; it's (1) a high probability that any command will be enforced, and (2) high probability that the commanded behavior is reasonable and worthwhile to carry out.

Another reason not to give too many commands is that children have more fun with their parents if they aren't being bossed around all the time. People tend to like freedom, all other things equal. The better time the child is having, the less irritated he is by unnecessary restrictions, the more he will want to please you by acting better.

Once researchers went to a bunch of parents, and said, "We'll watch you while you're with your children. Let's see if you can make your children act worse than they usually act." A group of parents actually went along with doing this, and sure enough, they got their children to act worse. Meanwhile, the researchers were counting everything the parents did. What do you think they did more often to get their children to act worse? They said things like "Put that down. Leave that alone. Sit down. Quit fidgeting so much. Tie your shoe better, it isn't tied right." When there is great directiveness, combined with great disapproval, the verbal environment is at its most unpleasant. Can you see why the children might have acted worse?

Here's another perspective on unnecessary commands. Imagine that you were to come to my office to get some advice about dealing with your child. Suppose when you walk in, I were to say to you, "OK! You sit here. You sit over here. Put both your feet on the floor. Take that coat off. No, don't put it down on the chair, hang it up. Look up at me here. Don't look at me with that sort of expression on your face." What would your prevailing emotion be, and how disposed would you be toward cooperation with me? If your answers are (1) angry and (2) totally uncooperative, the answers are probably just the same for children.

Exercise: Discriminating Necessary From Unnecessary Commands

This is to let you practice deciding whether commands are absolutely necessary or not. I'll give you an example of a command that somebody might give a preschool child, and you decide whether you think it's absolutely necessary. Compare your opinions with the opinions written at the end of the set of examples.

You might think this exercise is too easy. But it's good to practice asking the question anyway, the important question: is this a point where I want to give a command, or not? The difficulty in life is remembering to ask the question of whether a command is necessary, before you've already given it! Most of us come out with commands by reflex or by habit, not by some rational decision about what is necessary and what isn't. This exercise is meant to give you some practice at pondering whether commands are necessary or unnecessary; hopefully you can do the same sort of pondering about the commands you issue your child.

1. The child has a paper clip, and he starts to stick it in the electrical outlet. The adult takes it from him, and at the same time says, "No, we have to leave this socket alone."

2. A five year old is fidgeting around a lot while the adult is reading a story to him, but he is still paying attention. The adult says, "Hold still. Don't fidget so much."

3. A four-year-old child is playing with some toy people and toy animals. He decides that the lion can fly through the air, and is moving him around, saying, "Here goes the flying lion." The adult says, "Lions can't fly. Put him down on the ground."

4. A four year old child is looking at the material in some curtains. He is holding it in his hand and feeling it, and isn't pulling on it or mistreating it in any way. The adult says, "Johnny, put that down and leave it alone."

5. A four year old is picking up a puppy in a way that is hurting the puppy. The adult says, "Put the puppy down, right now."

6. A four year old is playing with toy people and a toy house. The people drive their car up on top of the house, and some of them stand up there. The adult says, "They shouldn't be on top of the house. Get them down from there."

7. A four year old child is playing with an adult, and reaches up and pulls the adult's hair. The adult says, "That hurt when you did that. Don't ever do that again. If you ever do that again, we'll stop the session and go back."

8. A four year old is playing with crayons and paper. He has drawn a person, and then he starts to scribble all over his own drawing. The adult says, "No, don't scribble on your drawing."

9. A four year old is starting to draw with a crayon on the wall. The adult says, "No, no. We don't draw on the walls, we only draw on paper." And while doing this the adult gently takes the child's hand and stops him from drawing on the wall.

10. A three year old is sitting around during one of the sessions with an adult, and he is exploring his shoes. He starts to take his shoe off. The adult says, "No, leave your shoe on."

11. A five year old has come in from outside, and still has his coat on, despite the fact that it is warm enough inside. The adult says, "Take your coat off."

12. An adult and a four year old are playing together. The child turns his attention away from the toys and lies on his back and looks up at the ceiling. The adult says, "Get up from there."

13. Two three year old children are sitting and having fun sticking out their tongues at each other, and giggling. The adult sees them and says, "Don't do that, that isn't nice."

14. A child is about to get a shot at the doctor's office. The child starts to whimper and cry. The adult says, "Stop crying."

15. The child is playing outside in a park, and puts a ball on the top of his head and tries to balance it, and makes silly noises while doing so. The adult says, "Quit acting so silly."

Here are my opinions on these, so that you can compare.
1. Absolutely necessary
2. Not absolutely necessary
3. Not absolutely necessary
4. Not absolutely necessary
5. Absolutely necessary
6. Not absolutely necessary
7. Absolutely necessary
8. Not absolutely necessary
9. Absolutely necessary
10. Not absolutely necessary
11. Not absolutely necessary
12. Not absolutely necessary
13. Not absolutely necessary
14. Not absolutely necessary
15. Not absolutely necessary

Exercise: Monitoring Your Commands

The hardest part of ceasing to give unnecessary commands is to interrupt the command reflex, and to reflect on whether a command is necessary or not. Here's a way to raise your own consciousness about unnecessary commands. For a couple of hours that you spend with your child, try to keep a list of every command that you give. How many of them are unnecessary? Which of them can you eliminate? If you find yourself tending to give unnecessary commands, do mental rehearsals of withholding unnecessary commands, and then monitor yourself again.

When to Use Commands, and When to Use Suggestions

Commands are meant to tell the child that he has no choice, that the adult is in charge and has decided that the child will do something. Suggestions are meant to tell the child that he has a choice: that he can decide whether he wants to do it or not. A command is something like, "Don't touch that skillet." A suggestion is something like, "Would you like to go outside?" If you want to give the child a choice, and you have decided that you can live with either way the child decides, make a suggestion; if you do not want to give the child a choice, and you are going to enforce the directive, give a command. I know that this sounds obvious, but again, the force of habit sometimes leads parents to confuse their children with the wrong type of message.

The first confusing tactic is giving a command when a suggestion is more appropriate. For example, the child comes into the house with his coat on, and the parent commands, "Take your coat off." The child ignores this. The parent now repeats the command. The child says, "No, I'm still cold, I want to warm up first." The parent has the choice of saying, "Well, OK, that sounds reasonable," and undermining the precedent that all commands are enforced, or saying, "No, it's time to take it off," and enforcing a command which never should have been given. (Between those two choices, I'd pick the first.)

The second confusing tactic is giving a suggestion when a command is more appropriate. For example, the child has been at a party, and the adult simply has to take the child home now. The adult says, "Would you like to leave now?" The child says, "No," and runs off playing. The parent says, "But I want to go now. Don't you?" The child says, "No." The child now has gotten the impression that he or she has a choice of whether to leave or stay. The adult has to undo that message now, and say something like, "Well, I'm sorry, you don't have any choice, we're both leaving now," in which case the child's reply might still be "No," just by inertia—the child has already said no twice before.

Exercise: Deciding, Command or Suggestion

Please read each of the following vignettes, and decide 1) whether the parent gave a command or suggestion, and 2) whether it would have been more appropriate to do something other than what was done.

1. A child is holding a younger child around the neck, in a way that is not hurting, but is greatly scaring, the younger child. The adult says, "Take your hands off him now."
2. At a birthday party, there are some extra balloons lying around that have not been blown up yet. An eight year old child is looking at it, thinking about doing something with it. The adult says, "Would you like to try to blow the balloon up?"
3. A preschool teacher has given the children a snack and has used napkins and paper cups. The teacher is cleaning up the napkins and cups, and says to one child, "Would you like to take this and put it in the trash can for me?"
4. A preschool teacher is going to do some vigorous play, and the teacher notices that one child has a big wad of chewing gum in his mouth. The preschool has a firm policy against the use of chewing gum in the midst of such activities, lest children inhale chewing gum and suffocate. The teacher says to the child, "If you're through with that chewing gum, you can put it in the trash can."
5. A parent says to his child, "Let's read a story, would you like to?"
6. A parent says, in an authoritarian tone, "Tell Uncle Pete what animals you saw today at the park."
7. The child starts to write on the desk. The adult says, in a tone of authority, "We write only on the paper; we don't write on anything else."

My opinions of the answers:
1. Command, and command is appropriate

2. Suggestion, and suggestion is appropriate
3. Suggestion, and suggestion is appropriate (If child doesn't want to do it, the teacher does it instead, and ignores child for a few seconds, or gets another child to help, and attends to that child.)
4. Suggestion, and command would have been better
5. Suggestion, and suggestion is appropriate
6. Command, and suggestion would have been more appropriate
7. Command, and command is appropriate

Arranging the Physical Environment to Help the Emotional Climate

If you have young children, don't have breakable or dangerous stuff in reach. Otherwise you'll constantly have to watch the child and command him to stay away from it. So to improve your emotional climate, go through the house and think of all the things that you have to command the child to stay away from. Put these things in high cabinets or on top of high shelves or lock them in closets or file cabinets. For a child who by temperament is extremely active and "into everything," these changes can drastically affect the way the house looks and is arranged. Sometimes a child with such a temperament makes it impossible to have a "house beautiful" decor. But it will be worth it to sacrifice decor for a few years, for the sake of not going crazy issuing the child many commands and having the child rebel against them.

Arranging the Physical Environment to Promote Sustained Attention

Suppose you want to use the responsive style, because you have found that the child acts much nicer when you do so. This means that you don't want to keep directing the child's attention back to something when the attention wanders. But you'd also like the child to practice sustaining attention to one thing for a while, rather than flitting from one thing to another. You can accomplish these goals by using the stimulus situation of the physical environment to bring out sustained attention; your responsive utterances will then reinforce the skill of sustaining attention.

You construct the room so that literally everything interesting in the room is on high shelves, out of the child's reach. You sit down on the floor with the child, and chat with the child until the child asks you to play with one unit of toys or books or whatever. (Every unit that you have on the shelves is something you want the child to pay attention to.) Then you get the unit for the child, and you track and describe, or reflect, or answer questions, or otherwise make responsive utterances in tones of approval. When the child tires of it and asks for something else, put the first unit away before getting the second unit down. Thus the child only has one unit of things in his reach, and those are just the things you want him to be paying attention to.

Using Alternative Activities to Distract, Instead of Commands to Stay Out Of

Imagine that the parent is taking the child to a place where there are several open doors that the child should not walk through. There are also some toys and books on a shelf out of the child's reach. In short, imagine yourself in a "waiting room." Consider these two options for the parent:

Option 1. The parent decides to rest his or her weary bones. The child starts going through the doors that the child isn't supposed to go through, and getting into the things the child isn't supposed to mess with. The adult says to the child, "Johnny, come back out of there! The child complies perhaps the first time, but then begins to ignore this command as he ventures forth exploring again and the parent again commands him. The parent starts to get irritated with the child's disobedience. The parent repeatedly commands the child, in an increasingly irritated tone of voice, "Get out of there and come back over here and sit down!" The child ignores this, and the parent gets so irritated that the parent goes and swats the child on the rear end. The child starts crying and screaming, and the adult is more frustrated with the child now than ever.

Option 2: The parent surveys the scene, and thinks: "If I want the child to stay out of all those rooms, it'll be a lot easier if the child has something else more fun to do than explore them." So the parent decides not to rest weary bones right away, but to get the toys down and get the child interested in them. The parent sits on the floor with the child, making "tracking and describing" comments while the child plays with the toys, and as the child begins to play more autonomously, the parent successfully rests the weary bones.

The principle here is that you can sometimes avoid a lot of commands to a child to "stay out of" something if you can provide an attractive alternative to "get into."

Caution! This principle does NOT imply that you should respond to the child's doing something you don't like by offering him something attractive and fun to distract him. You want to anticipate the child's being tempted, and get the child into something else *before* the child starts doing what you don't like. Otherwise, you run the risk of reinforcing the child for misbehavior. Consider this scenario.

Option 3. The parent and child have arrived at the same waiting room environment that they were in before. This time the child starts exploring the rooms, and the parent says, "Johnny, get out of there!" Johnny ignores for several more repetitions of the command. Then the parent says, "Johnny, if you'll come here, I've got some potato chips for us to eat." Johnny goes and eats them with his parent.

In this option the parent has offered a distracting alternative, but it is offered contingent upon the child's disobeying. The child is learning, "If I disobey, the parent will have to up the ante and offer me something attractive to make me obey." Thus the child is getting a powerful lesson in the advantages of disobedience.

Therefore the key idea is to distract the child with an attractive alternative before the child starts misbehaving, not after.

Using "Physical Guidance" as an Alternative to Repeated Commands

What do you do when you have made a command, and the child has ignored it? For example, you say to the child, "Come with me, it's time for us to leave," and the child treats you like background music.

Here's the type of dialogue that is NOT helpful. The parent says in a louder tone, "I said, Come ON!" The child says, "Why do we have to go now?" The parent says, "Because we have places to get to, now start moving!" The child says, "But I don't want to!" The parent says, "I don't care, you've got to, now get moving!"

What has happened in this dialogue? First of all, instead of practicing the disobedience of only one command, the child has practiced disobeying three or four of them. Second, the child has gotten reinforced for disobedience by the emotion the parent has generated and the attention the child has received. Third, the parent has modeled irritated and angry utterances for the child. The verbal environment has been polluted!

An alternative that is particularly appropriate for preschool children is what I call "physical guidance" to enforce the command. Physical guidance means as gently as possible, taking the child's body and moving it so as to enforce the command. There is no attempt to hurt the child, but only to move the child.

In the above example, rather than arguing or shouting, you simply take the child's hand or hands or if necessary pick the child up, and walk calmly out of the room.

For a second example, you have been playing with a child in a room. It is time to put the toys away before you leave. You say, "It's time for the toys to go back in the box, and for us to leave." The child says, "No, I don't want to."

Rather than giving repeated commands, the parent calmly dumps the toys in a box, puts the toys on a shelf, takes the child by the hand, and walks out the door. If the child is screaming and resisting, the parent calmly walks out the door with the child anyway.

You'll notice in this last example that the parent did not command the child to put the toys away, or try to use physical guidance to get the child to put the toys away. You can use physical guidance to enforce only the grossest physical movements, like going from one place to another, or moving away from something, or releasing an object which is then placed out of reach. If you think about it, these are the most frequent necessary commands for little kids anyway. For more complex tasks, where physical guidance would entail moving the child's hands or fingers rather than the whole body, I recommend thinking twice about whether you really want to issue the command in the first place.

You want your child to get a repeated, consistent experience that when you give him a firm command, he will have to obey it. If this experience is consistent enough, he will usually soon choose to avoid the embarrassment of being dragged kicking and screaming, and will cooperate. He will know that there is no "percentage" in resisting. You want to avoid the child's ever getting lots of attention from you by arguing back and forth over what to do. You want to avoid the child's feeling very powerful in successfully resisting your authority. These reinforce the child for disobeying. Intermittent reinforcement can produce a very strong habit of disobedience.

Disobedience Is NOT To Be Tolerated

I want to emphasize that a parent should never give a command, notice that a child disobeys it, and ignore that disobedience. Both for the parent's mental health, and for the child's developing self-discipline skills, it is important to establish the expectation that clear-cut commands from a parent are always obeyed. If the child does not obey such commands, there is physical guidance, a reprimand, loss of a privilege, repetitive practice in role-playing later on of compliance with the command, or some other communcation that the disobedience is not taken lightly by the parent. One of the main reasons for parents to eliminate unnecessary commands is so that the parent will have the energy to do one of these things each time the child fails to comply.

Chapter 7: The Quality of Talk with the Child

Chapter Overview:

How the people in your family talk to one another is not a trivial thing. It influences important outcomes such as life and death and success and failure. When two family members can talk in a way that both enjoy, their relationship is strengthened. Good talk is a vehicle for people to solve problems, learn about what problems need to be solved, gain thinking skills crucial for success, and communicate love and caring to each other. Good talk is usually characterized by people's taking turns responding to what the other said. I'll call this reciprocal interaction. When people don't talk too long and don't interrupt, they help this reciprocal interaction to take place.

Most adults who want a child to talk to them start grilling the child with questions. Often it works better to talk to the child about your own experience, then be quiet to give the child an opportunity to say something, and then respond enthusiastically if the child talks. We can call this modeling, silence, and responsiveness. When the child does start to open up, it's important not to respond with premature or unnecessary advice or reprimanding the child.

Six types of responsive utterances help you have good conversations with your child. Tracking and describing is simply observing and saying in words what the child is attending to. For example, the young child playing with a toy truck, and you say "There goes the truck, up the hill!" Or the adolescent is shooting basketball, and you say, "You're practicing the long ones." Facilitations are utterances like "Uh huh," and "Yes," and "I see," that communicate, "I'm listening; you can keep on talking." Reflections are statements that say, "If I understand you correctly, you are saying ______." When you reflect, you let the child know her message was understood; you also let her continue without directing her. Follow-up questions ask for some more information on the topic the child is already speaking about. Telling about your own experience models for the child how to tell about her experience. Positive reinforcement means giving approval for something the child said. If both parent and child learn to speak with each other with lots of these sorts of utterances, it is likely that very pleasant and useful and growth-enhancing conversations will take place often.

****

How the Quality of Talk Affects Psychological Health

The words conversation and talk sometimes seem have a connotation of triviality, as in "Let's while away the hours in amusing conversation," "a cocktail-party conversation," and "too much talk and not enough action." But the quality of talk among familiy members, as I've suggested before, can affect such non-trivial outcomes as suicide, homicide, divorce, hospital admission, and drug addiction, versus success and happiness and productivity. How can something so fleeting as spoken words have such concrete effects? Here are some mechanisms:

1. High quality talk between family members is "mutually gratifying activity": something that's fun, pleasant for both of them. The pleasure may come from humor, from intellectual stimulation, from progress on decision-making about life situations, from simply being understood by another person, from playful joint use of imagination together, or from any of several other sources. When family members do lots of mutually gratifying activities, they feel good about one another, they enjoy life, they don't want to kill themselves, they don't want to hurt each other, and they don't want to escape from something by drugging themselves.

2. Talk is the vehicle whereby people solve their problems together in nonviolent ways. Because of the miracle of language, I can politely say "Excuse me" instead of pushing you out of my way. In more complex problem-solving conversations, as we will discuss in future chapters, people can use talk to come up with creative and mutually satisfying solutions to their conflicts.

3. Talk is the vehicle whereby you will learn about something in the external world that is troubling your child. If the communication process is blocked off, you will not know and can't do anything about it.

4. Talk is the major way for the child to build his vocabulary and language fluency skills. These skills are of crucial importance for academic success, as well as psychologically healthy functioninly healthy.

5. Conversation provides a major opportunity for a child to practice the skill of sustaining attention to verbal information. This skill is another one that will be of crucial importance for the child's education.

6. Talk is probably the major way whereby family members communicate their love and caring for one another. I am referring not primarily to the sentence "I love you," but to the tones of approval and words of responsivity that communicate caring and positive regard in every conversation that goes on.

7. A major research study referred to the two major patterns of behavior problems in children as aggression and shyness. Fun talk going on between two people is the opposite of shyness, and somewhat incompatible with aggression.

Would you like to do an experiment? Think of two or three people you like, and two or three whom you dislike. For each, rate how much you like them, and rate the quality of the conversations you have with them. Specifically, how much approval goes on? How much unwanted directiveness goes on? Do you find that the quality of the verbal environment created between you and the other person predicts very highly the degree of like versus dislike? Is there anyone about whom you can say, "We have great conversations, that are a lot of fun for both of us. But we really can't stand each other." Probably not. Whatever helps family members to like each other more is conducive to psychological health.

When Two Reponsive Styles Meet: Reciprocal Interaction

In the last chapter I defined the responsive style as utterances which do not attempt to change the other person's direction of attention, but respond to it. What happens when you are responsive to the child, and the child is responsive to you? You and the child take turns responding to each other, just as the players in a tennis game hit the ball back and forth to one another. You talk back and forth, and each of you is saying something responsive to what the other person just said. It tends to feel good. We call this reciprocal interaction.

Reciprocal interaction contrasts with the situation when both people are talking, but neither is responsive to what the other said. Sometimes you hear people trying to communicate, with both talking at once—as if both were hitting balls to the other simultaneously, but not hitting any back. At other times they take turns speaking, but they are giving alternating monologues, not responding to what the other person said—as if our ping pong players took turns hitting balls in the other's direction, but still not returning any. Another departure from reciprocal interaction occurs when one person hangs on to the ball for so long that the other person doesn't get a chance to do any playing, and gets bored. Thus one person's delivering a long monologue is not responsive, and not compatible with reciprocal interaction.

Enemies of Reciprocal Interaction: Interruptions and Overlong Statements

Sometimes conversation produces a mounting hostility between people in a way that neither of them is fully aware of, when they can't settle successfully the issue of who has the "floor." People's interrupting one another and talking at the same time, in louder voices so as to prevail over the other, is a sure sign of this conflict. Avoiding interruptions and listening until the end will help the quality of the conversation, usually. However, sometimes the interruptor is merely responding to the other person's seeming that he will keep going forever if not interrupted. Here the main problem is "overlong statements" by the other person. Overlong statements give the listener the choice of interrupting or sitting and listening for way too long before having a chance to talk. As a general rule a statement lasting over a minute has fair chance of feeling like an overlong statement in conversations.

Conversation is a process of taking turns talking and listening, and it is crucial that this turn-taking process be worked out to the satisfaction of both. At times in family therapy sessions I have taken a piece of paper and written "the floor" on it, and have established the rule that one can speak only when holding "the floor"; you can ask for the floor by holding out a hand to the person who has it.

How People Try and Fail To Start Conversations With Children

Suppose you want to get a conversation going with a young child. Often the "natural thing to do" often doesn't work best. The natural thing to do is to be directive, and to ask questions, and to persist asking more questions if the first ones don't work. Example:

Parent: How was your day today?
Child: OK.
Parent: What did you do?
Child: Oh, not much.
Parent: Did anything fun happen?
Child: Not really.
Parent: Did anything unpleasant happen?
Child: Nope.
Parent: Well, tell me what did happen.
Child: I don't know.
Parent: How can you not know what happened to you?
Child: (Shrugs.)

An Alternative: Modeling, Silence, Responsiveness

How else can you help a child learn to chat better? Suppose the child is quiet or shy, or inhibited, or doesn't know what to do, and it's hard to get into a reciprocal interaction with him?

By doing three things, none of which are particularly directive, you can often get good interaction going where direction didn't do it. These three things are modeling, silence, and responsiveness to the child's utterances.

By modeling, I refer to showing the child how to interact with you. If you say, "Last night I saw the moon out really bright! It was pretty! I stood and looked at it for a long time," you're telling about your own experience, but you're also showing the child how to tell about his experience. Or for another example, suppose you are doing dramatic play with the child, and you put a little ball behind something, in the child's plain sight, and have a character say, "Now let's see, where did I put that ball? I can't find it anywhere," while the character looks for it. You are modeling how to have the characters talk in dramatic play, and how to enact a plot. The child is also being tempted to intervene and respond.

Or suppose you spread out several books on the floor where the child is sitting and say, "Hey, here's an interesting one. It's got a big butterfly on the cover!" You are modeling for the child how to take an interest in the things around him and comment on them.

Being silent for a while is very difficult for some people. Sometimes children can't get going with an adult because the adult is in too big a hurry. The child often needs some time to figure out what he's going to do. So after actively and enthusiastically modeling how to interact, you just sit there, for about 10 seconds. This seems like a long time, given our norms that there is almost no silence in conversations. But sometimes the child needs this long to understand that it is permissible for him to respond, or to figure out how he wants to respond, or to summon the courage to respond. If the adult does not tolerate silence, but barges ahead with nonstop utterances, the child never gets a chance to respond.

Responsiveness comes immediately after the child communicates with you. The adult hurries to give an enthusiastic approving response to what the child said or did. In the dramatic play example given above, if the child's character takes the ball and gives it to the adult's character, the adult might hurry to say, "Oh, thank you! You found it for me!." ("You found it for me" is the responsive utterance we defined in the last chapter as "tracking and describing.")

When you wait in silence for the child's response, you will often do well to busy yourself with something so that the child will not feel stage fright. What if, after waiting in silence, the child does not respond? Then you can deliver another model, or you can have more silence, using your judgment as to what will work better.

Exercise in Practicing Modeling, Silence, and Responsiveness

Put some toys on the floor, and sit down on the floor with an imaginary child—either another adult role-playing, or a child of your own imagination. Make up a model of some sort of utterance. Then wait and count to ten. No matter how good your model was, the imaginary child doesn't respond. Then do the same thing again. Do a third model, and now imagine the child responding. When he does, hurry to respond nondirectively, with some approval in your voice.

If you do this enough with real children, you will get a feeling for the rhythm of it. Concentrate on giving reinforcing responses after the child's communications, rather than on giving directives before the child's communications.

More on the Responsive versus Directive Style

When the child does volunteer a communication to the adult, lots of times adults respond in ways that squelch further communication from the child. One way is to give premature or unneeded advice.

Example of Premature Advice:

Child: This kid at the preschool is a real problem.
Parent: Well, just be nice to him and I'm sure that things will work out.
Example of Unnecessary Advice:
Child: I'm getting to where I can hit that tee ball almost every time. Not quite, but almost. I think my plan paid off.
Parent: Well, keep working on it and practicing.

At other times, the parent actually reprimands the child for trying to open communication.

Example of Reprimanding the Child for Starting to Talk:
Child: I forgot to do my math homework today.
Parent: You know you're supposed to keep on top of your assignments! I don't want to hear of your forgetting one more time, is that clear? Do you understand?

Let's examine five types of messages that work extremely well in producing a positive verbal environment for adults and children to occupy together. These are:

1. Tracking and describing
2. Facilitations
3. Reflections
4. Follow-up questions
5. Telling about your own experience. (Both follow-up statements, and new-topic statements.)
6. Positive reinforcement

If you become expert at each of these, and if you use them often in conversations with your child, you and your child will almost certainly have great times talking together. Let's talk about each of these techniques.

Tracking and Describing

"Tracking and describing" means that the adult watches what the child is doing (that is, tracks the activity) and verbally describes what is going on. For example, let's suppose the child is playing with toy people. The child puts first one person, then a second person, in a toy car, and rolls the car a short way. Then he takes a pipe cleaner and sticks it in the hole in the car and makes a noise like gas going in. Meanwhile, the adult is saying things like this: "Hey, the person's getting into the car!...Looks like the other guy can get in and go with him, huh?... Off you go! Have a good trip!...Humh, looks like they need some gas. ... There goes the gas, right into the gas tank. Now they're ready to go again.... Off they go!"

The adult can also track and describe much simpler activities. For example, the child is building a tower with blocks. The adult says things like, "There goes the next block, right on the top.... Looks like it's going to stay! ... Yes, the whole tower is still standing. There goes another... Over it all goes, onto the floor!"

Or the child is drawing. The adult says, "Look at that, that's a pretty color.... There goes the first part of it.... And now the second part goes on in a different color.... There goes the next part of the drawing."

Or the child is rolling a car back and forth with the adult. The adult says, "My turn to roll it to you. There it goes!... Now here it comes back to me. You pushed it right to me.... Oh, that time I tried rolling it and it turned over.... I'll try again."

Or a child is looking around in the woods with an adult. The adult says, "Time to see what's under that rock, huh? Hey, the dirt's formed just in the shape of the bottom of the rock! ... So you're putting the rock back, right where it was."

In these examples, the ellipses (...) are very important. The adult does not blab constantly, but does some tracking and describing and shuts up for a few seconds to give the child a chance to respond.

Why is tracking and describing so good?

1. One positive aspect of tracking and describing is its responsiveness and lack of directiveness. The child is not being asked to pay attention to something other than what he wants to pay attention to at the moment; therefore he gets to have fun acting out his fantasies or whatever else he wants. He gets a chance to practice exploring and using his own creativity and curiosity. He gets a chance to stretch his attention span, by paying attention to something as long as he can, without someone's distracting him from it.

2. At the same time, the child is getting a lesson in the use of language. The adult, in his comments, is letting the child hear how the very actions the child is paying attention to are encoded into language. The child learns to send words through his own mind so as to encode his own actions. This is a very important skill.

3. When the adult tracks and describes with an approving tone of voice (small approval is usually appropriate), he can give approval for what the child is doing, without interrupting it. When the adult tracks and describes with more approval for the more positive behaviors, and is silent in response to fantasies of antisocial behaviors, the adult is using differential attention at the same time that he is tracking and describing.

4. Tracking and describing, when done well by an adult, almost always seems to result in a pleasurable experience for the child. The more the adult pleases the child, the more the child will tend to reciprocate by pleasing the adult. If the adult can cultivate pleasure in tracking and describing while the child plays or explores, the two have a mutually gratifying activity to add to their repertoire.

What if the child starts picking up the habit of verbally describing what is happening, or doing his own tracking and describing? For example, the child says, "This airplane's going to fly to Florida. Here it goes, it's taking off!" The adult should very much encourage this habit in the child. It's a style of acting that is very much conducive to pleasant joint play with other children. When the child does comment and describe what is happening, the adult encourages that by taking great interest in what the child is saying, repeating what the child says in an interested way, or asking further questions about what the child has just said.

Facilitations

What does it mean to be a good listener for someone? It means that when the other person talks, you say things back that let the other person know that you are hearing them and trying to understand exactly what they are trying to communicate to you. "Facilitations" are one way that people let other people know they are listening. Here are examples of facilitations:

Humh!
Yes...
Is that right.
What do you know.
Umh humh.
Oh?
I see.
OK.
Umh.
Wow!
Really!

Facilitations don't add new content to the conversation—they just give the other person the message, "I'm listening, I'm hearing." Facilitate means "make easier," and facilitations make it easier for someone to talk to you.

Exercise: Practicing facilitations

Let one person be the talker, and another be the listener. The talker stops talking frequently, so that the listener can respond with a facilitation each time.

At first this exercise may so easy that you may be tempted to skip it. All the listener has to do is to keep saying "Yes," "I see," "Umh humh," and so forth. But you'll find that doing it well is more complicated than that. The listener should let the emotional tone of the facilitation be appropriate to the emotional tone of the speaker and to the listener's response; this is communicated by the inflection and intonation of the facilitation; this intonation is subtle and complex, when you examine it and think about it.

Reflections

The response to another person's communication that is most difficult, but which most separates the master communicator from the novice, is called a reflection (a.k.a. active listening, empathic reflection, empathic paraphrasing, checking out, restatements). You say back to the other person what you heard him saying, so that he knows you understood him.

Here's an example. The child says, "I hate that sister of mine." If the adult replies, "You shouldn't say those things about people," that is not reflection. If the adult says, "It sounds like she did something that really upset you, huh?"

that is a reflection. The adult is interested in knowing the child's experience, in knowing what it's like to be the child at that moment; the adult reflects back to the child what the adult thinks the child has communicated.

Why would anybody want to say back what the child has already said? Here are several good reasons:

1. Reflections tend to reinforce the child for talking with you. It is pleasant for a speaker to see that his messages are being heard.

2. Reflections tend to take the place of other responses that might punish the child for talking with you, such as criticisms or unwanted advice or other directive responses, anything that distracts the other person from the train of thought he wants to pursue.

3. Being able to practice keeping on his own train of thought without being pulled off it gives the child practice in sustaining attention.

4. When you reflect, you can check out to make sure you got it right, so that misunderstandings are reduced. People get more on the same wavelength. For example, when a young child says, "Car outside?" and the adult reflects by saying "You see a car outside?" the child might answer, "No, I mean are we going to ride in the car when we go outside?"

5. If your child hears you reflecting, he will start to imitate and do it himself, and he will become a better listener. He will probably have more friends, because people like people who listen accurately to them.

6. The child's hearing his messages reflected in just a little more complex or fluent language than the child was able to muster helps the child in language development.

Do these sound repetitive? They are very similar to the reasons for using tracking and describing. And when you think about it, reflection and tracking and describing are very similar to one another. Both involve letting the other person stay on a train of thought or activity without pulling them away, but just letting them know that you are taking it in. Reflection is to speech and tones of voice what tracking and describing are to physical actions.

Exercise: Reflection

If you would like to practice thinking up reflections, don't just read the following dialogue. Read the child's statement, and make up a reflection in response. Then compare your response with the one that is given. Keep going until the end of the dialogue.

Child: I played with Tom and his cousin this afternoon. (says this with an animated expression on his face.)

Adult: Sounds like it was pretty interesting to play with them.

Child: It was, I guess, but it was kind of weird, too, in certain ways.

Adult: There were parts of it that didn't feel so good to you?

Child: Tom is really nice, but his cousin is pretty weird. He keeps talking about

these strange things. Like he says he has a plane with a nuclear bomb in it and if I don't do what he wants he's going to blow up the whole city.
Adult: He tries to threaten you like that so that you'll do what he wants?
Child: Well, it's just little stuff, like give him a toy or something like that. I don't feel scared anything will happen if I don't do what he wants. And I know he really doesn't have a bomb and an airplane or anything like that. So it's not such a really big deal.
Adult: So you figure he's really just playing, so it doesn't worry you too much?
Child: Not too much, no, but he gets this really mean look on his face. And he keeps talking about all sorts of other mean things he'll do, like locking people up, and kidnapping people's parents, and all that sort of stuff.
Adult: So you know he's playing, but you still don't like the sort of playing that he does, because it has to do with a lot of mean stuff, and you'd rather play about other things?
Child: That's right. I like the way Tom and I play better when his cousin is not around.
Adult: When the cousin is not around, you and Tom have more fun together doing the sort of play you like better.
Child: Yes. Maybe if I just let the cousin alone and try to do some of that stuff with Tom, the cousin will join in with us. I don't know if his cousin will be up there very much, though. I think he's just visiting from out of town.
Adult: So the problem may solve itself by the cousin's going back to his home. But if he doesn't, you've got something in mind to try, huh?
Child: Yep....

This dialogue illustrates another advantage of reflection. It lets a child work on his own problems, use his own problem-solving ability, and start to feel good about his own ability to handle things. The adult is helping, by registering and underscoring the child's ideas, but is basically letting the child do his own work on the problem.

Here's another dialogue for you to practice with. I think it's best not just to read this, but to read the child's utterance, make up a reflection, then compare your reflection to that of the adult in this conversation.
Child: I think I did something sort of like one of the modeling stories today.
Adult: Hey, you did something kind, or something that you felt good about?
Child: Yep. There was this kid in class that no one wanted to sit beside at lunch. It seems like they never do.
Adult: So people don't want to be with this kid, huh?
Child: I don't know why they don't. He's from a different part of the world, and he looks and talks a little different. But he's a nice kid.
Adult: So he's not just like everybody else, but he's nice, and you're kind of at a loss as to why these other folks would not want to be with him.

Child: Uh humh. Well, anyway, so today he was sitting by himself at lunch and looking lonesome and I sat down beside him and said, "Do you mind if I join you?" and we had lunch together.
Adult: So the kind thing you did was to keep him company at lunch, huh?
Child: That's right. It doesn't sound like such a big deal. But I remember one time when I went to a new school, somebody talked with me, and it made me feel a lot better.
Adult: So even though it doesn't sound like such a big thing, you know how big a deal it can be when you're lonesome.
Child: There sure is a lot of difference between having one friend and not having any friends, you know? If there's just one person that you can talk to, it's all different.
Adult: Yes, I do know. Having just one person that's on your side makes you feel safe and secure, whereas it's not a good feeling at all when everybody else knows everybody and you don't know anybody.
Child: This kid that I sat with today is from India. They just came over this year, so that both his parents could go to school over here. He knows English really well, and he speaks another language too. I can't remember what it's called. He has an accent, but he can really talk better than lots of people that have lived here all their lives.
Adult: Sounds like he's a smart kid.
Child: I think so. I like smart people. I like to talk with them. Some people don't, I think. You know what I mean? I think some people get jealous, and act mean whenever they get the idea that they're talking with somebody that's smart.
Adult: But you don't feel jealous of smart people; you just enjoy hearing what they have to say?
Child: Well, I don't know that I never feel jealous. If there's somebody who's really, really smart, I sometimes feel jealous. But I enjoy them more than I'm jealous.
Adult: I see. It's not that you don't ever feel jealous, but your enjoying them wins out over the jealousy, so that you still like being around them.
Child: Right.

Now when people get into their minds that they want to use reflections, they sometimes do it in a way that backfires, and sounds phony. This is usually a consequence of just parroting back what the person said, rather than working hard enough to listen for what they mean. Here's an example.

Child: Sometimes my little brother is just like a fat pig!
Adult: So you're saying that sometimes your little brother is just like a fat pig, huh?
Child: That's what I said. Why are you saying it back to me?

Not parroting back what someone said, but listening for what they mean, requires more than just using synonyms for what they said. The following reflection still doesn't cut it.

Child: Sometimes my little brother is just like a fat pig!

Adult: You feel your little brother is like an obese swine?

Now let's listen to what it sounds like when the adult really thinks about what the child means rather than just what he says.

Child: Sometimes my little brother is just like a pig!

Adult: Like a pig. You mean he's sloppy, and leaves things all over the place?

Child: No, I mean he always wants everything of mine, and he won't share anything with me.

Adult: I see. So sometimes acts greedy like a pig, rather than sloppy like a pig. Sounds like that bugs you, huh?

Child: Well, it does some. But he's so little, I guess I can't blame him too much.

Adult: So you figure that since probably all real little kids are a little piggy, you won't hold it against him, huh?

Child: Yep.

One author who wrote about using reflections entitled his chapter, "Seek first to understand, then to be understood." If everybody used more reflections with each other, we would probably have a lot more understanding in the world.

Asking Follow-Up Questions

Another useful type of responses during conversations is called the follow-up question. A follow-up question asks the child to tell you more about something he just said. Here are some examples. The child says, "Saw big dog." You ask, "Oh, where did you see a big dog?" or "Was it a nice dog, or was he scary?" or "Whose dog was it?"

Here's another example. The child says, "I got a sticker." The adult says, "Oh, did you get that for doing something good?" or "What's that on your sticker?" or "I like that sticker, do you?"

In doing follow-up questions, you show your child how to be a good listener to what someone says, and how to be curious and to raise questions.

Exercise: Reflection and Follow-Up Questions

Read the sentences below that the child might say, and what I want you to do is first make up a reflection, and then ask a follow-up question. The examples are a little harder to reflect than the ones given earlier, because they are so concrete. But they can be reflected just the same, and the young child will be stimulated to talk more.

1. The child says, "We went to the zoo!" Sample answer:
Reflection: "You went to the zoo to see all the animals?" Follow-up question: "What animals did you see?"

2. The child says, "I want to take a plane trip." Sample answer: Reflection: "You think it would be fun to fly in a plane up in the sky, huh?" Follow-up question: "Where would you like to go?"

3. The child looks proud as he says, "I helped Tommy today." Sample answer: Reflection: "You did something to help Tommy? I'll bet you're proud of yourself." Follow-up question: "How did you help him?"

4. The child says, "Don't like snakes." Sample answer: Reflection: "Sounds like you think snakes are dangerous, huh?" Follow-up question: "Did you see a snake somewhere?"

5. The child says, "Jimmy is mean."

6. The child says, "I took a long walk yesterday."

7. The child looks very proud as he says, "I learned to write some letters."

8. The child looks excited as he says, "I taught Johnny how to tie his shoes today."

Telling About Your Own Experience

You can model for the child how to tell about his experience, by telling about your own.

What portion of your experience should you talk about? It's especially good to say things to the child that are positive and upbeat.

"Guess what I saw today. I saw a man outside painting his house. His house was blue, but he was turning it into a white house. I thought to myself, wouldn't it be interesting if he quit the job half way through, and he had a house that was half blue and half white!"

Or you might say, "I wonder what all those holes in those boards in the ceiling are for. Maybe they're just to look nice. Or maybe it has something to do with soaking up the sound, so people can't hear what goes on in other people's rooms as much."

Or you might say, "You know, I sure do like these shoes I've got on. They really are comfortable. They're looking pretty old these days, but they sure do feel good."

Or "I was able to help somebody out today. The person wanted to know how to get to the turnpike, and I told him. I guess I'll never know if he found it without needing any more directions, but I bet he did."

Or "I read something in a magazine that was interesting. Want to hear about it?"

Chat about something positive, something you're proud of, something interesting. If you do this enough, and leave some silence for the child to talk, the child will start doing the same sort of thing.

What about telling your child about your problems, and the unhappy things in your life? You don't want often to put a young child into the role of being your counselor or therapist. Particularly, it's not good for one parent to use the child as a sounding board about problems with the other parent! However, judiciously selected problems, ones that aren't terribly scary for the child, particularly those where a solution is within reach or has already been enacted, can help the child learn to talk with you about problems, and can give the child practice in problem solving and empathic listening. Young children can understand very concrete problems; older ones can understand those involving predictions of social effects rather than just physical effects. Examples:

"I have a problem. Want to hear about it? My guitar case is coming apart. See what's happening here? If this goes on much more, one day I'm going to pick it up and my guitar is going to fall out. I'm trying to figure out what to do."

"I'm thinking about a problem I have. Want to hear about it? I like getting strong, and the quickest way to do that is to work out with heavy weights. But it seems like these days, maybe because I've gotten older, when I lift heavy weights I hurt myself too often. My elbow hurts for a day or two, or my shoulder. I need to figure out some way of exercising where I don't hurt myself."

"I had a problem the other day. I was supposed to bring some food over to some people's house, to a party, but I forgot it until just before it was time to go over there. I knew that if I spent a lot of time getting the food, I would be late to their house."

A young or quiet child may not be able to do anything but listen as you continue to think out loud about the problem, or may not even be able to do that. But in that case no harm is done. The child is at least getting a model of how to pose problems and talk about them.

Exercise: Telling About Your Own Experience

Imagine yourself with your child, and imagine yourself talking about your own experience. Just make up something to say to your child, and imagine it going on.

What did you imagine yourself saying to your child? If you don't tell the child much about your own experience, give it a try in real life and see what happens. You may be very pleased with the results.

Positive Reinforcement

All of the responsive utterances probably positively reinforce the child's talking with you. Those that most obviously and overtly give approval to the child we will call positive reinforcement.

These are utterances such as the following:

"I'm glad you mentioned that to me."

"Sounds like you've done some good thinking about this."

"I like hearing you tell me about these things."

"Thanks for telling me about that."

For example: the child says to the parent, "It embarrassed me when Mrs. Smith kept talking about how I was so hard-working and polite."

The parent gets the urge to say, "You shouldn't feel embarrassed about that. You should feel proud." But the parent checks that impulse, and remembers that the first task is to make the child's disclosure comfortable. So the parent responds with a positive reinforcement followed by a follow-up question: "I'm glad you brought this up. Why was it embarrassing?"

The child replies, "Well, my friend Jean was right there, and Mrs. Smith wasn't talking about her that way. I didn't want her to feel jealous."

The parent gets the urge to say, "If you do something good, that doesn't take anything away from Jean. Jean will get complimented when she does something good." But the parent checks that impulse, and responds with a positive reinforcement: "I'm glad you're thinking about your friend's feelings."

The child continues, "I don't know how Jean really felt. It didn't seem to bother her, from anything I saw."

The parent responds with a positive reinforcement: "I like that you're thinking about the evidence for how she felt."

The child continues: "I guess it wasn't such a big deal. But at the time it was still embarrassing."

The parent responds with a positive reinforcement: "It's great to be able to decide when things aren't a very big deal."

Exercises: Telling About Your Own Experience, Facilitations, Reflections, Follow-up Questions, and Positive Reinforcements

Here's a very useful way to practice reflections. Get together with someone else, a friend, your spouse, or your child. The first person will think of something could tell about your own experience. The second person will respond with a reflection. The first person then tells more about his own experience, and the second person again responds with a reflection. Then after you've done that a while, switch roles. If you're doing this right, it should be very pleasant to have the other person listen very carefully to you.

Second, repeat this exercise, only now the second person uses a follow-up question instead of a reflection. Feel the difference in the quality of the interaction that comes when the listener questions rather than reflects. Which do you like better?

Finally, do it one more time, and this time the listener gets to choose between facilitations, reflections, follow-up questions, and positive reinforcements. But no new-topic questions, and no advice are allowed! And try not to overdo the follow-up questions.

If you and your child can get in the habit of having very interesting conversations with one another, you will have learned something that you and your child can do for the rest of your lives. This habit will vastly improve the quality of both your lives.

Chapter 8: Reducing Arguments

Chapter Overview:

Some arguing is normal. In fact some version of arguing is useful in developing skills of conflict resolution and independent thinking. But too much adversarial talk sets an unpleasant climate for a family. Here are some ways of reducing it. If there is something unwanted that you must impose on a young child, get it over with as quickly as possible, without trying to argue the child into accepting it as just. Use reflections and follow-up questions and other responsive utterances to make your talk less adversarial. If the child argues over whether the moon is bigger than the sun or other "academic" issues, you can simply state once what the truth is, listen responsively to the child's point of view, invite the child to listen to your point of view, and drop the matter if the invitation is declined. Or, instead of playing the game of "Let's exasperate the parent," you can lead the interaction into a game of "Let's be silly together." When the child wants something that you would like to give him, but for some reason you can't, you can "gratify the wish in fantasy." This means you speak about how you would like to give him what he wants; you create a fantasy of gratifying the wish, and you regret that it can't occur. When the child criticizes you, agreeing with part of criticism is a responsive utterance that models nondefensiveness, and often cuts short the adversarial feeling. Ignoring the bid for adversarial interaction and turning the attention elsewhere often works well. In response to hurtful statements the child makes, another option is simply telling the child that those statements are hurtful, without arguing or defending oneself. Another option is to play the game of "Let's have fun with a formal debate." Imposing a punishment for the child's hostile talk is of course an option, although it often has drawbacks.

All these are options you can use immediately after the child makes a bid for an argument. But it's at least as important to set a positive tone in conversation at other times, and make arguments less likely to happen.

Responding in these ways to a child is easier said than done. Parents can make it easier for themselves by noticing what thought patterns that stimulate their own arguing, and trying on new thought patterns. You can use fantasy practice to change habits. You do this by first listing vignettes where the child makes a bid to argue. Then you imagine each of these, and practice in your imagination the thoughts, feelings, and behaviors, you'd like to carry out. The more you practice in fantasy, the more likely you are to rise to the occasion in real life.

****

Let's apply the concepts already defined in the last two chapters to the goal of reducing adversarial proceedings between parent and child.

Of course, a certain amount of conflict and disagreement and even some anger and hostility is natural and normal in any relationship, and in fact without it, the child would get no practice at many essential skills, such as conflict-resolution and tolerating criticism. But an excessive amount of verbal hostility, especially when what is being practice is conflict non-resolution and intolerance of criticism, is a problem to be solved. Nonproductive hostile arguments are in the same "response class" as many of the behaviors that worry parents the most: physical fighting, sibling conflict, disobedience, and defiance of teachers at school. Getting more often on the same side as the child and less often being opponents is a move that can make the difference between happiness and unhappiness for many families.

Sometimes verbal hostility is the signal of a conversation that needs to take place: the sign of an underlying problem that needs to be explored and worked on. This book will later go into some detail about the process of joint decision making and problem-solving. On the other hand, sometimes verbal hostility is done for excitement when there is nothing more exciting to do. Sometimes it is the product of irritation from some other cause, directed toward an innocent bystander. Sometimes it's a habit picked up from unfavorable models. Sometimes the underlying conflict is clear, and the child simply wants his way on something it's not reasonable for the parent to deliver. And by several other mechanisms, it can result from causes other than an underlying problem that really needs to be discussed. When there is an underlying problem that needs to be discussed, responsive listening is the best way to find that out and start the process rolling toward productive conflict-resolution. Other strategies mentioned in this chapter can also be useful, especially when there is not a need for a problem-solving conversation.

This chapter will introduce few new principles, but will provide examples of the use of principles already introduced. We have been speaking so far about approval versus disapproval, differential reinforcement, and directiveness versus responsiveness as elements contributing to the interpersonal environment.

Now let's use these principles in examining some specific examples.

When in doubt, it's often a good idea to respond to bids for adversarial arguments by responsive listening. If there is an underlying conflict that needs to be discussed, you are more likely to discover this; if there is nothing much to discover, you've modeled nonadversarial responding which usually prevents an argument anyway. Let's first look at an example of how not to do this.

Interaction 1

Child: I think it was a mistake to come to this movie. The line to get in is too long.
Parent: The line isn't that long. We'll get in just fine when the other show ends.
Child: No we won't. It was a mistake.
Parent: Who was it that first wanted to come here anyway? It was you that was nagging me to take you.
Child: But I never mentioned this movie! You're the one who had the idea, after you read it in your magazine.
Parent: What is it with you with my reading the magazine? That happens to be a very good way of deciding what movies to come to.
Child: Nobody finds out about movies from reading magazines.
Parent: That's not true! Plenty of people do, and it's probably the best way.
Notice that in Interaction 1 each utterance that each person makes contradicts the last utterance that the other person just made. It's a reciprocal interaction, all right, but a rather mean game.

Interaction 2

Child: I think it was a mistake to come to this movie. The line to get in is too long.
Parent: When you see all these people in line, you can get the feeling we'll be in line forever, can't you?
Child: We should have gone to the other theater, not this one.
Parent: You think it would have been less crowded there, huh?
Child: I think that magazine of yours isn't right lots of times.
Parent: You mean the magazine that has movie reviews? You think sometimes it's wrong? I'm sure you're right.

***

With reflections, the parent in interaction 2 above restated a portion of the child's statement to see if was understood correctly. And with follow-up questions, the parent picked out some aspect of what the child mentioned to be curious about, and asked about it. Here the parent is using responsiveness rather than directiveness, and thus refusing to join in adversarial proceedings.

In following this strategy, you have to be careful that you don't just argue with the child in the guise of reflections and follow-up questions. Let's look at an example of that:

Child: You shouldn't have come this way. There's all sorts of traffic.
Parent: (In defensive tone) You think you know a better way? Well, what is it, Mr. Smarty Pants!

The difference between that reply and the following one is subtle, depending mainly on tone of voice:
Child: You shouldn't have come this way. There's all sorts of traffic.
Parent: (In an upbeat tone) It sounds like you may have a different way in

mind. If so, I'm interested in hearing what it is.

One might object that in the second example, the parent is reinforcing the child's argumentative tone by being so nice. The parent's strategy, however, is to model nonadversarial conversation, and to model nonadversarial ways of responding to provocation. The child has to know the alternatives to hostility, and the parent is showing the child one of them. The parent first wants to give the child lots of experience in having nonargumentative chats. If the insulting provocations don't drop out, the parent can try reprimanding them later. At that time, the reprimand will come in the context of predominantly positive interactions from the parent rather than be seen as just another argument.

Now let's look at a different strategy, where the rapid imposition of authority is the alternative to arguing.

Interaction 1

Parent: It's time for us to leave. Remember, we need to go to the doctor's office? Please turn off the television, and come with me to the car.
Child: I don't want to.
Parent: But you have to.
Child: But there are only five more minutes left in this show, and usually when we get there we end up waiting at least ten minutes.
Parent: But there's a lot of traffic today, and besides I hate to be late.
Child: There isn't either a lot of traffic. You just like to think up mean things to do to me, like telling me to turn off the program when there are only five minutes left.
Parent: (In a high-pitched tone, speaking quickly) Why would I want to do something like that? That's ridiculous. Besides, there are not just five minutes left, it's more like fifteen minutes.
Child: No it isn't. The real show ends in five minutes and then there are commercials the rest of the time. You don't do this with my sister, why do you do it to me?
Parent: I don't do a thing differently with your sister! Where are you getting that idea!....

Interaction 2

Parent: It's time for us to leave. Remember we need to go to the doctor's office? Please turn off the television, and come with me to the car.
Child: I don't want to.
Parent turns off the television, takes the child by the hand, and starts walking out the door.
Child: But there are only five more minutes left in the show! You are just doing this on purpose! You never do this to my sister! This is unfair! You're stupid!
Parent continues without replying, and they leave. The child looks sullen.
Parent (after a few minutes): I know you don't like having your show interrupted. I wouldn't like it either.
Child: You do it just because I don't like it. You just try to make me mad whenever you can!
Parent does not reply.

***

If you want to avoid giving lots of attention to nonproductive arguments, and when you know you will have to do something that the child doesn't like, it is best to make a swift end to things and not prolong the agony. In the second case, the parent got the conflict over more quickly, by imposing power right away. In the second case, the parent's reflection is responsive to the child's feelings, and an attempt to be on the same side as the child. The adult's delay in speaking is so that this responsive utterance will not reinforce the child's hostile utterances, taking advantage as much as possible of the "time gradient of reinforcement." The parent speaks in a calm voice so as to avoid the reinforcing power of excitement. This vignette does not have a particularly happy ending; the story ends with child still mad. This ending illustrates the point that all these techniques are aimed at long-term outcomes, not instant gratification.

One may ask, if the parent tolerates the child's hostile verbalizations, won't they just continue? Not necessarily. Commanding and punishing a child are not the only methods of influence in our armamentarium! One very prominent way is by modeling more positive verbalizations, refusing to reward the negative ones by arguing with them, and setting a positive tone for the relationship in general. The child can benefit from correction and disapproving comments and reprimands, but only when they are set in a background of a general climate of approval or tolerance.

Here's an example where the child wants to argue on an issue of fact where the child is totally wrong.

Interaction 1

Child: Which do you think is closer to the earth: the sun or the moon?
Parent: The moon is closer.
Child: No it isn't. The sun is.
Parent: Listen, I know that the moon is closer.
Child: Well you're wrong.
Parent: I happen to have studied astronomy for a whole year, in college. That's one of the most elementary facts that you learn, is where the planets and the sun and the moon are. The moon goes right around the earth. It's less than a million miles away from the earth, and the sun is several million miles away.
Child: No, it's the other way around. The moon is millions of miles away, and the sun is only a few thousand.
Parent: How do you know?
Child: I just know.
Parent: That's ridiculous!
Child: You're the one who's ridiculous!

I would bet that the child is not really very interested in which is closer, but is playing a game entitled "Let's see how long it takes to exasperate the parent." The child needs to enlarge his repertoire of interactions, so that he can play some games that are more fun for the parent to play also.

Interaction 2

Child: Which do you think is closer to the earth: the sun or the moon?
Parent: The moon is closer.
Child: No, it isn't, the sun is.
Parent: What makes you think so?
Child: I just know it.
Parent: The knowledge just came to you, huh?
Child: No, it didn't. I just know it.
Parent: Humh. Do you want to know why I think the moon is closer?
Child: No.
Parent: OK.

Here the parent in effect says, "I'm not going to play the adversarial game. I have another one, where I tell you a little about science, and you get to hear some interesting things and ask some more questions if you want. Do you want to play that game?" The child's response communicates, "No, I don't want to play that game." The parent's response communicates, "Then we don't play a game. Or we think of one that we both want to play." The parent does not get drawn into a game that is unpleasant for the parent to play.

There are various games that can be played with both people on the same side. One of them is "Let's be silly together."

Interaction 3

Child: Which do you think is closer to the earth: the sun or the moon?
Parent: The moon is closer.
Child: No, it isn't, the sun is.
Parent: Have you been to either one of them lately? I have.
Child: You have?
Parent: Didn't you know that I go to the sun every Sunday, and to the Moon every Tuesday? I ride that broom over there.
Child: I go up there too. Only I ride on my bicycle. It's a lot faster than your broom.
Parent: Well, which do you like being on better, the moon or the sun?
Child: The sun's a little too hot.
Parent: Yeah, I think so too. I like all that green cheese that's on the moon.
Child: There isn't any green cheese on it.
Parent: There isn't? Maybe I got lost and wound up some place different than on the moon. Maybe I rode the broom to Mars, or maybe to a green cheese factory in Alaska instead.

***

In this interaction the child still makes bids to play the arguing game, by contradicting what the adult says and challenging the speed of the adult's broom. But the adult is good enough at the silliness game that he or she can turn the game in that direction, and have it be fun for the child. In time, perhaps the child will learn to play the silliness game without bidding to play the arguing game.

Many arguments that children get into with parents are not over academic or scientific issues, but over the issue of "I want something that you won't give me." In this case "gratifying the wish in fantasy" is a useful way for you to respond, if you can do it honestly. First let's look at how not to do it.

Interaction 1
Child: I want some cotton candy!
Adult: I don't think there is any cotton candy sold here.
Child: But I want it! You said they might have it!
Adult: Do you know what the word might means? I didn't guarantee they would have it. You have to handle it when you don't get your way.
Child: No, I don't want to handle it!
Adult: Well, you don't have any choice, so quit bugging me about it.
Child: No, I want it. Why isn't there any!
Adult: I don't know. I'm not the one who decides to sell it or not. Why do you blame everything on me?
Child: I don't blame everything on you!

In gratifying the wish in fantasy, the adult states a wish or fantasy of being able to give the child what he wants. The message is that the adult would like to gratify the child if external circumstances didn't prevent it.

Interaction 2
Child: I want some cotton candy!
Adult: It looks like they don't sell it here. That's too bad, because I wanted to get you some. And I wanted some, too.
Child: But I want it! You said they might have it!
Adult: That's right, I was hoping I could get you some, because it's really good, and something you can get only at places like this. I wanted to get you a big pink or blue stickful of it.
Child: But they don't have it here.
Adult: I wish they did.
Child: Oh, well.

Here's another way to reply to provocative or critical statements. We can call it agreeing with part of criticism. It too is an utterance that falls on the responsive, rather than the directive, end of the continuum. In this type of response, the adult, when insulted or criticized by the child, refuses to get engaged in a power struggle, but acknowledges the possibility of his own imperfection in a nondefensive way.

Interaction 1
Parent: No, we don't have time to stop at the store today. We have to go home.
Child: (In a very angry tone of voice) Why is there never time!
Parent: What do you mean, "never time?" There's time to do the things you want lots of times.
Child: No there isn't!

Interaction 2
Parent: No, we don't have time to stop at the store today. We have to go home.
Child: (In a very angry tone of voice) Why is there never time!
Parent: (In a self-confident tone) Sometimes there isn't time for things we

wanted to do, and I don't plan things out well enough sometimes.
Child: Oh, well.

Interaction 3

Parent: No, we don't have time to stop at the store today. We have to go home.
Child: (In a very angry tone of voice) You're stupid. You're uglier and uglier every single day!
Parent: For that comment you lose the right to watch the cartoons today.
Child: That's not fair! You're a dummy!
Parent: For that second statement you don't get to watch the hockey game.

I believe that children who speak in very disrespectful tones to parents should find that such behavior quickly reduces their material standard of living to the level where their real needs are met but their supply of luxuries is cut off.

Here's an example of passing up a bid for an adversarial interaction by using the direction of attention principle, and turning attention to someone else.

Interaction 1

Child: But that's not fair. You guaranteed me last month that I could do that, and now you're saying I can't.
Parent: What? I never guaranteed you anything last month, and you know it. You're just making it up.
Child: No way am I making it up, and you know it.

Interaction 2

Child: But that's not fair. You guaranteed me last month that I could do that, and now you're saying I can't.
Parent: I don't remember it that way. (To spouse) How was your day today?
Other parent: Pretty good! I finished writing the article I was working on.
Child: I said you're not fair!
Parent: (To child) Maybe. (To spouse) Congratulations for finishing it! Did you mail the article off, today, then?

What if the child really does hurt the parent's feelings, and the parent feels dishonest trying to act as if the child's statements are not hurtful? Then one option is to simply tell the child that the statement is hurtful, again without arguing or being defensive. We might call this response an "I feel" statement.

Interaction 1

Child: You are a terrible parent. I wish that I could go and live with someone else's parent.
Parent: Nice, real nice thing to say. If you did, they probably wouldn't put up with you half as long as I have.
Child: Oh, yes they would have.

Interaction 2

Child: You are a terrible parent. I wish I could go and live with someone else's parent.
Parent: I'm sorry to hear you say that. When you say that, I feel hurt.

In this example the parent's response is of low energy and excitement level. It is at the responsive rather than directive end of the continuum. And it does not deliver disapproval to the child so as to get into the vicious cycle of disapproval of disproval.

Sometimes people just enjoy a debate. Arguing can be a fun game, if it's defined as one. An adversarial proceeding can be transformed into a paradoxically cooperative one by agreeing to have a debate, and having fun with it, just as people agree to oppose each other in a tennis game.

Interaction 1

Child: What sort of animal would you like to be if you could be any animal?
Parent: An otter.
Child: That's not a good choice. A lion is much better.
Parent: Don't call my choice bad. I'd rather be an otter than a lion. If you'd rather be a lion that's fine for you.
Child: It's still a bad choice. You just don't know anything about animals.
Parent: And I suppose you do, huh?
Child: Anybody knows more than you do.

Interaction 2

Child: What sort of animal would you like to be if you could be any animal?
Parent: An otter.
Child: That's not a good choice. A lion is much better.
Parent: Want to have a little debate? I'll talk for three sentences on why I would want to be an otter. Then you can have three sentences to tell the audience why a lion is much better to be than an otter. Then we can each have three sentences of rebuttal. Will you take me on?
Child: Sure, I'll take you on.
Parent: Ladies and gentlemen, any of you who have seen films of otters know how much fun otters have sliding down mud into the river. On a hot day, they get to splash around and cool off in the water. And they seem to really like eating fish. OK, now it's your turn.
****

How does one pick among the options listed above? Largely by gut feeling and intuition. But it's also helpful to respond on the basis of the child's apparent motive for the hostility or argumentativeness. If the child really has a conflict of interests with the parent, something that should be discussed, responsive listening is the best initial response. Future chapters will go into more detail about the remainder of the rational problem-solving process. If the child is motivated by a wish to resist a reasonable plan that the parent must carry out, quickly imposing the law works best. When the motive is a relief from boredom and having some excitement, ignoring or playing the games of silliness or formal debating may work best.

All of the ways of responding we've talked about so far have to do with what to do at the moment that the child delivers a provocation to argue. Let's remind ourselves that problems are almost never solved only by a decision of what to do in response to a negative behavior, but by the tone that is set throughout the whole rest of the time. Using the principles for creation of the interpersonal environment all the time, rather than just after a hostile comment by the child, will have the best results.

Cognitive Strategies in Avoiding Adversarial Interactions

So far I've talked about not replying, using reflections and follow-up questions, being silly, agreeing with part of criticism, imposing a punishment, turning attention to someone else, making an I feel statement, having a formal debate, and having as much positively or neutrally loaded conversation as possible that does not try to change the child. These are specific ways of using the principles of direction of attention, level of excitement and energy, approval versus disapproval, and responsiveness versus directiveness. All these are ways of behaving, of verbally interacting, in a way that precludes adversarial proceedings. But these things are easier said than done. What are some ways to "psych" yourself for responding in this way, rather than arguing with the child?

The art of influencing your own behavior and emotions by changing your thought patterns has become the object of much study in recent years, and it seems to be a very workable strategy. It has been the main strategy of "cognitive therapy."

In altering your own thoughts, a first step is to monitor and get in touch with what thoughts occur just before you allow the child to engage you in an adversarial interaction. Here are some possibilities:

He shouldn't be able to get away with saying something that's so obviously not right.

I can't let this pattern of talk go on without combating it.

Here's the logical counterargument to what he's saying; surely he will be persuaded by the logic of my argument.

He was not persuaded, even by such a brilliant argument! I can't believe it! Aaaugh!

My goodness as a person has been attacked, and unless I defend myself successfully the slur on my character stands uncorrected.

It is my duty as a parent to show him that he is wrong.

If I do nothing, and fail to nip this in the bud, he will do this with everyone else.

****

If you would like to motivate yourself for nonadversarial interaction, here are some thoughts that might do it:

My goal in the next few seconds is not to win an argument, but not to argue at all.

My goal in the next few seconds is to avoid reinforcing him for trying to be provocative, and the best way to do that is not to be provoked.

This is only a young child speaking; I don't need to defend myself. My job is to nurture him by modeling how to avoid hostility.

I'm going to make it easy on myself by not getting into this competition, but will just sit back and take it easy.

It takes two to play this game, and I'm not going to play right now.

He wants to play the arguing game; I'm going to see if I can get a different game going.

****

As I've mentioned before several times in this book, the strategy of fantasy practice is too useful to pass up when changing your own habits. Here's how you do it if you tend to get into adversarial proceedings with your child too much.

1. List a bunch of vignettes that you can recall, when the child succeeded in engaging you in an adversarial proceeding.

2. For these vignettes, see if you can reconstruct some of the thought patterns, some of the things you said to yourself, that got you hooked into hostilities.

3. Take the first vignette. Think through different ways you could have responded to the child, and choose the one you think would work the best. Also think through the ways of thinking about the situation, and choose what you would like to say to yourself.

4. Make a mental movie of the first vignette. Imagine yourself using the new preferred thought pattern, and imagine yourself using the new preferred behavior pattern. When you have handled the situation in this preferred way, imagine yourself congratulating yourself. Then in real life, congratulate yourself for doing the rehearsal.

5. Repeat this for the first vignette until you are really tired of doing it.

6. Do the same thing for all the other vignettes.

For more detail on this strategy, see the chapter on anger control.

All of the strategies we've mentioned so far are much easier if you can somehow reduce or successfully manage the stresses of your own life. It's hard to do anger control or think about techniques of argument reduction if you are feeling overwhelmed by endless unmet demands of life. In future chapters we'll think about strategies for relaxation skills and organization skills. If you use these, you're more likely to have the time and energy for effective improvement of the emotional climate.

But first we will spend time on another crucial factor contributing to the emotional climate: the quality of the models the child receives.

Chapter 9: Modeling in Real Life and Stories

Chapter Overview:

How do people choose their thoughts, emotions, and behaviors? We search somehow through our memories of what we've seen and heard. Sometimes we recombine bits and pieces of these to come up with a new response. Sometimes we simply select a remembered pattern and reenact it. Either way, the raw material we use to create our options is our memories. Thus what we see and hear is crucial in determining what we do. We thus cannot help but imitate at least part of what we see and hear. The more positive models your child stores away in memory, the more likely your child is to choose positive patterns. Thus a big part of the job description of a parent is to try to furnish lots of positive models to your child.

One way you can do this is by showing the child positive patterns with your own behavior. You can also show your child your thoughts, by saying them aloud. Each psychological skill has some distinctive thought patterns that go with it. In the family nightly review, you can report and celebrate your own positive patterns. Helping your child find playmates who will model positive behavior is very important. Also crucial is getting rid of almost all the negative models most chidren get through television and videos and videogames. Stories, written or told, are an important way you can present positive models. I define a "modeling story" as one showing positive patterns and as few as possible negative patterns. In a modeling story someone's getting hurt can be a problem to solve but never a solution to a problem or something funny. You're using a very powerful positive influence if you do create, tell, write, and/or illustrate modeling stories with your child. These can be made from real-life smart or good things the child and other family members do. They can also be made up.

Almost any child will learn to enjoy hearing stories read, if the parent follows several guidelines. Among these are using an enthusiastic tone of voice, picking stories short enough for the child's attention span, and reading in an environment where other stimuli do not compete.

****

The Importance of Modeling: Both Quality and Quantity

How does a child gain competence in the 62 psychological skills I have defined as central to happiness and productivity? There is an enormous amount to learn. The child can't possibly learn all that by trial and error. The child learns a huge amount of it by incorporating directly into his or her behavioral repertoire what the child observes in the world. This is imitation learning, or modeling.

Do children have to learn to imitate, or is imitation something they do innately? Some experiments by Meltzoff with infants demonstrated the innate nature of children's tendency to imitate. The researchers used as their subjects babies in the first hour of their lives, before they would have had a chance to get rewarded for imitation. The researchers made distinctive facial expressions at the infants. With some of the infants, the researchers opened their mouths; with others, they stuck out their tongues; with others, they puckered their lips. They videotaped what the infants did in response. Sure enough, the infants did more of the facial expressions that were done to them.

I think it's useful to get an image of the memory storage areas of the child's brain. Every time the child observes an interaction, that gets registered in memory. Some patterns are remembered well, and others are forgotten. Every time the child is faced with a choice of how to act (i.e. almost every instant) the brain engages in some sort of search process through the patterns of thinking, feeling, and acting that are stored in memory. Although there is much about the storage and search process that we don't understand, we can with some confidence say that the more positive patterns the child has stored in memory, the more likely the child is to land on a positive pattern when searching for what to do.

The implication is that adults who want to foster the psychological growth of children should see part of their job as pumping positive patterns into the child's memory bank as often as possible.

Other findings about imitation learning also stand to reason. The more the child admires the model, the more likely the child is to imitate. However, admiration is not necessary for imitation. Sometimes children imitate the aggressive acts committed against them by a hated abuser. This has been called "identification with an aggressor."

Modeling has been purposefully used to help children make up for deficiencies in psychological skills. Shy children have been helped to gain skills in making friends by seeing videos of other children learning to socialize. Children with fears of dental procedures, and various other fears, have learned not to be fearful by seeing models who coped well with the situation. Sometimes these models face the situation fearlessly from the beginning; sometimes they are nervous at first but learn to conquer their fear.

There is no psychological skill whose growth cannot be fostered by showing children models of it. Accordingly, in a world designed for the best development of children, models of each of the 62 skills would abound in our culture, in all sorts of media. Watching television for a randomly chosen several hours during the week could be counted on to provide positive models in each of the skills.

However, this situation is most definitely not the case in our society—quite the contrary is true. A later chapter is devoted to the problem of entertainment violence. Thus it is necessary for parents to go through a great deal of conscious planning to expose children to the quality and quantity of models they need.

What is a reasonable goal for models of positive patterns? Let's arbitrarily wish that psychologically skillful patterns would be modeled to children in at least the same quantity as violent acts currently are modeled to the average child by television. This would entail presenting somewhere in the neighborhood of 40 positive models per day to each child.

While this number is quite arbitrary, I want to emphasize that the number must be large. We can't expect children to get one or two positive models and have their lives changed in any appreciable way. Models are constantly being loaded into the memory bank, and a few good ones will get lost in a sea of mediocre or bad ones if the entire modeling "diet" is not attended to.

How can we achieve high numbers of positive models? Models come through the real-life people the child interacts with, the fictional people in stories, plays, tapes, television, movies, and so forth; and through the hidden people who are the authors of thoughts on how to live well.

Real Life Modeling Through Self-Talk Out Loud

Modeling research gives new meaning to the golden rule. Do unto your children as you would have them do unto you, not only because this is right, but also because they will certainly imitate your behavior.

When you think about the whole idea of imitation learning, some of the implications give us pause. For example:

When parents give their children lots of commands in a harsh tone, they are modeling in such a way as to influence their children to yell commands back to them in a harsh way.

When parents fight or loudly argue with spouses or other adults in front of the child, they are showing the child how to fight and loudly argue.

When parents try to get children to do what they should do by repeatedly nagging them to do it, they are modeling for the child how to nag and whine to get what he wants.

When parents handle frustration in an upbeat and rational way, they show children how to do the skill of fortitude.

When parents give verbal approval to a child, they are not only reinforcing the behavior the child did; they are also modeling the skill of expressing positive feelings to others.

When parents use the "self talk" associated with a given psychological skill in the child's presence, they are showing the child how to do the thought patterns associated with that skill.

Modeling For Children With "Self-Talk" in Real Life

Let's focus more on the last one. What do we mean by self talk associated with a given psychological skill? Perhaps that question is best answered by examples. Here's some distinctive "self talk" for the skill of fortitude:

"Well, I sure don't like it that this happened. But I can take it. I'm tough enough to handle it. Let's see, what can I do about this?"

Here's some distinctive "self talk" for a part of the skill of conflict resolution:

"Humh, you want this, and I wanted this other thing. Let's think about what options we have, and how we can best work this out."

Here's some distinctive "self talk" for the skill of feeling good about acts of kindness toward others:

"Hooray, I think I helped him out and made him feel better! I feel good about that!"

Here's some distinctive "self talk" for the skill of compliance with reasonable authority.

"Humh, is that a reasonable request? I think so. Sure, I'd be willing to go along with that."

Here's some distinctive "self talk" for the skill of sustaining attention to tasks:

"I'm getting there. I'm getting the job done. If I stick with it, I think I'm going to be able to finish it."

The central idea behind this idea of modeling through self-talk is that psychological skills are not just patterns of physical behavior. They are also patterns of thought, of what we say to ourselves while we are carrying out certain physical actions. They are also patterns of emotion, that are reflected in the tone of voice with which we speak our self-talk. By using self-talk, you can give the child an inside view on how to think and feel your way through situations skillfully, rather than just how to physically behave.

If you don't handle each situation skillfully, what then? Then you officially belong to the human race. You try to pick out situations that you know you can handle skillfully, and model the self-talk for those situations for the child. Meanwhile you work on your own psychological skills, and celebrate any positive examples.

Real Life Modeling by Reporting Your Own Positive Patterns

So far I've been talking about real-life modeling in that portion of your behavior that the child directly observes. Another way to capitalize on modeling is to report some of the positive examples you carry out in your child's absence.

When we spoke earlier about the nightly review, I mentioned that especially for older children, it's a good idea to include your own positive behaviors in the nightly review, as well as the child's. The child is not only less likely to be offended at being singled out as in need of an improvement program, but also the child gets to hear the positive models from your own life experience. The child is getting direct modeling of a very important skill, namely recalling and narrating life events, in addition to the modeling of the pattern you are celebrating. A word to the wise: if you want your child to be interested in your narratives, make them very concise.

Real Life Modeling By Playmates

Parents aren't the only ones that children imitate. Young children tend to imitate almost all that they see and hear.

Some colleagues and I did a study with Head Start Children who were paired on two occasions with two different randomly chosen classmates and videotaped while they were playing with each other. On the average, the two playmates' behavior resembled each other more than the child's behavior on one occasion resembled the same child's behavior on the next occasion!

The moral of the study is, when children are put together to play, they tend to resemble each other. The corollary is, try to help your child pick playmates well.

A Word About Television and Videos

What about imitation of television and other fictitious characters? This is such an important topic that I have devoted a separate chapter to it. But to be brief: children do imitate models that they see on television, whether those models are realistic or whether they are obviously fantasy characters as in cartoons. The moral is to choose your children's television and videotape models carefully. And to put it more stringently: avoid showing your young child examples of behavior that you don't want the child to imitate.

Most adults in contemporary U.S. society are very desensitized to hostility and violence in the media. Accordingly, it may be difficult, without conscious attention, to notice when characters in children's entertainment are being sarcastic or hostile or acting out slapstick violence. You may have to work hard to recognize those instances when it is meant to be funny that someone hurts himself. There is great need for raising our consciousness so that we notice when we are entertained by even small examples of hostility and harm to people, and questioning whether that is the way we wish to have fun.

Thus when you evaluate the quality of the interpersonal environment you are raising your child in, think about how the characters act toward each other in any piece of interaction the child watches, whether it be real life, television, video game, or any other medium. Sometimes parents can't understand why a child is misbehaving, when the parental models are so good; sometimes the answer is that the good models are simply "outgunned" by the sheer quantity and salience of models provided through mass media.

Using the Modeling Stories

By the phrase "modeling stories" I mean stories whose characters model the positive patterns exemplifying any of the psychological skills.

I have written and have had illustrated somewhere in the region of 200 modeling stories for young children. In addition, I have written a growing number of unillustrated modeling stories, some of which are included in an appendix to this book. Each of these is done with the express purpose of providing a model of one or more psychological skills. I have found these stories of immense usefulness in helping children develop psychological competence.

Of course, other people have also written stories whose characters model positive patterns of psychological skill. Here's what I mean by a "modeling story."

Features of a Modeling Story

Let's define a modeling story as one where the answers to the questions below are "Yes."

1. Does the protagonist act out an imitation-worthy positive example of at least one of the psychological skills?
2. Does the protagonist not act out negative examples of the psychological skills?
3. Do the characters in the story other than the protagonist also act in an imitation-worthy fashion? OR: If it is necessary for a supporting character to give a negative example, so that the protagonist can model an imitation-worthy response, (e.g. for a skill such as forgiveness and anger control) is the doer of the negative example portrayed in a way so as to inspire neither imitation nor hatred?
4. Is the problem of the story resolved by either a positive example of a psychologically skillful pattern, or by chance, BUT NOT by a violent act or by anyone's getting hurt or killed or gotten rid of? Do pain and death, even of an opponent, cause some mourning rather than rejoicing?
5. Are there no instances where someone's physically hurting himself, even mildly, or being verbally hostile to someone else is portrayed as fun and/or funny?

A couple of other features I think should be included in modeling stories as a set, although not necessarily in every modeling story.

6. Do the thoughts (self-talk) and emotions of the protagonist get revealed to the reader, as well as the overt behaviors?
7. Are there occasions when the external world and other people do not recognize and reinforce the protagonist's positive example, but the protagonist feels good anyway because of internal reinforcement?

Such criteria are rather seldom met in the works for children I see conveyed in the media. It is extremely common that the resolution to a problem comes by killing off the enemy characters or having them get killed due to an accident—movies from Star Wars to The Wizard of Oz to The Little Mermaid to the Disney version of Beauty and the Beast all portray a unidimensionally evil villain's being killed, followed by much rejoicing and happiness of the main characters. The plot of the "good" characters' destroying the bad is the near universal plot of "action and adventure" movies. We prepare children to solve problems by getting rid of villains, and then we send them out into a world where the opponents are just other people trying to get their needs met, and the best solution most frequently involves negotiation with the "villain" rather than destroying him or her.

Is it possible to hold children's interest without creating villains that they love to hate? It is a source of great pleasure to me and some renewed faith in human beings that young children can greatly enjoy the modeling story plots I have presented them in which people solve problems in reasonable ways and without destroying each other.

"Automodeling" of the Child's Behavior with Homemade Modeling Stories

By "automodeling" I mean taking the child's own positive behavior, and using it as a model for the child by presenting it to the child again. This principle was used when we spoke of the nightly review. Creating homemade modeling stories can make the review of the child's positive behavior much more effective and powerful.

For children who can't read yet, the modeling stories you create from the child's positive behavior should be illustrated. Suppose Fred is working on the skill of sharing attention, and one day when his mom spoke on the telephone for several minutes, Fred amused himself without interrupting during the whole time. Then you simply take a few pieces of blank paper, and on the first page you write, "Fred and his mom were playing. The phone rang." On the second page you write, "Fred's mom talked on the phone for a long time. Fred played with the toys and didn't interrupt." On the third page you write, "When she got off the phone, Fred's mom said, 'Thanks for sharing attention so well!'" Now the child can draw an illustration on each page. If the child is not in the mood to draw, you can illustrate them yourself. The illustrations do not have to be elaborate. Stick figures with the bare minimum of props can illustrate most homemade modeling stories. Then when you are done you can put a title on the first page, and staple the left sides of the pages together; in less than five minutes, usually, you can create an illustrated modeling story. A key skill of the adult is to capture the essence of the event in as few words as possible.

Once you have created this illustrated modeling story, you add it to the pile of illustrated modeling stories that can be read to the child any time the child wants. Now the child's positive behavior has become "history."

If you can have an ever-growing pile of illustrated modeling stories, and the child can enjoy seeing the pile grow, contributing to the creation of the stories, and enjoy hearing the stories repeatedly, you have a very powerful method of fostering the child's positive behavior.

As children grow older and learn to read better, the illustrations become less essential, and it is possible to put much more detail into the words of the story. One technique is to listen to the child's telling of a positive pattern that he enacted, and to be the child's secretary, writing down or typing out the narrative as he tells it. These can then be added to a growing collection of unillustrated modeling stories. As the child learns to write better, the child can write his own narratives of his or someone else's real-life behavior, or modeling stories created from the child's own imagination.

What's in it for the child to create such stories? Other than the intrinsic pleasure of creating a story, the attention and enthusiasm and excitement of the adult and of other people can be powerful reinforcers. An older child's modeling stories can be read to a younger sibling. A child's modeling stories can be shown to adult relatives and guests. A story that a child makes with one parent can be shown to the other parent. And the growing pile can be kept in one place, so that the child gradually sees his collected works become enlarged.

In the next chapter we'll talk about automodeling through dramatic plays as well as through written stories.

Side Benefits of Modeling Stories

The main purpose of modeling stories, of course, is to run positive patterns of thought, feeling, and behavior through the brain and thereby to make those patterns stronger. But there are obvious side benefits.

One of them is that if you read a lot to young children, you prepare them to learn to read. Young children also learn to talk better. If children can get into dictating or writing modeling stories themselves, they are practicing writing skills as well. The skills of reading and writing make up a vast fraction of what we hope children will learn in school; they can get a great deal of practice at it with modeling story activities.

And on top of all that, being read to is fun for the child, and is usually fun for you when the child responds positively. Thus reading together constitutes a mutually gratifying activity, and mutually gratifying activities strengthen relationships.

Sometimes a parent tells me, "My child doesn't like to be read to." If the child is between the ages of 3 and 8, I find it hard to believe that a child will not enjoy being read to if you follow the guidelines I list below.

Story-Reading Tips

1. Remove from the environment strong competitors for the child's attention. That means don't try to compete with television or with toys the child prefers at that moment.
2. Pick stories that are appropriate for your child's attention span. For the young child with a short attention span, the best stories are very short—the characters get on and off the stage in less than a minute—and the problem is presented and solved without a wasted word.
3. Put lots of expression in your voice.
4. Give the child lots of eye contact while you are reading. That way the activity increases the amount of attention the child perceives himself as getting; the book doesn't compete with the child for the adult's attention.
5. If the child stops paying attention, wait silently for the child to start again. If the child keeps paying attention to something else, quit reading without getting mad.
6. Use an approving tone at the end. You might say something like, "And that's the end of the story!" Your nonverbal tone communicates the message, "Hooray that you had a long enough attention span to listen to the end," without your actually having to say those words.

Here are a couple more tips that parents can use:
7. You can let the child sit on your lap and give the child lots of physical affection while he or she is hearing the story.
8. You can read the child stories at bedtime. Lots of children will do anything to put off going to bed. Why not use this to work for you, and let the child hear a bunch of stories? For example, "Well, Johnny, would you rather hear another story, or would you rather have lights out and go to sleep?"

If you do all these things, your child is likely to want to hear lots and lots of stories, and that's good.

Assignment: Try acting out reading to an imaginary child, doing none of these things, and then practice reading to an imaginary child doing all of these things. Have the imaginary child be beside you, and actually read aloud. Let someone else notice, or judge for yourself, how big a difference there would be in what the child would experience.

What if the child wants to hear the same story over and over? This is very likely to happen, and it's just fine. I have read the same story to some children fifty times or more. The child learns through repetition. So just be glad that the child is wanting to have that chance to learn. You have reason to feel good about yourself each time your child asks you to read to him. Your child's request means you have been doing a good job of reading to him in a way that is fun for him. On the other hand, don't feel bad about yourself if your child doesn't want to hear a whole story right away—some children take longer to warm up to this than others.

There's something else good that might happen with preschoolers with just a little bit of encouragement (but not pressure!) Your child may come to enjoy "reading" the story back you, by retelling it from memory as the pages remind the child what happened. This is an extremely positive habit for the child to develop, and the adult should respond in a very reinforcing way when the child does this, even if the child gives at first a fairly muddled version of the story. The act of retelling runs the positive pattern through the child's neuronal pathways in a more active way than the child's just listening to the story.

In order to use the power of prophecy (which we'll talk about later) to influence the child to do this some day if the child doesn't do it yet, you might remark, "Some day, maybe not today, you'll be able to look at the pages of the book and tell the story back to me! That will be fun, when you're able to do that!"

Chapter 10: Modeling and Practicing Through Drama

Chapter Overview:

If you use dramatic play with young children, you have a much easier job of increasing the number of positive models your child experiences. "Plays That Model Psychological Skills" are scripts I wrote, at least one for each of the 62 skills. You can simply put on these plays for your child, using puppets or toy people or animals. The ways you make plays interesting are very similar to the ways you make story-reading interesting. A second activity is to read the play, and then act it out with the child, with both you and the child acting out parts in the play. Some children will enjoy toy people and props; others will enjoy puppets; others will be able to act out dramas with their own bodies and imagined props. An added twist is to videotape or audiotape your production.

The most complex activity is for you and the child to improvise plays together. When you do this, it's good to use "advanced tracking and describing." This means you track and describe from the persona of a character rather than from your own persona. Speaking from the role of the characters is a major challenge to many adults. If you use the rhythm of modeling, silence, and responsiveness, you can help a shy child get started into improvisational drama. Once you get started, another part of your job is to insert positive models into the play. Ideally you'll model the skills of highest priority for your child. Keep in mind the balance between fun and productivity, and between directiveness and passivity. What if the child inserts violent acts into dramatic play? One way you can respond is to watch and wait, without reinforcing or punishing, and then to have a character model helping the victims. I provide at the end of this chapter a checklist you can use to self-monitor your play sessions with your child.

****

The more positive models your child is exposed to per day, the better. The use of drama enables you to increase your positive model count in a very pleasant and fast way, especially with young children.

The criteria for a plot that is a good modeling play are the same as those mentioned in the previous chapter on modeling stories. To recap: the main character models a positive pattern; the main character, with rare exceptions, doesn't model negative patterns; other characters model minimal negative patterns, and those that are absolutely necessary are presented without glamorization; the story's problem is not resolved by violence or injury; and hostility and injury aren't portrayed as fun or funny.

Here's an example of a script of one of the simplest modeling plays for young children:

Opening the Garage Door
First person: I need to get this garage door open. Unh! I can't get it open!
Second person: Do you need some help!
First person: Yes, please. I could use some. If we both lift I think it will be easy.
First and second person: Unnnh! Unnnnnh!
Second person and first person together lift the door up.
First person: Thank you! You really helped me!
Second person: It was my pleasure!
Narrator: And that's the end of the play.

This play is one of a couple of hundred I have compiled in a volume entitled *Plays That Model Psychological Skills.* With this book of the modeling plays, a lighthearted spirit, and for younger children some toy people or puppets, you can within a short time get a model of every one of the psychological skills into the memory bank of your child.

We will speak of three dramatic activities: putting on a play for the child (you are the actor, and your child is the audience); putting on a play with the child (you and the child are both actors of a prewritten drama); and doing joint dramatic play or improvisational drama, (you and the child are simultaneously making up the play and acting it out). The third activity is most complex, because you are mutually creating something, each having an influence upon the other's next lines.

Let's talk about the simpler of these two activities first.

Putting On Modeling Plays For Young Children

To do a modeling play, you first read the script and get the plot thoroughly in your memory. Then you get toy people and props set up, and then act out the show with the characters, playing the parts of all the characters in the show. You don't have to speak the lines exactly, of course; you can ad lib them.

The guidelines for helping children enjoy seeing modeling plays are very similar to those for modeling stories.

Guidelines for modeling plays

1. Pick a play of length and complexity not exceeding the child's attention span and comprehension ability.
2. Ask the child to sit in a chair out of reach of the toy people.
3. Have the play be very fast-moving.
4. Have an enthusiastic tone of voice.
5. Look at the child some, while putting on the play.
6. If the child stops paying attention, stop the play and wait.
7. Announce the end of the play with a tone of approval to the child.
8. At the end, put the toys on the floor and let the child play with them.

I have found it best if the adult clearly communicates when he or she is "putting on a show" and when the adult and the child are "playing together." That way the child isn't confused as to whether the child is supposed to play with the toys, or not.

When the adult is "putting on a show," the adult has a chair for the child to sit in that is out of reach of the toys. The adult says to the child, "I'm going to put on a little play for you. Why don't you sit right here, and watch. You can be the audience! Here goes the show!" Then at the end of the play, the adult clearly says something like, "That's the end of the play! Now we can play with the toys together, if you want."

It is a good idea to have the toys on the table while you are putting on the play, and then to put the toy people on the floor when it is time for the child to play with the toys together.

Don't start the play unless the child is looking in the right direction. If the child stops paying attention, stop the play. You may choose to ignore him until he starts paying attention again. Or, you may try to get his attention somehow, for example by saying, "Look at this." If the child gets thoroughly interested in something else, you may stop the play altogether, and do something else yourself. You may go into tracking and describing whatever the child is paying attention to, after a small wait.

It's not a good idea to continue the play when the child is not paying attention. You don't want the child to get into the habit of ignoring an adult who is speaking to him. This habit will be especially problematic when the child gets to school. On the other hand, it is important not to feel too frustrated if the child does not want to see the play. There is always another time for the child to pay attention to it.

The adult can make the plays attract the child's attention by making them very dramatic, and putting lots of emotion into what the characters say. Have the characters express their positive emotion with great energy. Keep the action very fast-moving, but still talk slowly enough that the child can process the language you are using. Have the plays be almost all dialogue, just as they are written; don't have a bunch of narration and description and explanation. In other words, have the characters talk to each other almost the whole time.

What if the child has a very short attention span? You can use the concept of hierarchy that we have spoken of repeatedly, and start out with very short plays, and gradually stretch your child's attention span by working your way up to longer ones. The very shortest plays, at the bottom of the hierarchy, I've called "microplays." Here's one of them.

Microplay: Nice Whistling

(First Character Whistles.)

Second Character: Nice Whistling! I like it!

First Character: Thank you!

Narrator: And that's the end of the play.

Does the child have to be staring at the characters in order to be considered paying attention? Not necessarily. Sometimes the child can be paying attention even when she seems to drift to something else. The adult will have to use his judgment to decide when the child is paying attention and when she is not.

What about the adult's using different voices for the different characters? This is a good idea, but it isn't necessary. Most play-performers find it a little difficult to keep track of exactly which character has exactly which voice. You don't really have to work this hard. If you do use different voices, though, watch to make sure that you continue to speak very distinctly. Sometimes when people use different voices their speech becomes hard to understand.

What if while you are putting on the play, the child starts moving the characters and speaking for them? Don't get angry at the child, because this is just the sort of thing you want the child to start doing in a few minutes. Check to see if you remembered to seat the child in a chair that is out of reach of the characters. Very politely ask the child to wait until the show is over. Say something like, "Johnny, please be a good audience and stay in your seat until the little play is over. Then we can both play with them any way we want to." If the child still can't keep his hands off the toys, then I would conclude that being an inactive audience is too difficult for the child's current level of self-discipline. While the child is developing more self-discipline, I would do lots of joint play with the child and insert my positive models into lulls in the drama.

When the show is over, you say something to indicate very clearly that fact, such as "That's the end! Now the show is over!" The adult might even have some of the characters who weren't in the show clap and cheer for the other characters. The adult might want to pat the child on the back and say "Good for you, you were a good audience!"

If, after the play is over, it's time for bed or some totally different activity, that's fine. However, a modeling play is often a good lead-in to more dramatic play. Sometimes the child will want to do the same play himself. If so, the adult should greatly reinforce that, with attention and interest. Or, the child may want to put on a play of his own composing, for the adult, or the child and the adult can move into joint dramatic play with each other.

Another variation on the theme that you might want to do from time to time is to challenge the child to remember and recreate the play. Before putting on the play, the adult might say, "Let's see if you can do something. I'm going to act out a little play, and then I want to see if you can act out the same play for me. OK?" Then, after acting out the play, the adult says to the child, "That's the end of the play. Can you do it for me now?" Then if the child does anything close to what the adult did, the adult responds with attention and approval. This activity is clearly in the category of "adult directed activity" rather than "child directed activity." It is important not to get too pushy with this. If the child does not respond to these suggestions, drop them and wait a few days before trying again. If the child doesn't like this or if it seems to turn play into work, forget it.

Meanwhile, here's another way to make it more likely that the child will get the positive pattern firmly into memory: simply do the same play a few times, over the course of a few days. As with stories, sometimes the child needs several repetitions before the plot is clearly in his mind enough to imitate. On the other hand, often one exposure permanently gets a plot into the child's memory.

Sometimes the child takes the general themes of the plays the adult puts on, and incorporates them into his own plays, without ever going through the step of directly imitating the adult's plays. If the child has people help people and solve problems and feel good about their solutions in his fantasy play, he is getting the sort of practice he needs, so there is no need to worry about whether he is directly imitating the adult's plays. He's getting practice at being creative when he makes up his own plays.

Most of the time the child will directly imitate the adult's plays without any particular encouragement to do so. The interest and enthusiasm of the adult's characters when he does do so is an added reinforcement for the positive patterns.

Videotaping Modeling Plays

I have made a low-budget videotape of modeling plays, the ones in *Plays that Model Psychological Skills*, in which the toy people enact the plays on the screen. If you want to increase the positive models your child sees, you can videotape some plays yourself; perhaps the child will view them repeatedly, as many children have chosen to do with my production.

Using the Plays With Older Children

Grade school aged children sometimes convince themselves (with the help of the advertisements that shape their opinions) that toy people are too juvenile for them. (This is a real shame, in my opinion, and a symptom that our society is pressuring children to progress to pseudo-sophistication too quickly.) Often puppets will be acceptable for grade school aged children where the sorts of toy people marketed to preschoolers will not be. But grade school children are also capable of acting out plays by using themselves as the characters, without props.

Here's one way of putting on one of the *Plays that Model Psychological Skills* in a way to challenge grade school aged children. First, the adult or adults and child or children all read the script. Then they figure out who will play the parts of which characters. Then, after a final peak at the script, people simply stand up and act it out. If there are any missing props, people simply pantomime their presence and speak aloud their thoughts about them so that the audience can know they are there. For example, with the play above about opening the garage door: the first person walks up to an imaginary door, remarks that he has to get the garage door open, bends over, grasps an imaginary handle, pulls on it, and grunts. The second person walks up and greets the first person, and so forth. Any other people in the group can be the audience.

In using this dramatic convention rather than toy people and props, it will occasionally be necessary for characters to point and ad lib a few descriptive words that help their fellow actors and the audience to know where imaginary objects are. For example, one actor says, "Wow, look at this airplane," pointing to where the imaginary airplane is. If the space for the "stage" is small, you can show your actors how to walk or run in place to portray walking or running in the drama.

Reading a play and acting it out like this is a real challenge to several important psychological skills. It is a great exercise in reading comprehension. It is a challenge to the ability to organize and remember sequences of interpersonal events. This ability is quite important: it is crucial, for example, if people are to benefit from thinking about what they did and said during the day, or what they will do and say tomorrow. Reading and acting out plays give practice in overcoming the stage fright that results from deficient skills of handling mistakes and failures. It gives practice in verbal fluency, as the child ad libs the lines of the characters. And of course, it gives direct role-playing practice in acting out whatever psychological skill the play is meant to model.

Since video camcorders are now widely available, it is quite feasible to use the play scripts and make movies of the plays that model psychological skills. You, your child or children, and/or your child's friends are the actors. This gives the child practice in enacting the psychological skill; it also gives a model of the psychological skill that the child is likely to view repetitively. This activity is fun, exciting, conducive to repetitive modeling and fantasy practice, and likely to be rewarded by other people who view the product. As such it is worth doing as often as possible, in any variations.

Another variation is to record audiodramas rather than video-dramas, using an audiotape recorder. If you and the child record enough of these, you can listen to them during automobile rides, and thus make useful some usually nonproductive time.

Jointly Created Dramatic Play

Now let's think about jointly created dramatic play, or improvised drama. With young children, this is best done with toy people. In this activity, each person contributes to the script of the play spontaneously, as the play goes along.

I'm of the opinion that a child is really missing out if he or she never gets a chance to do this. The advantages I mentioned previously for acting out prewritten scripts apply, and in addition there are the following.

First, this activity helps young children develop language, through all the talking they get to hear and practice.

Second, they get practice at sustaining attention to verbally encoded information, a skill that is an antidote to attention deficit problems.

Third, spontaneous dramatic play teaches the young child how to imagine interpersonal scenes that are not actually physically present. And that is a very big deal. Let's think about the skill of conflict resolution, or the skill of decision making about an interpersonal situation. Thinking of an option for the solution of a problem requires imagining the two people doing something they haven't already done yet. Predicting the consequences of that option also requires such imagining. Let's think about the skill of self-discipline and delaying gratification. A child works hard now, for an honor she hopes to receive in the future. That future honor is an imagined situation, one not physically present. Or, consider the skill of tolerating separation. The child comforts himself when his mother leaves, by the knowledge that his mother will return. That image of the mother returning is another imagined situation, not physically present. Imagining situations not physically present is at the heart of what thinking is all about. It is central to good functioning in most psychological skills.

Fourth, the child's creativity is stimulated, the ability to come up with ideas, the ability to do "divergent thinking."

And fifth, while the child and adult are having fun doing dramatic play, the adult has lots of opportunity to model important psychological skills.

Many adults find it hard to do dramatic play with a child. Indeed, I think the art of doing dramatic play with a child is a very complex set of skills, one that takes time and practice to develop. Doing responsive versus directive interactions is one of the biggest challenges for most adults. Many adults have a tendency to give commands and ask questions too much when they start to play with the toy people. An extremely useful antidote to such directiveness is tracking and describing, which we spoke about in chapters 6 and 7. In the version we spoke of, the adult simply names what the child is doing and paying attention to: for example, "The lion is pushing the car! He's pushing it all the way to the top of the house! ... Hey, here comes a man in an airplane. Oh, the lion's getting into the airplane." Let's spend some time thinking about an "advanced" version of it particularly useful in dramatic play.

"Advanced" Tracking and Describing from the Persona of Toy Characters

One of the major rules of doing fun dramatic play is: Speak from the point of view of imaginary characters, not from your own adult persona. Why? Because this lets the activity stay firmly planted in the land of make-believe, rather than wrenching back and forth between make-believe and real life. It allows the child to get into the fantasy and continue it longer.

There is a way to do tracking and describing while still following this rule. You simply have toy characters do the tracking and describing, by remarking to each other about what is going on. Let's imagine an example, where the child has first one person, then another, get into the toy car, and someone fills the car with gas. The adult "advanced" tracker and describer has two other characters speak to each other while this is going on.

First person: Hey, looks like he's getting in the car. Looks like a trip to somewhere; I wonder where.

Second person: Yeah. And look, another guy's getting in the car too. They're both going to take a trip, it looks like.

First person: (To persons in car) Looks like you're filling up your gas tank first, huh? ... You sure can't go very far without gas in the car.

Second person: (To persons in car) All full, it looks like. Now you're ready to take off again! (To first person) Off they go!

Having the characters do the tracking and describing accomplishes the same purposes of tracking and describing as previously, only now additionally, the adult strengthens the norm that the toy characters talk to each other. If this norm is set by the adult, the child is much more likely to have his characters talk. Furthermore, the adult may set the norm that the characters usually talk to each other in polite, enthusiastic tones of voice.

How to Start Joint Dramatic Play

If, after the example we just gave, the child characters spoke back to the adult's characters, and joined with them in action, and the child and the adult together spun out a plot together, that would be what I call spontaneous dramatic play, or joint dramatic play.

When this gets going, the adult can work positive models of any of the psychological skills into the spontaneous dramatic play. And the child tends to imitate these models in his own dramatic play. The adult's characters can reinforce the child for such positive patterns. And each time the child acts out the positive pattern in dramatic play, the child is doing a "fantasy practice" of the positive pattern. The more fantasy practices take place, the more likely the child is to act out the positive pattern in real life. In addition, joint dramatic play when done well is great fun for both people, and thus constitutes another mutually gratifying activity.

Many children need no help or encouragement to start doing fantasy play when given toy people and toy houses or airports or farms. But for those children who need a boost, I suggest that the rhythm of modeling, silence, and responsivity, as we spoke of in the chapter on conversation, may also be used with dramatic play.

I often do the modeling by starting a play myself. If the child picks up one of the characters and replies to something my character has said to another character, fine; if not I pick up the character myself and reply. Thus there is no way for the child to fail. If the child is too shy to do anything but sit and watch attentively, I will sometimes put on play after play, enjoying what a good audience the child is.

In getting the child involved, one of the most important things the adult can do is to wait for the child, and not to rush the child. The child often needs time to think of what to do. In other words, the adult often needs to keep his mouth shut, so the child can come up with something. If the child is feeling uncomfortable, the adult can do some more modeling; if the child is comfortable, the adult can watch silently.

Sometimes a much-needed step on the way to drama is to let the child simply manipulate the toys, while you do enough tracking and describing to keep the child interested.

Sometimes the child needs explicit permission to start the characters interacting. You can do this by having a character say something to another character, then handing the child the toy person, and asking that character a very simple question. If the child's character doesn't answer, don't put the child on the spot by insisting that the child answer. Instead, you get the child off the spot by answering for the character, yourself.

When the child does speak for a character, the adult responds very enthusiastically; the adult's energy, directed attention, and approving tones reinforce the child for getting involved.

This situation is a perfect example of when enthusiastic attention is better than direct praise. Here's a direct praise example:

Child's character: (to adult's character, both of whom are standing near the toy see-saw): Get on.

Adult: Good for you, you used your imagination and talked from the point of view of a character!

This sort of response would just interrupt the play and wrench everybody back to the land of reality from the land of make-believe. The shy child might see that evaluation is going on, and clam up to avoid doing something wrong. Here's enthusiastic attention in-

stead, from the point of view of a character:
Child's character (to adult's character, both of whom are standing near the toy see-saw): Get on.
Adult's character: OK, I'll get on, if you want me to. What's going to happen? Hey, we get to see-saw with each other!

Once you and the child are both speaking from the role of characters, you're in business.

Because speaking from the role of characters is so important, let me suggest an exercise on it.

Exercise: Speaking from the Role of the Characters

In the exercise below, I'll give you a sentence that the adult might say, out of the role of the character, from his own role. Translate that into something that the adult could say from the role of the character. When doing this exercise, it's helpful to have the toys out and to practice it with the toy people, moving the toy person up and down as he speaks.

1. The child's character is feeding the dog. The adult gets the urge to say, "Oh, I bet the dog likes that food." How could the adult say that from the role of a character?

Sample answer: the adult picks up the dog and moves him as he says, "Ruff! Ruff! Boy, do I like that food, Mr. Farmer! Thank you!"

2. The child has some people get in the car and has the car starts moving. The adult gets the urge to say, "Where are they going in the car?" How could the adult say that from the role of a character?

Sample answer: the adult picks up a character and moves him up and down as he says, "Hey, where are you guys driving to?"

3. The child has a character carrying a bed. The adult gets the urge to say, "He's carrying a heavy bed. Can he get it by himself?" How could the adult instead say something from the role of a character?

Sample answer: the adult picks up a character and moves him us and down while saying, "Boy, that looks like a heavy bed you're carrying. Could you use some help? I could get at the other end."

4. The child is commenting on what color the beds and chairs are. The adult gets the urge to say, "And do you know what color this table is?" How could the adult continue the conversation from the role of a character?

Sample answer: The adult could pick up a character and move him up and down while saying to one of the child's characters, "Hey, can you do me a favor? I haven't learned my colors yet. I'm just trying to remember. Can you help me? Is that table brown or yellow?" If the child ignores this, the adult can then turn to another person and repeat the request. The other person says, "It's brown!" The first person says, "Oh, thanks, I just wanted to get that straight." Then the adult sits still and waits for the child to make the next move.

5. The child is stacking some tables and chairs up to see how high he can stack them. The adult gets the urge to say to the child, "I wonder how high you can stack them before they fall over." What could the adult say instead that would stay in the role of a character?

Sample answer: The adult picks up a character and moves it up and down while looking at the stack, and says, "Wow, you're stacking those tables and chairs up really high. I'm going to stand here and watch and see how high you can stack them, if you don't mind."

6. The child has a piece of paper be a swimming pool, and says, "They're going to go swimming." The adult gets the urge to say, "Have they all learned how to swim yet?" What is something the adult could do instead that would be from the role of a character?

Sample answer: The adult picks up a character and moves him up and down while saying to one of the others, "Do you know how to swim yet?... I haven't learned how yet." "

7. The child is just starting, and the toys are out. The adult gets the urge to ask the child, "What do you want to have them do?" What could the adult do instead that would be from the role of a character?

Sample answer: The adult picks up a character and says to another one, "Hi! What do you want to do today?"

8. The child asks, "How do you get the house open?" The adult starts to say, "You turn the little handle on the top of the house, and then you can open up the house." What could the adult do instead that would be from the role of a character?

Sample answer: The adult has one character say to another, "Hey, we're trying to get the house open. Do you know how we do it?" Then the adult has the other character say, "Yes. What you do is to turn the handle up on top of the house, and then you can open it right up."

9. The child says about one of the characters, "He can't find his bag." The adult gets the urge to say, "He can't? I wonder where he lost it." What could the adult say instead that is from the role of a character?

Sample answer: The adult picks up another character and says to the one who lost his bag, "Would you like some help in finding your bag? I'll look for it too."

10. The child has the dog trying to jump over the fence. The adult gets the urge to say to the child, "You think the dog will be able to jump over the fence?" What could the adult say instead from the role of a character?

Sample answer: The adult gets a character and says to the dog, "Hey, Mister Dog! Have you ever tried to jump over that fence before?"

Now like all rules, there are times when the rule of staying in the persona of the characters should be broken. The adult should not speak from the role of a character when giving the child a command. For example, when it is time to finish up the dramatic play, the adult should say to the child, "Johnny, it's time for us to finish up now." It would not do to have a character say, "Well, it's about time for us to go to bed, why don't we all go to sleep and go in the box." The child needs to know that in the context of the dramatic play, the characters are permitted a very wide range of behavior, such as saying, "I'm not ready to go to bed yet; I'm going to play soccer out here." If the adult really wants the child to do something, he or she should communicate that to the child directly, looking at the child, calling the child by name. That way play is kept distinct from real-life commands, and the child isn't so likely to be confused.

While we're on the notion of staying in the land of make-believe: some adults wonder whether to call the child's toy character by the child's real-life name. I tend not to initiate this. If the characters have other names, it's clear to everybody that this is a play, a drama, a work of the imagination, and not something that the child is directly carrying out in real life. But if the child names a character for himself, and gets a kick out of having a character with his name, I certainly wouldn't squelch that.

The Balance Between Fun and Productivity

The adult should keep in mind a balance, between two goals: that of keeping the child thoroughly "hooked" on dramatic play, and that of eliciting and modeling high-priority skills. The attempts to influence the content of the child's fantasies should not interfere with the child's ability to experience true gleefulness and silliness in the course of this fantasy play. (After all, being gleeful and silly is one of the skills on the axis.) The adult should not be so impatient to get positive vignettes of one specified type into the fantasy play that the experience becomes boring for the child. I would hate it if any who read this chapter turn dramatic play with the child into drab lessons poorly disguised as play! This warning notwithstanding, if you look carefully for chances to do some sort of positive model in an unobtrusive way, literally scores of opportunities may come in a couple of hours of dramatic play.

Inserting Positive Models into Spontaneous Dramatic Play

When you are doing joint dramatic play, have your characters act out the most psychologically skillful patterns you can muster. Think of any positive examples of any of the skills on the skills axis. Think of anything kind or helpful that anyone can offer to do for anyone else. If the child has someone be unkind to someone else, have a character be nice to the victim rather than be angry at the unkind person. Or have the victim think rationally, out loud, about how to handle the situation. Review the examples of kind behavior in all the stories and modeling plays, and put as many of them into the spontaneous plays as you possibly can. Have people work hard and be forgiving of other people and be calm and cool when something bad happens to them.

What if the adult wants to carry out a positive model, but the character that the child is playing does not want to be helped? One option is to drop it and forget about it. Another option is for the adult to play two parts: the part of a person offering help, and the part of another person who does want it. For example, suppose the adult's character says to the child's character, "Would you like for me to get you something to drink?" and the child's character ignores this request. The adult might then have his character say to another character, "How about you, would you like something to drink?" and then have that character respond, "Sure, that would be really nice of you." Then the two characters played by the adult would finish their interchange quickly. In general, the adult should become very skilled at switching to play the part of a different character when it is useful.

I find it useful to get some plots of positive models in my mind, before the play starts. I plan that when there is a lull, my characters will start in the direction of these modeling plays. If the child joins in and changes the direction of the play, fine.

Skill-Oriented Choices Regarding the Plot of Dramatic Play

A given choice point in spontaneous dramatic play presents you with an infinite number of options. How do you choose what to have your characters do in the drama?

The first answer is that if you do something that is a reasonably positive model of any psychological skill, in a way that's fun for you and the child, you're way ahead of the game. You don't even need to read further in this section unless you want to be even farther ahead of the game.

The more advanced answer involves keeping in mind the four or five highest-priority psychological skills, the ones the child needs the most to learn. You try whenever possible to model one of those yourself or set the child up to enact an example.

Suppose a parent is involved in a play with farm characters, with a preschool child. Suppose the child, who is playing the part of the sheep, gleefully runs away from the rest of the characters; the farmer, played by the adult, says "Mr. Sheep! Mr. Sheep!" but the sheep replies, "I'm running away!" Let's think of different ways of responding depending upon which psychological skill we most want to model.

Suppose this child's highest priority skill is that of being able to ask for help, to trust and depend appropriately. The adult as farmer might go to another character and say, "Mr. Jones! I need some help! My sheep has run away. Could you help me find him?" The adult then can play the part of Mr. Jones, if the child doesn't want to, and be willing to help the farmer; the farmer can be comforted and grateful for the help, regardless of the success of the outcome.

Suppose, instead, that the highest priority skill for this child is that of tolerating separation, of overcoming the fear that his attachment figures will be harmed when he is away from them. The farmer in that case might attempt to get the sheep to come back, and when he is unsuccessful, talk to himself along the lines of "Gosh, I wonder what's going to happen to the sheep while he's away. I wonder if he'll be all right." The adult might then hand another character to the child and ask that character, "Do you think my sheep will be all right if I just go back to the barn and wait for him to come back?" If the farmer does go to the barn and wait, he might deliver a "soliloquy" in which he thinks about the separation: "I hope nothing happens to my sheep. But, I can't be with him all the time. He's big enough to take care of himself. He's been away lots of other times, and he's always made it so far."

Suppose instead that the highest priority skill for the child is that of being able to give in or to back down, or the related skill of being able to tolerate a wide range of behavior in the other person. The farmer might then say, "Well, OK, I'll let you have your way. I wanted you to come back and be with us, but I guess I can't have my way all the time." Then another character might say to the farmer, "Mr. Farmer, I think you're awfully smart to let that sheep have his own way! I bet he likes that!"

If the child needed the most to free up his ability to be silly, the adult might engage in a slapstick chase of the sheep. If the child most needed to develop language abilities, the farmer might ask the sheep some questions or make comments calculated so as to prompt the child to talk. If the child most needed to develop the ability to be assertive, the farmer's friend might ask the farmer in a very assertive way to please leave the sheep alone and come back to do some work they have to do. If the child most needed models of the skill of fortitude, the farmer might think out loud to himself things like, "Well, is this something I want to get upset about? I think I can handle this OK. Nothing terrible is likely to happen. And I've done all I can do, anyway." If the child most needed to improve in generating options for decisions, the farmer might muse about four or five courses of action that he could do at this moment. If the child most needed to get some patient nurturing behavior into his repertoire, the farmer might say, "I'll let the sheep run and play, and I'll just stay in sight to make sure he's all right. That way he'll have a good time, and I'll be sure he's safe. Yes, I can see him, even though he's a good distance away."

The Balance Between Directiveness and Passivity

One of the great things about joint dramatic play is that it's a cooperative endeavor, like most of those that are really crucial to existence (such as participating in a family, running a business, etc.) That means that sometimes one person, sometimes the other, and sometimes the two together determine the direction of what will happen. It is usually quite a lot of fun for both adult and child when you can get to the point where you are creating dramas together, with both contributing in a very cooperative way to the formation of the plot. In general, there should be a balance, such that no one person determines the plot for extremely long without the other person's having some input.

Watch out for being too directive. Don't have your characters want something of the child's characters often enough to be annoying. If your character wants the child's character first to help with something, then to receive some help, then to go to a certain place, and then to do a certain activity, your characters will be totally determining the course of action.

When the adult's characters are too directive, the child's characters start getting rebellious and oppositional, saying "No" very often. The child has them do this because he knows on some level that he will have more fun if he can make up the plot of the drama himself sometimes.

If the adult finds himself being too directive, he should consciously try to use more "tracking and describing" of the child's activity, and should be silent more of the time.

On the other hand, some adults may need to watch out for being too passive. If the adult does not often enough initiate plots for the dramas, or participate actively enough in them, the child may become uninterested in dramatic play, or may become so accustomed to determining all the action himself that he misses out on learning how to experience the "give and take" of constructing a plot jointly with someone else. Or, the child plays out all the plots he can think of, and if the adult doesn't infuse a new one every now and then, the child may "run out of gas."

If the adult finds himself being too passive, he should initiate more positive models and set up more situations where the child's characters can do something jointly with the adult's characters.

Responding to Violence in Dramatic Play

Suppose the child has characters hit and kick each other or run over other characters with cars. We are placed in something of a dilemma. On the one hand, I've emphasized that the catharsis theory doesn't seem to work, and enacting hostility through fantasy seems usually to present more of a practice of hostility than a release of it. For that reason, our models, our stimuli from our own characters, and our differential attention are designed to give maximal pull on the child toward prosocial, positive actions. On the other hand, I've advised staying in the make believe, joining with the child, and not being too directive, so as to support the child's use of the medium of dramatic play. So how do we discourage violent dramatic play, without getting heavy-handed and saying "We don't allow that sort of play in here."

One option is for the adult to sit and do nothing until a few seconds after the fantasied violent act. Without comment, the adult waits a few seconds before resuming. A second option is that the adult takes a second or two to tie his shoe, check to see what time it is, or some other activity that does not give attention to the child or to the act, for just a few seconds.

The reduced attentiveness of the adult fails to reinforce or encourage the rehearsal of violent acts. On the other hand, the adult doesn't express direct disapproval to the child, since the child himself has done nothing wrong: only the characters have, if anyone has.

Another very good way to respond is the way that a peaceful, civilized person in real-life usually responds to the aftermath of violent acts: by helping the victims. The adult's character is sad about the persons that were hurt, inquires how badly they are hurt and take them to the hospital, and cares for them. Then other people can come to see them, and act very sad that they were hurt. They do not get well quickly. This response teaches the child that violence really hurts people, people with friends, and causes them lasting pain and disability. At the same time, it models a caring response. Frequently, the child will get one of his characters involved in this caretaking and nurturing activity. This is part of the beauty of dramatic play: you do not have to convert the violent character to a good character in order for prosocial behavior to come out; you can simply let the violent character be forgotten and let the child assume another character.

Later one of the adult's characters might wish to ask the violent person why he did what he did. This response might let the child start thinking about why people are angry at each other and what they can do about conflict other than fight.

In later conversation with the child, (not interrupting an episode of dramatic play) I like to voice my opinion that somebody doesn't have to be very smart or imaginative to make a plot that will grab people's attention if people are fighting each other. To make a very interesting nonviolent plot, however, is a much bigger challenge. The ability to do this distinguishes the really creative people.

A special case of responding to violence comes when the child has actually been the victim of a violent act, and tends to recreate it in fantasy. Here the violent fantasy has a somewhat different function for the child than the usual violent fantasy play that is in imitation of television messages that "violence is fun." The child may be recreating the violent fantasy in order to achieve "mastery" over it—to get closure, somehow, on this memory. In this case I still would tend not to make the violent act exciting and fun, but would tend to sit and track and describe. If the child put me in the role of the victim, I would model with self-talk as many different adaptive thoughts as I could muster about what to do in such a situation—listing options and choosing among them, handling frustration, self-reinforcement for making the best of a bad situation, forgiving myself for being unable to come up with a perfect response instantly. That way I am at least giving the child different adaptive responses to rehearse in his own head when the memory of the incident recurs to him.

Self-Monitoring Your Play Sessions

I have used the following checklist to help adults become expert in playing with children. If you can consistently get 8 or above on all items, I'll bet children both enjoy and benefit from playing with you. You can use this checklist not only for dramatic play sessions, but the conduct of any sort of activity that is a candidate for a "mutually gratifying activity."

Checklist for Play Sessions

0=None
2=Only a Little
4=Some
6=Pretty Much
8=A High Amount
10=A Very High Amount

_____1. How much did you act and speak enthusiastically, with an upbeat attitude toward whatever you were doing together?
_____2. By how much did your utterances of approving feedback outnumber messages of critical or corrective feedback to the other person? (There should be at least 4 approvals per 1 criticism, to count a 10 on this.)
_____3. How well did you withhold unnecessary commands or requests and other directives, but instead let the other person follow his own lead whenever appropriate? (0=Lots of unnecessary directives given; 10=No unnecessary directives.)
_____4. How well did you encourage chatting with the other person? Chatting is nondirective, nonevaluative conversation. (Methods of encouraging it: telling about your own experience, facilitations, tracking and describing, reflections, follow-up questions.) (In the course of dramatic play, it's the characters who can chat with each other.)
_____5. How much reciprocal interaction, was there? (In this, each person takes turns doing or saying something in response to what the other just said or did.)

_____6. To what extent did the other person see positive models of psychological skills in your interaction? (This includes your real-life behavior and any symbolic models you communicated.)

_____7. If there was a problem or conflict of interest, to what extent did you do your part in staying rational and reasonable and curbing the display of excited hostility? (Steps in a problem-solving paradigm: problem definition, reflection, option-listing without evaluation, option evaluation, option choosing.)

_____8. To what extent did you avoid reinforcing, and effectively punish if necessary, any real-life negative behavior by the child?

_____9. To what extent did both people have a good time in this session?

Chapter 11: Modeling Songs

Chapter Overview:

It would be a shame for you not to harness the power of music in helping your child develop psychological competence. Music is a big source of pleasure, very closely linked to our emotions. I have written some songs meant to model psychological skills. I also include in this chapter a list of popular and folk songs containing elements of positivity. If you're religious, your hymn book has to include some "modeling songs" your family can enjoy. I recommend that you pick out some songs modeling important skills. Then don't just play them, but sing them to the child, and sing them together as a family. Don't be stopped by not having an instrument to accompany yourself, or by the fear of singing wrong notes. Our electronic media often compete too successfully with the custom of family members' singing together. With songs, just as with stories and drama, I recommend working to make yours a family of active participants rather than passive listeners. If you can your children can dance to modeling songs, you participate even more actively.

****

Music and songs are linked to the experience of emotion. Sometimes people with damage to certain areas of the brain that control spoken language can nevertheless recall and sing songs. Songs are more connected with the emotions than speech. Monotone speech, devoid of melodic content, tends to be unemotional.

Music also is an aid to memory. I can remember some songs that I heard only a few times in early childhood, with no exposures since that time. Apparently lots of other people find that catchy tunes stay tenaciously in the memory bank; this is probably why advertisers often put their messages into jingles. If memory for jingles is tenacious, it stands to reason that we should make available for children some of the important principles of living, in the form of songs and jingles.

Modeling songs, like modeling stories and plays, are meant to give positive models of psychological skills, no negative models, and no resolution of anything by violence.

I've composed and recorded some modeling songs in a collection called "Spirit of Nonviolence." If you want to sing along with these, it's a good way of getting what I feel to be positive patterns into the memory bank.

One of the great things about young children is that most of them usually don't care if somebody is a little off pitch. So don't feel self-conscious singing around a child. Unless they see somebody criticizing somebody else's singing, they usually will enjoy singing and have a great time with it. (On the other hand, if they've seen and heard enough of someone else's putting down someone's singing, they probably would reject the singing of the best singer in the world.) The important thing is not to worry whether anybody will win any singing contests, but to have fun with it. If you sing these songs in a way that looks like you are enjoying it, and use differential attention well, the child will almost certainly start singing joyously sooner or later.

One of the great things about modeling songs is that you can use them whenever and wherever you and your child are together. You can sing together at breakfast, at bedtime, or while you're walking somewhere together, or when you're working at home and your child is standing around near you, or when you're riding in a car together, or any other time you feel like. If you experiment, you can find out what seem to be the most fun times and places to sing together. If your whole family can start singing some songs together, regularly, that model psychologically skillful patterns, I think you will find a major effect. The words will be much empowered by the sight of everyone in the family singing these songs together.

A useful way of teaching a song is to play the recording of the song in the background, while doing something else, to get the melody into the child's mind.

Another activity is to play the "dance and freeze" activity. You and the child or children take a tape recorder and play the song, and dance around; when you press the pause button, you either "freeze" in the position you are in (variation 1 for the game) or sit down (variation 2), or lie down on the floor (variation 3). This gives the child practice in "revving up" his exuberance and then "revving down." This control of activity and energy gives practice in the skill of relaxation. In the process, the song is becoming familiar.

In the "dance and freeze" activity, is it necessary to teach the children to dance? No. My own opinion about "teaching" dance to young children is that the best way to start out is by putting on music, and then modeling moving around in time to the music in every way that you can think of, and inviting the child do it with you. If you know some dance steps, do them; if you have videos of people dancing in ways that you'd like the children to imitate, watch them with the child; but the essence is to just move with the music, and do it joyously, without generating any performance anxiety. This can constitute great practice in the skill of feeling glee, as well as exposure to the melodies of the modeling songs.

A Compendium Of Some Other Modeling Songs

If you are on the lookout, you can find many songs that model desirable, psychologically skillful ways of thinking about the world. Once you find those songs, see if you can make them belong to your family. Here are some "oldies" that have appealed to me.

The following can be found in the *Ultimate Fake Book*, Volume I, Hal Leonard Publishing Corp, 8112 West Bluemond Road, P.O. Box 13819, Milwaukee, Wisconsin 52313, 1985.

Button Up Your Overcoat, by B.G. Desylva, Lew Brown, Ray Henderson
(Kindness)

Climb Every Mountain, by Oscar Hammerstein II, Richard Rodgers
(Sustaining Attention to Tasks, Sense of Direction and Purpose)

Edelweiss, by Oscar Hammerstein II, Richard Rodgers
(Pleasure from Blessings)

Everything's Coming up Roses, by Stephen Sondheim, Jule Styne
(Pleasure from accomplishment)

Getting to Know You, by Oscar Hammerstein II, Richard Rodgers
(Social Initiations)

The Happy Wanderer, by Antonia Ridge, Freidrich W. Moller
(Pleasure from Blessings, Social Initiations)

If I Had a Hammer, by Lee Hays and Pete Seeger
(Kindness, Sense of Direction and Purpose)

It's a Good Day, by Peggy Lee and Dave Barbour
(Pleasure from Blessings)

If We Only Have Love, by Jacques Brel, English Lyrics by Mort Shuman and Eric Blau
(Kindness)

If Ever I Would Leave You, by Alan Jay Lerner, Frederick Loewe
(Loyalty)

It's Only a Paper Moon, by Billy Rose, E.Y. Harburg, Harold Arlen
(Trusting, Honesty)

Last Night I Had the Strangest Dream, by Ed McCurdy
(Conflict Resolution)

May You Always, by Larry Markes, Dick Charles
(Kindness)

Mockingbird Hill, by Vaughn Horton
(Pleasure from Blessings)

My Cup Runneth Over, by Tom Jones, Harvey Schmidt
(Kindness, Intimacy)

My Favorite Things, by Oscar Hammerstein II, Richard Rodgers
(Pleasure from Blessings)

Oh, What a Beautiful Morning, by Oscar Hammerstein II, Richard Rodgers
(Pleasure from Blessings)

On a Clear Day, by Alan Jay Lerner, Burton Lane
(Pleasure from Blessings)

On the Sunny Side of the Street, by Dorothy Fields, Jimmy McHugh
(Pleasure from Blessings)

September Song, by Maxwell Anderson, Kurt Weill
(Loyalty, Intimacy)

The Sound of Music, by Oscar Hammerstein II, Richard Rodgers
(Pleasure from Blessings)

They Can't Take That Away From Me, by Ira Gershwin, George Gershwin
(Separation Tolerance)

This Land Is Your Land, by Woody Guthrie
(Pleasure from Blessings)
Try to Remember, by Tom Jones, Harvey Schmidt
(Loyalty, Painful Emotion Tolerance, Intimacy)
Twilight Time, by Buck Ram; Morty Nevins, Al Nevins
(Pleasure from Affection)
We Shall Overcome, Traditional, Modified by Zilphia Horton, Frank Hamilton, Guy Carawan, Pete Seeger
(Purposefulness, Justice in Choosing Options)
The Way You Look Tonight, by Dorothy Fields, Jerome Kern
(Pleasure from Affection)
When the Red, Red Robin Comes Bob, Bob, Bobbin Along, by Harry Woods
(Pleasure from Blessings)
When Irish Eyes Are Smiling, by Chauncey Olcott, George Graff, Jr.; Ernest R. Ball
(Positive Aim)
Who Will Buy?, by Lionel Bart
(Pleasure from Blessings)
Whistle While You Work, by Larry Morey, Frank Churchill
(Sustaining Attention to Tasks)
A Wonderful Day Like Today, by Leslie Bricusse, Anthony Newley
(Pleasure from Blessings)
The World Is Waiting for the Sunrise, by Eugene Lockhart, Ernest Seitz
(Pleasure from Affection, Loyalty, Intimacy)
You'll Never Walk Alone, by Oscar Hammerstein II, Richard Rodgers
(Self-Nurturing)

The Following Are In the *Ultimate Fake Book*, Volume II
Alabama Jubilee, by Jack Yellen, George L. Cobb
(Gleefulness)
By the Light of the Silvery Moon, by Ed Madden, Gus Edwards
(Pleasure from Affection)
A Bushel and a Peck, by Frank Loesser
(Pleasure from Affection)
Ebony and Ivory, by Paul McCartney
(Conflict Resolution, Relationship Building)
I Gave My Love a Cherry, Traditional
(Trusting, Intimacy, Pleasure from Affection)
I May Never Pass This Way Again, by Murray Wizzell, Irving Melsher
(Kindness)
I Will Be In Love With You, by Livingston Taylor
(Kindness)
Jambalaya, by Hank Williams
(Gleefulness)
Moments to Remember, by Stillman & Allen
(Separation Tolerance)
My Way, by Gilles Thibault; Claude Francois, Jacques Revaux, Paul Anka
(Independent Thinking)
People Got To Be Free, by Felix Cavliere, Edward Brigati, Jr.
(Kindness, Toleration)
Sunrise, Sunset, by Sheldon Harnick, Jerry Bock
(Loyalty, sustained attachment)

Tomorrow, by Martin Charnin, Charles Strouse
(Positive Aim)
What a Wonderful World, by George David Weiss, Bob Thiele
(Pleasure from Blessings, Kindness)

The Following Are In *Rise Up Singing*, Edited by Peter Blood-Patterson, Sing Out Corporation, PO Box 5253, Bethlehem, PA 18015, 215-865-5366.
Somewhere, by Stephen Sondheim, Leonard Bernstein
(Kindness, Forgiving, Positive Aim)
John Riley, Traditional
(Loyalty)
Jock O'Hazeldean, Traditional
(Independent thinking)
Heaven Help Us All, by Ronald Miller
(Kindess)
Up On the Roof, by Gerry Goffin, Carole King
(Relaxation)
Lavender's Blue, Traditional
(Kindness, Intimacy)
Oh Had I a Golden Thread, by Pete Seeger
(Kindness, Purposefulness, Courage)
Over the Rainbow, by E.Y. Harburg, Harold Arlen
(Imagination)
What Have They Done to the Rain? by Malvina Reynolds
(Purposefulness)
Bringing In the Sheaves, by Knowles Shaw, George Minor
(Kindness, Delay of Gratification)
Garden Song, by Dave Mallet
(Delay of Gratification, Nurturing)
Man Come Into Egypt, by Fred Hellerman, Fran Minkoff
(Independent Thinking, Assertion, Purposefulness)
O Freedom, Traditional
(Assertion)
This Little Light, Traditional
(Kindness, conflict resolution)
All the Good People, by Ken Hicks
(Gratitude)
It's All Right to Cry, by Carol Hall
(Painful Emotion Tolerance)
Lean on Me, by Bill Withers
(Depending, Kindness)
My Rambling Boy, by Tom Paxton
(Loyalty, Separation Tolerance)
Pack Up Your Sorrows, by Richard Farina, Pauline Marden
(Nurturing)
You've Got a Friend, by Carole King
(Nurturing, Loyalty)
Waltzing with Bears, by Dr. Seuss, Eugene Poddany, Dale Marxen
(Humor)
Believe Me If All Those Endearing Young Charms, by Thomas Moore
(Loyalty)
I'm Looking Over a Four Leaf Clover, by Mort Dixon, Harry Woods
(Joyousness, Pleasure from Affection)
All I Really Need, by Raffi
(Joyousness, Kindness, Loyalty)
For Baby, by John Denver
(Nurturing)
Isn't She Lovely, by Stevie Wonder
(Nurturing)
Blowing in the Wind, by Bob Dylan
(Conflict Resolution, Purposefulness)

Love Will Guide Us, by Sally Rogers, Traditional Melody
(Kindness)
What the World Needs Now, by Hal David, Burt Bacharach
(Kindness)
Danny Boy, by Fred E. Weatherly, Traditional Melody
(Loyalty, Separation Tolerance)
Juanita, Traditional
(Pleasure from Affection)
All Through the Night, by Harold Boulton, Traditional melody
(Nurturing)
Day Is Done, by Peter Yarrow
(Nurturing)
Morningtown Ride, by Malvina Reynolds
(Nurturing)
Now the Day is Over, by Sabine Baring-Gould, Joseph Barnaby
(Nurturing)
Sweet and Low, by Alfred Tennyson, Joseph Barnaby
(Nurturing)
He Ain't Heavy, He's My Brother, by Bob Russell, Bobby Scott
(Kindness)
Morning Has Broken, by Eleanor Farjean, traditional melody
(Pleasure from Blessings)
Wild Mountain Thyme, Traditional
(Pleasure from Blessings)
Let There Be Peace On Earth, by Sy Miller, Jill Jackson
(Conflict Resolution)
Song of Peace, by Lloyd Stone, Jean Sibelius
(Tolerance, Conflict Resolution)
Study War No More, Traditional
(Conflict Resolution)
Baby Beluga, by Raffi
(Nurturing)
If I Only Had a Brain, by E.Y. Harburg, Harold Arlen
(Humor)
On Top of Spaghetti, by Tom Glaser, Traditional Melody
(Humor)
Shake My Sillies Out, by Raffi
(Humor)
There But For Fortune, by Phil Ochs
(Empathy)
You Can Get It If You Really Want, by Jimmy Cliff
(Sustaining Attention, Delaying Gratification)
Let's Get Together, by Chet Powers
(Kindness)
The More We Get Together, Traditional
(Social Initiations)
Funiculi, Funicula, Traditional
(Gleefulness)
Four Strong Winds, by Ian Tyson
(Separation Tolerance)
I Love the Mountains, Traditional
(Pleasure from blessings)

The following are not in any of the above-mentioned collections; they are where you find them.
Ja Da, Anonymous
(Gleefulness)
When You and I Were Young, Maggie, by George W. Johnson, J.A. Butterfield
(Loyalty, sustaining attachment)
Peace Train, by Cat Stevens
(Nonviolence)

Flow Gently, Sweet Afton, by Robert
Burns
(Kindness)
I Would Be True, Traditional
(Honesty, courage, fortitude, kindness)

Chapter 12: Entertainment Violence

Chapter Overview:

The positive models you can present through stories, plays, and songs are a drop in the bucket compared to the negative models the average child gets from the entertainment our culture creates and purchases. In the United States children see an average of at least 10 violent acts per hour of television watching. The rate of violent models they not only see, but enact, in the average videogame dwarfs that number. Young children are born imitators; they don't need to be taught to imitate. They naturally practice in their imaginations the patterns they see modeled on television and in movies. By repeated practice, they get desensitized to the normal revulsion to violence we'd like for people to feel. And when "heroes" get rewards for their violence—rewards such as being loved by the opposite sex, fame, money, or simply staying alive—your child is getting "vicarious" reward for hurting people. All these principles tell us that entertainment violence should increase real life violence. And in fact, hundreds of studies have found that it does so. One group is "laboratory studies." Experimenters have randomly assigned subjects to watch violent or nonviolent entertainment, and have then studied their behavior shortly afterward. Many studies find that people who watch people hurt each other for even a short time act more hurtfully than those who watch something more neutral or positive. A second group of studies has taken advantage of "natural experiments." Television came to different regions at different times. Studies have found that increases in violence have corresponded to the time at which television came to the region: the sooner television came, the sooner there was an increase in violence. In a third group of studies, experimenters have measured both how much violence children have watched, and how violence those children have used in real life, on two occasions several years apart. Children who watch more violent entertainment early on are more violent in real life later on, even if you statistically adjust for the real-life violence at the first measurement. Another study found that a group of youth were less violent in real life if they had helped make a videotape that argued against consuming violent entertainment. The evidence for the harmfulness of violent entertainment is quite impressive.

How then should parents respond to a culture that entertains itself in harmful ways? I recommend that all family members boycott entertainment violence. I recommend that you try to get your family members to view this boycott as part of your contribution to the world. I recommend that like-minded families bond together to support one another in boycotting violent entertainment. I go so far as to advise removing televisions and videogame machines from households. Some people's natural response to this is, "If we do that, what would there be to do?" If we try hard enough, we can recapture the skills

of doing fun things together without relying on electronic entertainment. I provide here a list of "mutually gratifying activities" other than television and videogames. See if people in your family can cultivate ways of having fun together rather than plugging in to their separate forms of electronic entertainment. If they can, your children will experience much fewer negative models, and will practice getting along with other people.
****

Medicine and psychiatry traditionally have viewed behavioral problems as located within an individual, and have seen the individual as the unit where cure is to take place. Increasingly, however, we have begun to see that many of the problems of violence and hostility and inhumanity that plague our society have causes not just in individuals, not not just in family systems, but in a whole culture. By the word "culture" we can refer to the set of influences that come toward a growing child other than from parents: e.g. from peers, the nature of schools, and other institutions, the economic system, and the mass media. One of the most pernicious aspects of American culture is that our favorite mode of entertainment seems to be watching people hurt one another.

Entertainment violence is conveyed by all of our methods of mass communication: television, movies, video games, mass produced toys, comic books, books, in-person performances, sports contests. The most of the evidence that has accumulated has to do with television.

In this chapter we are not just talking about the most extreme forms of violent media presentations, such as "slasher" horror movies, where there is lots of gore and blood. We are talking about the full range of portrayals of violence in the media, including the type of violence your child has been exposed to if your family is at all typical of families in general. We are including movies and television shows marketed for children, advertised as though they are extremely good for children. We are talking about the degrees of violence portrayed even in animated Disney Movies.

It could possibly be that the milder forms of violence, couched in comfortable and child-centered media, may be harmful partly because they insert violence in such a pleasant background. There have been several studies of cartoon violence, and the conclusion is that this sort of humorous, non-gory violence is harmful.

Some of these studies have involved cartoons such as Bugs Bunny and Woody Woodpecker that actually contain a great deal of violence, both verbal and physical. *Peter Pan*, a children's classic, contains 30 violent acts, including bombings, much sword fighting, characters forced to walk the plank, and characters thrown overboard. In *The Little Mermaid*, the good characters win over the evil when the prince drives a ship into the sea witch, probably killing her. In *Oliver and Company*, the good characters win over the evil when Mr. Sykes and his dogs are killed in a long fight and chase scene ending the film. Even in a relatively nonviolent film with many prosocial elements such as *The Wizard of Oz*, good wins by the (inadvertent) killing of the evil witch. (Actually two evil witches.) Many widely acclaimed and almost universally loved children's movies deliver a repetitive message about how human conflict is resolved. It is resolved

not by persuading or gradually winning over your adversary to your point of view;

not by coming to tolerate your adversary;

not by separating from or avoiding him or her;

not by appealing to a rule of law to resolve the conflict;

not by changing your own point of view;

but by the violent killing or hurting of your adversary.

Other movies marketed toward children are far more violent. In the 1990s a fad revolved around the Teenage Mutant Ninja Turtles. The full length film constructed around this fad contained some 194 acts of violence, of which 104 were committed by the heroes. The violent acts included much kicking, many concussion-dealing blows, and the portrayal of characters delighting in the infliction of violence. In this movie good triumphs over evil when a good guy makes the bad guy fall off a building into a garbage truck and be crushed by another good guy's pulling the garbage-crushing mechanism. Such movies make it seem almost priggish for someone to raise questions about the much smaller level of violence in children's classics.

And the fact that millions of children in the U.S. have seen such abominations as the *Friday the 13th* series, the *Nightmare on Elm Street* series, and the *Halloween* series, with graphic and gory and sometimes sexualized violence and sadism being the main attraction of the movies, makes it seem almost priggish to object to the violence in the Ninja Turtles!

But such objections are not priggish. They are based on a large body of research evidence. Many parents feel untroubled when their very young children repetitively view shows where good triumphs over evil through violence, as long as there is not a lot of blood and gore. This, however, is a symptom of how desensitized and jaded our society has become to violence.

The age and developmental level of the child makes a difference in deciding what sorts of fictional models are appropriate. As children grow older, their powers of reasoning and thinking obviously grow tremendously. They become capable of using the concept of *not*. When they become teenagers, if all has gone well they will be able to have antiviolence strengthened, not weakened, by seeing violence depicted in anti-violence works such as *Born on the Fourth of July* or *All Quiet on the Western Front or Galipoli*. They will be able to appreciate the fact that in works like *Hamlet* and *Oedipus Rex* the violent acts are tragic and horrible, with terrible consequences, and perhaps have their repulsion for violence increased rather than decreased. The teenager should have the maturity of thought processes to identify with certain characters in a work of fiction, and to want to become more like them, and to want to become less like other characters. The teen-ager is at least capable of seeing characters try non-imitation-worthy actions, have those actions produce bad consequences, and learn not to do those things. Again, there is discrimination involved—picking and choosing what is imitation-worthy and what is not.

I should emphasize the phrase "if all has gone well" when speaking about the capacity of teen-agers to discriminate what is imitation-worthy and what isn't. There are countless anecdotes accumulated wherein teen-agers or adults have imitated violent acts portrayed on the media. The case of John Hinckley, who tried to assassinate Ronald Reagan after repetitively viewing the movie *Taxi Driver* is one example. (The main character in *Taxi Driver* wins the attention of the beautiful woman, by positive effects he happens to produce by going on a totally irrational and gory shooting rampage resulting from a senseless attempt to assassinate a political figure.) The some fifty people who over several years killed themselves playing Russian roulette in imitation of a scene from the movie *The Deer Hunter* are more examples of cases where the capacity to make wise discriminations obviously had not developed enough. The violent movie *Boyz n the Hood* was obviously intended by the author to have an anti-violence message; however this message seemed to go over the heads of many audience members who cheered, rather than felt sadness, at the death of one of the adversaries, and who engaged in violence at or near the site of the movie.

For society as a whole, the research does not provide evidence as to whether violent movies with an anti-violence message are successful in reducing violence or actually increase it. All the evidence seems to point in the direction that the more violence people see, the more they carry out, period.

But for preschool children, the case against presenting any violence at all, even that which is embedded in an anti-violence message, is more clear-cut. The preschool child is very rapidly learning how to speak and act. The preschool child tends to indiscriminately imitate all that he sees and hears, whether the characters are good guys or bad guys, and whether the long-run consequences of the actions are positive or negative. There is very little power to pick and choose what is imitation-worthy and what isn't.

For this reason, in fashioning works of fiction for young children, we want as many imitation-worthy acts as possible, and we also want as few non-imitation-worthy acts as possible, regardless of who does them and whether good wins out over evil. Children do need to learn to deal with tragedy of life and to deal with bad people eventually, but the more their preschool years, particularly the early preschool years, can be filled with positive models, the better off they will be.

In thinking about how harmful a violent model is, it probably matters how easily imitated the violent act is. We particularly would like to avoid exposing young children to acts of violence that are very easy to imitate. In the *Wizard of Oz*, Dorothy's killing the witch by accidentally getting water on her is not an aggressive act that seems to inspire much real-life imitation in young children. The kicks and karate chops of the Ninja turtles, by contrast, are very much imitatable by young children.

What about the Motion Picture Association of America's ratings—the G, PG, and so forth? Is choosing a movie for a child just as simple as avoiding anything over PG? In my observation, these ratings are not a very good guide. The MPAA ratings do not seem to give much weight to violence. For example, *The Teenage Mutant Ninja Turtles* obtained a PG rating. *Indiana Jones and the Temple of Doom*, another PG, is an extremely violent movie, with one scene for example where a man has his beating heart pulled out of his chest, and then (the man remains alive for a while—anything can happen in the movies) he is lowered screaming into a pit of flames and is burned to death while a triumphant priest holds the now-flaming heart in his hands. (Footnote: a child was admitted to an inpatient psychiatric unit where I worked after the child had engaged in dangerous behavior in imitation of dangerous acts in this movie—fortunately not the heart-removing act.)

In other words, I have the audacity to suggest that people in positions of great responsibility who decide what is marketed to children, do not always have children's best interests in mind. Of course, that's putting it far too politely. One of the biggest mistakes a parent can make is to assume that all entertainments marketed to children are good for children. The marketers of children's entertainment get rewarded for producing revenue, not for producing psychologically healthy people.

As another example of this cynical but true point: Here's some copy that appeared on a box holding a toy called the "Teenage Mutant Ninja Turtles Footski Brain Sucking Sewer Machine." The box states that the toy is for children "Ages 4 and up."

The print on the box says,

"Cast off on the Footski, the Foot Clan's high-tech futuristic jetski! You're on the high-sewers as you patrol for brain-rich turtles. Yes, you're dredging for fuel! Because this mutant machine processes Turtle brains into Sewer Gas, making it the first self-contained jetski in the world! If you're running low on Sewer Gas, simply run over a Turtle and suck his mutant brains out. Not easy, you say? Well, think again. Simply sail through the sewers at top speed, and when you spot a Turtle—go for it! Capture and stun the Turtle with Electrifying Vinyl Leeches and the mutant brain intake valve does the rest! Pretty easy, huh? .... So the next time your Footski's low on gas, cruise by a Turtle... and just say, 'fill 'er up!'"

A picture on the box shows a Teenage Mutant Ninja Turtle figure (sold separately) being hurt by the leeches, with the following caption: "Electrifying Vinyl Leeches suck Turtle brains and cause migraine pain!" Another caption on another picture reads, "Detachable Turtle-seeking Torpedoes for those hard-to-get heroes! Sewer Side Scrapers to give you Turtle-peeling pleasure!"

One would think that most parents would not want children being given the message that inflicting migraine pain on someone and destroying their brains is great fun. Yet toys like this made huge amounts of money.

Evidence That Media Violence Is Harmful

Sometimes people ask me, with an attitude of some skepticism, does anybody really know whether the things that children see on TV and in the movies really make a difference in their real-life behavior? Has there really been any good research on this question? The answer is yes. There has been a tremendous amount of good research on this question. Literally millions of dollars of research money have been devoted to this question, by very competent social scientists. The was a surgeon general's report, with a follow-up report from the National Institutes of Mental Health, that have had as their main task simply the summarizing of all the work that has gone on. There is good evidence that media violence is harmful, and that it promotes real-life violent behavior. The next few pages will go over some of that evidence.

How do we know about the causal relation between media violence and real-life violence? What possible ways are there for us to get knowledge about this? There are two basic ways of knowing: deductive reasoning from prior principles, and inductive reasoning from a set of specific observations. To use deductive reasoning on the media violence-real life behavior question, we think about basic principles of human learning, and see if any of them predict a causal relation. To use inductive reasoning, we look at studies that have directly looked at the real-life behavior of people depending upon how much entertainment violence they have been exposed to.

Let's start with the fundamental principles, the fundamental methods of influence so central to this entire book. One is the principle of modeling. Psychologists have studied this principle in great detail in recent years, but it's one that has been known since antiquity. For centuries parents have known that children follow the examples that are set for them, not only in real life, but also in literature; Aesop's fables and biblical parables are examples of teaching tales adult society has used to help children learn how to live. Recently experiments have shown that shy and withdrawn children can learn to socialize better with their peers if they are shown a video of a child gradually overcoming inhibition about starting to make friends. Modeling through video presentations has been used to reduce dental phobias in children: when they see someone having a relaxed and pleasant time in the dentist's chair, they are not so scared. Modeling has helped children get over fears of swimming. (For a review of some studies of modeling, see Strayhorn, 1988, p. 87-92.)

Recent research has demonstrated that there is something innate in children that makes them imitate, even from the moment of birth. Meltzoff, who experimented with infants in their first day of life, made distinctive faces at the infants, and found that the infants made those faces back at the experimenter. There's something poignant to me about the innate trusting quality built into our brains, that makes us somehow know that we need to take our cues from older people and imitate what they do if we want to learn to handle a totally unknown world. Thought of in this way, it is an obscene violation of this trust to present children with models of violent and aggressive behavior. Aggression and other forms of hostility are the number one presenting complaint in child mental health clinics, and those in the business of presenting violent models to children are simply feeding the rosters of children with such problems.

A second basic principle of human learning is that the more one practices a behavior pattern, the more ingrained it becomes. Again people have known this since antiquity. One twist on this which has been studied in recent years is that practice in imagination, or fantasy rehearsal, is an effective way of ingraining a pattern. Experiments with piano players, ski racers, and people learning assertiveness skills have revealed that imagining a certain action makes the skill more easy to carry out in real life. (For a review of some of this research, see Strayhorn, 1988, p. 93-95.) For young children, dramatic play is the prototypical fantasy rehearsal method. The shameful counterpart to this is the inevitable production and marketing of toys for children based on violent characters in movies: Rambo dolls, Freddy Krueger dolls, and so forth, that enable fantasy practice to take place as a follow-up on the initial modeling.

The third basic principle is that behavior that gets rewarded is that which gets repeated: the principle of reinforcement. A twist on this one is that vicarious reinforcement also works. Characters in action and adventure movies are rewarded for their proficiency in violence, with sickening regularity. One could easily come to the conclusion that violence skills are the most important skills for our society. Often the reward for a male is the admiration of a sexy woman. Vicarious reinforcement also works in real life, when children perceive that the most admired characters in society, the Sylvester Stallones and the Clint Eastwoods and the Arnold Schwarzeneggers, are admired because of their presenting a persona of total proficiency in violence.

To summarize, if you think about the power of modeling, practice, and reinforcement in human learning, you would certainly predict that media violence should increase the likelihood of real-life violence. But prediction from first principles is not good enough evidence in and of itself. We have to go out and see if the predicted phenomenon is really happening.

Now let's look at some of the inductive evidence that entertainment violence is harmful.

One type of evidence is from "laboratory studies" in which children or adults are brought in to a researcher's offices, are usually randomly assigned to two groups, and are then shown either a violent or a nonviolent video or film. Then the people are put into some sort of setting where they have the opportunity to be aggressive or not to be, and their behavior is observed. In some studies, the measure of aggressiveness was how much a person was willing to deliver electric shock to another person as a punishment in what was presented to be a learning experiment. Other studies have looked at the real-life behavior of children, and have counted their episodes of imitation of the violent or nonviolent behavior. A pioneer in the study of imitation learning in children is Albert Bandura. Bandura showed children various models of either positive or negative behavior, and observed in various different ways that the children imitated the models.

In general, these laboratory studies have demonstrated very impressively that children do tend to imitate what they see. Study after study has demonstrated that when you present to children a filmed model of someone's doing something, children are in general more likely to do that something after having seen the film.

Another type of evidence comes from the "natural experiment." Rather than getting a small number of people into a laboratory and randomly assigning one group of them to one condition and one group to another, the natural experiment takes advantage of the fact that some real-life happenstance assigns people to different conditions, and measures the effects.

One recent important "natural experiment" study was conducted by Brandon Centerwall of the University of Washington. It was found that in the United States and Canada, there was a doubling of the murder rate some 10 to 15 years after television was introduced. Presumably the time lag occurred because children are most vulnerable to being influenced by television violence during early life, but most prone to commit murder when they are in adolescence to young adulthood. The doubling of murder rates in and of itself does not tell us too much—lots changed in society other than the introduction of television, to account for the increase in the murder rate. But there was much more to the study than this finding alone. The white population of South Africa had no television available until 1973, because of political reasons having nothing to do with the wish to avoid television violence. This population did not experience the doubling of the murder rate at the same time that the white population of the U.S. and Canada did. The white South African population did, however, experience a doubling of the murder rate 10 to 15 years after introduction of television there.

Centerwall also looked at the timing of the increase in the murder rate of various regions of the U.S. according to when television was introduced in that region. The time of introduction of television predicted a rise in the murder rate 10 to 15 years later with remarkable accuracy. The white population of the U.S. got televisions sooner than the black population, and the murder rates of whites rose correspondingly sooner than those of blacks. The conclusion of Centerwall's research is that of the approximately 20,000 murders that take place in the U.S. each year, some 10,000 of them would not occur without the influence of television!

Centerwall looked at murder rates because murder is something that our society very carefully records and documents. One would expect that if television had such an effect on the murder rate, it would also have a large effect on the rate of less serious violence, the type classified as disciplinary problems in school. And another important "natural experiment" documented just this.

A research team headed by Tannis MacBeth Williams heard of a certain town in Canada that they immediately realized held out great research opportunity. This town, because of being in a "geographical blind spot" (mountains blocked it from existing television transmitters) had very poor to nonexistent television reception. The researchers heard that a television transmitter was about to be put up in the town, so that suddenly television would be available. (They refer to this town as "Notel.") The researchers mounted a massive effort to study the people in this town and two other comparison towns that had had television for many years. For each of these three towns, the researchers measured the aggressiveness of children, children's reading ability, and other variables both before television was introduced into Notel, and two years afterward.

One of the most expensive, but also most valid, ways of measuring children's aggression is by having research assistants directly watch children and keep very careful counts of any time that they do something physically hurtful to another person or say something verbally hostile. This study used this method, as well as using teacher-ratings and peer-ratings of children's aggression.

The study found that both physical and verbal aggression increased much more in the children in the town receiving television for the first time than did the aggression in the children in the other two towns. The introduction of television into Notel was associated with a little more than a doubling of the rate of physically aggressive acts per minute.

What happened to reading ability? To paraphrase from this study: Before television was introduced into Notel, the second graders there were better readers than the children in the other two towns. But after television had been in Notel for 2 or 4 years, Notel second graders read no better than children who had grown up with TV. Notel children who had been in grade 1 when television arrived were poorer readers on the follow-up than the other two towns' children.

How can television reduce reading ability? One obvious hypothesis is that a child spends many hours watching television when he could be reading, looking at picture books, being read to, having a conversation, or doing something else that would increase his verbal ability more than sitting passively.

The results on reading ability are relevant to the general question of violence, since low reading ability is significantly correlated with violent behavior. Children who read poorly tend to have more minor problems with aggression, and among children and teen-agers who have very serious problems with aggression, there is a very high incidence of reading problems.

In another line of research, investigators have enrolled children in a study and have measured their aggressiveness and the amount of violence they view. One way investigators have measured aggressiveness is by asking school children which of their classmates punch other children. One finding that is almost universally agreed upon in the research community is that children who watch more violent television tend to be more aggressive. Freedman (1984) stated, "The research has involved many thousands of subjects, of both sexes, ranging in age from young children to older teenagers, from a wide range of socioeconomic and ethnic backgrounds, and from several countries. The relation between viewing television and aggressiveness is thus extremely well documented." Just to find a positive relation, however, doesn't prove that the television violence causes the aggression. Perhaps a certain type of personality both makes people more aggressive and also causes them to like violence on television. How do we make the jump from the agreed-upon correlation, to the conclusion of a causal connection?

One way that researchers have attempted to do this is to measure both aggression and viewing of violence at two points in time. When the researchers have two time points to look at, they can use a statistical technique called the analysis of partial variance to try to tell whether viewing causes violence or whether the violent tendencies cause the viewing. To do a study like this, you get a bunch of children and measure their viewing of violence and their aggressive behavior at a certain time—such as for example when they're eight years old. Then maybe ten years later, you find the same children, and measure both their viewing of violence and their aggressive behavior at that time. Then you see how much the early viewing of violence predicts the later aggressive behavior, while correcting for the early aggressive behavior. Another way of thinking about this statistical technique is that you are seeing how much the early violent viewing predicts an increase in violent behavior from time 1 to time 2. Finding this would suggest that the time 1 viewing is a cause of the time 2 behavior, not just a consequence of already existing violent tendencies. Several studies have found just this. Violent viewing predicts an increase in violent behavior over time. Several important studies that have used these methods, one of which was done by Huesmann and his colleagues. These studies in general have come out supporting the causal role of media violence.

Another set of evidence has come from experiments, based upon the principle of a wise professor who used to say, "If you want to understand something, try to change it." A group of researchers decided they would try to convince a bunch of children that television violence was unrealistic and not good to imitate, and to see what effect this had. They had the children make up an argument against television violence, and read it while being videotaped for other children to see. This intervention seemed to work in changing children's attitudes; what did it do to their behavior? If liking violent TV has nothing to do with behavior, you wouldn't expect this intervention to do much. On the other hand, if attitudes toward the violence on TV is connected with real-life behavior, you would expect the result that actually did occur: The children who underwent this intervention experienced positive effects on their own aggressiveness, as rated by their peers, relative to the group who underwent a comparison intervention in which they talked about hobbies. Thus successfully teaching children to disapprove of violent television seemed to be an influence toward less violence in real life.

The notion that media violence causes real-life violence has become less and less controversial over time. It has now been decades since the research has confirmed this conclusion. In 1972 and 1982 there were in the United States, Surgeon General's Reports on television and behavior, similar to the reports on smoking and health. To quote from the 1982 report: "Most of the researchers look at the totality of evidence and conclude, as did the Surgeon General's advisory committee, that the convergence of findings supports the conclusion of a causal relationship between televised violence and later aggressive behavior."

The American Academy of Pediatrics, the National Association for the Education of Young Children, and other organizations have issued policy statements condemning violence in the media.

There have been similar sorts of research on violent toys and video games as there have been with TV. To give an example with video games, a study by Shutte and other investigators randomly assigned two groups of children to play with either a karate video game or a nonviolent jungle vine swinging video game. The children were then observed during free play. To quote: "The children who had played the jungle swing video game later played more with a jungle swing toy and ... the children who played the violent video game later showed more aggression. The authors interpreted the findings as an indication that young children who play video games later tend to act similarly to how their video game character acted."

The notion that children imitate the acts of their video game characters is especially frightening if you have recently observed a typical video arcade. A high fraction of the "heroes" in video games are engaged in killing or knocking out large numbers of enemies, without even needing to discriminate whether they are enemies or friends. The means of killing enemies in these games seem to be getting more and more realistic.

When makers of violent toys and movies are challenged about the ethics of their productions, the response seems to come like clockwork: these are just a harmless way for people to get their aggression "out of their system."

As I mentioned at the beginning of this book, this "catharsis" theory is one of the major blind alleys in the mental health field. The notion that you get anger "out" by expressing it has undergone much research in recent years. When people act in symbolically aggressive ways they are more likely to be rehearsing aggressive acts and reducing their inhibition to aggression than to be getting the aggression out.

The notion that you get aggression "out" by performing aggressive acts either in real life or in symbolic activities is an interesting idea. We seem not to have this notion to such a degree about emotions other than anger. Do we get our shyness "out" by acting very shy, or do we only rehearse shyness? Do we get our friendliness "out" by acting friendly to people, or do we rehearse acting friendly?

There is much that can be said about the "catharsis theory" of anger versus the rehearsal theory and the disinhibition theory. The books by Bandura and by Tavris in the reference list discuss the catharsis notion thoroughly, and mention many studies that tend to weaken its credibility. But suffice it to say that watching people do or say hostile things, or for the child to do or say them himself, usually makes the child more likely to be aggressive, not less likely. "Practice makes perfect" and the concept of imitation are much more relevant than the notion of getting anything out of one's system.

Does this mean that a child should not be encouraged to beat on a pillow or do something else harmless to let his aggression out? Yes, it does mean that! Beating on pillows and screaming into pillows and other such remedies are almost never useful, in the long run, and may be harmful. Advising a child to beat on a pillow gives the child the message that he needs to "let out his anger" or else something bad will happen. This is in contrast to the notion that acting angry is something that we can choose whether or not to do, just as we choose our other actions. At times the most workable thing to do, in order to bring about the results we want, is to act angry. At other times, that does not bring about the best results. At times it works best to work ourselves up into feeling angry, and at (more numerous) times it works best to do just the opposite. But the child should get the message that he can choose what to do on the basis of what will produce the best results, not on the basis of having to rid his psyche of some poison that has accumulated in it.

What Is Obscene? The Facts on Closed Head Injury

Closed head injury is a blow to the head that doesn't cause an "open" wound. The notion that the public seems to have is that scenes of violence are not harmful unless blood is spurting everywhere, and that scenes of people giving each other terrific blows to the head are as American as apple pie and twice as harmless.

I believe a more realistic viewpoint is that the act of one person's hitting another person in the head is one of the most obscene acts that we can conjure up. The brain is the seat of the personality, and it is a delicate organ. It is easily injured by blows to the skull. One hard blow to the head can result in seizures for the rest of the life, or in permanent damage to the basic processes of thinking and feeling and behaving. Brain injury is a very prevalent horror in our society. Dorothy Lewis has looked at very violent delinquents, and has found a very high prevalence of brain abnormalities in them, the type that are often caused by blows to the head. Many of these delinquents gave histories compatible with the idea that their brains were injured by child abuse, specifically blows to the head. Studies of boxers reveal that brain damage is very frequently a consequence of the blows these men receive from other men's fists. Yet in movies like the Teenage

Mutant Ninja Turtles we see almost continuous blows delivered to heads, and we give the movie a PG rating.

If someone proposed to show movies to preschool children of rape scenes, and to sell them toys that showed characters in the act of rape, we would (I hope) have an outcry of horror and outrage. Yet the act of hitting the other person with full force in the head with a stick or chair or even sometimes a fist is an act capable of killing the person, giving him seizures for life, destroying his language ability, and totally depriving him of the most precious parts of his personality. It is an act as harmful as rape, and, I submit, as obscene.

Ways of Responding to the Media Violence Situation

Parents ask, how can I prohibit my child from doing what all the other children are doing? I don't want my child to think that I'm worried about his becoming a murderer, more than other children.

I think that one good way to explain the reason for boycotting violent entertainment is to tell children that watching a television show is like voting for more like it to be produced; buying a certain toy is like voting for more like it to be produced, and so forth. The more our money and attention and the example we set go toward patronizing violent entertainment, the more we encourage people to produce more symbolic violence. And the more of it is made, the more violent the world is. Therefore even if our own family value system is so nonviolent that there is no worry about any of our own behavior, a boycott of violent entertainment helps the world to become a better place. There is one certain way for violent entertainment to stop being produced, and that is for people to stop purchasing it.

In other words, I'm advocating that families enlist their children in a cause of social activism about the media violence issue. The thrust is to make the world better, not just to make ourselves better.

Some people, most of them not parents, raise the question as to whether parents have a right to take control of children's television diets. I think that it is not only the right, but the duty of the parent to take control of the child's television and movie diet. Suppose a parent learned that one of the child's babysitters regularly was visited by a boyfriend or girlfriend, and these two regularly yelled at each other, physically hit each other, and tried to stab each other in the child's presence. Most parents (I hope) would be horrified, and would quickly fire the baby-sitter. Nonetheless the "electronic baby-sitter" often models far worse behaviors than these. Parents have every right to decree to a child that certain shows should not be watched. The issue of freedom of speech and censorship in society at large is a totally different issue than the issue of what is best for a young, developing child. Just as you would want to be very selective in choosing a real-life baby sitter, it is baby sitter, it is important to be very selective in choosing media images to be your child's companions.

There is one practical step that will be very useful to parents in influencing children's television diets. I recommend not having multiple televisions throughout the house, and for a child never to have a private television set that stays in his own room. I would also recommend trading in large television sets for a set small enough that it can be picked up by a parent and removed from sight and put into a closet on a shelf. In other words, I recommend rigging the physical presence of televisions in the house in such a way that a parent can easily block or promote television-watching.

I would like to go one step further, and advocate the elimination of television from households, and using carefully selected recordings as the only video medium. I believe that the effect of this step in my own household has been extremely positive.

If children end up watching violent television and movies, despite all of parents' efforts to the contrary, how can parents minimize the harmful effects? Some research indicates that it may be helpful for you to explain to your children such things as that television is not like real life in many ways, that the violence on television is not a good way for people to solve their problems, that most people that they will encounter in real life are not totally bad like so many of the people on the television are, and that television violence is not good for our society. It may be useful for children to learn, if they don't already know it, that television shows are paid for by the commercials, and that the reason companies pay for television shows is to get people to buy their advertised products. It is probably useful for you to hear a description of the show from your child. Then the parent can react with hopefully genuine negative feelings (directed at the show, not at the child) to violent acts depicted on the shows. The parent can point it out if no one on the show seems to grieve or mourn persons hurt or killed. If the show manipulates your emotions such that you cheer and feel happy when the "bad guy" gets killed, it's good to look at this. How did the authors of the show bring it about that the image of a fellow human being's death produces pleasure? Are you glad they did that to you?

Is it a lie to tell children that life is not as violent as TV? Real life does contain violence, but television contains many times much more. This has also been the subject of research. The amount of shooting, killing, and hitting carried out by the average police officer in a year, or even in an entire career, does not begin to approach the number carried out for example by the heroes of a typical television cop show in a few episodes.

How does it alter the situation if a young child has a real problem with hitting or kicking or scratching or being verbally hostile? In that case, the parent should be even more comfortable with simply ending the child's opportunities to watch violence on the media.

If the child complains about this, then I would recommend that the parent take exactly the same attitude that he or she would if the child complained about not getting to have a steady diet of marshmallows and soda, or if the child complained about not getting to drink beer. If the child sees that the adult is not persuaded in the slightest by the child's protests, the protests will diminish in frequency.

Parents often tell me that they try to control the exposure to violence in their own house, but the child can then watch all the violent TV he wants to when he goes to a friend's house. What can be done about this? This is an illustration of the fact that the entertainment violence problem is a problem of the culture, not just of individual families. I think that this is a reason for parents to try to get to know their children's playmates' parents as well as possible, and to try to negotiate some high standards that will apply in all the households. This is really the difficult task of establishing a small subculture, superior to the general culture. It may not work, but it is certainly worth a try.

One would certainly expect that positive, or "prosocial" behavior can be learned through televised models, just as antisocial behavior can be learned. Eron (1986) mentions a number of research studies that have looked at this, and concludes that "prosocial television sequences do indeed lead to subsequent prosocial behavior on the part of the observer.... Moreover, ... antisocial behavior appears inhibited by prosocial portrayals." "Children who learn and perform prosocial behaviors are not likely to engage in aggressive behavior."

It is not hard for a parent with a camcorder and some good children's books to make his or her own videos for his or her own children! Your children will be very likely to greatly enjoy hearing your own voice coming over the video. I highly recommend this procedure. I have made a video of some of the "modeling plays" mentioned elsewhere in this book.

A good number of nonfiction videos are available for children—music videos, science instruction videos, and others. They may not grab attention as well as Tom and Jerry do. But that's OK. Because if a child does not want to watch prosocial or educational videos, the child gets some free time to find the fun things to do other than watching television.

Other arguments have been advanced, having nothing to do with violence, about reducing children's exposure to video media. One argument is that video media productions tend to be very "attention-capturing": with much action and rapidly shifting scenes, they capture young children's attention without their having to work much to concentrate. The child's habits, and some have argued, even their neuronal structures, may never accomodate themselves to the hard work of concentrating on less attention-grabbing media, such as textbooks, manuals, novels, or the process of writing their own thoughts. As a result, the argument goes, successive generations are becoming progressively less capable of sustained attention to less attention-capturing media.

The thought of eliminating television from a household sounds to some people so extreme and radical—it must be hard to believe that until the 1950's most households survived and found ways to occupy themselves without television. What can people do other than watch the tube? Let's remind ourselves of some, in the following table.

Menu for "Mutually Gratifying Activities" Between Family Members

Reading silently in one another's presence; reading aloud to one another, making up stories together; audiotaping stories; listening to audiotaped stories; putting on plays with each other; improvising plays with each other; conversation; debating current events, telling jokes, listening to or trying to solve each other's problems, singing songs together, playing music together, dancing, acting, taking walks together exploring objects: big things such as playground equipment; little things such as stopwatches, tape recorders, clocks, scales, boxes, pots and pans, toys

Doing Work Together: Cleaning and organizing, cooking, yard work, shopping, fixing things, paperwork, gardening

Academic activities: Doing homework together, reading nonfiction books to each other, doing tutoring activities or games, composing writings together; solving brain-teasers together

Playing Games: Games for infants and toddlers (repetitive sequences with suspense and celebration: e.g. peek-a-boo), board games, including psychological growth board games, card games, cooperative games: e.g. the shaping game, two-person solitaires, puzzles, thinking games such as Quarto, password, twenty questions, Scrabble, Boggle, Mastermind, chess, checkers, charades.

Computer activities: Edutainment games, using other programs, programming

Athletic Activities: Throwing back and forth, trying to make the target (basketball, darts, archery, horseshoes), traveling sports: skating, skiing, cycling, swimming, track, traditional sports contests

Outdoor Life: hiking, camping, canoeing, observing the natural world: stars, animals, plants

Pets: Taking care of them, playing with them

Arts and Crafts: Drawing, Painting, etc., making stuff that's useful, fun, or pretty

Religious worship as a family

Psychological skill games and activities: The classification of psychological skills exercise, The moral dilemma stories, discussing other moral dilemmas, the shaping game, the positive behavior diary, the Journey Exercise, social conversation role-play, the brainstorming game, joint decision role-plays, composing and enacting modeling stories and plays, readings on how to live well, affirmations for growth in psychological skills, the guess the feelings game, the celebrations activity, fantasy rehearsals, singing modeling songs, dance and freeze with modeling songs, biofeedback (heart rate, temperature are cheap), prisoner's dilemma game

Here are the sources for the research mentioned in this chapter.

Bandura, A. (1973). Aggression: a social learning analysis. Englewood Cliffs, New Jersey: Prentice-Hall, Inc.
Centerwall, B. S. (1989). Exposure to television as a risk factor for violence. American Journal of Epidemiology, 129, 643-652.
Centerwall, B.S. (1989). Exposure to television as a cause of violence. PP. 1-58 In G. Comstock (Ed.), Public Communication and Behavior, Volume 2. New York: Academic Press.
Eron, L.D. (1986). Interventions to mitigate the psychological effects of media violence on aggressive behavior. Journal of Social Issues, 42, 155-169.
Freedman, J.L. (1984). Effect of television violence on aggressiveness. Psychological Bulletin 96, 227-246.
Huesmann, L.R., Eron, L.D., Klein, R., Brice, P., & Fischer, P. (1983). Mitigating the imitation of aggressive behaviors by changing children's attitudes about media violence. Journal of Personality and Social Psychology, 44, 899-910.
Huesmann, L.R., Lagerspetz, K., & Eron, L.D. (1984). Intervening variables in the TV violence-aggression relation: evidence from two countries. Developmental Psychology, 20, 746-775.
Meltzoff, A.N., & Moore, M.K. (1977). Imitation of facial and manual gestures by human neonates. Science, 198, 74-78.
Meltzoff, A.N., & Moore, M.K. (1983). Newborn infants imitate adult facial gestures. Child Development 54, 702-709.
Meltzoff, A.N. (1988). Imitation of televised models by infants. Child Development, ;59, 1221-1229.
National Association for the Education of Young Children (1990). Naeyc position statement on media violence in children's lives. Young Children, July 1990, 18-21.
Pearl, D., Bouthilet, L, & Lazar, J. (1982). Television and behavior: ten

years of scientific progress and implications for the eighties. Rockville, Maryland: National Institute of Mental Health.
Schutte, N.S., Malouff, J.M., Post-Gorden, J.C., & Rodast, A.L. (1988) Effects of playing videogames on children's aggressive and other behaviors. Journal of Applied Social Psychology, 18, 454-460.
Strayhorn, J.M. (1988). The competent child: An approach to psychotherapy and preventive mental health. New York: Guilford Press.
Tavris, C. (1982). Anger: the misunderstood emotion. New York: Simon & Schuster.
Williams, T.M. (1986). The impact of television: a natural experiment in three communities. Orlando: Academic Press.

Chapter 13: Attribution and Prophecy

Chapter Overview:

Often prophecies are self-fulfilling. When people hold in mind an image of something they expect to happen, it's more likely to happen. Attributing a trait such as shyness or bravery to a child is in a sense a prophecy: you will continue to act shy, you will act brave. Accordingly, we want to use this form of influence with children in as favorable a way as possible. But this doesn't mean that we should lie, and tell children they are good at things that they aren't good at yet. We can use attribution after negative behavior by making a remark of the form, "If (or when) you get better at ________, a certain positive effect will happen." For example, instead of "You're irresponsible," "When you learn to keep your promises more faithfully, people will enjoy knowing they can depend on you." Attribution is also good to use after positive behavior: for example, "What an interesting question! Doesn't she have such an inquiring mind!" And "out of the blue," the parent can wonder and dream about the future positive behavior of the child: for example, "I wonder how you'll be making the world a better place when you're the age of that person over there? I bet by that time you will have learned many ways to do it." Such patterns of speaking and thinking help the child to grow into a general expectation of happy and productive and kind living.

The Phenomenon of Self-Fulfilling Prophecy

The phenomenon of self-fulfilling prophecy is interesting to think about. Sometimes it does appear that predicting something or expecting it to happen actually helps make it happen. If enough people expect the stock market to go down, then it probably will (in the short run at least). If it is widely predicted that a movie will be a blockbuster, then the movie's chances are helped by the prediction itself. If someone goes into a musical performance fully expecting that he will go blank in the middle of the performance and he will be greatly embarrassed and mortified, the chances of his doing so are enhanced by the anxiety itself. If a mother says repeatedly to a child, "You're going to wind up in prison before you're 18, just like that no good father of yours did," the chances that the child will fulfill that prophecy are probably increased.

When you say to a child, "You are shy," you are attributing to the child the trait of being shy. Whenever you attribute a trait to someone, you in a sense make a prophecy. When a child hears, "You are shy," the meaning he gathers is that he will continue to act however a shy person acts. On the other hand, if you should say to the child, "I think you can find some bravery within yourself to handle this," you are attributing to the child the trait of bravery. Attribution, then, is the process of talking about what traits and abilities child does or does not have.

Why might the prophecies that attributions make turn out to be self-fulfilling sometimes? Perhaps because someone comes to imagine himself as a certain sort of person, and tends to fantasy rehearse the thoughts and behaviors that go along with being that sort of person. Perhaps the belief that the person is a certain sort of way tends to make the child scared to try being a different way: for example if I am really shy, it makes sense that risking being socially outgoing may be more dangerous for me than for other people. Perhaps people get an image of themselves, and they feel secure when they do things consistent with that image, and feel uncomfortable breaking out of the mold they've created for themselves.

This chapter has to do with the question: how can we make attributions and possibly self-fulfilling prophecies in such a way as to be honest, yet maximize our chances of being helpful to the child?

We want to keep in mind the possibility that whenever you tell a child he's a certain way, he tends to become more that way. Telling him he's bad may make him bad. Telling people in his presence that he's a picky eater, may make him more of a picky eater. Telling him he's a nice boy and talking about all the nice things he's done may influence him to do more nice things. Telling him about how he's getting to be such a big boy as evidenced by his starting to like all sorts of more different foods may influence him to like even more different sorts of foods.

Using Attribution After Undesirable Behavior

Does the fact that attributions influence behavior mean that you have to tell your child that he's perfect in every way? Imagine saying, for example, about the very shy child, "Oh, he's so outgoing, he just goes up and talks to people, and is totally relaxed about it." This type of utterance would probably have the main effect of letting your child know that you are a bold-faced liar. Attributions need to be honest—as, by the way, do all other utterances made to the child.

However, if the child is not very good at doing something, you can still talk about the things the child needs to improve, but with the idea that the child can improve them rather than that the child has fixed traits that are undesirable. How exactly do you do that?

For any sentence that anyone says to a child that says, "You are bad in some way," you can change that into a sentence that says, "When you get better in this way, positive things will happen." For example, we can translate

"You're not nice."

into

"When you start doing lots and lots of nice things for your friends, they'll really like playing with you."

Here are some other forms attribution, forms to translate negative attributions into:

1. I really will like it when he (or you) ____.
2. I expect him (or you) to _____.
3. When you (or he) ______, things will be better, because _____.
4. He hasn't learned to _____ yet, but I hope he will soon.

It's helpful to practice saying things in that way rather than calling the child bad.

Here's an example of a translation:

"He's a picky eater. He just doesn't like anything but hot dogs."

How about translating that into, "I really will like it when he can eat all sorts of fruits and vegetables and different foods with me."

If you were the child, and you heard the second, don't you think you'd start eating those things sooner?

Exercise: Translating Negative Attributions into Talk About Future Progress

Please practice translating some more negative attributions into the forms listed above.

I'll give you the negative attribution, and you translate it into a sentence that makes a positive prophecy about the child's behavior and predicts a positive consequence when it happens.

"She's shy. She doesn't like new people." (Sample answer: If she starts liking new people more, she's going to be able to have a great time going to parties.)

"She doesn't like books." (Sample answer: "When she learns to enjoy books more, she's going to find that she has something that she can hang onto for the rest of her life.")

"You act bad in school." (Sample answer: "If you start acting better in school, I think you'll find that you enjoy it more.")

"He can't sleep by himself at night." (Sample answer: "When he starts sleeping by himself at night, it will be lots easier on his father and me, and I think he'll feel better about himself, too.")

"You're stubborn. You can't put up with not getting your way." (Sample answer: "You can really make me feel happy some day if you learn to put up better with not getting your way.")

"You just can't concentrate." (Sample answer: "If you learn to concentrate for a lot longer, you're going to be able to accomplish things you never thought you could accomplish before.")

"She doesn't like people with gray hair." (Sample answer: "I imagine that when she gets a little older and more grown up, she'll get more comfortable around people with gray hair.")

"He doesn't drink milk." (Sample answer: "He hasn't started enjoying milk yet.")

Do you see how the new statements say something totally different to the child about what he's like?

Here are some more negative attributional statements for you to practice translating.

"You knock things over too much—you're not careful."

"You don't know when to leave people alone."

"You can't be nice to people, can you?"

"There must be something wrong with him, that makes him be so mean."

"She is scared of the dark."

"She's bullheaded—she doesn't know how to change her mind."

"You just don't know how to get along with people."

If you use this principle to translate any negative attributions you get the urge to make, you will help your child. Plus you'll improve the emotional climate in your family. (When it comes as second nature to me to make attributional statements like the one I just made, I have reason to celebrate.)

Using Attribution, Part II: After Desirable Behavior

Attribution is perhaps even more important to use when you are reminded of a positive aspect of the child. Now you can honestly attribute to the child, not just the possibility of future development of a positive trait, but its current presence. This is something more than attention and approval and positive reinforcement.

Imagine that a child does something nice for someone else. It is very reinforcing for the adult to say, "I really do appreciate that nice thing that you did." But suppose the adult says, "It made me feel really good to see you doing that, because it showed me what a kind person you are becoming." This has more than reinforcement in it; it also attributes to the child the trait of kindness which is developing and unfolding more and more as time goes on. We would guess that the attribution may have an effect over and above the reinforcement.

The general rule is that every now and then, when you see positive things from the child, interpret them as signs of the unfolding of lasting positive traits in the child. But only do this when you honestly believe that it is the case.

Here are another couple of examples. The adult is teaching the child some math concepts, and the child catches on. A "pure reinforcer" would be "Right! Good thinking!" Reinforcement with an added attribution would be, "Right! I think you have a real talent for math!"

The adult is with the child at a birthday party. The previously shy child is running around having fun meeting new people. The child comes back to chat with the adult a while. A "pure reinforcer" would be, "Wow, you're really getting to meet a lot of new people!" An added attribution would be, "You're getting friendlier and more outgoing with people all the time, did you know that?"

A child is concerned about a child in the preschool class whose dog died. The child wants to make the other child a little card. The adult might say, "I think that's a really good idea. I like that, a lot." For an added attribution, the adult says to another adult, in the child's hearing, "He's really got the ability to think about how other people are feeling, doesn't he? He's growing up into a very loving person."

A child whose previous habit was to be extremely grumpy and irritable in a certain setting, goes back to that setting, and gets into an activity and sings and dances around and acts very happy. The adult says about the child, in the child's presence, "Did you see how joyous he was acting? He has a real joyous streak; he really knows how to have a good time."

Attributions Part III: Prophecies "Out of the Blue"

You don't have to wait until the child does something good or bad to make an attribution or prophecy. Consider the following examples.

A child has a problem with hitting. The parent and the child are taking a walk together. The parent says, "I just thought of something that made me smile." The child says "What was it?" The parent says, "I thought to myself that some day there will be a day when we both realize that you haven't hit anybody for months, not me, not your brother, not anybody at school. I'll say to myself, 'Wow, am I glad what a big boy I've got now!' That will really feel good. How should we celebrate when that day comes, I wonder?"

A child is afraid to go to bed by himself at night. One day he and his parent are taking a walk, and the parent says, "You know something? I think that some day very soon you will feel very safe and brave and confident every single night that you go to bed. Boy, will I be glad. I'll think to myself, 'I'm so happy that my son doesn't have to feel bad about going to bed!'"

A child hasn't learned to read yet. The adult says, "You may not believe it now, but some day, you're going to be able to pick out any book on this book shelf and read it easily. What a happy scene! I hope I get to see it myself. I'd be so happy for you, I'd think to myself, 'Now she can read anything she wants! Whole new worlds are open to her!'"

A child and an adult are in a car together. The adult says, "I wonder what life is going to be like for you in a few years, let's say when you're as old as that girl over there, who is about in fourth grade. I hope you'll have lots of friends that you have fun with. I hope people think of you and say, 'That's really a kind person, who loves other people.' I hope you'll be getting real joy out of learning lots of new things at school."

These prophecies have the effect of not only giving hope that the desired end will take place, but also defining the reaching of the goal as a very joyous occasion. If the child can start seeing a joyous vision of reaching the goal, the child is much more likely to reach it sooner.

Chapter 14: Consequences for Negative Behavior

Chapter Overview:

Punishment occurs when a child's behavior is followed by a consequence that the child doesn't like. It's meant to reduce the frequency of the behavior it follows. Punishing consequences can include reprimands, physical guidance, and natural consequences, as well as withdrawal of privileges and time out. I recommend that parents not use hitting as punishment; you can't punish by hitting without also modeling hitting. Punishment should be as mild as possible to do the job. It (as all other forms of influence) will work better if your overall relationship with the child is very positive. If you give punishment the child can escape by lying, you'll find yourself promoting lying. Don't feel the need to make it up to the child when you punish. Sometimes it's a good idea to let the environment do the punishing rather than doing it yourself; this is called natural consequences. Time out, or making the child stay in an unpreferred place for a short time, is often an effective and humane punishment; it tends to work if 8 guidelines are followed. We can view reprimands as some combination of punishment and instruction; when using them it's desirable to get the child alone, use an unexcited tone, and avoid making unenforceable threats. Another form of punishing consequences is the "withdrawal of friendliness and giving" by the adult: the nonverbal messages that put the child "in the doghouse" after antisocial behavior. When the child acts antisocially, the adult remains in authority and is not pleading or begging for cooperation from the child. My first choice for how to respond to negative behavior is to help the child take constructive action to undo any harm and prevent harm from happening in the future. Constructive action can be remembered by 4 Rs: accepting responsibility for the choice, making restitution if possible, redeciding on a more positive pattern for the future, and rehearsing that pattern in fantasy. I recommend that you, and anyone else that takes care of the child, sit down together and write out what your response will be to any common negative behaviors, of the child. That way your responses will be predictable and nondramatic, and you can tell whether your plan is working.

****

The Meaning of Punishment

How do we define the term punishment? Punishment is a person's getting something he doesn't like or doesn't want, in response to a behavior, which reduces (or is meant to reduce) the chance that the person will do that behavior in the future. Fines, frowns, irritated tones of voice, withdrawal of privileges, having a child stay in a room by himself, all fall into the category of punishment. But punishment doesn't have to be on purpose. Whenever something happens that a child doesn't like, the child is being punished for what immediately preceded that occurrence. For example, if a child climbs up a counter, and falls off and hurts himself, the child is receiving a punishment for climbing up the counter. Like reinforcers, punishments are dealt out by most environments fairly frequently.

Some people define verbal reprimands as something different from punishment. According to the definition I just gave, verbal utterances that are meant to make someone feel bad about what they did are punishment, just as a spanking or a time out is punishment.

It would be nice if we could totally rely on pleasant influences, use ignoring for negative behavior, and totally avoid punishment. As a general rule this isn't possible, and some fear-of-punishment motivation has to be mixed with desire-for-reinforcement motivation. Punishment is only one of our means of influence, and it is sometimes overemphasized, but that doesn't mean that it does not have a place in helping children develop well. However, punishment should be delivered in a very careful and well-planned way, and not handed out indiscriminately. Here is the reason:

The Trouble With Punishment

Remember our 9 methods of influence? When you deliver a punishment to another person, the influence is more complex than when a rat gets a shock from the bottom of his cage. It's true, the person gets an unpleasant stimulus in response to his behavior, which all other things equal tends to reduce the strength of that behavior. But also, the person is getting a model of someone's purposely making someone else feel bad. All other things equal, that will tend to strengthen "making others feel bad" behavior. And in addition, the experience of "someone purposely making me feel bad" is a stimulus situation that sometimes tends to elicit anger and the wish to retaliate. After being punished, a child usually has less strong a goal of making the punishing person feel good. Thus while the "consequences" method of influence may be working in the direction you want, modeling, stimulus situation control, and goal-setting may be working in the opposite direction from what you want.

The negative modeling, stimulus, and goal-setting effects of punishment are mitigated to the extent that (1) the behavior that is being punished is one that is truly wrong, (2) the methods of influence other than punishment have proven insufficient to do the job, and (3) the punishment given is the mildest possible that is capable of doing the job. Even very young children have certain powers of perceiving whether these conditions are met, I believe. And if they are not able to judge the justice now, they will be able to judge better in later years, looking back. The child's being able to see the justice in the punishment reduces the damage done.

Here is a summary of principles of punishment:

1. The only purpose of punishment is to reduce the frequency of undesirable behavior. It is not to get revenge, or to get out the parent's negative feelings.

2. The "last resort" nature of punishment means that in the long term, you should be content in using punishment only when you have created an environment where approval, responsivity, differential attention, differential excitement, and modeling are all used very well. In particular, don't try punishing a child into obeying superfluous commands—instead, stop issuing them. And if a child's negative behavior is in imitation of negative models that you yourself are providing, first eliminate those models (e.g. throw away games with titles resembling Mortal Combat or Street Fighter).

3. Use the mildest punishment that is effective in reducing the frequency of the negative behavior. Punishment that is too harsh risks a vicious cycle in which the child punishes the parent for punishing the child for punishing the parent for punishing the child. In addition, since punishment models trying to make someone feel bad, the harsher the punishment, the worse a model the child gets for trying to hurt.

4. Because punishment is unpleasant, people will attempt to escape it. The parent should make sure that stopping doing the undesirable behavior is the easiest way to escape the punishment, rather than some unwanted other way. For example: suppose parents regularly ask a child whether he did some forbidden act and punish him if he confesses. In escaping this punishment, it is easier to lie than to stop the behavior, and thus the parents are training the child to be a liar. For a second example: A child volunteers to answer questions about homework; when he gets questions wrong, the adult responds in a very disapproving tone of voice. It is easier for the child to escape the punishment by not answering questions than by learning to get them all right. Thus the adult is training the child not to take on academic challenges.

5. When you punish someone, there may be something of a withdrawal from the "emotional bank account": the reservoir of good will, cooperative spirit, and spirit of giving that exists between the two people. This is often quite a transient effect, especially with young children, and when the punished behavior is unreasonable and the punishment is quite humane. Nonetheless it's important to keep the emotional bank account replenished, such as by doing mutually gratifying activities and meeting the child's needs.

6. Don't feel such a need to replenish the emotional bank account that you regularly reward someone just after you punish him, or make the punishment last too short a time to be effective. If a parent regularly swats a child and then out of guilt hugs and kisses the child, the child is getting a very mixed-up message.

Physical Guidance

In a previous chapter I spoke of the use of physical guidance as a way of enforcing commands, and a way of avoiding giving repeated commands. I want to emphasize here as well that parents and caretakers should carefully avoid the pattern of either giving the same command many times while the child is ignoring it, or even worse, giving a command and failing to follow up at all if the child ignores it. This is a recipe for producing a disobedient child, one who gets used to ignoring the commands of authority figures, who is destined for major problems if this habit doesn't change.

Physical guidance is most useful with young children; it consists in physically moving the child's body so as to enforce the command or stop the negative behavior. For example, the adult says to a two year old, "It's time for us to have a diaper change"; the two year old shouts, "No!" and the adult gently picks up the child and goes and changes the diaper. A five year old is playing with an stapler in a way that poses some danger, just after having been instructed and shown how to use it correctly; the consequence is that the adult physically removes the stapler from his hands and puts it on a high shelf. A four year old refuses to leave a store when it is time to go; the parent picks the child up and walks out the door.

Physical guidance is punishment in the sense that children usually don't prefer this consequence. If they know that physical guidance will follow the ignoring of a command, they are more likely to obey the command.

Natural Consequences

Let's consider the following interaction.

Father: Are you ready to go to the park, Tilly?
Tilly: I sure am! Let's go!
(Father notices that Tilly is dressed in shorts on a chilly day.)
Father: Wait a minute—not dressed like that, you aren't. It's too cold to go out with shorts on.
Tilly: No it isn't. I've been outside. I'll be just fine.
Father: Absolutely not. Get some pants on, or sweat pants.
Tilly: I'm not going to do it! That's just stupid!
Father: For talking like that, you don't get to go, and you will have to stay inside all morning!
Tilly: I didn't want to go with you anyway! I'm going outside, and you can't stop me!
Father: For that defiance, you're going to time out. (Physically takes Tilly to time out; she screams and cries.)

Now in some ways, this sort of interaction may be exactly what Tilly needs. It is worth putting up with a great deal of negative emotion and confrontation and tears in order to be able to say, "My child is not spoiled." And the child who feels entitled to getting her way whenever she wants it has a very big problem.

However, with this particular conflict, whose problem is it if Tilly goes outside in her shorts and becomes too cold? Not the father's, but Tilly's. But in the interaction above, the problem became owned by the relationship. If Tilly's father has the luxury of letting Mother Nature deliver the punishment for Tilly's willfulness, why should he pass it up? Here's an alternative scenario:

Father: Are you ready to go to the park, Tilly?
Tilly: I sure am, let's go!
(Father notices that Tilly is dressed in shorts on a chilly day.)
Father: Do you know how cold it is outside? I don't think your shorts will be warm enough.
Tilly: I've been outside. I'll be just fine.
Father: OK. (Father picks up an extra sweater and an extra pair of sweat pants and puts them in his backpack, just in case.)
Later, at the park:
Tilly has been shivering for 15 or 20 minutes.
Tilly: I'm about ready to head back home.
Father: So soon?
Tilly: It is a little chillier than I thought it was going to be. I think you were right, Dad.
Father: I have an extra sweater and pair of sweat pants in my back pack, if you'd like to put them on.
Tilly: Thanks, Dad!

In this second scenario, Father waits to let Mother Nature impose her natural consequence, and then takes the role of the nurturing parent in helping his child. The result is a net deposit in the emotional bank account rather than a withdrawal.

Here are some other examples of natural consequences.

Harold is saving his money for a computer program. But he spends his money on junk food. His parents refuse to struggle with him, other than to predict the natural consequence, that he can't buy the computer program.

Jean refuses to eat breakfast. Her mother refuses to struggle with her beyond giving one reminder that it will be a long time before she gets a chance to eat again today. The natural consequence is the hunger that Jean feels while waiting for a late lunchtime to come.

Ted cares a great deal about his grades, but procrastinates on his homework. His parents refuse to struggle with him about his homework. He fails a test, and suffers the natural consequence of procrastination.

Mary's parents refuse to struggle with her about how she wears her hair, beyond one or two suggestions. The natural consequence of her refusing to do anything with it is that one day she overhears a peer talking to another peer about how ratty her hair looks.

Tommy mercilessly teases Growler, the neighbor's dog. The parents advise

Tommy to be nice to Growler or else leave him alone; they withhold punishment when he ignores them. When Growler nips Tommy, Tommy gets a painful but minor injury.

Alice stays up very late on Friday night, and her parents refuse to struggle with her. The natural consequence is that the next morning when her friend calls and invites her to do something fun, she finds it very unpleasant to wake up and she is too sleepy to enjoy what they do.

One-year old Melanie plays with the cabinet doors, and is gently closing the door with her fingers in the way. Her father calculates that the door is closing slowly enough not to do actual injury, and lets her close the door on her finger. She whines; on the next occasion she takes her fingers out before she closes the door.

When do you allow natural consequences to take place? As a general rule, the older the child is, the more you rely on natural consequences—since the child is headed toward more independent decision-making, anyway. As a second rule, you allow natural consequences to take place when the predicted consequence is in the "just right" zone of bad enough to teach the child something, but not so bad that permanent harm is done. Obviously there are many times when natural consequences should not be allowed! Here's an extreme example:

12 year-old Linda's parents refuse to struggle with her over her drinking alcohol and riding in fast cars with older boys who also drink. The natural consequence is that Linda is killed in a car wreck.

One of the major elements of parental judgment is when to use natural consequences and when to step in yourself.

Using Time Out

Time out consists in making the child stay:

in an unpreferred place

for a short time

without getting any attention.

It is given immediately after a child does something antisocial. Because it is something the child doesn't want, given after an undesirable behavior, to make that behavior happen less often, it is a punishment.

Many parents come to me saying that they have tried time out, and it doesn't work. I find that time out almost always "works" if a) parents can create and maintain a positive emotional climate, and b) parents can use time out just as described here. There are many ways of defeating the purpose of time out. You can easily use it in a way that accomplishes nothing. Let's go through the list of essential features. These features usually make the punishment not too harsh, but effective.

1. Give time out only for a very few of the most unacceptable behaviors, and have them very well defined. One way of defeating the purpose of time out is to give it too often, for too many differ-

ent things. I usually recommend that time out be given only for physical aggression, behavior physically dangerous to someone, destruction of property, or defiance of a very clear command.

2. As in the definition above, the child must get NO attention during time out. That means no visual contact, no verbal interaction, no communication, no acknowledgement of communication. For this to take place, in most cases, the child must be in a separate room, where visual interaction with other people is precluded. In some cases what is meant to pass for time out is that the child is asked to sit in a certain chair. If the child gets out of the chair, someone puts him back in it. While he is in the chair, he looks at people and is able to attract their attention. He asks if it is time for him to come out, and is told it will be just a little longer. All this attention may actually increase the net attention the child gets, rather than decrease it. The purpose of time out is defeated.

3. Make sure that the time out room cannot be locked from the inside, and that there is nothing the child can hurt himself with inside. A large, well-lit walk-in closet that has nothing in it is perhaps the ideal time out room. For grade school children, Gerald Patterson and his colleagues have found that the bathroom is often a good substitute. For children young enough that bathroom injuries are feared, I have found that the child's own room is often sufficient, even when there are toys in the child's room. If the child had preferred to be in his own room playing with toys, he would have been there already; thus the movement from somewhere else to the room is usually a punishment. If the child does find the things in his own room so reinforcing that time out does not work, those things can be removed to another place. In particular, a child's room in my opinion should never contain a television set.

4. Buy an extra kitchen timer and use it to signal the end of time out. Why a kitchen timer rather than a few glances at the watch? Because the kitchen timer makes the procedure more mechanical and therefore less reinforcing. You want time out to be a bore. You want as little novelty in it as possible. The kitchen timer removes the possibility that someone will need to be reminded. The kitchen timer allows the child to get the feeling more thoroughly that no attention is being paid to him during the time out.

5. Use time out for only a short time, about 2 minutes for preschoolers and five minutes for grade school children. Research has actually been done comparing short and longer periods of time out, and it has been found that longer periods of time out work no better than shorter periods. Because short time outs are much less hassle and invoke less resentment in the child and less guilt in the parent, they are definitely the way to go.

6. Before using time out, explain it when everybody is calm. This is done

so that the child doesn't think that he will have to stay in time out forever, and it won't be overly scary for him. It also gives the child a notion of exactly what will happen so that the child will be more likely to be cooperative with time out. The explanation usually best includes a role-play, acting out the sequence of events with the child. Alternatively, the explanation can involve a role-play with toy people. The adult can put on a play that demonstrates to the child exactly what will happen.

Here's what an explanation might sound like. "Johnny, I would like to explain to you something we're going to start doing to help you remember not to hit or throw things inside. It's called time out. Each time you hit or throw something, you will have to take a time out. That means that you will have to go to this room, right here, and stay there for two minutes, by yourself. I will set this kitchen timer for two minutes. You get to come out of the room when the kitchen timer goes off. Here's what it sounds like when it rings. Do you understand? Do you have any questions? OK, let's practice. Suppose you hit me. I'll take your hand and hit me, with it, just to act it out. I would say, 'You hit, so you go to time out.' Then you walk to this room, and stay inside, with the door closed. We'll act it out for just a second, instead of two minutes. OK? Now the bell rings, and when the bell rings you can come out. And that's it. This is to help you remember that hitting is not something that is to be done in our family, and we want to see none of it. If there's no hitting and no throwing things and so forth, then there will be no time outs. Now let's set the timer for two minutes, just so that you can hear how long two minutes are."

7. Have as few seconds, as few words, and as little emotion as possible transpire between the aggressive act and the beginning of time out. Example: the child hits the parent. The parent, in a monotone, says "You hit, so you go to time out." They walk to the time out room, the child goes in, the timer is set, and that's it.

Suppose, on the other hand, the parent screams at the child, "What do you think you're doing, hitting again? That's it. You're cooling your heels in time out. I hate it when you do that!" and so forth. Then we are back to what I have repeated so many times, that the emotion may reinforce the negative behavior and totally defeat the purpose of time out.

Another corollary of this rule is that there should be no negotiation before time out. If the child says, "I'm sorry, I won't do it again. Don't make me go to time out, and I'll be good the rest of the day. If you make me go there, I'll be mad and do it more," and so forth, all this falls upon deaf ears. The act of hitting sets off an invariate sequence of events that is done in exactly the same way each time with no possibility of anything different happening.

8. Don't fuss at the child after time out. One of the reasons why time out

works is that it gives people a chance to cool off, to get their negative emotions lowered, so that the vicious cycle of hostility is interrupted. Don't start it up again, but just let the time out be enough. If you do want to instruct the child about the ethics of behavior, do it later, as presentation of a lesson, rather than trying to combine it with a punishment.

Now here are the two big questions that always come up: First, what if the child won't go voluntarily to time out? And second, what if the child won't stay voluntarily in time out?

For preschool children, the answer to those questions is that the child is bodily carried to time out if the child will not go, and the door is held shut if the child will not voluntarily stay in. On the other hand, if the child will voluntarily walk in and stay, then the experience of physical guidance is obviated.

For grade school aged children, the child is not so easy to carry, plus the child's improved sense of time and consequences makes a different procedure possible. The parent says "That's a time out." The child says, "I'm not going." The parent says, "That's another minute, three minutes." The child says "No." The parent keeps adding another minute for each refusal, until about 10 minutes have been reached. At that time, the child loses a privilege for the day: no television, no bicycle, no access to his toys, etc.

Replies to Objections to Time Out

There are two sets of objectors to time out. One group wants to use corporal punishment, and sees the suggestion of time out as "wimpy." A second group on the other side of the spectrum wants to use nothing but concerned and nurturing explanations, and sees time out as "cruel." Let's reply to both groups in turn.

Admittedly, time out is much more difficult to give than a swat on the rear end. Here are the main reasons why it's better, though.

1. Hitting the child gives the child attention; a time out, if it's used well, makes the child not get attention for some time.

2. Hitting the child gives the child a model for hitting. It sends the child a message that the problems of the relationship cannot be solved without the use of physical violence.

3. Hitting tends to raise the level of emotion; time out gives people time to cool off.

4. Hitting a child can hurt the child. A parent who is angry can find strength just before the moment of impact that makes the hit cross the fine line to constitute injury.

Research has found that children who were physically punished more severely tend to have higher rates of delinquency, problems with social relationships, and school problems.

Now let me reply to the groups who feel that time out is cruel and inhumane.

I have had a couple of conversations with preschool teachers who complained of children's being physically aggressive with other children numerous times a day, over a period of months. At times the other children in the center have cried when going to the center, for the fear of this aggressive child. Yet at the suggestion that this child be confined in a room by himself each time he hits, there is recoil from the suggestion as though it constituted child abuse.

If explanations to the child that hitting is not nice and that it hurts people and people won't like him if he hits are sufficient to end the hitting, then obviously time out is not necessary. But if those explanations do not do the job, then which alternative seems more ethical: to inflict a nonviolent punishment upon the aggressive child a few times a day, with the expectation of ending the aggressive behavior within three or four weeks, or allowing the aggressive child to inflict a violent punishment upon his classmates or his teachers for an indefinite period of time? There seems to be an illogic about recoiling from time out while allowing the aggressive child's cruelty to other people to continue.

The physical harm done to other people by the aggressive child is not the only cost of allowing aggression to continue. Aggression tends to be contagious. When attacked by an aggressive child, a child uses violence to defend himself. If this defense is successful, the child's violent behavior has been powerfully reinforced. It requires little generalization for the child to start using violence as an offensive weapon to get his way. So the spread of aggression is one cost. But perhaps the greatest cost is to the aggressive child himself. The longer the habit of aggression continues, the more it becomes ingrained into his personality.

In my experience, if time out is given consistently, every time a child is physically aggressive, and if the suggestions of earlier chapters about creating a verbal environment are followed well, the rate of aggression (and thus the rate of time outs) steadily declines to near zero level quickly. Within a month or two after the program is instituted competently, especially if all the other methods of promotion of positive behavior are also instituted, the rate of physical aggression should be zero.

Exercise: Using Time Out

Read these descriptions of people using time out and decide what, if anything, the person did wrong.

Example 1. The child hits, and the parent says, "Go to time out." The child starts screaming, "But I wanted to go outside!" After listening to the child scream for a few seconds, the parent says, "Oh, go ahead, get outside and stay out for a while."

Here the parent is departing from the rule that no negotiation is allowed after a hit, and is reinforcing the child for screaming.

Example 2. A parent gives a child a time out. During the time out, the child says, "How much longer do I have to be in here? And the parent yells out, "A minute and a half more." The child yells out, "What did you put me in here for?" And the parent yells back, "I told you, that you're in there because you hit." What did the parent do wrong?

Here the parent is by definition not using time out, since during time out, the child receives no attention.

Example 3. A parent decides to start using time out. The child hits someone, and the parent takes the child to the room and makes the child stay in it. The parent sets the timer, but the child is screaming too loudly to hear the parent say that the child will only be in time out for two minutes. The child is very frightened, because the child thinks he may have to stay in the room for hours and hours. What did the parent not do?

Here the parent departed from the rule of having a thorough explanation before the procedure was instituted. In so doing, the parent gave some credibility to the critics of time out who would call it cruel and inhumane.

Example 4. A parent decides to use time out. After a week the parent reports that the child is in time out more than half of the day. The child has been made to stay in time out until the child will apologize, and sometimes the child won't do that for an hour or two.

Here the parent has departed from the rule that time out should last only a short time, 2 to 5 minutes, and the kitchen timer should signal the end of time out. The time out has become an ordeal for everyone, is probably doing more harm than good, and is done in an inhumane way.

Example 5. When the child comes out of time out, the parent starts saying, "I hope you've learned your lesson. You think you can just get away with anything, don't you? It's time you learned that other people have rights, that you're not the only one in the world, buster."

Here the parent is departing from the rule that you don't start fussing at the child after time out, but you start with a clean slate. The child is likely to start arguing back and a hostile interaction is likely to continue.

Example 6. The child starts screaming as soon as he gets into time out. The parent says, "I'm not going to start the two minutes until you get quiet." The child continues screaming for 20 minutes. The parent reminds the child on several occasions that the two minutes won't start until the child stops screaming. Finally after 50 minutes the child stops screaming and the two minutes are done.

Here the parent violated three rules: first, that the time out last only a short time, second, that there be no interaction during time out, and third, that the kitchen timer be set as soon as the child is in the room and the time out ends when the timer goes off. Although some experts advise starting time out only when the child stops screaming, I think this is a very bad idea. The purpose of the time out is to punish hitting, not screaming. If the child screams for two minutes, that's OK; the time out still ends after two minutes. If the child continues screaming after coming out of time out, then the screaming is ignored, in the "tantrum" paradigm. Screaming isn't punished as is hitting. If the child comes out of time out screaming and hits someone, then back he goes for another two minutes—for hitting, not screaming.

Example 7. A parent sends the child to time out. The parent gets distracted onto something else, and the next thing the parent knows, the child has been in time out for 15 minutes. What did the parent not do?

The rule violated here is that the time out should last a short time. I emphasize this repeatedly because it is so important that the child realize, either at the time or in future years on looking back, that the parent is not being unreasonable and harsh, that the punishment is mild, and that the punishment is given in a spirit of love rather than in anger or wish for revenge.

Example 8. The parent says, "You hit, so you have to go to time out." The parent sets a timer for two minutes. The child yells from the time out room, "I like being here!" The parent does not respond. The bell rings. The child says, "I like being here. I'm not coming out." The parent says, "Suit yourself," and goes on about her business.

In this example, the child used a "reverse psychology" maneuver that has stymied some parents. The child reasons, "If I act as though I like time out, the parent will figure it is no good as a punishment, and will stop using it." The parent in this example responded appropriately, by not being taken in by that routine, but continuing to follow the procedure to the letter. If the child doesn't seem to be put in great anguish by time out, then that's fine! The purpose of punishment is not to make someone pay for his sin by suffering; the purpose is to reduce the future frequency of the misbehavior.

What if there are two siblings fighting with one another, and the parent is not sure who started the fight? Then in my opinion the parent should keep in mind that "the world is not fair," and even though one sibling is probably always more to blame than the other, it's usually best to give both of them a time out, one in one place and another in another.

What about misbehavior that occurs in a restaurant, or in a grocery store? How do you give a time out there? I truly wish that there was a perfect answer to this question. One option is to give the child a time out that will be taken as soon as the child gets home; this procedure violates the principle that the consequence should occur within seconds after the behavior if at all possible. Another option is to use withdrawal of privileges as a punishment rather than time out for misbehavior in public places. If the child will comply with a time out in a car, that may be considered. If the public place is one where the child's attendance is optional, the child can stay home. Not all children are mature enough to handle all environments.

The fact that there is no perfect answer to this question reminds us that as long as the only reason a child has to avoid misbehavior is to avoid time out, the good behavior will not generalize. The task of the parent is to teach the child values, instill in the child an internal reward system for doing good and an internal punishment system for doing bad—in other words, to help the child have a conscience. Time out is not the final answer to this task. But it surely can greatly help to reduce misbehavior and to get the parent-child relationship on a footing where the more internalized learnings have a better chance to take place.

Giving Reprimands

A reprimand is a combination of punishment and instruction. In a reprimand, you look serious and disappointed and disapproving, and tell the child that you don't like what he did, and tell him why it's harmful.

Here are some tips for making reprimands effective.

1. Get the child away from other children.
2. Act serious and firm and disapproving, but don't act excited.
3. Tell the child what he did that you don't like, and why that behavior is undesirable or unacceptable. Don't attribute negative traits to the child.
4. Don't make threats you won't want to follow through on when you have time to think things over.
5. Be silent for a few seconds after the reprimand to let it sink in.
6. Let that be the end of your speech.

Let's go through these one by one. Why should you get the child away from other children? Because the other children can tease the child, or provoke the child into acting worse, or reinforce the child for getting reprimanded, or crack jokes that ruin the seriousness of the situation. You want to be in control of the situation yourself, and you're most in control when you and the child are alone together.

Why should you not act excited? Because as I've said many times before, excitement often tends to reinforce the child for doing something undesirable. Also: excitement tends to bring out responses from the child of fear or anger, and you don't want these emotions. What emotion do you want from the child? Let's face it: you want the child to feel remorseful, or guilty. Not so guilty that the child will be suicidal or will be in pain for a long time, but guilty enough to think twice before doing the harmful act again. Guilt is an emotion that is useful in inhibiting us from doing things that are unethical, and a certain amount of it is good. Guilt is a quiet emotion; anger and fear are loud emotions. For that reason, speak quietly when you reprimand.

You tell the child what you don't like and why it's harmful, because you're trying to educate the child. You say something like, "I don't like it when you keep grabbing the toys out of my hand. It isn't fun to play with you when you do that."

You don't make threats like "If you do this one more time you're never going to get to play with your toys, ever again," or something like that. Ever again is an awful long time. You want to preserve your reputation of honesty and dependability with the child, as one of your most precious possessions. For this reason you avoid giving threats that you don't carry through on. (However: if in the heat of anger you do make an unreasonable threat, renounce it rather than feeling duty bound to follow through.)

You wait a few seconds and are silent. This lets the child have a few seconds to feel uncomfortable and guilty about what he's done.

You let that be the end and get the whole thing over with fairly quickly, because you don't want to give the child a chance to get used to getting reprimanded. If you sit and fuss at him all day, pretty soon he'll learn to let it go in one ear and out the other. This principle of gradually decreasing reactivity as the child experiences something over and over is called habituation, or desensitization. It's one of the main reasons that you don't want to give reprimands extremely frequently.

Exercise: Reprimands

For each of the following things that people might say, please think about which of the above suggestions the person did follow and didn't follow.

Suppose the child goes up to another child and says "You look stupid." The adult first says, "Johnny, come here a minute," and leads the child to a place where the adult can talk to the child alone. Then the adult says, in a low tone, "I don't like it when you say that someone looks stupid. That makes people feel bad, and you know better than to do that." Then the adult waits a few seconds, frowning at the child, and then takes the child back in to where he was before. Which of the above suggestions did the adult follow, and which did he not follow?

Now suppose the child is clanging some toy pans together, and the adult asks him to stop, and the child ignores the adult. The adult physically take the pans out of his hand, and then takes the child and says to him, in a serious and controlled tone, "I asked you to stop banging the pans, because the noise was bothering me. You know better than to keep on when I've asked you to stop." Then the adult is silent for a few seconds, and then turns away and starts working again. Which suggestions did or didn't the person follow?

Now suppose the child is playing with another child, and purposely pours a glass of water on the rug. The adult yells, "What do you think you're doing! You do that again and you'll never get another glass of water in your life!! You don't know how to do anything right, do you? You just can't behave...." and then the adult keeps going like that for several more minutes. Which of these suggestions were followed?

Have you decided on the answers? If you have, compare them with these: in the first two examples all the suggestions were followed, and in the last example none of them were.

Does using a quiet, serious, rational, disapproving tone in reprimands guarantee that the adult attention will not be reinforcing? It helps, but some few children will be reinforced even by a quiet reprimand. If you find yourself using reprimands over and over, for the same misbehaviors, stop and consider that the strategy doesn't seem to be working, and consider doing something different! Sometimes what you need to reexamine the most is your nonverbal demeanor.

Withdrawal of Friendliness and Giving, and Nonverbal Messages

Let's imagine that you, an adult, were with a friend, let's say a coworker, and the two of you were trying to decide where to go for lunch. You wanted to go to one restaurant, and the friend had a very strong aversion to it, and suggested a couple of other places. Let's imagine you acted extremely spoiled and said, in a loud voice, "No! I want to go to MY place! Why won't you let me! You're stupid! I hate you!" Would you expect some punishment to come from the other person? Of course! I would expect that the other person would cease all smiles at me, to frown, and to get a very serious look on the face, a look that communicated, "What is wrong with you!" I would expect the other person to say, "Uh, I think it would be better if we didn't have lunch today," and walk away. I would further expect that the person would avoid me at work, and would perhaps not say hello to me, or give me a very perfunctory greeting, from then on perhaps, until I apologized profusely for my behavior and gave some very good excuse for it, and obviously seemed to feel bad about it. I would expect that until this reconciliation occurred, any requests I made to the other person would be denied.

What should we call this punishment? It's not corporal punishment, it's not time out, it's not exactly natural consequences, it's not withdrawal of privileges. It's not any of the usual options that parents think of when they are trying to unspoil a child. But it is what the real world usually gives out to people who act badly to another person: an effect on the relationship, a "being in the doghouse" with the other person, a permanent or temporary loss of the feeling that "I can count on this person for emotional support." We will call this punishment the withdrawal of friendliness and giving.

This sort of punishment has lots to do with attachment. The stronger the bond of attachment between the two people, the greater the dependency of one person on another, the more punishing is the withdrawal of friendliness and giving.

In this book whenever I have spoken about reinforcement, I have emphasized that non-tangible reinforcers, such as tone of voice and facial expression and emotional tone and attention, that say something about the relationship, are many times more important than material prizes. The same is true for punishment.

I think that the failure of punishment to "work" often results from the fact that the nonverbal messages do not "put the child in the doghouse," and leave it up to the child to obtain forgiveness and reentry into the more favored position of inclusion and social support. Sometimes with very spoiled-acting children the nonverbal messages are more of a pleading variety. The tone of voice says, "Please! You have the power to stop making me feel bad! Please use it, I need you to." This tone of voice and this interpersonal posture can be downright reinforcing for a child who wants interpersonal power, as almost all human beings do. It's as if in our example with two adults above, the insulted one were to say, in a childish tone, "Aw, come on. Please don't call me stupid and say you hate me. That's not nice. Please be nice to me, won't you?" This interpersonal demeanor is giving power to the other person in response to his negative behavior, and not withdrawing friendliness and giving. Parents who plead with their children need to become more comfortable with the unequal nature of the parent and the child, with being an "authority figure."

At other times the withdrawal of friendliness and giving are too temporary. For example, a child hits or verbally assaults a parent, and the parent withdraws friendliness and giving; the child quickly apologizes, and the parent hugs the child and all is right; but even at the time, the parent knows that this pattern has been repeated over and over and will probably repeat itself several times that very same day. The child comes to know that simply by saying the word "sorry," he can undo the withdrawal of friendliness and giving. It is not much of a punishment if you have total power to take it away instantly whenever you want to.

Often the inner state of the parent who can't withdraw friendliness and giving effectively is an intolerance of the child's anger and rejection, a need to get into the child's good graces, a fear of the child's not liking the parent. The parent must have clear in his own mind the following idea: "The child needs to be in my good graces; I do not need to ingratiate myself to the child." When children in my office have hit me, and I have delivered a punishment, I have heard their loud and angry protests upon receiving a punishment, only to have the child, far from acting rejecting, act even nicer to me than ever before when they see me on the next visit. There is something in most children that wishes to be on the good side of someone who is not afraid to incur their disfavor, and something that induces disrespect for someone who is afraid of incurring their disfavor.

At other times the parent undermines the withdrawal of friendliness and giving by linking this abstract condition to a concrete symbol that can then be discounted. For example, the six-year-old child acts spoiled and entitled and hostile for little reason, and the parent takes away a favorite stuffed animal. The child simply goes and gets one of her 15 other stuffed animals, and in a sassy way says, "I don't care. I'll just use another one." The parent thinks, "I guess that didn't work. I'm defeated on this one." And the withdrawal of friendliness and giving has turned into a situation where the child and parent are playing a game with each other to see who can come out on top. For children who have watched too many Saturday morning cartoons, the plot is all too familiar. The cat tries to get the mouse, but the little mouse keeps thwarting the cat in mischievous ways, leading the cat to go back and think of another way to come out on top. The whole scenario is defined as something fun and humorous on some level. It never occurs to the child to think that it is dangerous to threaten the quality of the most important relationship in their lives.

It's helpful for the parent to think about the meaning of the phrase "unconditional love," and which way of applying this is good or not good for the child. I believe that unconditional love is a wonderful thing if it means that the parent unconditionally continues to do and give what is in the child's long-term best interest—if the parent works unceasingly to make things come out well for the child. Unconditional love is a bad thing if it means that the parent's approval and friendliness and smiles and enthusiasm are not related to the child's behavior. It is harmful for a child to get the idea that he is entitled to pleasant behavior from others even when he treats them badly.

The Child Who Has Too Much

Suppose that family members withdraw friendliness and giving, and the child simply retreats into using video games, computer, television, recorded music, and other playthings until the period of withdrawal is over? The child can sometimes use his electronic friends to soften the impact of the disapproval of his real-life support system. For the child who is consistently misbehaving and for whom the temporary withdrawal of friendliness and giving have little effect, the next step might be to permanently end free access to a plethora of amusements, especially those that supply a fantasy playmate.

Let's think about how technology has changed things. Sixty years ago the toys in a young child's room were sports equipment, board games, dolls or toy people, kites, and books. Most of these required the cooperation of another person to be fun. Thus the withdrawal of friendliness and giving rendered a child not only psychologically "in the doghouse," but also with a shortage of pleasant interaction. Now, however, a child who is "in the doghouse" can often watch his own tv and play with his own videogame characters, or chat online with real people. The child can be entertained by these friends quite effectively.

I would therefore recommend that whenever there is an instance of serious aggression and hostility, the child's free access to television, computer, videogame player, and so forth be semi-permanently removed, one by one, until they are all unavailable. By semi-permanently, I mean until perhaps a year after the serious misbehavior has been totally absent.

I know that the logistics of this are quite difficult sometimes, especially when it is very desirable to allow other children or adults free access to these things. Nonetheless, when there is a serious misbehavior problem, it is often worthwhile to take drastic measures to solve it.

In my opinion all toys and playthings, and particularly communications through electronic media, are not an inalienable right of children, but a privilege that can be made conditional on the absence of serious misbehavior.

A Skill-Based Approach to Negative Behavior: The 4 R's

As a child gets older, and becomes more able to reason, time out becomes less and less effective. It's no longer so reinforcing for the child to be with everyone else, and it's no longer such an undesirable consequence to be alone. In fact, if the interpersonal environment doesn't feel good, it can actually be preferable for the older child to be alone.

As a child gets older, it becomes more and more possible that the child will respond to punishment by getting angry at the parent, staying resentful, and figuring out some means of retaliating against the parent. It becomes more and more possible that punishment is seen not only as something unpleasant, but an affront to one's emerging independent decision-making capacity. In short, things become more complicated, as if they weren't enough already for younger children.

Let's think for a minute about how adults ideally respond to their own mistakes and failures. Suppose that you have done something wrong or mistaken—what will be the most constructive response? Would it be giving yourself a time out, smacking your own body, or any other sort of self-punishment? I would suggest that the following four steps are more constructive. Step 1 is facing the truth: thinking very carefully about why the behavior was wrong, considering carefully what the harmful consequences were (including the harm to the precedents and customs of oneself and one's society), shouldering the pain of acknowledging without any self-deception your own responsibility for the bad action, and forming very clearly the goal of not doing that behavior in the future. A second step is making restitution to whoever was harmed by the action, preferably in greater degree than the original harm. A third step is to decide what, in the future, should be done instead of the harmful act. How would you like to refuse this behavior when tempted by someone else? How you would like to stay away from the temptation? How would you like to talk to yourself and act when the provoking situation comes up? Would you rather relax than to respond with heated emotion when the situation comes up? A fourth step is to rehearse the positive patterns, repeatedly, so that in the future you will be more likely to choose a positive pattern. In short:

1. Responsibility: Acknowledging the harm and your own voluntary role in it
2. Restitution: Making up for it, undoing the damage, if possible
3. Redecision: Deciding on a positive response for the future
4. Rehearsal: Practicing repetitively a positive response for future

These steps form actions that are usually not pleasant, but very constructive, in response to mistakes and wrong actions. They probably bring the best possible chance of making things better for the future. Accordingly, it seems logical to try to teach children to go through these steps, as early in life as they are capable of doing so. It seems logical to make consequences for wrong actions try as much as possible to promote these steps by the person doing the wrong action. Your goal, then, in devising consequences for negative behavior, is not so much the delivery of pain that will deter future negative behaviors, but the teaching of a pattern that will be an adaptive response for the child to use to deter himself from negative behaviors throughout the rest of his life.

This way of thinking tends to avoid the simplistic rat and pigeon model for human behavior, in which you suppress a behavior by delivering a punishment immediately afterwards. Because human beings have more complex brains, they can do such things as acknowledge responsibility for actions, list options, learn from experience, and rehearse the lesson.

Let's imagine some wrong actions and responses to them, as illustrations of this way of thinking.

Suppose that a teenaged boy, in a moment of jealousy over an ex-girlfriend, hits another boy in the face, doing some minor injury. The parents find out and are faced with the choice of how to respond. Some consequences that fit with the above model might be the following:

1. Making a written apology to the other person, in which the boy writes why the act was wrong, why he regrets doing it, and why he will avoid such acts in the future.

2. Making a monetary payment to the other person, in partial payment for any medical expenses or for pain and suffering the other person experienced. Offering to do something helpful to make up for it. Looking for chances to do kind deeds for this person, and reporting to parents when they are done.

3. Writing down the desired course of thought, feeling, and behavior when he in the future is exposed to a situation that might make him jealous. E.G. "I want to think to myself, I can handle this; this doesn't make me any less of a man; controlling myself and being gracious will make me more of a man."

4. Rehearsing that action by doing 50 "fantasy rehearsals out loud" in front of the parent, describing what he will do and think when encountering various similar situations in the future. E.G. "I'm seeing a guy from another school with a girl I really like, who wouldn't go out with me, and he makes a smart remark to me about how our football team got beat. I'm thinking to myself, this is a really provocative situation, because not only am I jealous, but he's also challenging me. But I am keeping my cool, and I just give him a disdainful look, and I say, that's not a problem for me, and walk on. And I congratulate myself for keeping cool and not letting him get to me."

Let's imagine an 11 year old girl who steals a very small item from a store. Some consequences that fit the model might be the following:

1. With the parent, making up 10 reasons why the act of stealing is wrong or bad, memorizing those 10 reasons, and reciting them back to the parent from memory.

2. Going, with the parent, to the owner of the store, and apologizing for the theft, returning the object, and making additional payment to reimburse the store for the security measures that the store has to take because people occasionally steal.

3. Writing down with the parent the desired thought and behavior pattern when she is in a store and she gets the urge to steal. E.g. "It's much more important to keep my reputation than get the thrill of stealing this thing. Even if I knew I'd never get caught it would make me a worse person to steal this. So I'm walking away, and I congratulate myself for using self-discipline."

4. Doing, with the parent, 50 fantasy rehearsals out loud of being in various shops and places where stealing is possible, but thinking to oneself the desirable thought patterns and avoiding the act.

For most wrong actions, the consequence should be a withdrawal of friendliness and giving; the state of friendliness and giving is restored when the child has won back the right to be a full member of the support system by doing some approximation of the 4 R's.

Enlisting Older Children in the Effort of Enforcing Justice

The older a child gets, the more the child is capable of taking a role in deciding how justice should be enforced: what the rules are, and what should be the consequences for following or breaking those rules. If, during moments where everyone is calm and rational, you ask an older child what rules are reasonable and just, and what are just consequences for breaking those rules, the child's judgment may be quite good. If these decisions are made by the family's sitting down together and agreeing upon them, the child is much less likely to rebel and revolt when it is necessary for consequences to be enforced.

Even when there has been no prior arrangment about a rule and the consequences for breaking it, it is helpful for the older child to meet with both parents and discuss and agree upon, if possible, what just consequences should be. If there has been agreement upon just consequences for offenses of similar degree, it will not be as hard to reach agreement upon the offense in question. If the child is not willing to accept any responsibility for having done anything wrong, and the parents feel that a great wrong has been done, then there are two problems: the problem of arranging appropriate consequences, and the problem of conflicting value systems or systems of morality and ethics. The latter is a much harder problem to solve than the working out of consequences when the child's ethical system is in synchrony with the parents.

For this reason, much preventive work should be devoted to developing an ethical system in the child. A separate chapter is devoted to this topic.

"Preprogramming" Responses to Undesirable Behaviors

Sometimes parents tell me that in response to a certain misbehavior they have "tried everything." They do first one thing, then another, and as nothing works, they try something else each time, deliberating or arguing among one another about what to do. I think that the child is sometimes reinforced for misbehavior by being in the powerful position of "Let's see what they'll try this time." Not only that power, but also the novelty of the adults' responses may prove reinforcing.

If you do the same thing each time, and if it doesn't involve a lot of excitement, the child might get bored with your response and not be reinforced for doing the negative behavior. It may be less important that the response is perfect, than that it is done consistently enough that it is predictable and thus boring.

Another very important consequence of a consistent response planned for a certain negative behavior is that the adults do not have to argue with each other each time the behavior happens.

This in itself can be worth the price of planning the response, even if the response doesn't work to reduce the negative behavior in the child.

For these reasons, it is a very good idea to make a written list of all the classes of negative behaviors that the child does at home, and have all the caretakers of the child come to some consensus on what to do when each of those behaviors takes place. If the plan they come up with doesn't work, they can revise it later, but for the time being, they agree to "go by the book." That way they can avoid arguing with each other about what to do at the time that the child does the negative behavior.

The list, for a first grade child, may look something like this:

Hits or other physical aggression: Time out

Says swear words: Out of the room for a reprimand.

Refuses to come with you when it is essential: Give clear command, then physically lead the child

Verbal hostility while receiving physical guidance: Withdrawal of friendliness and giving

Physical defiance while receiving physical guidance: Time out

Throws toys: Toys are placed on shelf out of reach for 20 minutes

Argues about "academic" issues (for example, argues that the moon is bigger than the sun): Use empathic reflections without arguing back

Takes his brother's toys away by force when his brother was playing with them first: physical guidance, toy taken out of the child's hand, put onto the floor, and child led out of the room for a reprimand

Has a tantrum when can't get his way: Put in ear plugs and ignore, never give him his way because of the tantrum, resume normal activities about 1 to 2 minutes after tantrum ends

Fighting at school: Any television shows or toys or video games involving violence in any way are permanently removed, one by one, for each aggressive act. Enforcement of 4 R's, including restitution to the other child.

Has toy people do violent things in dramatic play: Sit silently and watch until the violent acts are all over, then model nurturing responses to victims, sadness of victims' friends about victims

Doesn't get his way immediately, and screams, for something you were inclined to give him: Do not give him his way, even if you were inclined to do so before he started screaming.

Says something verbally hostile, such as to parents, "I hate you" Option 1: When there is an underlying substantive issue, use empathic reflections. Option 2: When the child is having an exaggerated response to a small frustration, use ignoring and withdrawal of friendliness and giving.

Asks a parent to do something, in a bossy tone of voice without saying please: Do not fulfill the request.

It's time to leave a place: Take him by the hand, say "It's time to leave, now, we must go." Walk out the door, quickly. If he resists use the basket hold to grasp him, lift, and take him out.
Refuses to leave a place: Do not argue with him, but physically take him.
Runs away when he is called: Catch him very firmly and quickly; withdraw friendliness and giving.
His mother is on the phone and he is interrupting: Go into a place where he doesn't have access to you. Reinforce him periodically with attention when he is playing nicely by himself. Avoid the protocol where you attend to him when he's acting up and go back to the phone call when he ceases to act up.
Doesn't want to stay at the table to eat: ignore. If he comes back and rejoins you, be pleasant with him; if he leaves, enjoy being with each other or relaxing. Save supper food for later and give it when he wants it, but no sweets.
Doesn't want to go to bed at bedtime: Start getting him up earlier in morning. Do a consistent bedtime ritual at the same time each night. Each time he gets out, take him back to bed with no reinforcement, no excitement.
Climbs on things or takes other risks with danger of hurting himself very seriously: Only one command to stop, physical guidance if he ignores, time out if he immediately returns.
Climbs on things or takes other risks with danger of very minor injury: natural consequences.
Defiantly disobeys after physical guidance: time out.
Starts running, jumping, screaming loudly, making lots of noise without hurting people or property: put in ear plugs, ignore until stops making noise.

The above illustrations are not given to imply that they are the answer to the problems listed. The "answer" usually consists in promoting positive behaviors, within a positive interpersonal environment, rather than coming up with the "perfect" response to the negative behaviors. Still, it is extremely useful for the adults to have their responses to the negative behaviors preprogrammed to such an extent that they can implement them calmly and deliberately, and without "dissension within the ranks."

When Preprogramming Isn't Enough: The Parent Council

One of the major purposes of preprogramming is to keep parents from having to battle with each other when the child misbehaves. Is the following sequence familiar? The child misbehaves; one parent gets angry, and in anger delivers or starts to deliver a punishment; the other parent, who feels less emotionally aroused, disagrees with that punishment and says so; now the parents get into a major argument with each other. The child is now subjected to a strange mixture of pleasant and unpleasant sensations, to which some children can become addicted: it's unpleasant to see your parents arguing and upset; it's pleasant to know that you have so much power to get such strong emotions going; and it's pleasant to experience the drama of being fought over; it's pleasant to have one person as your champion, defending you. Sometimes this little drama gets carried out over and over in families. It's not good for anyone.

Here's the alternative that I recommend. If the child does something to which the response cannot be preprogrammed, but something that deserves punishment, the very angry parent says, "That behavior is not acceptable. You will be punished for that." And for the time being, that's it. People allow themselves to cool off. Then the two parents get together, by themselves, and talk. They come to a consensus on what the consequence for the misbehavior should be. Then they call the child in to hear the verdict, which is presented with a united front.

Chapter 15: Contingency Programs

Chapter Overview:

Contingent reinforcement means that there is a high correlation between a person's behavior and the payoffs the person gets. Contingency programs are a very important solution to the dilemma that what is best to do is often not the most pleasurable. By linking pleasurable reinforcers to useful and good behaviors, we can help ourselves use self-discipline. My reading of the evidence is that contingent reinforcement programs do not usually reduce intrinsic motivation, that they can have an antidepressant effect, and that if run correctly they can be fun. Setting up a contingent reinforcement program is a long-term proposition. I recommend trying to make a gradual transition to the point where the child is self-monitoring and self-reinforcing. In order for contingency programs to work, the reinforcers must be highly desirable, must be withheld until the requirements have been met, must be not too hard and not to easy to obtain, and must be delivered without fail once earned. The interpersonal climate between the parent and the child must not be too hostile, and the parent should not make the offer of rewards contingent on bad behavior. I recommend the use of a global rating scale in which any, or all, of the sixteen psychological skill groups can contribute to an overall daily rating. I recommend that the parent start out by simply measuring the behavior, and considering after a few days whether the effort of doing this is sustainable over time. The next step is to give the child informational feedback on the ratings. The next stage is to make both daily reinforcers and less frequent reinforcers contingent upon the ratings. Then gradually the child is taught to self-monitor, i.e. give himself his own ratings. Then very gradually, the child learns to take control of giving himself and withholding from himself the reinforcers. The parent gradually shifts to a role of consultant and inspector of the program, and eventually the child takes over the program totally. This process takes place over a very long time, and "many are called but few are chosen" to be successful in completing all stages of it.

What Are Contingency Programs?

Suppose there is a child who needs to practice handwriting, and loves to play computer games. There is an adult living with him who needs to exercise more, and loves to drink coffee.

If the child plays computer games "for free" when he feels like it, and the adult drinks coffee whenever she feels like it, these rewards, or reinforcers, are noncontingent. They aren't tied to anything except the act of getting up and getting them. On the other hand, if there is a deal wherein the child gets 3 minutes of computer games for every 1 minute of handwriting practice he does, the reinforcer of the computer game is tied to the handwriting practice; it is now contingent reinforcement. If the adult makes a deal wherein she gets one cup of coffee for each 20 minutes of exercise, the coffee is now contingent reinforcement.

Contingency programs are ways of hooking up reinforcers to desired behaviors. The token economy is the most elaborate form of contingency program. In this sort of program, lots of positive behaviors let someone earn points, or tokens; many of the person's reinforcers require points or tokens to purchase.

The Problem: What's Best Isn't Always Most Pleasurable

The problem this chapter addresses is one faced not just by children, but by all people. The problem is that the best thing to do is not always the most fun thing to do. It's best to do homework, but it's more fun at the moment to watch a tv show. It's best to make up your bed, but it's more fun at the moment to play chase with your little sister. It's best to stick to an 1800 calorie diet, but the most fun thing at the moment is to eat 3 pieces of cheesecake. It is best in the long run for a writer to spend a certain half hour writing a book; it is more fun to play chess against the computer. This is the classic problem of self-discipline. Often it's necessary to choose the less gratifying option in order to get the best outcome in the long run.

A similar problem (if not the same one) is that the best thing to do is not always the most overlearned and habitual response. When a child asks for a cookie and doesn't get one, the response in the long term best interest of the child might be to say, "That's OK, I can handle it," whereas the child may be in a strong habit of whining or tantrumming. When the child is playing a checkers game and his little brother dumps the pieces onto the floor, it may be best in the long run to pick up the game and walk away without looking at the brother, but it may be most habitual to scream at the brother or hit him. When a husband hears his wife talk about a problem they are having, it may be best in the long run for him to listen carefully and see if he understands correctly the problem; it may be most habitual for him to yell angrily at her.

For every situation, there is something that "comes naturally" to do, because it is most pleasurable or most habitual. If you're going to do something other than this, you need self discipline.

Solutions to the Problem

One solution to this problem is to develop a very powerful internal reinforcement system, and to reinforce yourself at every step along the way for doing the best option. For example, you learn to say to yourself, "Hooray for me, I'm getting the work done that is most important to do!" That way you let the best option compete with the other one in the pleasure economy. An internal punishment system is also part of self-discipline: learning to say to oneself, "I'm indulging myself when I shouldn't be. It's time to get productive."

But often the internal reinforcement system needs some help. This is where contingency programs come in. If you can arrange it so that the external rewards that you really want come only when you do the self-discipline activities that are the best things to do, your reinforcement is contingent upon doing the self-discipline. The writer decides that she will totally avoid junk food, except that she will allow herself 100 calories of these goodies for every hour that she writes. The computer chess addict who wants to lose weight decides that he will allow himself to play computer chess only on those days when his weight is one pound less than it was the previous week. The woman with the cluttered office decides she will allow herself to purchase the new computer she has wanted only when she has uncluttered the office and kept it that way for a month.

All of these people will have a better chance of keeping their deals with themselves if they can make themselves accountable to someone else, and report in to a friend or family member as to whether they are keeping their promise.

I give these examples to point out that contingency programs are not just kids' stuff. They are extremely useful for adults as well.

Let's think of it this way. There is a lot of unharnessed motivating power lying around for most people. Why not harness that motivation in the service of self-discipline? Everyone has a list of self-discipline activities that he would be better off doing, and everyone has a list of pleasurable indulgences that feel good to do. Most people squander the tremendous motivating potential of the second list, by making those reinforcers noncontingent, or free. Making them contingent on those in the first list harnesses their motivating potential in the service of doing things that are best in the long run.

Pros and Cons of Contingencies and Extrinsic Reinforcement

An object to contingency programs is that offering tangible reinforcers may reduce the child's more "intrinsic" motivation to comply and cooperate. There are some studies suggesting that when children are offered big rewards for certain activities, and then those rewards are withdrawn, the children are for a while at least less inclined to do the activity than other children who were not rewarded for the activity. Some people have inferred from these studies that extrinsic motivation (such as money or toys) tends to reduce intrinsic motivation (such as inherent altruism or wish for a better relationship).

On the other hand, there's a theory that proposes just the opposite. A child, for example, gets candy or money or access to toys only contingent upon expending effort of some sort. After repeated experience of successfully achieving rewards for effort, the experience of effort itself becomes a "secondary reinforcer": something that is rewarding by virtue of being associated with rewards repeatedly. By this theory, extrinsic motivation strengthens, rather than weakening, intrinsic motivation.

Here's another theory. The more you act in a certain way, the more the brain gets used to acting in that way, and the more the synaptic connections grow themselves in a way that promotes acting in that way. Neurons that fire together wire together. In other words, practice of a desirable pattern enough times eventually gets those patterns wired into the brain. By this theory, if someone is acting with kindness and productivity long enough, even if their motives are purely external, the pattern of behavior may become so ingrained that it will remain when the external rewards are withdrawn.

Does the existence of the Nobel Prize and other awards strengthen people's motivation to achieve? It certainly appears so. Does getting paid increase people's desire to work? The evidence is very strong!

One thing is for sure: having a very noncompliant and negative child is not good for anybody in the family, most of all that child. It's a situation that must be remedied. In my opinion withholding the luxuries of life that the child considers necessities and giving them only in proportion to the child's cooperation is less drastic an intervention than, say, using physical punishment or using medication. I think these programs are very much underused, partly because they involve some persistent work on the parent's part.

Contingent Reinforcement as an Antidepressant

There is much research demonstrating that an absence of ability to control the rewards and punishments in your life is depressing. People, or animals, who have repeated experiences that teach them that nothing that they do matters, tend to get into a state of "learned helplessness." They conclude that nothing they do matters much, and there is not much point in trying anything. When they are put into new situations where what they do actually would matter, they tend to give up prematurely. They look depressed.

What is the opposite of those situations where nothing that you do matters? Contingent reinforcement. Contingent reinforcement means that your behaviors control the rewards and punishments that you get.

I believe that parents should use contingent reinforcement programs for children, not just to get them to do useful or good or skillful behaviors, but to help them be happier. People in general are happier when what they do matters.

I look upon contingent reinforcement programs as a type of game. Billions of dollars are spent each year on games – sports, video games, board games, and others. Why such expenditure of time and money? Games are an arrangement whereby reinforcers are made contingent on behavior. A basketball game, for example, is an arrangement whereby people get social approval, and sometimes money, contingent upon the behavior of getting a ball through one hoop and keeping it out of another. Why not just distribute the money and the social reinforcement, without worrying about where a rubber ball winds up? That doesn't work because the contingent nature of the reinforcement is destroyed.

The omnipresence of games is just one indicator of the appetite that human beings have for contingent reinforcement. Basketball is only one example of the fact that contingent reinforcement can be enormously pleasurable, even when the behaviors being rewarded are not particularly useful. When the behaviors getting the contingent reward are the ones that are really of highest priority for the individual, the arrangement is doubly beneficial.

When Do Contingency Programs End?

One of the biggest problems with contingency programs is that their effects seem to go away when the reinforcers are abruptly withdrawn. Don't start a contingency program hoping that with only a couple of months of effort you can permanently change behavior. It's more realistic to think that if a contingency program makes life better, you should be prepared to continue it indefinitely.

I mentioned the use of contingency programs by adults for several reasons. First, any adults who read this may want to try a contingency program for themselves. (I am at this moment looking forward to contingent reinforcement for today's writing.) Second, the description of contingency programs for adults provides a possible answer to the question of when a contingency program for a child might end: never. The self-discipline behaviors and the reinforcers may change, as the child gets older. And the role the parent takes in the program may change from that of an imposer of the program to that of a voluntary collaborator, then to that of someone to report in to and be accountable to, and finally to having no role at all. But it's possible to continue the strategy of contingency programs over a lifetime, and I highly recommend it. Making the gradual transition to the point where the child is in charge of his own self-run contingency program is, I believe, the best answer to the problem of the transience of effects.

Programs Between Parent and Child Alter the Behavior of Both

If you set up a contingency program for your child, your own behavior will be altered. What comes most naturally for most parents is to rely fairly heavily on fussing, nagging, reprimanding, and otherwise saying unpleasant words to the child if the child doesn't do what he should. Doing this usually requires generating some unpleasant emotion on your part. But if you run a contingency program right, you shouldn't have to yell at the child or generate lots of negative emotion to give disincentives for bad behavior. What you do is simply to announce that the bad behavior is lowering the number of points that the child is getting for that time period. Or you announce that the bad behavior will receive a consequence of loss of reinforcers, that you will later decide upon. If the reinforcers are those the child intensely desires to get, you will motivate the child without generating nearly as much distress in yourself.

Similarly, if the contingency program involves your noticing and counting (or at least registering in your mind) your child's positive behaviors, you behavior will be changed by that. Tuning in much more to the positive behaviors of your child and saying more enthusiastic things about them is sometimes one of the side effects of trying to keep track of them.

Reasons Why These Programs Sometimes Don't Work

Most parents who have worked with behavior problems in their children have tried some version of a program like this; many times it "hasn't worked." To conclude, however, that because one program didn't work, all of them will not, is something like concluding that because one book wasn't good, all won't be. There is tremendous difference between programs in how they are rigged up. The following suggestions outline some traps that you should avoid falling into.

Giving Up

By far the most common reason why reinforcement programs don't work it that people cease to use them. They are long-term efforts, and few people can sustain them. One of the worst reasons to discontinue a contingent reinforcement program is that the child refuses to work for the reinforcers. If this happens, the last thing the child needs is for the parent to say, in effect, "Oh, all right, if you refuse to work for these reinforcers, I'll give them to you for free." Another bad reason to discontinue a reinforcement program is that the child is behaving better. If the medicine is helping, it's important to continue it.

Offering Rewards, Contingent on Negative Behavior

Sometimes people feel that they are using a reward program when they do something like the following. The child starts whining and screaming and slapping at the parent. The parent says, "If you can settle yourself down, we can get some ice cream on the way home." The child settles down and the child gets some ice cream.

What has happened here? What has been rewarded? The parent hoped to reward the behavior of settling down. But what really has been rewarded is the whining and screaming and slapping. The offer of ice cream immediately followed those negative behaviors, and the offer is in itself a reward. The moral is: whatever you do, don't offer rewards when the child is acting bad. You will defeat your purpose and end up with a worse child than if you did nothing.

To give a more fanciful example of this principle, suppose that I were giving a speech to a bunch of adults, and I were to see two of them talking to each other. Suppose I said, "I really want everyone to be quiet for this speech. I'll give you $1000 if you two will stop talking to each other right now." They stop talking, and they get the money. I continue this whenever any other people talk with each other, to get them to stop talking. What would happen? How many seconds would elapse before everyone in the room would be talking with one another, in hopes of getting a similar reward for stopping? Suppose someone told me, "You are increasing the amount that these people talk, not decreasing it," and I replied to them, "No, when I give them the money, they do stop talking. It works." I would be engaging in a massive self-delusion, but one that people have done on countless occasions in dealing with children. The reinforcement for stopping negative behavior works to stop the negative behavior for a few seconds but it increases it for the rest of the time. To repeat the moral: you don't put the child in a position where he can successfully practice extortion. You don't improvise a reward system in the middle of a negative behavior. You have the negative behavior meet only with negative consequences. If the child can get anything positive by acting negative, you and he will suffer greatly.

Reinforcers That Aren't Desired Intensely Enough

Another major reason contingency programs don't work is that the rewards that are at stake are too easily done without.

For example, the child is supposed to work for a special outing to McDonald's once a week with his parent. The outing is nice, but is something the child can easily do without. Or a child is working to be able to play with his video games; meanwhile he has similar computer games that he can play with any time. Or suppose what's at stake is all electronic games, but when the child loses them he's still free to watch television. Or the child is working for some money, but he already has most of the things that money can buy him anyway. Or the child works for stars that are put up on a chart or stickers, that have a certain novelty value but after a few days lose their appeal. All these don't get close to the types of reinforcers I'm talking about, which are luxuries the child perceives as dire necessities.

To repeat: if you want a point program to work, the child has to be working for things that the child feels he absolutely has to have, not the luxuries. (Of course, what you may consider the necessities of existence may be along the lines of food, clothing, and shelter; the child's definition of necessities in this culture will probably include entertainment, junk food, and acquisition and use of fun objects.) You have to have the baseline existence for the child, the life style where the child is acting maximally bad, a life style where several things the child considers necessities are totally withheld.

If up until now you have provided pleasure and entertainment to the child in any way you could, for free, the first step in such a program will not be welcomed by the child. It consists of taking away the child's free access to some of those things the child was most dependent on for pleasure before. Examples include television, videos, movies, music recordings, videogames, computer, junk food, gifts, the right to play with some of the toys he already owns, outings to interesting places, access to the internet, and money. If you have been giving these for free, you can start to give them contingent upon good behavior.

If this seems drastic, it is because we are living in a culture where many children consider it an inalienable right to have entertainment items of all sorts, and sugar is the most basic of foods. But if you are to use it this program to best advantage, you must be decisive and thorough in removing the child's free access to certain luxuries.

If you feel guilty about removing the child's free access to these things, assuage your guilt by reminding yourself of what you're NOT removing free access to. The child can have free access to a cheerful conversation with you, to your friendly attitude toward him, to your positive reaction to anything he does good at any time, to free provision of all the true necessities of life. It's an existence that many children in the past and in the present would love to have.

Reinforcers Get Stolen Without Being Earned

Another reason programs like this fail is that the parent fails to keep the child from stealing what he's supposed to work for. For example, the child is supposed to work for the right to watch television. But there are 3 televisions in the house, and to keep the child from sneaking into a room and watching what he wants would require a full-time surveillance worker. Or the parent takes away the use of a certain toy, but the child finds out where it's kept and goes and gets it when the parent isn't looking. Or the child is to work for the right to have any sweets or desserts, but when the parent isn't looking the child goes to the freezer and helps himself to some ice cream. Thus before starting such a program you have to either 1) have a child who is exceptionally honest and dependable and mature, or 2) get ways of locking up the reinforcers so that you can totally control the access to them.

The toys that are withheld are put into boxes that can be put in closets under lock and key, and brought out for limited times when the child has earned the right to play with them. The junk foods the child previously had lots of access to are locked up in a cabinet or kept in a locked refrigerator you have purchased. The television the child had free access to is given away and replaced with a small one that can easily be picked up and locked away. The computer the child had free access to is traded in for a laptop or a model that requires a key for access, or you install a software program that requires a password for the use of the computer.

If these seem like drastic steps, so be it. If you have to get a locksmith out to put locks on several of your closets, to keep toys in them when they are not accessible to the child, then so be it. Much is at stake. The benefits of having a workable program far outweigh the drawbacks of getting rid of a big television and paying a locksmith and so forth. The last thing that you need is to set up a program where the child gets to play the "frustrate the authority" game successfully. You don't want to be running around the house telling the child to put things down because he doesn't have enough points to deserve them. Unless the child is dependable and disciplined enough to avoid the reinforcers until he has earned them, you want methods of withholding reinforcers that rely on locks and keys and physical impossibilities, not upon the good will and cooperative spirit of the child. You can move gradually toward the stage where the child is regulating his own access to reinforcers, using his own self-discipline to avoid them until earned. But this movement can take years to carry out.

Lack of Unanimity Among Parents

Obviously if the child is going to have the reinforcers successfully withheld, all the adults who have access to the reinforcers must be fully engaged in the program. You can't have one parent trying to withhold reinforcers while the other is trying to give the child a special treat. This just results in the adults in the family getting into conflict with one another. You have to have a way of seeing for sure whether the child has earned a reinforcer, and have this communicated in a fairly foolproof way from one parent to the other.

Making the Reinforcers Unattainable

A third reason some programs like this fail is that they require the child to be too good for too long, so that the child doesn't have a prayer of getting the reinforcer. For example, let's say the program is as follows. The child gets a star if he has been good all day, and if he has a star every day for 7 days in a row, he gets the reinforcers. The child soon learns that any lapse means he has to start all over again, and he gets demoralized and resigns himself to never getting the reinforcer.

Making the Reinforcers Too Easily Attainable

A fourth reason for failure is the opposite of the third one; the rewards are too easy to get, and the child can get most of them while still maintaining the troublesome behavior that the program was set up to end. You have to have the program set up so that if the child acts very bad, he doesn't get the rewards.

Thus you have to be vigilant in how you rig up how many points you get for good behavior and how much reinforcers cost. You have to revise the relationship between behaviors and reinforcers as often as necessary, to make sure the reinforcers are not too hard or too easy to get. You keep adjusting things until it's just right, and then when the child changes, you adjust some more. This is a lot of work.

Too Much Hostility

The fifth reason that contingency programs fail is that the relationship between the parent and the child is too full of hostility and rejection. A child who is mad enough at a parent can continue to act bad much of the time, because he wishes to punish the parent. There are certain things that tend to improve relations between parents and children, and these should be done vigorously at the same time the contingency program is going on, and should not be withheld by the program. Please see the advice in this book on the emotional climate, and ways of speaking with children.

Let review the high points of creation of a positive emotional climate here. Make sure that you are not expecting something of a child that is way too difficult. Suppose someone asked you to solve a math problem that was at least 5 courses over your head. No amount of incentive could induce you to do it; you're dealing with "can't" rather than "won't." The same is true, for example, with asking a very restless and active 5 year old not to touch anything for a long time at someone's house. Second, try to have a high ratio of verbal approval to disapproval (try not saying much of anything about the bad behavior except to announce the loss of points). Don't give unnecessary commands; don't have a high fraction of your utterances to the child consist of commands. Too much bossiness can lead to resentment and rebellion. Do a lot of responsive utterances like "facilitations" and "reflections" and "tracking and describing." Don't spend time arguing with the child. Use differential reinforcement, particularly by making your attention and excitement follow the good behavior and not the bad behavior. Excitement is often reinforcing, even when it takes the form of yelling at the child to quit being bad. If you're yelling at the child's bad behavior, work very hard to stop, and try to generate excitement over the positive. Give the child models of positive behavior to other people in the family and to him. If a conflict comes up speak very rationally. If there is any activity that parent and child truly enjoy doing together, i.e. that gives the parent pleasure as well as the child, I would tend not to withhold it. If the child enjoys hearing stories of positive models of psychologically skillful behavior, I would not withhold those. I would not withhold time with the parent spent in chatting. If you enjoy going with the child for a chat and a walk around the block, don't withhold that.

Haggling Over Points

Another reason why such programs sometimes fail is that the parent can't hold himself or herself back from trying to justify to the child the reason for certain decisions about how many points are given or taken away or how much certain things cost, and the parent and the child spend large amounts of time haggling. The parent finally gives up on the program because such haggling is so aversive. The antidote to this is to set up the rule at the beginning that the parent's giving or taking away points is always final, and that any protest of this on the part of the child results not in an explanation or argument, but a further loss of points by the child. The parent must be an authority and must not negotiate with the child as an equal. The purpose of this program is to put more influence into the hands of the parents. The parent must be comfortable with being decisive and not giving in to the child's protests.

Nondelivery of Rewards

A final reason why programs like this fail is that the child earns the right to do something or get something, and the parent does not deliver. For example, the child earns the right to get a certain toy, but the parent keeps putting off the trip to get the toy over a matter of weeks. Or the child earns the right to have a special outing somewhere with the parent, but the parent can't find the time to do it with the child.

Stages in Instituting Contingency Programs

I recommend doing contingency programs with children in 3 stages: measurement, informational feedback, and feedback with contingent reward and punishment.

First, you simply measure whatever it is that you are trying to increase, without even giving the child feedback. If you have a rating scale that you are using each day, you fill it out and add up the points, just for yourself. You take enough notes about the child's good and bad behaviors so that you can remember how good or bad a day it was in whatever aspects you are rating. You want to get a number that summarizes how desirable the day was. You want to make sure that better days get higher ratings and worse days get lower ratings.

One thing to watch out for is getting into a rut where you use the same rating each day, even though the child's behavior varies somewhat. You want to let your ratings reflect the variance in the child's behavior.

Here is a generic rating scale that can be used with almost anybody, at school or at home.

Daily Global Rating Scale

0=Very bad day. Very big problems, severe difficulties.
2=Bad day. We should be quite dissatisfied with a day like this.
4=So-so day. Not good enough to be called good, but not bad enough to be called bad. Not good enough for us to feel pleased.
6=OK day. If this sort of day were repeated every day, it would be ok, acceptable.
8=Good day. If this sort of day happened every day, it would be cause for celebration.
10=Very good day. If this sort of day happened every day, it would be cause for very major celebration.
Today's date:___________

Today's rating: _________

The items below are meant to help communicate why the rating was what it was. If you have time, you can put a plus or a minus sign next to any of these that particularly raised or lowered the rating. If something not on this list raised or lowered the rating, you can write it in and put a plus or minus sign next to it.
Productivity: doing useful things, useful work
Joyousness: cheerfulness, pleasantness
Kindness: being nice, sharing, consideration, courtesy
Honesty: Telling the truth, keeping promises, not cheating or stealing
Fortitude: frustration tolerance, putting up with hardship
Good decisions: Thinking before acting, solving problems with other people well
Nonviolence: No hitting, kicking, hurting of any sort
Nonhurtful talk: Not being rude, not doing unkind teasing
Friendship-building: Having good chats, letting people know him, being a good listener.
Self discipline: Being able to do what's best rather than just what he feels like
Loyalty: Being true to people he has long-term relationships with
Conservation: Not wasting things, being thrifty
Self-care: Doing things that are good for himself
Compliance: Obeying parents or other proper authorities

Positive fantasy rehearsal: Practicing good acts and not bad ones in fantasy
Courage: Doing things that take some bravery

This global rating scale takes only a few seconds to fill out if you are rushed. If you have more time, you can make annotations about how the trainee did in each of the 16 skill groups. If you want you can agree that the global rating is going to focus only on one skill, or on two or three skills.

One of the strategies in such a program is that you, and the child, go over many concrete examples of each of these skills, so that you can have a very clear knowledge of what each of them means. The more examples of each you have run through your mind, the more likely you will be to notice a positive example on the child's part when you see it.

It's a good idea to write down a list of the particular positive examples you are most looking for from the child, and to expand the list as you go along. For example:
Kindness:

Looking for: Saying "good morning" in a pleasant voice. Sharing things with sister. Helping a family member carry something. Complimenting someone on something. Teaching someone how to do something. Helping with a chore. Saying please and thank you and yes please etc.

Not looking for: Taunting sister. Tempting sister with attractive play-things and then not letting her have them. Speaking disrespectfully to any family member. Hitting or any other physical aggression. Yelling in anger.

Thus for each skill, you have the concrete, specific examples of what you want and what you don't want. Each day when you fill out the rating scale, you write down any positive or negative examples, and you add them to the overall list of concrete desirable or undesirable behaviors.

After filling out the rating scale a few days, you stop and consider: am I going to have the energy to do this over a long period of time? If not, then you need a different type of program. It's best to drop it before even communicating with the child about it.

Ratings Versus Counts

In ratings, you give a number that summarizes how good a day it was in any respect you want to measure. A different way to quantify the child's behavior is by counting certain behaviors.

I have found this most useful when the highest priority skill is compliance. You can watch carefully for the child's response to each directive that you give, and give immediate feedback as to whether the response is a comply or a noncomply. You can use wrist counters that are sold to golfers in sporting good stores to keep track of the complies and noncomplies. The total score for each day is the number of complies minus the number of noncomplies.

If you are working on compliance, your first task is to make sure that you give your commands well. Here is a quick summary of the art of giving commands:

1. Give commands one at a time. Don't say, "Go upstairs and brush your teeth and get dressed and don't forget to brush your hair." Instead, say "Please come upstairs with me so that we can get ready to go. Good, you did it. Now it's time to brush your teeth please. Great, you moved right away to do it.... You finished it! Now please take your shorts off so you can put these blue pants on. OK!"

2. Be very specific and concrete. Don't say, "Settle down." Instead say, "Please speak quietly. Please use about the same loudness that I'm using now."

3. Speak in a calm, firm voice, without yelling. If at all possible, speak in a friendly, upbeat tone, as though you expect cooperation.

4. Make sure you have the child's attention first. For example, when the child is watching television, don't just call out, "Time to get dressed." Instead, walk in, address the child by name; if the child doesn't look up at you, touch the child's shoulder to get his attention first.

5. Be very polite, despite being firm. Instead of "Get over here!" say "Come with me, please."

6. Explain the reason for the directive if it feels right, even if the child already knows. For example, instead of "Get that helmet on," you can say, "I love my son, and I don't want your brain hurt, so I have to insist that you put your helmet on."

7. Make a very clear distinction between commands and suggestions. That way the child won't be practicing disobedience if he chooses not to follow a suggestion.

8. Do not yell a command from one room to another; get yourself in the child's presence.

9. Never give a command without watching to see whether the child complies or not.

10. Don't give commands that you predict the child isn't going to obey and you aren't going to enforce.

One advantage of counting behaviors it is that the number arrived at by counting is more objective. Another advantage is that specific behaviors may get reinforced more effectively. A disadvantage is that the behaviors that you haven't decided to count, but are nevertheless important, don't influence the rating. And counting is a good bit more work than rating. This is the main reason that I have never seen a parent maintain counting-based measures for a very long time.

Communicating Results to the Child

If you are able to continue with some method of quantifying the child's behavior every day, and if you feel you can continue this indefinitely, then you are ready to go forward. Step 2 is to start communicating the results to the child each day. You sit down with the child once a day and let the child know what the rating or count was, and what behaviors raised the rating and what behaviors lowered it. You are wanting to work toward the time when the child can accurately self-monitor, and know how good a day he has had before you tell him. But the first step is simply to communicate the ratings.

If at this stage the child is interested in the ratings, fine. If he isn't, that's ok too. If the child is interested in guessing what rating he got, before you tell, that's great. If not, that's ok too.

The third step is to tie the ratings to reinforcers. What the child has access to each day depends upon his ratings for the previous day. You can make contingencies for any category of reward that the child gets: for example junk food, electronic entertainment, other toys, outings, money. You divide these into two groups: daily reinforcers, and less frequent reinforcers.

Daily Reinforcers

For the daily reinforcers that you want to make contingent upon the behavior, you make a table of what the child gets for each degree of achievement. For example:

Money: 0 or 1=Lose money
2 through 5= get 0
6 or 7= get .25
8 or 9= get .50
10= get .75

These quantities should be adjusted according to how what the child is expected to buy with her own money versus what is bought for her. The more the child buys with her own money, the more contingent monetary reinforcement is.

Electronic entertainment:
0-2=No access to phone, tv, computer, video games, radio, cd player, etc.
3-4=Phone and tape player only
5-7=Phone, tape player, computer
8-10=Access to all for reasonable amount of time.

Junk food:
50-100 calories of junk food for every point above 5.

Less Frequent Reinforcers

Now suppose the child asks you for a doll or a cool pair of athletic shoes or the chance to order a pizza and have it delivered to the house, or a trip to a fun place. If what is asked for is outside the family's budget or in conflict with your value system, the answer is simply no. But otherwise, you can consider answering, "We'll put it on the chart!"

By the "chart" I mean a grid with lines that make rows and columns of rectangles; I like grids with fifty blocks per page. You have one chart taped up somewhere at any given time. If the reinforcer is a big one, you write it in a block far away from those already colored in. If the reinforcer is a small one, you write it in a closer block.

Here is how you might fill in the blocks:

0-5=no blocks filled in
6=1 block
7=2 blocks
8=3 blocks
9=4 blocks
10=5 blocks

So at the end of the 24 hour period, the child gets his rating on the skill in question, and together you fill in blocks. You write the date in the blocks, and the child colors them in with a crayon, if desired. As more blocks get filled in, the child sees himself gradually getting closer and closer to the reinforcers written on the chart. And when the block with the reinforcer written in it is colored in, the child gets the reinforcer.

Helping the Child to Self-Monitor

If such a program is successful, the next step is not to fade it out, but to very gradually transfer the measurement function and the taking and denying of rewards function to the child. Transferring the measurement function to the child means that you teach the child to rate himself accurately, or in other words in a reasonable approximation of your ratings.

To teach the child to self-monitor, you ask the child to repeatedly go through the process of 1) rating himself, 2) comparing his ratings with yours, and 3) getting reinforced for accuracy. You might work this into the point system by adding a point or two if the child comes pretty close to your rating.

Accurate self-observation is very useful, if not essential, for self-improvement; it's interesting how many children seem to be fairly oblivious to how well they are doing. Rating themselves, comparing their results to someone else's rating, and getting reinforced for accuracy day after day, month after month, and year after year has the best chance of growing these self-monitoring skills.

Helping the Child to Give Himself and Withhold From Himself the Reinforcers

The ability to give yourself or withhold from yourself reinforcers depending upon your performance requires lots of self-discipline and motivation. It will probably be successful only when the child has been instructed about self-discipline for a long time and has thoroughly learned about adult-type contingency programs. Such a program will probably be more successful when the child has had lots of experience with self-discipline exercises involving voluntarily resisting temptations. Such a program also is only likely to be successful with highly honest children.

You move to such a program by making more and more assumptions of the child's honesty. You come to depend more upon the child's self-reports of behavior (which is appropriate as the child gets older and less of his behavior is directly observed). You stop having the reinforcers locked up, but depend upon the child's cooperation in following the rules of the contingency program. You go to a stage where the child self-monitors, and computes how much of the reinforcer he deserves, and you simply say, "Fine, go have it." You are now functioning as someone to be accountable to rather than someone to exert total control over the reinforcers.

The last stage is one where the child simply rates himself and withholds or gives himself reinforcers depending upon his ratings, with only periodic and infrequent reports to maintain accountability, or without any reports at all. When the child can do this, he has "arrived" at habits of self-discipline and following his own rules that will greatly help him in doing anything regarding self-discipline.

Chapter 16: Decision-Making Skill

Chapter Overview:

People who have experience, skill, and information that lets them make a confident decision in a situation have a crucial antidote to psychological distress in that situation. The first step in decision making is to identify the problem: to realize that you're in a choice point, and to tell yourself in words what the situation is. Next you decide how high the stakes of the decision are: whether the decision is worth lots of time and energy or only a little. For very important decisions, it is useful to write down what the questions are. A next step is getting more information, if you need it. This information can come from reading, consultating with experts, asking questions, and making systematic observations. A next step is brainstorming a list of possible options for the solution, trying to get as many ideas as possible. Then comes ruling out certain options, narrowing the field. Then you predict the consequences of the best options, and think about how much you like those consequences. Thinking about both how much you like a certain outcome and how likely it is to happen allows you to use the powerful idea of "maximizing expected utility." To maximize expected utility, you consider the different outcomes that could happen with a certain option. You rate how much you like that outcome (its utility) and also how likely it is to happen (its probability). Considering both the utility and the probability (or multiplying them together, if you think in numbers) gives you a score for how much that possible outcome pulls you toward or away from that option. You add up that sort of score for all the possible outcomes of the option, and you get a score for how desirable the option is. You compare that to the score for the other options, and pick the option with the best score. Although this sounds complicated, people intuitively juggle probabilities and utilities routinely in everyday decision-making. Another way to help your mind use and integrate your information is to use a rating scale. You list the things you want, and make a scale to rate how much any option would give you each of those things. Usually the option with the best total score is the best. When you think about consequences of options, be sure to take into account long-term precedents for future actions. That is, an option may work out OK for now, but if it sets too bad a precedent for the future, you should forego the present benefit. When the stakes of the decision are low, it saves time if you "satisfice" rather than "optimize." Satisficing means picking the first "good-enough" option, whereas optimizing means trying to find the best one. Some common reasons for bad decisions include misjudging the stakes, inferring from too small a "sample size," making the "sunk costs error," or by distorting reality with too much "postdecisional regret" or "bolstering." If you make good decisions, but lack the will to enact them, think of ways to use the nine methods of influence upon yourself.

****

Decision-making and problem-solving are absolutely crucial psychological skills, both for children and adults. This chapter and the next will focus on principles of "individual decision-making" and "joint decision-making," respectively. The first is the process by which one person decides what to do; the second is the process by which two people decide jointly on actions that will affect them both.

Anxiety and Decision-Making Under Uncertainty

Most of the time when people are anxious or depressed or in turmoil or suffering other ill effects of stress, they are not sure what to do. They have the feeling, or the certainty, that something is wrong, but they are very uncertain as to what they can do about it. In my observation and experience, once people have made a clear-cut decision either 1) that there is something they can do, and they have to put their effort into doing it, or 2) that there is nothing they can do, and therefore they have to put their effort into tolerating the situation, there is a great relief of tension.

The "serenity prayer" says, "Grant me the courage to change the things I can change, the serenity to tolerate the things I can't change, and the wisdom to know the difference." Much of the time when people are in great distress, they're not sure whether, and how, they can affect a situation. They would hate just to try to tolerate a situation, and later find out that there was something they could have done to vastly improve it. They would hate to spend huge hours trying to change something, when it is obvious that nothing they're going to do is going to work. Once they're sure what to do, it's much easier, even if the work they have to do is unpleasant or if it's difficult to tolerate the outcome that they have no control over.

Let's look at an example. Suppose a person is responsible for the care of an elderly parent, who has lost his ability to reason for himself, and who has a terminal illness. The person is responsible for deciding when medical life-support systems should be applied, and when they should be withheld. This is a stressful decision, in any case. But if the parent has written a "living will" that specifies very clearly what he wants done, the situation is not nearly as stressful as if he had no idea what the parent would have wanted.

Suppose that someone is having a conflict with a coworker. The person has had little experience with this sort of situation before, so that he is unsure whether the best strategy is to apologize, take the conflict to his supervisor, ignore the coworker, sit down and talk with the coworker in a certain way, or ask for a transfer to another department. Such uncertainty is stressful; when the person is sure that he has made the best decision he can, given the information he has or can get, the stress is likely to go down.

A couple have a child with behavior problems. They are not sure whether the answer is more punishment, less punishment, more toleration of the child's behavior, a different school, or any of many other options. Because of the uncertainty, they tend to argue with each other about what strategy is best. Once they get enough information to become convinced that a certain strategy is best, they experience a great reduction in stress. (If the strategy works, they experience even greater reduction in stress.)

A person is the first to arrive on the scene after a very bad accident has occurred and someone has been badly hurt. If the person knows no first aid and has no idea what to do, the situation is likely to be much more stressful than if the person is an expert in first aid for accident victims. To the doctor in the trauma center who handles accident victims all day every day, there may be no distress, or even pleasure, from taking on the job of helping the accident victim. The distress is proportional to how well equipped the person is to make the decisions necessary to cope with the situation.

Perhaps it would be a good exercise for you to stop reading for a moment and to think on the circumstances in your life in which you have felt the most distress. Were they also the times in which you were uncertain about what should be done about a situation, times when there was a high-stakes decision to make but little or no confidence that you could make the right one?

Easing Decisions Through More Information and Improved Process

Let's talk about two ways to make decisions easier. One way is to get more information that bears upon the decision. And the second way is to learn to make more systematic and logical use of the information you do have, so that you have the highest expectancy for the outcome of your action.

Players of the game of bridge have an expression that summarizes these two ways: "One peek is worth two finesses." A "finesse" is a way of playing the cards that maximizes your score, given that you are uncertain what cards one of your opponents holds. But if you get a "peek" and actually see what cards your opponent holds, you know even more about how to play the cards.

One very useful way to organize the information you do have, when making a difficult decision, is to sit down and use pencil and paper or a keyboard to write, and keep track in that way of the thoughts you have about the decision. If someone asked you to multiply 628 by 321 (without a calculator or computer) you would not think of doing it without using pencil and paper as an aid to your memory. But most people try to make decisions that are much more complex than this arithmetic problem, without ever writing anything down. The problem is that we can only hold a limited amount in memory. If you don't use writing as a memory aid, you tend to remember one aspect of the situation, and this gives you the urge to act in one way; then you remember another aspect of it, and this gives you the urge to act in another way. By writing you can better integrate all that you know about the situation.

Writing Or Stating a Situation Summary

When you start to analyze a decision, one of the first things to do is briefly to summarize the situation, who is involved, what your goal is, what the immediately obvious choices are, and what is at stake. This is just a concise summary of the situation you are facing. Here's an example of this sort of concise summary:

"We live near a family who have a son the same age as my son. This boy is fairly aggressive, and has some other bad habits I don't want my son to pick up. I would rather my son not play with him, for that reason. But I don't want to make this child more desirable for my son to be with by making him a 'forbidden fruit," and I also would like to avoid alienating his parents, with whom I have been friendly so far."

We can call this the stage of problem-identification. Although simply formulating the situation and the nature of the decision is the simplest of the steps in decision-making, it may indeed be the most crucial and most difficult, especially for children. Many decisions are not made correctly for one major reason: they are never really identified and addressed. If you were to ask many children for the first time the question, "What decisions have you faced lately," you would probably get either a blank look or a reply that no decisions have been made, when of course every waking moment involves some sort of decision of how to respond.

How High Are the Stakes?

A reasonable next step is to make a decision about the decision: How much is at stake in this decision, how important is it, how much time and effort does it deserve? Some decisions deserve a great deal of time and energy, and some deserve almost none. As you read the following, think about how much time and effort you think each would deserve:

Which type of apples to get at the grocery store
Whether to have another child
Whether to buy a house or to rent an apartment
Whether to get married to a certain person
What to wear to work on a certain day
Whether to take a certain course in school
What sort of television to buy
Whether to take the bus or walk to a certain place
Which restaurant to go out to on a certain night
Whether to buy self-sticking envelopes or the type you have to lick
How to strengthen my "social support network," how to have more mutually

rewarding relationships with other people

People seldom put enough effort into decisions such as "What shall I do with my time," "What are my goals." Where do I want to put my effort? Should I watch the evening news each evening, as I am doing, or is there something I could do that's more rewarding to me? How should I spend my day today? What sorts of things do I want to do with my children? What activities are best for my spouse and me to do together? How can I be of greater service to humanity? How can I make my family life better?

Few of us put time and effort into the decision process in proportion to how important the decision is. Some of us err by making important decisions impulsively, some by obsessing over small decisions deserving little more than a random choice; most of us make both sorts of errors. If you have, you have a good chance of making your life better by apportioning your time and energy better.

Posing More Questions

If a decision is important enough to warrant some time and energy, a next step is to pose to yourself questions helpful to know in making the decision. For example, with the decision about the aggressive playmate mentioned above, some relevant questions might be:

How aggressive is this playmate? How often is he aggressive?

Exactly what are his other bad habits, and how bad are they?

How impressionable is my son, and how likely is he to be influenced by the other child?

Are children on the average influenced very much by the behavior of their playmates?

How closely do his parents supervise them when they're together over there?

How closely can I supervise them when they're together here?

Are his parents of the sort that would be interested in changing their son's behavior?

Is it possible to prepare my son so that he would be less influenced by the other child?

Are there graceful ways to reduce the time they spend together?

How important to us is the relationship with this family?

How important to my son is the relationship with this child?

After the questions have been raised, the next step is to go through them again and think about the answers. And this may trigger more questions to add to the list. If the decision is very important, it will be useful to write down what you know about the answers. If the decision is not as important, it may suffice just to think about the answers to the questions without writing.

Getting More Information

Another decision about the decision should be made at about this time. When the relevant questions have been raised, the next question is, "Can I, and should I, get more information, in any way, that will help me know the answer to this question, and thus make the decision better?" Here is where the "One peek is worth two finesses" strategy comes in.

Here are some examples of getting more information:

Someone who is deciding whether or not to accept a recommendation regarding a surgical operation gets a second opinion from a highly regarded surgeon, and goes to a medical library and reads articles and textbooks about the condition he has.

The person who is worried about the playmate's influence on his or her child invites the playmate to do something with his child and himself, so as to get a bigger sample of the playmate's behavior.

A person who is getting his house remodeled phones the references of prospective remodelers.

A person thinking of using a certain babysitter decides to watch the babysitter interacting with the children for a couple of hours before ever leaving the children alone with the babysitter.

A person who is worried by whether the babysitter is supervising the children adequately decides to come home for brief periods of time unexpectedly to see what is going on at those times.

A couple who disagree with each other about what to do about the child's behavior problems consult an expert on that topic, and ask for readings that shed more light on the topic of how to solve behavior problems.

A doctor who is not sure whether a child needs stimulant medication for hyperactivity gives the drug on some days and gives placebo on other days, and gets behavior ratings done each day by parents and teachers. At the end of the trial he compares the ratings for drug days and placebo days.

A person who is hiring a secretary gives prospective candidates a test in the skills they will need on the particular job they are applying for.

A teacher who is not sure which of two ways of instructing children works the best sets up an experiment in which children are randomly assigned to the two methods. After instructing them, the teacher gives a test to see how well each member of each group learned the things that were taught.

These examples illustrate several ways of getting more information: reading books and articles on the topic, consulting an expert or several experts, getting information from friends or acquaintances, asking systematic questions of the person who wishes to transact something with you, doing an experiment yourself, giving a test, making systematic observations yourself, enlarging the "behavior sample" you have observed.

Brainstorming and Listing Options

Another important part of the decision-making process is brainstorming as you "list options." This means that you address the question, "What could I do in this situation?" It is very helpful at this point to aid your memory with writing. It's also helpful not to censor your options, but to let as many different ideas come into your mind as you can. A wild or unreasonable option might suggest another one that turns out to be just the one you want.

For example: A parent is deciding what to do about his or her child's problems of not doing well in school. After "peeking" at some information by talking with the teacher and talking with the child, the parent lists the following options, some of which are options for "peeks" at more information, and some of which are options for making things better:

Get the child a tutor

Learn how to tutor the child myself

Reward the child with money for doing better

Persuade the teacher to give a daily report card so that I can celebrate days where the child tried hard

Have the child tested to get more information on his or her ability level

Transfer the child to a different school

Transfer the child to a different type of class

Have the child go to school only a half day, to avoid turning him off to academic work even more than he has been, and teach the child at home the rest of the time

Get the child a better table and lamp and quiet work place for him to do his homework

Do some of my work from the office while sitting near him at night, so that he won't be so lonesome while doing his homework

Get a book on study skills, and read it and teach it to him

Consult an expert on whether medication would help the child; read about this question too

Consult a child psychiatrist about how to make things better

Ask other parents about their ideas on how to help the child achieve more, especially the parents of children who are doing well

Explore more with the child whether emotional problems are getting in the way of his schoolwork

A very useful exercise is to take a decision that you are facing, and to list as many options as you can about what to do about it.

Predicting Consequences

Then with options listed, a logical next step is to try to predict the consequences of the options that are being seriously considered.

Here, as in almost all stages of the decision process, there is uncertainty. You can never know with total certainty what will happen if you try a certain option. So for that reason, it's useful to think of several different consequences that may occur for any option you are considering, and to think about how likely each consequence is. It's often important to remind yourself to think of long-run consequences as well as short-run consequences.

For example, a teacher at a preschool sees two children bickering with each other and saying hostile things to each other. The teacher is trying to predict the consequences of going to the two children and directing them to do something that will distract them from their conflict. As the teacher thinks of possible consequences, the following come to mind:

short term:

they will go to the new activity, and their hostility will cease (fairly likely)

they will refuse to go to the new activity, and their hostility will continue (a little less likely)

they will go to the new activity, and another similar conflict will arise very soon (a little less likely)

longer term:

their hostility will be reinforced by my attention to them, and they will have their tendency to be hostile increased (very likely)

they will have less of a chance to practice hostility because I interrupt the activity, and their tendency to be hostile will decrease (somewhat likely)

they will get the message from me that hostility is not acceptable, and this will decrease their tendency to be hostile (somewhat likely)

other children will notice that I pay attention to them for this behavior, and the other children who want my attention will have their tendencies to be hostile increased (fairly likely)

Sometimes when listing possible consequences of an option, it's useful to divide them into positive and negative consequences, or advantages and disadvantages. Sometimes a very useful guide in making a decision is to write down the advantages and disadvantages of each major option you are considering. In the example above, it's not very hard to tell which possible consequences are advantages and which are disadvantages.

In the example above, the teacher judged the likelihood, or the probability, that each consequence would occur, in terms like "very likely" and "fairly likely." There is, of course, a more precise way to do it: using numbers. If I guess that there's a .5 or 50% chance that something will happen, that means that if the situation were repeated over and over, I would expect the thing to happen about half the time. I'm guessing that there is about the same chance of the thing happening as that of getting "heads" when flipping a coin. If I guess that there's a one in six, or one sixth, or 17% chance that something will happen, I'm guessing that there is about the same chance of the thing's happening as that of rolling a "one" when rolling a die.

Why think in terms of numbers, when all you're doing is taking a wild guess anyway? Even a wild guess, when you understand what the guess is, is better than one where you're not sure what's meant. And when you use numbers, you can also think about how "wild" your guess is, how wide your range of confidence is.

Suppose you are thinking of taking a trip in a space shuttle. An engineer tells you, "I think there's a pretty good chance the shuttle will blow up." Suppose instead that the engineer were to tell you, "My best guess is that the chances are 75% that the shuttle will blow up." Which statement gives more information about whether to take the shuttle flight or not?

Summing Outcomes' Utility Times Probability, for Each Option

Once you have predicted consequences and have taken your best guess at how likely each possible consequence is, the next important step in decision-making is to decide how much you like each possible consequence, how much you want or don't want it to happen. The word that has been given to this "goodness" or "badness" of a consequence is "utility." If something is more desirable, more preferable, it has higher utility. It is usually of higher utility to live than to die, to be healthy than to be sick, to get money rather than to lose it, and to experience pleasant things rather than unpleasant things.

Here's a concept very central to living: the idea of making a decision by picking the option with the highest "expected utility."

Expected utility means how good you would expect things to come out, on the average, if you were to do this option many times in just the same circumstances; if you were to let the random elements in the outcome average themselves out over time.

If you know exactly what will happen if you do a certain option, you don't have to do as much calculation. For example, if it's one hundred percent certain that option A will produce a very good outcome, and it's also totally certain that option B will produce a so-so outcome, option A obviously has a higher expected outcome than B. The challenge comes when you aren't certain about the outcomes, but all you can do is estimate probabilities.

For example: you are introduced to a stranger who extends his hand for you to shake. You have a choice of whether to shake the hand or not. If you refuse to shake it, you have a chance of offending the stranger and the person introducing. If you shake it, you have a chance of catching a dreaded illness from him and dying, or of being dragged off and kidnapped or mugged.

Even if you've never heard the formula I'm going to give, you intuitively know how to make such decisions. You have to take into account how likely the different outcomes are, as well as how bad they are. You weight the goodness or badness of each possible outcome for an option by multiplying it by the probability of its actually happening. You do this for the various outcomes possible for each given option, and add them up. This gives the "expected utility" for the option, and the option with the highest expected utility is the one to choose.

Expected utility = sum of (utility of outcome * probability of outcome) for all possible outcomes.

I intuitively think, yes, I could catch a dreaded illness and die, and that would be very bad. But the probability is so low that this takes away very little from the expected utility of the option of shaking hands. I also judge the probability of getting mugged or kidnapped low because I'm much bigger than the stranger and I'm in a crowded public place. If I refuse to shake hands the chance of offending is high, and this takes away a good deal from the option of refusing to shake hands. So I shake the stranger's hand.

Here's another example. Someone offers you a chance to make a bet on a coin flip. If you pick "heads" or "tails" correctly, you win $1. If you pick incorrectly, you lose $10. The chance of your guessing correctly is 50%. Should you make the bet, or shouldn't you? (We'll temporarily forget about your feelings about gambling in general or the long-term consequences of setting a precedent in favor of gambling.)

Without even multiplying probabilities by utilities, this sounds like a bad deal, doesn't it? (When you do multiply probabilities by utilities, you find that if you were to accept this deal many times, you would on the average lose $4.50 each time. You get that by adding a half times 1 and a half times minus 5.) On the other hand, by raising a utility or probability, we can turn it into a good deal. What if your chance of winning, rather than being 50%, were 99.9%? Or what if the amount you would win if you guess right, rather than being one dollar, were a million dollars? Maybe these examples will convince you that if you're like most people, you have been intutively multiplying probabilities by utilities and adding them up all your life, even if you haven't been aware of it.

Here's another example. Suppose that a friend tells you the following. "I've been having some pain. There's an operation that has a good chance of taking away the pain. But there's also a chance that I'll die during the operation. What do you think I should do?" Now what would you want to know before you would have any idea what to advise your friend?

Most people would want to know how bad the pain had been. If it had been very mild, the benefit of relieving it would be smaller; if it had been very severe, the benefit of relieving it would be larger. The "benefit" we are talking about here is a utility. Most people want also want to know, how big is the chance that the operation will relieve the pain? And how big is the chance that you will die? The bigger the chance of relief, and the smaller the chance of death, the better an idea it is to get the operation. These chances are probabilities.

These examples illustrate that in making decisions, most people have some sort of rough way of estimating and calculating with utilities and probabilities, even if they don't use those words.

So what I've said is that in making a decision, you take any given option. You list the possible consequences of that option. You figure out how well you like each consequence, or assign a "utility" to it. You guess how likely it is that that consequence will occur, or assign a probability to it. You give a score to each consequence, that is higher the better that consequence is and the more likely it is to happen—and you do this by multiplying the probability by the utility. Then you add up the score of all the possible consequences of the option, to get a score for that option. Then you do this for any other options, and you pick the option with the highest score.

Does anybody ever really do this in real life? How useful is this way of thinking?

Like most of the things suggested in this decision-making chapter, you don't have do it all the way to benefit from it. Just having the notions of utility and probability in your mind may help you in systematically making a decision. If you have a very important decision to make, you may wish to actually do the multiplying and adding.

In general, I think that this notion of "maximizing the expected utility" is one of the most important and profound principles that anyone has ever figured out. It is worth quite a bit of effort to understand it.

If You Want to Use Numbers: Preference Probabilities To Rate Utility

Now there's one problem. How do you assign numbers to utilities? We know how to assign numbers to probabilities. You just guess how likely a certain consequence is to happen. If you can "peek" at information about this, about what has actually happened when people have tried the option many times, you can make a better guess. But how do you assign numbers to utilities? Here's another idea. It's called a "preference probability," a way of measuring utility.

Let's suppose that you are deciding whether to get an operation. To simplify things let's suppose that it's absolutely certain that this operation will relieve all your pain. It's absolutely certain that if you don't get the operation, you will continue to have pain at the same level it is now. The only problem with the operation is that it might kill you. (We assume you'd rather stay in pain than die.)

There are three possible consequences. You can keep the same level of pain you've got, you can be totally relieved of pain, or you can die. How do you assign utilities to these consequences?

A useful approach is to anchor yourself by the best and worst alternatives in the decision. In this situation, dying is worst. Let's assign the number 0 to it. Being totally relieved of pain is best. Let's assign the number 1, or 100%, to it.

Now, what number do we assign to the utility of staying in pain? It's better than dying, and worse than getting total relief. Thus it's somewhere between 0 and 100%, but where? Here's a way to assign the number. Suppose that we offered you a lottery. We take 100 cards and put them into a hat. We write "pain relief" on some of them, and "die" on the rest of them. Which would you rather do: keep your pain, or take your chances at the lottery? Maybe your pain is so bad that you would take your chances on the lottery if you had only a 10% chance or better of getting pain relief. If so, we could say that .1, or 10%, is the utility of living with the pain. On the other hand, let's say the pain were mild enough or that you are good enough at standing pain that you would not want to risk the lottery for anything less than a 99% chance of getting rid of the pain. In that case, 99%, or .99, is the utility of living with the pain.

What you do in this process then, is to define the utility of all consequences between the best and the worst one. You do this by imagining a gamble between the best and worst consequence, and asking yourself what probability of getting the best consequence would make the gamble an even swap with the intermediate consequence.

Let's go back to that operation. How does assigning these utilities help you decide?

Let's say the person decides that he hurts bad enough that taking a gamble on living without pain versus dying would be an even swap with living with the pain, if the odds of living were 80% or greater. He then "peeks" at information, by asking his doctor, reading articles, or whatever other means, and assures himself that in fact the probability of his living is 98%. When he multiplies probabilities by utilities he gets an expected utility of .98 for getting the operation, (1 utility of pain relief times .98 probability of this consequence, plus 0 utility of dying times .02 probability of dying) and an expected utility of .80 for refusing the operation (1 probability of living with pain if no operation, times .80 utility of this consequence). Thus he's better off getting the operation.

Someone may say, I don't see why these "preference probabilities" are necessary. He decided he wanted the operation if the chances were greater than 80%, and they were, so he got it. Why do you need to multiply things out? You could do it without multiplying things out for such a simple situation. But if there are more outcomes and the situation gets more complex, you can't keep track of it all without multiplying things out.

Using Rating Scales

Now let's go to a different sort of problem in assigning utilities. Here the problem is that there are different aspects of a given consequence, and you want to decide how to weight them.

For example, you are trying to decide which child-care worker (a.k.a. babysitter) to hire, out of several different possibilities. A number of different aspects of such a person are desirable to you. You think about one person, and how the person is very enthusiastic, and you lean toward choosing that person. Then you think of another person, and how that person is probably more mature and less impulsive, you lean toward choosing that person. You think of another person, and the fact that this person charges less attracts you. When you think of certain aspects, you lean in one direction, and when you think of others, you lean in another direction. The problem is that your memory can't hold all aspects of each consequence in mind all at the same time.

A solution to this problem is to make for yourself a rating scale. This is to look like the rating scales used for research purposes. You have one item on the scale for each important aspect of the situation you're evaluating.

Here's a sample rating scale that may be made up by our hypothetical searcher for a child-care worker.

My Child-Care Worker Search Rating Scale
0=Very Bad
2=Bad
4=So-so
6=OK
8=Good
10=Very Good

_____ Enthusiastic and fun way of dealing with child
_____ Big repertoire of mutually gratifying activities with child
_____ Child seems to have positive feelings about person
_____ Quality of conversation, language use modeled for the child
_____ Kindness
_____ Knowledge of safety precautions
_____ Knowledge of first aid techniques
_____ Nonimpulsiveness, good judgment
_____ Honesty
_____ Refrains from unnecessary directives
_____ Good at responsive interactions
_____ Uses appropriate assertion
_____ Ease of transportation to and from here
_____ Price the person charges
_____ Wide range of times available
_____ Uses differential attention and excitement well

The simplest way is to use a scale like this is to assign a rating to each item, add up the scores, and pick the option with the highest score. This method makes every item just as important as every other. Research has found that this simple method usually works just about as well as adjusting the weights of the items so that the ones that are more important get weighted more heavily.

Suppose that when you simply add up the ratings, you have the gut feeling that you like a different option better, one that didn't get the highest score? Then maybe you need to make the rating scale more precise by assigning different weights to the items, according to their importance. Each item score will be multiplied by the weight when the total score is calculated. The more important items will have higher weights, so that they will contribute more to the total score. Let's say that our searcher for a child care worker decides that "price the person charges" is least important. This item gets an arbitrary weight of 1. All the other items will be weighted according to how much more important they are than the person's wage. Knowledge of safety precautions gets weighted 4 times as high, as does honesty; appropriate assertion skills gets weighted 2 times as high. Now our searcher notices that safety precautions are weighted twice as important as assertion skills; if this still rings true, then the weights are left as they are; if not, they are adjusted.

Then he scores the scale again, this time multiplying each item score by its weight and adding up all the products. He picks the option with the highest score. Again, if the option with the highest score somehow doesn't seem most desirable to him, he fiddles with the weights and the ratings until the total scores are in accord with his feelings.

One may ask, if he's going to go with his gut feelings, why go through this process in the first place? The process of figuring out the important aspects of the situation, assigning the proper weight for each aspect, and rating each choice according to those aspects and summing the score may change his gut feelings, because it causes him to focus systematically on first one, then another of the important aspects of the choices.

You can use a rating scale for most other sorts of decisions: buying a car, hiring an employee, choosing a job, deciding whether or not to have another child, or even choosing a spouse. (When Elizabeth Browning wrote the poem that started "How do I love thee? Let me count the ways," could she have been referring to a rating scale?)

What if there are not a bunch of other options for comparison? For example, suppose someone gets only one job offer, and is choosing whether or not to take it? It still helps, in evaluating an option, to have some standards for comparison, even if at this moment they are only hypothetical, if similar options will present themselves later. The person evaluating a job offer may compare it to all other jobs he has had.

Including Precedent-Setting As Part of Outcomes

When evaluating the utilities of consequences, there is one aspect that is often overlooked. People often overlook the consequence of the option on the precedents they set for their own behavior and for other people's behavior. If the option involves violating some important principle, undermining the precedent of that principle can be harmful even though the other consequences of the action are positive.

For example: A person knows that he can drink alcohol in moderation and not suffer ill consequences. However, he takes into account in his decision making the precedent he sets for other people who admire him, including his children; he is not so sure that alcohol will never be a problem for them. When he takes into account the chance that he could set a precedent for them that drug use is permissible, he decides not to use alcohol.

A person calculates that if he were to cheat on his income tax return, he could claim ignorance of the situation if he were audited, and would lose nothing more than having to pay the back taxes. If on the other hand he is not audited, he saves the money he does not pay. So far, the utility equation seems to be in favor of cheating. However, when he takes into account the fact that by cheating he is undermining his own habit of honesty and is weakening a personal precedent for honesty that he might have had, this consideration shifts the balance in favor of paying the extra tax.

A legislator is deciding about laws regarding euthanasia. It appears that there are some cases of terminal and painful illness where actively giving drugs to end someone's life is the most merciful thing to do. On the other hand, allowing this may undermine society's precedent against murder. When this aspect of the outcome is taken into account, the decision is not so easy.

Satisficing Versus Optimizing

How should one make low stakes decisions? What about the choice of which envelopes to buy, which parking place to take, whether to get red apples or golden apples, and so forth?

Some useful concepts in thinking about decisions are "optimizing" and "satisficing." Optimizing means that you go through the process of generating all the options you can, gathering information, predicting consequences, estimating utilities, and choosing an option by maximizing the expected utility. Optimizing means trying to pick the very best option. The only trouble with optimizing is that it takes time and energy. But if the decision is important, time invested in optimizing may be the best time you can spend.

Satisficing, on the other hand, is a strategy for less important decisions. When you satisfice, you search through options until you come to the first one that is "good enough." You then stop searching, enact the option, and get on with the next thing in life.

Here are some examples of satisficing. A person is in a town on a business trip. He wants to get a quick lunch at a restaurant while he is planning important things that will go on in the afternoon. He walks down the street until he finds the first restaurant that looks acceptable. Without gathering any more information on any other options, without rating any of those options on the ten aspects of restaurants he finds desirable, he sits down in the restaurant. He looks quickly at the menu; he stops reading as soon as he sees something that looks acceptable, and he orders it for lunch.

A mother is picking out a story to read to her child. She looks through the books until she finds one that she feels like reading, and without bothering to compare it to all the other books, she says, "Here's a good one!"

Two people are spending an afternoon together, and they are deciding what to do. One scans through options in his mind; the first option that strikes him as fun is to go for a walk in the park. He suggests that. It's also a "good enough" option for the other person, and they do it without contrasting it to all other possible options.

Satisficing is one way not to spend a lot of time and energy on a decision. Another way is doing abbreviated optimizing. You can list some options, not necessarily all possible ones. You can think about the most likely consequences, not all possible ones. You can make an intuitive appraisal of utilities rather than using preference probabilities or a rating scale. You can spend no time peeking at new information. The principle to keep in mind is that you want to spend time and energy in proportion to how much the decision deserves it.

The Small Sample Size Error

Errors in decision-making can be committed by spending too much, or not enough, time and energy on a decision relative to what the decision deserves. The person who obsesses over what color scarf to buy, or the person who quits his job in a moment of anger at his boss, is likely to be making this type of error.

Even when the decision is carefully considered, a frequent error is making a conclusion based on too small a sample of data, i.e. not enough peeks.

A person concludes on the basis of one thirty-minute interview, and a great deal of thought, that someone is a wonderful candidate for a job. A person concludes on the basis of knowing someone for a month that that person is a wonderful marriage partner. A doctor decides after trying a medication with a child for one day that the medication is not helping and discontinues it. Someone knows one person who had an operation, and suffered no ill effects of it; the person concludes that the operation is very safe. Someone is cheated by a person of a certain race, and concludes that all people of that race are dishonest. Someone's Aunt Hattie smoked a pack of cigarettes a day and lived to be 90; the person concludes that smoking is safe. These are all examples of the "too small a sample size" error. No amount of thinking can substitute for adequate numbers of data points in making a conclusion.

The Sunk Costs Error

Another interesting error is the failure to ignore "sunk costs." Sunk costs are the time, money, and effort that have been put into something so far, that will never be recoverable no matter what option you choose. Because they are the same for all options, they help you in no way in making the decision, and should be ignored.

For example, suppose that a person buys a movie ticket, not knowing much about the movie. He intensely dislikes very violent movies. After the first fifteen minutes of the movie, he can tell that this one is very violent, and he hates watching it. He overhears someone who has already seen it, who says things that confirm his impression that it will continue to be this violent. We assume that he cannot get a refund.

Should he walk out? He calculates that he will very much more enjoy his time if he does than if he doesn't. He decides that leaving will maximize utility relative to staying. Therefore he should leave.

But wait. We don't know how much he paid to get into the movie. If he paid nothing, he would feel no hesitation in leaving. Suppose, instead, that he paid 10 dollars for this performance. He thinks, "If I leave I will just be throwing away 10 dollars."

If he lets this thought influence him, he is making the "sunk costs" error. The essential point is that at the time of his decision point, his $10 is already lost no matter what he does. Whether he had paid $500 or $1, that money is gone. The only question now is whether he wants to spend the remaining time of the movie doing something more valuable, or something less valuable to him. A good way of putting his decision is, "Would you rather pay $10 to do something you don't like, or pay $10 to do something you like better?" He will be rational to forget about what he paid to get in, and walk out.

Here's another example of the "sunk costs" notion. A person owns shares of stock, that have gone down in price. She is trying to decide whether to hold them or sell them. She concludes that the money she could recover by selling now she will probably grow more in some other investment, and she decides to sell. But someone says to her, "How much did you pay for the stock?... You've lost money? If you sell now you'll lock in your loss. Are you sure you don't want to hang on longer? It's likely to go up eventually."

If she lets this sort of thinking influence her, she is making the sunk costs error. The money that she paid for the stock is a sunk cost, no matter what she does. The only question is whether the money recoverable now would be employed in this stock or somewhere else.

Here's another example. A nation is fighting a war. As people study the situation more, they realize that fighting the war was not a good decision in the first place. More to the point, they realize that the losses that they would entail from now on by continuing to fight would exceed the gains that they and other people would get by continuing to fight. This is true, people decide, even if you take into account the undesirability of the precedent of failing to finish something that was started with a great show of commitment.

But when it is proposed that they simply pull out their troops and stop fighting, some people argue "But we've already lost thousands of lives in this war. If we pull out now, those lives will have been wasted."

If the country decides to keep fighting on this basis, it is making the "sunk costs" error. The lives that have been lost have been lost whether or not the fighting continues.

Postdecisional Regret and Bolstering

Postdecisional regret occurs when someone makes a decision and does something to signal a commitment to it. As soon as the commitment is made, all the disadvantages of the options decided upon come into great prominence in the person's mind, and he regrets his decision.

Some people get into a habit of postdecisional regret so strong that they can predict that whatever decision they make, they will regret it afterward. Since the expectation is of regret, some people with this pattern fear making decisions, and tend to postpone them whenever possible. The decision process is very painful if this pattern is strong enough.

Bolstering is the opposite. When a person makes a decision, sometimes he then successfully convinces himself that the option he picked was obviously the best one, or only good one. He is much more confident after making the commitment than before. After making the decision he is sold on all the advantages, and ignores the disadvantages. He has an advantage of not being plagued by doubts as he does the work necessary to enact the course of action he decided upon.

Is postdecisional regret always bad, and is bolstering always good? Not necessarily. If someone made a bad decision that further information reveals all the more clearly to have been a bad decision, bolstering can distort the truth and keep someone on an unwise course. Postdecisional regret can work on the side of rationality when further information, or more careful reexamination of the information, reveals that the decision was wrong.

Too much bolstering leads a person to be set in his ways and stubborn; too much postdecisional regret leads a person to be wishy-washy and tormented.

Here's a technique that people can use when making a decision that may help them avoid too much postdecisional regret and too much bolstering after the decision is made. The technique is very vividly to project yourself into the future, in your imagination. Imagine that a certain alternative has been chosen, and that a firm commitment to it has been made. Imagine the setting you will be in, and the other people who will be in the setting; imagine yourself doing the things you will be doing. Create as detailed a "movie" as you possibly can about the ways things will go if you decide upon the option. It may be useful to use writing as an aid to memory, and to write your own description, your own movie script. If in your movie your natural tendency toward postdecisional regret or bolstering starts to come forth, you know you are doing a vivid job of imagining.

Having done this, then do the same thing with the other option. Create just as vivid an image of what will happen with this option. Let the movie go in as great detail as you can. Note your feelings in this situation. If you feel postdecisional regret or bolstering operating, take note of it.

Then come back to reality and remember your movies. Did postdecisional regret operate in both, so that for each option you ended up wishing you'd taken the other? Did bolstering operate in both, so that for each option you felt like this was by far the best choice to have made and that there could never be a good argument for deviating from it?

If you decide that you are overusing postdecisional regret or bolstering, you can set as a goal for yourself not distorting the truth so much. You can consciously try to focus your attention more on the advantages of the decision you made (if you are trying to do less postdecisional regret) or to focus your attention more on the criteria that would make you reverse your course (if you are trying to do less bolstering). You can monitor how well you are able to change your postdecision patterns. You can celebrate to yourself when you are able to do more as you want to do.

What if when you do your mental movies, you decide that both options will work out just fine, and that both will lead to happy, but different, outcomes? This prediction may often be true. Fortunately, there are very often many right answers to a decision. Sometimes if someone is equipped with an optimistic and cheerful spirit and a willingness to work to make things better, he or she can make the best of many different decisions. However, sometimes some options make it very difficult for the heartiest spirit to remain hearty.

When the Problem is Enacting the Decision, Not Making It

Suppose that someone has made all sorts of good decisions. He's decided to quit smoking, to avoid yelling at his child when he misbehaves in order not to reinforce him with excitement, and to get to bed early enough that he's not irritable the next day. His problem is doing these things that he's decided to do. He just doesn't do them, even though he's unwavering in his decision that they are best.

If the problem is enacting the decision rather than making it, the "methods of influence axis" is useful to think about. The methods of influencing a child are the same ones you can use to influence yourself. For example, affirming to yourself repeatedly that the new pattern is your goal, setting up a hierarchy of small steps toward the goal, reinforcing yourself for moving closer to the goal, enlisting the aid of other people in reinforcing you for steps toward the goal, monitoring your own progress, making the stimulus situations more conducive to progress, reading instructional materials that remind you how to make progress, repetitively practicing the desired pattern in fantasy and role-playing as well as real life, and observing models of the desired pattern are likely to help you carry out the pattern you have decided upon.

Here's a summary of the decision-making techniques recommended here.

1. Make a decision about how much effort and energy this decision requires.
2. On very important decisions, write your thoughts, to keep up with them in all stages of the decision process.
3. Start with a concise description of the situation and the goal and the choices and what is at stake.
4. Be careful not to avoid decisions about your goals and your use of time.
5. List questions, the answers to which would give you more information with which to make an important decision.
6. Seek the answers to those questions, by reading, asking questions, and making observations, so as to get information that will help you with the decision.
7. Brainstorm options for what to do about the situation, without censoring them.
8. Try to predict the consequences of the most prominent options.
9. When predicting consequences, give thought to long-run consequences as well as short-run consequences, and to precedents and habits as well as effects on this situation only.
10. Get in the habit of guessing the probability that a certain consequence will occur, expressed in numbers.
11. Rate the utility of the various consequences. "Preference probability" is a way of rating the utility of outcomes other than the best and worst. A preference probability is the odds of getting the best outcome, rather than the worst, that you think would make an even swap between taking a gamble on the best or worst and taking the intermediate one.
12. Pick the option with the highest expected utility. Expected utility is a sum you get by taking the utility of each consequence, multiplying it by its prob-

ability, and adding up those products for all possible consequences.
13. To help yourself weight all the important aspects when judging the utility of an outcome, make up a rating scale for yourself, and get a summary score for each outcome. Most of the time you can just add up the scores for each item; sometimes you will want to weight the items so that some are more important than others.
14. On unimportant decisions or decisions where there is a great deal of time pressure, you may wish to "satisfice," or take the first acceptable option you come across. Or, you may wish to do a much abbreviated version of the "optimizing" process described above.
15. Make sure that on important decisions you get enough data before deciding.
16. Don't let "sunk costs" influence you when deciding what's the best course of action.
17. If you find that you have a prevailing pattern of too much postdecisional regret, or too much bolstering, try to change these patterns over time, the same way you try to change any other habit.
18. Make mental movies of your guess of what outcomes certain options will lead to. Notice your tendency toward postdecisional regret or bolstering and practice in fantasy using less of those patterns if you decide that's what's best.
19. If the problem is getting yourself to enact the decision you know to be best, use the techniques of self-influence listed in the methods of influence axis.
20. Keep in mind that for some decisions, there are many right answers, meaning many options that will lead to a happy outcome given a cheerful and optimistic and hard-working attitude.

Chapter 17: Joint Decision-Making

Chapter Overview:

When people decide together what to do, they are doing joint decision-making, or conflict resolution. If you want the best relationships among people in your family, everyone should learn these skills. Part of the way to make joint decisions is simply to use the same techniques I discussed in the previous chapter, for individual decisions. People can help each other generate options, predict consequences, and judge how well they like outcomes. But there's much more to it than that. Here are some other guidelines for joint decisions and conflicts. Deal with conflicts as they come up, one at a time, rather than allowing too many unsolved frustrations to build up on the agenda. Keep in mind that the goal is solving the problem, not getting anger "out." Form the mental image of two people on the same team, working together to land upon the best solution to the problem, rather than on opposite teams working against each other. Often reflect the other person's point of view, making sure you understand it right, and letting the other person know his points are being understood. Slow down the rhythm of the conversation, so that you don't interrupt each other, and even spend time thinking in silence before replying. This process takes patience, but it's better to get somewhere slowly than to get nowhere fast. Often summarize what the two people agree on, and seek to enlarge those areas of agreement. At the beginning, think of interests rather than positions. To do this, define the problem in some way other than by demanding one certain solution. Exercise judgment about when to tolerate the other person's behavior and not engage in conflict-resolution conversation at all. Focus on improving the future, not blaming for the past. Use writing as an aid in memory, especially in complex joint-decisions. In addition to these guidelines, think of the following: (1) Defining. Each person defines the problem, without blaming the other or telling the solution. (2) Reflecting. Each person reflects the other's point of view. (3) Listing. They list at least 4 options. (4) Waiting. They don't criticize options until they're through listing. (5) Advantages. They consider the advantages and disadvantages of the best options. (6) Agreeing. They pick an option to try. (7) Politeness. They don't raise their voices or insult each other or interrupt. Merely reviewing such guidelines is not enough; repetitive practice with hypothetical and then real problems will help the family change its customs.

****

The previous chapter talked about how one person can make rational decisions. This chapter deals with two-person problems: situations where two people decide jointly on options that affect them both.

The process of conflict-resolution literally makes the difference, daily, between life and death. In teaching conflict-resolution, I have often asked people to practice with conflicts written about in the newspaper which in real life resulted in a murder of one of the individuals. But conflict-resolution is important for an even more prevalent reason. The way in which conflicts get resolved in any family, workplace, or other organization has is one of the main determinants of how people feel about each other, the interpersonal environment. Do people feel chronically angry at one another? Do they come to dislike or hate each other? Do they have a motivation to do things together, or to avoid each other and escape to a separate subculture (e.g. the drug-using youth subculture)?

There have been several books written on the process of negotiation, problem-solving, and conflict-resolution between people. One of them that I wrote, entitled *Talking It Out: A Guide to Effective Communication and Problem-Solving*, goes into detail in classifying the types of messages that people send and receive during conflict-resolution conversations. The plan of this chapter is to summarize some of major guidelines about problem-solving, and then to present some scripts that purport to model a process whereby problems are approached rationally. Systematic and thorough study of the process of rational problem-solving can reap great rewards.

Seeing Conflict Resolution as Joint Decision-Making

Conflict resolution or two-person problem solving involves the same process of decision-making as was outlined in the previous chapter, only two people participate together. Ideally, they pool their knowledge and creativity to make a decision together. Getting information, brainstorming options, predicting consequences, estimating probabilities, and assigning utilities of outcomes is a very rational, intellectualized activity. But calculated thinking helps to produce good decisions.

Beware the Catharsis Theory, But Avoid Buildup of Frustration

As mentioned in earlier chapters, the catharsis theory is that you have to get your anger "out." However, the anger that one "gets out" at the other is likely to make the other more angry, in an escalating spiral. Anger is something one does and not something one has; one can decide not to do it; in joint decision-making it is usually wise not to do much of it.

There are various kernels of truth in the catharsis idea, however, which explain why the idea does not die. One such kernal is that in families, where people's irritating or disturbing behavior is often repeated many times over, it is often useful to make joint decisions before the memory of many such situations has built up so high that it is difficult to contain one's anger. It is useful to make joint decisions about little issues peacemeal rather than letting them coalesce into major dissatisfactions. For example, it is easier to make a joint decision on "How should we spend the next week end" rather than "You never have spent enough time with your family." It's easier to come to a joint decision on "What should be our routine about washing dishes" than "There has never been any organized system of housekeeping in this household, and it drives me nuts!" I would argue that what is building up when problems are swept under the rug is not anger itself, but the memory of unsolved problems; the larger that mass becomes, the larger the anger when someone reviews them.

People Versus the Problem, and Not Against Each Other

In most conflict situations, people see themselves as in competition with the other person. Who will win? Or will there be a compromise? How much of the pie will one or the other person get? There are many situations where such a view is by and large correct. But in families, people sink or swim together. That which makes one person very unhappy usually gets back to make another unhappy sooner or later. There is a way of viewing problems that is far superior to the competitive model. In this view, the situation provides constraints, and the two people have to work together to find the best option. Given the constraints of the problem, there exist various options for handling it; each of those options makes a certain addition or subtraction to the long-term utility of each person involved. How close can the two people come to the option that maximizes total long-term utility? The two people are cooperating to find the best option they can, rather than fighting each other.

If people can view the problem in this way, they will tend to focus on solving the problem, and not on attack and defense of people. They will discuss advantages and disadvantages of options, not the good and bad points of the other person. They will try to locate disagreement in their understandings of what an option entails, and in issues of predicting outcomes or valuing consequences, rather than in the features of the other person's personality.

Empathic Reflections Can Turn Away Wrath

In the chapter on conversation with the child we defined a reflection as an utterance where someone listens carefully to what the other person says, and paraphrases it to make sure she heard it correctly, for example by saying, "So what I hear you saying is __________."

Here's an example of a reflection.

First person: Why do we have to go over to your mother's again? We never do anything fun.

Second person: So you're saying that all the time at my mother's isn't enjoyable for you, and it's taking away from other things you'd like to do?

Here's an example of not using a reflection:

First person: Why do we have to go over to your mother's again? We never do anything fun.

Second person: You don't seem to understand how much my mother needs for me to be there now.

Empathic reflections can reduce unnecessary anger. This is because usually in heated arguments there are two sources of frustration and anger: one is whatever the argument is about, and the second is that one can't seem to get the other person to hear the point one is making. In the first example above, the second person was willing to hear the first person's point, and wait until later to make her own point; in the second example, the second person couldn't wait. In the second example there are likely to be two competitions at once: the first is over how often there are trips to the mother's house, and the second is over whose point gets attention first.

The Time Rhythms of Rational Conflict-Resolution

If you listen to most heated arguments, you get the feeling that there is a huge rush, that time is running out and there is none to spare. People interrupt each other because they just can't wait to make the point that's on their mind. They speak quickly. There's no silence between people's utterances. It's as though there was a deadline for the solution of this problem, and it's already passed.

The trouble with this sort of rhythm in the conversation is that there is little time to listen, and little time to think. People stimulate each other to greater anger, and don't allow each other the time to cool off and think calming thoughts. It represents being "penny wise and pound foolish" regarding time expenditure on conflict resolution. If an issue is important enough for people to get upset with each other about, then it's important enough to allocate enough time to approach it patiently.

It takes time to stop and remind oneself that the end of the world will not occur if this conflict doesn't get resolved one's own way. It takes time to make sure one understands the information coming from the other person. It takes time and patience to generate creative options for solving the problem at hand, and time to think carefully about the probable outcomes of those options. If these activities are to be done at all, the required time must be allocated to them.

Some people object that the process of rational joint decision-making is too time-consuming. But it makes much more sense to move forward slowly than to move backward quickly. And it makes more sense to spend time on joint decision-making than to spend large amounts of time and money on divorce or meetings about children's misbehavior or other side effects of poor conflict-resolution. Rational conflict-resolution may feel like a slow and tedious process sometimes, especially when one is used to a much faster rhythm. But it is infinitely less wasteful of time, in the long run, than is irrational conflict-resolution.

If people want to resolve conflict expertly, they should get in mind a rhythm where people don't interrupt each other, and where in fact there is some thinking-silence after each utterance. The rhythm for each person is listening, thinking, speaking, and thinking. The more time in the conversation you allocate to thinking, the better.

Look For the Areas of Agreement, and Enlarge Them If Possible

Sometimes people see the cup as 90% empty when it is 90% full. For example, Steve and Cindy Jones are each concerned about exposures to violent images; they agree that their son Paul should not own a videogame player, and that there should not be television reception in the house. They agree that each of the videos they have bought for him to watch are of positive influence. They disagree about what to do about letting him visit a friend where the television is constantly playing in the background. They both agree that this is a problem and that they would rather not have it occur; one feels that the benefit of visiting this friend outweighs the cost, whereas the other does not.

When reviewed in this way, it appears that this couple is of remarkable unanimity about the issue of violent entertainment. However, in the moment of a heated discussion about the particular area of disagreement, that area of disagreement can seem to enlarge to take up the whole psychological space, and the areas of agreement can be overlooked. The other person can be seen as adversary rather than ally.

There have been instances in which divorcing couples have in general agreed about the terms of property settlement, about how the children should be treated, about how custody should in general be shared; but because there was not agreement about the particular times of transfer of the children, an adversarial quality grew up, and the areas of disagreement grew and grew.

For this reason, third party mediators in disputes have found it useful to write down what the areas of agreement are between the two parties, and frequently to review those areas. Very frequently people will agree on the general goals of the decision. Reviewing the areas of agreement can have a major positive psychological effect.

Focus on Interests and Don't Get Locked Prematurely into Positions

The "interest" of a person is what really maximizes long-term utility, what makes the person happier, the general goal of the person. The "position" is a stance in a negotiation of saying, "I deserve to have this particular option." A classic story about the difference involves two people who both wish to have a portion of an orange. One feels a greater right to it, and wants a 60-40 split; the other wants a 50-50 split. These are positions. But then someone explores with the people what their interests are. What do they plan to do with the orange? One plans to use the orange peel to make a cake, and the other plans to eat the fruit. As soon as they think of their interests rather than their positions, a new way of resolving the conflict becomes apparent; the solution where one gets the peel and the other gets the rest will produce a "win-win" solution instead of a compromise.

Here's another example of positions versus interests. Two countries are negotiating about disarmament, and one country takes a stand for at least 10 inspections a year, whereas the other wants a maximum of 3. Yet neither side has defined exactly what an "inspection" consists of, who will do it, and how it will be carried out. The two sides become prematurely locked into their positions about how many inspections, and lose sight of their interests, which are the security of knowing some things about what the other side is doing and the privacy of not having certain information revealed to them.

Let's look at some other examples. A parent and teenager are in conflict about the teenager's messy room. The parent's interest is that the teenager become skilled at organization, so that he can be successful in life. The teenager's interest is in getting independent enough from the parent that he will feel comfortable in moving out of the house soon. If these are the interests, there are ways of achieving each of them other than through the issue of cleaning the room, more ways for each party to gain satisfaction, and thus more ways for a successful resolution of the conflict.

A husband and a wife are in conflict over who should sweep up the dust in the house. The interest of the wife, it turns out, is not the minutes of labor involved in carrying out this particular chore, but the symbolic acknowledgement from the husband of how much work she is already contributing to the household. The interest of the husband is not getting exposed to the dust involved in this particular task, which activates his allergies. Once they name and recognize their interests, they can figure out a different task (e.g. doing the tax-related paperwork, taking out the garbage) that will be a win-win solution.

The less the interests of the two people are in conflict with each other, the more possible it is to arrive at a win-win solution. The more the interests are directly in conflict, the more necessary it is for compromise or for one person to sacrifice for the other. A husband and wife, for example, are in conflict over spending versus saving. It turns out that the interest of the wife is a greater long-term security and less present gratification. The interest of the husband is more present gratification and less long-term security. Sometimes interests are directly opposed, and there is no getting around that. However, in families, there is an overriding interest in preserving harmony between family members, which can prevail over any particular interest, as long as one person is not consistently the sacrificial lamb.

Sometimes Toleration, Not Conflict-Resolution, is Called For

It irritates person A that person B jiggles his foot while sitting. Should person A exercise conflict-resolution skills, and negotiate with person B? Or should person A exercise toleration skills, and learn not to worry about a behavior that doesn't tangibly harm him in any way? I think he should exercise toleration, and turn the attention to something more worthwhile to worry about. You may disagree with me about this example (perhaps depending upon whether you are a foot-jiggler like I am). The point is that if people negotiate every little habit of the other person that is unpreferable to them, and seek to change habits that are often very difficult for the other person to change, they set themselves up for disappointment and frustration.

Focus on Improving the Future, Not Blaming for the Past

In rational conflict-resolution, people are very future-oriented, talking about what they can do to make things better in the future, rather than talking about whose fault it was that something went badly in the past. What has happened in the past is already done and unalterable. Does this mean that it should be forgotten about and not mentioned? Sometimes. Sometimes, on the other hand, figuring out how somebody's behavior caused something bad to happen helps in learning from the experience, and bettering the future. People don't need to shy away from the hard fact that something they've done has been a mistake or harmful, when that fact helps to improve the future. The important point is that analyzing past mistakes is useful only insofar as it improves the future. Recasting thinking toward the goal of improving the future—rather than getting caught up in assigning blame for the past as an end in itself—can represent a new and liberating way of thinking about problem situations.

Use Writing as an Aid to Memory

In the previous chapter I spoke of using writing as a way of aiding memory when making complex decisions. When two people make complex decisions together, the same notion holds. If people really brainstorm about a problem, they may come up with many possible options, some of which may be forgotten if they are not written down. It may be useful to make a rating scale for the various options, as suggested in the last chapter. Like arithmetic problems, life problems often require an aid to memory.

Joint Decision-Making Criteria

In learning and practicing the fine art of joint decision-making, keep in mind the following seven criteria.

Checklist for Joint Decision-Making

1. Defining. Each person defines the problem from his or her point of view, without blaming, and without telling what the solution should be.

2. Reflecting. Each person reflects to let the other person know he understands the other person's point of view.

3. Listing. They list at least 4 options.

4. Waiting. They don't criticize the options till they've finished listing.

5. Advantages. They think and talk about the advantages and disadvantages of the best options.

6. Agreeing. They pick an option to try.

7. Politeness. They don't raise their voices or put each other down or interrupt.

The habit of speaking about problems in this way is extremely worthwhile.

To introduce or define the problem without blaming or dictating the solution is often the hardest step. Introducing a joint decision in this way helps people to be rational and to think of interests rather than positions.

Taking the time to use reflections to make sure you understand the other person's point of view promotes self-restraint, and reduces misunderstanding.

Why at least four options? And why not discuss them as soon as they are put onto the table rather than after all are listed? Because doing these things makes people less possessive of a certain option. At the moment that I put an option on the table, I somewhat possess it, but not fully. Then when the other person criticizes it, and I defend it, there is much more sense of possession. The more attacking and defending takes place, the more the two people get locked into positions. On the other hand, when both brainstorm about options for as long as they can, and each puts more than one option on the table, there is no one option that is either's "baby." Sometimes people even forget who suggested a particular option. The more obvious reason for listing many options, and for postponing the evaluation until the listing is over, is that when more options get listed, there is a greater chance of finding a creative one that will be an agreeable solution.

Speaking about the advantages and disadvantages of options, rather than the good and bad points of the other person's personality, helps keep the decision in the realm of rational evaluation rather than combat.

Entering the conversation with the expectation that there will be agreement upon something helps to increase morale. Sometimes the agreement is only to gather more information or to postpone a decision, but this is better than no agreement at all.

Politeness, as operationalized by not raising the voice, not interrupting, and not insulting the other person, enables people to preserve an emotional climate where rational choice is possible. When politeness starts to disintegrate, it is usually time for the two people to attempt to agree on postponing communication until they have both cooled off.

Is it necessary to meet each of these criteria to be successful in solving problems in real life? Of course not. But there is evidence that effective problem-solving conversations tend to resemble this process more than they resemble the disorganized arguments that are on the other end of the spectrum. The more of these criteria are met, the more likely the conflict is to be solved in a satisfying way. If your family has very successful problem-solving using some other process, more power to you. If you want to improve the process, you might give these a try.

Experience also suggests that one person can unilaterally move the process of a conversation toward the meeting of these criteria. The more rational one person is, the more the other tends to be.

Learning to Have Rational Joint Decision Making Conversations

The skill of joint decision-making and conflict resolution is learned just as any other; the nine methods of influence all are helpful. In particular: the more models of rational conflict-resolution conversations you can hear and see and experience, the easier it will be to enact them. The more you can practice such conversations, the stronger the habit will become. And the more people can reinforce each other for behaving this way in real life, the more likely they will be to do it again.

The rest of this chapter consists primarily of some modeling scripts of rational problem-solving conversations. I highly recommend getting the format and rhythm and feeling of such conversations thoroughly into your memory bank. If you can record such conversations onto audiotape and listen to them while driving, you and other family members can acquire an "ear" for them.

Here's an option to consider strongly. When two family members resolve a conflict in an unsatisfactory way, (for example by getting extremely angry and yelling) that conflict gets written down on the list. It is then the responsibility of the family members to construct a rational problem-solving conversation similar to the ones below, to tape record that conversation, and to listen to it several times. This is the form of "consequence" for maladaptive

behavior mentioned in a previous chapter when speaking of the 4 r's (taking responsibility, making restitution, redeciding on a better way, and rehearsing the better way). Making the new conversation and listening to it repeatedly constitutes the redecision and rehearsal.
****

The Modeling Scripts

The problem is that the son is starting to use profane words at home; neither of the parents likes this.
Father: I want to discuss with you what we talked about earlier today, about our son's swearing. I think we need to make a plan about this that both of us can feel comfortable with.
Mother: OK, now is a good time for me to think and talk about this. He has been doing it more often lately, I'd say about once a day for the last week. It bothers me when he talks like that, and it worries me that he's going to get into bad habits. I think we want to get it so that he almost never swears, particularly when he's with adults.
Father: You're saying that he's doing it more often, and it bothers you to hear it, and you're also worried that this habit will cause him problems with other people. You want him to get rid of it almost altogether, especially when he's with adults.
Mother: Yes.
Father: My point of view is that I would rather he didn't do it also. It bothers me less than it does you, I think. I think that he may be able to swear sometimes, and not do it when it's important not to, just like most people I know. But like you, I guess I'd rather he didn't do it at all.
Mother: So you aren't as bothered as I am by it, and you think he may be able to learn to turn it on and off depending on where he is. But it still bothers you, and you would rather he didn't do it.
Father: Yes.
Mother: Shall we think of some options of what to do?
Father: Yes. One is that we could make him stay by himself in a room for two minutes every time he swears, just like we've done for hitting. In other words we could use time out.
Mother: If we do that, we could give him a list of the exact words he would get a time out for. Or we could do it without giving him a list. Another option is that we could just ignore it when he swears, and not give any emotion or attention that might reward him for doing it.
Father: Another option is looking serious and giving him a reprimand whenever he does it.
Mother: Another option is having one serious talk with him at the beginning of whatever we do, and explaining to him that we don't like it and why we don't.
Father: We could offer him a reward of some sort if he can go a certain length of time without doing it.
Mother: Or, we could give him a certain number of points at the start of the day. Each time he does it he could lose a point, and if he loses all his points he gets a privilege taken away from him.

Father: We could try to have more fun with him and disapprove of him less often so that it will mean more when we do disapprove of him for swearing.
Mother: Or, we could start out with mild consequences and gradually increase them. For example maybe the first time he gets a reprimand, then a privilege lost, then something else.
Father: We could include into some of our regular discussions of moral dilemmas and some of our ethical readings that we do as a family, some things having to do with use of respectful language.
Mother: That's a good idea. We could combine some of these, particularly the options that don't tempt us to fight or argue with him. One way to do this would be if we first sat down with him and explained why we don't like it, and allowed him to ask questions, and so forth, and told him we are not going to mention anything when he does it, but we want him to quit it. We could include the subject in the ethics sessions we have as a family, and then not say anything, but withdraw some friendliness and giving if he swears. That's a combination of several of the options we mentioned.
Father: Shall we talk about the advantages and disadvantages?
Mother: Yes.
Father: I like the combination plan you just mentioned. The main advantage of that is that we don't have to hassle with punishing him. Plus, we have a talk with him, so he knows how we feel and why. Plus, we don't reward him for swearing by getting emotional or paying attention to him.
Mother: The disadvantage is that by not punishing it more drastically and explicitly, we may be giving him a message that it's OK.
Father: I think actually that explaining how we feel about it and withdrawing friendliness and giving are probably more effective messages that it's not OK than something like a time out or a small penalty. Those little punishments seem to trivialize the issue, it seems to me. Plus, the ethics discussions and our talk with him will make more clear our feelings about it. So I think the plan we're talking about has less of that disadvantage than most of the others. Withdrawal of friendliness and giving is a pretty heavy duty punishment.
Mother: Those are good points. What do you think about forming a back-up plan in case the first plan doesn't work, and telling him what the back-up plan is? I'm inclined not to, just because of what you've said about withdrawal of friendliness and giving as a more intense punishment than time out and taking away points.
Father: I'm also inclined not to announce a back-up plan. The punishment may be exciting to him, and that might make him want to keep on swearing just to see what happens when the excitement starts.
Mother: So shall we agree to have a talk with him, explain that we won't react but we still don't like it, withdraw some

friendliness and giving when he does it, and see how that goes for a couple of weeks?
Father: Sounds good to me. Want to plan how we are going to have our talk with him?
****

A Situation Between Parent and Child
Parent: I want to talk with you about a problem we have, about reminders for homework. Is now a good time?
Child: Yes, I suppose so. You mean the problem of my not doing it when you want me to?
Parent: Well, the problem that it gets done, but only after I've had to hound you for a long time, keeping on reminding you with your saying you'll do it later. I don't like nagging at you, and I'm sure you don't like being nagged at.
Child: So you're saying that you want to find a way for my homework to get done without your nagging at me?
Parent: Exactly.
Child: It's not as though I don't want to do my homework. It's that I think I'm old enough to pick when I want to start it, without any reminder at all from you. I appreciate your interest, but I don't think I need any reminder at all.
Parent: So you're saying that you can handle it totally by yourself?
Child: Right.
Parent: I'd like to believe that, but I remember a few times when you didn't get reminded, and you didn't get something done, and you felt really bad about it the next day.
Child: You don't stop reminding me because there have been some times that I've forgotten.
Parent: Right.
Child: But the point is that I've gone on to make good grades. I've always made good grades. I may miss a little assignment here and there, but not everything is all that important. I come through when it's really important.
Parent: So the times when you haven't been organized have been on assignments you knew weren't terribly important.
Child: That's right.
Parent: So should we list some options?
Child: Yes. One option is that you could stop reminding me and stop checking on my work altogether.
Parent: Another option is that I could check to make sure that your homework's done just before you go to bed, but not remind you before then. Or for another option, I could check a little earlier, so there would be time to do it if it hadn't been done, like maybe 8 pm. The rule would be no reminders before then, and I would check then and only then.
Child: Another option is that you could not do any reminders or any checking until the next report card. If the report card is still all A's at that time, you don't check or remind until the next report card.
Parent: Those sound like some good options to me. Shall we talk about their advantages and disadvantages?
Child: Sure.

Parent: I like the one you just mentioned, about leaving me out of it as long as the grades are good. But until the report card is a long time. I'd feel more secure with a shorter time of feedback.
Child: The advantage of my having a longer time is that I may screw up here and there, and I need a longer time for it to all average out in the end. I don't want you to scrap the whole thing if I get one bad grade on one assignment.
Parent: I can see that. What's the disadvantage of having me check, without reminding?
Child: I just feel that I'm ready to be more independent. I'm too old to have you checking my homework any more. Plus it would eliminate the whole issue of us struggling with each other about my homework. You shouldn't have to be dealing with that. It's my problem, and if I don't do it, I'm the one who will suffer. I don't like getting bad grades, you know that.
Parent: How about this for a compromise, one more option? It will be about six weeks until the next report card. How about if I stay out of it altogether for 3 weeks, and we average all the tests and homework and papers during that time? Then if the average is high enough, I'll continue to stay out of it.
Child: The disadvantages of that are that we won't know exactly how to weight the different scores. And also how high an average is high enough? But the advantage is that you will feel more secure about it, and that's important. Let's do it for 3 weeks and see what happens.
Parent: OK. We can decide at the time how high an average is high enough, and we can guess at how to weight the scores. Let's give it a try.
Child: OK. I'll put it down in my calendar, for 3 weeks from now, that's Wednesday November 14. I'll save everything that's graded until then, and we'll look at it together.
Parent: OK, good luck.
Child: Thanks, and thanks for being reasonable with me.
Parent: You're welcome.

A Situation Between Two Siblings
Brother: I'm looking forward to seeing something on TV today. Some folks from my school are going to be in a contest where they answer school-type questions, and it's going to get broadcast.
Sister: Wow, that's interesting. You know, it's a coincidence, because I was wanting to watch something on TV today too. There's an all-time great movie, that one of my friends and I are planning to see.
Brother: Hmm. What time is the movie?
Sister: Two in the afternoon.
Brother: Uh oh. That's what time the contest is on. And we only have one television set. I really wanted to watch that contest.
Sister: It's important to you to be able to see your classmates in action, isn't it?

Brother. Yes. And it sounds like you were looking forward to having your friend over and being together.
Sister: Not only that, but watching this particular movie. My friend and I both have been looking forward to it a lot.
Brother: So the important thing for you was not just to visit, but to watch this particular show.
Sister: That's right.
Brother: Humh, let's think of some options. Want to?
Sister: Yes. If worse comes to worst, one of us could just not watch our show. We could flip a coin to decide who.
Brother: Or another possibility is to watch the contest, and then pick up with the movie in the middle after the contest is over.
Sister: Another possibility is that you could go over to a friend's house to watch the contest. Or I could go over to my friend's house to watch the movie.
Brother: We could see if the movie is available in the videotape rental places. That way you could see it when the contest is over.
Sister: That's an option. It's possible to tape one show while watching another one, on the videotape recorder. I did that once before, a long time ago. I'm not sure I remember how. You could tape the contest and watch it later.
Brother: Yes, or you could tape the movie and watch it later.
Sister: I think we've got some good options. Want to figure out which one is best?
Brother: I think by far the best one is for us to get the vcr manuals out and figure out how to record the contest while you're watching the movie. That way I'll be able to see the contest, and I'll also be able to lend the video to my friends who want to see it but missed it.
Sister: That sounds great to me. I think I remember where the manuals for the VCR are. How about if I get them for you, and we can figure it out now and see if it works? That way if it doesn't we'll have time to decide on another option.
Brother: Sounds good. Let's give it a try.
****

I think it's useful to practice with hypothetical situations, during a time set aside for practice. Here are some hypothetical two-person problems for couples to practice with, involving children.

The three year old boy is hitting his older brother.

The six year old turned his father's computer on and accidentally erased a file.

The teacher sends home reports about how the child disrupted the class. One parent wants to be punitive, and especially wants the other to do something punitive. The other behaves much too gently to suit the other parent.

When the father comes home, the mother tells the father about bad things that the children did and expects the father to do something about them. The father wants the mother to deal with these things, since he wants to have a pleasant time himself with the children when he comes home.

The child has a habit of coming out of his own bed to ask for something or to just be with the parents several times after he has gone to bed. One of the parents is "soft" with the child, and will hug him and speak gently to him. The other is more irritated with this behavior, and favors more punitive measures.

The father likes to play golf on week ends. This reduces the time that the father has available to be with the children.

The child is having trouble with separating from his mother. The father thinks that the mother should just separate and let the child cry it out. The mother thinks that that strategy is cruel.

One parent believes that spanking a child is justified in order to get the child to behave; the other believes that spanking is violence and never justified. The one who believes in spanking tends to blame the other one's philosophy when the child acts up.

The child ran out into the street on one occasion.

The three year old child broke a living room ornament that was very precious to one parent.

The one and one-half year old soils his diapers when both parents are home. Each wishes that the other would change the diapers.

The child insists on his mother's doing things with him instead of his father.

One parent wants the child to start going to religious services from an early age. The other wants to take it easy, and save the religion for later in life.

The four-year-old child refuses to say his prayers at night. Both parents would prefer that he do so; one would prefer a more strict strategy and the other would prefer a more permissive strategy.

Both parents are trying to argue less with the child. Should they monitor each other's behavior, and signal each other when they get into an unnecessary argument with the child, or leave each other alone, and work independently on this? Or should they adopt a different option?

One of the parents has a child by a previous marriage. The child is defiant to the stepparent, saying "You aren't my parent." The child will obey the biological parent.

One of the parents has a child by a previous marriage. The ex-spouse of that parent wants to be able to drop in and see the children on a free and easy basis. This is OK with the biological parent, but it's not OK with the step parent.

One of the parents has a child by a previous marriage, and the child goes to visit his biological parent on a regular basis. The child comes back from the visits more defiant toward both his parents.

One of the parents has a child by a previous marriage, and the child goes to visit his biological parent on a regular basis. Upon return, the child tells the parents things that he did that seem overly dangerous.

The mother had an alcoholic father. The mother feels it would be much better if the children saw absolutely no drinking in the house, so that they would be less disposed to drink themselves. The father wonders whether it might not be better for them to get a model of how to drink in moderation.

The parents are trying to keep the children from playing with violent toys. However, the parents of one of the parents just gave a very violent toy to the child.

The parents are trying to keep the children from watching violent movies and television shows. However, when they visit their friends, they see violent movies and television shows, and the purposes of the parents seem thwarted.

The preschool aged child has a habit of being very disruptive in order to get attention, when a parent is talking on the telephone. Both parents tend to interrupt the phone conversations to deal with the disruption, but they are concerned that this reinforces the disruption.

Two siblings do a lot of arguing with each other in hostile and unpleasant ways. They don't physically hurt each other, but they seem to be creating a negative interpersonal environment.

Chapter 18: Teaching Joint Decision-Making to Children

Chapter Overview:

Here are some ways you can teach children to resolve conflicts and make joint decisions. First, you can "walk children through" the problem-solving process by asking questions and making suggestions. For very young children these should be very concrete. For older children, you can ask questions that prompt each of the steps of decision-making. For example: "Please tell me more about the problem." "What did you hear him saying?" "What options can you think of?" "What else?" "What do you think would happen if you did that?" "So what do you think is best?" It's much easier for a children to resolve conflicts rationally in real life if they've practiced in role-playing. You can practice with toy people or puppets, or with no props. If the child handles a conflict poorly, you can have the child practice several repetitions of a good handling of the situation, as an alternative to traditional punishment. The brainstorming game is another way of practicing problem-solving. Participants get points for thinking of options in problem situations. In the problem-solving game, they role-play conversations and get points for meeting the 7 criteria for problem-solving conversations. With both these games, you can add situations from your family's real life experience. This helps your child to contemplate real life situations after they've occurred, and to let such contemplation influence future real life decisions. If you create a custom where your child thinks and talks about what's the best thing to do in situations she encounters, you've given your child a gift of great value. The decisions game is a simulation meant to help children juggle probabilities and utilities in decision-making. All these games can be done by children as young as first or second grade.

****

In this chapter we'll discuss 5 strategies for helping children learn problem-solving and decision-making skills:

1. "Walking children through" the decision-making process.
2. Doing problem-solving role-plays with the child.
3. Doing the brainstorming game.
4. Doing the problem-solving game.
5. Doing the decisions game.

Walking Children Through the Problem-solving Process

Children can start to learn the process of understanding a problem, getting information, listing options, and choosing among the options early in life. You can use questions and suggestions to guide the child through the process.

Preschool teachers of children as young as two years old have "walked children through" these processes. The teachers have supplied the entire language of the process at the beginning; later they have had the pleasure of hearing children using such language on their own.

For example: a child is playing with something, and some other child wants it. The adult says, "Johnny, if someone is using something you want, please tell them, instead of just taking it." Johnny stands and looks blank. The adult says something like, "You say, 'I want a turn.'" Johnny still looks blank. The adult says, "Would you like for me to tell Jimmy?" Johnny nods. The adult says, "Jimmy, Johnny would like a turn. Jimmy, are you finished with it yet?" Jimmy shakes his head no. The adult says, "Then Jimmy, you need to tell Johnny you're not finished yet." Jimmy says, "I'm not finished yet." The adult says, "Johnny, you need to ask him for a turn with that toy when he's finished." Johnny says, "Can I use that when you're finished?" Jimmy nods. In a minute or two, Jimmy has put the toy down, and the adult notices. The teacher says to Jimmy, "Jimmy, remember Johnny wanted a turn? Could you please tell him you're finished now."

In this example from the early stage of the process, the teacher is doing a lot of modeling and prompting, supplying the lines for the children to speak.

In a later stage, or with older children, the teacher may use more of a Socratic question-asking process to prompt the children, rather than supplying the lines. Two children are physically struggling over one toy. The adult takes the toy in her hand and puts it behind her back. She first asks one child what happened, and then asks the other. She asks each child to repeat back what the other said. The teacher may then summarize the problem: "You have a problem. We have two boys and one car. What can you think of to do to solve this?" If the children can list options themselves, fine; if not, the teacher can feed them an idea. Both children have to agree before the toy is returned to either of them. Occasionally, the children cannot compromise, and lose interest in the whole process, and walk away to do a different activity. But gradually, the children become more able to talk with each other about what sorts of solutions they want to adopt.

The following are some nearly verbatim utterances made by a preschool teacher in walking some children through the problem-solving process:

"She said she wasn't done with it. Would you like to use it when she's done?"

"Does she know you want it when she's done?"

"How could she know you want it?"

"He really wants the big rolling pin."

"Can you ask her to share it when she's finished?"

"Do you want me to help?"

"_______ really wants that rolling pin when you're done."

"What would you like to do while we wait for it?"

"You waited, there it is."

With still older children, who have had more instruction in the problem-solving process, the questions of the adult may be prompts for the various stages of the process.

"What's the problem?"

"What's your point of view?"

"Can you say back what you heard him saying?"

"What options can you two list?"

"Let's try thinking of some more options before you get into figuring out what to do. What other options can you think of?"

"Now you've listed _____, ______, ______, and _______ as options. What do you both think about the advantages and disadvantages?"

"So what can you both agree to try?"

Question: why does the attention that the children get from the adult in the course of this process not reinforce the conflict behavior, so that you see conflicts increasing, not decreasing? I hypothesize that the above-described process works best in an environment where there is a large adult-to child ratio, and where children are not feeling so chronically deprived of adult attention that they are motivated to get into conflict to obtain it. I would bet that in environments where adult attention was in very short supply at all times, one might run a risk of reinforcing conflict by attending to it so thoroughly.

Exactly the same process of walking the child through the problem-solving process can be used when a child has an individual decision to make, a one-person problem.

Doing Decision Role-Plays With the Child

In this activity, the adult and the child make up a puppet show together. In the one-person problem version, one of the puppets has a problem, and the other is taking on the role of listener and facilitator. In the conversation, the one with the problem defines the problem and tells about the situation. The facilitator does empathic reflections and follow-up questions while the one with the problem gives more information about the situation and his reactions to it. Then the facilitator invites the problem-owner to list options for what to do about the problem, and they both think of options, naming at least four of them. When they can't think of any more, they talk about the advantages and disadvantages of them, and the one who owns the problem decides which option he wants to try.

Here's an example of a play like this.

The problem is that someone has moved into a new town, and doesn't know anyone, and is lonesome.

First person: How are you liking your new town that you moved into?

Second person: It's ok, as a town, I guess. I live in a neighborhood that was sort of like the one in the old town. There's a park not too far away. School is ok, I guess.

First person: Sounds ok, but you don't sound real happy with it, though.

Second person: Well, actually, there's a problem.
First person: Oh? What is it?
Second person: Well, since I've just moved into this town, I don't know anybody, and don't have any friends, and all the things that I used to do with my friends, I can't do because I don't have any.
First person: So the new town is really lonesome for you, huh, without knowing anybody.
Second Person: Yep. I think I need to figure out how not to be so lonesome.
First person: Let's see. How not to be so lonesome. That sounds like a challenging problem. Do you want to think of some options?
Second person: I could talk on the phone with my old friends a lot more.
First person: That's an option. And you could write letters to us.
Second person: Yep. Or I can watch to see if I see any kids my age in my neighborhood, and if I do, I can go out and meet them and find out their names and telephone numbers. Then I can call them up and invite them to come over and play with me.
First person: Yep. And you could go out to that park that's near your house, and see if there are any kids your age there.
Second person: I can ask my parents if any of the friends that they've made have any children, and if so could they maybe invite one of them over to get together with me.
First person: You can introduce yourself to other people that you go to school with, and invite some of them over to your house to be with you.
Second person: Or, I could get out the books I like to read the most, and read them when I'm lonesome.
First person: That's about all I can think of right now. Can you think of any others?
Second person: Nope. I need to think about which one has the most advantages. I think all these have some advantages, and I probably should try all of them. The one that I want to do first, though, is to talk with my parents about inviting somebody from school to come over here.
First person: That sounds like it has some good advantages, because you'll get to know the people at school anyway.
Second person: I think I'll try that one first. And also I think I'll write a letter to my old friends.
First person: I bet they'll like that one. People really like to get mail.
Second person: Well, those sound like some good ones to try. Thanks for problem-solving with me.
First person: You're welcome.

The temptation in this sort of conversation is to list an option, then list a disadvantage that shows why it won't work; then list another option, then list a reason why it won't work, and so on. When you get to the end, you just feel frustrated, like there is no solution. The thing to do is to list the options first, and then talk about the advantages and disadvantages once they are all listed. The separation of the listing process from the evaluation process has been found to be very important in the whole problem-solving process.

Here's an example of a role-play of a two person problem.

Tom: Hey, Bruno, we have a problem, because the music that you're playing in your apartment is keeping me up when I'm trying to sleep at night.
Bruno: Hmmh, so my music is too loud for you. What time do you go to bed?
Tom: About 9:00.
Bruno: Well, we have a problem. I like to listen to my music from about 9:00 to midnight, because I get up late in the morning.
Tom: So just the time when I want it off is when you'd most like to have it on, huh?
Bruno: Yes. Well, what can we do about this problem?
Tom: Well, you could turn your cd player down low.
Bruno: You could put some ear plugs in your ears, or turn a fan on so that the music won't come through so much. Or maybe I could get some earphones for my cd player.
Tom: And maybe you could just hold off between nine and ten, because after then when I'm already asleep, I don't get waked up usually.
Bruno: Want to think about which one to try first?
Tom: Yep.
Bruno: The last one you mentioned has the advantage that I would just have to turn down the music for one hour. I think I could handle that.
Tom: If you bought earphones, and liked to use them, that would totally solve the problem, and an advantage is that you wouldn't even have to look at the clock.
Bruno: Yep. The disadvantage is that right now I don't have the money for the earphones, plus I like to move around a lot in my house while I'm listening.
Tom: So do you want to try the one where you watch the clock and turn it down low between nine o'clock and ten o'clock?
Bruno: Let's give it a try. If it doesn't work we can talk again later.
Tom: OK. I'll let you know in a couple of weeks how it's worked.

When doing these role-plays with children, it's very important to communicate that while you want to have fun, you do not want to have fun with slapstick violence. Otherwise many children, particularly those raised on violent cartoons, will simply have the characters get into a physical fight and laugh at their fighting.

An option mentioned in the previous chapter is to incorporate problem-solving role-plays as part of the consequence for unfortunate handling of conflicts. For example, two siblings get into a fight with each other. Rather than simply imposing a punishment, the parents ask them to role-play an appropriate conflict-resolution conversation about the problem they fought over, several times. Thus they are "redeciding" upon a more appropriate response to the conflict, and "rehearsing" this response, the 3rd and 4th of the 4 r's we went over in the chapter on consequences for misbehavior. (The first two were accepting responsibility for the behavior, and making restitution for it.)

Doing the Brainstorming Game

The material necessary for this game is a set of pages of paper with a situation for individual or joint decision written on it, with a list of some 6 to 10 options as to how the problem could be solved. I have written such a list; it is included in *The Options and Consequences Book.*

Here's the way the game is played. You have two sides, with anywhere from one to several people per side. You randomly pick which side will be the option-generators first. The other side then randomly picks a problem page and reads the problem to the other people. Then the option-generators get a minute (or whatever other time limit you want) to think of all the options they can for the solution to the problem. Someone takes notes so their options can be remembered. Then when the time is up, the options the option-generators listed are compared with the ones listed on the problem page. The players get one point for each nonviolent and nonhostile option they listed; they get an additional point for each option they listed that was also listed on the problem page supplied.

The problems are situations for individual or joint decision. In individual decisions, you are supposed to take the point of view of the main character in the vignette, and think only of options for what that person could do. For joint decisions, you might imagine that you are a mediator for the two people that have a conflict. You think of any options that the two people could possibly both accept.

Here's a noncompetitive way of playing the game. You simply take the problem pages and list options for a minute, and see how many points you can come up with. Then you write down that score on the page, and that becomes the score to try to beat the next time you do the same problem. You also keep track of the highest score you've gotten so far in a particular session of game-playing, and that is the score to try to beat when you do the next problem. Another strategy is to compete against Mr. X. You take turns generating options. If you can come up with more than 6 options, you win; if you run out of ideas before then, Mr. X wins.

The Problem-Solving Game

This game uses the same sort of problem pages used in the brainstorming game. But instead of just listing options, two people act out the process of problem-solving. When they get done, people decide whether they did each of the following things during their conversation:

Criteria for Joint Decision-Making

1. Defining. Each person defines the problem from his or her point of view, without blaming, and without telling what the solution should be.

2. Reflecting. Each person reflects to let the other person know he understands the other person's point of view.

3. Listing. They list at least 4 options.

4. Waiting. They don't criticize the options till they've finished listing.

5. Advantages. They think and talk about the advantages and disadvantages of the best options.

6. Agreeing. They pick an option to try.

7. Politeness. They don't raise their voices or put each other down or interrupt.

When they get through role-playing the situation, you give each person either 0, 1, or 2 points for each of these seven criteria: 0 if they didn't do it, and 2 points if they clearly did it. They get 1 point if they almost did it (for example, if the person put the other down slightly). Thus each pair can get anywhere from 0 to 28 points. The points go to the two-person team, not the individuals. (This of course is meant to foster viewing the two people as collaborators against the constraints of the problem rather than as competitors against each other, as mentioned in the previous chapter.)

For one person problems, you can have one person be the problem-owner, and the other be the facilitator, and go through the following steps:

1. The problem-owner describes the problem
2. The facilitator does a reflection to make sure he or she understands the problem.
3. They list at least four options.
4. They don't criticize options until they are through listing.
5. They think about the advantages and disadvantages of the options (in terms of what the consequences would probably be, and how good or bad those consequences would be.)
6. The problem-owner decides what option he or she would like to try first.
7. The facilitator does not tell the problem-owner what to do, but only helps by listening and listing options and mentioning advantages or disadvantages; they do not argue over what is the best idea.

Each criterion gets judged as getting the team 0, 1, or 2 points. The maximum score in this version is 14 points.

Here's a sample problem page from the game.

****

Two Person Problem

Pat and Lee live together. Pat's favorite food is a dish made of fish and sauerkraut. When Pat cooks it, it makes a smell all through the place, that Lee thinks is horrible.

1. Pat could cook the dish on an outdoor grill.
2. Pat could get a big fan that would pull the smelly air out of the house.
3. Pat could cook the dish only when Lee is going to be out of the house for long enough that the smell has time to go away by the time Lee gets back.
4. Pat could try to find a neighbor that really likes it, and go over to that person's house to cook it and eat it together.
5. Pat could find a restaurant that makes the dish, and go out and order it there.
6. Pat could go ahead and cook it and Lee could put up with it, and in return Pat could do something nice for Lee.
7. Pat could not cook it any more, and in return Lee could do something nice for Pat.
8. Pat could try putting it in an air-tight container and cooking it in a microwave oven, and see if that works in making it smell less strongly.
9. Pat could cook up a whole bunch of it and freeze it in little packets, and then heat up each frozen packet in an air-tight container in a microwave.
10. Lee could try to gradually get used to the smell.

****

Generating Your Own Problem-Pages

The problem-pages that I supply in *The Options and Consequences Book* can be a useful start on the brainstorming game and the problem-solving game. In order to get the maximum benefit, you can enlarge the set of problem-pages by making new ones yourself, with problem stated and options listed. Real-life problems encountered by family members get transferred to problem pages. The process of movement from fantasy situation to real life, and from real life back to fantasy situation, as described before in the use of the modeling stories, plays, and songs, can also be used with the brainstorming and problem-solving games. Making more problem pages can give practice in the crucial activity of problem formulation and definition, which is often even harder than listing options and choosing.

The Decisions Game

The decisions game is meant to provide practice in juggling utilities and probabilities and predicting expected outcomes, as described in the chapter on decision-making. The cards that are used in this game are printed in the book I wrote entitled *Exercises for Psychological Skills.*

Here is the sort of decision you are faced with by the pages that make up this game. You have to choose either option A or option B. Then you will roll a die. You will get a certain number of points, depending upon how the die comes up, as specified in the option you've picked.

If you choose option A:
for a roll of 1, 2, or 3, you get 0 points
for a roll of 4, 5, or 6 you get 14 points
If you choose option B:
for a roll of 1, 2, or 3, you get 2 points
for a roll of 4, 5 or 6, you get 4 points

In the chapter on decision making, we spoke about the expected utility of an option as being the utility of each outcome times the probability of each outcome, summed across all possible outcomes. This game is meant to give practice in thinking in that way. Interestingly, the game can be played by first or second grade children, who can make good and reasonable choices in this game, even though they don't understand the concepts of probability, multiplication, or expected outcomes.

In the example above, the mathematical decision theorist would think in the following way. For option A, there's a .5 chance of 0 points and a .5 chance of 14 points; .5 times 0 plus .5 times 7 yields an expected outcome of 7 points. For option B, there's a .5 chance of 2 points and a .5 chance of 4 points; we get an expected outcome of 3. Thus option A has a higher expected utility, and is a better choice.

I've played this game in a several ways. Here's the competitive version:

You deal from the deck of pages any number of them that you want to use for your game, and put them in one pile, face down. One player draws a page from the deck of pages, and reads or has read to him the conditions for option A and option B. The player then decides whether to pick option A or B, and indicates the choice by putting a piece of paper over the option not chosen. The two options will each tell you how many points you get for given results of a die roll. Then you roll the die. Then you get points (on a tally sheet) or chips according to how many points you get from the results of the die roll. Then it is the other person's turn. The other person uses the same page from the deck, so that each page gets played by each person. But the other person has to use the option not chosen by the first player. The next round, the second person gets to pick the option that each person will play. You keep playing until the allotted time is over.

Another way of playing, that is good if you want to have more than 2 players, is to have each player pick which of the two options she would like to play, for each page, and roll the die and get points.

Competing Against Imaginary Character Version:

In this version, the players compete against "Mr. X." For each page, the players decide together which option they like the best, and play it for themselves; then Mr. X gets the other option, and they roll the die for him.

All of these versions are complicated by the fact that utility isn't exactly equal to points. If there is one play left in the game and option A maximizes the expected number of points, but option B represents your only chance to win, then option B is the better choice. That's because any number of points on this play less than the amount needed to win have no utility. Thus the mathematics illustrated earlier will have to be modified for the "end game" situation.

A Variation That Teaches More About Expected Outcomes

The concept of an expected outcome means what you would expect to get on the average if you made the decision over and over. The expected outcome calculations illustrated above don't predict the score on any given roll very well. However, if you change the method of play so that instead of rolling once, you roll 5 times, and get points for each of the 5 rolls, it becomes much more apparent that in the long run the option with the higher expected outcome gives more points.

Why the Game is Applicable to Life

The task of living life is to make decisions in such a way that you maximize expected utility, where utility is not points, but whatever is accurately deemed to be worthwhile and valuable. Being consistently good at maximizing the expected utility of your decisions is almost guaranteed to maximize your chances at a good life, assuming that the things you define as utility are really values worth striving for.

It's good to be able to think separately about the utility of an outcome and the probability of that outcome. This skill helps in avoiding unnecessary anxiety. If a fear is unrealistic, then someone is usually overestimating either the probability or the disutility of a bad outcome. If someone is afraid of the roof of his well-constructed house caving in, then he is bothering himself because he is overestimating the probability of the bad thing. If someone is devastated at the possibility that some stranger on the street won't approve of his wrinkled shirt, then he is overestimating the disutility of the outcome. Having appropriate emotional reactions to events depends upon the ability to estimate both probabilities and utilities with some reasonable degree of accuracy.

It is very interesting to me to see that young children can often make very appropriate decisions in the decisions game, without knowing any of the mathematical concepts involved. This observation proves that there is some sort of informal, intuitive calculator of expected outcomes that we use in life, even if we don't have any idea what probability means or how to multiply

Chapter 19: Ethics

Chapter Overview:

A child who has a "behavior problem" is usually acting unethically. What keeps children from acting badly toward other people? Rewarding or punishing children provides immediate and visible effects, but more important in the long run is for them to develop an ethical belief system. Children's moral thinking progresses as they develop, in a series of stages. As these progress, the child moves from a conception of "I should do whatever feels the best right now for me," to "I should do what will have the best long term effects on others as well as myself." Morality is not just about thinking, but about feeling. As children develop they should learn emotional associations: feeling good about making others happy, and feeling bad about making them unhappy. Many parents make no systematic effort to teach ethics to children. Here are some fundamental ways in which people have taught ethics: regularly saying out loud key principles; taking time to reflect quietly on these principles; valuing and repetitively reading a set of writings on living well; valuing and learning about ethically heroic acts people have done; doing rituals that affirm ethical principles; discussing what is right or wrong in specific situations; working together in ethical service projects. Some specific ways of using these techniques include composing and regularly reading a family value statement, reading the affirmations regarding psychological skills contained here, compiling or finding and reading aloud a set of writings on living well; gathering and reading aloud from a set of biographies of individuals whose acts are exemplary of family values; linking readings or discussions to regular events such as meals or bedtime; discussing ethical dilemmas; and engaging as a family in efforts to help other people. You can gather situations for ethical dilemmas from the real-life problems occuring in each of your lives, and from contemporary social issues. You can also refer to a list of questions I provide about what is good, just, and ethical. You can try to decide jointly, ahead of time, what family expectations are with respect to ethical behavior, and what sorts of results it would produce if those expectations were violated. By all the techniques listed in this chapter, one can be proactive in preventing the unethical behavior your child will be tempted with by his culture, rather than hoping that unethical behavior will not occur and only reacting when it does.

****

The Nature of Moral Development

We have been dealing, throughout this book, with the question of how to help children behave well. Behavior has everything to do with morality and ethics, and any program to improve behavior that neglects children's ideas about morality and ethics is lacking.

Consider the fact that hitting, disobedience, hostile language, failure to work, lying, stealing, and most other problems people complain of children having involve decisions that are ethical in nature. The child with a "conduct disorder" does not just have a psychiatric problem, but an ethical one.

Young children can behave with kindness out of a desire to get attention from their parents for kind acts, or a fear of punishment for doing unkind acts. But the ultimate behavior of an adolescent or adult depends in large part upon a child's developing a belief system, a system of ethics that is strongly held.

In this view, the ultimate answer to aggression is not just having effective rewards and punishments, but the child's developing a commitment to the idea of kindness and nonviolence. The ultimate answer to stealing is not imposing a consequence of making the offender do work around the house, but the child's developing a commitment to the idea of truthfulness.

Very important research has taken place on the question of how moral ideas emerge in children. Thinkers such as Jean Piaget and Lawrence Kohlberg saw a progression in children's ability to think about ethics. To simplify some of these ideas: Many children start out with a hedonistic view, i.e. doing what gets the best consequences, or an authoritarian view, i.e. thinking of rules as unbreakable. They may pass through a stage where they bargain with other people to exchange favors, and through a stage where they wish to be a good person in other people's eyes. Ideally children progress to a point where they recognize certain ethical principles as valid, and choose to commit themselves to those principles. This sequence gradually unfolds, in the best of circumstances, over the years encompassing preschool and adolescence.

But morality is not just "reasoning," it is also the building of emotional connections. We feel emotions that are in accord with our ethical beliefs. When we do something kind, and when we strongly believe in the value of kindness, we feel good. When we do something harmful, we feel guilty. When we lie, and we strongly believe in the value of truthfulness, we feel guilty.

Which comes first: the emotional association, or the belief? This is an interesting question. Do people adopt ethical beliefs so as to be consistent with the association learning they have picked up from their parents? For example, having internalized approval for kind acts and disapproval for hurtful acts, and having picked up habits of kind behaviors from observing kind models, do they later adopt an intellectual belief in the importance of kindness? Or do they first adopt an intellectual belief, and then do the feelings and behaviors come as a consequence of it?

My own guess is that the intellectual belief systems that people adopt are very strongly influenced by the behaviors they have learned and by the emotions they have internalized. Nonetheless, research has also shown that directly seeking to influence children's moral reasoning by discussions of ethical issues can positively influence behavior. The bottom line is that thoughts and beliefs, behaviors, and emotions all influence one another.

The Pros and Cons of Teaching Values to Children

I believe that almost all parents should undertake some systematic way of teaching ethical values to children. Why?

It's impossible not to have some system of values. The child will develop a system of values somewhere. If kindness, truthfulness, productivity, learning, joyfulness, and resiliency are not somehow promoted, the predominant influences of peer culture or television or whatever else the child is exposed to will usually prevail. If the parent does not systematically promote a value system, the parent may find that the values of youth, physical beauty, wealth, fame, sexual prowess, proficiency in aggression, and glibness may be the highest values the child learns, absorbed from the culture of the day. I mentioned earlier in this book that the parent who fails to take up the task of teaching values to the child on the theory that "The child should be able to make his own choices" is not reckoning with the fact that the culture is constantly sending out very powerful influences upon the child's choice.

What about the idea that the child has to learn from his own experience, and therefore it's no good to teach character and ethics? Imagine if this idea were applied to science and mathematics. We would probably wait a lifetime for most people to rediscover from scratch the Pythagorean theorem, and several more for one of them to reinvent calculus. Successive generations should not be forced to reinvent the wheel over and over, but to build upon the highest and best discoveries of previous generations. This notion applies just as much to ethics as it does to science and math.

There is a downside to the parent's trying to teach ethics and values to a child, sometimes. If the parent's relationship with the child is so problematic that the child is likely to reject whatever the parent teaches, it might be best to delegate something so important as ethical instruction to someone who can start anew in the relationship-building process. If the parent on an ongoing basis provides enough negative models of ethical decisions that the child would experience ethical teaching from the parent as hypocritical, perhaps in that case too the important task is best delegated elsewhere. And finally, if the parent has no taste for the task, and finds it abhorrent or unpleasant, it is probably best delegated.

What Elements of Moral Instruction Have Been Used Successfully?

Let's think about some of the ways in which people have taught children ethics and morality.

One way is through repetition of key concepts. The pessimistic philosopher Schopenhauer is quoted as saying, "There is no absurdity so palpable but that it may be firmly planted in the human head, if only you begin to inculcate it before the age of five, by constantly repeating it with an air of great solemnity." This idea is actually cause for optimism as well, for it implies that the great truths may also be taught by beginning early to repetitively pronounce them with an air of earnest or enthusiastic belief.

Benjamin Franklin repeated daily to himself the following prayer:

"O powerful Goodness! bountiful Father! merciful Guide! Increase in me that wisdom which discovers my truest interest. Strengthen my resolutions to perform what that wisdom dictates. Accept my kind offices to thy other children as the only return in my power for thy continual favors to me!"

By the act of repeating this prayer to himself, Franklin provided himself with daily reminders of ideas key to the skills of decision making (discovering my truest interest), delay of gratification (resolution) and feeling good about kindness to others (kind offices).

Another element used in moral instruction at its best is arranging time for quietness and stillness, with an agenda of reflection on ethics and values. When I was a boy I went to a summer camp where there was a custom called "Morning Watch." Between getting dressed and going to breakfast, everyone in the camp went to a quiet outdoor amphitheater and sat silently for 20 minutes, reading their own chosen religious or philosophical writings or sitting silently and meditating. The experience stands in stark contrast to that of the child who awakens to a stimulus load of television cartoons and video games.

The simple act of closing the eyes when praying or meditating has the effect of shutting out extraneous stimuli, fostering concentration on the messages being affirmed.

Another element of moral instruction is the very high valuation of a standard set of written words on how to live. The religious texts of humanity have been used for this purpose for many centuries. For families outside a traditional religion, it may be tremendously useful to decide upon and gather a set of writings containing eloquent verbal expressions of the highest ethical and moral values for the family.

Still another element of religious instruction has been the valuation of heroes who in real life or in myth have embodied concrete examples of the values the family holds most dear. Especially for families outside a traditional religion, it is important to compile a set of biographies of people who have embodied kindness, honesty, productivity, learning, joyousness, and so forth.

Another element of moral instruction is that of rituals, carried out at regular intervals. Regular prayers are an example of these. I imagine that it is better that prayers or affirmations be done regularly, in the same way at the same time, rather than only spontaneously, whenever the spirit moves people to do it. Why? In order to take advantage of the tremendous force of habit in human affairs. Once the habit of regular ritual is started, it becomes a force that can resist disorganizing influences.

Another element of moral instruction that has been most useful is of ethical situations and ethical issues among groups of people. Why is discussion among people such an important element? Because people are social animals. They enjoy interacting with one another, rather than simply hearing the word handed down. Children and adolescents often define ethical beliefs with reference to the beliefs of a peer group, or at least a group of other human beings. Discussion is a pleasant way for people to practice trying on different verbalizations of their belief systems.

And finally, a key element in moral instruction has been the actual performance, as a group, of moral actions. For example, a religious group participates together in work to help needy people. Or a family regularly participates in a charitable endeavor.

Let's summarize the elements we've talked about so far:

1. Repetition, aloud, of key concepts, with an attitude of reverence or enthusiasm.
2. Arranging time for quietness and stillness, to think about these concepts.
3. The high valuation of, and frequent reference to, a standard set of writings on how to live well.
4. Valuation of real life or mythical heroes embodying the valued character traits.
5. Rituals carried out at regular intervals.
6. Discussion, among groups of people, of ethical issues.
7. Group efforts to make the world a better place.

Some Suggestions For Using These Elements in Families

If you think about these elements, many of them have already been incorporated into the psychological skills training methods articulated earlier. The modeling stories and modeling plays represent the valuation of fictional characters embodying valued character traits. The nightly reading of modeling stories and the nightly review represent rituals. The talking about smart or good things the child has done, and the use of attribution necessarily entail repetition of key concepts.

There is no real difference between the concepts of "values" or "character traits" or "ethical habits" and the concept of psychological skills, as the term skill is used here—not, at least, with the term skill being used as broadly as I use it. The habit of being honest even when it is difficult, for example, can be viewed as a psychological skill, or it can be viewed as a character trait.

Let's think about how families might incorporate some of the other techniques of ethical instruction, mentioned above, that have not been mentioned in previous chapters.

1. Repetition of Key Concepts, Aloud, With an Attitude of Reverence

One way to do this is to adopt a short statement of family values, that the family repeats at some time when they are all together. For example, each time they sit down to a meal together, before eating, one of them reads a statement like the following:

"Let us rededicate ourselves to helping make the world a better place, starting with ourselves and our family. May our actions be productive, joyous, and truthful, and may they contribute toward nonviolence and kindness."

It may be an extremely useful exercise for a family to compose a statement such as this, together: to collectively ask themselves the question, how can we concisely express our values? New statements may be composed at regular intervals.

Below is a set of "affirmations" I have written, one for each of the sixteen psychological skill groups mentioned earlier. These may be useful in linking value statements to the organizing concepts of this book.

1. Productivity. I want to work hard to make the world a better place. I want to better myself and prepare myself in the skills I need for this great goal.
2. Joyousness. I want to take pleasure in joy in the wonder of life and living. May I have a heart that is grateful for being able to take part in the great adventure of life.
3. Kindness. I want to treat people as I would like to be treated. May I work to make people happier, and to be unselfish and forgiving.
4. Honesty. I want to keep my promises and tell the truth, without lying, cheating, or stealing.
5. Fortitude. I want to be strong when things don't go my way. I want to put up with hardship when necessary.
6. Good decisions. I want to think carefully and systematically when important choice points arise. In my joint decisions with other people, I want to work thoughtfully to find a just and good option.

7. Nonviolence. I want to hold sacred the right of people to live without being hurt or killed by others. I want to work for the day when this right is available to all.
8. Respectful talk (not being rude). I want to consider carefully the effect that my words have on others, and let my words support and nurture people.
9. Friendship-building. I want to build and maintain good relationships with other people, for my sake and for theirs.
10. Self-discipline. I want to do the best thing, even when it is not pleasant. I want to give up pleasure and tolerate discomfort when necessary to achieve my higher goals.
11. Loyalty. I want to value the continuity of relationships. I want to stand by those who have earned my continuing loyalty.
12. Conservation. I want to use scarce resources wisely, without wasting them. I want to protect the earth for future generations.
13. Self-care. I want to be appropriately cautious, and protect my own health and safety and welfare.
14. Compliance. I want to comply with authority when it is right and reasonable to do so.
15. Positive fantasy rehearsal. I want to rehearse in my imagination the thoughts, feelings, and behavior patterns I consider good and right. I want to avoid taking pleasure in images of another person's misfortune.
16. Courage. I want to overcome unrealistic fear. I want to be courageous enough to do what is best and right, even when that involves some risk.

One family used these in a most creative way, a way I have come to recommend to other families. The affirmations were cut out and put into a container. Before mealtime, a child would pick one of them out. The family would at least read the affirmation, and would sometimes add a discussion of examples of it.

2. Arranging Time for Quietness and Stillness, to Think About These Concepts

One way to accomplish this is to have one or two minutes of silent meditation, just after the readings of the value statements. Another way is the arrangement of a family "morning watch" or "evening watch" along the lines of that which I described above. The family members sit together silently for a period of time to read or think. This custom stands in stark contrast to the hectic mishmash of television, hurry, and confusion that characterize many morning and evening rituals for families.

3. The High Valuation of, and Frequent Reference to, a Standard Set of Writings on How to Live Well

One way of accomplishing this is to keep one shelf in the house dedicated to writings on how to live well, writings that people have found useful. These may be religious writings, philosophical writings, or writings from psychology or the self-improvement genre, or whatever. The activity of choosing, of separating the wheat from the chaff, of continually refining the body of written work, is an extremely useful activity.

Establishing the custom of regularly reading a brief selection from one of these works may be extremely valuable. As the child learns to read, the child may take some pride in moving into the position of reader.

Over several years I have put together an anthology of readings on how to live well that have struck me as particularly useful. At some point soon this may be available for anyone else who wants to use it.

4. Valuation of real life or mythical heroes embodying the family values.

One activity that can be done with children is to find pictures of real-life people who have done things that we highly value, to write out brief descriptions of what they did, to attach these descriptions to the pictures, and to display these in the house. It may be useful to think in terms of what psychological skill these individuals most embodied.

The collection and reading of children's biographies of people who did smart and good things is another important way of creating heroes embodying the family values.

5. Rituals Carried Out at Regular Intervals

Reading from the set of valued writings at mealtime or at morning or evening watch, the nightly review, the nightly reading of modeling stories—linking these activities to the "activities of daily living" such as eating and going to bed can make their regular occurrence much more likely.

6. Discussions of Ethical Issues

Researchers on moral development have found that it is good for children to discuss moral dilemmas, to weigh the pros and cons of various actions and to search for the principles for making good decisions. An example of a dilemma used in such discussions is the problem of the man whose wife has an illness, curable by a drug, but otherwise fatal; the only way he has available to get the drug is to steal it. What should he do?

A set of illustrated stories available from me pose moral dilemmas constructed for younger children, which pose a conflict between self-interest and interest in the welfare of another person. For example, our protagonist is in the lead in a very important cross-country ski race. Another competitor gets hurt. No one else stops to help the person who was hurt. Should the person stop and help the hurt person, and forfeit his win of the race, or should he go forward, probably winning the race?

Such hypothetical situations provide useful material for regular family discussions, either at mealtime or at other regular times for the family to come together. Another possible family activity is to add gradually to the list of moral dilemmas, by incorporating situations that family members encounter in real life. As the list gradually grows, it becomes more and more directly relevant to the subculture in which the family functions.

Discussing ethical issues that face society in general provides a chance to refine one's powers of reasoning about right and wrong. Here are some sample questions for family discussion.

1. Sometimes scientists wish to do research on animals, in a way that cannot be done without making the animals sick and experience pain. When, if ever, do you think they should be allowed to do this?

2. What do you think about the ethics of legalizing or illegalizing abortion? Does your answer take into account lots of different effects that such a decision might bring about?

3. Every year as deer season opens, thousands of hunters go out into the woods to hunt deer. Some people argue that hunting involves not only killing, but taking pleasure in killing, and that all taking pleasure in killing is wrong. What do you think?

4. Suppose a law says that you have to fill out several forms and make social security tax payments as an employer, if you pay anyone to do anything over a certain amount of money. Someone neglects to do this, for someone who babysits for her child, and for someone else who cuts her grass every couple of weeks during the summer. Then that person is nominated for a high government position. Do you think that this should keep the person from getting the job?

5. Someone proposes, "I have a way to end the drug problem. Set up roadside searches, and do random drug testing on everyone who passes in their car. Give large fines to all who test positive." What do you think about this method of solving the drug problem?

6. Someone proposes, "I have a way to improve the population problem, and the problem of poverty as well. You have the government pay people to get sterilized. Those that will take the money in exchange for getting permanently sterilized are just the sorts of people we don't want having children." What do you think about the ethics of this plan?

7. A city government is trying to decide whether to legalize gambling casinos. The opponents point out that casinos are a waste of time and energy and resources that could be used on better pursuits, such as educating children. They also point out that a certain fraction of people get addicted to gambling and lose all their family's money. The proponents point out that for many people gambling is fun, that lots of jobs would be created by the casinos for people who might otherwise be unem-

ployed, that tax money would be generated to support city services, and that no one has to gamble who doesn't want to. What stand would you take, if you were on the city council?

8. What do you think about the ethics of capital punishment?

9. A government wants to provide for the people who are poor and can't support their children. So they set up a program where the lower your income is, the more money you get. People worry that they are rewarding people for not supporting themselves, and doing them more harm than good by encouraging dependence on welfare. How would you set up a welfare system in the most ethical possible way?

Another variant upon the discussion of ethical dilemmas is grappling, on a regular basis, with questions that have to do with what is really valuable and good in life. The following is a set of questions I have found useful to raise to children periodically.

Questions for Discussions of What Is Valuable in Life

1. Who is someone that you admire for making the world a better place, or making things better for at least one person? What did that person do?
2. What do you think is one way that you could someday make the world a better place, or make things better for at least one person?
3. What qualities of people are most important to you? In other words, if you were hiring somebody for a job, or thinking about getting married to someone, or thinking of being a roommate with someone, what qualities would you like to see in that person?
4. What do you think is one of your best qualities? In other words, what skill or characteristic of yourself is something that you are proud of?
5. What is a quality that you would like to develop more of in yourself? In other words, what is a skill you would like to get better at?
6. What is something that you think people are spending too much time and energy and money on, today, that you think they are wasting their time on? In other words, what do you think is something that is absorbing people's interest that is not valuable enough to get so much interest?
7. What is something that you think people aren't spending enough time or energy or money on, today, that deserves a lot more than it is getting? In other words, what do you think is something that should absorb a lot more people's interest, something of great value, that would make society better?
8. What's a decision you've made lately, or something you've chosen to do lately, that you're glad about? In other words, what's a choice of yours that you can celebrate?
9. What's something you've done lately that you wish you would not have done? In other words, what's a choice where you wish you would have chosen something else? What would you have chosen to do instead, looking back?

10. If you were going to give rules or guidelines about how people should act with each other, how they should behave with each other, what rules or guidelines would you give? In other words, suppose someone from another planet asked you, "How should I act here on Earth?" What would you tell them?
11. One of the problems that the world has is that sometimes people are violent and mean to each other: sometimes some people hurt other people, some people sometimes kill other people, and some people seem to enjoy hurting other people's feelings. What do you think is one way that this problem can be solved?
12. Another problem the world has is that whole countries sometimes get into wars with each other. There are big fights and many people are hurt or killed. What do you think is something that could be done to solve this problem?
13. Another problem the world has is that there are some people that are very poor, and don't have enough food to eat, or a home to keep warm in, or enough clothes to wear. What do you think is something that could be done to solve this problem?

Discussion of Family Rules or Expectations, and Consequences for Breaking Them

What unfortunate ethical decisions are some members of your child's peer group or older peers carrying out? If you can list these and hold serious and meaningful discussions of the ethics of these behaviors before they have ever taken place with your child, you will stand a much better chance of being on the same ethical wavelength as your child. As mentioned in the chapter on consequences for misbehavior, if you and your child have similar ethical systems the dealing with adolescent transgressions is much easier.

Here are some sample topics for such discussions.

1. A teenaged girl slips out her window in the middle of the night, and goes for a walk with a boyfriend. They do not do anything wrong or harmful. But her parents do not know that she has gone, or where she has gone. She slips back in after an hour, and her parents have not noticed. She sleeps until the morning. What do you think about the ethics of her action? What sort of family rule do you think should apply to such a situation, and what do you think should be the consequences of breaking it?

2. A teenaged boy goes to the home of a friend, whose parents are not at home. There are other people his age using drugs and drinking alcohol at this place. He chooses not to use drugs or

alcohol himself, but he hangs around with his friends and talks. His parents hear about this from the parent of another boy. What do you think about the ethics of his action? Do you think a family rule should apply to this sort of situation?

3. A boy at a high school is picked on by a group of other boys. They call him a faggot, hide his possessions, laugh at him, and try to trip him, occasionally succeeding. After several weeks of this he confronts the leader of the group that is doing this to him, and punches him in the face, breaking his nose. What do you think about the ethics of his action? Do you think a family rule should apply to this, and if so, what do you think the consequences should be of breaking the rule?

4. A boy is horsing around with another kid at school, and he shoves him into a locker and locks the door. He walks away, leaving someone else who comes around about 5 minutes later to get the other kid out of the locker. When confronted about this he says that it was all in fun. What do you think about the ethics of this action? Should a family rule apply, and if so, what should be the consequences of breaking it?

5. A girl has started to have "make out" sessions with a boyfriend. There is no danger of pregnancy, because they do not do have intercourse. Her mother asks her if she is involved in any sort of sexual activity, and she lies and says that she is not involved in anything at all, not even kissing. She does this because she thinks this should not be her parents' business. What do you think about the ethics of her actions? What rules and consequences, if any, do you think should apply?

6. A teenaged girl has gotten her driver's license. She is driving with friends who urge her on to go faster and faster, and she succumbs to the pressure. A police officer hears the squealing tires, and she gets a ticket for speeding and reckless driving. She attempts to pay the ticket without her parents' finding out about it, but while cleaning up in her room one day, her mother sees the ticket. What ethics apply, and what rules and consequences should apply?

Family Group Efforts to Make the World a Better Place

Working together on a project, or several projects, designed to make the world a better place, is another very important way of transmitting ethical beliefs to children. Here are some options for projects family members can do together: Helping someone learn to read. Building a house for a family in need. Working in an organization to persuade people to boycott entertainment violence. Chipping in money to sponsor a poor child in a developing country, and writing letters to that child. Being in campaigns to improve the environment. Working for political causes the family has decided are ethical. Teaching psychological competence to other families or children. Volunteering in a nursing home. Volunteering in distributing food to the poor, as in a soup kitchen. Volunteering in a shelter for victims of violence. Providing child care for those in need. Helping to organize tutoring projects. Teaching vocational skills or recreational skills. Participating in educational campaigns against drug use. I am sure that you can add more options.

If you can help your family members make "mutually gratifying activities" out of efforts at improving the human condition, surely your children will learn something very important. Just as children's ethical beliefs influence their behaviors, their ethical behaviors influence their beliefs.

Where can a family find time to do things together to improve the human condition, when they are already so frantically busy that they can't find time to be together? Many upper middle class families that I see find themselves so busy with parents' competing in the business world and children's competing in the sports world that there is hardly any time for contact between family members at all. On the other hand in the average family there seems to be a great deal of time allocated to television, movies, and videogames. Huge numbers of adolescents seem to drift without being tempted by anything useful to do. Making time for efforts to improve the human condition requires setting priorities and sacrificing some easier and more tempting activities, which is what ethics is all about.

Why Should These Suggestions Be Taken Seriously?

I wish that I could say that the suggestions in this chapter had been subjected to lots of scientific study, and that experiments with random assignment to groups and careful measurement of outcomes had conclusively proved their usefulness. But I haven't run across one such study of training family members to use all or most of the techniques mentioned in this chapter. These are some of the oldest and most time-honored techniques for the ethical instruction of children, yet as far as I know they have not yet come under scientific scrutiny.

In the meantime, I see over and over again good, ethical parents, whose families have never repeated aloud any key ethical concepts; have never had a specific quiet and still time for thinking about what the highest principles are; have never referred within the family to a standard set of writings on how to live well; have never identified any real life or mythical heroes or heroic acts embodying the highest values; have never carried out regular rituals that remind the participants of the highest principles; have never spent time discussing what is right and just; and have never worked together on a project meant to improve the world. Meanwhile, the rest of the culture—television, video games, the peer culture—are promoting values of shallow opportunistic materialism and hedonism. Then when the child or adolescent steals or gets involved with drugs or does acts of violence, there is a need to react to the situation and try to fix it quickly. The proactive solution is to work day in and day out, year in and year out, to lay a foundation of ethical beliefs that will withstand the onslaught of an unethical culture.

Chapter 20: Fortitude and Anger Control

Chapter Overview:

Fortitude, or frustration tolerance, is the skill of handling unwanted situations in a rational way. This skill is crucial for two reasons. First, as a parent you need to get as skilled in this as you can, because children very frequently deliver frustrating situations to parents. Second, you will want to be able to teach this very important skill to your children. Theorists used to focus on whether to let anger out or keep it in. We now realize that it's possible to choose not to create so much anger or other negative emotion in the first place—if you desire this enough and want to work at it enough. And how do you work at it? You review often the benefits of developing this skill. You generate a list of situations of the sort that you wish to handle better. You put into words the "automatic thoughts" you have been having in these situations; you notice and classify them. Changing these thoughts can lead to different emotions and behaviors. You decide on new thoughts, emotions, and behaviors that you'd rather do in the situations. Then you do many fantasy practices of using the more desirable patterns. You monitor how you handle provocations that come up in real life. You celebrate it when you handle a situation well, and run those positive patterns through your mind for future benefit. For situations that you didn't handle well, you redecide how you would have like to handle them in the future, and use them in fantasy practices. Examining your individual thoughts may lead to another productive activity, namely examining your belief systems that generate thoughts. Beliefs about how much you want to be able to control the other person, and about the other person's motivation in frustrating you, may have a big influence on your thoughts, and on your entire patterns of responding.
****

Anger control and frustration tolerance are crucial skills for all people. They are even more crucial for parents. Parents need to tolerate the frustrations their children deal out to them. And parents need to teach their children to handle the frustrations of life. This chapter will give the basics of the art of fortitude. The next chapter will focus on how you can teach fortitude to your children.

Sometimes the best thing that can happen to a child is for the parent to gain skills of fortitude. The responses I've advocated to children's misbehavior involve a great deal of rationality and calm firmness. If you avoid yelling and getting excited when a child misbehaves, but speak to the child in a voice that is lower, slower, and quieter than usual, you can avoid reinforcing, stimulating, and modeling hostility. At times the best choice is totally to ignore the child's misbehavior and go on about your business as though nothing had happened. At other times the best choice is to give the child a time-out, but again to do it in a very calm and deliberate way. And at other times you want to withdraw friendliness and giving for a period of time, but not in an excited way. And at other times you want to summon the rationality and thinking power to help the child through the 4 r's in response to the child's misbehavior. It's difficult to do any of these well if you have lost your temper. This is one reason why anger control and fortitude skills for adults are so important. In addition as you become more expert yourself, you will find it easier to teach your child.

Anger In, Out, or Uncreated?

What is the goal of the anger control program that is suggested here? Is it that I "hold my anger in" rather than "let it out"?

For many decades therapists and researchers thought in terms of either letting anger out or holding it in. The notion was that any amount of anger was just fine; how you responded to your anger and what you did "with it" was the crucial variable. However, realistically speaking, feelings of extreme fury and rage do make it more difficult by far to simultaneously choose behaviors that are calm and rational. More recently we have become aware of a third and much better option, for use when angry behavior is a problem or when very angry feelings are not useful: not to create so much anger in the first place. In other words, the goal is learning to tolerate the frustrating situation without "doing" so much anger.

You may not be familiar with the idea of our "creating" our own anger, or with the idea that anger is something we "do" rather than "have." Do external situations that happen to us cause our anger to take place, regardless of what we do? When you think about it, it's not the external situations themselves, it's not the things that happen to us alone, but our interpretations of those events, our thoughts about them, that make us angry. Coming to this realization is one of the first steps in anger control.

For example, suppose that there are two people waiting for a bus. One of them is thinking, "This is pleasant weather we're having today. That breeze feels good on my face."

A second person is waiting for the same bus, and is thinking, "That stupid bus company! It's so inefficient! I waste so much time standing here waiting for these buses! If the company were run right they would come on time!"

Now, isn't it likely that the second person will be feeling more angry than the first person at this moment? They are both experiencing the same external event, but their thoughts are what make the crucial difference in how they respond to it emotionally. If it were only the situation, and not our thoughts about it, that created our anger, then everyone who experienced the same situation would react the same way—and this is clearly not true.

Does this mean that we should always choose not to get angry? Aren't we sometimes justified in getting angry? The question is not whether anger is justified or not, but whether it is useful to you or not. There are some times when anger is definitely useful. For example, if I am a public speaker, and I am trying to convince an audience that a great wrong is being done by a certain political decision, it may help me to have anger in my voice as I speak about the outrageous things that have been done. I might be much more effective than I would've been if I had given a dry intellectual argument to my audience.

As a second example, there are some parents who are in the habit of letting their children "walk all over them", for example, hit them, without imposing any consequence that teaches the child not to hit. Some of these parents might benefit from developing a certain low-level controlled anger that helps them to feel OK about applying a firm and humane punishment.

The capacity to feel negative emotions of all sorts did not evolve for no reason. Anger helps us to keep other people from taking advantage of us. Fear helps us to avoid dangerous situations. Guilt helps us not to repeat harmful actions. But too much of these emotions can lead to blind destructiveness or paralysis from terror or self-hatred. The goal for negative emotion is to have just enough of it to accomplish useful goals, but not so much that the accomplishment of goals is blocked. When any of these emotions take away the ability to make good, rational decisions, it's time to turn down their volume.

For many people the crucial shift in learning fortitude skills is to stop asking the question, "What do I do with my anger," and replace it with "What are the most effective thoughts feelings, and behaviors I can come up with in response to this situation?" If you can chose those patterns, and feel good about your choice, you've done all you need to do.

Therefore it's useful to take inventory: to think back upon frustrating situations, and to ask, for each, "Was the degree of negative emotion that I felt useful in helping me deal with the situation?" If the answer is no, some work on fortitude is in order.

How Does One Work on Fortitude?

The way in which one "works" on fortitude should have a familiar ring by now. You do some goal-setting by selling yourself on the benefits of gaining more fortitude. You allocate time to working on the goal. You generate a list of situations from your own life or from imagination (or from the list at the end of this chapter) that includes just the sorts of situations you want to handle better. You remember and watch to see what sorts of automatic thoughts you have been in the habit of thinking in these situations, and how you have felt and behaved. You decide on new patterns of thought, feeling, and behavior that you like better. Then you do repetitive fantasy practice of using the new and better patterns in the situations you've generated. You go out and experience real life, and notice how you handle new frustrations that come up. If you handle them well, you celebrate and rehearse those positive handlings. If you handle them undesirably, you add them to the situations list, decide on a better response, and rehearse the better response repeatedly. Thus you cycle back and forth between real life experience and redecision and rehearsal in fantasy.

Let's go into some more detail on how to do these things.

Goal-Setting and Selling Yourself

If fortitude is a really important goal, then it is useful frequently to remind yourself of the benefits of achieving it. Repeatedly sell yourself on the benefits, so that there's no question in your mind that you want it. It is extremely hard work to do this program, and unless you are really sold that it will help you, it is difficult to keep up the motivation to do all the work.

Let's review some of the disadvantages of outbursts of negative emotion and advantages of fortitude. Among the disadvantages of angry outbursts are being a bad model for family members and other people, having to endure angry outbursts from other people that are in imitation of your own outbursts, making the person whom you're angry at feel more pain than would have been necessary to keep them from doing the undesirable behavior, losing friends, risking losing a job, getting your blood pressure up, looking immature, and running the risk of hurting someone else emotionally if not physically. Another important disadvantage is saying things in the heat of anger that will not be forgotten and will very much impair relationships. Among the advantages of fortitude are a feeling of being master of circumstances rather than having them master you, setting a good model for others, noticing greater fortitude in family members, feeling less frustration and more inner peace yourself, having better relationships, "voting with your behavior" for a less violent world, protecting your vocal cords, and being more successful in all human relationships. If you are seriously undertaking the pursuit of fortitude, you might spend time revising these lists for yourself, and memorizing them.

The point to aim for in the pursuit of fortitude is where in provocative situations you can regularly think, "I handled this situation effectively!" Handling a situation effectively is making things come out favorably in the long run. It is not getting your anger out, or making yourself feel better in the short run, but causing the most favorable events possible in the external interpersonal world.

Many of our frustrations are caused by other people. What does it mean to respond effectively to the things other people do that we don't like? When a child misbehaves, effectiveness for the parent means that you do something that makes it less likely that the child will misbehave in the future, while causing the least possible amount of unhappiness in your child or yourself. Applying a mild punishment such as time out for hitting is an example of responding to a situation effectively. You have done something to make the hitting less likely to happen next time, but you have not subjected your child or yourself to a needlessly large amount of suffering. Ignoring some whiny behavior is another example of making the whining less likely to occur next time, without causing much unhappiness to the child or the parent.

If you can realize that you have accomplished the goal of making the misbehavior less likely to occur while minimizing the pain that anybody feels, you deserve to feel very good about yourself. Even more importantly, it is extremely useful for you to feel very good about yourself in such a circumstance. Your self-congratulation for handling a situation in that effective way is what keeps you going and enables you to handle the next situation equally effectively.

If you're like most people, you'll notice that not all of the behavior that makes you angry qualifies as misbehavior or unreasonable behavior. Sometimes the child makes parents angry just by asking a question, in a totally appropriate way, or by crying at an appropriate time, or something else that's totally normal. Not all anger comes from bad behavior. Sometimes a parent's anger, for example, is more a consequence of the stress the parent is going through than anything bad the child did. Sometimes we have our irritation level gradually increased by lots of people, and one person's minor provocation becomes the "straw that broke the camel's back." People frequently get angry at one person and aim that anger at someone else. Thus fortitude involves handling other people's reasonable behavior, as well as their unreasonable behavior.

Generating the Situations List

In this step, a pencil and paper (or computer and keyboard) are almost mandatory. You generate a list of provocative situations: things that have happened or things someone has done that have made you feel more anger or pain than you would prefer. Record as long a list of these provocative situations as you can. If you need some help in coming up with situations, look at the sample list at the end of this chapter. When a real-life situation comes up, add it to the list. Make sure you include enough concrete details to give yourself a clear mental image. I would recommend at least a dozen situations for starters.

Noticing the Automatic Thoughts

Now that you have these images, you can go through them one by one, and replay them in fantasy, observing very carefully to notice the automatic thoughts that tend to inflame you. What are you telling yourself, and what are the unspoken thoughts, that you can put into words if you try hard enough to? As you examine the thoughts, think in terms of the twelve thought categories we've spoken of before:

awfulizing vs. not awfulizing
getting down on oneself vs. not getting down on oneself
blaming someone else vs. not blaming someone else
goal setting
listing options and choosing
learning from the experience
celebrating luck
celebrating someone else's choice
celebrating your own choice

It's particularly useful to search out the "awfulizing" thoughts and try to verbalize them. If you have found yourself feeling that when someone has spilled juice on the floor it is just awful, and a catastrophe beyond your endurance, try to put those automatic thoughts into words, no matter how silly they seem: "It is just terrible, in fact it is close to the end of the world, that my child has spilled that sticky apple juice on the floor one more time. I just can't stand it!"

If you find yourself blaming someone else to avoid getting down on yourself (a very common pattern with anger control problems), try to put those thoughts into words. For example, "If this were my fault it would mean I was a terrible person. But it's all his fault, he's the terrible person, not me!"

The point of verbalizing the automatic thoughts is to be better able to hold them up to the light of reason, to be able to realize logically that nobody has to be branded a terrible person as a result of this incident, that on the grand scale of triumph to tragedy, what produces lots of anger is often a rather trivial setback in life.

It's very important not to berate oneself for thinking automatic thoughts that seem silly when verbalized. Instead, it's useful to celebrate greatly when you notice yourself awfulizing or getting down on yourself or blaming another person. The celebratory thought is, "Hooray! I've noticed exactly what I'm doing! The more I have awareness of this, the more control I'll be able to exert in changing it!"

Redecision: New Patterns of Thought, Emotion, Behavior

Pick a situation and spend time deciding exactly what response would be most effective. For example, if the situation is a provocation your child offers, think about whether this behavior is one that is best responded to by ignoring, by physically guiding the child into the desired response, by giving a reprimand to the child, by giving a time-out, by temporary withdrawal of friendliness and giving, and so forth. Decide exactly upon the demeanor that you wish to have while responding in this way. You want to visualize as accurately as possible the tone of your voice, the speed of your physical motion, the loudness of your voice, and so forth. Again, the overriding criterion is, what is most useful in making things come out well in the long run, while inflicting minimal amounts of suffering. Or, if you decide that the provocative behavior of the child isn't really a misbehavior at all, but in fact a normal and healthy behavior for a child your child's age, then your criterion for effective response is that which helps you enjoy the behavior and not even wish to punish it.

Deciding on the thoughts you want to think in the situation is also a very important task.

One very important type of thought is that of recognizing that you are at a choice point: becoming aware that you have an opportunity for a success or failure at anger control. This thought may go something like this: "Here's another provocative situation. This is a chance to practice fortitude. I hope I can succeed at it."

Another important type of thought is deciding the general style of response you would like to come out with: "In this situation, I want to stay rational, I want to keep thinking, I don't want to lose control. It's fine to be assertive but I don't want to start yelling or stop listening."

Another way of thinking that can be very useful is to let flash across the mind an image of a previous success in anger control. Each success is a resource for future successes; calling to mind a memory of a previous success mobilizes the thought and feeling patterns most useful in repeating that success.

Ideas useful in anger control are "hot thoughts" and cool thoughts." Hot thoughts are those that tend to inflame anger; cool thoughts are those that tend to produce rational, deliberate action. "What the @#$%! do you think you're doing!?" is a hot thought. An example of a cool thought is "Here's another provocative situation. I want to see how well I can handle it this time. I'll relax and take it easy, and if I can handle it effectively I'm going to feel really good about myself."

Here is a sample of cool thoughts.

Observing and describing to oneself the situation:

I want to understand what's happening here.

What does the other person want? What do I want?

What's the motive of the other person? What's my motive?

What are the constraints of the situation?

Recognizing a choice point:

This is an opportunity to practice good anger control.

I have a chance to chalk up another success if I play my cards right.

This situation will put me to the test.

Now's the time to see whether I can do it or not.

Deciding the general way I want to respond:

I want to be assertive, but not to yell.

I want to keep thinking, and come up with creative options.

I want to act so as to preserve the quality of the relationship.

Calling to mind a previous success:

This is like the situation a few days ago that I handled successfully.

I am imagining my successfully handling that situation, and watching a mental movie of it.

Thinking myself through the situation:

How awful will it be if this doesn't come out the way I want it to?

How high are the stakes here, compared to life and death matters?

This isn't the end of the world.

This is no big deal.

If there is some imperfection in my own behavior, it doesn't mean I have to punish myself.

I'm not obligated to punish the other person for all his imperfect behavior.

What options can I think of to solve this problem?

What would be the likely consequences of this option?

What should my negotiating tactics be?

What can I learn from this for the future?

"To err is human, to forgive, divine."

Thinking about my behavior:

I'm being assertive but not aggressive.

I'm ready to concede unimportant things, and I'm sticking up for the important things.

I'm being criticized, but I'm listening, asking for more information, and telling my own wants and feelings.

I'm relaxing my muscles.

I'm letting my jaw muscles get loose and relaxed.

Celebrating:

Hooray, I'm rising to the occasion!

Good for me! I'm succeeding in one more frustrating situation!

I did it! I handled this situation in the way I want to!

I responded to this with style!

Some of these cool thoughts had to do with relaxing muscles and getting one's body more relaxed. Does it help to practice this so as to be good at it when you need it in a provocative situation? Of course. Relaxation is a skill that is very useful for a number of purposes; it's discussed in greater detail in its own chapter. To practice it, let your attention go in turn to each group of muscles in your body. First tense the muscles, to become sensitive to the feeling of tension. Then practice relaxing each muscle immediately after you tense it. After that, you can graduate to a stage where you avoid purposely tensing. You simply notice the tension in your muscles, let that tension off, and make your muscles as loose as you can. Several other relaxation techniques are also useful. If you consciously relax for fifteen minutes a couple of times a day, you will gradually increase your ability to relax so that you will be able to use it in provocative situations.

Not Just Thoughts, But Belief Systems Are Important

Certain types of thoughts organize or generate other thoughts. We call these beliefs. For example, if a parent believes, "This three year old child should always act in ways that make rational sense," you will probably get more angry at the child than if you believe, "A three year old is very immature, and it's natural to see very immature and irrational behavior from such a young child." It may help you to do a lot of thinking about just how much you do expect from a child of certain ages, and to temper those expectations downward in the interest of anger control.

Another belief system relevant for parents has to do with the meaning of the child's disobedience to you. Suppose you believe, "If the child disobeys, I am looking like a wimp and the child is making a fool of me, on purpose." You will, with such a belief, get much more angry than one who believes, "The ability to obey reasonable authority is a very important psychological skill; I want to teach my child to respect my authority in the way that's most likely to work well."

A strongly related belief system has to do with how much you feel you have the right or obligation to control your child's behavior. Suppose you believe, "I should be able to demand the behavior I want from my child, and get it, in any situation that I encounter." Then you are likely to be embroiled often and regularly in power struggles with your child. On the other hand, if you believe, "The child is his own person, and he has no obligation to do anything that I or anybody else asks him to do unless he decides it's best," then you'll probably have problems of spoiled and bratty behavior. If you believe, "I'm a fragile person. I can't take it when the child has a tantrum. To protect myself, I need to appease the child to get him to behave right," then you'll almost certainly have problems with spoiled and bratty behavior. If you believe, "I want to train my child to obey me so that I can exert control on the things that are important; I want to give the child as much choice as is reasonable, and have that choice gradually increase as the child gets older," then you are likely to be somewhere in the happy middle.

What is your belief system about your child's motivation for disobeying you? If you believe that she does it in order to thumb the nose in your face and to manipulate you and make you look stupid, you will probably respond to rule-breaking with anger; if you believe that every human being to some extent resists being controlled by any other human being and wants to stake out her own areas of autonomous decision, you may still decide that the child should obey, but you won't take disobedience so personally. If you believe that your own negative emotion may excite the child in a way that might reinforce the child's negative behavior, then you'll have an additional very powerful motive for learning fortitude.

It may be useful to go further in examination of your philosophy. What do you believe about freedom and liberty, and do those beliefs have to do with your reactions to children? Personally, I believe that one person should impinge in coercive ways upon the freedom of another person to choose her own behavior only when there is a good reason to do so. (By coercive ways, I mean giving commands and enforcing them with physical guidance or the threat of punishment. These are in contrast to noncoercive means of influence, such as models and differential attention, which I believe should be used whenever the goal of the influence is ethical and just.) The other side of the coin, however, is that with young children, there are very frequently good reasons to impose control through coercive means! (Example: A certain amount of coercive behavior control gets imposed almost every time a certain one-year-old is subjected to a diaper change or put to bed.) A certain pragmatic weighing of the costs and benefits of trying to control another person, and by what means, rather than a rigid belief system, may help you greatly in achieving anger control in dealing with a child.

Practicing the New Patterns In Fantasy

Once you've decided exactly the sequence of thought, feeling, and behavior you want to practice, an extremely important way to practice handling provocative situations is by fantasy rehearsal out loud. As mentioned at various places in this book, this consists in speaking out loud, describing yourself encountering an imaginary situation, describing your thoughts and feelings and behaviors, and continuing until the end of the scene. You talk in terms of "I" and what I "am doing now" while doing this fantasy rehearsal.

Here is a summary of steps in carrying out a fantasy rehearsal.

Steps in Practicing Fortitude
1. Situation: Describe the situation. What are the sights, sounds?
2. Thoughts:

Here's an opportunity.

How bad is what happened? When I compare this to the worst that has happened to people, how does this stack up? Not awfulizing.

Not getting down on myself. Not blaming someone else.

Listing options and choosing.

Learning from the experience.

Let me remember a time when I handled a situation like this well. I want to see and hear it in my mind.

I want to relax.

It will be an accomplishment if I can tough this out and handle it well.

I want to speak to myself and to others in a calm voice.

3. Emotions:

If I feel mad, that doesn't mean I can't act reasonable.

I imagine myself feeling the way I want to feel: confident, excited, determined, resigned, calculating, proud of the way I'm handling this, or ...

4. Behavior: I'm doing the option that I chose. I'm doing something that makes sense.

5. Celebration: Hooray, I did a good job!

Here's an example of a fantasy rehearsal out loud.

Situation: "I'm in the house, sweeping the kitchen floor, and my child comes up to me and says 'You're ugly!'"

Thoughts: "OK, this is an opportunity for some practice in anger-control and fortitude. I want not to reinforce him with a lot of negative emotion. I want to stay cool, just as I did so well the other day when he hit me. Let me remind myself, this isn't the end of the world. I want to relax my muscles, and let my jaw feel limp. I don't need to get revenge on him. I don't want to get down on myself that my child would do such a thing as this. What's the best response? A quiet temporary withdrawal of friendliness and giving is the one I want to choose.

Emotion: "When I relax and stay in control and figure out the best thing to do, that makes me less angry. But I still feel disappointed that my child would say something like this to me.

Behavior: "Now I'm not speaking; I'm looking at him with a disappointed, disapproving frown, as I continue my work, and then I look away and go on about my business. I'm resolving that if he asks me for some ice cream or something else in the next 15 or 20 minutes, as he's likely to do, the answer is a quiet and distant no, no matter what he does."

Celebration: "Hooray! I handled this in a way that I like. I don't like the situation I got dealt, but all I can control is the way I respond, and I like that!"

The good news is that if you do enough of these fantasy rehearsals, you can change your habit patterns in almost any way you want. The bad news, however, is that it takes many, many rehearsals. How many rehearsals does it take before a piano player can play scales correctly, or a dancer can do a dance step well, or a tennis player can hit an excellent serve? Rehearsals are numbered in thousands. Millions of people do thousands of rehearsals for sports skills, and feel—often correctly—that their time is well spent. Almost no one does thousands of rehearsals for fortitude skills, but in my opinion it would be much more worthwhile to do so.

It's helpful actually to speak the words aloud while doing a rehearsal. Once you've done fantasy rehearsals out loud, you can also simply sit quietly and see a mental movie of yourself carrying out the response in the way that you want to, with the desired behaviors and the desired thoughts. You can perform these rehearsals at any time you wish: when you are waiting for a bus, when you are waiting for a stoplight, when you are waiting to be served in a restaurant, at any time. The more of these imaginary rehearsals you can get under your belt, the more success you are likely to have.

Cycling Between Monitoring Real Life and Rehearsing in Fantasy

As you do all this practicing, the simultaneous step is to experience real-life provocative situations. It's useful to expand continually the list of provocative situations, drawing on those you encounter in real life. Every situation can be used in one of two ways. If you handled it well, then you want to run that memory of the positive handling through your mind often, celebrating and congratulating yourself for your positive response. This is a pleasant way of doing fantasy practice. If you handled the situation poorly, then you redecide how you would have liked to have handled it instead, and use that new image for more fantasy rehearsals.

Other Important Maneuvers to Increase Your Fortitude

This cognitive rehearsal strategy is not the only thing that will help with anger control and fortitude. There are other very important maneuvers people can do. One is getting enough social support from other people in your life. Social support, i.e. having friends (who may also be relatives) to count on and be with in pleasant ways, is a general antidote to overly great negative emotion. Another related maneuver for parents is getting enough time away from the child so that you can relax and not resent the fact that you have to spend so much time with the child. The techniques of personnel selection with babysitters are very important. Another is to regulate the general demands on you, so that your to do list is at handleable level. Knowing how to say "No" to additional commitments that make the time demands unhandleable is a very important step.

A Starting List of Provocative Situations

Here is a list of hypothetical provocative situations for parents, to get started in practicing fortitude.

There is a piece of mail that has come for you, that is a fairly important one. It is left out, and when you look for it a day later, you find that your child has first scribbled on it with crayons and then torn it up.

It is important that you arrive on time at a certain place, with your child. You ask your child to get dressed. But your child is watching television, and he sits and ignores you and continues watching.

You are eating supper, and your child whines that the food is no good and he doesn't like any of it and wants something else.

You are working on writing something on a computer word processor. Your child comes up and turns the power off, so that you lose everything that you were writing for the last 20 minutes.

You have a watch, and your child asks to see it. You tell the child he can see it if he will be extremely careful with it. He promises. Then 5 seconds after he takes it into his hands, he drops it and breaks it.

You are very tired after a very harrowing day. You are keyed up when you go to bed, but finally you fall into a relaxing sleep. Just at that moment your child wakes you up wanting something he could get for himself.

Your child is not supposed to come into your bed at night. One night you feel something wet in the bed and you discover that the child has not only come into your bed, but that he has wet your bed.

You and your child have been eating at a fast food restaurant, the type where you dump your paper and any uneaten food in a trash can when you leave. Your child dawdles over his food and does not eat. You tell the child that you will have to go soon, so if he wants his food, he should eat it. It comes time to go and you can't take the food with you, so you start to throw the food away. Your child starts screaming "No! Don't throw my food away!" Other people look at you as though you are doing something terrible.

Your child is playing with a friend whom he has invited over to the house. Your child has a toy, and you suggest that he share it with his friend. Instead, he grabs it next to his chest, and says, "No, you can't make me."

You have someone visiting your house, someone whom it is important for you to impress. Your child comes up and acts so nasty to this person that the person is very turned off.

You are doing some work in your house, and your child says to you, with no justification, "You're stupid." when you ignore this, the child says it a couple of other times, and when the child gets no response he hits you on the leg.

Your child whines at you and pleads and cajoles, asking for a certain food. Eventually you get it for him, specifically what he asked for. After taking one bite, he says, "I don't like this." He leaves the table and goes off and whines that he wants to see a videotape.

Chapter 21: Teaching Fortitude and Anger Control

Chapter Overview:

Sometimes you can teach children the same steps of learning frustration tolerance that we discussed in the previous chapter. An important preliminary step is to make sure that violent or angry behavior is not adaptive in real life for the child—that the child doesn't need this to defend himself against physical assaults from other children.

You can use the same principles we discussed in the previous chapter, even if your child is too young for or not interested in the formal practices described there. You list the situations that have provoked the child to tantrums or overly angry or violent behavior in the past. You also think of frustrations the child has handled successfully. Thus you come up with a list of potential positive examples to watch for. Then you watch for positive examples of fortitude. When you find them, you give immediate enthusiastic interest, tell another person about them, mention them in the nightly review, include them in the positive behavior diary, and turn them into stories, plays, and songs. You also expose your child to models of fortitude through stories and plays. You model fortitude in real life through you own self-talk, out loud. You cue the child when opportunities to practice fortitude are going to arise.

When a child screams and wails over some minor frustration, bear in mind that a tantrum is usually a way of getting someone else to do something. Usually the child is trying to get you to grant a request or give some attention. Therefore, if your child gets into the habit of screaming over trifles, you should ignore the screaming. Ear plugs help in doing this. If the tantrum occurs just after you have given the child a command (a reasonable and necessary one!), then enforce the command with gentle and unemotional physical guidance. If the young child escalates the tantrum to destructive or aggressive or dangerous behavior, then you use a short time out. You keep separate in your mind that you use ignoring for screaming and time out for actual destructive behavior. When at other times the child uses more appropriate ways to ask for attention or to start social interaction, you reinforce these. You define success by what happens over a course of days or weeks, not minutes.
****

This chapter reviews some ideas covered more thoroughly in other chapters, including those on differential reinforcement, and giving enthusiastic attention for the positive examples. In addition, the chapters on relaxation and on problem-solving are very relevant to the goal of this chapter.

Many children 7 years old or so will be able to learn exactly the same steps of learning fortitude that were mentioned in the previous chapter, if they are taught them concretely enough. How do you teach concretely? First of all, you do it by modeling these steps with situations from your own life, showing the child how to do it. Thus even if fortitude is not a skill that is high on your priority list, you can model for your child how to work on this skill using situations from your own life, and then encourage the child to do the same thing with situations from his own life.

An important preliminary step for the parent is to determine whether conditions exist that make what looks like poor anger control adaptive and useful for the child. For most adults, it is seldom that you must physically defend yourself against physical assaults; unfortunately this is not true for many children in our schools and neighborhoods today. As you enter a program of teaching anger control to your child, it is also important to attempt to insure that the child is able to inhabit a nonviolent environment, where anger control is indeed useful and more adaptive than violent self-defense. Insuring this may often take the form of various sorts of conversations with school teachers, bus drivers, parents of other children, and sometimes keeping a child off a bus or withdrawing the child from a school.

The following is a program for increasing fortitude with children too young to go through the same steps mentioned in the previous chapter.

A Program for Tantrums

By tantrums I refer to a child's screaming, crying, shouting, and perhaps getting on the floor and kicking his legs, in response to a frustration. If the child hits or kicks somebody, then that's no longer just a tantrum—it's physical violence. Tantrums are in my experience not difficult for parents to eliminate if they will follow the directions in this chapter.

The goal, however, should be not just to eliminate tantrums, but to help the child increase his fortitude. Fortitude is a very important skill. It's the one that is the antidote for lots of problems with children that parents complain about. The child who whines when he doesn't get his way, or has a tantrum, or gets aggressive, or gives up, can by definition reduce these problems by learning fortitude.

We can use each of the nine methods of influence to foster the growth of fortitude in the child. Let's think about the following: reinforcing the positive examples of fortitude, modeling fortitude, signaling when the practice opportunities are coming, and avoiding reinforcing the examples of poor fortitude.

In reinforcing fortitude, you use the same procedure I outlined earlier for any other psychological skill. Let's review it here briefly:

Make a potential positive examples list. Take a piece of paper and make a long list of very concrete situations that provoke the child to have tantrums or to exhibit intolerance of frustration. Make the list very concrete: for example, the child asks for some ice cream and is told no. Or another child grabs a toy away from this child. Or, the child is given a doll and wants another doll and is told that she can have only one. Any response to these that does not involve a great deal of negative emotional display is a positive example of fortitude. Think of any positive examples of fortitude the child already has in his repertoire, and put that on the potential positive examples list. One of the major stimuli to anger in children is the perception that they are being treated unfairly. As you generate your situations list, think of situations where the child experiences the unfairnesses that everyone must learn to tolerate.

Then watch for real-life actual positive examples, and respond with attention, approval, and excitement when you see them. Enter them in the positive behavior diary. Tell a third person about them in the child's presence. Go over them verbally in the nightly review. Write them in the positive behavior diary. Act them out with toy people and make real-life modeling stories from them, and sing songs about them.

For young children, you can prime the pump by acting out plays where the main character handles frustration well, and then another character remarks "Boy, he really put up with not getting his own way!" Alternatively, the character himself says to himself, "I'm glad I was able to put up with not getting my way." Read to the child stories that model fortitude and cooperation. If you're using the ones I wrote, stories such as "Mary Had a Good Time Anyway," "Helen and the Strawberries," and "Hank Doesn't Get to Go to the Zoo" are examples of stories modeling fortitude. If you're using my modeling songs, "I Can Take It" is meant to model cognitions of fortitude.

In real life you can model the "self-talk" associated with fortitude. For example, the parent is driving with the child and the traffic light turns red just when the parent wanted to go through the intersection. The parent remarks, to no one in particular, "I sure wanted to go ahead and go then, but I'll have to wait. But I can handle that, with no problem." Or the infant sibling of the child spills food over the floor, and the parent says, for the benefit of the older child, "I would rather not have to clean that food up off the floor. But, I can take it, just fine. This is a time where I have to put up with not getting my way."

Another technique useful in teaching fortitude is signaling to the child when a practice opportunity is coming up. When the child is going to receive a frustration, the parent can label the situation as such. This way, the child gets a signal that he gets a chance either to perform well or to perform poorly. For example, the child passes a candy machine and says "Mommy, buy me a candy bar!" The mother might respond, "Now you have a chance to practice putting up with not getting your way, because we can't get a candy bar now." That way the child knows that if he responds by saying, "Okay, I can handle that" or something like that, then the parent will be pleased and that the event will be recorded.

Now let's think about how the parent responds to poor fortitude and tantrums. If the child responds with physical aggression when frustrated, for example by hitting or kicking, then refer to the earlier section on time out and other consequences for aggression. If the child responds by yelling or screaming or nagging or whining, or tantrums, the following suggestions may prove useful.

Tantrums are almost always a technique the child uses in order to get his way. The parent should meditate upon the following sentence, repeating it over and over again as a mantra: "Never again will the child get his way by having a tantrum." A second thing to remember is almost as important: a tantrum is a request for attention. If it regularly fails to get the child the attention he wants, and if other more polite ways of asking for attention do succeed at getting the child attention, then the child will choose the methods that work rather than the method that does not work.

The automatic, consistent behavior of the parent while the child is having a tantrum, every time there is a tantrum, is first simply to glance and notice if the child is hurt or otherwise in need of immediate care, and then to go about his or her business as if the child were not there.

But how do you go about not paying attention to a tantrum when the child is yelling so loudly that he is literally hurting your ears? I recommend going to the drug store and buying some ear plugs. When the child starts screaming loudly, walk to where the ear plugs are kept and put them in. This gives the child a visual signal that you intend to ignore the screaming and not give in to it. It also makes it much more pleasant for you to ignore the screaming.

When the parent is ignoring the screaming during a tantrum, the parent should not be telling the child to be quiet. Any commands, any verbal interactions with the child constitute attention. If the tantrum is in response to a request that must be enforced by physical guidance, then the parent uses physical guidance gently, without excitement, and without any unnecessary words directed to the child.

When the tantrum has been over for thirty seconds or so, the parent then takes the ear plugs out and resumes interacting with the child as if nothing happened. If you decide that the child should get what he wanted, don't give it until at least ten minutes after the tantrum is over. That way at least some time separates the tantrum from the reinforcer. The reinforcer follows a period of non-tantrum behavior.

The child will be able to handle the ignoring much better if she has been told ahead of time that this is the procedure. The parent should sit down with the child and say something like, "We want to help you get out of the habit of screaming so much when you don't get your way. To help you with that, I'm going to do something different. When you scream, I'll notice and make sure that you're safe, but otherwise I'm not going to talk to you or get anything for you or do anything for you while you're screaming.

I think it's very important to use ignoring for tantrums and not to use time out. Why? If you put the child in time out for screaming, it doesn't make sense to end the time out before the child stops screaming. And what if the child screams for an hour? That's way too long, especially when ignoring of tantrums works so well when done consistently.

Suppose the child escalates the maladaptive behavior, and does something destructive or aggressive or dangerous. Then the child goes into time out and comes out after two minutes. If at that time the child continues to scream, but does not do anything destructive or aggressive or dangerous he gets ignored; if he does something aggressive or destructive or dangerous again, he goes back to time out for another two minutes. By aggressive or destructive or dangerous I mean actions such as hitting someone, tearing a book, throwing a hard object, brandishing a fist at someone, kicking a chair, or pushing over a piece of furniture.

I have seen children who bang their heads or scratch their faces in a bid for getting their way and getting attention from adults. In general, I have seen the same principles, and in fact the same strategy work for these sorts of problems as for tantrums. However, when the child's safety is at stake, I would advise parents to get expert guidance. With head-banging or other self-injurious behavior, you want the program to work quickly. With some head-bangers it's useful to use a special helmet as part of the program.

Since tantrums are ways of getting attention and getting one's requests granted, it is very important that the child be reinforced for positive ways of getting these things, when it is reasonable to do so. These are the behaviors that compete with the tantrums. The skill of appropriate social initiation, getting attention in good ways, is just as much the opposite of tantrums as fortitude is. What sorts of positive examples of social initiations are we talking about?

Let's list a few: coming up and asking a question, telling about something that happened, asking the parent to look at something he did, offering to help with something, requesting something from the parent in a polite way, acting silly or funny in a nondestructive way, singing or dancing around, looking at what the parent is doing, wanting to be read to, wanting to be played with.

What if the child's problem with fortitude is manifested in a more verbal way? What if instead of screaming, the child keeps on and on, nagging at the parent, arguing about why he should get his way, giving millions of reasons, in a way that is very exasperating to the parent?

A certain amount of persistence in pressing for one's way is an adaptive skill to have—it's the skill of assertiveness. However, enough is enough. The main thing for the parent to remember in this case is that it takes two to have an argument. The parent is under no obligation to respond to each of the child's responses. There is no problem with explaining to the child once or twice or three times why he cannot get what he wants, and then letting the child receive only silence in response to his further arguments. In the interest of modeling politeness, it might be nice for the parent to say, "I'm not going to say anything more about this." Then the parent silently attends to other business while the child whines and nags and argues. It is helpful to tell the child at some time when all are calm that this will be the nagging protocol, and to act out the new strategy with toy people—again, the "extinction burst" may be less severe in this case. For other techniques on arguing, please refer to the chapter on arguing that was presented earlier.

In all these strategies, you measure success not by what happens over a course of minutes, but by what happens over a course of days. If the tantrums or nagging gradually get less and less frequent, the strategy is working. The first time the child gets ignored, the child might increase the volume of screaming or the intensity of arguing. It's important to stay the course, and not to give up when the child temporarily escalates the unpleasant behavior.

In thinking about the nagging child, where do you draw the line between maladaptive nagging and backtalk, on the one hand, and appropriate use of persuasion, on the other hand? This is not a black-and-white distinction. The art of persuading others to see your point of view, by the use of logic and reasoning and citing of facts, is a very useful and important skill. To rely on verbal means of influence as opposed to physical force is at the basis of civilization and government. Therefore you certainly don't want to quash all conversation on the pros and cons of doing a certain thing. If the child has a particularly good point, a particularly compelling reason, for wanting you to do things a certain way, and if the child presents it in a polite and articulate way, then there is nothing wrong with reinforcing that behavior by giving in to the child's reasoning.

In any of these strategies, it is important for the parent to keep a calm and relaxed emotional tone. Excitement on the parent's part is often rewarding for the child, (as I've said many times before) and if the parent can eliminate all excitement from the parent's response, the child will more quickly get over the tantrums. Many of these things that parents are being asked to do are very difficult. The techniques mentioned in the previous chapter make it easier, over time.

Sometimes you might get in touch with with something from your past experience that makes a certain behavior particularly distressing. For example, a child teases in a way similar to how your brother teased you when you were a child. Sometimes it is useful to include in the imaginary rehearsal a "self-talk" reminder that the present situation is not the same as that of the past.

Chapter 22: How Not to Spoil

Chapter Overview:

When you are assertive with your child, you insist, in a firm, deliberate, and nonhostile way, that your decision will be carried out. One of the biggest benefits of assertion is that you don't reinforce the child's negative behavior by giving the child what he wants whenever he acts upset or angry. Thus you avoid teaching the child to be a chronically upset and angry person. As a rule, you grant the child's request only when the child wants something reasonable, and asks for it politely. Here are several reasons parents are nonassertive, and spoil their children: a general habit of being nonassertive with everyone; guilty feelings over not spending enough time with the child; the child's precious status as an only child or a hard to conceive or adopt child; guilt over divorcing; vying with a divorced (or married) partner for the child's affection; loneliness and insufficient social support of the parent and dependence on the child for friendship; reaction against the parent's experience of a harsh upbringing; social pressure from a community where most of the children are spoiled; unusual tolerance on the part of the parent; a carryover of habits appropriate for infants to the post-infancy years; and competition with the other parent for the child's affection. If you want not to spoil your child, examine your thoughts about how awful it is when the child is distressed. It's useful to conduct a mental debate on the topic, "Resolved: the good parent often does things that frustrate the child." Some points on the side of the affirmative: the young child doesn't have the judgment to make the correct decision all the time; it reduces anxiety in children to know that someone wiser is in charge; fortitude takes practice; young children's distress tends to be short-lasting; with consistent enforcing of a rule, the protest and distress rapidly diminish; if the child doesn't learn fortitude, other people, and even the parent, will have trouble liking him. What skills, other than fortitude, become deficient in the child whose caretakers can't be assertive? Option-evaluating, empathy, compliance, positive aim, delay of gratification, pleasure from kindness, handling criticism, and relationship-building skills all suffer. You can avoid this depressing outcome by enforcing reasonable requests of the child, and not granting the child's unreasonable or impolite demands. Differential reinforcement is the key: the child gets his way by acting nice and does not get his way by acting unpleasant. But what is reasonable for the child to expect of you, and for you to expect of the child? The best way to answer this question is to ponder examples of specific situations. Fantasy practice will help you respond in the way you have decided upon as reasonable. By explaining to your child in clear words what the "new deal" will be when you begin to be more assertive, you can reduce the time it takes your child to get over the hump of protest and negativity.

****

This chapter complements the chapter on anger control for parents, and other sections on eliminating unnecessary commands. It's important not to be too bossy with your child, on the one hand, because too many unnecessary commands lead to a child who is both disobedient and bossy. It's important not to speak often in harsh and hostile tones, because your child will imitate these tones and because too many harsh tones spoil the emotional climate. On the other hand, it's also important to be able to stick up for your own rights and those of others beside the child. It's important that the child not often practice habits that bother people a great deal. If the child is to succeed in school and work, it is important that the child develop the habit of respecting reasonable authority.

By assertion skills we refer to the art of insisting on one's own decision, even though it is opposed by another person: the art of being firm, of not taking no for an answer, of making it very clear what you want, of making it clear that you mean business, of acting in an authoritative way. We refer to turning down requests, of not doing something someone would like you to do, or insisting on doing something someone would NOT like you to do. Assertion is different from aggression: assertion is done in a rational, deliberate way, without violence or threat of violence.

A major portion of assertion skills in a parent is the art of "nonreinforcement of negative behavior" and "nonreinforcement of negative emotion." The parent who spoils a child tends to give the child whatever the child wants when the child acts or feels irritable or angry.

In an earlier chapter we spoke of request-granting by parents. My advice was to grant requests based on consideration of two variables: the reasonableness of the child's request, and the politeness with which it is requested. Granting reasonable polite requests tends to reinforce these, and declining the unreasonable and impolite ones tends to extinguish these. One spoiling way to grant requests is for the adult to grant them based on his own energy level, and on the intensity with which the child demands, rather than on reasonableness and politeness. The child learns to escalate the intensity of a request so as to increase the chance of its getting granted. A second spoiling way to grant requests is simply to grant all of them, reasonable, unreasonable, polite, or impolite. A large fraction of what any human being desires must go ungranted, and the child who doesn't get used to this fact of existence is headed for trouble.

In the chapter on commands we also spoke of limiting commands to the child to those that are very reasonable, but enforcing those commands without fail. This is also an important part of being a nonspoiling parent.

By setting limits we refer to the act of making a very clear decision as to what is permissible and what is not permissible, deciding exactly where the line is drawn, and communicating that very clearly.

What is the relation between parents' appropriate assertiveness and children's fortitude? The child develops fortitude skills by practicing dealing with frustrating situations. If your child whines and cajoles and complains when frustrated, and if you respond by giving in, two bad things happen. First, the child misses out on practice in fortitude. Second, the child gets reinforced for intolerance of frustration.

Let's look at some examples of non-assertiveness on the part of the parent, where assertiveness is called for.

The parent says, "It's time for bed." The child says, "No, I don't want to go to bed," and acts fussy and angry and whiny. The parent backs off. A few minutes later the parent says, "It's really getting to be bedtime." The child does the same thing again. Each time this happens, the child is practicing using negative emotion and behavior to oppose the authority of the adult. Plus, the child is not getting effective practice at tolerating the frustration of stopping a pleasant activity and going to bed without procrastinating.

The parent and child are out for a walk together. The child says, "I want to go over and see that over there." The parent happens to have an appointment, so the parent has to conclude the walk without delay and get to the appointment. The parent says, "We have to get back." The child whines and complains so much that the parent gives in for a few minutes. The parent resents the child's selfishness, however, and as the parent is late for the appointment, the parent feels irritated toward the child.

The parents report that the child won't "let" one parent pour the child's breakfast cereal in the morning, but will only "let" the other parent do it. The parents accede to the child's order out of fear that the child won't eat enough and will be cranky later.

The parents report that the child won't "let" them have a conversation with each other. When the child interrupts them, they feel obligated to attend to the child, for fear that the child will get more upset and have a tantrum if they don't.

The parent picks out clothes for the child to put on, and the child whines and rejects them. The parent tries something else. The child rejects these as well. The parent asks the child what the child wants. The child chooses some clothes, then changes her mind, then spends a lot more time choosing, then changes her mind again. Meanwhile the parent is getting more and more irritated with the child. This builds up until the parent yells at the child.

The parent and child are at a party. The parent says, "It's time for us to leave now." The child ignores this request, and the parent gets into a conversation with another adult for a while.

Now let's think about what an appropriately assertive response of the parent would be, in contrast to an aggressive response, for some of these examples.

The child refuses to go to bed. Aggressive response: parent yells at the child, "What do you mean you're not ready! You go when I tell you to go, if you don't want to get punished." Assertive response: parent takes child by the hand, and while leading the child toward the bedroom, says, "Come on. First we'll get your pajamas on, and then when you've brushed your teeth we can read a few stories before good night."

The child wants to see something while the adult and child are on a walk. Aggressive response: parent roughly grabs child's arm and says in a harsh voice, "Get over here, you little brat! Move!" Assertive response: "We can go see it another time. Right now I have to get back, to make an appointment." The child whines, "No, I want to see it now." The parent ignores this response and continues to walk with the child toward home. Or, the parent calmly informs the child, "When I say it is time to leave, your job is to comply. It's very important that you do your job."

The child yells, "I don't want you pouring my cereal. You don't do it right! I want [the other parent] to pour my cereal." Aggressive response: parent yells, "That's enough of that! You're not going to get any breakfast at all, period!" Assertive response: parent explains, "What you're asking for is not polite, and it's not reasonable. I'll give you your breakfast, and you can decide for yourself whether you want to eat it or not." The child says, "I'm not going to eat it!" The adult replies, "That's up to you," and ignores the child for a few minutes, attending to other family members or the morning newspaper.

The child ignores the parent's words, "It's time to leave now" when they are at the party. Aggressive response: The parent hits the child. Assertive response: The parent physically takes the child by the hand and leads the child out the door. If the child starts to scream and resist, the parent gets the child out the door even more quickly. The parent says, "The rule is that when I say it is time to leave, you must comply right away. Before you go to any more parties, we will role-play this at home and practice it twenty-five times." The parent makes a habit of consistently enforcing the command to leave, immediately after giving it.

Let's think about some of the motives that lead parents to be nonassertive with the child when assertion is more appropriate.

Some parents are in a general habit of hardly ever being assertive with anyone, and this habit simply generalizes to the child. These adults fairly frequently might feel that they are being taken advantage of by other people, or might find themselves strongly resenting something someone is doing while feeling powerless to oppose that action. They might find it hard to say "No" to anyone even when it is appropriate, or to ask someone not to do something, even when that something is inappropriate and offensive. The image of someone's disliking them or being angry at them or thinking badly of them is often intensely unpleasant, in a way that is out of proportion to how much is really at stake. If so, the parent might benefit from some work on the art of appropriate assertion with adults as well as with their child. Many people have helped themselves be much happier by getting better at the art of assertion. This skill, however, should be developed in consort with other conflict-resolution skills: skills of conciliation, of listening to another's point of view, of generating just solutions to interpersonal conflict, and so forth.

On the other hand, certain parents find it particularly hard to be appropriately assertive with their child, even though they find it easy to be assertive with other people. Here are some reasons this may be true.

Sometimes working parents spend a great deal of time in their professions and do not have much time to spend with their child. They want the time they do spend with the child to be pleasant, plus they feel a guilty about having so little time to spend with the child. For this reason, when the child begins to display negative emotion, they tend to give the child whatever the child wants in order to make the child happy again.

Sometimes it may have been difficult to conceive or adopt a child, or the child may be the only child; the child is thus precious and extremely highly valued to the parents. Their impulse is to do what the child wants and never to disappoint the child in the short run (even though the child is losing out on important psychological skills in the long run.)

Sometimes a divorced parent feels guilty about putting the child through the pain of the divorce, and wants to spare the child any more pain, including the pain that would come from enforcing a rule, even though the rule is appropriate.

Sometimes two divorced or divorcing parents each want the child to like him or her better than the other parent, in the fantasy or real circumstance that the child will choose between the two parents.

Sometimes a parent is going through a temporary or permanent lonely time and is feeling unsupported by other people, and needs to have the child on his or her side, and thus does not want to incur the child's negative opinion by frustrating the child, even when the frustration is appropriate.

Sometimes a parent experienced a very harsh childhood, with a parent or pair of parents who had an aggressive style. In order to avoid repeating this with his or her own children, the parent avoids appropriate assertion as well as inappropriate aggression.

Sometimes parents find themselves living in a community where the norm is to give children whatever they want and to spoil them, and the parents can't resist the social pressure of what the other families are doing.

Sometimes the parent is simply an unusually patient and tolerant person, who really doesn't mind sacrificing for the child by giving in to the child and not sticking by limits. The parent does not suffer from the child's low fortitude, but the child and the other people who come into contact with the child do suffer.

Sometimes a parent is convinced, with very good reason, that proper parenting of an infant is to try to discover what the child wants and give it to her as soon as possible. The parent continues this paradigm of "I'll meet any need, in response to any distress," into the toddler and preschool years, where this pattern induces spoiled and bratty behavior after having induced trusting and happy infancy.

If you talk about the child's "letting" or "not letting" you do something, think about whether you are spoiling the child. If you frequently make requests of the child with the question, "OK?" at the end, examine whether you are in an appropriate position of authority. If you live in an upper-middle class suburb in the United States, examine whether you are spoiling your child, since spoiling seems to be an endemic problem in such regions.

In thinking about changing one's habits, it's a good idea to pay attention to the situation that evokes a habitual response, and the thoughts, emotions, and behaviors that then follow. (I use the mnemonic STEB to remind myself to think of situation, thought, emotion, and behavior.) If we want to change any one of these elements of our response to a situation, we will make it easier if we can also change the other two in a way that is compatible with our new, more desirable response.

For example, suppose that someone recognizes in herself a behavior pattern of inappropriately giving in to the child when the child whines or complains. Are there any unspoken thoughts that are relevant? Is there some emotional conditioning that is relevant?

Often when someone fails to be assertive when appropriate, the underlying thought, or belief, is something along the lines of "It would be terrible if this person did not like me or had bad feelings about me." That thought is often closely connected with an emotion of fear that may be hard to recognize: fear of being disliked by the other person. The giving in and appeasing the other person serves to get rid of the fear.

At other times, the thought is more along the lines of "When my child is unhappy, that means I'm being a bad parent." Again, the thought makes it sound like a terrible thing for the child to experience negative feeling from frustration. Maybe the parent's feeling in this case is guilt rather than fear. Another variation on this thought is, "When the child is unhappy and upset he is getting emotional scars that will hamper his ability to be happy."

In learning to set and enforce appropriate limits with the child, it will often be useful for parents to look inside themselves, and to see if they find the thought that it would be especially terrible to disappoint the child, and to see if they find some fear that keeps them from doing this.

Parents who find themselves thinking or feeling these ways are not doing anything terribly out of the ordinary. The sorts of thoughts I have described happen very frequently in parents who are very psychologically healthy. It is easy to get into these patterns of thinking, partly because there is a kernel of truth in them. If the child consistently hates the parent, that indeed is a very bad outcome, one worth putting much energy into avoiding. If the child is upset all the time, without ceasing, that is a terrible thing; the parent might have good reason to doubt that he is taking care of the child properly. So it's easy to sometimes generalize the appropriate worry and guilt and fear that one would feel over sustained and consistent negative feelings in a child, so as to feel this way toward the moments of anger and distress that are an inevitable, necessary, essential part of growing up for all children.

Suppose that a parent studies his or her own thoughts, emotions, and behaviors, and decides that yes, he is overestimating how bad it is for the child to be distressed, and yes, he is failing to be appropriately assertive with the child for that reason. What is a good step for the parent to take in changing that pattern?

A good place to start is with thoughts and beliefs. Consider this debate topic: "Resolved: the good parent often does things that frustrate the child." You may want to pretend to prepare for a debate, where someone else will argue the opposite side of the question. Can you defeat the idea that a good parent never causes an instant of distress in the child? If you can't, you may not have the arguments necessary to convince yourself when the time comes to enforce an appropriate limit.

In preparing for this debate, here are some things to keep in mind.

First, a child by his very inexperience and immaturity does not know what is best for him, in many circumstances. He needs "someone older and wiser telling him what to do" much of the time—if he didn't need this, he would be able to get his own apartment and live on his own. The fact that he wants something doesn't mean that it is good for him, as evidenced by the fact that some children would choose a steady diet of potato chips and pop and a steady television diet of violent cartoons if given free choice.

Second, when the child is young and doesn't really know how the world works, perhaps on some level he often realizes that. When the child is allowed to be in charge of things he should not be in charge of, then, the child often feels the feelings appropriate to the realization that he is in over his head. The child is often much less anxious when adults are willing and able to exert appropriate authority and take charge.

Third, the child can't learn fortitude well if the adult is afraid to withhold whatever the child wants. In order to learn any skill you must practice it.

Fourth, the bad feelings that children have over the minor frustrations of life that adults inflict upon them tend not to last a long time. The child who screams "I hate you" while being dragged to the bath tub may have very loving feelings only ten or fifteen minutes later. This is part of the nature of children, especially young ones.

Fifth, if a certain reasonable rule is enforced consistently, the child usually stops getting distressed over it. Why get distressed over it if the distress isn't going to get reinforced by someone's giving in to you? For example, when a consistent bedtime routine begins to be enforced, there is often much protest at the beginning of the "new deal." Once it becomes a routine, however, that clearly will repeated every night despite protest, the protest drops out, and with it the negative feelings of the child. The child actually begins to feel a sense of security in the routine. Thus paradoxically, by being willing to produce a certain amount of necessary distress in the child, the adult reduces the long-run distress that the child feels.

Sixth, if the adults cannot set and enforce appropriate limits, and the child gets into the habit of getting his own way through negative behavior even at times when this greatly infringes upon other's rights, the child will become very much disliked by other people. It is extremely important that the child learn at least enough fortitude that other people don't come to reject him.

Seventh, if an adult goes on long enough without being appropriately assertive with the child, the adult will usually come to resent the child's selfish behavior and come to feel that the child is taking advantage of him or her. This state of being reduces the positive feelings that the adult has for the child. And this is the last thing that the child needs. Whether the adult manifests this resentment by sullen behavior or by "blowing up" at the child, it is not good. The adult owes it to the child to influence the child to behave well enough that the adult likes to be around the child!

I think these arguments leave you well-armed in your debate with "Mr. X" over whether or not to be appropriately assertive with your child. But to look at the situation more thoroughly, let's review the psychological anatomy of being spoiled.

The Psychological Anatomy of Being Spoiled

Poor problem-solving, anger-control, and organization skills in adults tend to lead to the same skill deficiencies in children. But problems with assertion in parents toward children tend to lead, not necessarily toward unassertive children, but to spoiled and bratty behavior.

Spoiledness and brathood are not in the official psychiatric nomenclature; sometimes it is difficult for people to recognize this state in children.

I preached earlier that psychological skill concepts are more useful than derogatory labels in thinking about children's problems. I want to practice what I preached, and translate the concept of spoiled brathood into psychological skill concepts. What skill deficiencies lead to a child's acting spoiled? There are several:

1. Option-evaluating. This is the skill of deciding whether a given option for solution of a two-person problem is just or unjust. For the spoiled person, the reasoning is, "I want this, therefore I deserve it." Or, "I prefer it, therefore it is just." There is a certain tone of voice children use in protesting, that seems to say, "But it's totally just that I get what I want." One day I had told a 9-year-old child at church a couple of times that I was leaving and needed to take one of my possessions home with me, and therefore he would have to give it to me. He protested, "But I want to keep playing with it," in a tone of voice that seemed to say, "You must not understand. If you understood that I want it, that would be sufficient reason in and of itself for you to give it to me." Getting skilled at option-evaluating means that you can tell the difference between what you want and what is reasonable for someone to give you.

2. Empathy. The confusion of wishes and justice is connected with a habit of seeing a problem from only one point of view. "I want it, therefore it's just," leaves out the counterargument of "The other person wants something else, therefore that's just too. Humh, they can't both be just. How can I decide what's reasonable?" Thus the skill of looking at hypothetical interpersonal situations from both people's point of view is a very useful one for a child engaging in bratty behavior.

3. Fortitude. Prototypical bratty behavior is engaging in a great deal of negative emotion in response to a frustration, with the expectation that someone will give you your way and the frustration will be removed. Deficiencies in the whole group of fortitude skills can develop, including handling mistakes and failures and handling criticism.

4. Compliance. Going along with the reasonable requests of a legitimate authority (such as parents or teacher) is very difficult, and instead there gets to be a game of "let's thwart the authority figure." Sometimes the child plays this game with perverse gleefulness, sometimes with sullen resentfulness, sometimes with angry defiance. It often is not as fun, particularly in the short run, to engage in adult-directed activity, and follow directions, than to do child-directed activity, and follow your own lead. However, to feel that it is automatically horrible and totally unpalatable to follow someone else's direction is an error leading to spoiled behavior.

5. Positive aim. What does it do to the human spirit to be able to get what you want, get someone to do your bidding, through thousands of repetitions, by exhibiting (and feeling) intense negative emotion? What happens to you as tantrum after tantrum gets reinforced by someone's giving in to you? I believe that with enough repetition, one can learn that "it's useful to feel bad." The development of the skill of positive aim, of trying consciously and unconsciously to make things better, not worse, and to feel better, not worse, can be disrupted. This can lead to a miserable existence.

6. Delay of gratification and sustaining attention to tasks. When there is the repeated pattern wherein you don't immediately get your way, you display negative emotion, and someone gives you what you want, you miss out on the learnings that it's possible to "hang in there" with unpleasant experience and get a greater reward by "toughing it out." Thus it becomes hard for the spoiled child to attain the happiness from accomplishments that only are achieved through sustained work.

7. Kindness and pleasure from kindness. The spoiled child can often be kind and giving when there is nothing else to do, and when the kind behavior entails no sacrifice on one's own part. But being truly skilled in kindness entails patient and unselfish sacrificing of one's own immediate wishes.

8. Handling criticism. The child who has developed a sense of overblown entitlement may develop either of two habitual reactions to criticism: to ignore it, even when it is constructive and absolutely necessary, or to become righteously indignant upon receiving it.

9. Friendship-building. If spoiling is bad enough, people in general have a hard time tolerating the child's frequent negative emotion and demanding, entitled behavior, and the child finds himself without friends, and rejected. Then the skills of trusting and socializing and relating to people in general begin to suffer greatly.

The person with very great skill deficiencies in all these areas is usually a very miserable person indeed. Of course, all different degrees and combinations of skill deficiencies can be seen in different people.

Summary of How Not to Spoil

After detailing such a depressing litany of skill deficiencies that can develop as a result of being "spoiled," let's review quickly how to avoid these, how not to spoil the child.

You will avoid spoiling to the extent that:

1. When you want reasonable things from the child, you enforce them.

2. When the child makes unreasonable or impolite demands on you, you don't grant them.

3. The child has a chance of getting what he wants by being nice, polite, and cheerful, and almost no chance of doing

so by being hostile or whiny or feeling bad about trivial things.

Here are some "mantras" to meditate on in learning not to spoil the child:

Mantras For Meditation on Not Spoiling Your Child

1. Spoiled behavior is learned. It happens more often, the more it "works."

2. I don't need my child to approve of me. My child does need to learn good behavior.

3. I will not try to get bad behavior to go away by appeasing the child.

4. I will not reinforce my child for undesirable behavior by giving what he or she wants.

5. When the child gets very upset over not getting a minor luxury, I must not rescue the child.

6. I grant the child's requests for non-necessities only when they are BOTH reasonable AND politely stated.

7. Disobedience is not to be tolerated.

8. I give one clear, firm command and if it is not obeyed I use physical guidance or impose a consequence.

9. I am prepared to withhold for as long as necessary any or all luxuries from my child.

10. My child must speak to me with respect and politeness—not because I need it, but because my child needs to practice it.

11. The fact that my child's peers all have something does not mean it is good.

12. The fact that my child wants something is not sufficient reason for me to give it.

13. I will model for my child how to avoid acting rude even in adversity.

14. I will model speaking with respect and courtesy, especially to family members.

15. When my child speaks disrespectfully, I teach or impose a consequence rather than reciprocate.

16. I must indoctrinate my child in the value of doing useful and helpful things for others. Useful work, courteously done, is the opposite of spoiled behavior.

17. I must get my child to do useful work, regularly, for the family and other people, for the child's good.

18. Both my child and I must say please, thank you, you're welcome, and excuse me when appropriate.

19. Differential reinforcement. Differential reinforcement. Differential Reinforcement.

There above summary avoids settling a Great Judgment Call: What ARE "reasonable" expectations for your behavior, on the child's part? What ARE "reasonable" expectations of the child's behavior, on your part?

These judgments have to be made on a situation by situation basis. But we can practice on situations, and you can add more situations to this list as they accumulate. You can almost always come to a better conclusion by pondering and discussing than you can by making a snap judgment. So let's do an exercise.

Exercise: Reasonable Requests, Reasonable Expectations

Decide what you think about what is reasonable in these situations, and compare your judgment with mine.

1. A 9 year old child has forgotten a major homework assignment, until late the evening before. He asks the that the parent write a note to school excusing him for a day for sickness, so that during that day he can get the assignment done. (My judgment: reasonable for parent to deny request.)
2. A 2 year old orders her seated parent, "Don't sit in that chair. Sit over there." When asked why, the child repeats the request. (My judgment: reasonable for parent to deny request—politely.)
3. A 5 year old has gotten lots of the parent's attention for a couple of hours. The parent gets a phone call, and the child calls the parent and demands that the parent pay attention to the child during the phone call. (My judgment: reasonable for parent to deny request.)
4. A 14 year old has made some money babysitting. She wants to get some contact lenses in addition to the glasses she already has. Her parents don't feel that she needs contacts when the glasses are working OK; she proposes to use her own money to buy them. (My judgment: reasonable for her to get her way, unless family economic circumstances are very dire.)
5. A father is, as usual, tired from working all day and would like to lie on the couch and watch TV all evening. The 4 year old child says, "Will you please play with the toy people with me?" (My judgment: reasonable for the child to get her way.)
6. The parent has prepared some supper that consists of spaghetti, salad, green peas, bread, and milk. The 7 year old child says, "I want a hot dog!" (My judgment: reasonable for parent to say, "Supper has already been made, and this is it; you can take it or leave it.")

7. The 4 year old child asks for a parent to tie her shoe. When the father starts to tie it, the child says, "No! I want my mommy to tie it!" (My judgment: reasonable for parents to say, "No, your daddy will do it.")
8. A parent has to make an exchange at a department store. As they pass the toy section, the 6 year old child sees a ball, and says, "I want the ball!" The child has about 3 similar balls at home. The child whines and cries, "Please get it for me!" It only costs a dollar or two. (My judgment: reasonable for the child to leave the store empty-handed.)
9. A 6 year old boy has been having trouble with aggressive behavior toward peers. The parents tell him, "Because you've been having problems with being violent, we're getting rid of all violent toys and videogames, we're eliminating television, and we're having only totally nonviolent videotapes." The child has a major tantrum, and complains bitterly that all his friends have them and want to play with them and he can't have friends if he doesn't have them. The child also argues that those toys are his property, and the parents can't steal them from him. (My judgment: reasonable for parents to stick to their "non-guns" and get rid of violent stuff.)
10. A 7 year old child has just been assigned a 3 minute time out, in a room other than the rest room. The child says, "But I have to go pee!" The parent ignores this. (My judgment: reasonable for parent to deny request for 3 minutes.)
11. A parent is playing with fingerplays and rhymes with a 2 year old child. The child delights in a certain one, and wants the parent to repeat it; the parent does so. Then the child says, "Again?" and wants the parent to do it a third time. (My judgment: reasonable for the parent to repeat things like this many times, if she has the patience for it, in the interest of the child's attention span and repetition-tolerance skills.)
12. A 10 year old child proposes that instead of doing his homework first thing when he comes home, he play with his friends at that time, since they're most available then; he will do his homework after supper. (My judgment: reasonable to experiment with this plan and see how it works.)
13. A 12 year old wants to be taken out to a certain restaurant rather than eating at home. He very persistently argues that he is really in the mood for the certain type of food you can get only there, and it has been a long time since he has been there, and he isn't in the mood for what they have at home, and it doesn't take long to get to the restaurant. (My judgment: reasonable to stay home.)
14. A 9 year old has some athletic shoes that are not worn out. But he argues that he will suffer a great decrease in popularity at school unless he obtains shoes that have a pump attached to the tongue of the shoe, and also movement-responsive electric lights that are built in to the soles of the shoe. (My judg-

ment: reasonable to make do with the regular athletic shoes.)

15. An 11 year old comes home with a compact disc, purchased with his own money, of music whose lyrics explicitly endorse violence toward women. The 11 year old wants to listen repeatedly to the compact disc and put a poster of the musicians up on his wall. The parents get the urge to insist that the disc and poster be returned to the store, or thrown away if not returnable. (My judgment: parents' urges are reasonable.)

16. A 16 year old gets a ticket for driving under the influence of alcohol. The parents get the urge to eliminate the privilege of driving the family car, or any car, for 1 year after this offense, to be extended to one year after any future evidence of drinking alcohol. The adolescent thinks that this is way too harsh a punishment. (My judgment: parents' plan is reasonable.)

17. A 10 year old has found it very difficult to learn reading and writing. The child would like to get some tutoring in reading and writing, from a parent or someone else. The child would also like the parents to arrange with the teacher to make it possible for the child to succeed in the meantime in science and social studies homework by reading the textbook to the child, and writing down from the child's dictation answers to homework questions. (My judgment: this plan is reasonable, and in fact has worked well several times I've seen it in action. It's unlikely that the child would come up with this plan by himself, however.)

18. A 15 year old is in a school play. She wants her father to come, and he has promised to see it. But shortly before the play he gets invited to a party that will allow him to see some people he enjoys. (My judgment: reasonable to skip the party and see the play.)

19. A 12 year old would like a parent to participate heavily in the scout troop. If the parent does this, it will require a substantial time commitment. The parent will have to take time out of recreational activities that are more preferred, such as hunting (which the child doesn't like) and playing golf (which the child is not good at). (My judgment: reasonable for parent to make this sacrifice for the child.)

20. An 8 year old says to his mother, in a bossy tone of voice, "Get me some milk!" When the mother says, "You didn't say please," he says in a very loud voice, "Oh, all right! Please! I want you to get me some milk, right now!" The parent says, "I'm sorry; the answer is no," and does not listen to any further requests for a while, no matter what the manner and the tone of voice. (My judgment: parent's behavior is reasonable.)

21. A 10 year old is reluctant to help in chores around the house. The parents decide that the child will get no money from them whatsoever except in return for the child's work, and that the child will have to save for most of the nonessentials that the child wants to buy. (My

judgment: parents' behavior is reasonable.)

22. A two year old gets for a present an ornament to be hung on a Christmas tree, that is highly breakable. The child wants to take the ornament off the tree and carry it around, with a high likelihood of shattering it soon. The parent gets the urge to take the ornament away, but then thinks, "After all, it was given to her. And she'll probably cry if I take it away." (My judgment: reasonable to give one quick calm explanation, take it away and put it out of reach, and ignore the subsequent crying.)

23. The parents are at a party, and it becomes time to go so that the children's bedtime can be kept. The parent says, "It's time to leave now." The child has been playing with other children, and the child says, "But I can't go now, I'm in the middle of something." (My judgment: reasonable for the parent to insist that the child interrupt whatever it is, immediately, and leave. It is more important to maintain a precedent of leaving places immediately when the parent requests, than it is to finish up a particular activity. On the other hand, if the parent wants to plan ahead and observe the child's play for five minutes, watch for a good stopping point, and then give the command that must be obeyed immediately, that's reasonable too. The crucial thing is that once the command is clearly given, it must be immediately obeyed.)

As these situations indicate, my bias is for parents to make substantial investments of time in being with the child and patiently engaging in child activities; not to indulge the child with material things; and not to accede to the child's emotional demands for nonessential preferences about the immediate situation. My strong belief is that the parent should exercise judgment about what is reasonable before giving a command; once the command is given, the parent's job is to make sure that it is obeyed, and obeyed quickly, or to deliver consequences that will make the command more likely to be obeyed in the future.

Using Fantasied Situations to Practice Appropriate Assertion

If you want to start using more appropriate assertion with the child, the next step is to make a list of as many situations as possible where you've failed to be appropriately assertive. Included on this list situations that might occur in the future. These will be the situations that you will use in fantasy rehearsal and role-playing practice.

Then, for each of these situations, decide what sorts of thoughts, emotions, and behaviors you would LIKE to carry out in the future. Usually the thoughts will be of the "not awfulizing" or "not getting down on yourself" variety: e.g. "It's not terrible that the child is distressed for a few minutes. It will be good in the long run. I am being a good parent, not a bad one." Usually the emotions will be rather calm. And the limit-enforcing behaviors might involve 1) ignoring the child's inappropriate demands, 2) physically guiding the child, e.g. by taking the child by the hand and leading the child, to enforce a command, 3) calmly stating a consequence, e.g. "If you don't want the cereal you don't have to eat it, but you're not getting any more," 4) giving the child a reprimand, 5) giving the child a time out, 6) withdrawing a privilege, 7) withdrawal of friendliness and giving for a time.

After you have decided upon a desirable, appropriate response for each of the situations listed, then is the time for fantasy rehearsal or role-playing rehearsal of the appropriate responses.

As discussed many times in this book, fantasy rehearsal consists in vividly imagining the situation and imagining your own response, making a mental movie of the scene running as you want your own response to be; fantasy rehearsal out loud consists in describing this movie out loud as it is running. In role-playing you act out your response with someone else. As you continue practicing in fantasy and role-play, you monitor your real-life behavior. You watch very carefully to see if situations like the ones on your list come up. You try to do the sorts of responses you have practiced, and you notice exactly what goes on both inside yourself and with your child. If you did what you wanted to do, remember to celebrate and congratulate yourself immediately. If you did not do what you wanted, add this situation to the list and use it for fantasy rehearsal.

The whole procedure, of course, is very similar to that described in the fortitude chapter. The task of the person who is overly aggressive is similar in lots of ways to that of the person who is not assertive enough: to practice calm, deliberate, and rational responses to situations involving conflict between two people.

"The person who is overly aggressive" and "the person who is not assertive enough" are, of course, often the same person. I have made mistakes in both of those directions, many times. The human condition for most of us involves thousands of times in our lives when we make mistakes in each of those directions. If we can simply increase the rate with which we respond appropriately to conflict-type situations, we will be making a very important step.

Once a parent becomes more appropriately assertive, should the child's behavior should start to improve immediately? Unfortunately, there is almost always a "getting over the hump" phenomenon where the child protests more than before, because the child is not getting his way. Once the child learns that the "new deal" is steadfastly in place, and no matter how much he protests the limit will still be enforced, then the child's behavior improves. But you should expect a few days of increased struggle when the "new deal" of steadfastly enforced limits is put into place.

Thus there may be reason to expect that "things get worse before they get better" when starting to enforce a limit. The behaviorists call this an "extinction burst": the misbehavior that was formerly rewarded by the parent's giving in is no longer rewarded, and is undergoing "extinction"; but before the behavior is extinguished it bursts forth with greater frequency.

In my experience there is a way for parents to shorten the time of "getting over the hump" during which "things get worse before they get better." The useful strategy is to communicate to the child the "new deal" in symbolic ways, rather than simply letting the child infer it from your new responses. If you explain very thoroughly to the child, and act out for the child several times in role-playing or with toy people, exactly what will happen from now on, the child may not have to test so many times.

If the time of "getting over the hump" seems to last more than a week or two, the parents should look for other problems. Maybe the rule is not appropriate, or maybe the child is continuing to be reinforced for protesting, or maybe there is some person who is letting the child continue the "old deal" rather than consistently sticking to the new one.

Chapter 23: Courage Skills

Chapter Overview:

The first step in dealing with fear is to assess the realistic danger of the situation. If you're in actual danger, the task is reducing the danger, not reducing realistic fear. But we can develop fears that are out of proportion to the danger. Sometimes this happens by response generalization: the fear spreads from a dangerous situation to a nondangerous one. People can also learn unrealistic fears by imitation of others or by being reinforced for fearful behavior. In getting rid of unrealistic fears, exposure is key: you have to get yourself into the scary situation so that you can learn to master it. Some ways of making this less painful are as follows. You go gradually along a hierarchy from less scary to more scary situations. You practice in fantasy before doing the real life exposure. You get factual information about the dangerousness of the situation. You remind yourself of how nondangerous the situation is as you expose yourself to it. If your child talks to you about fears, be a good listener, using reflections and avoiding premature or false reassurance. You can teach a child a variety of coping strategies in dealing with scary situations. One is to use self-talk to remind himself about the nondanger of the situation. Another is to get support from friends and allies, either in imagination or in real life. Another is to take scary fantasy characters and make fantasies about them in the daytime that gradually change them into allies. You can help your child greatly by minimizing movies and other media exposures that introduce new scary and violent characters into your child's memory bank. Learning muscular relaxation, recalling previous successful experiences in dealing with fear, putting oneself into the role of someone protecting a real or imagined weaker character, and highly valuing bravery will also make the task easier. You should keep in mind the principle of differential reinforcement: fears, as well as every other human response, are to a large extent under reinforcement control. You want to celebrate your child's bravery, and give unrealistic fearfulness the minimal reponse compatible with kindness.

Even young children can learn to clarify their thoughts about how bad something is, and how likely it is to happen. It's a great exercise for children to think about hypothetical situations, and to decide how bad a thing might happen, and how likely that bad thing is to happen. Learning to evaluate danger in a deliberate way will help your child in learning both courage skills and carefulness skills. You want the child to learn that the reasonable response to danger is to try to protect oneself, and the reasonable response to fear when there is little or no danger is to "tough it out." Children can learn to use very similar steps of fantasy practice that were described for fortitude: describing the situation, thinking rational thoughts, imagining feeling the desired emotions, imagining the "toughing it out" behavior, and celebrating success.

****

There is a very important first decision that we need to make when anyone is afraid. Is the person in actual danger of harm—either physical, social, or psychological? If a child is in actual danger, then the child's fear is doing just what fear is meant to do: alert people of the presence of danger and motivate the person get out of danger. Not all fear is bad. Being afraid of driving at 120 miles per hour is something we all hope adolescent children will have. Being afraid of playing Russian roulette gives someone a better chance of surviving. If a child is greatly fearful of being left with someone who is abusing him, that fear is realistic. If the child is afraid to eat something that he had a very bad allergic reaction to, that fear is realistic. If the child is afraid of a pair of large ferocious Rotweiler dogs, we wouldn't want to "cure" the child of fear for these dogs. If the child is afraid to watch a gory horror movie, we don't want to cure the child of this, either: here the child is in psychological danger from seeing such violence. If the child, a novice dancer, is scared to go dancing in a group of people who are very expert, and very angrily impatient with novices, the child's fear of negative social consequences is realistic.

So the first thing the parent should do when the child is afraid is to gather information about whether there is a realistic part of the child's fear. The parent should study whatever it is that the child is afraid of, and make sure that it isn't actually endangering the child. If the child is in actual danger, then the task of adults is to protect the child from danger, not to get rid of the fear.

Things get complicated, however, when realistic fear sometimes "spills over" to produce unrealistic fear. For example, the child who learns, very realistically, to be afraid of the ferocious rotweilers down the street may also be very afraid of the gentle cocker spaniel next door. The child who was afraid of the bully in the park who threw rocks at him may also become afraid of the nice child in the park who wants to play gently with him. When the child is afraid of things that resemble the actually dangerous thing, even though these new things aren't really dangerous, we call that "response generalization."

Response generalization is thus one way that unrealistic fears can get started. Another way is less direct. Sometimes children can learn fears by seeing someone else look very frightened in a certain situation. The child can get the idea that the situation is very dangerous and fear it himself, even though he has never experienced anything bad directly. For example, the child sees his friend looking deathly afraid of robbers at night, and infers a sense of danger: he learns by observation.

Children can also learn to be fearful by being rewarded for fearfulness. For example, suppose that a child is afraid to play with peers, with his mother around, and he runs to her and looks frightened. Suppose she talks to him and cajoles him and asks him what he's afraid of and looks very concerned. If the child has been feeling a little short on attention, the attention he gets for being afraid rewards his fearfulness. The efforts to help may inadvertently make the fear get worse or come more frequently.

Or suppose that a little boy wakes up in the middle of the night scared, and because he is scared he gets to come in and sleep beside his mother. The good feeling he gets from doing that may tend to make the fear come more frequently.

One sort of reward for fearfulness is "bargaining" with the child about the fearfulness. For example, the child acts very afraid of going to the doctor's office, and the parent immediately offers the child to get the child some ice cream on the way home—in the spirit of, "If you'll do it anyway, you'll get rewarded." But the offer of the ice cream may reward not the "doing it anyway," but the fearfulness, because the offer of the reward came immediately during the fearfulness and seems clearly related to it. The child learns that getting afraid is a good way of getting some free treat.

I'm not saying that the child actually calculates and says to himself, "Hmm, if I act afraid, I'll probably get something," and then deliberately becomes fearful. But fearfulness can still be under reinforcement control. You can teach animals to do things more often if they get rewarded for them, even though the animal doesn't consciously formulate the connection in his mind (at least not in language, we assume). Probably lots of things that people do are the same way—we do more often those things that get us a payoff, without really fully realizing why.

Secondly, I'm not saying that the child who has been inadvertently rewarded for fear is putting on an act of being afraid: the child actually is afraid. We can learn to feel emotions more often, just as we can learn to do behaviors more often.

Let's assume that we have satisfied ourselves that a child's fear is not realistic, that the situation that the child fears is not actually putting the child in danger. Then what do we do to help the child get over the fear? Treatment of fears has been going on systematically for several decades now, and there have been various programs devised. If you look at what all these programs seem to have in common, there seems to be one essential element to all of them: exposure. That is, the programs that work lead the person to expose himself to the situation he is afraid of, until the fear can wear off.

With adults who want to get over a fear, convincing them to voluntarily expose themselves to the feared situation is the order of business. But a child may not want to expose himself to the situation. He may cry and protest so much when he has to, that parents often don't have the heart to make him expose himself to it.

For that reason, there are several techniques developed so as to make exposure less painful. One way is by going gradually along a hierarchy. The child who is afraid of dogs might do well to start with a stuffed dog, then to a very cute and small dog, before learning to handle being around larger dogs.

Another way is to practice the exposure in dramatic play with the child before practicing it in real life. For example, the child who is afraid of darkness may in play with a therapist experience a scene in which the lights are turned out in imaginary activity rather than real life.

Another way is to provide information to the child about the nondangerousness of what he fears. Sometimes this is more effectively done through storytelling or looking at pictures than through direct verbal instruction. For example, a child who is afraid of butterflies may be shown a book about butterflies and see pictures of people with butterflies on them, while he is being told that the people are very gentle with the butterflies and the butterflies are gentle with the people.

When instructing a child about the nondangerousness of a feared situation, is it good to stress how it won't hurt, and can't kill the child? If you find out that the child is already afraid that he will be hurt, or that he will be killed, or that some other specific bad outcome will happen that won't happen, it is important to be honest and straightforward to the child that the outcome won't happen. For example, a child is afraid that he will stop breathing and die while he is asleep if he doesn't lie on his back, and the parent tells him that he doesn't need to worry about that, he can't die by that means, that the body is built such that it won't let that happen, etc. On the other hand, if the child is not already afraid of something, sometimes adults put ideas into their heads by what they say. For example, the child is going to get his blood pressure taken, and someone volunteers the statement, "It won't hurt!" Sometimes the child becomes afraid just by someone's raising the possibility of getting hurt, especially if someone said, "It won't hurt" before he got a shot. It would have been better for the person to say, "This will feel like a balloon is being blown up and squeezing your arm. It will get tight, and then quickly get loose."

How does an adult find out whether the child does have an idea that something bad is going to happen to him, or not? By listening to the child. When the child starts talking about the subject, the parent listens and reflects what the child has said, and waits for the child to tell something else, or asks follow up questions at times.

Now suppose that the child does realize that the feared situation is not dangerous, but is still scared. What can be done to help the knowledge have an effect? One coping method in the face of a feared situation is to remind oneself that the situation is not dangerous. It's one thing to know something; it's another to remind oneself of it frequently enough that it is right at the center of one's attention.

One way to teach a child to use this coping method is by dramatic play. The adult models a character facing a scary situation, and all the while saying his thoughts, e.g. "This is scary, but I know that it's not dangerous, and that I am perfectly safe. I may not like doing this, but I know that nothing bad will happen to me. If I can put up with it, I'll be really proud of myself.... I did it. Hooray!"

Another good coping method was illustrated by the self-talk above: "self reward." It was self-reward when our protagonist said, "I'll be really proud of myself... I did it. Hooray!" If the child can learn to reward himself for exposure to the frightening situation, that makes it much more pleasant.

Another way of making it less scary to face a scary situation is to use that universal antianxiety agent, social support. Facing the scary situation with some supportive person makes it easier. Even imagining yourself having a supportive companion with you can make it easier. So in dramatic play, the model might say, "I'm going to face this all by myself, but I'm going to imagine that my guardian angel is with me, walking right here beside me, making sure that everything comes out OK."

Sometimes the problem is that the child has imaginary people around, all right, but they're ghosts or robbers or people intent on murder. One strategy is to take the characters who are persecuting the child and put them into daytime fantasies where they gradually get reformed, and gradually get turned into allies who will help the child and others rather than persecute them.

If the scary fantasy characters are violent characters the child is constantly seeing on TV and in movies, then this task is virtually impossible. It's possible to change a scary character and turn him into an ally if the only input is your own imagination; movies and television however would keep bringing the villain back to his accustomed violence. This is one of several reasons why children should not watch violent TV and movies.

Here's another tried and true coping response that makes it less unpleasant to face a scary situation: muscular relaxation. Becoming limp and loose and relaxed tends to reduce fear. Thus model characters in dramatic play can give themselves instructions about relaxation: "This situation is scary. One thing that helps me to face it is to relax my muscles, and to let my face just get real loose and limp...."

Another important coping strategy is to recall a previous instance in which you successfully handled a scary situation. By doing this you activate the mental scripts, and possibly the neuronal circuitry, that enable you to handle scary situations.

Still another coping mechanism in dealing with fears is to get into the role of the protector with some real or imaginary character who is weaker than you. The small child who is heard comforting her Teddy bear and telling him not to be afraid, that she will take care of him, is using this coping mechanism.

How can we help a child become more motivated to expose himself to the situations he unrealistically fears? One way is to let your conversation promote the goal of being brave. Talk with admiration of brave people, talk favorably about times in your life that you did something brave, so that bravery becomes something that is highly valued within the family group.

I mentioned trying not to reward the child with lots of individual attention in response to the child's being scared. If it is necessary to give the child attention, or if it feels inhumane not to, what sort of attention is best? Planning and discussing how to cope with the situation is best done at a time and place when the child is not scared. That is, it's best to plan ahead, and practice before the situation actually occurs.

When comfort is provided for the child who is scared, especially avoid the type of attention where the adult seems to plead with the child to get less scared. If the child is given individual attention, it should be the sort in which the adult is very calm and relaxed, and gives the message that the child will get over being scared in his own time, and that time will come sooner or later.

Now suppose the child does expose himself to the feared situation, and successfully handle it. How does an adult reward the child for the skill of handling situations that previously were unrealistically feared? In the same fashion that I've already recommended for increasing other skills, such as enjoying kind acts, tolerating frustration, sustaining attention to tasks, and so forth. That is, make a written list of the things the child is unrealistically scared to do or see, and review this list frequently. Whenever the child does any of the things on the list, whoever sees it gives enthusiastic attention, involving anything from praise and congratulations to enthusiastic tracking and describing to a spontaneous parade with singing and marching. When one family member has seen the child do something brave and someone else hasn't, the one who has seen it should tell the other one about the brave behavior, in the child's hearing, whenever possible. At the end of the day, go over with the child all the brave things the child has done during that day. Act out the brave things with toy people, make home-made modeling stories about them, and sing songs about them.

All these suggestions tend to reduce the pain of exposure to scary situations. But it's still difficult to see a child experiencing any pain whatsoever, and particularly it's hard to use my parental authority to have a child do something painful. Not all fears need to be tackled immediately. The child who is afraid of the dark, for example, will do just as well having a night light for as long as she wants. The three year old child who is afraid of going in a swimming pool may be best "treated" by being allowed to stay away from swimming pools for a couple of months or years, after which time the fear may no longer be an issue. That's why it's a matter of judgment when to tackle a fear and when to simply let the child avoid the scary situation until she's a little older. In most cases it's not hard to decide whether it's possible to put off dealing with the fear, or whether it's causing so much pain that it should be dealt with now.

When it is necessary to subject the child to some uncomfortable exposure in order to help her get over the fear, consoling thoughts for the parent are that 1) the child's pain will be reduced in the long run by getting over the fear quicker, 2) the fear of the specific situation may be reduced by the child's seeing that the parent is not afraid that the child experience it; and 3) the child may gain a certain amount of security in the knowledge that the adult, who is older and wiser, is in control of major decisions, and not the child.

Disutilities and Probabilities and Fear

In the chapter on teaching children decision-making, and especially the section on the decisions game, we spoke of the fact that an option under consideration is good or bad depending upon the product of a utility and a probability: how good an outcome is, multiplied by the likelihood that it will happen, for each possible outcome of the option. Similarly, a situation is dangerous or not dangerous depending on the product of a disutility and a probability: how bad a thing may happen, and how likely is that to happen?

Many times when people are very scared, they focus on how bad it would be if something happened, but they don't appreciate how unlikely it is that the thing will happen. For example, the person with a phobia of bridges appreciates how bad it would be if the bridge collapsed at the very moment that he went over it, but doesn't appreciate how unlikely this event is. At other times, people appreciate that something is likely to happen, but don't appreciate how trivial a setback it would be. For example, someone with a social phobia anticipates that at a party, at least one of the people he meets will not be terribly impressed with or attracted to him. This indeed is likely for most people, but assigning a very high disutility to this is "awfulizing." Thus it can be very useful for people with anxiety to learn to think explicitly and separately about how bad things are and how likely they are to happen. In the next section I'll present a sample set of instructions to children to help them understand these ideas.

Teaching Children to Deal With Fear of Nondangerous Situations

Children with phobias, children with more general anxiety problems, those with extreme shyness, and those with obsessions and compulsions, all have in common that situations that are not gravely dangerous evoke more fear or bad feeling than they should. But distinguishing between fear that is unrealistic, and the many realistic fears that exist in a world where real danger abounds is a difficult cognitive task for a small child. The following is a brief teaching program to help young children distinguish between fear where there is real danger—in which case protecting yourself is the first priority—and fear where there is no real danger—in which "toughing it out" is the thing that will help the most. Children as young as first grade can understand this script.

***

Let's talk about what DANGER means. The more likely it is that something really bad will happen to you, the more danger you're in.

Suppose someone says, "A very large fly could maybe fly over and untie my shoe." How much danger do you think the person is in? Would you say a whole lot of danger, pretty much, or only a very little bit?

I would say only a very little bit, because if it did happen, it wouldn't be very bad. And also there's hardly any chance that it would happen. So that person isn't in danger. Not from the fly untying his shoe, anyway.

Suppose, though, that someone was in a country where a war was happening. This person's town was getting bombed, and the house next to them just got blown up. This person feels very scared. How much danger is this person in?

I would say he's in a lot of danger. That's because getting blown up is very bad, and for this person it looks likely to happen.

Now let's see if you can listen to these situations and tell how much danger the person is in.

Suppose that someone is scared, at the idea that while he's away from home, his pencil will fall off his desk. How much danger is he in?

Probably none, because it probably isn't very likely to happen, and even if it did happen, it wouldn't be very bad.

Suppose that someone is very scared, because he has somehow gotten signed up to fight in a boxing match, and he isn't good at boxing. Also, the guy he's supposed to fight has knocked out almost everybody he's ever fought. How much danger is he in?

He's in a lot of danger, because there's something that's very bad, which is getting knocked out, and it looks like it has a high chance of happening, unless something changes.

Suppose that someone is scared, because he's riding in a car, and the person driving the car is going very fast, maybe 100 miles an hour, and the tires are screeching and they are just missing running into other cars and telephone poles. How much danger is this person in?

He's in lots of danger, because there's something that's very bad, which is having a wreck and getting hurt or killed, and it looks like it has a high chance of happening, unless something changes.

Sometimes there is something very bad that could happen, but there's still no danger, because there is such a small chance that it will happen. Here is an example.

Somebody is very scared. He says, "I'm scared that while I'm walking by this building, the whole building will fall over on me." The building looks just fine. Is this person in a lot of danger, a little danger, almost no danger, or what?

I'd say no danger. Maybe it's possible that a perfectly OK looking building could fall over on somebody. But it's so unlikely that that will happen, that I would say the person is in no danger.

Sometimes there is something that is very likely to happen, but there's still no danger or almost no danger, because the thing isn't very bad. Here is an example.

Somebody is very scared that maybe there will be somebody in his school who will have a birthday, and not invite him to the birthday party. How much danger is the person in?

Almost none, or none, because even though it is likely that that will happen, it's not such a bad thing. It's not very harmful to the person.

Suppose that somebody is out in the woods. There are a bunch of hunters with guns who are shooting a lot, and they are trying to shoot deer. The hunters have a lot of beer with them and they are drinking a lot of it, and some of them are so drunk that they can't even walk straight. The person feels scared that one of them might shoot him if he doesn't get farther away from them. How much danger is the person in?

I would say pretty much danger. It's very bad to get shot, and it sounds like the chances of it are high enough to be scared about.

Suppose that someone has hurt his back. His doctor has warned him, "Don't try lifting anything heavy for a while, or you'll hurt your back even worse." Someone says to him, "Can you help me carry my piano somewhere?" The person says, "Sure, I'll help you." But then he remembers about his back, and all of a sudden he feels scared for just a moment, that he'll hurt his back again. How much danger is he in, if he tries to lift the piano?

I would say pretty much danger if he tries to lift it, because hurting his back again is pretty bad, and it sounds really likely that he'd hurt it again.

On the other hand, if he says to the person, "I'm sorry, I just remembered I can't lift it, because of my back." Now how much danger is he in?

Now he's in almost no danger of hurting his back again. He escaped the danger by doing something about it.

There are several types of danger. Sometimes danger has to do with actually hurting your body or getting sick or getting killed. Sometimes danger has to do with losing friends and having people not like you or admire you as much. Let's think about which of these types people are in, in the situations below.

A person has to give a speech in front of the people in his school. He has forgot to prepare his speech, and doesn't have anything to say. He feels really scared. What sort of danger is he in? Is it the danger of hurting his body, or the danger of losing friends? How much danger do you think he's in?

Four or five of a boy's friends say to him, "We dare you to jump off that bridge into the river. We'll all think you're a coward if you don't do it, and we won't like you any more." The person starts to do it. But then he looks down, and sees how far it is, and realizes that he doesn't know how deep the water is, and thinks that if he lands wrong, he could wind up dead or in the hospital. He feels very scared. What danger is he thinking about now? Is it the danger of hurting his body, or the danger of losing friends?

Then the same boy thinks about saying no to the dare, and he thinks that his friends might make fun of him and not like him. He also feels scared of this. What danger is he thinking about now—is it the danger of hurting his body, or danger of losing friends?

If the bridge is very high up, and nobody knows how deep the water is below, which danger do you think is bigger? What do you think this boy should do?

Somebody is going to play at a basketball game. He thinks to himself, "If I make a mistake, and miss a really important shot, maybe people won't like me as much." What danger is he thinking about? Is it the danger of hurting his body, or the danger of losing friends? If the boy is a pretty good basketball player, how much danger do you think he's in? Would you say a whole lot of danger, pretty much danger, or only a very little bit of danger?

Suppose somebody feels perfectly good, and doesn't have a cold at all. But he worries that he's going to sneeze and get mucus all over his nose and his lip, and people will look at him and they won't like him as much from then on. Is he worried about the danger of hurting his body, or the danger of losing friends? How much danger do you think he's in: a whole lot, pretty much, or only a very little bit?

If you feel scared and there is danger, the thing to do is to try to protect yourself from the danger. If you feel scared and there is almost no danger, then the thing to do is to "tough it out." To tough it out means to be tough and be brave and let the scared feelings gradually go away. You think about the other times that you handled scary things bravely, and do the same thing this time.

Why should you tough it out if there's no danger? It's not because it's wrong or bad not to tough it out. But if you tough it out, and you get over the fear and the bad feeling without doing anything to protect yourself, then the next time the fear and bad feeling doesn't last as long, and gradually you get over it. Plus you get more practice in toughing it out, and you get better and better at toughing it out for when the next time comes along.

I'll give you some situations, and you decide whether the person should protect himself from the danger, or tough it out.

A person is out on a golf course, on a high hill. It is starting to thunder and lightning. The person knows that lightning has hit the golf course before. He doesn't want to get hurt by lightning, and he feels worried. How much danger do you think he's in? What do you think he should do: protect himself from the danger, or tough it out?

Someone has done his homework really well. He knows his lesson really well. But he's afraid that his teacher will ask him a question, and he'll miss it. Is he worried about hurting his body, or losing friends? How much danger is he in? He gets the urge to protect himself from the danger by staying home from school. Do you think he should protect himself from the danger, or tough it out?

A boy is learning to play the piano. He is all by himself. He starts to practice the piano. But then he's afraid he'll make a mistake. He feels scared. How much danger do you think he's in? Do you think he should protect himself from danger, or tough it out?

A girl has a neighbor with a very ferocious and very big dog. The girl is walking along the street, and the big dog comes running after her, growling and showing his teeth. The girl feels scared. How much danger do you think she's in? Do you think she should protect herself from danger, or tough it out?

Another girl has a fear of animals. This girl has a friend who has a very lazy and very cute little cocker spaniel dog, who is very nice and who hasn't bit anybody in his whole life. The girl is afraid of the dog anyway, and gets the urge to protect herself by leaving the friend's house. How much danger do you think the girl is in? Do you think she should protect herself from the danger, or tough it out?

A boy shook hands with somebody at a party. The person did not seem the least bit sick. When the boy went to the bathroom later, he washed his hands really well. Still later, the boy thinks that maybe he might catch a disease from touching the person's hands, and gets the urge to try to protect himself by going and washing his hands again. How much danger do you think the boy is in? Do you think he should protect himself from the danger, or tough it out?

Somebody sees a picture hanging on the wall, and it doesn't look straight. He makes it as straight as he can. It still doesn't look exactly straight, and this bugs him and makes him feel bad. How much danger is he in? He gets the urge to protect himself from the danger by straightening the picture again and again. Do you think he should protect himself from the danger, or tough it out?

Somebody is at home. He remembers a time earlier in the day when he coughed. He thinks he might have coughed on someone. He can't remember for sure. He feels a very bad feeling. How much danger do you think he is in? Do you think he should protect himself from danger, or tough it out?

Someone is walking on a path in the mountains at a time and season where rattlesnakes are sometimes found. He hears a rattling sound in the trail in front of him. He finds himself feeling scared. He gets the urge to protect himself from danger by stopping and looking very carefully to see if there is a rattlesnake, and then walking way around the snake if there is one. How much danger do you think he's in? Do you think he should protect himself from danger, or should he just tough it out and walk straight ahead and not let himself get off the trail?

Here are some things to do when you get a scared or worried feeling.

1. You answer the question, what am I scared or worried will happen? In other words, you figure out what harm or danger you are worried about.

2. You figure out how much danger you're in.

3. If you're in danger, you try to protect yourself from the danger.

4. If you're in almost no danger, then you tough it out.

5. While you tough it out, you remember other times that you toughed it out, to help you do it again. You also think thoughts that will help you not feel so scared.

6. When you finish toughing it out, you congratulate yourself that you were brave enough to tough it out.

Here's a story of someone doing these things.

One time a boy felt worried, and he wanted to wash his hands. He asked himself, "What am I worried about? He realized that he was worried that he would catch a disease. He thought to himself, "How much danger am I really in?" He realized that he hadn't been around anyone with a very serious disease that he could catch. And he realized that even if he got a disease, the chances are he would get well fairly quickly. So he decided he was in almost no danger. He decided that since he was in no danger, he would tough it out and not wash his hands. He thought back on times when he'd wanted to check and see that a picture was straight, and how he had just toughed it out then. He remembered how good he felt about himself when he was able to tough it out. He waited and just felt bad for a while. Finally he noticed his distress going down, and after a while the distress went way down. He said to himself, "Hey, I toughed out another one!" He felt good. He went to his mother and said, "I got the urge to wash my hands because I felt scared of a disease even though I was in almost no danger, but I toughed it out, and now I feel OK."

Here's another story of someone doing these things. A man was driving his car. When he got home, he felt worried and scared. He asked himself, "What am I scared will happen?" And he figured out that he was worried that he had hit someone with his car while he was driving. He said to himself, "How much danger is there, either to this person or to myself?" He decided that if he really had hit someone and the person was lying by the road hurt, someone would have stopped and helped the person by now. But then he decided that the chance that he really could have hit someone without even realizing it was very low. So he decided that there was almost no danger. He still had the urge to drive back and see, as if that would protect himself from the danger. But he decided that since there was really almost no danger, he would tough it out. So he didn't drive back. He thought of other times that he had been tough and brave before. He relaxed and he reminded himself that the situation he was in was not awful. After a while, he felt better, and he said to himself, "Hooray, I toughed out another one!"
****

Some Steps in Fantasy Rehearsal of Courage Skills

The following steps summarize much of what was spoken of in this chapter. The person who wishes to increase courage skills can learn to go through these steps for hypothetical situations in fantasy, and then in real life, try to enact the pattern practiced in fantasy.

Steps for Practice for Scary Situations
1. Situation: Describe the situation. What are the sights, sounds?
2. Thoughts:

Here's an opportunity.

What bad could happen? How bad is it? How likely is it? How much danger am I in? If I'm in danger, I want to protect myself. If I'm not, I want to tough out this situation.

Let me remember a time when I handled a situation like this well. I want to see and hear it in my mind.

I want to relax.

Not awfulizing.

Listing options and choosing.

It will be an accomplishment if I can tough it out.

3. Emotions:

If I feel scared, that doesn't mean I'm in danger.

I'm feeling brave, confident, happy, relaxed, excited, or having fun.

4. Behavior: I'm doing the option that I chose. I'm doing something that makes sense.

5. Celebration: Hooray, I did a good job!

Chapter 24: Courage At Separations and Bedtimes

Chapter Overview:

If a parent leaves a preschool child in the care of a total stranger or group of strangers, it's normal for the child to feel scared. You can prevent a great deal of misery by overlapping caregiving: you allow the child to get to know the substitute caregiver while you are present. This practice also lets you learn more about how good the substitute caregiver is. In group care situations, when the substitute caregiver is kind, sometimes the child still feels realistic separation fear because of mistreatment by other children. The child can also fear separation because of worries that something bad will happen to you. If the child senses that you are in danger, have an open discussion with the child. Being open about any danger you are in, and creating a nonsecretive climate, will allow the child to be reassured when you get out of danger. When unrealistic separation anxiety persists, the next strategy is to expose the child to separations along a hierarchy of difficulty. You start with using dramatic play to practice separation. Then you move to real but very brief separations; you gradually increase the time of separation. You celebrate each successful step. and you are very dependable about the time of reunions. At the moment of separation, don't ask your child's permission: you are announcing, not asking. And your nonverbal demeanor should be confident, cheerful, and unworried, so that the child will get the message that all is well rather than that something horrible is about to happen. You should never tell children you will just be gone briefly when you will be gone a long time; you should never sneak away from the child without saying goodbye.

Harmonious sleep and bedtime customs will result in a less cranky child, and perhaps more importantly, a less cranky parent. Sleep requirements range from about 13 hours for 2 year olds, to about 8 hours for 18 year olds. Going to sleep at night is easier if the child has gotten lots of exercise and has not slept too late the previous morning. Put together a nightly ritual that addresses all reasons for getting out of bed (such as being thirsty or needing to go to the bathroom) before the moment of bedtime separation occurs. Use differential reinforcement throughout the bedtime ritual, paying attention when your child complies and ignoring when he resists. If you put the child to bed at the same time each night, biological rhythms can make the child ready for sleep when the time comes. Setting a timer to make a light come on at wake-up time lets the child know when to go back to sleep and when it's time to arise. If you use differential reinforcement, you don't let your child sleep with you whenever the child is scared or upset. Such a custom comforts in the short run but actually fosters negative emotion in the long run. Provide for the child the same conditions to fall asleep that the child will encounter when he wakes up in the middle of the night. That way the child can fall back to

sleep after awakenings. This means don't let the child fall asleep on a couch, in your arms, with you sitting in his presence, with music playing, with a television on, with a pacifier in the mouth, or with bright lights on. You want the bed and the low lights to signal sleep. If a child can't fall asleep without you, and stays in bed and screams, then set up a schedule of checking on the child every few minutes without picking the child up and without being very reinforcing. If the child comes out of the room, one system that has worked well has been to take the child back to bed each time he gets out, in a nonreinforcing way, however many times it takes until the child stays in bed by himself and falls asleep. Monitoring with a talley sheet and celebrating successes the following morning helps such a program to work. Finding out about underlying fears the child has is best done by the listening techniques described in an earlier chapter. One of the modeling stories illustrates the technique of transforming scary images at bedtime into more handleable images during daytime fantasies. The nightmares get replayed with a happy ending, and the scary characters get reformed and converted to allies. The child practices the self-talk of mastery of bedtime fears during the daytime. Tackling nighttime fears can result in some temporary distress from the child; it is almost always better to get that distress over with and learn to master the situation than to prolong the agony by avoiding it and reinforcing distress.
****

Let's first talk about how to solve and prevent the problem of children's becoming overly distressed and upset when the parent leaves.

It's important to realize that a certain amount of anxiety when left with total strangers is normal and desirable. Suppose a parent is leaving, and introduces a three year old child to a caretaker the child has never met before; thirty seconds later, the parent leaves. Probably most three-year-olds will experience some distress and fear. And probably it is adaptive to do so. John Bowlby pointed out how fear of separation probably conveys a certain survival advantage upon young children. Children without separation anxiety, who would be totally fearless wandering off from a parent in a crowd, or who would feel no discomfort with strangers, over centuries of evolution have been at greater risk of death.

Parents these days spend a lot of time teaching children not to go with "strangers." But preschool teachers or doctors or mental health practitioners or babysitters are strangers from the child's point of view, until the child gets to know them.

So how does the parent help a person move, in the child's point of view, from being a stranger to being a nonstranger? The key is overlap. The child gets to know the person, with the person and the parent both present. The parent introduces the child to the person and hangs around in the background, or jointly plays with the child, while the child gets to know the person.

Babysitters can be hired to come over for an hour or two and play with the child, while the parents or parent is still at home. The next time, when the parents go out, the babysitter comes over an hour or so before the parents go out. That way the child has plenty of experience with this person with the parents around before being asked to spend time with the person without the parents around.

Or the parent takes the child to the preschool, and takes along a book or some work to do. The parent sits in a corner somewhere and works, while the child does whatever is natural. The parent is available for the child to come and check in with at times. When the child has gotten to know the children and the new caretakers well enough to feel confident, separation is much more easily accomplished. For some children, the time to comfortable separation is a matter of minutes; for others it's a matter of days or even weeks. The more friendly and engaging the substitute caretakers are, and the more the child takes to them, the shorter the time is.

Sometimes using this principle of overlap in and of itself prevents or solves the whole problem of separation anxiety. Of course, the parent during the overlap period is not just letting the child get used to the substitute caregiver, but also noticing the quality of the caregiving. If separation anxiety develops or persists, one of the major hypotheses is that the child experiences something unpleasant during the separation. If the child is being mistreated, the task is of course to end the mistreatment first, and only second to use the procedures to decrease unrealistic fears. Especially if the child develops separation anxiety after having been at one time comfortable with the substitute caretaker, or develops separation anxiety in one caretaking situation and not another, the parent should more thoroughly investigate the caretaking situation.

Having the child in the care of a very kind caregiver does not automatically prevent mistreatment at the hands of other children. A situation with a caregiver who is so gentle and loving that she does nothing to deter an aggressive child from terrorizing other children is a very plausible cause of separation anxiety. If the child is being regularly mistreated by another child, the substitute care is not good. It must be improved or terminated.

If the child is afraid for the safety of the parent, that can be another reason for separation anxiety. I have seen separation fears in children whose mothers have been threatened by ex-spouses. If there is really any danger that the parent is in, and the child suspects this, then paradoxically, it is important for the child to hear this honestly. Why do I say this? Won't that make the child more anxious? In the short run, hearing about the danger may make the child more anxious; however, when the danger ceases, the child will be able to trust that the danger is over. If the child is assured that there is no danger when there obviously is some, then the child learns not to be assured, and can be set up for long-term worrying that there is some danger he isn't being told about.

Now if there is no clear-cut explanation found for the separation anxiety, and we are left with chalking it up to temperament or the child's disposition, there are procedures that almost always help. The same procedures also help if in the past there was a reason for the child to fear separation, and now there is no longer, but the child is still scared.

The basic strategy is simple. It consists of 1) giving the child exposure to separations and reunions in some form, repeatedly; 2) having a step-by-step progression from the easiest to the hardest separations, taking baby steps rather than giant leaps; 3) celebrating handling separations well when the child does so; and 4) being dependable in making sure that reunions take place when they are promised.

What sort of exposures to separations and reunions are the easiest and least traumatic to use in the first step? At the bottom of the hierarchy are the separations in fantasy play rather than in reality. The parent may engage the child in fantasy play with toy people, and in the course of play, have a character say good bye and drive off to go somewhere for a while. Then the character returns after a few seconds for a happy reunion. If you are lucky, the child may become fascinated by the plot of separation-reunion and start acting it out himself, repeatedly. The more practice the child can get with these pure fantasy separations, while the parent is in the room, the better.

For the next baby step, the parent makes the fantasy play more realistic, by designating one character as the substitute caregiver, one as the parent, and one as the child. The parent acts out a play for the child in which they are all three together; the parent leaves the room for five seconds and then comes back. The parent then rejoices that the child tolerated the separation. The parent tells the child that before long they will act out this play in real life, to let the child practice separating from the parent. If the child is apprehensive, they stick with practicing just with the toy people, until the child gets bored with the activity.

Then the substitute caregiver, the parent, and the child can practice having the parent leave for five seconds, without the parent actually going out the door, but just pretending to go out the door. The parent counts to five, and then pretends to come back in the door. The parent says, "Hey, good for you, you put up with separating." After practicing in this manner, the five second separation is then carried out in reality. The parent says goodbye to the child, walks out the door and closes it, counts to five, and comes back inside for a joyous reunion with the child.

Next, the time that the parent is gone is progressively lengthened. The time goes from five seconds to fifteen, to one minute, to two minutes, to four minutes, and so forth. This is continued until the child is staying with the substitute caregiver with the parent out of the room for half an hour or forty-five minutes, and then to however long a time the substitute caregiver has for the child.

During the time the parent is gone, the substitute caregiver is engaging the child in fun activities—such as dramatic play or some other activity already established as a mutually gratifying one for child and caregiver.

What if the child starts crying and screaming during the separation, in this program? If you have made the steps on the hierarchy small enough, you don't have to arrange a reunion because the child is crying and screaming—you just wait until the end of the time, when the parent is due to show up anyway. You congratulate the child for being to wait out the time even though the child was scared.

In planning this program, you want to try your hardest to have the parent return before the child gets distressed. In particular, you do not want to plan, "We'll separate, and if the child cries, we'll have a reunion; if not, I'll stay away." The problem with this is that the reunion is a reward for the scared child, and to arrange a reunion contingent upon the crying and fear is rewarding the crying and fearfulness and making it more likely to occur another time. It is much better to reward success at tolerating a lower level of separation than to reward failure at tolerating a higher level. In other words, you would do better to have the child separate successfully for two minutes than to separate for twenty-five minutes and then be reunited because of crying and distress.

In doing this program, a kitchen timer is a good way of helping the child realize when the reunion will take place, and that it's a function of time and not distress.

Here are two very important aspects of separating from your child. First, you shouldn't feel the need to wait for the child's permission for you to separate. Second: don't sound scared or worried yourself, if you want your child not to be scared. Suppose you say, in a worried tone of voice, "Mommy's going to leave for a while, OK?" Then suppose the child screams, "No!" Suppose you say, "But it'll just be for a little while." The child screams back, "No, I don't want you to." During all this time the child is being rewarded, with the parent's attention and compliance, for being distressed about separation. If you will say good-bye, say when the reunion is, look very confident and nonguilty, and turn around and leave without looking back, the child gets a very different message from you about how non-awful the separation is.

When you do not seem upset and distressed about the separation, even when the child is upset, the child gets the message that "Nothing dangerous is happening now. You feel upset, but I don't, and you can reasonably guess from the fact that I don't feel upset, that nothing horrible is happening."

It doesn't hurt for you to say this in words, but the most important thing is your nonverbal communication. If you have a relaxed, cheerful facial expression, and a relaxed and cheerful tone of voice in the goodbye, then the child will get the message in the most important ways.

It fairly often happens that children whimper and whine—or scream—when their parents separate from them, but are playing happily with other children within three or four minutes after the separation. Often the parent worries much longer than the child does. Some parents have called the caretaker by phone to see how the child is, so as to preclude that worry. Sometimes it seems to help in walking away confidently to know that an answer will come in a few minutes.

What if you are the foster or adoptive parent of a child who has been severely abused, removed to your family, gets very attached to you, and does not want to let you out of sight? The important principle in cases like this is that appropriate trusting and depending is of even higher priority for the child to learn than appropriate separation. Usually it is a good idea just to gratify the child's need for closeness and protection for a period of time, and then begin the step-by-step process of separation very slowly. If the child has for whatever reason a need for improvement in the skills of trusting and depending, it may be a good idea to put separation and independence on the back burner for a while. It is a judgment call when to do this. Often necessity dictates that the child separate, ready or not. But if there is the luxury of avoiding certain separations with children who have fears of trusting and depending, it may be in the child's interest to do so.

In dealing with separation, parents should keep in mind that the child's ability to trust you is much more important than the goal of making a particular separation go smoothly. For this reason the parent should never say, "I'll be back in just a couple of minutes," when the parent plans to reappear in five hours. Here's something else very important not to do. Don't stay in a preschool room and let the child start contentedly playing with peers and substitute caretakers, and then sneak away without saying goodbye. This strategy is likely to backfire, as your child's reason to trust you is undermined. The strategy tends to promote anxiety in the long run. In the future the child is more likely to watch you nervously to make sure that you're still in the room.

What about treatment with medication for separation anxiety? Antidepressant drugs have been used successfully for adults with panic attacks and for children with separation anxiety. If the above measures fail to resolve the separation anxiety problem, you may want to discuss the possibility of undertaking a careful trial of such medication. However, since I have used this option only if the above-mentioned measures fail, at the date of this writing I have never used antidepressant medications for separation anxiety with young children.

Bedtime and Sleep Problems

There are two main reasons why it is important to get into a harmonious sleep and bedtime procedure for your child. The first reason is that the child behaves better, is less irritable, and is happier when he gets enough sleep. The second reason is that the parent feels better about the child and about life in general and has lots more energy when the parent doesn't have to struggle with the child about the issue of sleeping and going to bed and get waked up a lot.

Average Sleep Requirements

How many hours of sleep (counting naps) does the average child need, in order to be at his best? Richard Ferber (whose book, Solve Your Child's Sleep Problems, is an excellent source on this topic) feels that two year olds on the average need about 13 hours, three year olds need about 12 hours, four year olds need about 11 1/2 hours, and five year olds need about 11 hours. From ages 6 to 10 requirements go from 10 3/4 to 9 3/4 hours, and by 18 they reach 8 1/4 hours. Sleep requirements vary from child to child, but these are guidelines.

At about four years of age most children are able to do fine without a nap. But sometimes some experimentation will best tell whether the child's sleep schedule is best when it includes a nap or when it does not.

Decreasing Resistance to Bedtime

Let's think about how the parent can make it more likely that the child will comply with the command, "Now it's time for you to get ready to go to bed," or more specifically, "Now it's time for you to take your shower and get your pajamas on," "Now it's time for you to brush your teeth," "Now it's time to get in bed."

One useful strategy is to arrange things so that the child really is sleepy by bedtime. If the child has been in the habit of sleeping late in the morning, getting the child up sooner will help the child be ready for bed earlier. But if you are trying to reset the child's sleep schedule, remember that it often takes several days for the sleep rhythms to get into a new pattern.

Another thing that will help the child comply with the command to get ready for bed is for the child to have gotten plenty of exercise so that the child is tired.

If the child appeals to the need to go to the bathroom or get a drink as reasons to get out of bed once in it, then it's important to build into the bedtime ritual doing all these things before the child goes to bed.

Another very important thing to keep in mind in all dealings with preschool children is the principle of differential attention we have spoken of many times before: a behavior that gets more interest and attention from the parent is more likely to be carried out. You want to arrange things so that the child gets more attention for complying with going to bed than he would for refusing to go to bed.

We have earlier discussed building into the bedtime ritual the reading of modeling stories and the nightly review. Hopefully, these are very reinforcing activities for the child. If these occur after the pajamas are on and the teeth are brushed and the child is sitting with you in the bedroom, these activities will reinforce the child's compliance with the ritual of getting ready for bed.

If the child greatly enjoys the modeling stories, and wants to hear lots of them, to put off going to sleep, then take advantage of that opportunity to get lots of positive models into the child's memory bank. Just let the child get ready for bed earlier, and take advantage of the chance to lengthen the child's attention span and go through many positive modeling stories. However: once you make a definitive statement that there are no more stories and it's time for lights out, stick by it; otherwise, the child is getting rewarded for not taking seriously your definitive statements. However, the longer you go on with "Would you rather hear another story, or would you rather have lights out?" and letting the child choose another story, the more positive models you are presenting.

As a general rule, it's better if you have approximately the same length of time with stories each night. The more the whole bedtime ritual gets into a predictable routine, the better. It's best if the moment where the child is left alone to go to sleep is at very close to the same time each night, so that the child's circadian rhythms can adjust to the schedule and create biological readiness for bed just at bedtime.

Here's something else that will help the child comply with the initial command to start the ritual: The parent accompanies the child to bathing and toothbrushing and has pleasant conversation with the child during that time. Thus the child is getting more attention by complying than by not complying. If on the other hand, there are a group of people in the living room, and the child is commanded to leave them and go off by himself to do the bedtime ritual, the child is in effect starting the ritual with a "time out" from the reinforcement of interaction with other people.

What if the child refuses to comply with your very clear command that it's now time for him to get a shower and get into his pajamas, or whatever else is the first step in the sequence of bedtime behaviors? Then you respond in the same way that you do to noncompliance of other sorts. For young children, usually the best option is physical guidance.

Regularity in Biological Rhythms

It is important to have regularity in the child's schedule of eating, napping, and especially the time of bedtime. We all have biological clocks that are meant to help us to be ready to sleep when it is time to sleep, and be alert and awake when it is time to be awake. These biological clocks influence the secretion of hormones and other important physiological events in our bodies. But the clocks can't get set unless there is some regularity of sleeping and waking and eating and exercise. It's useful to keep a time log of your child's naps and bedtimes and awakenings, to see how regular or irregular the schedule is. If sleep is a problem, it is often worthwhile sacrificing convenience in your schedule to get your child on a schedule of falling asleep at regular times.

How do you train your child not to wake up at irregular times in the morning, thinking that it's time to start the day? When you think about it, a toddler or preschooler has no way of knowing whether it's time to get up if he wakes at 4 am. In the winter it may look just as dark when it's 7 am. You can give the child a very clear cue about when it's time to rise, by setting a timer (available in electronics stores) to make a light come on in the child's room at getting-up time. The rule for the child is that the child stays in bed and tries to relax until the light goes off. If the child is sleepy enough, the child can sleep through the light. But the absence of the light gives the child a clear signal that it's not time to wake up yet. If the child is in the habit of waking very early, then it might be a good idea to start the light signaling system by setting the timer for when the child usually gets up, and then extending the time 15 minutes later each day.

The Child in the Parents' Bed?

Suppose the child wants to sleep all night long with both parents or one parent. What is wrong with this? If there are two parents, their private time with each other is impinged upon by the child in a way that at least one of them is likely to resent. If there is one parent, the child can get to feeling too much like a husband or wife and not enough like a child. It's usually better for everyone if the child can learn to feel comfortable sleeping in his own bed. It's not as though sleeping with the parents causes drastically horrible results; it's just irritating, usually.

Suppose the child wants to come into the parents' bed and sleep only when he is scared or upset or out of sorts. What's wrong with allowing this to occur? The answer is that it's such a potent reinforcer for most children to be able to sleep with the parents, that the movement into the parents' bed will reinforce the fear or upset or being out of sorts. If you do want to let your child come into your bed with you, I would suggest doing so when the child has slept all night long in his own bed, getting up time has arrived, and snuggling in bed is a good morning celebration rather than a middle of the night rescue.

Associations to Falling Asleep

Suppose the child wants to fall asleep in bed with his parents or on a couch, and the parents then put him in his own bed once he's asleep. What's the problem with this arrangement?

The answer to this question, and the principle behind it, is very important in solving and preventing sleep problems. First of all, it's important to realize that all adults and children usually wake up some during the night; most of the time we go right back to sleep and often don't remember waking up.

Second, it's important to realize that falling asleep is very dependent on what we learn to associate with falling asleep: the sound and sight of the room, the bed, and so forth. We learn to fall asleep in response to certain stimuli that are associated with falling asleep.

Now, if a child learns to fall asleep in his own bed, with the room looking just as it looks when he wakes up in the middle of the night, he is learning associations to falling asleep. He is also learning not to be scared of that scene. The stimuli are the exact same ones he will find when he wakes up in the middle of the night. Thus, it is more likely that he will fall back asleep without having to get up.

On the other hand, if he learns to fall asleep somewhere else, he does not get practice in falling asleep in his own bed. It is therefore more likely that when he wakes up in the middle of the night, he will be scared and call out to his parents.

So for any child who wakes up scared in the middle of the night, it is important for him to start falling asleep with the room and the bed looking just as they will look in the middle of the night.

This principle also implies that it's better for the child to fall asleep without music on. It also implies that toddlers not fall asleep with a pacifier in the mouth.

This principle also dictates that if the child cries out in the middle of the night for his parents, and the parents check on the child, the parents should get out of the room before the child falls back to sleep, rather than waiting for the child to fall asleep and then leaving. If the parent is always or usually present when the child falls asleep, the child fails to learn to fall asleep in the room by himself. Thus each time he wakes up, which is at least once a night, he needs his parent present. If he is to learn to fall back asleep without the parent there, he needs to practice without the parent there.

By the same principle, letting a child have a television set in his own bedroom is asking for—or demanding—sleep problems. Don't even think of letting a child sit in bed watching television as the child goes to sleep. In the first place, television is in the business of stimulating and exciting people. In the second place, when you sit in bed and watch television, you are undermining the conditioned association between the bed and sleeping and resting.

For this reason I prefer that even when reading bedtime stories or singing songs to a child, the child not be in bed. Sitting together on a rocking chair or next to each other, or at most sitting on the side of the bed helps to make a clear-cut demarcation, so that the child's body knows that when he lies down in the bed, it's time to drift into sleep.

A night light is very useful for most children, so that they will be able to see a little bit. Having bright lights on at the time of falling asleep is not a good idea, because you want the stimuli that are associated with sleeping to be different from those of waking life.

When the Child Can't Fall Asleep By Himself

When a child calls out for a parent in the middle of the night, the parent should just ignore the child? No—a rule like that goes too far in the other direction. The child may need something, or there may be an emergency of some sort. However, in responding, the parent should keep in mind the balance between modeling loving and caring, on the one hand, and reinforcing the child's distress, on the other. If the parent comes in and leaves the child in the bed while checking to make sure everything is OK, and leaves the room fairly soon, there's usually not too much worry about reinforcing the child's distress.

If it's obvious that the child is afraid of falling asleep by himself, then the child usually does one of two things:

1. Stay in bed and scream.
2. Get out of bed and come into the parents' room.

Let's talk about dealing with each of these patterns.

Helping the Child Who Stays in Bed and Screams

The child who screams and gets parents' company, like the child who comes out of bed and gets parents' company, has been reinforced for these behaviors. You want to start a "new deal" where the child will no longer get the reinforcement he has come to expect. As we have gone over several times before, you expect an "extinction burst" before the child catches on to the fact that the behavior really will no longer get the reinforcement.

And as we have mentioned previously in several contexts, you can get over the extinction burst more quickly if you communicate to the child verbally, some time in the daytime, what is going to happen, and if you act it out, either with your own bodies or with toy people. The exact sequence of events should then come as no surprise to the child.

Now one way to go about the "new deal" is simply not to go into the room at all, but to let the child scream until the child falls asleep. The main problem with this plan is that most parents find it very painful and difficult to carry out. They feel too cruel and heartless.

Accordingly, a better option for most parents is to work out a schedule where they go into the child's room every once in a while, not to pick the child up, not to engage in extended interaction with the child, but simply to check and see that the child is OK and to let the child know that he hasn't been abandoned. As time goes on in any one night, and as time goes on from one night to the next, the time between visits gets stretched out longer and longer, from maybe 5 to 15 minutes for the first night, to 30 to 45 minutes for waits on the 7th night or more, if you have to last that long.

One might ask, isn't this graduated schedule of progressively longer times between visits reinforcing the child for progressively longer and longer periods of crying? What lets programs like this work is that the child is not getting the reward that he really wants, which is to be able to sleep with the parent or have the parent sleep with him. Yes there is a minor reward, but it usually isn't rewarding enough to make it worth continuing to scream very long.

Helping the Child Who Comes Into His Parents' Room

Now let's talk about the child who doesn't stay in bed and scream, but who actually gets out of his bed, and gets into the bed with his parents, or who gets out of bed and wakes his parents up.

A program for dealing with this problem is illustrated in one of the modeling stories, "Cindy and the Scary Bedtime Problem." With or without the story, "Cindy and the Scary Bedtime Problem," the parents act out, explain, and try to predict as concretely as possible what the "new deal" will be for the child before enacting it.

The parents put a blank piece of paper on the wall in the child's room. If the child gets out of bed to come to the parents, the parent simply takes the child back to bed, with as little eye contact and conversation as possible. The parent also puts a tally mark on the chart. If the child can get fewer marks on any given night than he did previously, the parents compliment the child the next morning and make prophecies such as "The way you're going, it won't be long until you stay in bed all night, and don't have a single mark. Boy, will we celebrate when that happens."

Then, if the child does stay in bed all night, the following morning the parents should sing, dance around, blow horns, or do anything else they can think of to celebrate the child's accomplishment in a way that will be fun for the child.

The program sounds very simple, and it is. However, the parents should be prepared, upon starting this new deal, that the child might come out of the bedroom just as soon as the parent takes the child back to bed, many times.

The parent should be prepared to simply keep walking back into the bedroom, leading the child, over and over, for an hour or two if necessary, even if a hundred and fifty tally marks are made. The wonderful thing is that on the hundred and fifty-first time, the child will fall asleep in his own bed, without the parent there, and will have accomplished what he could not accomplish before. Even this is worth some celebration the next morning. The parent should also be prepared to do the same thing after two or three hours if the child wakes up in the middle of the night.

While doing this, it is important that the parent's interaction with the child be non-hostile, non-reinforcing, but just bland, and somewhat robot-like. The parent can occasionally (i.e. once every 20 minutes or so) make a "positive prophecy" such as "Before too long you'll get brave enough to stay in your own room." Once the procedure is begun, the parent must have absolute determination to continue it until the child finally lies down and goes to sleep in his own bed. For this reason it's often best to initiate the procedure on a week end. The advantage of this procedure is that it just requires persistence and does not call upon the parent to be punitive or to shut the child in a room.

Dealing With the Underlying Fears

What about the strategy of trying to figure out what the child is scared of, and helping the child to reduce the fear? This can also be a very helpful strategy. This is one that is also illustrated in the story "Cindy and the Scary Bedtime Problem." Sometimes the child can manufacture fear because he knows that being scared gets him something he likes very much, namely to sleep with a parent, and the kindest way to help the child get over his fear is to allow him to practice confronting it, so that he can master it. At other times there are other reasons for the child's fear that should receive attention, such as misconceptions the child has about dangers that occur in the night, and so forth. It is a matter of individual judgment for each case when to have the child confront the feared action of staying in bed by himself, and when it is best to do a good deal of exploring what is actually feared and learning to master those fears.

Suppose that the child actually fears some real-life event: such as that he will quit breathing in his sleep, or that someone will come in and kidnap him, or that someone will hit him while he is asleep, or so forth. Then it is important to listen to the child and encourage the child to talk about these fears, so that the adult can come to understand them. In encouraging the child to talk, it is much better to have a "shaping" strategy where the disclosures that the child makes are greeted with warm reinforcement, rather than a "prying" strategy where the adult interrogates the child.

Another way of finding out about these fears is by participating with the child in dramatic play where toy people have beds and bedrooms and so forth. A therapist, by observing the child's play, can sometimes learn about the child's fears of events happening during the night.

If the child fears real events, then as in all other fears, the first question the adult has to address is whether there really is any danger that the child is in. If the child's fears are realistic, then the first priority is modifying the environment so that the child is safe.

If the adult determines that the child is safe, then an important step is to communicate to the child that the child is safe. Verbal explanations may help. Stories and dramatic plays may be more effective in communicating with the child, and a therapist may help in figuring out how to do this.

Suppose the child fears fantasy characters that he knows aren't real, but which are scary anyway. How can someone help the child with this? As illustrated in the story "Cindy and the Scary Bedtime Problem," it is a useful strategy to teach the child to convert the formerly scary characters to characters that are friendly and protective to the child, to allies rather than persecutors. The way to do this is to practice in one's mind spinning stories about the characters during the daytime, stories wherein the characters come to play the role of ally and protector. In the role of therapist I usually try to help the child do this through dramatic play or by constructing stories especially for the child.

When doing this sort of thing with a child, sometimes I find it helpful to consider the idea that the child is afraid of some of his own impulses, and the scary characters symbolize these impulses. If I get the notion that this is true, then I use this information in trying to construct stories about the characters where the characters transform those same impulses into useful actions rather than destructive actions. That is, I will try to take as much of the child's psychological reality into account as possible while making stories and plays designed to help the child fear the fantasy characters less.

At other times, however, the hypothesis that the child fears his own impulses doesn't get much confirmation, and it turns out that the child is simply afraid of violent characters portrayed in movies and TV shows. Both dreams and the fantasies a child has while lying in bed awake draw upon the images the child has in his memory bank. Having very mean and vicious actions and very horrible outcomes stored away in one's memory bank increases the likelihood that they will come to mind. As mentioned several times elsewhere, I strongly recommend that parents help children to boycott entertainment violence.

Here's a good way to practice the procedure of separating from the parents at "Good night" time, if the child is afraid to separate at that time. You do it in the daytime, when the fears of the night are far from the child's mind. The parent makes a game out of the practice, and tries to have it be playful. The parent does not have the child change clothes—the child stays in his daytime clothes. The parent and child role play the scary moment of bedtime, at which the parent leaves the room. They go into the child's room, and the child lies down on the bed, and the parent says good night and gives the child a good night kiss or whatever, and leaves. The child pretends to get a little scared, by saying out loud to himself, "I'm getting a little scared. But I'll think about something brave: let's see, I'll pretend that I'm forty feet tall, and I see somebody that is having some trouble in a flood, getting swept away by the water, and I just reach over and fish them right out..... Now I feel better: congratulations to me for getting myself unscared."

This will work best if the parent first plays the part of the child, and acts out the sequence for the child, while the child listens outside the door. Then they switch places, and the child practices while the parent plays the part of the parent. Then they practice again, and the person playing the part of the parent actually goes far away in the house. Each time at the end of the play there is celebration.

The more the child can practice the mastery of bedtime during the daytime, the less scared he will be at actual bedtime.

What about the ethics of enforcing the child's sleeping in his own bed? Should the parent sacrifice whatever is necessary to prevent the child from having to go through the pain of learning to do this? My observation is that if the suggestions of this chapter are followed consistently, skillfully and lovingly, everyone is happier within a few days, including the child. Many children are very proud of themselves, and feel a boost to their self-esteem, from conquering their fear. The temporary discomfort the child feels in the process is worth the discomfort saved from that time on.

These bedtime problems, when they are not dealt with, can often result in many hours of hostile or unpleasant interchanges between parent and child; that is much worse for the child than having to put up with the temporary discomfort of learning to sleep in his own bed. The resentment toward the child felt by the parent who is waked up regularly is usually much worse for the child than the child's temporary discomfort. These suggestions contain some of the best ways I know for making the child's discomfort as temporary as possible.

Chapter 25: Relaxation Skills

Chapter Overview:

In this chapter we'll review seven ways to practice relaxing yourself. All the techniques have some things in common. They should be practiced often and regularly, not just when there is unusual anxiety or tension. That way you won't get a conditioned association between the use of the technique and the feeling of tension. It's helpful to work hard at remembering to practice, but once you sit down to relax, don't put yourself under so much performance pressure that you feel tense about wanting to relax. You'll benefit from practicing in a comfortable place, free from nerve-jangling interruptions. You can relax more easily if you've had enough exercise. And any of the techniques will work better if you imagine that it is doing good things for you. The first technique is simple rest—just getting comfortable and not using any particular technique for fifteen or twenty minutes. Second is progressive muscular relaxation. In this, you practice tensing and relaxing all the muscle groups of the body. Third is meditation using a mantra: usually this consists in saying a word over and over to yourself. Equally important in this technique is maintaining a passive attitude, of letting whatever thoughts also tend to come into the mind come, without opposing them. Fourth is using pleasant imagery: conjuring up a pleasant place and safe and happy events. Fifth is biofeedback: you use a device to measure your muscle tension, skin conductance, finger temperature, or something else that goes up or down with relaxation or arousal. Then you see if you can move the number in the direction you want by using some other relaxation technique. Sixth is cognitive restructuring: attempting to substitute more rational thoughts for the awfulizing or self-downing or blaming thoughts that get one unpleasantly aroused. Seventh is images of kindness: you imagine people being caring and gentle and nurturing with one another. I include in this chapter a scripts that you can use for cultivating relaxation skills.

****

This chapter will explain several techniques that people have found useful in promoting relaxation. These techniques are useful for adults and children alike. Increasing the skill of relaxation has produced positive results in outcome studies of a wide variety of stress-related problems. I regard relaxation as a skill of such wide utility that it should be taught to the general public in the course of health education.

I will go over seven different techniques, as follows: simple rest, progressive muscular relaxation, meditation using a mantra, relaxation assisted by pleasant imagery, biofeedback, cognitive restructuring, and images of kindness. First, however, I will go over some of the aspects that all these relaxation methods have in common.

One of the most important suggestions for all these techniques is that the technique should not be used like a pain pill and employed only when anxiety and tension are at their worst. Instead, they should be practiced on some sort of regular basis, for example for fifteen minutes a couple times a day, and should not be neglected on days when one is already feeling relaxed. The reason for this suggestion is based on simple conditioned association learning. If one does a certain maneuver only when tension is at its worst, that maneuver soon becomes associated with the feeling of tension. This of course is just the opposite of what is desired in a relaxation technique. So whatever technique is used, it should be practiced especially when it is not immediately needed.

A practice schedule that for many people is most useful is three or four seconds of relaxation, thirty or forty times a day. With practice, you can learn to relax yourself thoroughly but quickly.

A second suggestion common to all the techniques is that one should try to relax, but not try so hard that the goal of relaxation becomes just another test where one may succeed or fail. It's important to think of the relaxation practice periods as times where it is impossible to fail, where every possible outcome is OK and nothing to worry about, even if some occasions turn out not to be relaxing at all.

A third suggestion that all these techniques have in common is that the physical setup of the environment should be arranged so that interruptions may not intrude, and one's physical position is conducive to relaxation. Taking a telephone off the hook or putting a do not disturb sign on an office door and lying down on a mat are examples of what can facilitate this.

The fourth suggestion is that using any of these techniques is easier if you have gotten adequate exercise. Exercising thoroughly may be thought of as a relaxation technique in and of itself. I think that for many young children, the biggest barrier to their being able to relax is that their bodies have not had enough chance to move as much as nature intended for them to. If a child has been cooped up in a classroom all day with little chance to walk or run, the last thing that child wants is to learn to be still and calm, until the child has burned off some energy through movement.

The fifth suggestion for all these techniques is to imagine that using the technique will gradually bring about the desired results. This suggestion comes from countless studies of the placebo effect: countless times it has been documented that when people expect a positive effect to occur from a drug, a positive effect actually tends to occur. What do people do when inducing a placebo effect in themselves, that one can consciously and purposely mobilize? One factor might be the belief that the remedy will indeed produce positive effects. In the case of relaxation for certain tension-related problems, according to many outcome studies such a belief does not require any self-deception to adopt. A second factor, perhaps separate from the belief, is the mental image of the desired results' occurring. In other words, one who doesn't believe can always imagine.

Now for the first technique, which is simple rest. For some people this might work just as well as the more elaborate techniques I'll mention later, as it has in at least one controlled study. This technique is simply a combination of the suggestions that I've already mentioned as common to all the techniques. You simply take out fifteen minutes a couple of times a day, get into a place where it's possible to relax, and sit or lie down and don't try to do anything in particular—you just rest. Whatever your mind wants to do, let it. Try to relax but don't try so hard that you induce performance anxiety. You peek at your watch whenever you want do, and when the allotted time is up you get up and go about your business. So much for technique number 1.

The second technique is progressive muscular relaxation. This is the technique that was first used by Jacobsen in the 1930's. It's the one that Wolpe used with great success in desensitizing phobias. It rests on the following theory: first, that one can learn, through practice, a high degree of control of the tension in the skeletal muscles; and second, that relaxing those muscles is conducive to emotional relaxation as well.

There are two stages to learning this technique, one involving purposeful tension and relaxation, and the second involving purposeful relaxation alone. The goal in the first stage is to sensitize your mind to the perceptions of muscle tension, and to give yourself practice in undoing tension. You for example tense your forearm muscle by gripping with your hand; then you let off the tension and pay careful attention to how it feels to uncontract your muscle fibers. Once the muscle has got back to the normal state of relaxation, you try to go even further in the direction of relaxation than you have already gone. You do the same thing with all the major muscle groups of the body, contracting them, paying attention to the tension, and then relaxing them as far as you can. I think that it's helpful when doing this procedure not to induce a high degree of tension, as though you were doing isometric exercises, but to induce a very mild and slight degree of tension, so that you will become expert at discriminating fine differences in muscle contraction. When doing these exercises pay particular attention to the muscles around the head, since they seem to be particularly associated with emotion. The clenching or unclenching of the jaw, the tension of the muscles of the forehead, the tension of the neck muscles and the muscles around the mouth should get a good deal of this first stage discrimination practice.

In the second stage of progressive muscular relaxation practice, you don't contract the muscles to begin with, but you just let your attention go to the various muscle groups and try to reduce the degree of muscle contraction in each of them. Many people like to time this relaxation with their breathing: that is, every time you breathe out, you let your muscles get a little more limp and loose. You do this for fifteen minutes a couple times of day, and hopefully enjoy the pleasant sensations that the relaxation induces.

When Joseph Wolpe pioneered this technique to desensitize fears, he would first ask the person to relax, and then alternate the relaxation activity with imagining the situations that trigger unrealistic anxiety, starting with the last scary scenes and gradually working up to the more scary ones. If there are particular imagined scenarios that tend to make you more tense, one option is to gradually desensitize oneself to those scenarios.

The third technique is meditation using a mantra. This is the technique that was given a great deal of publicity in the early seventies under the name of transcendental meditation. In those times people were given a Sanskrit word to say to themselves while meditating; researchers found that using the word "one" as a mantra worked just as well. Some people may not like the word "one," and may want to choose a different mantra. A mantra is simply an auditory or visual image to which one returns one's attention during the relaxation practice. Some people have used an imagined spot of light as a mantra. Others have used as a mantra paying conscious attention to their own breathing. Perhaps the mantra functions as a means of turning the attention away from other thoughts such as worrisome ones. To use this technique, then, you prepare to relax, and then turn your attention to the mantra. It's important not to worry about how relaxed you become. It's also important not to feel compelled to keep repeating the mantra. If you realize that your attention has been on something else other than the mantra for a few minutes, don't worry about it, and let your attention gently return to the mantra.

The fourth technique is relaxation assisted by pleasant imagery. Here you don't have just one image that you keep returning to; you have your imagination carry out something similar to a pleasant dream. You go in your imagination to a very pleasant place, where pleasant things happen. You create images of safety and security, where any stories have happy endings. The goal of practice of this technique is to be able to drift into a pleasant and relaxing fantasy at will. This technique is limited only by the bounds of your imagination.

The fifth technique is biofeedback. It's not used by itself, but is a way of seeing how well other techniques work. In our list of nine methods of influence, the last is monitoring progress. Biofeedback is a way of objectively monitoring the extent to which relaxation is taking place, by measuring certain aspects of bodily functioning that usually change with relaxation. If you find that doing certain things with your mind is very effective in bringing about those changes in the body, you have a clue to do those things more often when you want to relax.

What happens physiologically when people relax? Obviously one change is that their muscles become less tense. The tension of muscles can be measured directly by an EMG (electromyogram) biofeedback device. You put electrodes over a muscle and read out how much tension there is. The cheapest EMG biofeedback device I've been able to get hold of costs somewhere in the neighborhood of $250. Another parameter that changes with relaxation is galvanic skin resistance, or the electrical conductivity or resistance of the skin. As people get more nervous they get sweaty palms, and the sweat tends to increase electrical conductivity. You can obtain a device measuring such conductivity for about $60. Temperature of the hands and feet also change with relaxation, getting warmer as someone becomes more relaxed. (This is the basis of the saying, "I'm getting cold feet." It's also the basis of "Cold hands, warm heart," in that the cold hands represent nervousness about wanting to make a good impression.) A device to provide feedback on finger temperature can be had for about $30. (You can obtain information and prices from Bio-Medical Instruments, 2387 East Eight Mile Road, Warren, MI 48091-2486, phone 800-521-4640.)

Biofeedback is best done, I think, in a spirit of playfulness. First you measure a parameter, then you try some sort of relaxation technique, and as often as you like, you check the parameter and see what's happened so far. There are devices that will give continuous feedback in the form of tones or lights; as you get more relaxed you lower the tone, for example. It's also fun to get yourself nervous purposely by thinking of stressful events and seeing if you can get the biological parameter to go in the opposite direction.

For some people with performance anxiety, who see the biofeedback devices as giving them a passing or failing grade on their relaxation examination, it might be best not to monitor functions continuously, or not to monitor them at all until they have gotten over their attitude about failing.

The sixth technique is cognitive restructuring. This is based upon the notion that feelings of tension and anxiety result from anxiety-provoking thoughts, that sometimes are not even noticed enough to be remembered unless one consciously keeps a log of them. such thoughts include self-statements such as "This situation that I'm in is terrible," "Something awful is about to happen if I don't watch out," "I'm going to fail terribly if I don't watch myself, and that will be terrible," "I'm putting in a performance that I should be ashamed of,"

"I'm not doing well enough," "I should do better than this," "This other person should be acting better and the fact that he isn't is terrible," and so forth. Sometimes the beliefs underlying such thoughts are things like "Nothing short of perfection is good enough," or "Everything has to be just right in order for me to feel good." Such cognitive patterns in general tend to estimate highly the awfulness of situations and the blameworthiness of oneself and others. The opposites of such cognitive patterns are self-statements like, "This situation is unpleasant, but it is not terrible," or "My performance was not perfect, but the only way I learn is to try things repeatedly," or "Sometimes it's a waste of time and energy to want everything perfect," or "I'll decide what the highest priorities are and put energy there, and not worry if the lower priorities fall by the wayside," or "The purpose of this situation is for me to try to do some good for somebody or learn to do good rather than for somebody to evaluate my worth as a person," or "I can put up with a very wide range of other people's actions," or any of hundred of other thoughts that tend to reduce the awfulness of situations and reduce blameworthiness of oneself and others. By becoming aware of when one is exaggerating awfulness or blameworthiness and substituting thoughts that don't do so, one can greatly reduce negative emotion, including tension.

In using cognitive restructuring you may become aware of certain sorts of situations that tend to trigger the thoughts of awfulness or blameworthiness—situations of interpersonal conflict, rejection, disapproval, criticism, failure, frustration, being alone, not knowing how to do something, or whatever. Once these connections are understood, one can then practice in imagination facing these trigger situations but doing so with the more desirable cognitive patterns in mind.

The seventh technique is images of kindness. It's a special case of using imagery. It's based on the idea that for most people the most important form of pleasant imagery is not necessarily the place one is in, but the quality of the interpersonal environment. A major antidote to anxiety is a positive emotional climate among people. Therefore the essence of this technique is to envision people who give each other messages of acceptance and approval, the same sort as are desired in the cognitive restructuring technique. You gradually cultivate the ability to envision very wise, loving, nurturing, and forgiving people, acting in kind ways.

These techniques all have much potential, provided that one persistently uses them. They do require some systematic effort and allocation of time before gains begin to appear. Like all other things of that sort, most people who think they would be a good idea do not ever carry them out. However, the increase in quality time and energy brought about by improving the skill of relaxation far outweighs the time required to devote a substantial effort to one or more of these techniques.

A Relaxation Instruction Script

The following is a script combining some of the techniques mentioned above. I believe it is appropriate for a wide range of ages, from kindergarten aged children through adults. You can tape record it and play it while practicing relaxation, or just read it until it is very familiar and then recall the strategies while relaxing in silence.

******

The ability to relax your body and your mind, whenever you want to, is a skill that is very useful in many different ways. It allows you to calm yourself so that you can think better. It makes it easier to go to sleep. It lets you undo any tension in muscles that would be uncomfortable or painful. It has been found helpful in preventing several physical problems, including headaches and certain types of stomachaches. It gives you practice in controlling your own mood. It allows you to get rid of restlessness. It allows you to better handle and enjoy being by yourself. It is very useful in reducing fearfulness, when you want to do that. It can prepare you for getting good and thoughtful ideas. It helps you in resolving conflicts with other people that come up. It is a skill that is worth working on for a very long time if that's what it takes to master it.

One of the most important ways of relaxing is to notice any tension in your muscles, and to reduce that tension, and let your muscles stop pulling. As you sit or lie down comfortably, it often feels pleasant to let your muscles relax themselves. The more relaxed your muscles are, the more your mind will tend to drift in ways that are calm and peaceful also.

Here is one way that you can practice relaxation of your muscles. You can think about the different muscles of your body, and go through the different muscle groups one by one. You can notice the tension that is already in the muscles, or you can tense those muscles just a little bit. Then you make that tension go away, as totally as possible. If you can notice the difference between full relaxation and even a very small amount of tension in a muscle, you have a very important skill. Because as long as you can notice tension, and even make tension greater, you have the power to make that tension go away. All you have to do to produce relaxation is the opposite of what you do to create tension. When you let off the tension, you let the muscles get very loose and relaxed. You do this for all the muscle groups in the body. You notice what happens when you relax muscles. You feel the difference that happens when you relax. When you've done this enough times, you'll know very well how to tense and relax all the muscles of your body.

You will not have to tense the muscles at all hard, but only very lightly, or maybe not at all, to feel the difference that happens when you relax the muscles.

You might start with gripping your hands into fists, not hard, but very lightly. Even if you do it very lightly, you can feel a tension in the muscles of your forearms and hands. Once you feel that tension, you can let it off, and let your forearms relax and get very loose. Pay attention to the feeling of relaxation, and how it is different from the feeling of tension.

You might next make your upper arms a little tense by trying to make a muscle as though you were going to feel the muscle in your upper arms. You do this by pulling so as to bend your arm at the elbow, but at the same time trying to straighten out your arm. Feel the tension in your upper arm muscles. Then you can let off the tension and let those muscles get loose and relaxed.

You might next make your shoulders a little tense by starting to shrug your shoulders a little, the way people do when they say, “I don’t know.” Then you relax those shoulder muscles.

If you want to make your neck muscles tense, try to pull your head forward, and at the same time pull it back, so that the muscles are pulling against each other. Then when you feel that tension, you can relax those muscles, and let those muscles be very calm.

If you want to tense the muscles that are at the side of the face, the jaw muscles, you do it by biting so as to clench the teeth together, while at the same time trying to open the mouth. This produces tension in the jaw muscles, the muscles on the side of the head, and the muscles on the upper part of the neck. Then you can relax those muscles by letting your jaw relax. When you do this usually your jaw will be hanging open just a tiny bit.

If you want to tense the muscles of the upper part of your face, you lift your eyebrows and at the same time try to push your eyebrows down. Then when you feel that tension, ever so slightly, you can let it off.

If you want to tense the muscles of the lower part of your face, you push your lips together a little bit, and pull the corners of your mouth back as though you were smiling, and then you try to pull your lips back as though you were trying to whistle. Then you let all that tension off, and you feel the relaxation of the muscles of the lower part of your face.

Many people find that relaxing the muscles of their face and jaws and neck is just what makes them feel the most calm and peaceful. You might try it if you want to, thinking about the muscles of your jaws, your upper face, your lower face, and your neck.

Some people like to think about their breathing as they are relaxing, and let their muscles get a little more relaxed each time they breathe out. So the rhythm is breathe in, relax out. Breathe in, relax out.

Now you might experiment with how to make the muscles tight in your back. If you try to arch your back like you are bending backwards, you can tense the long muscles that run down your back. Then when you feel that tension, you can let it off. If you pull your shoulders back, you can feel tension in the muscles in the upper part of your back, and then let that tension off.

You can also experiment with tensing and relaxing the muscles of your chest and your abdomen, or belly. To tense those of your chest, pull your arms as if you are going to clap your hands together, then relax that tension. To tense the muscles of your abdomen, if you are lying on your back, pretend that you want to sit up, and feel just a little tension in those muscles. Then you can let them off. Or if you are sitting in a chair, you can tense your belly and back muscles by trying to lean forward, while at the same time trying to lean backward.

You can make the muscles in your upper legs tense by trying to bend the leg at the knee and trying to straighten it out at the same time. Then you can let off that tension, so that your upper legs are very relaxed. You can tense your lower legs by trying to push your toes down and trying to pull your toes up at the same time. Then you can let off that tension too, so that your lower legs are relaxed.

There are many muscles in the body, including some I didn't mention. It can be fun to experiment with finding out how it is that you make a certain muscle tense. Over time, you will become very much able to tense or relax any muscle in the body any time you want to.

After you go through and actually practice tensing and relaxing your muscles, you can just let your attention go first to one muscle group and then another, seeing if you can make that muscle group any more relaxed and loose and limp than it already is.

You might want to think about your breathing again, and feel the air going in and out, and each time you breathe out, feel some part of your body getting just a little more relaxed than it was before.

The skill of getting your muscles relaxed is one that will be very useful to you, for the rest of your life. It's one that people can gradually improve at over time, simply by noticing what sort of effort tends to tense what muscles, and what sort of relaxation of that effort relaxes those muscles. You will start to find which particular muscles are the most important ones for you.

Relaxing your muscles is only a part of the interesting and pleasant things you can do while you are relaxing.

Another very useful way of relaxing is to practice imagining beautiful and relaxing scenes, nice and pleasant places to be. You may want to think of the following scenes, briefly, when I mention them, and then come back to them later when the tape stops and imagine them more thoroughly. Different scenes are relaxing for different people. How does it feel when you imagine a beautiful sunset? How does it feel to imagine the sound of wind gently blowing among the tree leaves? How about the image of a bunch of beautiful flowers? How about the sight and the sound of a waterfall? How about listening to rain fall on a roof? How about imagining waves rolling in where you are relaxing on a beach? Or the image of how you feel just as you are awakening on a morning where there are no responsibilities you have to carry out? Or the image of sitting in a cool room, with a warm blanket around you, looking at a fire burn in a fireplace? Or what's it like to imagine yourself drinking cool water when you are very thirsty? Or watching snow drifting slowly to the ground? Or can you imagine a rag doll, and imagine that your body is that loose and relaxed? What's it like to imagine watching white clouds drifting by on a day in the spring? Or can you just become conscious of the chair or the bed that is holding you up, and feel yourself being held?

Sometimes the most relaxing images are not just of places, but of people, and people acting kind and gentle and loving and giving with one another. These images let people feel peaceful and relaxed.

You can imagine stories of people's being kind. For example you may want to imagine that someone is searching for something, and someone else in a very calm and kind way helps that person find it. When they find it, the people feel good about each other. If you want you can fill in your own details about where they are, what is being searched for, where they look, and what it looks like when they find it. You can do this in a different way every time if you want, or the same way every time you do it, or sometimes one way and sometimes another. You are in control of your own imagination and you can lead yourself wherever you choose.

Or you may imagine that someone leads someone else on a very interesting and pleasant journey, showing that person something that is very fun or interesting to see. If you want you can imagine your own details, about where the first person takes the second, what sorts of things they see and experience. You can imagine the faces of the first person as that person enjoys what they are doing, and the face of the other person feeling good about giving the other a pleasant experience.

Or you may imagine that someone teaches someone else something that person really wants to know. The teacher is very kind and patient. The teacher wants to let the learner learn at his own pace, and does not rush him. The learner is very grateful to the teacher. The teacher is also grateful to the learner. The teacher realizes that people who allow themselves to be taught are giving a nice gift to the teacher, a pleasant memory that the teacher will have for a lifetime. You can fill in your own details of where they are, what is being learned, and how they are learning it.

Or you may imagine that someone helps someone with a job of some sort. As you do it, imagine that the two people feel very good about one another. You can see and hear what they are doing together and what sort of words they are saying to each other, if they are saying anything.

Or you may imagine that people are being kind and loving to each other by playing together. They know in the backs of their minds that the most important thing when they are playing with each other is to be kind and caring with each other. They each take pleasure whenever they can see that they have helped the other feel good. If you want to let a story about this come to your mind, you can imagine where they are and what or how they are playing and what they are saying with each other.

Or you may imagine people showing their love and caring about each other by noticing and commenting on the other person's good acts or accomplishments. You can imagine that people rejoice and feel good when their friends and loved ones have successes. If you want you can imagine exactly what someone is doing and how someone else feels good about it, and how that person lets the other person know his pleasure.

Or you may imagine people sharing things with each other, making it so that there is enough to go around. You can imagine whether they are taking turns with some toy or tool they want to use, or whether they are sharing something to eat or drink, or someone else's attention and time, or something else.

Or, you may imagine one person showing love and caring for another by being a good listener when the other speaks. As one person tells thoughts and feelings, the other very patiently tries to be understanding.

Some people enjoy recalling the things they have done in real life that they are glad they have done. Some people like to think back about the kind things they have done for other people, or the work that they have done to educate themselves and make themselves better or the work they have done to make the world a better place, or the times that they have lived joyously, or the times that they have made good decisions and carried them out. They may want to celebrate the times that they have been honest, or the times that they have been strong and brave.

Some people enjoy thinking about the ways in which they are blessed, and feeling gratitude for those. If they are able to have any material things that make life easier, if they are able to eat and drink so that they do not have to be hungry and thirsty, if they have someone who can take care of them when they need it and be of support to them, if they have friends or loved ones that they can care for and support, they may want to feel gratitude for these blessings.

You can let your mind drift, and think about any stories or images of these things that you want to. You are perfectly free to let your mind drift in any way that you choose. Sometimes people enjoy not choosing, but simply letting the mind drift wherever it wants to go, and observing what happens.

In fact sometimes it's a very pleasant experience just to imagine that your mind is a blank screen, and to simply wait and see what comes on it, and to observe it with interest and curiosity, not trying to control it in any way.

You can practice relaxing your muscles, imagining relaxing scenes, thinking of stories of people being kind to each other, or you can simply let your mind drift and see where it takes you. Or you can let your mind drift and not observe it, but simply rest. You can guide your own experience to make it pleasant, relaxing, peaceful, and enjoyable to you. As you do so you have reason to celebrate practicing such an important skill.

****

I believe that images of kindness are more central to the relaxation process than most people have realized.

Fitting a Relaxation Technique to One's Personal Tastes and Style

The art of relaxation training has grown to the point where one can choose a technique that is consistent with one's particular outlook and world view. Those who have a no-nonsense scientific outlook will probably prefer biofeedback and progressive muscle relaxation. Those with more of a dramatic and imaginative style may prefer use of imagery. Those who like mysticism may enjoy meditation with a mantra, with all the elements of eastern philosophy; those who reject anything mystical may benefit from the use of the word *one* as a mantra, divorced from all suggestions of mysticism. On the other hand, perhaps in the long run one grows more from using a technique that is not so totally consistent with the prevailing personality style. In the absence of data on this topic, it's only logical that individuals experiment with what seems to work best for them.

Chapter 26: Organization Skills

Chapter Overview:

Mental health professionals have, I think, greatly underemphasized organization skills. Much of the conflict and irritation and anxiety and nonproductivity that plagues humanity result from people's disorganization. By organizing, I mean having routines, grouping related things together, using writing as an aid to memory, and most importantly, making plans and following them. Someone who wants to organize unfortunately has to allocate time to the following activities: putting objects and papers where they should go; thinking and writing about goals and tasks and priorities; scheduling activities; and keeping financial records.

Each important object should have a "home," as close as possible to the place where it will be used. The fewer objects you choose to own, and the more you put them in their homes after each use, the less time you'll spend looking for them and being cluttered by them. To organize papers, you get file cabinets and file folders, arrange the files alphabetically, and take the time to put the papers in their files. To organize time use, the first step is thinking about your goals. Write your goals, sell yourself on achieving them, decide where you will find the time to accomplish them, get a concrete picture of what attaining the goal is like, decide how to monitor progress toward the goal, and make a detailed plan about how to achieve the goal and overcome the obstacles. Executing this plan often requires using the nine methods of influence with yourself as well as with other people. In writing goals, don't leave out goals of maintaining relationships with specific people who are most important to you.

To organize the way you allocate time to the tasks necessary to achieve goals, use a notebook that can be carried at all times. A master to do list goes in the front; an appointment calendar goes on the right pages; a daily to do list goes on the left pages. If you establish systems and routines for the tasks you do repeatedly, you can zero in on a system that minimizes hassle. Making an error-reduction checklist saves you worry over the question, "Have I forgotten anything?" In organizing communications with other people, keep the "signal to noise" ratio as high as possible. Often the crucial decisions in maintaining organization have to do with turning down new commitments for which there are not adequate time and energy. A "minimalist" system of organizing money is simply to calculate your net worth periodically, and to save these figures. If your net worth is rising sufficiently in the long term, you can avoid hassling with a detailed budget.

****

Why is a chapter on organization skills a part of this book? It is here for several very compelling reasons. First, a great deal of the interpersonal conflict and distress and hostility between family members, hostility that harms children, comes from disorganization. Someone forgot something important, someone lost something important, someone didn't put things away, and other people are upset by it. Or one person's totally arbitrary gut feeling about how much money is available to spend (arrived at with no calculations) is different from another person's equally arbitrary gut feeling. Second, a great deal of the individual tension and unhappiness and anxiety that prevent parents from feeling good are the results of disorganization. A parent has many tasks that he can't keep up with; he ruminates on them instead of sleeping; he is irritable with the children the next day. Or the parent feels so bad about being behind in everything that the children get models of tense and worried behavior too often. Third, many of the suggestions this book makes—the positive behavior diary, the use of ethical readings, etc.—are difficult to carry out if the positive behavior diary and the books of ethical readings are misplaced or people are in too big a rush to use them anyway. Fourth, a very substantial fraction of children's school problems have to do with children's low organization skills. Very frequently, in my observation, that children have been treated with stimulant medication for attention deficit disorder without hyperactivity, when the only real complaint was of disorganization, and when the child had never had any systematic teaching in how to get organized. Fifth, organization skills are among the most important ones for children to develop if they are to be successful in life. For these reasons and others, it is difficult to overemphasize the role of organization skills in mental health; in most mental health treatment these skills get no attention at all.

Lack of organization skills by people in charge of safety of others has cost countless people's lives. Lack of organization skills by people in positions of financial responsibility has cost the jobs and the life savings of countless people. Organization skills can make the difference between success and failure, poverty or wealth, for an individual and his or her family.

The key to organization is making plans, and following those plans. The plans have to do with managing 1) objects, 2) paper, 3) time and tasks, and 4) money.

Organization skills are necessary because we do not have infinite memory. If it were possible to remember the position in which every piece of paper were placed, there would be no need for file cabinets; if we could remember every appointment there would be no need for an appointment calendar. But because the complexity of life grows to exceed what we can hold in memory, we need customs and habits that are brain-extenders, ways of enlarging our effective memory or minimizing the drain upon it. Or put another way: having good organization skills can make us act in smarter ways without having to get a brain transplant. Put another way: poor organization skills can result in smart people's doing stupid things.

There is, however, a price to be paid for organizing. Things don't automatically get organized just because you know how to organize them. It takes a certain amount of time, every day, to put things in order, to plan tasks, and to do the other jobs of organizing. Unless that time is allocated and spent, it will not do any good to know the principles of organization. Furthermore, the jobs of organizing are not nearly as much fun as some other things you could be doing. Thus it takes self-discipline to spend time planning and organizing rather than just going ahead and doing.

Here are some of the basic principles of organizing.

1. Benefit from having routines: for example, try to make a routine time and place for doing certain activities, and try to have a routine place for certain things to be kept. And most essentially, there should be routine times allocated to organization itself.

2. Group related things together, whether they are ideas, or papers, or objects.

3. Put things in writing, so that you don't have to rely on your memory.

4. On complicated or important tasks, make plans of what is going to happen, and then carry out those plans, rather than trying to plan and carry out the plan at the same time.

Setting Aside Time for Organizing

Organizing yourself consists of several activities that take time to do. These are:

1. Taking your physical objects, deciding where they should go, and putting them there.

2. Taking pieces of paper, deciding where they should go, and putting them there.

3. Writing your goals, writing the tasks you want to do, ordering their priority, estimating how long they will take, and scheduling when you are going to do them. Also, looking at what is written in the to do and appointment book frequently enough to remind yourself to do them. And, celebrating the accomplishment of tasks.

4. Keeping records of monetary income and expenses, and making calculations about these.

None of these tasks do themselves, no matter how much you know about organization. How much time per day is someone willing to spend on these tasks? If the answer is zero, then there's no need to resort to attention deficits as the explanation for disorganization. In order to be organized, you must be willing to spend a certain amount of time each day organizing.

Organizing Physical Objects

I mention this area first because it is one that children can start learning beginning in toddlerhood. The basic principles are simple:

1. Make a "home" for each object, where that object will go when it is not being used.
2. Group related objects together, and make their homes as close as possible to the place where they will be used.
3. Establish customs of putting objects back in their homes as soon as they are not being used any more, rather than when the space becomes so cluttered that there is no more room.
4. Don't acquire so many objects that it becomes a needlessly complex task to keep them organized. In other words, de-clutter yourself.
5. The task of putting many objects back in their homes (such as many toys, dishes, etc.) like most other tedious tasks, is more fun if people do it together, rather than alone.

No one has time to waste on looking for objects like keys, wallet, appointment book, pen, glasses, coat, and so forth. With objects like these it is a good idea to have only two or three places that you permit them to be. For example, dad's keys when not being used are either in a certain pocket or in a certain box, and nowhere else. Mom's glasses are in a purse when not being used, and the purse is either at her side or at a certain place on a table. If she can resist the temptation to put them down anywhere else, she will not have to look for them.

In deciding upon a "home" for an object, I often think to myself, "If I forgot what the home for this object was and wanted to pick the most logical place to start looking for it, where would I look?" This often is the answer to where its home should be.

Organizing Paper

In this world of paperwork, it's difficult to overestimate the importance of having a file cabinet with organized files. The best way to organize files is to have a title for each file folder, and to put them all in alphabetical order. At regular intervals, you process incoming paper by taking each piece and either doing something with it, filing it, or throwing it away.

Let's suppose that the piece of paper is something that you want to do something with at a later time. In that case you file it and at the same time make an entry in your to do book and appointment calendar that will remind you what to do with this piece of paper, and where it is filed.

Two useful file categories are the "to do" file and the "holding" file. The to do file is one for the papers corresponding to tasks that you can do as soon as you can get to them; the holding file is the one for tasks that can only be done at some specified time in the future.

Suppose that someone writes you a letter, and you want to reply to it whenever you can. That would go into the to do file. You would put on your master to do list, (which we'll talk about in the section on tasks) "Reply to Mr. X's letter (to do file)."

Suppose that you get in the mail a plane ticket that you will use in three weeks. Then you would put it in the holding file. You would make an entry in the "master to do list" (at the beginning of the appointment and to do book) something like "11/21: flight to Cleveland,(ticket holding file)." On the day for 11/21 in the appointment book, you would write down something like "3:27 pm, US Airways fl. 43 to Cleveland, arrive 4:30 pm. Ticket holding file." Now this piece of paper has been processed and you don't have to remember anything additional because of it—all you have to remember is to look at your notebook, which you already do anyway.

What about things that should happen by a certain time, for which other people are responsible, things that should be taken care of without action from you? For example, what if you send back a piece of merchandise, and you are supposed to get a refund within a couple of weeks? Or what if someone promises you over the phone that a certain very important job will get done by such and such a time? In such cases it's good to do just the same sort of thing that we spoke of with the airline tickets. When you send in your piece of merchandise for the refund, keep a copy of the mailing slip or notes on when it was sent and where, and put these in the holding file. Then make an entry on your master to do list something like this: "Verify receipt of refund from X-store, see notes holding file." If the refund comes, then you can look at the holding file and make sure that the refund is in the right amount, and check this item off your to do list. If the refund does not come, then you are reminded of this by seeing the unchecked item on your master to do list.

Or in the case where someone has promised to do something very important by a certain date, during the conversation you take notes on what will be done by what time. Then you file those notes in your holding file, and make an entry on your master to do list, for example "By 11/30, printer to return galleys of book. Holding file." And on the to do list for 11/30, write in something like "Call printer if galleys not back by today—holding file." Now you have something to remind you in case the person that you're dealing with has not gotten himself organized.

Managing Time and Tasks: Goal-Setting

One of the great benefits of organizing oneself comes from setting goals for the future, and systematically working toward them. This enables you to be "proactive" rather than simply reactive to the events that come up. When you are proacting, you develop a vision of a desired future and try to bring that vision into effect. There are several aspects of being proactive that are worth thinking about.

Let's use an example that should be familiar to you from earlier portions of this book. Let's suppose that you want to help your child improve in some vital psychological skill, such as enjoying acts of kindness to others or tolerating frustration. The first step is setting the goal: realizing that you want the outcome to take place, realizing that things would be much better if your child could get more pleasure out of kind acts or tolerate frustration better. In order to know what you're going after, however, it's not sufficient to have just a vague image of what you want: it has to be very concrete. Rather than just thinking, "I want him to be able to tolerate frustration better," proper goal setting involves getting an image of specific, concrete examples of what you will be seeing and hearing if the goal is achieved. "I want him to be able to think to himself 'I can take it' and congratulate the winner when he loses in a game," is one of many concrete examples of fortitude that you might bring to your mind in making your goal concrete. A second part of goal setting is heightening your desire for the goal by dwelling on the benefits that would occur if it were achieved. Simply acknowledging "Yes, I suppose I'd like that to happen," is not sufficient for setting a goal: it is important to sell yourself, to convince yourself how important it is that the goal be achieved, because to achieve it you will have to do lots of work. In selling yourself on the goal of helping your child learn fortitude, visualize the reduced level of conflict that the child would experience with a sibling, or the increased success in school work, or the increased pleasantness of your interactions with him, or whatever other benefits you can imagine. If you can't convince yourself that the goal is worth the work, maybe some other goal is more important to you. Another important part of goal-setting is generating some optimism: summoning the basic faith that given enough work, you can achieve the goal at least to some degree. If you believe that there's really nothing you can do that will affect anything, it's hard to do the work necessary to achieve it. If you believe that the child is the way he is because of fixed traits that will never change, or that you are the way you are for the same reason, it's a good idea to work on changing these attributions. Some people have been able to radically change their lives for the better, and those people are made out of the same type of protoplasm that everyone else is made of.

But you can't accomplish everything. Every goal that you work on means that you are choosing not to work on certain other goals. For this reason, it is crucial to invoke a well-grounded value system, to decide what goals really are most important. Is it more important to get along better with your child, or to become the best-dressed person in your social circle? Is it more important that your house be immaculate, or that your child be able to have more fun in it? Is it more important that your child succeed in his schoolwork, or that he succeed in athletics? Is it more important that the child learn to read at this time, or that he develop a positive feeling about eventually learning to read? Sometimes the choices are very difficult. Is it more important to foster progress toward world peace, or to increase good feeling in the family by for example spending time in lighthearted recreation? Is it more important to preserve harmony with a spouse, or to enjoy one's favorite hobby? Sometimes people can choose "both of the above" when making goal decisions; sooner or later, however, something has to be eliminated because of limited time and energy.

One approach to choosing worthy goals is to value those that make oneself, and other people, most happy in the long run—those that make the world a better place. (This is called utilitarian thinking.) Another approach is to choose goals using a principle that you would like for all people to use. (This is called the "categorical imperative.") Many religious principles contain elements of these two ideas.

After setting the goal, getting a concrete picture of what its achievement would look like, selling yourself on the importance of achieving it, and generating optimism that it can be achieved, what's the next step? You need to devise some way of measuring or monitoring the progress toward the goal. For a track runner or competitive swimmer, such measurement is relatively easy: the time that it takes to cover a certain distance. As the time gets smaller and smaller, progress toward the goal is being achieved. For enjoying acts of kindness or tolerating frustration, the measurement has to involve more judgment. But giving some sort of score to how well the child did in these tasks, or keeping a record of how many and what sort of positive examples you are seeing, will help in the crucial task of monitoring progress. For those parents who have used the "positive behavior diary," this is a rough tool for monitoring progress.

The next step is making a plan as to how the goal will be achieved. What are you going to do to bring about the desired result? Do you want to present real-life models to the child, present symbolic models, arrange practice opportunities, provide reinforcement contingencies, and in what specific ways? For plans having to do with people, it's good to think about the nine methods of influence listed in an earlier chapter, to remind yourself how to bring out change in people's habits.

When planning, it's useful to anticipate some of the obstacles that might obstruct progress toward the goal, and figure out how to get around these obstacles. For example, an obstacle might be that a relative who spends time with the child tends to undo some of the positive work that you are doing with the child; a way to get around that obstacle may be to include that relative in the program of training that you are taking, or find a way for the child to spend less time with that relative. An obstacle in the way of your being able to enthusiastically attend to the good things the child does may be that at a certain time of the day you are irritable because of fatigue; a way of getting around that obstacle might be to schedule a 20 minute relaxation session alone before being with the child.

In planning how to overcome obstacles, the decision-making and problem-solving steps outlined in the chapter on these topics are extremely helpful.

The next step is to execute the plan, to do the work that was planned, while frequently monitoring progress toward the goal. If progress takes place, make sure to celebrate it thoroughly. Effective celebrations renew your energy for further work. If progress does not take place after a reasonable amount of time, return to the problem-solving or decision-making process, and decide how to modify the plan. (It is often difficult to decide what a reasonable amount of time is—whether to stay the course or change tactics. Information on how long it takes for the solution to work is crucial in making this decision.) Persist in this process until the goal is attained.

It is extremely useful to write down your goals. What things would you like to accomplish in your lifetime, and in the foreseeable future? What would you like to accomplish in the next year? If you take the time to answer this question in writing, your time will be extremely well spent.

In setting goals, it's sometimes useful for someone to think of the following categories: career, financial security, strength of support system, relations with family, child-rearing, relations with friends, health and fitness, personal development, and contributions to humanity.

When goal-setting, people often neglect the goals of cultivating their own relationships, their own social network. Who are the people most important to maintain continuing closeness with? Most of us spend time with people based on proximity or chance rather than a conscious effort to be with the ones most important to us. Think about writing goals for maintaining close relations with certain specific people, listed by name.

If you write your goals and post them in front of you, and look at them as you plan your daily activities, you will have a means of keeping yourself centered upon what is really important to you.

Organizing Time and Tasks: The Logistics

Once you have devoted time to figuring out what goals you have, the task is to translate those goals into daily activities that foster their accomplishment.

No organized person should be without a small notebook for keeping track of appointments and tasks to be done. I like to use as 4 inch by 6 inch 60 sheet spiral notebook, one for each month. In setting it up, you can leave the first three sheets for the master to do list, which we will talk about later. After those pages, write the consecutive days and dates of the month on the next 30 or so pages. These fronts of pages will be used for appointments; the back of the page preceding each dated page will be used for the daily to do list. Thus when you open to a given date, the appointments are on the right hand page and the daily to do list is on the left hand page.

In the front of the notebook is the "master to do list." This is where you write down everything that needs to be done, of any sort. In other words, whenever there comes to mind anything that you need or want to do, write it down on the master to do list.

Then each day, you make a daily to do list. On the appointment page, you have written down any activity that is scheduled for a certain time, whenever the appointment is made. Each evening you can review what you are scheduled to do the following day. Then, for the time that is not scheduled, you can look at the master to do list, and also your list of long range goals, and put onto the daily to do list the additional things that you want to get done the following day. You write these on the daily to do list page. Throughout the day, you then refer to these two pages.

There's something else very useful to do when you make a to do list: to order the priority of your "to dos." After you write the items for the daily to do list, number them in order of priority. That is, write the numeral 1 by the most important item; write 2 by the next most important, and so forth.

Why should the activities be numbered in order of priority? Because you never know exactly how long things are going to take, so you never know whether you are going to get through all the items on your to do list. But if you get the most important ones done, then you at least know you are putting your effort into the areas that will pay off the most.

Another reason for doing the items in the order of the priority list is that by doing so you train yourself not to put off the unpleasant or difficult activities. When a task's number comes up, you do it, like it or not.

Here's a game useful to play with yourself. After making your daily to do list and ordering the priorities, you look at your scheduled activities, and figure out how much time you have to devote to your to do list items, and predict how many you will get done. Then, put a mark by the last item you predict you will finish. Then at the end of the day, see how your prediction compared with your actual accomplishment.

There's a major benefit of seeing how your prediction compares with the actual accomplishment: you gradually get better and better at predicting how long something will actually take to do. Being able to predict well then allows you to make plans both in the long run and in the short run. It enables you to make commitments to other people that you can more easily keep.

When you finish an item on the to do list, check it off, congratulate yourself for finishing it, and try to feel good about what you have done! If you can train yourself to feel good when you finish an item, you will get much more done.

When you're making a to do list, it's better to break down large tasks into small parts, so that you will be able to check off an accomplishment and feel good about it more often. For example, rather than having one item for "Do income taxes," you could have separate items for "Sort out papers in tax file," "Find canceled checks for deductible items," and so forth. Breaking a job down into small parts is often a very important step in overcoming resistance to getting it done.

What if as the day goes on, you decide that some task not on your to do list is what's most worth doing? The to do list of course can be changed at any point during the day. Priorities can be rearranged. Some people write newly-arisen tasks on their to do list and check them off, sometimes even after they've done them, just to aid in self-reinforcement.

When you do a task so automatically and routinely that you don't need even to think about whether and when to do it, your reward is not having to write it down. For example, suppose that each evening at a certain time, a parent sits down and looks at the child's homework. If this gets to be so routine that it is never forgotten, then it can be eliminated from the to do list.

Establishing Routines

Which of the following sounds more pleasant for you? To do laundry when you notice that no clean clothes are left, or to schedule laundry at certain regular times each week? To pay bills and process paperwork when you wake up in the middle of the night wondering if the phone will be cut off, or to have a certain scheduled time once a week for bills and paperwork? To write your daily to do list whenever you can remember it, or to have a certain routine time in the daily schedule for writing it? To call the doctor and try frantically to get a new prescription the day that blood pressure medicine runs out, or to schedule a routine way of renewing it regularly? To wash the dishes when there are no clean ones left, or to wash them routinely after every meal or once a day? In the first instance the stimulus to do the task is some sort of unpleasant circumstance; in the second instance the stimulus is a regular habit or something on an appointment calendar.

In many families these tasks become the source of much irritation and feelings of frantic emergency, because there are no routines. It will be useful for family members to sit down together with pencil and paper and decide together what routines they wish to adopt, and to write them down, and review them frequently. If the routines save time and energy and effort, keep them; if they cause discord and contention, make a different plan. What's the routine for laundry? for dishwashing? for homework-doing? for cooking and mealtimes? for bedtimes? for buying of supplies? If some job causes hassle repeatedly, raise the question of what the system is for accomplishing it, and try to arrive at a system that will eliminate the hassle.

Reducing Error in Tasks

Before a pilot takes off in a plane he refers to a list of things to check, and checks each thing that could possibly cause trouble during the flight. The same thing can be done, mentally or on paper, with any other task: you make a list of all the things that have to be done right in order for the job to be successful, and you don't call the job finished until each one is checked off. Your checklist should cover all the conceivable errors that you can think of.

An example might be the task of childproofing an area of the house where there are infants or toddlers. The checklist might have items such as the following: 1) Are there no matches and lighters available to the child? 2) Are no firearms available? 3) Are there no knives, ice picks, or other sharp objects available? 4) Are there no poisonous substances or medicines available? 5) Are there no heavy objects that can be pulled over or pulled down onto the child? 6) Are electrical outlets plugged? 7) Are there no opportunities for the child to get to a place high enough to be seriously injured if he fell? 8) Are there no objects small enough to be swallowed or choked upon? 9) Are there no plastic bags that the child could suffocate from inhaling? 10) Is the temperature of the hot water from the faucet turned down enough that exposure to it would not burn the child badly?

There's a big difference between error-reduction using a checklist as mentioned above, and compulsive checking rituals of a nervous worrier. The error-reduction method that I'm advocating is one wherein you can focus on one type of possible error at a time, and feel secure that all have been checked once you've gotten through the list. The compulsive checker is often trying to think about too many aspects of the job at one time, and can't remember what has been checked and what hasn't, and tries to make up for this disorganization by repetition.

Organizing Communications With Other People About Tasks

Be as light as possible in your demands on the other person's memory, just as with your own. Other people also have many things they want to do with their available memory space.

If the procedure you want someone to do is a little much to hold in memory, write it down for them. Writing it down also prevents a good bit of telephone tag and a good bit of misunderstanding of verbal messages.

Keep unnecessary information to a minimum. If we call the most important points the "signal," and unimportant points the "noise," then you want your utterances to have the highest ratio of signal to noise that you can have.

Suppose someone asks, "Why didn't you buy the computer paper today?" and the important point that the other person wants to communicate is that the store was out of computer paper. If the person says, "Because the store was out of paper," that utterance has a high signal-to-noise ratio.

The following utterance, on the other hand, has a low signal-to-noise ratio: "Well, I went down to the place on about 2:00, no, I think it must have been about 3:00 in the afternoon; that's right, it couldn't have been 2:00 because I was still in a meeting until just a little before 3:00—anyway, when I got there, the place we always get paper down on Meyran Avenue, I looked all over the place, and at first it was hard for me to believe that they would have been out, because I've been going there for at least a year, and I don't think there's been one other time that I couldn't find any, but I asked the clerk, who wasn't in a very good mood today...." In this example, the essential message is buried in a sea of irrelevant detail.

Deciding To Take on a New Commitment to a Task

Here is an important principle that accounts for a good fraction of human unhappiness: People continue to take on new commitments to tasks, until they are performing incompetently in at least one, if not all, of them. Or as expressed by Laurence Peter and called the Peter Principle, in organizations, people rise to their level of incompetence. If people are performing successfully, other people will ask them to take on new things to do, and often offer rewards for doing them. People tend to say "Yes" to such commitments. A psychotherapist who establishes a reputation for very thorough and competent work tends to get more and more patients referred to him, to the point where he can't keep up with who is who. An executive who establishes a reputation as a competent and thorough director of an organization gets invited to be on more and more boards of directors, until she doesn't have time to understand an organization she is directing. A full-time mother who establishes a reputation for organizing activities for parents and children to do together takes on so many projects that there is little time left to relax informally with the child. A couple enjoy their first child so much that they have two more, and find that with their other commitments they can't give any of their children the time and attention they deserve.

Each person has only a finite amount of time and energy. As the commitments proliferate, something has to be sacrificed. Sometimes the task that gets sacrificed is spending quality time with family. Sometimes it's enjoying time to oneself. Sometimes it's the task of getting adequate sleep. Sometimes it's the least urgent commitment someone has made to someone else, or sometimes the least urgent 5 commitments.

Just as organizing objects is easier if you can avoid owning so many of them, organizing tasks is easier if you think carefully before taking another one of them on. Are you on top of things now? Is your stress level in a very comfortable zone? How much time will the new commitment take? With that time no longer available, will you still be on top of things and in a comfortable level of stress? This is the way to think before taking on a new commitment. The way not to think is simply to say, Would this be interesting or worthwhile or profitable? You think not only of the returns, but also of the investment of time and energy needed to reap the returns.

Organizing Money

The disorganization of money is certainly responsible for the failure of businesses, failure of marriages, and other very unpleasant outcomes, just as is the disorganization of time and tasks and the other areas.

Most of the works I've read on managing money ask people to spend a lot of time making a very detailed budget, figuring out how much money does and should go to each category of expenditure. But it seems that very few people in the real world can consistently muster the energy to do this. Perhaps the labor that such a task requires isn't justified by the payoff. Is there a simpler and easier way to get a handle on what is handling financially in one's family?

Many families have no real money management system at all, and would do well to adopt the following "minimalist" approach to financial organization, rather than taking on a very detailed and laborious system.

This minimalist system doesn't require that you add up expenses and income. It doesn't require that you categorize expenses into groups. It isn't even necessary to record your expenditures and income in order to use it, although records are necessary for taxes and perhaps other purposes.

In the most minimal of minimal systems, you simply calculate your family net worth each month. You assemble the statements that list your assets: bank account, brokerage account, and whatever. Most financial institutions these days will give your account status over the phone or internet. You add the assets and subtract the debts (e.g. credit card debt, loans, etc.) to get a total net worth figure.

The change in net worth from one month to the next represents the same number you would get if you were to keep a detailed record of all your expenses and all your income, and compute the total of income minus expenses. If you own stocks and bonds, any fluctuation their prices are also included as income or expense. You don't count the value of consumption items such as china or cars or anything else except a house when calculating net worth.

If the general trend of the net worth figure over the long term is upward in the amount that you want it to be, you don't need to waste a lot of time on further recording and calculation.

If you want to go one step beyond this system, then you can calculate separately the change in net worth due to earned income minus expenses, and the change in net worth due to investment income and investment value fluctuation. You take your earnings and put them into checking accounts, and you make your expenditures from checking accounts, and you see what is happening to the total checking account number, separately from the brokerage account number. You make transfers to or from the brokerage account after the month's calculations have been made. Making these separate calculations allows you to answer the question of whether you are spending more than you are actually earning by working.

Of course expenditures vary from month to month, and there may be some months where the change in net worth is negative, balanced by other months where the number is very positive. But by adding those monthly figures you can find out how much in the red or the black you are for whatever time period you want. If you are in the black by a sufficient amount to prepare for retirement and future emergencies and future college expenditures and so forth, then you are finished with this minimalist money organization procedure. If you are not sufficiently in the black, then you need to add income or cut expenditures. If you need to cut, then there usually needs to be discussion between family members on what expenditures are cuttable and what are not. In the minimalist procedure, you simply go out and cut whatever you can cut, and see what happens. If this doesn't work, then you go to the detailed budget figures, keeping track of food, clothing, phone, electricity, etc. But your reward for sufficient thrift is not having to do this.

Organization Skills Checklist

Are you willing to allocate time, regularly, to putting objects in their homes, filing papers, writing to yourself about goals and tasks, and organizing money?_______

Do you declutter your life by acquiring and keeping no more objects and papers than you really need?______

Do you have a "home" for each object, especially the important ones? _____

Do you have adequate file space to keep organized files of all papers you want to keep?_____

When you get a piece of paper that calls for some action later on, do you file the paper and make a note in your master to do list of what you have to do, with a

note in parentheses of where the piece of paper is filed? _____
Do you have a written list of your long-term goals? ______
Do you periodically ask what is really important in life, and revise your goal list accordingly? _____
Do you have one, and only one, "appointment and to do" book that is almost always near you? _____
Does the appointment notebook have in it adequate space to write daily appointments and daily to dos, and to see both of them without having to turn pages? ____
Do you keep a master to do list, of all tasks to be done?_____
Do you make a to do list each day?_____
Do you put numbers by your tasks to be done, to order their priorities?_____
Do you check each task off the list as you do it?_____
Do you remember to feel good when you check a task off the to do list?_____
Do you make error-reducing checklists for important tasks, i.e. lists of all the things that need to be right for the job to be complete? Do you check them before finishing the task?_____
Do you create regular routines, and do recurring tasks according to a schedule rather than waiting for some negative consequence to prompt you to do it?______
Do you communicate complicated procedures to other people in writing rather than straining their memories? ____
Do you have a high "signal to noise ratio" when you communicate to other people? _____
Before taking on a new commitment, do you carefully consider whether you will have the time and energy to do it well, and say no to it if the resources aren't there?_____
Do you calculate, each month, the change in your net worth, and adjust your use of money according to what those numbers tell you?______

Chapter 27: Teaching Organization Skills

Chapter Overview:

Many children are bright enough to do well in schoolwork, but are too disorganized to do so. Should you avoid organizing a child for fear of removing the child's motivation to organize himself? I think not. Some children find it more difficult to learn organization skills than others do. The most humane procedure is to start by doing as much of the organizing yourself as is necessary for both your lives to be comfortable. Gradually work toward your child's doing more and more of the organizing. The bottom of the hierarchy is organizing for the child, while talking to yourself out loud to model for the child. The next step is that you and the child can take turns organizing and while the person who watches tracks and describes, with an approving tone. Or, you and the child can do organizing tasks together, to make them more pleasant and less lonely. Next the child organizes, without you present, and you inspect the results; the final step is that the child is totally on his own. Children can learn organization of papers by using file folders, with their school bags as rudimentary file cabinets. When enough papers accumulate, a child should start to use a real file cabinet. A parent can help a child organize his use of time and tasks by interviewing the child about goals in various areas, using the outline presented here if desired. Children may be taught to use a to do book and appointment calendar just as described in the previous chapter. School logistics consist of getting books and papers and other things, as well as oneself, to the proper place at the proper time; this task for many children is more difficult than the schoolwork itself. In mastering school logistics, you and the child write a task analysis, i.e. a detailed breakdown of the steps of the logistic procedures, and the child goes through them several times in fantasy practice. When the child forgets books and papers and assignments, the competence-oriented consequence is neither nagging nor some arbitrary punishment, but more fantasy practice of the logistics. The same procedure of task analysis and fantasy rehearsal can help with older children who have difficulty in the task of getting dressed and going somewhere. Preschoolers can learn to plan by being asked what their plans for play activities are, being helped to carry out their plans, and then reviewing how they carried out their plans after doing them. Preschoolers with problems in dressing can be helped by a program which emphasizes differential reinforcement for getting dressed and ready.

****

The Importance of Organization Skills for Children

I have seen numerous children who were more than smart enough to succeed at school, who were nonetheless not succeeding, or succeeding only with very painful struggles, because of poor organization skills. Doing the homework posed little problem compared to remembering what homework to do, remembering to bring the book home that was necessary in doing the homework, remembering to take the homework paper back to school, and keeping up with the paper long enough to turn it in. Disorganization on these tasks can literally make the difference between a hellacious school experience and a pleasant one.

Here's a checklist for students on disorganization of school tasks:

Do you often have trouble leaving books or papers at home that you should have taken to school?

Do you often not have with you the papers and books that you need in class?

Do you often not write down your assignments well enough to let yourself know exactly what all the assignments are, when you sit down to work on them at home?

Do you often leave books or papers at school that you need to do homework with?

Do you often forget to do some of your homework?

I have also heard of endless battles' going on in homes between parent and child about crucial organization tasks. Here are some questions for parents:

Is there unpleasant conflict between you and your child about the child's cleaning up his room?

Is it a source of irritation that the child doesn't put away playthings and other objects?

Is it very difficult for the child to remember to do anything without being reminded?

Is the task of getting dressed and ready to go somewhere on time a source of conflict and hassle for you?

Does your child have a clear sense of goals and direction, or is your child somewhat aimless?

Organizing For the Child Versus Teaching the Child to Organize

A Chinese proverb says, Give a man a fish, and you make him happy for a day; teach him to fish, and you make him happy for a lifetime. Here's my addendum: If the man has nothing else to eat and it will take him a few months or years to learn to fish, it's better to give him fish for a while! Sometimes teaching a person to fish may best take place by letting that person watch you fish over a very long time.

I've become convinced that some children find it much more difficult to organize than others do, because of biologic differences in their brains. If this is true, it should be of no surprise to anybody: there are differences among people in musical ability, mathematical ability, coordination skills, and other talents; why not for organization skills? There are some children who are quite talented at reading and math, for example, but who are very untalented at organization. Some children are best conceived of as having a "learning disability" in organization skills. They need very systematic teaching over a long period of time, in skills that other children pick up much more easily, if they are to learn these skills.

For all learning, this book has emphasized that it's important to stay in the "challenge zone": the region where the tasks are not too hard, not too easy, but just right. Accordingly, when children have widely differing abilities, it's a good idea to accommodate so that the child can be working at the challenge zone in the different abilities. For example, for children with troubles in learning to decode printed words, but good abilities in comprehending spoken language, a parent can read textbooks to the child, and at the same time work on decoding at a lower level of difficulty.

For organization skills, it is often the most humane and workable procedure for the parent to organize for the child, and to help the teacher organize for the child, while at the same time gradually trying to work with the child on learning better and better organization skills.

What sort of teaching do you do when the child needs help in organizing? Here's one strategy for doing this: organizing for the child, with the child, out loud. The parent and child together put objects away, organize papers, and manage time and tasks, with the parent speaking out loud the sorts of "self talk" that the child will eventually need to internalize if he is to become organized.

Organizing Objects In a Joint Activity

For the child who is at the bottom of the hierarchy in this skill, the parent can simply ask the child to watch and listen while the parent puts things in their homes. The parent says, "Watch what I do, and see if you can later do the same thing." The parent models self-talk such as the following:

"OK, there's lots to put away. But I'll pick up one thing at a time, and decide or remember where its home is, and put it there. First a dirty sock. The dirty clothes go in the hamper, no problem. Now a sweater, still clean. The home for this one is on the shelf in the closet, there it goes back home. Now a book, back this goes to its home on the bookshelf."

Next the child picks up objects one by one and does the same sort of self-talk and putting away, while the parent watches and listens. The parent gives reminders as to where the home of the object is, if necessary, and the parent celebrates with the child the completion of putting each object in its home.

Parent and child can alternate back and forth in these roles as long as necessary; the parent is alternately modeling and giving the child practice opportunities. The parent will get much better results by reducing commands and by doing a lot of tracking and describing in a positive tone of voice.

At some point the putting-away activity no longer presents a challenge to the child's cognitive organization skills, but only to self-discipline skills. The child knows how to do it, but doing it alone is not as much fun as doing something else. It's wise to avoid large conflicts by not jumping immediately to the stage of expecting the child to organize objects by himself, but to have this activity continue to be a joint one that parent and child do together. When the process has become automatized enough, they can have pleasant conversations while doing it and it can even be a "mutually gratifying activity."

Organizing School Papers

Most children at the time of this writing transfer things from school to home in a backpack. The backpack can hold folders in which papers are filed, and be the location for a rudimentary filing system. It can hold folders, one for each school subject, in which class notes, papers given out by the teacher, and completed homework assignments are kept. Another useful folder for the backpack is the "To parent, to teacher" folder, where notes home to the parent or signed forms to be sent back to the teacher are kept.

If the child arrives home each day with a disorderly array of papers in the backpack, parent and child can sit down together and go through the same steps with papers as they did with objects; the "home" for each paper is its folder. In time the child may learn to put papers in their home as soon as the opportunity presents itself.

When the child accumulates more papers to keep than can be kept in the rudimentary system just mentioned, it is probably time for the child to receive the gift of a file cabinet. I think that in the information age, the first file cabinet should be celebrated as a rite of passage. The parent will demonstrate for the child how to use file folders and organize papers.

Organizing Time and Tasks: Goal-Setting With Children

What do you want to accomplish in the next few months, the next couple of years; what do you want to accomplish during your life? Most children I know have never been asked these questions, and when they are asked, they are at first rather blank. The question is an abstract one. But it's an extremely important one; unless you know where you're going, the choice of which road to follow gets made in a very arbitrary way.

A parent or other adult can be helpful to grade school aged and older children by being a combination interviewer and secretary to them and arriving at a written list of the child's goals.

Here are some more concrete categories and questions that will help the child answer the more general question.

School Achievement and/or Learning

Are there any subjects you would like to get stronger in?

Would you like to get school work better organized?

Would you like to get better grades in general?

Would you like to be able to study better?

Is there something you would like to learn about, or learn to do?

School Behavior

Are you making life pleasant for your teacher? Would you like to do this more?

Are you making life pleasant for your classmates? Would you like to do this more?

Do you have a good reputation at school for behaving reasonably? Would you like to do this more?

Athletics and/or Health and Fitness

Any accomplishments you want to make in sports?

Any sport you want to get more skilled at?

Any particular sports skills you want to get?

Do you want to get more exercise? If so, how?

Do you want to improve your eating habits? If so, how?

Are there other health habits or attitudes you want to strengthen, such as non-use of alcohol or tobacco or others?

Hobbies and other skills

Do you want to take up any new activities, such as playing a musical instrument, learning to use a computer well, reading and learning about a new subject, hiking, cycling, etc.?

Are there particular skill goals you have in any activity?

Or do you have a goal of simply spending time enjoying some activity?

Relations with family members

Are you pleased with the way you get along with each person in your family?

Whom in your family would you like to get along better with?

What would be happening less often, and what would be happening more often, if you got along better with that person?

Is there someone in your family you would like to spend more time doing fun things with?

Social Life, Relations with friends

Would you like to make more friends?

Would you like to have a best friend that you are closer to?

Would you like for your time with a friend to be more fun?

Would you like for people you don't know really well to like you better?

Personal development

What would you like to do to improve yourself?

How would you like to make yourself a better person?

What psychological skills would you like the most to get better at, at this time? (Looking carefully at the menu of psychological skills will be helpful in making this decision.)

Religious or philosophical life

Would you like your religious life to be improved in any way?

Do you have a philosophy of life that is fully developed and very helpful to you?

Service to Humanity, Making the World a Better Place

Would you like to be of more service to humanity?

Would you like to be of service in some particular way?

Would you like to learn more about how to be of service to humanity?

Are you interested in a cause such as nonviolence, reducing poverty, or improving the environment?

******

When you and your child together have arrived at a list of the child's goals, and have narrowed them down to the ones that are of the very highest priority at this time, the next task is for the interviewer/secretary to ask, for each goal, "Do you have any ideas right now about what you could do to accomplish this goal?" If the child is interested in making better grades, what would help this: spending more time studying, learning organized study habits, getting some tutoring, or what? If the child is interested in getting along better with a brother or sister, what could the child do to accomplish this?

Once these goals and activities have been identified and written down, then you and the child can get together regularly and go over the goals, and remember what activities have been done to work toward accomplishing them, and celebrate any steps that have been taken. Of course, it's important not to lose the paper or computer file where the goals and activities lists were written down!

The Child's To Do and Appointment Book

In the previous chapter we spoke of a method of having one monthly book where both "to dos" and scheduled appointments could be listed. For a child who has trouble with organization, developing the habit of using such a book should occur as early as possible. The school assignment book can be the predecessor for this.

My recommendation is to use the same sort of 3 by 5 or 4 by 6 blank spiral notebook as was mentioned before. On the page that is on the right as you open the page, the scheduled events are written down; on the page on the left, the to dos for that day are written.

Homework assignments are both scheduled events and to dos. Turning in the homework assignment is scheduled for a certain time; doing the assignment is on the to do list. Reminders of special events happening at a certain time fall into the category of appointments. For the child who has trouble remembering what class to go to at what time, the daily class schedule can be put into the appointment calendar page.

If the child is old enough to have chores that occur regularly, and particularly if these don't occur daily, these should be written into the to do list. For example, if the child takes on the task of taking out the garbage for pick-up once a week, this can be written into the to do list for every date on which the task should be done.

For a long time the parent will have to sit down with the child and do the to do and appointment book together. The parent should constantly have in mind the notion of hierarchy, and do as much or as little of the task as is necessary for the child to be at the "challenge zone." The parent and child should look at the book for at least two purposes, that of making the to do list for the next day, and that of checking off and celebrating the tasks that were done that day.

The goal of the to do and appointment book is that the child who is poor at remembering things will not have to remember them nearly so well—all the child will have to remember is to look frequently at the appointment book. And the child who is good at remembering things will be able to free up memory space for higher purposes.

Organizing School Logistics by Task Analysis and Fantasy Rehearsal

If the answer to any of the questions about school organization tasks at the beginning of the chapter was "Yes," the child will benefit from working on the skills of organizing school logistics. By "logistics" I'm referring to tasks other than learning. Logistics do not include how the child does in reading, and studying, and remembering, and writing. Logistics do include how the child gets from one place from another with the things she's supposed to have, and how she keeps track of what she's supposed to do.

As with almost all other problems children have, there are two approaches: one to try to make the challenges the child is given less difficult, and the other to try to teach the child to cope with the challenges with more skill. Logistics are much easier for children if they stay in the same classroom rather than rotating to several different classrooms; if the teacher sends home a photocopied schedule of all the homework assignments for the week rather than depending upon students to write them down; if there is a small number of textbooks that will consistently need to be brought home and brought back to school for at least a month or so rather than a different combination of textbooks every day; and so forth. With younger children particularly, it seems wise for schools to make the logistics easier so as to leave more energy to spend on the learning itself. However, this book is written for parents, and you will often have little control over how easy or difficult the school makes the logistics. Therefore the rest of this section will focus on improving the child's logistic-organization skills.

How do you work at getting the logistics of school down to a smoothly flowing system? Here's how I recommend that you do it.

First, you help the child write down, or write down for the child, the logistic steps the child goes through in a school day. Writing down these steps will help the child to get an image in mind of exactly what must be done at what times.

Second, you revise this written list of steps, as many times as you need to, so that it really makes sense to do things according to this system.

Third, the child reads over the list of steps and get the list firmly in memory.

Fourth, the child does "fantasy practices" of the steps, so that he will be likely to do them in real life. He can do "fantasy practices out loud," in which he talks his way through the steps, and he can do "mental movies," in which he sees in his mind himself carrying out the steps. Each time he fantasy-practices a step in this way, he should celebrate in his mind.

Fifth, he goes out in real life, in a real school day, and carries out the same steps. Each time he does one, he celebrates and congratulates himself.

Sixth, the child can go over with you how well he did in the steps. You celebrate with your child the ones he did well.

That's an overview of what the plan is. Now let's talk about writing down the steps.

Writing down the steps has been called doing a "task analysis." You take a procedure or complicated process, and break it down into its individual parts. Let's illustrate task analysis with a very simple task, one so simple it will seem silly to even do it. Here are the logistics of getting a drink of water from the kitchen sink.

1. Walk to the kitchen cabinet.
2. Open it.
3. Get a glass.
4. Walk to the kitchen sink.
5. Turn on the cold water.
6. Let it run until it's cold.
7. Stick the glass underneath the stream of water.
8. When the glass is full, take it out.
9. Turn off the water.
10. Lift the glass to the lips and drink the water.
11. Go back to step 5 if still thirsty.
12. If not still thirsty, put the glass in the sink and walk away.

(I could have had the drinker wash the glass out, dry it, and put it away, but I'll let the drinker be lazy, so we can keep it simpler.)

When I wrote this, I forgot a step, right between steps 3 and 4. Can you figure out what it is? It's not easy to write a task analysis and remember all the steps the first time. Writing the task analysis forces you to think really hard about what the steps are. If I were editing and revising this task analysis, I would have a step where the drinker closed the cabinet door, so this person wouldn't get hit on the head by the open door! Thinking about these steps and writing them down helps you to get a very clear image of exactly what goes on in the process.

If you've ever written a computer program, you'll recognize that writing a task analysis is like writing a computer program. Of course we don't want to waste time writing task analyses of processes that are already no problem, like getting a drink of water. But a task analysis of the logistics of schoolwork will be very helpful. The goal is for the child to program his brain to do the logistics of schoolwork without having to hassle about them.

Let's do an imaginary task analysis for someone who has a locker in the hall, switches classes every period, and finds it convenient to stop by the locker between each class. This student likes to carry a book bag to all classes.

Let's start the task analysis as the school day begins.

1. I pick up the book bag that I left on my desk last night, and check one more time to make sure all my books and papers and my assignment book are in it. I take it with me to school.
2. Before the first class, I stop by my locker. I check what books and pencils or pens and paper I need for the first class, and put it into the book bag.
3. At the first class, I turn in my homework paper when asked to do so. When I get a homework assignment, I take the assignment book out of the book bag, open my assignment book to the date that it is today, write the name of the subject, and write the assignment carefully. (If there is no homework, I write "none".) I check to make sure I wrote the assignment correctly. I return the assignment book to the book bag.
4. I do steps 2 and 3 before all the other classes.
5. Before going home, I stop at my locker, and open my assignment book. I look at each assignment, and make sure the books or papers I need to do each assignment are in my book bag. I take the book bag home.
6. At homework time, I sit at my desk, read the first assignment from my assignment book. I get out of the book bag what I need to do it. I do it. I check it off in the assignment book. Then I put the completed paper back in my book bag, in the file folder for that subject.
7. I do the same thing with the other assignments until all are finished.
8. I go to my parent, and let him or her check the assignment book and take a look at each completed assignment. I celebrate the completion of tasks. Af-

terwards I put the assignment book, the books, and the completed assignments back into the book bag.
9. I return the book bag to the top of my desk.

What if the child doesn't like carrying a book bag? Or what if he likes having his assignment book in his right hip pocket rather than his book bag? Or if he has a home room and a desk, instead of a locker? What if his schedule is a little different on different days of the week? Just make these changes in the task analysis.

When I have done this with children, I have acted as secretary and questioner, and have had the child walk me through the logistic steps of the school day as I type out the task analysis.

As the child gets the task analysis onto paper, he has an opportunity for the child to think about ways to change or improve the process. For example, if there are two classes, one right after another, in a building a good distance from the locker, maybe it makes sense to plan for those two classes at the same time and skip coming back to the locker between them.

After the task analysis is written out in the most sensible way, the child is then to read over it enough times that he is thoroughly familiar with it, and can remember the steps. In other words, the child memorizes it, not word for word, but so as to remember the steps. The child practices saying the task analysis back to the adult from memory.

After the child commits the steps to memory, he can practice in imagination going through the steps in "fantasy practices." There are three ways to do fantasy practice: fantasy practice out loud, making silent mental movies, and practicing manipulating materials with your hands. Thus fantasy practice can involve hearing, seeing, and touching and moving things.

Here's what a fantasy practice out loud would start out sounding like for the task as analyzed above.

"It's morning, and I'm about to leave for school. I'm seeing my book bag on my desk, and I'm checking to make sure that all my books and homework papers are in it. I'm picking it up and taking it with me. Now I'm at school, and it's before my first class. I'm stopping at my locker. I'm pulling my assignment book out of my locker, and looking at it. I see what I need for my first class, and I'm making sure I've got that book in my book bag. Now I'm at my first class, and the assignment is written on the board. I pull my assignment book out of my book bag, and I write the name of the subject, and copy the assignment. I'm checking it very carefully; yes, I've got it right...."

Here's a second way to do fantasy practice. The fantasy practice out loud used a lot of words. The "mental movie" uses visual images, the pictures you make in your own mind. To do this the child just sits silently and sees himself doing all the things that he mentioned doing in the fantasy practice out loud. As he does this, you can check for the vividness of the images. Can he see the exact color of his book bag? Can he see himself in class, and can he see exactly where he is reaching, to get his assignment book?

The third way to practice is to actually get the book bag and some books and your assignment notebook and some papers and a pencil. The child goes through the physical motions of picking up the book bag first thing in the morning, and checking it; opening an imaginary locker by twisting the dials on a combination lock; pulling out the assignment book and looking at it; putting a book for the first class from the locker into the book bag; pulling out the assignment book and writing the subject name, making a mark or two with your pencil for the pretend assignment, and so forth. In this way the child's body gets used to the motions that it will go through in doing the logistics in the steps that you have listed. You can play a game with your child: can the child act out the steps so well that you can name each one as you see it?

As you practice in each of these ways, try to make sure that after each step of the process, the child remembers to congratulate himself. You encourage the child to say, "Hooray for me, I did this step well!" or to see himself receiving an award, or to feel himself receiving a pat on the back. Learning to reward yourself and getting in the habit of doing this is a very important part of being successful in this new learning.

Then the child goes out into real life and practices what he's already practiced in fantasy. As he does each step in real life, he should try to remember to celebrate and congratulate himself.

How much fantasy practice is sufficient? Many, many repetitions are often required. Whenever a problem comes up with forgetting things, rather than nagging the child, you go back to the task analysis and do more fantasy practice repetitions.

You can help your child by going over all the steps at the end of the day and asking the child if he's done them; if he has, then the two of you can celebrate together.

If you find that the way the process is set up in the task analysis just doesn't work very well in real life, then you and the child can revise the task analysis and improve the process. Then the child practices the new plan in imagination.

After a while if the child gets such good habits of organization that he no longer has problems with the logistics of school, then his reward is that he can quit doing fantasy practices of this, and can start practicing something else.

A Task Analysis of Getting Dressed and Ready To Go Somewhere

A school bus will come at 730. It takes about 15 minutes to get showered and dressed, about 15 minutes to eat breakfast, about 5 minutes to brush teeth, 5 minutes to make sure everything's organized for school, 10 minutes to relax and plan the day, and 5 minutes to wait at the bus stop. What time should the whole process start? This arithmetic problem is within the capacity of grade school children past a certain age, assuming that the child actually engages in the problem. But for the child actually to get ready to go sometimes elicits much nagging from a parent and much unpleasantness for parent and child.

The complex tasks of getting ready can be broken into simple parts in a task analysis, just as was done with the logistics of school work. The steps listed above probably a detailed enough task analysis for most purposes. These can be written down and rehearsed. When there is a problem, the desired response is not a lot of yelling and nagging, but acknowledgement of the problem and lots of fantasy rehearsal of doing the process more smoothly the next time.

Your role in such a process is hopefully more that of an interviewer and secretary than of a slave-driver. You and the child can sit down together and plan when the process should start and what should be accomplished by what time, and post this schedule where the child can see it. You also can take the role of the "reinforcement officer" rather than the nagger. If the child is on schedule and performs an appointed task by the appointed time, you cheer. This role will probably take you at least as much time and energy as the role of nagger, at least for a while, but it will be infinitely more pleasant. After the child gets enough practice, your effort can be reduced.

The Degree of the Parent's Involvement in These Tasks

Sometimes the child has absolutely no motivation to participate in any of these organization tasks. To what extent should the parent let the child suffer the "natural consequences" of disorganization, in order for some motivation to develop in the child, and some receptivity to the help the adult will offer? Versus, to what extent should the parent simply use his or her authority to insist that organization tasks be done, and try to make them as pleasant as possible, before the child suffers real life consequences? Like all use of natural consequences, this is a judgment call; the answer will be different for different families.

Helping Preschoolers Get Used to Planning

The teachers in one prominent preschool project asked children, every day, to make a plan as to what they wanted to do with a certain amount of time—did they want to build something in the block area, did they want to play with the musical instruments, did they want to look at books and listen to audiotapes, did they want to help a teacher make salad, etc. Then they did what they had planned, and afterwards, they were reminded of their plan and had the opportunity to talk about how it had worked out. The skill of goal-setting and goal-monitoring, I think, was being fostered, and I think that might have had some influence on the good things the program seemed to bring about.

You can use this same principle by asking young children what they plan to do in the next period of time, remembering what they say, and checking with them at the end of that time whether they did what they planned. If the child actually carried out a positive plan, that is cause for celebration. If they did something different than what they planned, that is no cause for mourning; you can explore why they changed their mind, with an attitude that flexibility is a virtue.

Dressing Problems

A fairly frequent problem with preschool children is resistance to getting clothes put on in the morning. There can be several reasons for this sort of problem. First, the child may hate the preschool or day care center to which he goes after dressing, and resistance to dressing is a way of resisting leaving home. Second, the child may have a somewhat compulsive streak about clothes, and be so fastidious that the decision to put one thing on rather than another is something the child tends to dawdle over and put off. Third, and probably most commonly, the dawdling over dressing is an effective way for the child to get some attention from the parent, even though the attention is an exasperated sort.

The following program is for the child who already has clearly demonstrated that he or she knows how to dress himself or herself. It is probably very useful for the second and third types of problems listed above; if the problem is that the child hates preschool or school or day care then this program won't solve that basic problem.

The guiding principle is differential reinforcement. The parents should follow a set procedure that guarantees that whatever the child does, the child gets more desirable consequences from dressing than from refusing to dress or arguing about dressing.

In carrying out this program, you stop rewarding the child with attention for dawdling in dressing. Thus we are into another "extinction" program, partly, and we want as before to use as much verbal explanation and acting out of the "new deal" to reduce the extinction burst as much as we can.

Thus the parents sit down and explain the program to the child, telling the child exactly what will happen in each circumstance, and acting out the procedure with toy people. This is done some time other than the first thing in the morning, at a time when people are calm.

If the choice of which clothes to wear is a big issue, then the first step is to decide upon them the previous evening, and lay them in the child's room so they will be ready the following morning. If the child can decide on his or her own time, or if the child with the parent can decide in a reasonable length of time, fine; if not, then the parent simply decides and gets them out and puts them somewhere where they will be available the next morning. In any case, the decision is made and is not reneged upon in the morning.

In the morning, the parent sets the alarm for a little earlier, so that there will be time for the parent to get dressed and get ready before taking on the task of dressing the child, and also so that there will be some more time for fun activities after the dressing.

Oftentimes when dressing is a problem, the order of morning activities is that the child eats breakfast first, watches television or videotapes second, and gets dressed just before leaving. The dressing is therefore an interruption to the television watching and a prelude to leaving home to lose the parent's company. In such circumstances, it's no wonder that dressing would be resisted.

The new deal is upon first arising, dressing is the first thing on the agenda, before breakfast and before watching videotapes or hearing stories.

One of the things that you do with the extra time from getting up a little earlier is to stay with the child while the child dresses. If the child starts dressing appropriately, i.e. putting on one garment after another without engaging you in an argument over what garment should be worn, then you remain in the room, speak to the child in a pleasant tone of voice, and perhaps "track and describe" what the child is doing as the child dresses: e.g. "There goes on your shirt. There goes the first button... and now you've got it all buttoned up!" This should be done in a very calm, gentle, and approving tone. If the child continues dressing appropriately, continue this, and at the end of the dressing, you clap, celebrate, compliment the child, tell the other parent, and enter it in the positive behavior diary. Afterwards, you continue to spend some pleasant time with the child at breakfast. Or, if the child is in the habit of watching videotapes while you take care of some other business, then that happens after the child is dressed.

This is the procedure if from the beginning the child starts dressing appropriately. What if the child from the beginning balks at dressing, either by refusing to put on a garment, or arguing over what garment to put on? Then the immediate consequence of this is that the child loses your one-to-one attention. You get out of the child's room within five seconds of the negative behavior. In those two to five seconds, you set a timer for five minutes, and you say, "Let's see if you can get dressed by the time the timer goes off." Take the timer with you, rather than leaving it with the child; this way the child can't fiddle with the dial. At the end of the time, put the timer where the child will come after getting dressed: e.g. downstairs at the breakfast table.

Go to the timer before the time is up. If the child arrives dressed by the time the time is up, the child gets compliments and applause and attention and approval, just as if the child had cooperated from the beginning. The message is that either of these procedures is OK. You allow the child to pick the preferred method of dressing: in privacy, or with lots of attention.

What if the child does not get dressed by the time the timer goes off? Then you calmly and resolutely use physical guidance, physically dressing, the child, attempting to accomplish this task within five minutes and with no excitement during the whole dressing. If when you start to use physical guidance, the child says "No, I'll put my clothes on," then the parent in a quiet and calm voice says, "You can do that tomorrow, maybe; it's too late today." Otherwise the parent speaks little during the dressing, and does not give much eye contact to the child. The parent attempts to dress the child as quickly as possible so that the total quantity of attention the child gets through this is as low as it can possibly be.

What if, when the parent dresses the child, the child then takes off a garment that the parent has put on the child? Then there are no videotapes and no stories read, and no breakfast before the child puts the garment back on. The child is ignored during this time. If the child still doesn't put the garment back on, the parent physically puts the garment back on the child and they leave, without the child having had breakfast that morning.

In this program the child who dresses cooperatively gets lots of attention, and the child who refuses to dress cooperatively gets very little attention. Given this paradigm, usually within a few days the child gets into the pattern of either dressing cooperatively or letting the parent dress him passively, either one of which is OK.

Chapter 28: School Problems

Chapter Overview:

When there are academic or behavioral problems at school, yelling at and punishing your child usually don't work well. Most of the time this accomplishes nothing but to import into your own relationship hostility originating at school. However, there are a number of constructive actions you can take. Unless you have only one choice about school placement, the first step on the decision tree is for you to observe what goes on in the classroom, perhaps with the help of a checklist presented here, and decide whether the environment is right for your child. Another step is to see whether work inhibition due to fear of mistakes and failures is the culprit. Fear of failure often develops when the child is initially less competent than other children in something, and the child's first attempts are punished by disapproval or humiliation. Once a fear of failure is in place, the child can get into a vicious cycle: the child doesn't try to practice because he fears failing, and becomes more likely to fail because he doesn't practice enough. Then the child can learn "avoidance maneuvers" to get away from having to perform: physical complaints, disruptive behavior, or withdrawn behavior. To undo the fear of failure, you first find the point on the hierarchy of difficulty where the child succeeds on at least 80% of the challenges. Then you celebrate all successes and stay in that zone long enough for the child to enjoy his successes and his work. You move up the hierarchy of difficulty only when the child is able to have at least 80% successes in the new level of difficulty. It's often helpful to teach the child to identify the thought patterns that make it so painful to fail, and the replacement thought patterns that make failures handleable and successes pleasant. It's often useful for the child to examine his own thought processes while doing some academic work. The child may also benefit from learning the terms for avoidance maneuvers and toughing out fears of failure. In overcoming fear of failure you help the child define success as a persistent best effort and not as a right answer. Other techniques include relaxation practice, modeling and letting the child practice positive self-talk while doing academic tasks; practicing the shaping game; and reading modeling stories such as "The Boy Learns About Champions' Mistakes."

Some children provide challenges to education systems by having what I call "widely varying abilities": they are a quick study in some areas while learning more slowly in others. These children are more at risk for fear-of-failure type demoralizations, because their high abilities in some areas lead people to believe they are just being lazy in others. The same approach outlined for the child with fear of failure is necessary for the child with widely varying abilities. You locate the correct level of difficulty for each separate ability area and celebrate the movements up each separate hierarchy.

If a teacher has the time and energy, it is often quite helpful for a teacher to contribute to the child's positive behavior diary by sending home notes of the child's positive acts. It's often useful to teach a child to self-monitor school behavior by asking the child to rate himself and compare his ratings with the teacher's ratings. Problems of disorganization and attention deficit are dealt with in separate chapters.

****

I heard a story that once a teacher sent a note home to a parent as follows: "At school your child is talking too much, has a very messy desk, and is not finishing his work. Please do something." The parent sent the teacher the following note back: "At home your student is not cleaning up after himself, failing to do his chores, and interrupting family members too much. Please do something."

What can a parent do to affect a child's behavior at school? (In this chapter the word "school" is also meant to encompass preschools and day care centers.) We'll address this question in this chapter. In the spirit of prevention in which this book is written, we'll be thinking not only about responding to problems once they have started, but heading them off before they arise.

The Option of "Doing Nothing At All" Is Better Than This Strategy

There have been times that I have advised parents to stay out of a child's school problems and let the teachers handle them independently. First let's recall the strategy of "Yell at the child when the child does something undesirable." This is a notorious member of our band of ineffective strategies listed in Chapter 1. Sometimes a teacher, having tried fussing and yelling at the child at school, and seeing that that strategy is not working, calls the parents and complains about the child's behavior, and the parents fuss and yell at the child at home. The most frequent consequence of this is that bad feelings at school get transported into the home and the relationship with the parents.

The First Step on the Decision Tree: Is This Placement Right?

Sometimes the best answer to problems at school is to decide that a given school isn't right for a given child, and to remove the child from the setting. Likewise sometimes the best prevention is not to put the child into the setting at all. I have had several patients with major problems in a certain day care or preschool or classroom, where the problems disappeared or drastically improved when the child went to a different setting.

How does a parent know what a setting is like? The one best way that I know of is to take a half day off, and to go and sit in the classroom and watch what goes on, and take notes. Fifteen or twenty minutes will not do: you have to get a large enough behavior sample to have valid inferences. By spending a few hours in the setting you will get a "gut feeling" for whether you want your child in this environment.

As you review your notes, look at the following list of relevant variables to help you evaluate the setting. Checklist for School and Preschool Settings

0=Very bad
2=Bad
4=So-so
6=OK
8=Good
10=Very Good

_____1. How favorable is the ratio of adults to children?
_____2. To what extent is the group of children small enough?
_____3. To what extent is the physical facility a place my child will enjoy staying in for the number of hours she will be there?
_____4. To what extent were the children presented with opportunities to do activities that are challenging, enjoyable, varied, and developmentally appropriate for my child?
_____5. To what extent was there an appropriate balance between times requiring a single focus of attention for all children, and times where different children pursue different activities?
_____6. Did the teacher model for the children the attitude that the activities available to do are potentially enjoyable and are to be carried out with gusto?
_____7. How much did the teacher catch the children doing positive examples of skills, and respond with enthusiastic and energetic attention and approval?
_____8. To what extent did the teacher present positive models to the children, in stories, plays, reviews of children's real life behavior, or in the teacher's own real life behavior?
_____9. To what extent did the teacher avoid unnecessary requests and commands and other directives? (0=Lots of unnecessary orders given; 10=No unnecessary directives.)
_____10. How much did the average child during the average day have a chance to have a conversation with someone—teacher or student?
_____11. To what extent did the teacher use "tracking and describing" or reflections or other responsive utterances?
_____12. In the times when the child did something undesirable, how well did the adult choose between ignoring, using a reprimand, using time out, and so forth?
_____13. To what extent was the teacher's response to undesirable behavior calm, quiet, deliberate, and disappointed rather than loud, fast, and hostile?
_____14. To what extent was the behavior of the other children that which

you would like for your child to imitate?

_____15. How much smiling and laughing and other positive emotion took place among the children?

You will, I hope, recognize that most of the variables listed here are the same sorts of factors that we spoke of in relation to the interpersonal environment of the home. Most of the items have their effect through approval versus disapproval, differential attention, differential excitement, responsiveness versus directiveness, and positive models versus negative models.

First let's talk about adult-child ratios. I have spent some time teaching groups of preschool children. I very strongly perceive the difference between 5 children in a group and 8, and between 8 and 12. The quality of the children's experience, as I observe it, suffers as the numbers go higher. When we put together one teacher and 25 or 30 kindergarten children, we are almost guaranteeing suboptimal learning and interpersonal experiences. Some highly talented teachers manage to make positive environments out of such a situation, and they are accomplishing an amazing task. I am convinced that putting children together in as large herds as our society does for a large portion of the day is not such a good idea—especially for the children who deviate from average in any way.

The size of the entire group of children is a variable apart from the ratio of adults to children. If there are 4 adults with 20 children, but the 20 children are in a large mass, the effective adult-child ratio is not as favorable as 1 to 5. On the other hand, if the children are divided into small groups, where each group is effectively interacting with an adult, the effective ratio of 1 to 5 may really hold.

If your child is in grade school, the size of the entire institution is relevant to your thinking, especially if the child changes classes and teachers for various subjects. Sometimes young grade-schoolers find themselves in institutions with hundreds of other children. They sometimes find that when the bell rings, they must enter a sea of humanity in the hallways and exit from it again for the next class, with the correct books and papers. There is no one teacher who is the caregiver for the child. My opinion is that the benefits gained from allowing teachers to specialize in subject matter areas is greatly overshadowed by the interference with development of stable and comfortable relationships, and the premature demands upon organization skills. It is not asking too much for teachers to be expert enough in all grade school subjects, so that children can be in a self-contained social circle with one major substitute caregiver.

In looking at the physical facility, I'm not just referring to whether things are in good repair. Is there enough space for each child? Is there space where you don't have to worry about the children's knocking something over or getting hurt? Is there a space, and enough space, for children to run—i.e.

can they go outside and cover some ground at regular intervals? (Sometimes the problem of active children is that they don't get enough chance to run off energy.)

In looking at the activities available, ask yourself whether your child would have a good time with the activities that are available or suggested. This answer may be very different for one child than for another. In a preschool, are the children led to do dramatic activities, to play, to sing, to dance, to hear stories, to make things, to draw things, to explore novel objects, to build things? One of the most frequent missing items in early childhood environments is a sufficient number of toy people for the children to do dramatic play with. In an elementary school, are there projects, are there discussions, or are there only worksheets?

Another aspect of activities for children is whether they are at the "challenge zone" for each particular child involved: not too hard, not too easy, but just right. For developing children, that zone changes quickly, depending upon the particular activity. Is there some mechanism whereby the teacher can find out if a given activity is too hard or too easy for a certain child? And if that proves to be the case, is there some plan as to what to do next? We will speak of finding the correct level of difficulty at greater length later on.

Also when evaluating activities: especially for young children, there should be a high enough ratio of "gross motor" activity, i.e. running and jumping and riding bikes and otherwise burning off energy, to the types of activities where you have to be more still.

When I speak of "times requiring a single focus of attention for all children," I mean for example activities where if one child doesn't sit still and be quiet and pay attention, that child disrupts the whole group. If the teacher is lecturing to the group, or reading a story to the group, or asking questions of the group, or holding a group discussion, then this condition holds. These activities can be quite useful, as long as the teacher does not try to hold the attention span of the group longer than the children with the shortest attention spans are capable of attending. Otherwise, you begin to get lots of off-task behavior and lots of reprimands and commands from the teacher trying to keep everyone focused. By "times where different children pursue different activities" I refer to times when several children can be talking and moving around without disrupting other children's work. Examples are times when there are different learning centers in the classroom, and some children read, some listen to tape recorders with headphones, some work at a computer, some build things, some talk with each other about a joint project. The best preschool and kindergarten teachers I know feel that the clock starts to run out for most groups after about 15 to 20 minutes of group activity. As grade levels increase, so does the attention span; still if children are asked to "sit still, be quiet, and pay attention" for much longer than you think your child can do this comfortably, anticipate difficulties.

I have seen classrooms in which the teacher or teachers looked rather depressed, hardly ever smiling or laughing or speaking in a very animated tone. If the teacher does not model for the children how to approach the activities with gusto, it is much less likely that the children will approach them with gusto. And this is really important in preventing behavior problems: the more the children have fun activities to compete with poking one another or withdrawing, the fewer behavior problems you will see.

In further scrutinizing the teachers' behavior, many of the same variables we have already talked about for parents are of utmost importance: noticing the positive examples and reinforcing them with attention and approval and excitement; presenting positive models; avoiding unnecessary commands; promoting conversation; tracking and describing; promoting reciprocal interaction; responding with calm deliberateness to negative behaviors and excitement to positive behaviors.

In thinking about whether the approach to negative behavior on the part of children is appropriate, I would emphasize that a positive setting is one where physical aggression gets consequences capable of almost totally eliminating it. If the child who hits and kicks other children gets some individual time with an adult who gently explains to him why his behavior is not good, and if such aggression continues many times a day over weeks or months, the environment is not suitable for any of the children.

The next variable has to do more purely with children's behavior rather than teachers' behavior. Parents should face the fact that children learn behavior from one another. If the children in the setting are modeling high rates of verbal hostility, for example, then no matter how good the teachers are, it is likely that a child without a lot of verbal hostility in the repertoire would pick it up. The operative question is, How imitation-worthy are the behaviors of the children in the setting?

Finally: do the children in the setting look happy? Laughing and smiling are the most prominent signs of this, but animated, curious, intensely involved facial expressions are as good. Listless, bored, frustrated, and angry looks are a red flag.

How do prospective settings for your children measure up to these criteria? Observing in the setting and thinking about each of these variables separately will help you to understand what your child is dealing with, if not to change it.

Work Inhibition and the Skill of Handling Mistakes and Failures

The phrase "fear of failure" is perhaps a little too narrow for the very major problem I want to talk about. I want to talk about the vast numbers of children who are inhibited from trying to learn certain things because failing would feel too bad for them in some way. Sometimes "hatred" is a more appropriate term for what the child feels rather than "fear": hatred of the task, hatred of the self, hatred of the person making him do the task. Sometimes the negative emotion is experienced as disgust or physical discomfort, and sometimes the child is not able to describe any negative emotion at all, but the presence of an aversion to the task is inferred by the child's avoidance of it.

The fear of failure is sometimes hard to recognize in children. You usually don't see a fearful look on the face as you do with fears of thunderstorms or bees. And whereas some adults can come to you and say, "I'm afraid of failing, and because of that I don't want to try," a child doesn't usually do that, particularly a young one. The child may have ways of getting out of the task that are so effective that you don't even see the child looking uncomfortable.

It may take some time before a child develops enough trust, verbal fluency, confidence and self-insight to be able to tell you, "I hate trying to do this because failing at it would be so bad for me." If the child can't talk with you in this way about it, you can get some clues by seeing whether the child:

seems to tense up and look unhappy when asked to do certain academic tasks

refuses to do certain academic tasks

erases work over and over in an attempt to get it perfect (some children erase holes in their paper)

scribbles over or tears up her own work productions

seems to lose work productions regularly and on purpose

gets distracted onto almost anything else, easily, when asked to do certain tasks, (especially if she has a good attention span when doing something she enjoys)

tells you that she hates doing the task

gets disruptive, inhibited, very unhappy, or complains of feeling sick when certain tasks are coming up

does tasks well when there is no pressure, and fails the same tasks in a situation where performance is measured

quickly guesses answers when called upon, with little or no thought about the questions, as though to get out of the spotlight as soon as possible

tries something, fails once, and doesn't want to hear or see anything else about it after that

The fear of failure doesn't stop operating once someone is no longer a child. For example, millions of adults avoid reading and studying about challenging topics because they have formed the idea, "I'm not good at this, I'll fail at it," and their lifetime achievement is greatly reduced. Or their ability to do new pleasurable activities is reduced: an adult is interested in singing, but won't take singing lessons for fear that in the initial attempt, his teacher will laugh at him. Or someone thinks he can do a certain job well, but stays in a more boring job because of fear of failing at the more exciting one. Or a smart high school graduate doesn't go to college for fear of failing at it.

There is a certain rationality in fearing failure at times. If someone untrained in brain surgery should somehow get the chance to try to remove a brain tumor, that person would do well to avoid trying because of fear of failure! Here there is much to lose, much danger, by trying and not succeeding. On the other hand, when trying and failing hurts no one, but simply allows the teacher to see where the learner is on the hierarchy, and allows the learner to find out what the limits on his current ability are, then avoiding trying because of fear of failure is irrational.

How do kids get a fear of failure? If some villain wanted purposely to induce a fear of failure, here's how that villain could do it. Put the child in a situation where she is being measured in relation to other people, in something she isn't immediately perfect at. Have her try. When she doesn't do perfectly, draw lots of attention to the imperfect aspects and disapprove of them heavily. If there is a whole group of people who can witness this disapproval, or even more powerfully, take part in it, then the effect is achieved all the quicker.

Oftentimes well-meaning people follow this recipe. In fact, it goes on probably to some extent every day in almost every school in the country for at least a few children. What is intended as corrective feedback for not doing well turns into punishment for attempting the task in the first place. The child soon develops a conditioned aversion to trying it.

Sometimes there is fear of failure without any identifiable humiliation from teachers, peers, parents, or anyone else. Perhaps very subtle facial expressions can convey disapproval in a way that affects the child. Certainly some are constitutionally more susceptible to fear of failure than others. But once a child has a fear of failure, the important goal is to get him over it, not to discover where it came from.

Once the child has a conditioned aversion to the task and a fear of failing at it, the conditions are ripe for a very harmful vicious cycle to take place. When it comes time for the child to work on the task, he quickly does something to get out of doing it, to avoid trying this challenge. And the more the child succeeds at avoiding the challenge, the less practice the child gets. If other children are practicing and this child is avoiding practicing, the other children are getting farther ahead of him. As he compares himself to them as time goes by, he gets a stronger and stronger negative emotional reaction to his perceived inferiority, and it's associated with this task. He wants more and more to avoid trying at it, and becomes more and more incompetent relative to his peer group.

It's time now to introduce a new term for the things the child does to get out of trying a challenge because of the fear of failure: avoidance maneuvers. Avoidance maneuvers let someone get out of the arena where performance will be evaluated and there is the possibility of another failure. Children can avoid taking on challenges by getting headaches or stomach aches, being disruptive, withdrawing and being inhibited, getting depressed, being distracted onto some stimulus other than the task at hand, acting as though one is too stupid to learn, and many other ways: that is, the whole panoply of symptoms. Often these avoidance maneuvers are what bring the matter to people's concern. People observe that the child is disruptive, unhappy, inattentive, or hypochondriac. The root cause, the fear of failure, is often not identified.

An even more devastating vicious cycle can then get going. Teachers come to recognize the avoidance maneuvers as ways the child tries to get out of doing work, and start to disapprove of them and punish them in addition to disapproving of the failure itself. But if the work inhibition and fear of failure are strong enough, the child may avoid the punishment for the avoidance maneuvers by developing even more powerful, though ultimately self-destructive, avoidance maneuvers: behaviors bad enough to get him suspended from school, being truant from school, refusing to go to school, and if old enough, dropping out of school altogether.

Undoing the Fear of Failure

In the fear of failure problem, as in any other vicious cycle, it's important to start as soon as possible.

In chapter 3 I defined notion of hierarchy, a series of baby-steps to a goal. This notion is nowhere more important than in working with the fear of failure. Whatever task the child is failing at is made up of a set of subskills. It is possible to list in order of difficulty the steps toward mastering each of those subskills. At some point on that hierarchical list, the child can do the tasks with total success. Ideal instruction will drop back to that point on the hierarchy, and let the child practice succeeding. You find an activity where the level of difficulty is pleasant for the child, and let the child stay in that zone for lots of successes to build up.

How do you locate that point on the hierarchy? You first have in mind, or written down, what the tasks on the hierarchy or hierarchies are. You start at a level that is easy for the child and ask the child to do the tasks; you gradually work your way up in difficulty until you find the zone that is not too hard and not too easy, the ideal instructional level. There are many individually administered standardized achievement tests that make it easy for a teacher or tutor to do this, if only the tests are harnessed for this purpose.

A brief word about the use of tests. Too often, I think, individually administered tests are given by someone other than the person teaching the child, for example a psychologist, and the child's performance is communicated in numbers that don't communicate to the teacher what sorts of tasks are in the "challenge zone" of not too easy and not too difficult work. For tests to be best used, the person doing the teaching should see the specific sorts of items that are too hard, too easy, and just right for the child.

How do we know when the tasks we are giving a child are not too hard, not too easy, but just right? As a general rule, most children keep their morale up if they can succeed 80% of the time. If the child greatly fears failure, you want to start out closer to 100% success.

Once you've found the correct level to work at with a given child, then what? You play the shaping game. You gradually move up those hierarchies, celebrating every step up the ladder.

As long as you're in the very easy zone, the child may have no problem. Sometimes, though, as soon as you approach the challenge zone, the child gets scared and starts back in on the avoidance maneuvers. Sometimes success experiences in the easy zone are not sufficient to help the child become unafraid of challenges.

In this case some direct conversation about the fear of failure problem will usually help the child. You might enter into a dialogue about this problem, by saying, "Johnny, you know some children sometimes don't like to try things that look unfamiliar, or things that are hard, because they're scared someone will laugh at them or tease them if they miss something. Do you ever feel this way?" If the child can talk about this, listen with rapt attention.

Sometimes the child needs to be taught the ways of thinking that will help him handle failure when it does occur, as it certainly will many times as the child moves up the hierarchy.

And what are those ways of thinking? We listed them, earlier in this book, when talking about the skill of handling mistakes and failures.

Awfulizing vs. Not awfulizing
Getting down on oneself vs. Not getting down on oneself
Blaming someone else vs. Not blaming someone else
Goal-Setting
 Listing options and choosing
 Learning from the experience
Not celebrating vs.:
 Celebrating one's own choices
 Celebrating someone else's choice
 Celebrating luck

If the child is old enough to learn words for these concepts, you can teach them to him. The Journey Exercise is a way of teaching children these concepts in a pleasant way. This is a story where the characters model the twelve types of thoughts, so that the reader or listener can practice identifying them. The Journey Exercise is printed in my book, *Programmed Readings for Psychological Skills*. If the child is too young to learn the names for these concepts, then you model the adaptive thought patterns for the child in stories, plays, and real life.

One of the "modeling stories" I've written has to do very explicitly with the fear of failure; it's called "The Boy Learns About Champions' Mistakes." I consider this a central part of the anti-fear-of-failure program also.

Here's a true modeling story about dealing with failure. (This is quoted from Alan Lakein's book, *How to Get Control of Your Time and Your Life*.)

"Take the following extraordinary personal history of failure: Lost job, 1832; defeated for legislature, 1832; failed in business, 1833; elected to legislature, 1834; sweetheart died, 1835; had nervous breakdown, 1836; defeated for Speaker, 1838; defeated for nomination for Congress, 1843; elected to Congress, 1846; lost renomination, 1848; rejected for land officer, 1849; defeated for Senate, 1854; defeated for nomination for Vice-President, 1956; again defeated for Senate, 1858; but in 1860 Abraham Lincoln was elected President of the United States."

Once the child knows how to choose among the twelve cognitive patterns listed above, and once the child understands the relevance of these patterns for overcoming the fear of failure, the child can start a very useful strategy. The child does some academic work (at the correct level of difficulty!) When a challenge comes up, the child monitors her thoughts. If the child can recognize that she is awfulizing or getting down on herself or blaming, the adult should celebrate the recognition of those automatic thoughts! The first step in changing them is to be able to recognize them and talk about them.

Now the child has encountered a challenge that makes her feel some aversion. If the child gets an urge to do an avoidance maneuver, the child should also identify that urge, name the avoidance maneuver that comes to mind, and celebrate that insight. But the child resists that urge, and tries to do the more effective thought patterns. She keeps trying, perhaps on the current task, or perhaps backs up and does a more appropriate preliminary task. She celebrates not avoiding. If she makes some progress, she celebrates that as well. It is useful for the child to have in her vocabulary the terms for fear of failure, avoidance maneuvers, and toughing out the fear. You "tough out" the fear when you don't let yourself do an avoidance maneuver, but face the scary situation head on. Each time this sequence of events happens, the fear of failure is a little closer to being conquered. And carrying out this sequence in fantasy practice is also effective, in addition to carrying it out in real life.

Throughout this process you may use the power of attribution and prophecy in helping to deal with the fear of failure. For example, the child misses something, and doesn't want to try any more. The adult says, "OK, for now, let's go to something different. But let me tell you something important. Some day, probably not long from now, I hope you're going to be able to try hard problems and miss some of them and will be able to just keep on trying, without feeling bad at all. That's one of the things I hope you'll learn from the work you're doing."

You can let your use of language help the child see that overcoming the pattern of avoidance maneuvers is highly desirable, by talking about the ability to keep trying in terms of "being tough" and "using self-discipline." For example, the child has the urge to quit in the middle of something, and you say, "I guess you're getting the urge to avoid this. But I think you're tough enough to try it a little longer. If you can try longer, that will be a great example of self-discipline, whether you get it right or not." If the child does keep working on something after getting the urge for an avoidance maneuver, this should be celebrated. "You got the urge to give up when the going got tough and you missed some, but you kept going anyway! That's being a winner! That's using self-discipline."

Of course, most children need a good deal of guidance through this process. Someone should be quite skilled at working with children before taking it on.

Relaxation skills are the physical antidote to fear of failure, just as not awfulizing and the other thought patterns listed above are the cognitive antidote to it. Another chapter goes into relaxation techniques in great detail. It's possible to teach muscular relaxation to children.

Once the child gets good at relaxing, then it's possible to do the same strategy that I just spoke of with regard to thought patterns, where you sit with the child and alternate between academic work and some self-monitoring and self-control, this time with respect to muscle tension rather than thought patterns. When the child feels herself getting tense, she recognizes that, and celebrates that recognition. When she feels an urge toward an avoidance maneuver, she quickly relaxes (quickly, lest the relaxation itself become an avoidance maneuver), and then goes back to the task or a preliminary one. She keeps with it until there is something to celebrate.

Here's an important message to give to the child: staying on task is something to celebrate, whether or not the task is successfully finished. Simply trying for a reasonable length of time is by definition a success. By staying on task, the child has practiced exposing herself to the fear of failure. This is a brave act.

When doing this sort of work with a child, it's important to make good decisions about when to move quickly to an easier point on the hierarchy, a task preliminary to the task the child is having trouble with. Having successes in these preliminary tasks gives the child the prerequisite skills for the later task, and should also build up a momentum of confidence and willingness to take on challenges. How do you know what the preliminary task is? And how do you know when to move to a preliminary task and when to let the child struggle just a little more with the task at hand? These are judgment calls. They require some skill on the part of the person working with the child. These skills, I think, are honed by the adult's studying the subject matter to get clearly in mind what the various hierarchies are. Looking at the progression of skills on standardized achievement tests, the ones that go in order from easier to harder questions, is very helpful in understanding what is easier and harder than what, and what is preliminary to what. When in doubt, with the child with great fear of failure it's best to err on the side of giving too easy work than too hard.

Here's another helpful procedure in working with the child with fear of failure. First the child simply watches while you model doing academic tasks, speaking your thoughts aloud, modeling the sorts of thought patterns the child will need to use, particularly the celebrations or self-reinforcements. For example:

"OK, let's see. I've got some numbers to add, 8 plus 4. If I remembered that right off the bat, that would be great, but I don't. But that's OK. Now how can I figure it out? I just start at 8 and count four more. 9, 10, 11, 12. So 12 is the answer. I think I got it! Let me check it. 8 plus 1 is 9, 8 plus 2 is 10, 8 plus 3 is 11, 8 plus 4 is 12. Yep, I think I got it right! Hooray!"

Or:

"Let's see, here's a word I'm trying to read. If I remembered it right off, that would be easy, but I don't. But that's OK. Maybe I can sound it out. Vuh aaa nnn ih sss .. oh wait, the sh says shh. Vuh aaa nnn ih shhh. Vanish! Hey, I was able to sound it out!"

Or:

"Let's see, here's another word I'm trying to read. I don't remember this one right off either. Let's see if I can sound it out. Eh nnn ah uh guh hhh. Ehnauhguh? Hmm. That doesn't seem to make a word. Let me try again.... I can't put these sounds together to make a word I know. Oh, well, that's not the end of the world, I'll just ask somebody what the word is. Not all words can be sounded out. Can you please tell me what word this is? Enough? How did they get a fff out of these letters? OK, I guess this is one of those that was pretty hard to sound out. But that's OK. Maybe I'll remember it, if I take a good look at it. Congratulations to me for working on this!"

In these monologues, the adult models for the child the process of "not awfulizing," picking an option, and celebrating successes.

The next step is to do it with a somewhat shorter monologue, and then ask the child to do some problems in the same manner, imitating your monologue.

It is a fairly complex skill for an adult to do this sort of work with a child. Many adults are not well equipped to do the sort of work I've been describing. In fact, many are still at the stage where the main issue is whether they can work with the child on academic work without getting angry at the child, getting into an argument, criticizing the child, getting quite upset, and doing lots of awfulizing and getting down on oneself and blaming someone else. If you're at this stage, don't get down on yourself or awfulize, but acknowledge it, and find someone else that can do these things with the child, and let the child alone with respect to academic work. However, if you do have time to gradually learn the skills of working with children in this way, it's a great thing to be able to do.

The steps that I have outlined so far presuppose that the child's fear of failure is in control enough that the child is capable of participating in adult-directed activity at all. (Adult-directed activity, as mentioned in a previous chapter, occurs when for example an adult gives test questions or tasks, and a child gives answers. Child-directed activity, on the other hand, occurs when the child plays with things or examines things or intiates activities, and the adult is responsive.) Some children have such a large fear of failure that they can't, or won't, participate in adult-directed academic activity at all, or only for very short periods of time.

In such a case, I think that it's usually best for the child to do a great deal of child-directed activity, and to gradually work up to the more adult-directed activities. In the meantime, the child can learn a great deal by simply being read to, watching videos and listening to tapes, exploring things, asking questions and having them answered, and the other sorts of informal learnings that can take place in the context of child-directed activity. Once the relationship has become strong enough with the adult, the child can be challenged to do little bits of adult-directed activity, interspersed among periods of child-directed activity. The adult-directed activities should be chosen so as to be fun and easy. Gradually the child becomes desensitized to the fear of adult-directed activity, and in time some of the more structured approaches to undoing fear of failure can be used.

One adult-directed activity that is extremely useful for children old enough to understand it is the shaping game, described in a previous chapter. The child's experience of shaping, and learning to do self-shaping, and any teaching adults' learning to do shaping, are by and large the antidotes to fear of failure.

The fear of failure (skill deficiency in handling mistakes and failures) often coexists with the fear of being controlled (skill deficiency in submission, giving in to the will of another when appropriate). The procedures mentioned above hopefully will also help in the desensitization to the fear of being controlled.

The Child With Widely Differing Abilities

The notion of "widely differing abilities" is the phrase I like to use when thinking about what are called "learning disabilities." Children with widely differing abilities are particularly vulnerable to developing fear of failure problems, for reasons I'll explain.

If a child is uniformly a quick study, across the board, in all academic pursuits, then the child is unlikely to receive punitive feedback on performances; if the child is uniformly a slow learner across all academic pursuits, then in most schools the child will become recognized as such and less will be expected of him. He gets little punitive feedback if educators are at all sensitive and humane. However, what if the child has an excellent vocabulary, and excellent listening comprehension, so that he impresses people as a "smart" child, but has extremely poor writing skills? What if when he starts to write, the concentration required just to make the letters properly is such that it pulls his mind off whatever he was going to say in the first place? He may turn in extremely sloppy papers after having just demonstrated excellent understanding of the subject in his verbal performances. A teacher who has to juggle information on 30 children, or if the children are rotating from class to class, perhaps on 120 children, may be so subject to information overload that it is difficult for the teacher to come to the conclusion that the child simply has a lot of natural ability at some things and a lot less natural ability in other things. Sometimes instead the teacher concludes that "He can do it; he's just lazy. He needs someone to get tough with him and not let him get away with goofing off." And sometimes other students, who might envy the child's performance in his areas of strength, revel in laughing at him and teasing him when his areas of weakness become apparent.

Now let's go back to our hypothetical child who had good natural abilities in verbal fluency and listening comprehension and poor natural abilities in writing. If he starts feeling embarrassed and upset when he delivers a written performance, he may start developing a fear of failure associated with writing that leads him to practice writing much less than his peers. His success experiences in listening comprehension and verbal fluency lead him to practice for example listening to documentaries and talking about them more than his peers do. So now he gets better at what he practices, and he gets relatively worse at what he doesn't practice. Now there are practice effects that lay themselves down upon the natural ability effects, and the abilities that varied widely to begin with get even more widely varied. In addition, when the child is tested, and an area comes up that the child knows he's not good at, he may get anxious and tense and the stage fright can interfere further with his performance. Thus in another way, initially widely varying abilities appear to be even more widely varying.

For this reason, when you look at a child at any given point in time and see widely varying abilities, it is hard or impossible to tell how much of that variation is due to the child's biologic makeup, how much is result of unfavorable learning experiences, and how much is due to stage fright. Getting negative emotional connotations associated with the things you aren't good at creates a "multiplier effect" that can widen the differences between the child's abilities as indicated by the child's performance on tests.

Thus a major challenge with children of widely varying abilities is to prevent or cure fear of failure and avoidance maneuvers.

The strategy for solving and preventing fear of failure and avoidance maneuver problems with the child with widely varying abilities is exactly the same one outlined above as with any other child. That is:
You identify the correct level of difficulty, the "challenge zone" for the child, on each hierarchy for each type of academic work that the child is doing; you celebrate the child's successes and help the child to celebrate them; you avoid punishing the mistakes and failures, and encourage the child to not awfulize, not get down on himself, not blame, choose options, learn from the experience, celebrate the act of trying, and relax, when mistakes and failures take place.

For the child with widely varying abilities, however, getting the right point on the hierarchy for the various abilities can require some quite individualized instruction. It is literally possible that a child could be understanding science concepts written on a high school level, when these are read or spoken to him, but he may be decoding reading only on a second grade level. His spoken language, when dictated into a tape recorder, can be on high school level, whereas his written language can look like that of a first grader. In shaping the ideal educational environment for such a child, these widely varying abilities are recognized by, and are just fine with, the teachers, and the teachers will figure out ways for the child to take on tasks just at the challenge zone for each of his widely varying abilities. Thus there is "teaching to the strengths" AND "teaching to the weaknesses;" in each of them, the child gets success experiences.

The process that I am describing takes so much work that it is probably much better carried out within the context of individual tutoring than in a large class. It is hard for me to imagine how a teacher could carry out the process well for more than 10 or so children of widely differing abilities at the same time, unless by some highly unlikely quirk the children all had abilities that varied in the same way.

Asking a Teacher to Contribute to the Positive Behavior Diary

If you have used the positive behavior diary and the nightly review, and these have helped with the child's behavior at home, a very helpful addition may be to enlist the teacher's aid in recording positive behaviors from school.

The teacher watches the child's behavior during the day, and for young children, jots down a brief concrete narration of the most positive thing the teacher remembers the child's doing all day. The teacher sends this home with the child. As parents, you respond to this in the same way that you respond to any other item on the positive behavior diary: by celebrating it with the child, recounting it to someone else in the child's presence, mentioning it in the nightly review, making an illustrated or unillustrated modeling story out of it, putting it on as a play with toy people or acting it out without toys, or making a song that recounts it.

For children old enough to write, the teacher might do a group variant upon this procedure: the children get their pencils and papers out, and the teacher goes around and whispers individually with each child a positive behavior that the child has done that day. The child writes it, and the teacher comes around and signs it. In addition to serving all the purposes of the positive behavior diary, this gives the child practice in writing narratives.

Teaching Children to Self-Monitor

Some children seem to have very little insight into what they are doing at school that is causing problems. The skill of becoming aware of how their behavior is affecting others is deficient. The following strategy sometimes proves useful with children who need more skill in self-observation and self-monitoring.

The following is an all-purpose brief questionnaire that a teacher can use to give daily feedback to the child and the parent.

Daily Global Rating Scale

0=Very bad day. Very big problems, severe difficulties.
2=Bad day. We should be quite dissatisfied with a day like this.
4=So-so day. Not good enough to be called good, but not bad enough to be called bad. Not good enough for us to feel pleased.
6=OK day. If this sort of day were repeated every day, it would be OK, acceptable.
8=Good day. If this sort of day happened every day, it would be cause for celebration.

10=Very good day. If this sort of day happened every day, it would be cause for very major celebration.

Today's date:____________

Today's rating:__________

The items below are meant to help communicate why the rating was what it was. If you have time, you can put a plus or a minus sign next to any of these that particularly raised or lowered the rating. If you have more time, you can write down the positive or negative example. If something not on this list raised or lowered the rating, you can write it in and put a plus or minus sign next to it.

1. Productivity: doing useful things, useful work
2. Joyousness: cheerfulness, pleasantness
3. Kindness: being nice, sharing, consideration, courtesy
4. Honesty: Telling the truth, keeping promises, not cheating or stealing
5. Fortitude: frustration tolerance, putting up with hardship
6. Good decisions: Thinking before acting, solving problems with other people well
7. Nonviolence: Not physically hurting anyone, not threatening or trying to hurt
8. Respectful talk: Not being rude, not doing unkind talk
9. Friendship-building: Having good chats, letting people get to know you, being a good listener.
10. Self discipline: Being able to do what's best even when it's not pleasant
11. Loyalty: Honoring commitments, sticking up for people when good to do so
12. Conservation: Not wasting things, being thrifty
13. Self-care: Doing things that are good for yourself
14. Compliance: Obeying parents or other reasonable authorities
15. Positive fantasy rehearsal: Practicing good acts and not bad ones in fantasy
16. Courage: Doing things that take some bravery

Other:_____________

Other:_____________

***

One of the advantages of such a scale is its simplicity: the child gets one number, which is arrived at without having to add anything up! The child learns the meaning of the numerical ratings quickly.

After the child has simply gotten feedback on his ratings for a few days, you move to a stage where every day, at the end of the day (or more often if the teacher has the time to do it) the child rates himself and the teacher rates the child independently. Then the two compare their answers. The first goal is simply that they will agree fairly well. When the child is able to reliably realize when he has done well or poorly along the dimensions that are important for him, at least lack of self-awareness is not the barrier to his improvement. Other psychological skill deficiencies, of course, may continue to be barriers.

Some teachers may feel that they have time for this strategy and/or the positive behavior diary, and others may not. If there is not time to do these daily, then perhaps they may be done less frequently. If a teacher with an average sized class load is able to do these strategies consistently over a long period of time, that teacher deserves quite a bit of accolade and gratitude from parents.

The Problem of Disorganization

Some children's largest problem with respect to school is staying organized. Doing the work is not so much the problem, as remembering what work to do, remembering to bring home the right book to do it with, remembering to get papers from school to home and back, and so forth. This problem is dealt with in a separate chapter on teaching organization skills to children.

The Problem of Attention Deficit Hyperactivity Disorder

I can't close a chapter on school problems without mentioning attention deficit hyperactivity disorder. The subject is so large, however, that I'll be devoting a couple more chapters to it, one to learning-based and situational approaches, and another to pharmacological treatment.

The Option of Homeschooling

We're lucky that more and more options become available over time. Homeschooling is for many families a wonderful option for promoting a child's psychological and academic development. The combination of individual attention and individualized academic programs is hard to beat if it is done well. The results I have seen with homeschooling have been quite encouraging.

For parents who feel that they cannot homeschool but who feel that school is going very badly despite everything they can devise, the option of "cyberschooling" may be considered. The child enrolls in a school, stays at home, and communicates with teachers via telephone and internet.

Chapter 29: Tutoring

Chapter Overview:

If we want a child to be psychologically healthy, we need to figure out a way for the child to have positive experiences with learning. It is also important for parent and child to learn well the "dance" of adult-directed activity, as well as child-directed activity. Tutoring the child provides good opportunities to practice both these dances. The main reason for a parent not to get involved in academic work with a child is to avoid power struggles and conflicts that make the child dislike academic activity. If you've done well enough what the rest of this book suggests, and if you're lucky, you may have the sort of relationship where you can tutor your child successfully. If the child asks you to do academic activities with her, and reminds you when you forget, you know you're on the right track. Sometimes, however, it's best to hire a tutor.

You want to help a child realize that there's a reason to learn reading and writing, and it isn't just because someone tells him to. The written word exists so we can remember thoughts worth thinking. We can think about most of education as learning 3 processes: 1) inputting ideas and information, 2) thinking, and 3) outputting thoughts and ideas and information. Reading, learning vocabulary, spelling, writing, and using mathematical symbols are "codes" used in the input and output of ideas. Because there is so much information worth knowing, the educator should be careful not to waste the child's time on low priority information. The child and adult should grapple together on the question of what is worthwhile. If a child has trouble cracking some codes—e.g. learning to read, write, spell—then your task is not to get so bogged down in the code that the child loses the pleasure of working with ideas. What you do is to keep the input, processing, and output of ideas at the challenge zone for the child, while simultaneously working at the challenge zone for code-cracking. What this means is that if the child can absorb ideas more complex than he can read, you read to the child. If he can say ideas more complex than he can write, you take dictation from the child. You do these things until the child can learn to read and write well enough to do his own input and output. As much as possible we want the child to figure out how to do things rather than telling him how and getting him to memorize it. We want the child to write his own thoughts as much as possible. Listening and speaking are the foundation for reading and writing.

School grades often punish a just the children who need the most to be rewarded for their progress in learning. If the child is progressing, and enjoying his progress, then there is reason to celebrate, even if other children are progressing faster.

When you tutor a child, your first priority in any session is to whet the child's appetite for the next session. Teaching the child habits of learning is also of higher priority than teaching any particular subject matter: these include habits of concentrating and trying to remember, cultivating curiosity, being brave about making attempts, monitoring one's own performance, trying for continued improvement, rewarding oneself internally for a success, learning from the experience of failures and mistakes, tolerating repetition, enjoying trying to meet challenges, and not taking pleasure from "frustrating the authority."

To be a good tutor, you practice the following skills: assuming an enthusiastic attitude, explaining and demonstrating activities, gauging whether an activity is too hard or too easy for the child and adjusting the difficulty level smoothly and quickly; getting excited about the child's successes, being informative in response to mistakes, being patient in response to off-task behavior, gauging how long to stay on any one activity, and taking pleasure both in adult-directed and child-directed activity. The tutor finds a balance, a happy medium, in various dimensions: easy and hard challenges, already fun and not-yet-fun activities, learning new material and practicing old material, and moving versus sitting still.

Not all education should be "fun" in the way that a cartoon or a Ferris Wheel is fun. You can explain to the child that it's good to cultivate a more subtle pleasure: the confidence of possessing the self-discipline to accomplish something worthwhile.

An important tutoring activity is simply to read to the child, and chat with the child about what you've read. Another very valuable activity is for the tutor to be the child's transcriptionist. Another is helping the child enjoy "brain teasers." When you do this, you seek "good" problems that are at the challenge zone for the child. Critical Thinking Books and Software produces enough thinking challenges as to cover the correct level of difficulty for almost any learner. You can promote thinking skills by playing various games with children: twenty questions, password, checkers, chess, scrabble, boggle, blackjack, quarto, charades, one of these things is not like the other, guess the category, and what does he like are useful thinking games. When you're helping a child to crack the reading code, you can do some fun activities: reading letter stories to the child, reading alphabet books to the child (occasionally saying the sounds of the letters rather than their names), singing the letter sound songs, and playing the blending game. The which-picture game and the which-sound game give further preparation for reading. The sounding and blending exercise, an activity meant done with a tutor, teaches decoding skills. Many other activities and materials are available for the parent who wishes to take a large part in his child's academic learning.

****

This is a book on fostering psychological health. Why a chapter on teaching academic skills to children? This subject is probably greatly underemphasized in mental health writings. Children spend a huge fraction of their existence trying to learn academic skills, and a great portion of their happiness depends upon the success of this venture.

I listed pleasure in working toward academic competence as one of the psychological skills for good reasons. Children who do better academically have fewer conduct problems. It's not difficult to think of reasons why there might be a connection between academic work and conduct. For the child who can't read well, almost everything he's asked to do in school is difficult and tedious; he fails at many tasks, and he experiences teachers as people who ask him to do things he can't do and then are displeased when he doesn't do them. For the child who can read well, school becomes a place where he can show what he can do and win the admiration of teachers.

Here's another reason why academics are so important for psychological health. The process of teaching the child academic skills is a setting whereby the important "dances" of adult-directed activity and child-directed activity can be practiced.

In adult-directed activity, the adult has the idea about what to do, tells it to the child, and the child does it. For example, the adult points to pictures and asks the child what they are. Or, the adult shows the child pictures of two objects and asks the child which word begins with a certain sound. The adult is very pleased when the child gets the right answer, and models for the child the right answer when the child misses. The child is complying with requests initiated by the adult.

On the other hand, if the child sees something in the room and goes over to look at it, and talks with the adult about it, that is a child-directed activity. Or the child makes up a game and show it to the adult, who plays it with the child. Or the child just chats with the adult and the adult listens and chats too. If the child plays with toys while the adult "tracks and describes," that too is child-directed activity.

There are big advantages to each of these types of activities. One of the major theses of this book is that both parents and children should get good at both of them.

An advantage of adult-directed activity is that if the child can learn that it can be fun to follow someone else's lead, the child has learned something very important. This piece of learning is very important for the child's ability to comply with adult requests, which is a very important ability. The ability to comply with teacher requests is of crucial importance in the child's success at school. And finally, if the teacher has a body of material that he or she wants to teach the child, it usually requires a great deal of adult-directed activity to cover it, rather than just hoping that the child will happen upon it of his own accord.

Advantages of child-directed activity are that the child learns to be creative, the child usually enjoys taking the lead, the child gets practice at leading, the child lets the adult get to know him better, the child gets models from the adult as to how to follow someone else's lead, and the child usually finds the activity pleasant enough that there are deposits in the emotional bank for the relationship.

Thus both of these dances are important. There are times when the adult must take charge and see that something happens for the child, as for example when the child has to go to the doctor, when the child has to go to bed, when the child has to stay out of the street, and so forth. It is crucial that the child be able to comply. On the other hand, a child who has learned to do nothing but comply has problems with social interactions and with taking initiative.

When we spoke about reciprocal interaction and responsive utterances, we did so in the context of child-directed activity. But these are also present, ideally, in adult-directed activity. The prototypical adult-directed activity involves the adult's telling the child some information, asking the child a question, and then responding to the child's response. When the child responds, some enthusiastic tracking and describing or reflection or approval or praise by the adult furnishes the responsive utterances that make the directive ones palatable.

The world isn't so simple that all academic teaching is adult-directed, and all dramatic play is child-directed. There are various academic activities that are child directed, and various parts of dramatic play that are adult-directed. Ideally, both of these activities contain a balance between the two. But academic activities are usually weighted more toward adult-directed activity, and dramatic play more toward child-directed activity.

The Decision to Get Involved in Academic Activities With The Child

If a parent helps a child become more prepared for academic tasks, is there a danger that the child will be "bored" and misbehave more when he or she goes to school? Various observations suggest that this concern should not keep us from helping children with academic skills.

One famous study looked at children who showed up at kindergarten already knowing how to read. These children were followed throughout several more years of schooling, and they continued to do better than their peers, on the average. There is no evidence that they were harmed by already knowing a fair amount of what they would be taught.

There seems to be a very positive correlation between how well children do in school and how well they behave. This fact suggests that it is much more harmful for a child's behavior to be behind his classmates than to be ahead of his classmates.

Imagine yourself as a child. It is easy to imagine yourself having a good time at school simply showing off what you already know. You get an assignment, you do it quickly, you do well on it, you get approval from the teacher, you feel good. On the other hand, it is much less easy to imagine yourself having a good time at school when almost all the tasks you are assigned are over your head. You get an assignment, you don't know how to do it, you act up in order to make it seem like you don't want to do the assignment rather than that you don't know how to do it. There is nothing more "boring," and at the same time unpleasant, than being expected to do a task that you don't know how to do.

Because the danger of "boredom" and unpleasant feelings is so much greater from knowing too little than from knowing too much, I recommend that parents err on the side of helping the child be on top of his academic skills.

What about the argument that a parent might use one system of teaching a child something, that would interfere with the teacher's system of teaching it, and confuse the child? I think it's just as likely to suppose that people learn things better, not worse, by approaching them from two different systems. At any rate, I have not seen evidence that this consideration should stop us from helping a child with academic skills.

What about the argument that a parent might do academic activities with a child in a way that is unpleasant for the child, and create a bad taste in the child's mouth for learning, that will interfere with the child's future learning? Now we've landed on the single best argument for parents' staying out of children's academic life, at least until the parents and children have learned better to do the necessary interactions. I have seen examples of parents and children who get into nightly battles, struggles, nagging, rages, weeping episodes, and other highly negative emotional experiences while trying to work together on academic material. The saddest moments for parents come when they realize that the battles have succeeded only in teaching the child to dislike the activities, and their efforts have been counterproductive. This is a demoralizing realization, to say the least. For this reason let's emphasize that it is better not to do any of the activities to be described here than to do them in a way that brings unhappiness to parent or child. If you work on doing the rest of the things this book advises, sooner or later the interaction skills and the emotional climate should permit joyous tutoring.

How positive is the emotional climate between you and the child? How would you rate your own current style of approval, differential attention, differential excitement, responsiveness versus directiveness, and positive models? If you and the child can routinely spend an hour or two together in playing, chatting, doing errands, or hanging around the house, with a positive emotional tone prevailing, then you and your child can probably enjoy doing academic work together. If not, then I would recommend working on the interpersonal environment first. The academic activities can wait, or can be delegated to someone else. That person—tutor or teacher— can sometimes be in a very advantageous position from being able to start afresh with the child and not be encumbered with the authority and power struggles that have taken place between parent and child. That person can also have a tremendous advantage in having spent lots less time with the child, having energy supplies that are less drained, and being more fresh and ready for the interaction.

If you do undertake academic activities with your child, it is very important to monitor the signals that the child gives. If the child smiles a lot, if the child looks forward to the activities, if the child reminds the parent about them when the parent is tardy, and if the child gets a lot of pleasure from getting right answers on questions, you know you're onto a good thing.

Tutors have a tremendous advantage over classroom teachers in making academic activities fun. A tutor has only one child to work with at a time; a teacher has a whole room full of children at once. If an activity is too easy or too hard for the child, the tutor can immediately adjust the level of difficulty or go on to a new activity; the teacher does not have this luxury. The teacher must put a high priority on keeping order; the tutor can let the child do a lot of talking and having fun without fearing that things will get out of hand.

When I see so many children who don't learn well in school, so many children who openly hate school, and when I see so few eager learners, I mistrust anyone who would tell all parents to stay out of academic teaching lest they interfere with what the schools are doing.

The children who are able to learn well in the large group settings that most schools represent, usually, are those children whose families have already brought them up the hierarchy of academic skills to the point where they can pay attention to academic-like material, (or "verbally encoded information) before school even starts. Those children who have had little one-on-one experience in being read to, engaging in conversations, doing dramatic play, and experiencing verbally encoded information in other pleasant ways before school starts, require absolutely masterful kindergarten teachers and first grade teachers if they are to learn.

Parents can choose any degree of involvement in children's academic education, from "let the teachers and the child work it out with no interference" on one end of the spectrum, to homeschooling on the other. All points on this spectrum have proved useful for various families.

The Purpose of Reading and Writing

What are reading and writing for? Why should anyone want to learn such activities? For many school children, the answer to these questions is, "Because somebody is telling me that I have to." Unless the child has direct experience that gives some other better answer than that, the process of learning these skills will be not nearly as rich and fulfilling as it would be if it were connected to some other source of motivation.

So what is the alternative answer—why read and write? The best answer I can come up with has to do with memorializing things, and retrieving those memories. We write things down because we don't want them forgotten. We read them because we want to get into our minds this memorial that we or someone else has created.

Writing is worthwhile, therefore, in proportion to how much the thoughts are worth remembering. Reading is worthwhile in proportion to how much the recovered thoughts are worth thinking about. If the child doesn't have any inkling as to why the thoughts are worth remembering or thinking about, the education game is lost.

What makes certain thoughts, encoded into words, worth remembering and thinking about? Perhaps they are entertaining, as in a story that has a funny or suspenseful plot. Perhaps they teach us something we are curious about, as in a science book that tells why we get sick and how we get well. Perhaps the words have some beauty, and appeal to our esthetic sense, as in a beautiful poem. Perhaps the words tell us how to do something we want to do, or how to solve a problem, as in directions for putting together an appliance. Perhaps they fulfill our wish for socializing, as in reading a letter from someone we know. Perhaps we want to encode them because they are ours and we want to keep owning them, as in a story that I make up and want to keep. Or maybe they do something else I haven't listed. But the point is that insofar as possible, we want the child to be able to see and experience, without our even having to explain it, what the point is of encoding and decoding thoughts via words. This means that we look for writings that children can resonate with, and help them to look for writings that they can resonate with. This means that we help them write the answers to questions that they are really curious about, to write stories and poems and essays and articles that they would want to read again some time, rather than to write just to fulfill an assignment.

What Is To Be Learned?

Let's expand on the question of the purpose of reading and writing, by asking what we want a child to learn in the academic realm.

The answer is to make the world a better place—the child's own world, and the world of the people around her. In order to accomplish this, we can divide the task up into the following pieces:

1. We want the let the child get some information—science, history, literature, mathematics, psychology, eco-

nomics, philosophy, the arts, technologies, trade skills, whatever—so as to have a sampling of the thoughts most worth thinking, the ideas most worth knowing, that people have come up with yet. We can't give the child complete knowledge. But a sampling gives the child a basis for further interest in these areas. People are most interested in the things they know the most about. Thus creating the motive to get information is very important, but it can't be separated from actually getting some information.

2. We want the child to be able to input this information. One way of receiving such information is by direct observation. But there are major codes that we should help the child crack in order to receive such information:

2.1 The language code. The child needs to develop the vocabulary, and the listening comprehension ability, such that the child can receive and understand information, particularly when it is heard in words.

2.2 The reading code. The child needs to be able to decode the written word.

2.3 The mathematical code. The child needs to be able to understand what mathematical symbols mean.

3. We want the child to be able to process information, to think, to be creative, to rearrange bits of information in his head and come out with something new or useful or good. This includes solving problems, and thinking. Of course, the codes that we use for input and output to the world are also useful in communicating with ourselves while thinking.

4. We want the child to be able to output this information. In order to do this, there are these major codes:

4.1 The vocabulary code, knowing words for communicating.

4.2 The linguistic code, knowing how to put words together to express ideas.

4.3. The spelling code, the sometimes very arbitrary conventions for making words from letters.

4.4 The mechanical process of getting language written down: the ability to handwrite or type.

4.5 The code of numbers and mathematics.

4.6 The codes of art, music, dance, photography, building or fixing things, and other means of expression other than by the written or spoken word.

Practical Implications of the Previous Two Sections

What are the implications of the aims I've listed for academic education? Here are some corollaries of looking at academics in this way.

1. One of the major concerns of educators should be the question: of all the bits of knowledge and information and ideas that one can possibly learn, which are the most worth dealing with? Some are worthwhile because they give us happiness; some are worthwhile because they help us give other people happiness. In my opinion, educators who induce children to memorize the

capitals of the states and the state flowers and birds in the United States are wasting children's time, effort, and memory space. Someone else may have a different opinion. But unless an educator really believes that the information being taught is vitally worthwhile, he is undermining the trust of the child that vital time and neuronal storage space is not being wasted.

2. The educator should communicate to the child the question of what is most worth doing and thinking about, so that the child can grapple with this question. The educator should frequently get the child's thoughts on what is most worthwhile. If a child is unmotivated to read or write a certain assignment, perhaps either the instructor has come up with something unworthwhile to do, or else has failed to adequately communicate and transmit to the child an appreciation for why it is worthwhile. The child is by definition an immature being and may not have an appreciation for why learning certain things is worthwhile. But the educator's responsibility is to nurture this judgment as the child grows.

3. If the child has unusually great difficulties in cracking one of the codes, we should avoid punishing the child for that, and we try to keep the input, processing, and output of worthwhile thoughts moving for that student through whatever channels the child can use, while working on cracking the code in the channels the child can't use. For example, with the child who hasn't learned to read, we spend part of the day reading to the child, and part of the day teaching the child to decode. For the child who can't seem to connect brain and hand to write, we spend part of the time teaching the child to write, while spending other time each day taking dictation from the child's spoken words.

4. We should give lots of practice and challenges to the child's thinking and problem-solving skills, rather than simply asking the child to memorize facts and procedures. For example, rather than simply ask the child to memorize that area of a rectangle is length times width, we give the child several rectangles marked off in squares and ask the child to infer the rule. (Of course, the child must have been prepared by previous learning such that such a task is in the "challenge zone.")

5. Assignments to children should often involve inputting worthwhile information, doing some thinking and processing with it and other information, and outputting a new product in a worthwhile form. For example: read a bunch of modeling stories that illustrate the skill of delay of gratification; think of a new story that illustrates this same skill; write it.

6. Since speaking and hearing language is the foundation for writing and reading language, lots of activities involving speaking and listening should be done, not just those involving reading and writing.

7. If we can measure, over time, the child's abilities in to do the above-mentioned tasks, and find that they are progressing nicely, then there is reason to celebrate the child's success, even if the child is not making good grades. Failure to make good grades in school can come from higher performance by other children in this child's comparison group, slow development in the skill of organizing the turning in of assignments; use of unreliable measurement systems by teachers, and various additional reasons other than the basic academic competences mentioned above. For example, if a child gets better and better at decoding reading each year until he finally can sound out almost any word given to him, a great success has taken place, even if he has been far enough behind his peers each year that he has consistently gotten a c or d in reading most years.

8. If we can appeal thoroughly enough to the child's sense of what is really worthwhile, we can dispense with many of the extrinsic rewards and punishments that seem to drive much of the educational world: grades, rewards for good grades, punishments for bad grades, comparisons to other students, punishments for not turning homework in, etc. Even if those extrinsic rewards and punishments cannot be done away with, we should often appeal to the motivation to do something because it is worthwhile.

Priorities In Conducting the Activities

It's very important to keep in mind what the first priority is for any session that an adult holds with a child in helping the child develop academic skills. For example, in a session where the adult is trying to help the child recognize the sounds that come at the beginnings of words, is the first priority that the child learn those sounds? No. In a session where the adult is trying to help the child learn some new words, is the first priority that the child learn those words? No.

The first priority for any session with the child is that the child will have his or her appetite whetted for the next session. It does you little good to teach the child the alphabet if the child is forming a strong opinion that working with letters is extremely unpleasant. You want to be producing not a child who can recite something back to you, but a learner who is on the road toward enjoying learning for the rest of his or her life. You want to produce a curious individual, someone who wants to find out things. You want a child who will be eager to have learning sessions with you. Of course, if this is taking place, you and your child are developing a positive relationship with each other, which is a goal of utmost importance.

A second priority always to keep in mind is to help the child learn habits of learning. Whether the child is learning to play the piano or play tennis, to read English or to read music, to solve equations or do a science experiment, certain habits of learning will always be helpful.

One of these is the habit of concentrating and trying to remember while someone (either in person or writing) is explaining or demonstrating how to do something.

Another habit is that of feeling OK about taking the first practice at doing something, without fearing looking silly or fearing failure at it. This is the habit of bravery about making attempts, without fear of ridicule.

Another habit is that of monitoring your own performance, and comparing it to the desired performance.

If the performance is a positive one, it's important to be able to say, "Hey, I did it! Hooray!" and otherwise reward yourself internally for a success. If the performance fell short of what you desired, it's important to be able to say, "OK, here's what I need to do differently the next time," and learn from the experience, rather than to come down on yourself or get very frustrated or try to escape the situation.

Another habit is to have lower standards for oneself when one first begins to learn to do something, but to gradually increase one's standards with more practice.

An extremely important habit is repetition tolerance: the ability to tolerate a huge number of repetitive practices of the skill, doing it over and over in various different ways, not just until one can do it right, but until doing it right becomes "second nature" or almost automatic. This habit is related to the skill of sustaining attention to tasks.

Another very important habit is learning to enjoy the "Meet the Challenge" game: "You give me a task, and I'll enjoy trying to do it and pleasing you by succeeding at it." If the child can have lots of fun experiences at this game, he is greatly helped, because this is the pattern repeated over and over by successful students in school. It's the same game that happens when a parent says to a one-and-a-half year old, "What does the dog say?" and the child replies, "Woof woof!" and the parent smiles and says "Right!" and the child smiles. It's the same game that is played by a graduate student getting a Ph.D., who writes a dissertation in such a way that makes the committee say "Right!"

The opposite of this game is the "Frustrate the Authority" game: "You give me a task, and I'll get out of it somehow or fail at it, in a way that exasperates you, and I'll enjoy seeing you frustrated."

If a child masters these strategies, the child can learn almost any subject matter. A child can start developing good habits in these strategies from a very early age.

Skills for Tutors

Before we go into the specific teaching activities that a adult can do with a child to increase academic skills, let's think about the skills that the adult has to develop first if the tutoring is to be successful. What are those skills?

First, you need to be able to assume an enthusiastic attitude from the very beginning, a way of using your tone of voice and facial expression that says, "I'm looking forward to doing these things! This is really going to be fun for me!" If you act this way about the activities, the child will pick up on that attitude and will be much more enthusiastic about them himself, other things equal.

Next, you need to be able to explain and demonstrate the activity to the child in a way the child can understand. The best explanations are usually very brief. The more you can communicate what the child is to do by demonstrating it, the more likely you are to hold the child's attention.

Next, you need to be skilled at watching a child's reaction to an activity and seeing whether it is too hard or too easy for the child. If the child doesn't seem to be able to figure out how to do it, even when you've explained it well and demonstrated it yourself, the activity is probably too hard; if the child gets it every single time and doesn't seem to feel particularly challenged by it or proud of his successes (even when he is proud at other times and thus demonstrates a capacity to feel proud of his successes) the activity is probably too easy. A good rule of thumb is to rig the activity so that the child can be successful on at least four-fifths of the attempts he makes at whatever he is being asked to do.

Next, you need to know, for any given activity that you are doing, ways of making it harder and ways of making it easier. That way once you have perceived that the activity is too hard or too easy, you can very quickly adjust and get at the right level of difficulty, the "cutting edge" level of difficulty.

Next, you need to be able to get really excited about the child's successes. Your excitement when the child does well at something will be a very potent reward for the child that goes a long way toward making the child want to have the next session.

Conversely, you need to be able to respond in a matter of fact, informative way to the child's mistakes, never in a way that shows irritation with the child or humiliates the child.

Next, you have to be able to be patient when the child gets off task. At the beginning, you need to have more tolerance, and to be able to sit and wait for the child to return to the activity with you. As time goes by and the child gets more skilled at the tasks, the child's ability to stay on task will increase. But at the start you may need to just sit and meditate a while, fairly frequently, not punishing the child for getting off task, but not rewarding the child with your attention, and rewarding the child with your attention when he or she comes back to the task.

Next, you have to have a feeling for how long to stay on any one activity.

Even a child with a very short attention span can get lots of useful work done if you use this strategy: Have several different activities for the child to do. Arrange them in order of least pleasant to most pleasant. That way the more pleasant activities reinforce the completion of the less pleasant ones. Set goals in each activity that will allow the child to finish before the attention span for that activity runs out.

Finally, you have to be able to take pleasure in both adult-directed activity and child-directed activity, and to figure out the best balance between the two at any given stage of your work. If the child finds one type of activity particularly difficult or unnatural, start out with small amounts of it and gradually increase it as the child gets more comfortable with it.

More on the Notion of "Balance" in Tutoring

We've talked about balance between adult-directed activity and child-directed activity. The notion of balance is important in other respects, too. In several ways, the tutor has to do "not too much, not too little, but just right" amounts of something.

One way has to do with the balance between too hard and too difficult tasks. By the "challenge zone" of the child's skills we mean activities that are not so easy for the child as to be boring, and not so challenging as to be over his head, but in the "just right" region in the middle. (Robert Kreigel coined this term, and also spoke about the "panic zone" when the material is too hard, and the "drone zone" when it is too easy.) When there is one tutor working with one child, the adult can figure out what that "challenge zone" is, and pick activities that are just right for the individual child. This is much harder to do when working with a bunch of children of different ability levels at the same time. As mentioned earlier and later, the tutor, in order to be an expert, must have in mind ways of making any activity harder or easier to adjust it to be at the "challenge zone" of difficulty for the child. When we talk about specific activities later on, we will talk about ways to make each of them harder or easier. If the tutor can regulate the difficulty so as to spend time in the challenge zone, the task of "motivating" the child is incredibly easier.

Another important balance is the balance between activities already fun for the child and activities which you hope will become fun, but aren't now. For example, suppose that a child starts out tutoring liking to chat with you, liking to throw a ball back and forth outside, liking to make interesting things come up on a computer screen, liking to play with toy people, and liking you to read to him. Suppose that at the beginning he doesn't much like going over letter sounds, trying to read, and answering questions you ask him. Your hope is that eventually he will come to enjoy the more academic activities, because he will get better and better at them. But at the beginning, perhaps he has experienced nothing but failure and criticism when he has done them, and he has a bad taste in his mouth for them.

The thing for the tutor to do, in this case, is to try to have enough "already fun" activities in the session so that the child develops a very positive taste for the tutoring sessions, while having enough "later to become fun" activities so that the child makes some progress toward learning to enjoy them.

Again, how to draw the balance is an individualized decision. The great thing about individual tutoring is that you can make this decision for the one child you are working with. In some cases it may be the best idea for a tutor to have several weeks of "already fun" activities only, particularly if they are activities from which the child is learning something—such as your reading to the child, or the child's fiddling with a word processor. But other children would prefer to play the whole session, but can benefit more from systematic teaching.

The Sandwich Technique: Alternation Between Tutor's Choice and Child's Choice

Here's a tried and true way to arrange a balance between adult-directed activity and child-directed activity, and between already fun activities and someday-to-be-fun activities. The child and the tutor take turns deciding what to do, for fifteen-minute intervals or longer. For example, for the first 15 minutes the tutor decides, and they do the some reading activities. The second 15 minutes the child decides, and they play with the word processor. The third 15 minutes the adult decides, and they do some more reading activities; the fourth 15 minutes the child decides and they play with toys.

The idea of this alternation is first that the play reinforces the work, and second that the child gets a chance to develop a more rich relationship with the tutor than would be possible with only activities chosen by the tutor.

The tutor says, "We'll set the timer [or keep an eye on the clock] and we'll do what I want us to do for fifteen minutes. Then you get to pick what you want us to do for the next fifteen minutes, within certain boundaries. Then it'll be my turn, and then your turn again."

This alternation does not have to occur for all children; it's a judgment call. Some children enjoy the highest-priority learning activities enough that there seems to be mutual agreement on doing them, so that the child is looking forward to them and the tutor is looking forward to them too; in such circumstances there is probably no need for an alternation. This is the ideal circumstance.

Some children have long enough attention spans that alternation of 30 minute intervals is better than 15 minute intervals. Sometimes the best thing for the tutor to do with a young child is to alternate in a less formal and agreed upon fashion.

And sometimes there can be such mutual agreement on activities that are deemed worthwhile by both tutor and child that there is no need for alternation.

Still More Dimensions for Balance

Another balance is that between learning new material and practicing with old material. The principle of balance between learning new material and practicing with old material is a result of the fact that there are at least two types of memory. Totally unfamiliar material gets stored in short term memory. If you keep loading more and more unfamiliar material into short term memory, the new material will crowd out, or interfere with, the material that you just loaded in. However, if you load a few bits of new information into short term memory, and then practice them over and over, they begin to get consolidated into longer term memory. Then you can load a few more bits of new information into short term memory, practice them, and then go back and practice the first ones again.

Different children require different balances between practice of old material and introduction of new material. A very fast learner may be able to take in lots of new information relative to the practice of the old. A very slow learner may need huge amounts of practice with the old material relative to introduction of new material. The tutor makes this judgment based on the child's responses. If the child is catching on quickly and getting all the questions right, you can try moving in the direction of faster introduction of new material. If the child misses more questions, you move toward more practice with old material. Just as with finding the correct level of difficulty of the material based on the child's responses, you also find the proper level of difficulty for the rate of introduction of new material based on the child's responses.

Another area where balance must take place has to do with attention span. For some children, you may need to break up the activities into short bursts, because the child gets bored with any given activity quickly. For other children, you can keep on the same activity for much longer at a stretch. Again, you want to meet the child where he is, and try to gradually stretch out his attention span.

One more area where the tutor should find the best balance for any given child is between staying in one place and moving around, between being still and exercising one's body. Some children can do activities that require them to stay in one place for a long time; others get very restless very soon.

If you are dealing with a child who seems to need and like to move his body a lot, why fight it? This is one of the great advantages of tutoring versus classroom instruction. You can take a break and go outside and run for ten minutes with the child in the middle of the session, and then restart the session with the child refreshed. Or you can just run up and down the stairs for two minutes. Or you can go outside and take a walk and play some educational games as you go (for example, the blending game or the which-object game to be described below, for children who are just starting to learn to read).

I think many of the problems of schools come from failure to take into account children's needs to move their bodies. I hear frequently of children's being asked to experience a full school day without any time for running. Don't make this mistake if you are tutoring.

Fun, Self-Control, and Repetition-Tolerance

Tutors sometimes prejudice a child that an activity isn't fun. The tutor might say, when introducing an activity, "OK, it's time to do so and so. This is kind of dull, but let's do just a few of them, OK?" Or the tutor might say, during the course of an activity, "Only just a few more to go, and then you get to do something else." Or the tutor might give the message while praising the child, by saying, "Wow, you put up with doing that for a long time. Most children would not have gotten tired of doing this a long time ago." In all of these utterances, there is the message that the activity is unpleasant in and of itself. It's usually best not to bias the child, but to give the child the chance to find a way to enjoy an activity. However, there are different types of enjoyment that can be cultivated.

Some educational theorists would have us believe that a child's curiosity motivation should be sufficient to keep the educational process going. I agree that it is important to appeal to curiosity as much as possible. This is done by teaching things that have some relevance to life, by first allowing a child to discover why it is useful to learn something before asking him to learn it, by teaching skills in the context of the applications that allow them to do people good, and by allowing the child to find out for himself all he possibly can rather than memorizing answers that someone else gives. But there is another important source of motivation that children should learn to cultivate. This is the knowledge that you can learn things that you want to learn, even when your curiosity temporarily wanes, because you have enough self-discipline to keep repetitively practicing. This is the discovery, or the reminder to yourself, that your own self-discipline is equal to the learning challenges you are faced with.

The tutor wants to convey the message that getting more competent at activities important for success should be intrinsically rewarding, or should produce a certain type of good feeling inside. I use these phrases in distinction to the word "fun." The word fun conveys to many children a certain sort of amusement-park type pleasure, the sort of pleasure from "edutainment" type computer games. But this is not the only type of pleasure available from learning, and not the most important type. The pleasure I'm focusing on now is more subtle: the pleasure from knowing that they have done something difficult and have mastered it, the pleasure of growing competence, the pleasure of knowing that they can if necessary tough out a tedious and repetitive activity to learn what they want to learn.

Let's face the fact that not all educational activities can be "fun," especially for the child who has trouble remembering certain types of information and needs lots of repetition to cement them in memory. For certain children, for example, reading comes with difficulty, and there needs to be very repetitive practice, as for example in the sounding and blending exercise to be described later. No one should pretend that this activity is a rollicking good time.

But children over 6 or 7 will benefit from having it explained to them something like this: "This activity is not fun like a cartoon is fun or like a video game is fun. It's work. It requires you to use self-control to keep your mind on it. It requires you to develop something called repetition-tolerance: the ability to keep practicing, over and over, and not have to quit right away because you're bored. You feel good not because you're seeing a bunch of action and excitement, but because you know inside yourself that you're getting better and better at something important, and because you know the self-control and repetition-tolerance you're developing are going to help you in everything you learn for the rest of your life. It's a more grown-up way of feeling good. It's a way of feeling good that you develop and cultivate over time."

As time goes by, you can monitor that more subtle way of feeling good. You can say, after a repetitive practice activity, "I know that was not fun for you the way a cartoon is fun or cake and ice cream are fun. But I'm curious. Are you able to feel any of that good feeling inside about getting better at this, and about getting more self-control, and about getting more repetition tolerance?" If the child is able to cultivate that source of pleasure, something very important will have happened. If the child looks frequently inside herself for this type of pleasure, often she will find it.

Some Specific Academic Activities For Young Children

The following description of tutoring activities is not meant to be comprehensive. This is just to give an adult a taste of some activities which can be done by an adult and a child. If you are interested in more comprehensive descriptions of activities, a more comprehensive manual on tutoring is available from me.

Reading to the Child and Talking About What Was Read

So much has been written on the value of reading to children that it would seem unnecessary to even mention it. However, the following points are not always obvious.

First, it is important to keep reading to children even after they can already read. Reading aloud is a social activity that has offers rewards unattainable by reading alone. Also, reading aloud allows the adult to find the challenge zone for the child's input and processing of information, limited only by the vocabulary and language codes, but not limited by the reading code. Many children can understand and enjoy understanding much higher level material than they themselves can read.

Second, reading aloud to a child is more exciting when combined with the detective task of tracking down a book on some specific question or some specific subject that the child is curious about or thinks worthwhile at the time. If the child is searching for information, and finds it, the child will be a much more eager participant in inputting it than if the child's job is to passively listen to whatever the adult chooses to read to him. Thus spending time in a library (or on the internet) together tracking down information on a certain topic is a useful one to combine with reading aloud.

Third, the notion of processing and outputting ideas rather than simply passively inputting them implies that adult and child will benefit from thinking together and talking about the books they read. How does a young child learn to think and talk about the ideas that books stimulate? Partly by observing the models of an adult thinking and talking about the ideas. Here is a set of prompts for adults to chat about books:

(Reminders) "That operation the veterinarian did reminds me of an operation I got. What happened was that..."

(Motivations) "I wonder why the little boy didn't like the way the babysitter looked. Maybe it was because ..."

(Curiosity about next step) "That told us that the sky is blue because the blue light is scattered differently by the air molecules. But it didn't tell us why that is so. I wonder why?"

(Restatements) "That was pretty complicated. I'm going to see if I can say what I remember of it. Tell me if you think I understand it right."

(Alternatives) "That boy who kept going down the different trails in the cave, faster and faster—I think he should have done something else instead. I think he should have taken out his pen and paper, if he had one, and made a little map of the passageways, as he went along."

(Worthwhileness) "I'm glad I read this, because it gave me a good model of sharing and generosity to think about." or "Let's see, that explained how you multiply numbers together. Let me remember why it is that people would want to multiply numbers together."

(Concrete examples) "That quotation was saying that people can overcome big obstacles if they work hard enough. I remember hearing about a guy whose legs were injured so much they thought he couldn't walk, and he worked and worked so hard that he became a championship runner."

(Abstract principles) "The man in that story was so greedy for more land, that he died trying to get more and more. I think the author is trying to tell us that we should learn to feel satisfied at a certain point and not always keep wanting more and more wealth."

The adult who models these sorts of comments about things that he and the child are reading together will at some point or another find the child making similar sorts of comments. Then, of course, the adult should listen carefully to the child. Listening carefully means using reflections, facilitations, and follow-up questions. Reading aloud with someone and discussing the book informally is a great way to get educated.

You Act As the Child's Secretary

In a set of extremely useful activities, you allow the child to process and output information through the spoken word. You accomplish the task of transforming spoken language to written language, memorializing the child's output.

In one variant of this activity, the child makes up a story, possibly with some help from you. You write or type the story for the child, and let the child keep it. You or somebody else can read the child's story, or read it to the child, immediately or later on.

It helps in doing this activity if you are a fast writer or typist. Otherwise you can use a tape recorder to record the story when making it up for the first time, to avoid slowing down the process so much that the child loses interest. The tape recorder can keep up with the child, no matter how fast the story is told. The child will get to listen to the story on the tape recorder as well as hearing it read after being written down; both of these are fun for the child.

How do you help a child make up a story? If you were to say, "OK, I want you to make up a story," many children would not know how to begin. On the other hand, with the following procedure, almost all children can come up with a story.

You say, "Let's make up a story together. I'll start it off. Once upon a time, there was a _________ " and then look expectantly at the child. If the child doesn't answer, say, "Just say anything that comes to your mind." Suppose the child says, "A boy." You say, "OK! There was a boy, and one day something happened to this boy, which was that ________." Again it is the child's turn. In this way you prompt the child, letting the child fill in all the significant details, while you only provide some filler.

I tell children beforehand that I have certain principles that obligate me to boycott entertainment violence. Thus I give the child fair warning that if the child dictates a violent story I may choose to edit it with the child before printing it, or may just save it on disk and not print it. Then I use my judgment with any particular violent story, as to whether there is redeeming social value or not.

This doesn't mean that only stories that are blandly good are written down, in the way I do things. The child's story can be very bizarre or wild, and the more the child's imagination gets stimulated the better. Images of violent or cruel behavior are not be encouraged, but there is plenty of room for very imaginative images within this constraint.

Another variant of story-making requires getting a bunch of pictures cut out from magazines. You randomly pick out pictures, and make up stories about the pictures you pick. Then you can tape the picture onto the page with the story, as an illustration for the story.

In another variant of the adult's taking the child's dictation, the adult elicits from the child a nonfiction article, not a story. For example, the adult simultaneously reads and writes a question such as "Should people be able to do medical experiments on animals, even if the animals are hurt or killed, when those experiments will help human beings very much?" Then the adult looks to the child for an answer. If the child says, "I think they should," the adult writes this down. Then the adult says, "Why do you think so?" When the child answers, the adult transcribes what the child has said. The adult functions as an interviewer, asking all sorts of follow-up questions, and taking down the child's answers. At the end, the adult may have elicited a coherent essay from the child. As with stories, it is printed and read.

In another variant, the child tells real things that happened to her—the stories of her life.

In another variant, the child tells thoughts about questions of her own choosing. This is an extremely valuable exercise, because the child is challenged to decide what is worthwhile to think about, as well as to think about it.

Other variants borrow from the other psychological skill activities mentioned elsewhere in this book, and described more thoroughly in *Exercises for Psychological Skills*. The child can dictate problems for the brainstorming game, solutions for these problems, and ideas on which solutions will work the best. The child can dictate dialogues between two people, replicas of dialogues created by the problem-solving game. The child can dictate stories meant to be models of specific psychological skills. The child can tell stories of events in life, and thoughts about them, as in the Guess the Feelings game, and tell what sorts of feelings she had. The child can dictate fantasy rehearsals.

Some Activities for Thinking Practice

If you can help the child get "turned on" to the pleasure of solving "brain teasers," you will have accomplished a very important educational goal. You will have created another reason for the worthwhileness of certain activities: the pleasure of trying to find a solution given the constraints. There are many "good students" who think and solve problems in order to get grades, but who have not cultivated the pleasure of problem-solving for its own sake. The world and life offer huge numbers of problems to be solved; if the child can learn to take pleasure in tackling them, the child's life will be changed.

What are the most essential ingredients in the task of "turning on" a child to brain teasers? I would list two. First, of course, the problems must be at the "challenge zone" for the child, not too hard and not too easy. Any bookstore will have books of brain teasers that are hard, for adults; less ubiquitous are easy brain teasers, on the level for preschool, kindergarten, and early grade school years.

The second ingredient is that the problems be "good." What makes a good problem? Many good ones are in the form of a story. They should not require any more mathematics than the child already knows. And most good ones have a certain quality of "once you know the answer, it seems that it should have been obvious," quality, a "you'll kick yourself if I tell you the answer" quality. With enough of a "good" quality, children themselves will communicate the problems among each other, as riddles. Here are some examples of problems of such a quality.

A bear walks 10 feet South. Then he realizes he forgot something, and turns around and starts walking in exactly the opposite direction. After that he doesn't change direction, but after going 11 feet he realizes he's walking South again. What color is the bear?

A man is running outside. It starts to rain. He doesn't have an umbrella, or a raincoat, or anything else to keep the rain off him. But still his shirt doesn't get wet. How can this be?

A poor but smart man wants to marry the king's daughter, and she him. The king would ordinarily just dispose of him, but his daughter persuades him to give the man a chance. The king is superstitious, and believes in giving fate a chance to work. So he decides that tomorrow in the great hall, in front of the fireplace, (where a roaring fire always burns) the man will draw one of two pieces of paper out of a hat. One will say "daughter," and the other will say "dungeon," and the drawing will determine how the man will spend the rest of his life. The princess overhears the king's dishonest assistant making a plan to write the word "dungeon" on both pieces of paper, and thus seal the man's fate. But she tells her friend, and she also tells him a strategy to use that will ensure marriage for them. What strategy did she figure out?

An adventuress comes to a cave where there are two doors. One has a deadly dragon behind it, and the other has a pot of gold behind it. The adventuress can become rich, but if she opens the wrong door she will be killed. There are two people guarding these doors. She has found out that one always tells the truth, and the other always lies, but she doesn't know which is which. The guards know whether the other is a liar or not, and the guards also know where the gold is. A wizard tells her, "You may ask one question of one of the guards. If you pick the right question, you will be sure of making the right choice." What question should she ask?

The trouble with problems like these is that they can be difficult, even for adults. Children who are not at the beginning good problem solvers tend not to have anywhere close to 80% successes at these. (The answers are as follows. The bear is white, a polar bear, because the only place where two opposite directions could both be south is the North Pole. The man's shirt doesn't get wet because he isn't wearing a shirt. The princess figured out that the man should pick a piece of paper, fumble it so that it lands in the fire, and then be able to prove that it said "daughter" by pointing to the remaining slip that says "dungeon." The adventuress should ask one of the guards, "If I were to ask the other guard which door is in front of the gold, what would he say," and then take the other door.)

What is needed is a hierarchy of brain teasers, ordered from easy to hard, so that if a problem is too hard, you can pick another much easier, and move around on the hierarchy until you have landed in the challenge zone for the child.

The Critical Thinking Books and Software Company (www.criticalthinking.com) markets a wealth of books and puzzles covering a wide range of difficulty. The task of the tutor is to move quickly up or down the hierarchy of difficulty depending upon the child's response to the initial challenges.

Games for Thinking Practice

Much practice in thinking can take place through playing games. Again, the games should be at the challenge zone level of difficulty for the particular child. The following are some games, mostly very familiar ones, both fun and useful. If the child's experience of the latest video game crowds out the experience of these, his education is incomplete, in my opinion.

Twenty Questions. The first player thinks of something: e.g. a person, a thing, a place. The other players try to guess what the first is thinking of, by asking yes or no questions. If you want to be true to the title of the game, you can limit the number to twenty; otherwise you can keep going with patience as the only limiting factor. In this game, the child learns skills of strategies of zeroing in on correct answers by first asking general questions, and only going to specific ones as the field has become narrowed down. The inexperienced thinker will start out by asking, "Is it a dog?" Whereas the more experienced thinker will start out by asking things like, "Is it something that is or was ever alive?"

You can make this game easy by limiting the field of possible answers, for example to things in the house. You can make it very difficult by imposing no limits on the possible answers, and allowing answers ranging all the way from "self-improvement" to "The Golden Rule."

Password. The first player knows the password, and is trying to get his partner to guess it; this player gives a clue to his partner by saying a different word. The partner guesses, and if she doesn't guess correctly, another clue is given. The game provides good exercise in vocabulary and searching for words and in seeing things from another person's point of view. The competitive version is with 4 players, with two teams alternating in their guesses. The less competitive version has any number of players all guessing in turn after each clue.

Checkers, chess, and Connect Four. Games such as these have been used in cognitive therapy programs designed to teach children to think and predict consequences before acting. They are pure skill games, i.e. with no luck involved. They are simulations of the aspect of life in which you must think of what you could do, what the likely response would be to that, what you would do in response to that, and so on, for each option you are considering. You can play these games with more than 2 players, having pairs or threesomes decide together which move should go next.

Scrabble, Boggle, and other games of making words from letters. Boggle involves some dice with letters on them; you generate a random configuration and make as many words as possible out of the letters that come up. Scrabble also draws upon the ability to think of words—an important skill in most intellectual activity—and to spell them.

Blackjack. When played with betting of chips, and where the decisions involved are not only whether to hit or stick but also whether to fold or call or raise, the game is a very intricate exercise in calculations and probability estimations. When played in a much simpler way without betting, the game gives practice in adding and subtracting and making probability-based judgments.

Quarto. This game helps a child learn to think in terms of different variables, spatial images, and to think several moves ahead before acting. There are sixteen wooden pieces in the game, representing each of the possible combinations of two conditions for each of four variables: short or tall, dark or light, round or square, and hollow or solid. There are sixteen squares on a board, and the object of the game is to line up four pieces that share any characteristic in common.

Charades. Creativity, acting skills, and skills of predicting how things will seem from another's point of view are some of the skills this game of acting out familiar titles or phrases promotes.

One of these things is not like the other. At least one IQ test I saw was predominantly made up of questions of the form, "Which of these 4 or 5 things is least like the others?" There is a reason why such questions appear on IQ tests, since the activities of examining different phenomena and inferring commonalities and differences and classifying things as in or out of different sets are fundamental to a great deal of intellectual work. If you and your child can make up questions of this sort for each other in a fun way, especially while using otherwise wasted time such as on car trips, you can get in some great thinking practice. Here are some examples, starting easy and getting a little harder. Which of the following is not like the others: a book, a letter, a knife, a magazine? A belt, a pen, the equator, a ribbon on a birthday package, a lasso? An elephant, an egg, an Exxon station, a cake, and an economist? A circle, a square, a rectangle, a pyramid? (Answers: the knife (others are things you read), the pen (others are things that go encircle something), the cake (others are things whose words start with short e, and the pyramid (others are flat shapes rather than solid).

Guess the category is a similar game, where the challenge is to infer the common feature of some specific examples. One person thinks of a category such as "things you wear on your feet." Then the clue-giver gives clues such as shoes, slippers, socks, stockings, boots. As with password or any other guessing game, you can have two teams which alternate in giving clues, and see which team can guess it first; or you can simply have one person give clues and the others guess.

What Does He Like? is a game that in a simple version can be played with cards in an ordinary deck, with the face cards removed. One person gets in mind a certain rule that determines what the man from outer space likes and what he doesn't like. For example, for the youngest child, he doesn't like red cards and he does like black cards. You pick cards and put them in two piles, saying "He does like this," and "He doesn't like this," following the rule. When the child can infer the rule, he can tell you ahead of time whether he likes the next card or not. By doing so he doesn't give the rule away to any other players who haven't guessed it yet. To make the tasks more complicated, you can have rules that involve ands and ors: he likes cards that are red or an even number. To play this game in a more challenging version, you make a deck of 64 cards, with all the possible combinations of the following: triangles, circles, plus signs, or stars; one, two, three, or four shapes; shapes colored red, green, brown, or blue. Thus each card has three characteristics: number, color, and shape. You can have rules such as "He likes cards that are either stars or red or brown," or even more challenging ones. In this game you are looking for the elements shared by the cards in the "liked" set, which are not present in the cards of another set. This search for crucial variables is central to scientific work.

Some Activities on Cracking the Reading Code

The activities I've listed so far feel more like play than work. They will be fun for almost all children if they are carried out at the child's challenge zone. The task of learning to decode words for most children involves some plain work. The following activities, however, will allow some fundamental code-cracking knowledge to be introduced in a fun way, so as to minimize the frustration.

Reading the Letter Stories

The "Letter Stories" are part of the larger set of "modeling stories" that I have written. The letter stories have characters who are letters. The letters can speak normally to each other, but to human beings they can only speak their sounds; they communicate words by getting together and blending their sounds. They do acts of helping and rescuing by speaking words to people.

In this activity, the adult simply reads the letter stories to the child. There is no drilling or question-answering.

In a way that is hopefully fun and playful for the child, the child gets exposed to the "fundamental idea" that reading occurs by sounding and blending, as each letter says his sound separately, and the letters then blend to form the word. The child also gets to hear the sounds that many of the letters make. Finally, since the communication of the word usually saves someone from a disaster, the child gets reminded that words and the ideas they communicate can be very important: figuring them out is not something that will be done purely to please a parent or teacher.

Reading Alphabet Books to the Child

These books go through the alphabet and in some sort of interesting way, name a bunch of words that start with each letter. A good example is Dr. Seuss's ABC, which starts out "Big A, little a, What begins with A? Aunt Annie's alligator ... A ..a.. A."

It will be necessary at some point for the child to know the alphabet and recall what sounds each letter makes. But the more the child has been exposed to these facts in a fun, informal way, the more the child will have memory traces that will make the memorization come quicker and be less tedious.

I would advise not drilling the child and asking questions about alphabet books, but simply reading the books to the child as many times as the child wants. If the adult wants to try some game in which the child participates, for example by calling out the name of the letter when he sees it, the cardinal rule should be that the game should be dropped instantly if it is not fun. You want to preserve a precedent for the child that being read to is pure pleasure.

Here's a variation on reading alphabet books. Instead of saying the letters by their usual names, you say their sounds. You say "buh" and "duh" rather than "bee" and "dee" and so forth. You give the child exposure to the sounds the letters make, which are as important as the names of the letters.

When doing this, say "I'm going to read this book, but instead of saying the names of the letters, I'm going to say the sounds of the letters." That way the child will gradually get used to the distinction.

The Letter Sound Songs

I have put together some songs that are meant to teach the child what sounds the letters make. (A CD of these songs, entitled *What the Letters Say*, is available.) The theory is that learning the sounds the letters make can be fun and interesting if the child hears these songs sung to him, dances around with them, plays the dance and freeze game with them, and hears them played, without any drilling or memorizing. Later the child can drill and memorize if necessary, but the memory traces will already be in the mind from the totally recreational activity of listening to the songs.

If you sing these to the child enough, and occasionally point to the written letters as you are doing so, the child will find it easy to remember the most frequent sounds that the letters make.

The Blending Game

Sounding out words has two parts: being able to say the sounds the letters make, and then blending together those sounds to make a word. The blending game is meant to exercise the second of these skills. The blending game is an important part of the set of foundation reading skills known as "phonemic awareness." Phonemic awareness is the ability to take words apart into their separate sounds, and put sounds together to make words.

I can do this game either with pictures, or with objects in the room, or objects in the car or things we see while we are out for a walk. In the very first time of playing the game with a very young child, I say, "There's an easy way and a harder way of playing this game. In the easy way, I just say a word, and you point to it." Then if I'm doing the game with objects in the room, I say, "Can you point to the desk?" When the child does it, I say "Right!" If I'm doing it with pictures, I put out two or three pictures, and find something in one of them, and ask the child to point to it.

When the child is comfortable with this way of doing the game, then I say, "Now let's make it a little harder. Instead of saying the word in a regular way, I'm going to break it up into pieces. Let's see if you can guess what I'm trying to say."

Then if I were playing with objects in the room, I would say, "Can you point to the fluh oor?" or "Can you point to my nnn ose?" You start out by just breaking the words into two parts, with the beginning sound split off from the rest of the word. As time goes by and the child gets more skilled, you break the word into more parts: rather than duh og, you say duh aw guh. You pronounce each sound just as it is pronounced in the word, so that you are not spelling the word for the child; you are breaking it down into its sounds.

As the child gets better and better at this, the child can learn to recognize the word without having anything to look at in order to choose from. If you name the category, this will make it easier for the child. For example, if you say, "Here are some animals. How about chuh i kuh en? Right! Chicken! How about buh aaah rrr? Right, it's bear!"

As the child gets better and better at this, the child can play the game with you, giving you words to figure out.

Another variation of this game is the Blending Game with Stories. Here's how that variation sounds. "I'm going to read you a story, and as I do it, I'll take some of the words apart. Let's see if you can put them back together. OK?

"For example, let's say I read this. Once upon a time there was a boy named Jerry. Jerry was at a puh-ar-kuh. You would guess park. OK? Jerry saw a little boy, who was playing near a fountain. The boy leaned over the fountain to reach for a lll-eee-fuh. Can you guess it? Yes! A leaf. The boy leaned over too far, and he fell into the water!"

When doing the blending game with stories, it's important not to take the words apart too frequently. If you do, you lose the flow of the story.

The blending game presents a good example of an activity that the adult can make harder or easier depending upon whether the child is finding the game too hard or too easy. How can we summarize ways of making it harder or easier?

Options for making it easier:

Have pictures or objects that give a clue as to what the word is.

Have only two pictures, so that the child knows that the word is one of the two ahead of time.

Name the pictures ahead of time, so that the child has heard the word pronounced regularly.

Use easier and more familiar words.

Break the word into fewer parts rather than more parts; for the easiest task, just split off the beginning sound from the rest of the word.

If you still aren't getting enough successes, at times say the words normally and let the child point to the pictures.

Options for making it harder:

Have more pictures or objects to choose from.

Don't have a picture at all.

Break the word up into more parts—up to a part for each sound in the word.

Use less familiar words.

Say letters along with the sounds, making the task harder by throwing in that extra information: for example "In this word b says buh, a says aaa, and t says tuh."

Have the child give you the words to guess.

The Which-Word Game

This game, another phonemic awareness exercise, falls squarely into the camp of an adult-directed activity. In it, you give the child two words, and ask him which word begins with (or ends with, or has in the middle) a certain sound. For example, "The two words are *boy* and *fish*. Which one starts with buh?"

What's the purpose of this activity? It helps the child learn to take words apart into their sounds, and to discriminate what sounds make up a word. These skills will greatly help the child when the child gets ready to sound and blend words.

It's often most fun to do this while pointing at pictures that illustrate the words. Otherwise, you can use objects in the room, or you can just name words without using any pictures.

At the beginning of this activity, when you want to make it as easy as possible, you very much emphasize the first sound when saying the words beforehand. "Here's a BUH-icycle, and here's a LLLL-ake. Between BUH-icycle and LLLL-ake, which one starts with BUH?"

If the child gets the question right, you give some quick excited approval. If the child gets the question wrong, you reply like this: "No, the one that starts with BUH is Bicycle. If lake started with BUH, it would be Buh-ake, or bake!"

As time goes by, you can start simply saying the words regularly, without emphasizing the beginning sounds. "Between ink and church, which one starts with ih?"

The activity is easier when the beginning sounds of the two words are fairly different from one another. Thus telling the difference between "tuh" and "duh" is harder than telling the difference between "tuh" and "chuh."

When the child has mastered the game with the beginning sounds, then start doing it the same way with the ending sounds of the words. "Between booK and tie, which one ends with KUH?"

Finally, go for the middle sounds. "Between HAT and HORSE, which one has an ă in the middle?"

The best tutor has in mind ways to make this activity harder or easier so as to be right at the "cutting edge" for the child. How can we summarize ways of making this activity harder or easier?

Options for making it easier:

Use two pictures.

Use simple words.

Make the sounds that you are contrasting very different from one another.

Emphasize greatly the sounds you are asking about when you pronounce the words.

Ask about the beginning sounds rather than ending or middle sounds.

Stick with the same beginning sound for several questions in a row.

If all else fails, tell the child the answer to the question before asking it. For example, "Buh-icycle starts with BUH, and LLL-ake starts with LLLUH. Which one starts with BUH?"

Options for making it harder:

Don't use pictures.

Use less familiar words.

Make the sounds you are contrasting fairly similar to one another.

Pronounce the words normally rather than emphasizing any sounds in them.

Ask about the ending or middle sounds in the words.

Skip around from sound to sound rather than staying on the same sound for several questions in a row.

The Which-Sound Game

In the which-sound game, the child is given a word, and picks the correct beginning (or middle, or ending) sound. You can do it looking at a picture. You say the word and give the child two choices as to which sound the word starts with. For example, you say "Here's ant. Does ant start with ă or does it start with tuh?"

Here are ways to make this exercise easier:

Pick sounds that are much different, like short a and t.

Emphasize the beginning sound or even split it off from the rest of the word when saying the word.

Ways to make it harder:

Pick sounds that are similar, like short a and short e and short i.

Don't emphasize the beginning sound.

Ask for the ending or middle sound instead of the beginning sound.

Let the child name the sound without being given two choices.

The Sounding and Blending Exercise

This is a procedure for practicing decoding words. The child first learns to say the most common sound of each of the 26 letters. Then the child practices sounding and blending three letter words, all of which end with the letters *a* and *t*. Then the child practices with *ab* words, and *ag* words. The lists gradually progress. Longer words and more sounds are gradually introduced, and the child practices with lists of words that give concentrated rehearsal in a certain sound.

When starting a new list, it's helpful for the tutor to sound and blend each word and let the student sound and blend it immediately afterwards. By doing this when the lists are difficult, you can get close to errorless performance by the student. This makes the student's task much more pleasant.

You explain to the child that this activity isn't meant to be great fun; you do it for the payoff it brings. You explain that the purpose of reading is to get meaning from words, not just to call them out. But once you've learned to decode, then the pleasure that you get from reading for meaning can be fully felt. By doing the work now, you get access to all the things that are encoded in written words for the rest of your life. So as you do the exercise, you take pleasure in knowing that you have self-discipline. Doing this exercise for many hours can help many children avoid huge amounts of frustration in their later education, by becoming facile at the art of decoding.

And the exercise can even be fun, especially for children who need lots of practice to crack the code, and for children working with tutors who celebrate successes with true joy.

More Complete Instructions for the Parent

This chapter is not a complete manual for tutoring a child. There are many more curricular materials available, for the parent who wants to get into the child's education in a big way.

The reading instruction activities I've described here are discussed in much greater detail in my book entitled *Manual for Tutors and Teachers of Reading.* A wonderful set of resources for tutors of grade school children is three books by Peggy Kaye: Games for Reading, Games for Math, and Games for Learning. The first two are published by Pantheon Books, a division of Random House. Games for Learning was published by Noonday Press, a Division of Farrar, Straus and Giroux. Another source of great ideas for learning activities is *What Do I Do Monday?* by John Holt.

Chapter 30: Attention Problems: Learning-Based Methods

Chapter Overview:

When we say a child has attention deficit hyperactivity disorder, we by definition imply that he needs improvement in certain skills: sustaining attention to tasks, delaying gratification, getting relaxed and calm at will, thinking before acting, and making decisions carefully. Any child who receives drug treatment for this problem should have a systematic plan for working daily at these skills, as soon as parent and child are capable of instituting it.

When we think about things children do and situations they're in, we should consider how stimulating those environments are. The more skilled a child is in sustaining attention, the more that child can enjoy a less stimulating situation. To develop this skill, the child should have enough practice with less stimulating situations that his skills are challenged. It could be that when our culture furnishes so much stimulation from television, video games, and other electronic miracles, we help produce a generation on the average less skilled in attending to low stimulus tasks. Progress in electronic information-handlers hasn't changed the fact that most of the useful work of the world involves low stimulus tasks.

Here's a concentration exercise useful in learning to sustain attention. Think of a question. For a long time allow to come into your mind many possible answers. After each answer, return to the central question, rather than going from one idea to the next without "returning to the center." This exercise is also basic if you want to write nonfiction, or just to think in an organized way.

Some children probably have their hyperactivity reduced by getting very large doses of regular exercise. It isn't easy to see this, because many children only get more aroused by a small dose of exercise. It would seem logical to teach hyperactive children relaxation. Most children with very high activity levels find relaxation training unpleasant unless they have gotten large amounts of exercise beforehand. The "dance and freeze" activity is a good way for young children to practice regulating their degree of arousal: you dance wildly, and you freeze when the music stops.

If you want a child not to be impulsive, help him get large doses of practice in deciding what to do in made-up situations. The *what's best to do* exercise and the *brainstorming game* represent opportunities for this activity. In addition, you can teach your children to review the choices they have made during the day. You and they can rejoice about their good choices, and rehearse them. You can use bad choices as grist for the mill: the child describes the situation, decides on a more desirable response mill: the child describes the situation, decides on a more desirable response pattern, and practices that new pattern.

Most children with ADHD, like other human beings, need to improve in lots of psychological skills. These children need what other people need: work on the skills of highest priority for them at the time.

****

Attention deficit hyperactivity disorder is a very frequently assigned diagnosis. It is diagnosed not by a test, but by observing what the child does in real life. It's defined by its symptoms: a short attention span, a high activity level, and impulsive behavior. How short does the attention span have to be, how active does the child have to be, and what separates impulsiveness from ordinary human fallibility? These are all judgment calls, based on somehow getting an intuitive feeling for what "average" children are like, and comparing any given child to the average child. There's evidence that genetics influence these symptoms. And there's evidence that drugs such as methylphenidate (Ritalin) and amphetamine (Dexedrine, Adderall) reduce the symptoms, sometimes a little, sometimes quite dramatically. I'll talk about drug therapy in the next chapter. But in this chapter I want to stick to the main orientation of this book, and speak about psychological skill approaches to ADHD symptoms.

The best approach to short attention spans, hyperactivity, and impulsive behavior is not simply to give medication by itself. Some learning-based treatment, either instead of or in addition to drug therapy, should be part of the treatment.

And for every child who is given an official diagnosis of ADHD, there are many others who do not warrant the diagnosis, but who could also stand to gain by improving in the psychological skills that are the opposite of ADHD. In fact, few human beings of any age could not stand to benefit from improving in the skills that will be mentioned in this chapter.

People Are Unique

People tend to put other people into pigeonhole categories, and then act as if all people in a category are the same. Having known many children who have the diagnosis of ADHD, I can tell you for certain that they are very different from one another. Their profiles of skill deficiencies and skill sufficiencies are quite varied. Some don't know how to initiate social conversation with other people, but butt in very obtrusively; others are very successful at social initiations. Some are deficient in taking pleasure from kind acts, and are quite selfish; others are very kind and giving. Some tend to down themselves for mistakes and ignore their own successes; others celebrate successes well and regret mistakes appropriately; still others seem oblivious to the whole notion of success and failure. Some are quite deficient in conflict-resolution, and others are surprisingly masterful at this. Many have major difficulties in organizing their papers and other possessions, and in organizing their use of time; a few are about as well organized as most other children their age. And so on. One of the major reasons for a psychological skill axis is to help in thinking about what skills each particular person can most benefit from learning. You make such judgments from the data of the life situations and their handlings, and not from one label that the person has been given.

What ADHD children as a group tend to have in common, however, are the skill deficiencies that are pretty much required by definition for the diagnosis to be given. What are those?

Psychological Skills That Are the Antidotes to ADHD

What skills are the opposite of a short attention span? Foremost are sustaining attention to tasks, concentrating, persisting, and self-discipline. Fortitude is closely related also, since people tend to drop tasks when they become frustrating.

What skills are the opposite of hyperactivity? Foremost are regulating your own degree of arousal, getting relaxed and calm at will, and self-discipline.

What skills are the opposite of impulsive behavior? High on the list are thinking before acting and careful decision-making.

ADHD characteristics tend to last for many years. Sometimes drug treatment is given for many years. Accordingly, it would seem that in the ideal treatment for ADHD, children would work on the above-mentioned skills systematically, daily, over a course of years. Yet very few do.

There are few biological dispositions that cannot be overridden at least to some degree by strong enough motivation and logging in enough hours of systematic work. Most families and most children with ADHD do not know how to work at and practice the skills that will allow them to undo their symptoms without medication. Let's review how such work can take place. (I use the word "review" because most of the basic principles I'll discuss have already been mentioned elsewhere in this book.)

Let's think first about the skills of sustaining attention to tasks.

Characterizing Environments by their Attention-Grabbing Quality

Many children who have big ADHD problems and who take medication are able, even when not on medication, to attend well to video games. Why? Because there is rich and colorful and rapidly changing visual stimulation; because the audio input is either music or vocal utterances of high excitement: rapid, high pitched, and of wide range; the imaginary stakes are high, involving often life and death, and for that reason emotion tends to be evoked; there are very frequent opportunities for the child to be an active responder in a very concrete way; there is very clear-cut and instantaneous feedback to the child's responses; the feedback is about very important (imaginary) consequences, again usually life and death; and there is usually somewhere upwards of 80% successes on all the maneuvers that the child tries; the demands upon the child's memory and complex information-processing functions are low.

At this point I'm not yet assigning a positive or negative value judgment to attention-grabbing environments; I'm trying to define a concept that will be useful to us.

Let's rate other environments on the same variables that I just listed. We can form a summary score of the "attention-grabbing quality" of the environment. Most action and adventure movies would rate very high, although it would get low marks for the "child as active responder" variable. On the other hand, a book on a desk, no pictures in the book, but words and symbols describing how to do mathematical procedures, would rate as very low on the attention-grabbing scale. Taking a walk along a suburban sidewalk and having a conversation with a parent would probably rate fairly low. Playing an interscholastic basketball game would rate very high, especially if there are cheerleaders, it's an important game, you are very skilled at the sport, and the score is close. Listening to a lecture by an extremely brilliant professor would probably rate fairly low, especially if there were no slides or videos. Reading what you are reading now (which is putting great demands upon your memory and complex information-processing ability) rates low, but not as low as reading the writings of Kant. Listening to an audiotape of "Barney" songs rates higher for most young children than listening to a tape of Debussy, but watching a videotape of Barney songs rates even higher. The Saturday morning cartoons rate very high, and the average religious service rates very low. Most movies rate very high, and most textbooks rate very low. Attending a rock concert would rate very high, and practicing piano scales would rate very low. Working in most jobs would rate fairly low. Doing housework would rate low. Going to gambling casinos would rate high. Thinking about how to better the world would rate low; watching a wrestling match would rate high.

Now let's start making some propositions about this concept. First: the higher one's skills of sustaining attention to tasks, the more one is able to be content and satisfied in, and even prefer, a situation that rates low in attention-grabbing quality. Second: in making progress in this skill, one can move along a hierarchy, where the first steps are attending to highly attention-grabbing situations, and the more advanced steps are attending to situations that are low on the scale. Third: in order to progress in this skill, one must work at attending to materials low enough in attention-grabbingness that one's skills are challenged. Fourth: there are more attention-grabbing stimuli available to today's generation of children (because of electronic and video technology) than there were to any previous generation. Fifth: it could be that the profuse and ready availability of highly attention-grabbing stimuli is creating, or has created, a generation that is on the average less able to attend to low attention-grabbing stimuli. (Many teachers will endorse this supposition.) Sixth: in doing the work that is really useful for the world, including the education of other human beings, scientific research, production and delivery of food and other necessities, creating organized systems for people to work together, and so forth, there is a great need for the ability to enjoy sustained attention to low attention-grabbing stimuli.

A Concentration Exercise

When I was a boy, I read a very helpful book on Yoga that contained a concentration exercise. This exercise is quite useful to children with priorities in the skill of sustaining attention.

You start with an idea, a concept, a question, or anything else that can trigger other thoughts. You draw a circle with this inside it, and lots of arrows going outward from the circle. Now, for each of the arrows, you think of an idea that the concept triggers. You keep going until nothing immediately come to mind. Then you keep searching for ideas, thinking of more about this central question, resisting the urge to give up and go on to something else. You also resist the urge to go off on a tangent from one idea to the next without returning to the concept in the center of the circle. Thus we can refer to this as the "returning to the center" exercise. Returning to the center is a mental maneuver that most people with ADHD are not skilled at.

Although the spatial image of returning to the center is of a circle with lines emanating outward from it, an equally good way to do the exercise is to put the central concept at the top of the page, and list the offshoots of it on successive lines down the rest of the page. In other words, you simply make a list.

In the yoga book, there was an example for concentration on the concept of "cow." The question is defined as, "What is anything you can say about a cow?" The thinker might start with a list something like this:

Gives milk
Usually lives on farms
Eats grass and clover
Makes mooing sound
Hide can be brown, black, or reddish
Hide sometimes used to make leather

If you do this exercise, you will perceive the difference between the way you think while doing it, and the more tangential course that our thoughts often take. This course may be represented as follows:

Cow — Gives milk — A milk shake would taste good — I saw Mary Jones last time I got a milk shake — Mary Jones's brother plays the guitar — I saw somebody break their guitar on stage —They're smashing up that vacant house on the corner...

Letting the thoughts drift from one to another without any "return to the center" has many useful purposes, and is not to be discouraged; the point is that the style of thought with "return to the center" is also useful and should be in the repertoire. Let's give another example of it.

Suppose the question is, "How can violence be reduced?" You can do the same concentration exercise, sitting and thinking about the question, writing down one possible answer after another, but always returning to the main question after every possible answer. The list someone would make might look like this:

How can violence be reduced?

Teach joint decision-making skills

Reduce availability of guns

Reduce violent models in the media

Form a world court or world government

Educate people better, for useful work

Teach parenting

Improve dispute-resolution systems in community

Reduce the demand for illegal drugs

Remove children from violently abusive parents quicker

Teach people about peace heroes and heroes of kindness

Provide fictional models of peace and kindness

Help teachers promote kindness in classrooms

Remove violent criminals from rest of society

Put more law enforcement officers into action

Promote a universal second language for reducing misunderstandings between nations

*****

Returning to the central question and continuing to search for items to add to the list is the essence of the yoga exercise.

If you make the exercise a little more complex, you can after doing this arrange the ideas in some rational order; you can generate a list of ideas underneath each of the ideas previously generated, and more ideas underneath them, as far as is desired to go. This then comes to resemble writing an outline for an article or book.

Teaching children to organize their own thinking and writing is a useful antidote to skill deficiency in concentration.

The brainstorming game, described in a chapter on problem-solving, is another activity where this concentration exercise may be carried out. You might impose a certain minimum time for thinking about each decision situation, and gradual increase that time as the learner grows in self-discipline. Learning to tolerate and keep searching during the time when no more ideas come easily is at the essence of learning concentration skills.

Many children have the problem that the mechanics of handwriting and figuring out how to spell words gets in the way of their using writing to organize their thoughts and to concentrate. If so, an adult can often help by being the child's secretary. The child dictates the list, the outline, or the essay.

Self-Monitoring Exercises

If a child is not aware of how well he is doing, it is difficult for him to celebrate success or make plans to improve. A useful exercise is to make a simple rating scale, explain it to the child, explain that accuracy in observing himself is the first goal, and not perfection; do together a certain limited period of an activity—for example a tutoring session; then to rate, and have the child rate, how he has done in the skills in question. Then the adult and the child compare their ratings, and talk about the specific examples of behavior that contributed to the ratings. If the child gains from this the ability accurately to assess his own behavior, an important skill has been gained. Here's an example of the simple rating scale:

0=Very bad
2=Bad
4=So-So
6=OK
8=Good
10=Very Good

_____1. How well did I keep on task?
_____2. How well did I act cooperatively?

Using Exercise as an Anti-Hyperactivity Agent

I once lived in an apartment in Chicago above a couple of friends who had a Labrador Retriever dog who had hyperactivity problems. The dog would race back and forth across the floor, jump up and down on people, and in general exhibit motor restlessness very similar to that of some hyperactive children. I began to take this dog with me on long runs and bicycle rides through the park. When we returned from a several mile journey, I noticed that the dog's behavior had been transformed. She was now capable of acting like a "normal" dog.

For certain restless children, it appears that a small dose of exercise only arouses them more. And a degree of exhaustion capable of reducing the restlessness produces sleep or irritability, not relaxation. However, I suspect that the children who respond in this way make up a small subset of all children. For most of them, a very large dose of exercise several times a day seems to be what the body was built for, and this schedule is most compatible with being able to sit and work during other parts of the day.

One of the worst aspects of some schools is the ignoring of children's needs to move. I have spent many hours observing in classrooms, sitting while the children are sitting. I have emerged from many of them after two or three hours of sustained sitting with minimal breaks, and have felt the urge to do calisthenics or sprint through the parking lot, from sheer pent-up physical energy.

Review of Relaxation Strategies

It would seem that relaxation skills would be the logical opposite of hyperactivity, and children with ADHD would benefit greatly from learning such skills.

It also would come as no surprise to find that many ADHD children would find the low attention-grabbing nature of traditional relaxation training even more unpleasant than schoolwork.

I think that because being still and relaxing is downright unpleasant for many ADHD children, muscle-relaxation or imagery techniques for relaxation are best done after the child has gotten a good bit of vigorous exercise, or else is lying in bed going to sleep.

An alternative activity for teaching relaxation skills is the "dance and freeze" activity, especially the version where the participants alternately dance wildly when the music is on, and then flop as if lifeless on the floor when the music is turned off. This helps the child with difficulties in regulating the degree of arousal gradually gain the ability to "rev down" after "revving himself up."

Biofeedback as an Aid to Relaxation

Children enjoy the gadgetry of biofeedback. Temperature biofeedback seems about as good as any in monitoring the general state of relaxation of the body, and has the advantage that finger skin temperature can be monitored extremely inexpensively. You simply tape a thermometer probe onto the finger tip; fairly inexpensive thermometers give accurate enough readings. It is worth a try to "turn on" the child to attempting to learn to control his skin temperature through relaxation.

It can be a fun game for a child to try to make skin temperature go down, by trying to imagine scary or performance-anxiety eliciting situations, and then trying to make the temperature go back up again by imagining safe, secure, pleasant images and relaxing the muscles. Doing this exercise requires some patience on the part of the child, however, because skin temperature does not respond instantaneously to changes in thoughts — it takes half a minute or so.

Decisions About Hypothetical Situations as an Antidote to Impulsiveness

The opposite of impulsiveness is to think before acting. This entails imagining several options, imagining how things may come out with each of the options, and choosing accordingly, as extensively detailed in the chapters on problem-solving. The essence of such reflectiveness is to make a decision about a situation in the mind before carrying it out in behavior. To get a child to practice this skill, you figure out some way of making it fun for the child to think about hypothetical situations, and promote the child's thinking about very large numbers of hypothetical situations over time.

The "What's Best To Do" exercise is simply practice in deciding what's the best thing to do in hypothetical situations. You look at a written list of situations, and you enlarge the list based on life experience. The analysis of hypothetical situations can be an activity that family members can do as a group, discussing what choice points presented themselves and contributing ideas on options and predicted outcomes.

The Review of the Day's Choice Points With Celebration Or Redecision-Rehearsal-Celebration

The following procedure is recommended for anyone who wishes for personal growth. You review your own choice points of the previous day. You first think about the smart or good choices you made, the imitation-worthy actions you took. You rehearse them by running them through your imagination, and you celebrate them by saying "Hooray," or "Good for me." You think about the unwise choices you made, the things you regret doing or thinking or feeling, and you decide (or redecide, since you already decided once) upon the best alternative pattern you can come up with. Then you rehearse that pattern in your mind, imagining yourself doing it, and imagining yourself celebrating when you have done it. Then you celebrate having done the work of accomplishing such practice.

In this way almost everything you do can become either a focus of celebration or a focus of redecision and rehearsal and celebration.

Writing down the choices to celebrate or the imagined new and more desirable patterns will add to the usefulness of this exercise. Many children can greatly benefit from an adult's functioning in the role of secretary, transcribing the child's statements and preserving them on paper or computer disk to review later.

Children with ADHD can use growth in psychological skills just as can everyone else, and even more because their handicap interferes with the development of some very important ones. Therefore whereas many people can do perfectly fine without these all-purpose self-improvement techniques, ADHD children should start as early as possible in developing customs of personal growth.

Cross-Reference to Other Skills Often Deficient in ADHD Children

Attending to Verbally Encoded Information. One way to think about "attention deficit hyperactivity disorder" is that children getting this label are not able to pay attention to "verbally encoded information" for a very long time. By verbally encoded information I mean conversation, written material, math problems—words and symbols. One would guess that having lots of practice in paying attention to verbally encoded information, especially the sort of practice that is fun and rewarding for the child, the child would gradually get better at these skills. This theory would predict that the more time the child spent listening to stories read or told, having a conversation, or engaging in imaginative dramatic play, the more the child would tend to learn to pay attention to verbal information longer. This would be especially true if the child got practice at sticking to these activities for longer and longer periods of time. This is one of the reasons why I have emphasized chatting with the child, reading stories to the child, and doing dramatic play with the child for longer and longer periods of time.

Kindness and cooperation. Another set of skills that children with attention problems often need to work on are those involving cooperation, kindness to others, consideration of others' needs. Teaching these skills has been the subject of a large part of this book.

Compliance with adults' requests. Much of this book has dealt with increasing this skill; my emphasis has been upon the elimination of unnecessary commands and requests, improvement of the interpersonal environment, and enforcement of 100% of commands from an early age with physical guidance.

Using words to think about the world. A central skill antidote to impulsivity is using self-talk when deciding what to do. This skill is modeled for young children in the modeling stories and modeling plays, whenever a character reveals her thoughts. You practice this skill whenever you do a "fantasy rehearsal out loud."

Fortitude. This skill usually requires a very great amount of work for children with ADHD problems. It's alluded to many times in this book. See especially the chapter on fortitude and the chapter on responding to positive examples (regarding ways of responding to positive examples of fortitude).

Individual and joint decisions. Careful decision making and rational problem solving require a great deal of patience and self-control, which are often in short supply in children gaining the label of ADHD. The chapters on problem-solving will be useful.

Ethical decision skills. The development of an ethical and moral value system is difficult enough for any child; for those with a tendency away from careful, patient, calm, painstaking thought and reflection, this is even harder. See the chapter on ethics for further ideas on this.

Organization. Many of the criteria for ADHD have to do with keeping one's time and tasks organized. Check the chapters on these skills for these.

Peer relationship skills are the hardest to come by with some children with the ADHD label. Check the chapter on peer relationship skills, plus the chapter on conversing with children: the same skills that adults use in conversing with children will be of great help to children in getting along with their peers.

If I were to expand this list to include every skill I have ever deemed worth working on in an ADHD child, I would have to include the entire skills axis (even courage skills, despite that fact that some ADHD children have too little fear, and very poor carefulness skills). The conclusion emerges that what is best for a child with an ADHD label is periodic evaluation of the strength of the full range of psychological skills, and concentrated work in those which are most in need of work. And this, of course, is just what is needed by any other child.

With some children these learning-based methods may be sufficient, without medication, to overcome the problems of short attention span or hyperactivity or impulsivity. With others, the learning-based methods in conjunction with medication can accomplish the job where medication alone cannot.

In any case, I emphasize that for any child with skill deficiencies sufficient to consider medication, it is important to have in place systematic learning-based strategies to promote progress in those skills. I would go so far as to say that daily work on these skills, over a course of years, is what every child with an ADHD label should have. Is this because carefully controlled studies have shown that such work drastically improves the long-term outcome with ADHD children? It is more from a supreme confidence, gained from observing all sorts of human endeavors, that people get better at skills by practicing them, trying to get better at them, observing models of them, reading or hearing instructions about them, and using the rest of the methods of influence axis to improve them, than by ignoring them.

Chapter 31: Attention Problems: Pharmacological Methods

Chapter Overview:

Although this book has emphasized learning-based approaches, some children with ADHD symptoms are helped by medication, notably methylphenidate and amphetamine. These medications have several short term side effects that are usually not very troublesome. The most worrisome possibility to me is the long term effect these drugs may have on the brain. No harmful long-term effects have been conclusively proved. But some animal research suggests that the question of long term effects should be raised. Also, since cocaine shares some pharmacologic properties with methylphenidate and amphetamine, the fact that long-term cocaine users seem to get more of certain psychiatric problems raises hypotheses that the stimulants may not be totally benign. On the other hand, for some children the benefits of these drugs can be truly life-changing. In order to tell for sure how much the drugs help, I sometimes do controlled trials of medication versus placebo, with blind ratings by parents or teachers, with statistical tests done to see how significant the difference is between active drug and placebo. Some children respond to amphetamine who don't respond to methylphenidate, and vice versa, and some children have side effects with one drug, and not another. A different class of drugs, the tricyclic antidepressants, are effective for ADHD. These incur a risk of effects on heart conduction which in rare cases apparently have been deadly. Clonidine, originally used in adults for high blood pressure, tends to reduce emotional outbursts and is often especially helpful during the times of rebound from effects of stimulants. Bupropion was originally marketed for depression, but has some efficacy as a drug for ADHD.

****

Throughout this book I have spoken of learning-based techniques for promoting psychological growth. However I have seen some children drastically affected for the better by receiving medication for attention deficit hyperactivity disorder, as defined by short attention span, high activity level, and impulsiveness.

It's true that almost all children have these problems to some degree. But some children have them worse than others. The children that have these problems enough to where it makes their lives a good bit less happy and successful are the ones we think about treating with medication.

The learning-based strategies I've mentioned so far just don't work quickly enough with many children. Many children seem to get help from medication that they don't seem to get by any other means. There isn't a commonly used laboratory test that detects ADHD, although some recent research studies have begun to detect differences in brain functioning that may account for these symptoms. The more severe are the child's problems with paying attention, sitting still, and thinking before acting, the more likely medication is to help. Some children are helped tremendously by medication. Some who were almost impossible to live with and deal with before medication become pleasant to be around.

Medical Illness As A Cause of ADHD Symptoms

Can medical illness be responsible for attention deficit-hyperactivity problems? It can, but seldom is ADHD cured by treating a medical illness. Hyperthyroidism, with overproduction of thyroid hormone (which regulates the speed of the body's processes), can be confused with hyperactivity. Lead poisoning of the child, for example through the child's eating dust from leaded paint, can produce the ADHD symptoms. There is evidence that other brain insults can result in ADHD symptoms: maternal use of alcohol or tobacco during pregnancy, trauma to the brain, and possibly exposure to pesticides and herbicides. Hyperthyroidism is more likely with a family history of thyroid problems, diarrhea, intolerance of heat, changes in hair texture, tremor and changes in the appearance of the eyes. Lead toxicity is primarily signaled by something in the environment that could be a source of lead: lead paint in the house, lead pipes, eating meat killed with lead shot, ingesting lots of dirt.

Why "Stimulant" Medication?

The first line medication for people with ADHD is often called "stimulant" medication. People often ask, why would someone want to give stimulant medicine to someone who is already too active? The medicines are called "stimulant" because they seem to reduce the need or ability to sleep and increase alertness. The effects include lengthening of the attention span and lowered activity level. Just as with adults, the child's capacity to work at things—particularly boring tasks— for a longer period of time is increased.

The most commonly used "stimulants" are methylphenidate, (Ritalin, Metadate, Concerta), and amphetamine (Dexedrine, Adderall). These are given much more frequently given than another stimulant, pemoline. Liver toxicity has been reported with pemoline and it's necessary to monitor liver functioning with blood tests periodically.

Methylphenidate and amphetamine, unlike several other psychiatric medications, show their positive effects almost immediately—with a half hour after the medication is given—and the effects seem to go away when the medication is eliminated from the body. If the benefits are to linger, one has to keep taking the medicines. ADHD tends to be a long term problem. Some people never grow out of it. Some people therefore take stimulant medication for years and years.

The half life of methylphenidate is around two and one-half hours; the effective duration for most people is about four or five hours. Various preparations (methylphenidate sustained release, Metadate CD, Concerta) prolong the release of methylphenidate from the capsule or tablet into the digestive tract, so as to make one dose last in the region of seven, ten, or twelve hours depending on the preparation. These preparations make dosing of methylphenidate more flexible. The half life of amphetamine is longer, closer to 10 hours. There are sustained release preparations of Dexedrine and Adderall that make the duration of action of amphetamines still longer.

Theoretically, the short half life of methylphenidate should be an advantage with respect to long term side effects: the person taking it gets to spend more sleeping hours with very little medication on board, with the brain having more time to restore the status prior to the taking of the medication. Whether this is definitively the case is a question for future research.

Side Effects of Methylphenidate and Amphetamine

Suppose that medical causes of hyperactivity are unlikely and learning-based methods of dealing with it have not worked sufficiently. Suppose that a parent is considering a trial of medication. Many parents are justifiably worried that medication is being used too much, on too many children, and that it might hurt their child more than it helps. It's reasonable to avoid giving any sort of medication unless the benefits outweigh the risks. For some children, the benefits seem to far outweigh the risks. For others, the opposite is true. The task of the doctor or therapist, with a lot of help from the parents and teachers, is to make an individualized determination for any given child about whether the medicine helps more than it hurts.

Let's talk about the risks of the medication. Any of the stimulants we named earlier have several side effects. As I already mentioned, when they are working the child sometimes has less appetite and doesn't go to sleep as readily. However, these aren't usually big problems.

Perhaps because it suppresses appetite, some studies have suggested that methylphenidate makes children grow less than they would otherwise. However, the studies that have accumulated on this topic have concluded that the effect on the child's eventual height that the medication has is on the average negligible, and not worth worrying about. Nevertheless, it is common practice when a child is put on medicine to monitor the child's height and weight to make sure that the child continues to grow as he or she should.

A problem called Tourette's Disorder is thought to be a hereditary disease. In this disease, the person has twitches of various muscle groups, for example jerks of the mouth or muscles around the eye or shoulders or a leg. The person also has what is called "vocal tics": involuntary noises like grunts, spoken words, barks, and so forth. If a person has Tourette's Disorder, stimulant medication usually makes it worse, at least for the time that the person is on the medication. Thus the medication isn't usually given to people with Tourette's Disorder, or to people who have muscle twitches, or a definite family history of Tourette's disorder. More recent research, however, is suggesting that methylphenidate may even be helpful and useful for some children with Tourette's Disorder.

Methylphenidate and the other stimulant mediations can cause motor tics (that is, twitches of muscles) without vocal tics. Eye-blinking, mouth movements, and other facial movements are the most common tics that are side effects of this medication. Usually these tics go away fairly quickly when the medication is discontinued, but sometimes the tics can linger for quite some time. Sometimes a tic appears while a child on medication and does not go away after medication is withdrawn. In such cases it is likely that the child would have had the tic even without medication, since tics are not uncommon in children without medication. But it is impossible to say that no children have permanent tics caused by stimulant medications.

If a person is on any drugs of the class called "monoamine oxidase inhibitors" that person should not get stimulant medication, because the two sorts of drugs can interact to produce very high blood pressure and other bad effects. It is unlikely that a young child would be taking a monoamine oxidase inhibitor.

For reasons unknown to us, some children get stomach aches or head aches when they start on stimulant medication; many of them have these side effects "wear off" after they have been using the medication for a few weeks. If these side effects are very troublesome, however, it is usually a reason to lower the dose.

The stimulant medications sometimes can raise the child's blood pressure and pulse rate a little bit. Almost never is this a problem. Nevertheless, the child's blood pressure and pulse rate are commonly monitored to make sure that this is not a problem.

If the dose of stimulant medication is way too high for the child, the child can start to act "crazy": get delusional ideas, see or hear things that aren't there, and do strange things. This problem usually only comes when people are trying higher doses than the usual dose range. In the rare circumstance in which this problem occurs, it is not permanent, but goes away fairly quickly when medication is discontinued.

Another side effect that is troublesome in some children is weepiness, bad spirits, irritability, or depression. If the drug controls the child's behavior but makes him miserable, we have hardly gained anything. Fortunately this rarely happens.

As drugs go, the stimulants are probably fairly safe ones when taken as directed. There are not irreversible side effects as far as anyone knows. These drugs have been in very widespread use for several decades, so it appears unlikely that a gross side effect has been overlooked.

It is very difficult, however, to rule out the possibility of long-term behavioral side effects from stimulant medication. If someone is on stimulants for a number of years, and then discontinues the medicine, does that person experience more hyperactivity or short attention span or impulsivity than if she had never been on the drug in the first place? In other words, does "behavioral dependency" develop? Or does the long term use of these medicines cause an increased incidence of some problem like depression? Worries about these problems are triggered by the study of long term abusers of cocaine. Cocaine is in the stimulant class of drugs, like methylphenidate and amphetamine. Much further research with methylphenidate and amphetamine is necessary before we can say for sure that behavioral toxicity over the long term certainly does not occur. We do know that in animals given this sort of medication over long periods of time, there are changes in neuronal functioning that do not go away immediately when the medication is withdrawn. Methylphenidate should be safer than most other psychotropic medications with respect to long-term brain changes, because of its short half life. The brain gets to recover each night from whatever changes were induced in neurons during the time the drug was on board. Unfortunately, finding out the long-term behavioral effects of the medication on humans involves research designs difficult to carry out.

Benefits of Stimulant Medications

The benefits, when they occur, are a rapid improvement in the symptoms of attention deficit-hyperactivity: longer attention span, lowered activity level, and reduced impulsiveness. People who deal with the child can experience great relief when this occurs, and the child himself can feel much better about himself and the way relations with people and school tasks seem to go so much more successfully. When symptoms have been very severe, and the change is very positive, the medication can seem to be a godsend.

With such effects, you would expect that the medication would improve school grades. Some research is suggesting an improvement in grades from before these medications to after; other research fails to demonstrate a long-term effect. Again, long-term research is difficult to do.

Here's a very important question: does the medication help all hyperactive children? The answer is no. It has been estimated that 70 or 80 per cent of children who are tried on stimulant medication respond positively to it. That means that there is about one chance in four or five that any given child won't be a responder. For this reason we can't know for sure that a hyperactive child will benefit from medication. Since children usually stay on medication for many months or years if they are deemed to need it, it is very important to tell very accurately whether a child really needs the medication.

Controlled Trials of Medication

How can we tell whether a child really needs medication? Should we get several opinions from very distinguished experts? A motto I have come to adopt is that An ounce of carefully conducted clinical trials is worth a pound of expert opinions. In other words, the proof of whether a child needs medication is seeing very carefully what happens when we give it to him, as compared to what happens with placebo.

We are lucky when we give such trials, in that we don't have to wait a long time to see the drug's effects. Methylphenidate, for example, starts having its effect within half an hour, and its effect wears off after about five hours. So we can give the medication one day, and expect that the effect will be gone by the following day.

This means that we can take the days in a month and randomly divide them up, and give active drug on some days, and placebo on the other days. In order to give a placebo controlled trial, you take the active drug tablets and put them in capsules and give them on the "active drug" days. You take pieces of vitamin pills, and put them in capsules, and give them on "placebo" days.

Then, you keep track of how the child does each day during this trial. If the child does a lot better on the drug days than the placebo days, then we figure that the drug has worked. If the child does better on the placebo days than on the drug days, we figure that the drug has been harmful. If the child does no differently on drug days and placebo days, we figure that the drug has done no good. Only when the drug has been helpful do we continue to use it.

Keeping track of how the child does each day means filling out rating forms. In my way of doing things, usually either the child's teacher or the parent or both are given rating forms whereby they can use numbers to say how big a problem the child has had with various symptoms or behaviors that day. On those forms are written any side effects that are noticed or that the child complains of.

Why, in such a trial, do we have to use placebo tablets? Why not just give the drug on some days and not give it on other days? Placebo is something that is used in ALL drug experiments, because it is humanly impossible not to have some sort of expectation or opinion about the drug that is likely to affect how someone feels after taking it. For example, a child who starts the trial with the notion that taking the drug isn't a good idea might purposely act worse on the days when drug is given. Or a teacher who is philosophically opposed to the use of medication might without even realizing it give the child better ratings when the child is not on the drug. Or a parent who hopes very strongly that the drug will work unconsciously gives higher ratings on the drug days. Giving placebo, so that it is difficult or impossible to know for sure whether drug has been received, enables the trial to be more objective, more independent of people's hopes and fears. The need for placebo absolutely does not mean that the child or the rater is not trusted. It is that all human beings give more objective ratings under the blind conditions possible with placebo control.

Now, if the drug has its effect in half an hour or so, why do we need to give a trial for a month or so? Why not just give one dose and see from that whether the child gets better or worse? The reason we can't do this is that there are lots of other things that determine how good a day the child has, other than the medicine. Suppose the child was having a really bad day because a friend had upset him, or because his parents had had a fight. If we happened to try the medicine on that day, we might get a false impression that the medicine didn't help. On the other hand, if we tried the medicine on a day when the child got lots of positive attention and fewer demands were placed on his patience than usual, we might get the idea that the drug helped, when actually it was the circumstances that helped.

The way we deal with this problem is to randomly assign the drug to several days, and the placebo to several other days. If we do this over enough days, it becomes very likely that the bad and good circumstances will even out in the long run, so that the placebo days and the drug days get approximately equal exposure.

The same person fill out the forms each day, as much as possible. That way we don't have a great deal of variation from the fact that different people have different definitions of how severe a certain problem was.

When the trial is done, how do we tell whether the drug helped or not? We do a statistical test to see if the child did better or worse on drug or placebo, by an amount that is greater than we would expect by chance alone. If the results are too close to call for sure, we might decide to add some more days to the trial.

If it comes out that the drug didn't help, then that drug at that dose is not given any more. Sometimes it is reasonable to try a different drug, or the same drug at a different dose.

How do we work the logistics of the placebo-controlled blind trial? I write a prescription for the active drug, and the parent brings this bottle of pills to the office. Then the parent gives the pills to me. I then sort out the active drug and the placebo pills into envelopes, according to a random schedule. The parent will then be handed a stack of envelopes, with dates written on them. If the drug is to be given at school, there will be a similar stack of envelopes for the teacher to use. Each day, the parent or teacher opens the envelope with that day's date written on it, and gives the child the pills in that envelope at the appointed times.

The drug is absorbed just as well, apparently, whether it's given on a full or empty stomach. At a meal or after a meal seems to be a better time than very much before the meal, because you'd rather the drug's action not suppress appetite during the meal.

If the child cannot swallow pills, then you can crush the pill up in ice cream or pudding, or dissolve it in fruit juice, or roll it up in a stick of chewing gum, or put it in the blender with ice cream and milk to make a milk shake. If it is crushed or dissolved in food, it's important that no remnants of the pill be left uneaten. It's also important that you be honest with the child that you are giving him or her the pill in this way, so that the child's trust won't be reduced. And since the drug is unstable in water, it should not be stored in solution, but given as soon as it is dissolved in something.

Rebound Effects

When the effects of the drug wear off, sometimes the child seems to be more active than ever during that time, in a "rebound effect." If this is too big a problem, the dosage schedule or activity schedule can sometimes be changed around so that the drug is wearing off at a time when the demands on the child's patience are the least.

Dosages

For young children, a usual dose is five or ten milligrams of methylphenidate, given two or three times a day. For some older children and adolescents, 15 or 20 milligrams per dose may be the best. However, some older children and adolescents may do just fine on 10 milligrams per dose. If the child's major problems occur in a school setting, taking the drug at breakfast and lunchtime is usually the best schedule. If the child's problems occur both at home and at school, a third afternoon dose, around four o'clock or so, will allow the positive effects of the drug to persist into the evening's activities with the family.

With the various sustained release preparations of methylphenidate on the market, dosing can be arranged more flexibly. For each child it is necessary to experiment to find the ideal dose and the duration of action of any given preparation.

Other Drugs

Some children respond better to amphetamine than to methylphenidate, and vice versa; for this reason researchers have concluded that children who don't respond to one should be tried on the other. I have seen some children who had tics with methylphenidate and not with amphetamine.

In recent years clonidine and guanfacine, both of which were originally marketed for high blood pressure, have proved useful for certain children with ADHD. These are not stimulant drugs; they act on the alpha adrenergic system. They may have their beneficial effects on ADHD children by lowering the arousal and the "fight or flight" reaction mediated by adrenalin-like chemicals in the body. Sometimes children who have very emotional outbursts are helped by taking guanfacine or clonidine in addition to methylphenidate or amphetamine. These drugs also have opposite side effects of methylphenidate on appetite (they seems to stimulate it) and on sleep (they – particularly clonidine-- make you sleepy, if given in a large enough dose). There have been a very few reports of heart problems, with death, in children who have taken the combination of clonidine and methylphenidate. Although it appears very unlikely that the medications caused the fatality in most of these cases, these reports have understandably dampened many clinicians' enthusiasm for the combination. In addition, as is probably true with all or most psychoactive drugs, tolerance to clonidine and guanfacine develops over time so that you sometimes have "the devil to pay" when you want to discontinue them.

The tricyclic antidepressants, among them desipramine, imipramine, and nortriptyline, are still another class of medication that has also been useful for ADHD symptoms in children. Unfortunately, there have been a few cases of sudden death in children on desipramine; this makes us nervous about using this medication and others in its class in the fairly hefty doses usually needed to have an effect on ADHD symptoms.

The serotonin reuptake inhibiting drugs such as fluoxetine (Prozac), and sertaline (Zoloft) do not seem as effective for ADHD as the stimulants. Withdrawal symptoms with the serotonin reuptake inhibitors can be quite problematic. Bupropion (Wellbutrin), a drug that like the stimulants is thought to act primarily on norepinephrine and dopamine, seems to have positive effects on ADHD with some children. In one controlled study bupropion was found to be as effective as methylphenidate on most measures. The stimulants are still considered the first line drugs for attention deficit disorders, however.

Chapter 32: Skills for Peer Relations

Chapter Overview:

There's hardly a psychological skill on our list that won't help a child make and keep friends. In this chapter we'll focus on some of these skills, and some of the subskills of social initiations and social conversation. We'll also look at some activities to practice these skills. Children should learn to smile appropriately, do greeting rituals, and use eye contact comfortably. They need to learn how to decide what to find out about other people and tell about oneself so as to be not too intimate and personal, not too guarded and bland, but in the "just right" range. Other important skills of social conversation include using facilitations, reflections, follow-up questions, and telling about your own experience, and keeping a reasonable balance between talking and listening. Learning when to ask another person to shift attention to you is another important social conversation skill. Helping and complimenting, having fun activities in the repertoire, winning and losing well, not cheating, tolerating unfairness, handling teasing, and using tactfulness are important peer relationship skills. Children will benefit from learning to offer a guest a choice of activities, avoid bossiness, help others with academic work, have calm responses to frustration, overcome shyness, congratulate themselves for kind acts, and be aware of other people's feelings. For each of these skills there is at least one type of exercise or activity that an adult and child can use to practice it. Children should be aware that there are other determinants of popularity, such as sports prowess, physical attractiveness, and adhering to arbitrary marks of a certain subculture, but the more enduring skills will be more lasting ways to attain good relationships. A child can learn about peer relations by observing other people and herself. I provide a questionnaire in this chapter that a child can use to self-monitor the 24 social habits just mentioned.
****

Situational and Learning-based Strategies for Peer Relations

Being rejected by peers is extremely unpleasant for a child, as it is for adults. Children who are rejected and stay rejected tend to have lingering problems years later. A child who is not as popular as he or she wishes may benefit from some of the ideas in this chapter on friend-making and friend-keeping.

Before launching into learning-based strategies, however, we should remind ourselves of a point made at the beginning of this book. Sometimes the first priority is not to give a child new learning, but to improve the situation he is in. Sometimes no amount of skill learning will be sufficient to protect a child from victimization by peers. Sometimes school-wide interventions are needed to reduce the amount of bullying that students experience there. Sometimes the bullying and harrassment a child receives at school is so vicious that the parent should simply remove the child from the environment. All children need to be protected from physical and verbal abuse. Only in such an environment will the learning-based strategies in this chapter have a good chance of working.

Twenty-four Tips for Peer Relations

The learning-based strategies for dealing with peer relations are the same that I have recommended throughout this book: look at what skills need to be fostered with highest priority, and foster them with every method of influence that can be mustered.

The art of making and keeping friends is extremely complex, and it requires, or at least is assisted by, almost every psychological skill on the skills axis. It is particularly helped by social initiations, social conversation, empathic listening, conflict resolution, toleration of a wide range of others' behavior, humor, gleefulness, and pleasure from one's own kindness.

The following is a list of "tips" on how to make and keep friends, and a list of ways that a caring and skilled person can help someone else practice the skills that are entailed in enacting these tips. In my experience the caring and skilled adult is often a therapist; some parents may be also able to help their children by doing some of the following exercises with them.

1. Smile. Simply smiling at someone is an act of kindness that tends to make people feel good. Smiling when you first see someone lets the person know you are glad to see them. Smiling at them when they do or say anything that justifies smiling lets them know you like them. People like being around someone who looks happy and friendly. Often they reject people who they think have sent rejecting messages to them.

Exercise. Do a "smile experiment." Walk around in some place where there are people you know. Look at every person whose path meets yours, and give them the friendliest smile you can, and maybe say hi. Notice the results. One's own family is a good place to do this experiment.

2. Use greeting rituals. Another way to be kind to people and initiate social contact and to let them know you are glad to see them is by greeting rituals. A greeting ritual well carried out consists of saying hi to a person in an enthusiastic, using the person's names, and asking them how they're doing or what's happening or something that will let them have a chance to talk if they want.

Exercise. Role play seeing a friend, and exchanging a four-stroke greeting ritual. This means that there are a total of at least four greeting statements exchanged. Then, adult and child practice, for a whole week, in the following way. Each time the adult and child see each other, they practice at least a 4-stroke greeting ritual. The following is an example.

Hi, ______! How are you today.

Hi, ______! Good. It's good to see you. How have you been?

Been doing all right. What have you been up to?

Mainly homework and hockey practice have been taking up my time. How about you?

3. Use eye contact. When people are talking to you, look them in the eye fairly much of the time, but not all the time.

Exercise. Practice having a staring session. Chat with someone, while looking them right in the eyes the whole time. Then practice again, and look them in the eyes most of the time but not all the time. Have the other person do the same thing. Figure out what feels the most comfortable to you.

4. Know things to talk about and find out about. What do people find out about each other as they get to know each other? I find useful the mnemonic PAPER, to help remember these things: Places, Activities, People, Events, and Reactions to any of the above. To be more concrete:

Places: Where do you live? Where did you live before you came here? Where do you go to school? What place do you like the best? What classroom are you in?

Activities: What do you like to do? What's your favorite game? What's your favorite sport? Do you like to play music or sing? Do you like to write? Do you like to read? What books have you read lately? Have you taken a vacation lately? What did you do? What's your favorite food to eat?

People: Do you have brothers and sisters? Who else is in your family? What are they like? Who are your best friends? Who else is most important to you?

Events: What's been happening in your life lately? What's on your mind the most lately? Has anything happened lately that made you feel sad or happy or scared or surprised? Has anything really interesting happened lately?

Reactions: What was that like for you, when that happened? How did you feel about that? How is it for you, having a little sister? How do you like it, playing soccer? That event you mentioned, were you expecting it to happen? Did it surprise you when it happened?

In a "getting to know you" conversation, people tend to ask each other questions to find out these things; they also spontaneously tell these things about themselves. They seek to have a balance between finding out about the other person and telling about themselves.

Another related skill in deciding what to talk about is recognizing which of these areas is most personal and least personal. Sometimes people turn others off by disclosing or asking too personal material too quickly, before the requisite degree of trust has had time to build up.

Exercise: Two people each role play, and make up the character they are playing as they go along. They tell each other about themselves (i.e. the personas they make up), and they find out about the other. They have fun making up the aspects of the character they are creating, and simultaneously practice finding out about the other and disclosing. They find out and tell the answers to the PAPER questions.

Exercise: People divide up into pairs, and find out about the PAPER questions, only instead of role-playing they find out about the person's real life. Even close family members and friends can often find out things they never knew before by doing this exercise. Being interested in learning about another person is one of the major ways in which people communicate to others that they care about them. It is thus a very important skill.

Exercise: Make a list of questions that you could possibly ask people about themselves, ranging from "Where do you live" to "Who's in your family" to "What do you like to do" to "What's the most embarrassing thing that ever happened to you" to "How do you feel about living with your mother and not your father?" Then put these in order, from "least personal" to "most personal", from "most acceptable to ask or tell someone you don't know well," to "least acceptable to ask or tell someone you don't know well." Do some thinking about how quickly or slowly one should move to more private areas of subject matter.

5. Use facilitations. When people are talking to you, use "facilitations" to help them enjoy talking to you. Facilitations are things like: nodding your head, raising your eyebrows, or saying: humh!, Um humh!, I see, Is that right, What do you know, Oh, Yes, Wow, I understand.

Exercise. This is a silly exercise to do for a minute or two. Two people chat with each other, using nothing but facilitations! The conversation might start out like this:

First person: Humh!
Second person: Is that right!
First person: I see.
Second person: Yes?

Exercise: The second exercise is not so silly. In it, one person speaks normally, about something on his mind, and stops speaking frequently. The other person does a facilitation every time the other stops speaking.

6. Use reflections. When people are talking to you, use "reflections" to help them know you understand what they are saying. Reflections are statements that check out what the other person is thinking or feeling. Example: First person says, in a happy tone of voice, "My family is getting to go to Disney World next month." Second person says, "Hey, it sounds like you're pretty happy about that, huh?"

Exercise: Practice with a dialogue in which someone uses a reflection each time the other person talks, such as the one illustrating reflections in the chapter of this book on conversation. The adult reads the dialogue, and the child's job is to do a reflection each time the narrator stops talking. The adult then reads the reflection that is a sample answer, and continues with the narration.

Exercise: In this second reflection exercise, one person speaks and stops frequently. The other does a reflection every time the other stops. After three or four utterances they switch roles.

7. Use follow-up questions. When people are talking to you, use "follow-up questions" to help them know you are interested. Follow-up questions are questions that ask for more information on something the other person was already talking about. Example: First person says, "My family is getting to go to Disney World next month." Second person says, "I never have been there. What sorts of things are you going to do there?"

Exercise: One person speaks and stops frequently. The other does a follow-up question every time the other stops.

8. Tell about your own experience. Think of things to tell people about your own experience (or that you have read about or seen or heard about) that are funny or interesting. If anything funny happens, remember it so that you can have fun telling people about it. Tell them something short at first and something longer if they seem interested.

Exercise: Try to think of 1 thing funny or interesting to tell the other person about, and do it.

Exercise: Talk about your own experience while the other person practices doing reflections, facilitations, and follow-up questions.

9. Have a balance between listening and talking. When you are talking with someone, try to keep a good balance between your telling about your experience and their telling about their experience. If you do nothing but listen, the other person will run out of things to say, maybe. If you do nothing but talk, the other person will get tired of listening to you. Try to have it even out in the long run.

Exercise: Get a chess clock, which has two clocks and two buttons on it. Or accomplish the same thing with two stop watches. Have a conversation with someone. Each time one person talks, his clock runs; each time the other person talks, his clock runs. The game is for both people to try to have it come out that one person gets no longer than a minute ahead of the other person.

10. Don't intrude. When some other people or one other person is playing with something or doing something, try not to interrupt them by distracting them from what they're doing, unless you know they will want to leave it and do what you are asking them to do. Instead, watch what they're doing, and make a positive comment of some sort or another on it, and join in with it if the person seems to want some company.

Exercise. One person plays the part of someone who is playing with something or working with something. The second person comes up, look for a while at what the person is doing, and then makes a comment and tries joining in with the other person. Depending upon the other person's response, decide whether to join in or leave the other person alone.

11. Help and compliment. Watch for any opportunity to help somebody with something or compliment somebody on something, and do it whenever you get the chance, whether you want that person to be your friend or not. Don't worry about whether they thank you or not, but just feel good that you were able to make somebody else feel good.

Exercise: The child keeps a little diary, with the help of the adult, on every time that he complimented or helped someone. The child acts out these events for the adult.

12. Know fun activities. Know how to do several games, including some games that you can do any time or place, such as password or twenty questions, and see which people enjoy doing them. Get good at explaining to people how to do them. Not everyone will enjoy doing them, but some people will. Also get a bunch of other activities that you can have fun with people at, like hiking or sports or anything else.

Keep on the lookout for some jokes, riddles, brain teasers, or magic tricks that people have fun with. See what people's reactions to them are, and do with other people the ones that people seem to enjoy the most.

Exercise: Any library will have books of jokes, riddles, magic tricks, and brain teasers. Find one fun thing in each of these categories and practice it together.

Exercise: The adult and the child practice playing games with each other. When they do so, they also practice the next few suggestions as well.

13. Be good at winning and losing. When you play a game or sport with someone, remind yourself that the purpose of playing is not to win, but to have a good time. If you win a point, be joyous. If the other person wins a point, congratulate the other person. If you lose a point or a game, maybe have fun suffering the "agony of defeat" in a dramatic way, or maybe have fun suffering "defeat with honor." That way anything that happens, you will enjoy. People have fun playing with someone who has fun.

14. Don't cheat. When you play a game with someone, always follow the rules of the game and don't try to cheat. Remember that it's much more important to help the other person have a good time than it is to win.

15. Handle cheating or other unfairness. If the other person cheats while you are playing a game, have fun catching them and getting them to do it by the rules. If they keep on cheating, don't worry about it, but find a way to have fun anyway. If a referee or other players make bad call, learn to handle it.

To practice this while the adult and child are playing games, they can agree to play a game where the adult cheats and the child practices handling it. This experience may touch off a conversation about how games are in the long run much more fun if nobody cheats.

16. Work at handling teasing. Handling teasing is an extremely complex social skill. "Just ignore it" is frequently given advice that only sometimes works. Other options at the moment of the tease include an articulate criticism of the teaser, a friendly something funny to say back to the teaser, a sincere effort at forgiveness and friendliness, a vague nonviolent threat, a calm response to the effect that, "You'd like me to get upset over what you're saying, wouldn't you?" and a wide variety of other options. In the long term, the best option is often finding a core of loyal friends who will join you in disapproving of the teaser or in supporting you so that you aren't hurt by an occasional teaser. Sometimes the best solution is to organize a school-wide program to prevent bullying. (Refer to the writings of Dan Olweus for descriptions of these and research on their effectiveness.) Sometimes the best solution is to make a rapid exit from an environment where cruelty and rejection prevail.

Exercise: The adult and child can read together the modeling stories in *Stories that Model Psychological Skills* (a book I wrote) having to do with the skill of handling teasing and criticism. For each way of handling it that seems useful to the child, they can act out the story with each other. They can also pursue other stories of successful handling of teasing, and perhaps compose some together.

17. Cultivate tactfulness. Most of the time, avoid bluntly telling people that they are wrong. If you disagree with them, and you want to tell them, do it diplomatically, by saying something like, "Here's another way to think about it. It could be that ..." However, sometimes its fun to debate with people, and to flatly tell them they're wrong, and let them tell you you're wrong. Pick carefully when to do this, however.

Exercise: One person makes very outrageous and definitely wrong statements, and the other practices disagreeing with the other person in the most polite and tactful of ways. Example:

First person: Orange juice is poisonous! If you drink it, you'll die!

Second person: Humh, that's interesting to hear you say that. I had some this morning, and so far I've been feeling fine. Maybe some of it is poisonous and not all of it, do you think?

18. Offer a guest a choice of activities. When you have someone over to your house, think of several things that you and the person can do that would be fun for the person and for you. Take the person around and show them the things. Let them pick what they want to do, which they will usually do by just starting to do it. When that happens, do it with them.

Exercise: The adult first role-plays the child, and the child plays the part of the guest. The adult shows the guest all the things that they can do, and lets the guest pick. Then they switch roles, and the child practices being the host.

19. Don't be bossy. If you have a friend that you're playing with, don't tell them what to do all the time. Let them do what they want and join in and do it with them. That's part of being a gracious host.

Exercise: The adult and the child play together, just as the child would play with another child. Every five minutes, they stop and both of them rate how bossy the child was during the previous five minutes: not at all bossy, just a little bossy, pretty bossy, or very bossy. The aim is that the child can accurately rate himself, and also that over time the bossiness rating will go down to not at all or just a little.

20. Help others with schoolwork. Work really hard on your schoolwork so that people will admire you for doing well, and offer to help someone who isn't doing so well with their math problems or something else.

Exercise: The adult can role-play the part of another child who is having some trouble with a school subject. The child practices being a helper to that person, explaining the things the other person is confused about.

21. Practice a calm response to unwanted things. If someone does something that really makes you mad, don't blow up at them, but tell them calmly what you don't like, and don't hold a grudge for very long. Remember that no one is perfect. On the other hand, if someone you know acts badly to you almost every time you're with them, look for a different friend.

Exercise: Make a list of irritating things that friends or acquaintances have done. Then have the adult role-play the child, and decide how to talk to those people in those situations, and act out the conversation. Then the child role-plays himself while the adult role-plays the friend.

22. Tough out shy feelings. If you feel shy about being with people, try to hang in there until the shy feeling goes away; it will if you do all the things listed above long enough. If you feel shy, try to get your mind off what people think of you, and try to focus on how you can make somebody else happy or be nice to someone.

Exercise: List the situations that make you feel shy. Try to go into one of those situations and be as brave as you can, and keep as oriented as you can to making other people happy.

23. Congratulate yourself for kind acts. Try to do as many nice things for people as you can, every day. Write them down or remember them, and congratulate yourself for doing them every so often.

Exercise: The child recalls the kind things he has done, especially for peers, while the adult writes them down. Then the child practices congratulating himself, first out loud, then in his mind, for these things.

24. Cultivate awareness of other people's feelings. The more skilled you become in picking up on how other people are feeling, the easier it becomes to make decisions on how to act toward them. You will not always want to do things that please them or make them like you. But it's not good to be oblivious or unknowing about how one's actions are affecting others.

Exercise: The "Guess the Feelings" Game gives practice in the skill of awareness of other people's feelings, and the skill of self-disclosure. One person tells something that happened to him, and what he thought and said to himself in the situation. The other person guesses how he felt in the situation. This is a cooperative game, so that rather than trying to stump each other, the two people try to express the situation and their thoughts so clearly that the other person will be able to guess the feeling easily.

Example:

First person: I had in mind that I really wanted a vanilla ice cream cone. So I went to buy it, and they said they were out, that all they had was chocolate, which I'm allergic to. I had two thoughts: one was, "Aw, that's too bad that they don't have it; I really wanted it," but the other was, "That's good, I'm trying to lose weight, I needed to pass up that ice cream cone anyway."

Second person: Sounds like you felt disappointed, but you also felt a little glad, or relieved, that you wouldn't get the extra calories.

First person: Right!

Other Determinants of Popularity

The above-mentioned twenty-four tips fall into the category of social skills. We should not kid ourselves that they are the only determinants of popularity, especially in contemporary youth culture. Success in competitive sports (especially for boys) and physical attractiveness (especially for girls) are major determinants of popularity. To some extent, each of these are able to be influenced, e.g. by lots of practice and work on sports, and lots of attention to clothes, hair styling, weight control, etc. My own opinion is that in a world filled with violence, poverty, illiteracy, and ecological disasters, the time and effort spent by the culture on sports and physical attractiveness are deplorable. But obviously these pursuits seem to tap into something basic to being human.

Within any given subculture, other elements contribute to popularity. Being an adolescent puts very complex demands upon people. When adolescent culture provides few guidelines for measuring what is worthwhile and good and worth pursuing, there evolves in any subculture an unwritten code for distinguishing the "cool" from the "uncool", and the goal of peer acceptance takes on an importance greater than it will have at any other time in life. Adhering to certain customs of dress, use of certain slang terms, enthusiasm about certain entertainment figures, or, unfortunately, enthusiasm about certain recreational drugs, can be parts of the code for winning social acceptance. The danger for most youth is that the more enduring human relationship skills become subordinated to the search for the keys to the arbitrary code of what is considered cool for their particular subculture. It is very important for the youth to realize that being liked by their peers is not the highest value that should drive their life. It is often important for the youth to learn that their are other subcultures that they can enter, later or at present, where the definition of what is socially acceptable is totally different, and superior, to the definition prevailing in their current group. Parents may often take a role in helping a child find those subcultures.

Other-Monitoring and Self-Monitoring to Improve Social Skills

The above-mentioned 24 peer relationship skills are here converted to a questionnaire, as follows.

Relationships Questionnaire

Please rate how well you or someone else does the following things, using the following scale.

0=Very bad at this
2=Not good at this
4=So-so at this
6=Fairly good at this
8=Good at this
10=Very good at this

_______1. Do you smile at people often, at appropriate times?
_______2. Do you greet people by name often, and always when they greet you?
_______3. Do you give people eye contact in a comfortable way?
_______4. Do you know things to tell about and find out about when getting to know another person? (Mnemonic PAPER is helpful.)
_______5. When you have a chat with people, do you use facilitations, such as "Uh hum!" and "I see," and "Is that right?"
_______6. When you have a chat with people, do you use reflections, such as "So you're saying _____, is that right?"
_______7. When you have a chat with people, how well do you use follow-up questions?
_______8. How well do you tell about your own experience, selecting interesting things to tell people about?
_______9. In conversation, how well do you keep a good balance between listening and talking?
_______10. How well do you decide when to interrupt someone, when to distract them from what they're already doing?
_______11. How well do you find opportunities to help people and compliment people?

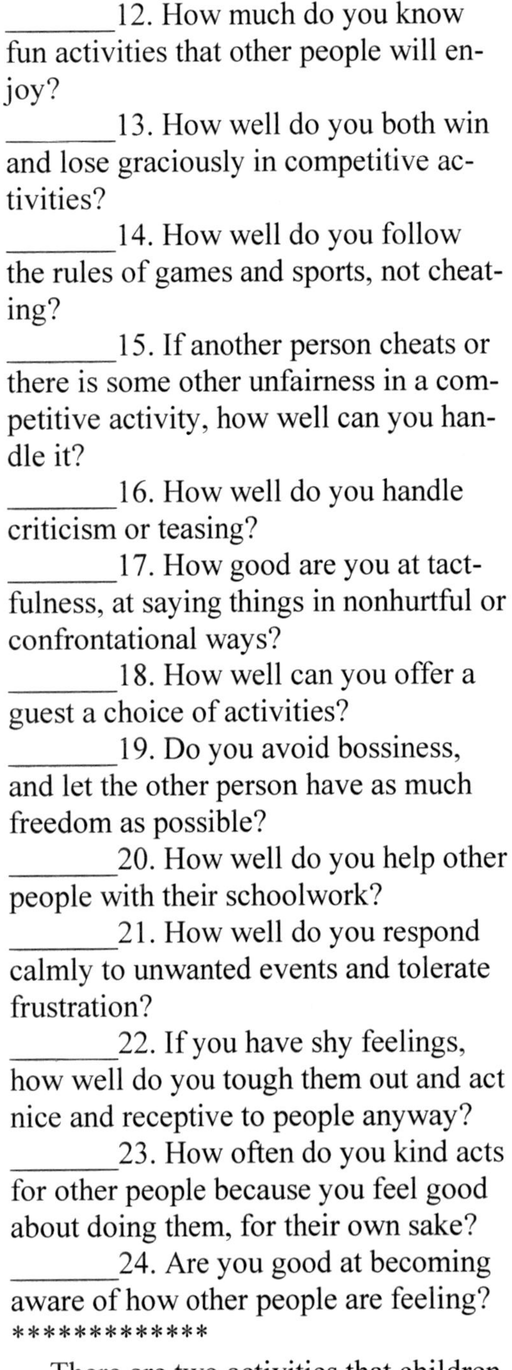

_______12. How much do you know fun activities that other people will enjoy?

_______13. How well do you both win and lose graciously in competitive activities?

_______14. How well do you follow the rules of games and sports, not cheating?

_______15. If another person cheats or there is some other unfairness in a competitive activity, how well can you handle it?

_______16. How well do you handle criticism or teasing?

_______17. How good are you at tactfulness, at saying things in nonhurtful or confrontational ways?

_______18. How well can you offer a guest a choice of activities?

_______19. Do you avoid bossiness, and let the other person have as much freedom as possible?

_______20. How well do you help other people with their schoolwork?

_______21. How well do you respond calmly to unwanted events and tolerate frustration?

_______22. If you have shy feelings, how well do you tough them out and act nice and receptive to people anyway?

_______23. How often do you kind acts for other people because you feel good about doing them, for their own sake?

_______24. Are you good at becoming aware of how other people are feeling?

****

There are two activities that children can do with this questionnaire. The first is "other-monitoring." They go out and notice popular and unpopular children in their class or elsewhere in their social network. They notice how the popular and unpopular children do at these things, and see for themselves whether these things have anything to do with popularity in addition to such things as sports skills and physical attractiveness. They become gradually better at discriminating when someone is doing a good job of these things and when the person is not.

The second activity is self-monitoring. The child periodically sits down with the questionnaire and rates himself on how well he has performed on these skills. The child recalls what results have occurred when he has or has not done these things well. The child shoots toward higher and higher scores on the scale. Most peer groups will contain at least a few members who respond positively. If the child's peer group does not appreciate these skills, the child's present and future family members almost certainly will!

Chapter 33: Eating Problems

Chapter Overview:

In this chapter we discuss principles that help prevent the major eating problems of preadolescent children: overeating, undereating, and picky eating. What are the goals for a child's eating? First, that the child take in adequate calories, protein, vitamins, and minerals. Second, that the child not get too many calories. Third, that the child should gradually cultivate a taste for a diet rich in fruits, vegetables, and grains. Fourth, that the child should have healthy attitudes toward eating, with a healthy mix of skills of pleasure from blessings and delay of gratification. Fifth, the interpersonal aspects of eating in the family should be pleasant, with neither the child nor the parent feeling overly controlled by the other.

A study of the protein and calorie requirements of children at various ages reveals that the protein requirement is not too hard to achieve. However, it is also not hard to meet a child's daily calorie requirement with foods that are "empty calories." If the parent lets the child meet the caloric requirement with empty calories, it will be a futile battle to try to get the child to eat more nutritious foods in addition.

Most of the time a child's innate hunger drive and satiety mechanism will direct the child to take in a number of calories in the average day not too far from the daily caloric requirement. Sometimes what interferes is the parent's own habit of nagging the child to eat more. Sometimes you can cure eating problems by stopping trying to control the child, but just seeing what happens when the child is allowed to do what comes naturally. But doing what comes naturally doesn't automatically create a diet that is well distributed among food groups, or prevent obesity in children who get very little exercise.

At the table, you can create a "stimulus situation" of pleasant conversation. You can model enjoying eating nutritious food. You can practice differential attention by ignoring when the child rejects nutritious food and attending when the child eats it. These measures influence eating behavior without having the disadvantages of urging and nagging. For the picky eater, or the child who wants only junk food, a useful maxim is that "hunger is the best sauce." It doesn't work well to plead with the child to eat, or command the child to eat. It also doesn't work well to let the young child eat any empty calorie food he wants at any time. I recommend allowing the child to eat a certain amount of sweets or fats each day, not as a reward for eating more nutritious food, but in a small enough quantity that the child's hunger drive will still motivate the child to meet the rest of the caloric requirement with more nutritious food. When the child reaches grade school age, or perhaps earlier, the child can start receiving instruction about basic principles of nutrition, so that the child can start taking pride in choosing a

nutritious diet for herself. Such instruction should include attitudes of moderation and avoidance of extremism. If someone tries to impose on a child, or the child imposes upon herself, an overly restricted diet, the child often gets a "deprivation fear" that leads to overeating. Similarly, if you try to get people to eat more than they want, you often produce a "fear of stuffing" that leads the person to undereat. It is useful, but not essential, to have structure in meals: a certain consistent mealtime, and certain rituals, rather than everyone foraging through the refrigerator and the cabinets at random times. But each family can find its own balance between flexibility and rigidity. If you can't get schedules together to conduct rituals at bedtime, you can do them at another time. It's helpful for parents to separate their role and the child's role about eating: the parent's role is to offer nutritious food, and to withhold whatever food the child shouldn't eat; the parent should make an unlimited quantity of at least one food available, each day, to make sure that the child's own satiation mechanism is limiting food intake. The child's role is to decide how much of whatever is made available he wants to eat. The smart parent avoids the job of urging the child to eat more, or eat less. Defocussing eating, and cultivating mutually gratifying activities, is often the most helpful strategy when parent and child are in conflict about eating. If the child is overweight, the first strategy I would recommend is to foster a substantial increase in exercise by cultivating long walks or sports activities as mutually gratifying activities between parent and child. If that doesn't do the job by itself, I recommend training the child to do the calculations necessary to consume only three or four hundred calories fewer than those expended each day, for a very gradual and non-depriving weight loss program.
****

I'll talk in this chapter about principles relevant to 3 types of eating problems, those particularly applicable to children in the preschool and grade school years: undereating, overeating, and picky eating. Most of the principles mentioned in this chapter are applicable to all three sorts of problems. Adolescent eating problems such as bulimia and anorexia nervosa are outside the scope of this chapter, although cultivation of healthy attitudes toward eating via the guidelines given here may help prevent such problems.

Goals Regarding Children's Eating

Let's think about the goals of food intake for a child. If you want to get subtle and complex about the study of nutrition, you can think of many components of the ideal diet. But to a first approximation, adequate nutrition means getting adequate calories, protein, and vitamins and minerals. If any of these requirements are not met, the child's growth will suffer or deficiency diseases will result. A second goal is important in cultures where food is abundant. The child should not get too many calories relative to exercise; if this requirement is not met, obesity will result. Third, the child should gradually cultivate the habit of choosing a wide variety of foods, especially fruits, vegetables, and grains, and those without a great deal of added fat. This sort of diet will be in the long-term best interest because low fat is good for the arteries; because the fiber in fruits and vegetables and grains helps prevent constipation and certain other conditions; and because choosing a wide variety of foods exposes the person to nutrients that are as present not well defined.

In the table on the next page are approximate protein and calorie requirements for children of various ages, assuming that the child is of average weight. (Source: Food and Nutrition Board, National Academy of Sciences—National Research Council, Recommended Dietary Allowances, 10th ed., Washington, DC: National Academy Press, 1989. Adapted in Tamborlane, W.V. et al., The Yale Guide to Children's Nutrition, New Haven: Yale University Press).

Age	Protein Grams	Calories
Under 6 months	13	650
6 months to 1 year	14	850
1 to 3	16	1300
4 to 6	22	1800
7 to 10	28	2000
11 to 14 females	46	2200
11 to 14 males	45	2500
15 to 18 females	44	2200
15 to 18 males	59	3000

If you worry a lot about the whether the child's food intake is adequate, you may do well to keep a food diary for a few days and with some tables of food composition, compute how much protein and how many calories the child is getting. You may be surprised to see how junky and skimpy a diet can be and still provide adequate protein. For example, if a 6 year old child eats nothing in a day other than the following, the protein requirement is still met: 3 ounces of pretzels, 4 ounces french fries, a cup of chocolate milk, 6 honey-coated graham crackers, 2 slices of white bread toast, and a Payday candy bar. Note: I am NOT recommending this diet. But it illustrates that adequate protein nutrition is fairly easily attainable.

On the other hand, doing some arithmetic can also help us understand how easy it is to meet the child's entire caloric requirement from rather "empty calories." A two and a half year old child requires about 1300 calories a day. Suppose that the child doesn't like water, and drinks her entire fluid requirement (about a quart and a half, or 1.5 liters, per day) in the form of apple juice. This has supplied about 570 of the daily calories, close to half the daily calorie requirement, in the form of the sugar in the juice. Suppose that some time else in the day, the child has in addition 2 one-once brownies with nuts (for 275 more calories) and 3 ounces of potato chips (for 450 more). The child has now consumed approximately her entire daily caloric requirement, with just these three foods.

Why is this so important? Because our hunger and satiety centers in the brain are set so as to keep us from going too far above and below the daily caloric requirement. If the child mentioned above gets 1300 calories from juice and brownies and potato chips, the parent will be battling against the satiety mechanism if she tries to get the child to eat "good for you" food in addition. On the other hand, if all that is available for the child is unlimited quantities of "good for you" food, the child will almost always come around, eventually, (meaning in two or three days) to eating it in an amount that approximately meets the daily caloric requirement. In any given day it is usually possible to have some empty calories, and enough more nutritious food to meet all nutrition requirements.

In addition to goals for nutritional intake, there should also be goals for children's ideas and attitudes toward food, eating, and exercise. Let's list some here.

1. . We eat and drink for two reasons: first, because we need to if we want to stay alive and grow and be healthy; second, because it feels good. Both of those are good reasons. Our bodies are built so that it feels good to eat and drink, and it feels bad not to; that way we don't forget to do these important activities!

2. Hunger and thirst are signals that tell us when we need to eat and drink. To a first approximation, responding to our own wishes to eat and drink, or not, and doing what comes naturally, will be good for us.

3. Moderation and balance in eating is good. It is good not to eat too much or too little. It is good to eat moderate amounts of lots of different foods.

4. Foods may be "good for you" without tasting as good as some others. Thus it's necessary to educate yourself and use some conscious choice and thinking about what's best to eat, as well as doing what comes naturally.

5. Using conscious choice about what's good for you and how much food is good for you does not mean that eating should cease to be one of life's pleasures.

6. In a culture where food is abundant, eating is an important and nice pleasure

in life, but should not be the central focus of life, as compared to, say, having good relationships, achieving things, and making the world a better place.

Finally, the realm of food and eating brings up interpersonal goals. Neither the parent nor the child should be overcontrolling of the other. That is, the parent shouldn't have to constantly threaten or cajole the child about eating, and the parent shouldn't have to constantly go out of her way to cater to the child's whims in order to get her to eat. The realm of eating should be one that is comfortable for all concerned. Food should not be the frequent subject of arguments and discord and bad feeling between people. The parent should avoid giving the child the "entitlement syndrome": the idea that I deserve to have whatever I want whenever I want it. To achieve such goals requires that parents cultivate psychological skills useful in other areas of parenting as well. The skill of nonbossiness and tolerating a wide range of other's behavior is useful in not being too controlling regarding a child's food intake. The skills of assertion and tolerating another person's disapproval are useful in avoiding giving the child too much junk food or giving the child the entitlement syndrome. Skills of tactful, well-timed instruction and persuasion are useful in teaching the child nutrition facts and attitudes. Skills of conversation, listening, playfulness, expressing gratitude, and humor are useful in setting a positive atmosphere at mealtime.

To a First Approximation, Trust the Body

Many parents worry themselves unnecessarily for fear that their child is eating too little or too much. Such worry can lead some parents to be overcontrolling, with constant commands to the child to eat more of this or to stop eating. Or, such worry can lead an unassertive parent to be a hostage to the child's whims, a short-order cook at every meal, fearful that if the child isn't given just exactly what she wants, she will not eat and in the long term waste away. Sometimes parents see a child eat very little or very much at one meal, and think something like, "If she continues to eat this little, she will starve to death," or "If she continues to eat this much, she will turn into a blimp."

To counteract this nonproductive worry, parents should remind themselves that most of the time, overeating or undereating tends to average out over the course of a few days, if the child eats as much as, and no more than, she wants. If you are in doubt, measure the child's height and weight, and check a table of percentiles. If your child is within the normal range for height and weight, or is above or below to the extent expected by virtue of having big or little parents, you know that something is happening right.

I have had several parents tell me that the child was in the normal range, but they felt that they had to continually fight with the child in order to keep the child there—either to persuade the child to eat, or to keep the child from eating too much. My advice is to quit fighting with the child, let the child regulate her own food intake, and to measure height and weight regularly to see whether or not the child wastes away or balloons up once the parent gives up a tight control of eating. Almost always the result of this is that the child stays in the normal range, and the parent discovers that the worry and conflict were unnecessary.

Centuries of evolution have built in to people the wish to take in enough food. There is a hunger center in the brain that automatically makes children want to eat when they need to. In the vast majority of cases it can be trusted to assure that adequate caloric intake will occur, on the average, over several days, given availability of reasonably palatable food.

Sometimes physical illnesses can interfere with appetite. If the child seems to have lost his appetite, or to have a much higher than usual appetite, take the child to your pediatrician so that appropriate examination can be done. In the vast majority of cases, however, nothing physical is found that explains problem eating.

Sometimes the root cause of problem eating is the very means that is meant to correct it: nagging the child.

Nagging and Urging Are Self-defeating

When the child is eating what the parent conceives of as too little, the natural tendency of many adults is to start urging or even nagging the child to eat. "Eat the rest of your food!" "Let me see you clean your plate!" "You can do it when you've finished eating your ________." "Quit playing and eat."

But such nagging communicates to the child that eating is a job for him to do, rather than something to be enjoyed. Also, if the child is rebellious and likes to get attention by saying "No," (as nearly all children do at some time or another) then urging the child to eat allows the child to rebel by refusing to eat.

If you find yourself nagging your child to eat, and want to break the habit, one way is to try not to use the word *eat* at all while at the table. You eliminate sentences like "Eat your peas," or "You won't grow if you don't eat," or even "You're doing a good job of eating," at least until you've broken the habit.

Another thing wrong with commanding the child to eat, offering rewards for the child's eating, and so forth, is that these sorts of behaviors give the child the impression that eating is work, rather than that eating is pleasure.

Let's make up a fanciful example to illustrate this point. Suppose that you had an experience much like a child has, and found yourself in a world in which you were learning new words. Suppose you heard someone saying "OK, go ahead and glimp!... You're not glimping enough! Glimp more! ... Listen, I'll give you something nice if you'll just glimp some more." Now, having heard nothing else, if you were offered the choice between glimping and not glimping, which would you do? It sounds like glimping is hard work and no fun, doesn't it?

When the child has been commanded to eat, and the child refuses to eat, sometimes adults have actually physically placed food in the child's mouth, against the child's will. This is almost always a very bad idea. This is an unpleasant experience for the child, and tends give the child bad associations with the whole process of eating.

What harm is there in pleading with the child to eat, or offering to reward the child by doing something special for him if he will just eat? This sets up a situation where the child has power over the adult based on his refusal to eat. In other words, as long as the child refuses to eat, the adult will do what the child wants, or give the child lots of attention. Thus although the adult thinks that he is rewarding the child for eating, he runs the risk of really rewarding the child for not eating. The child may figure out that not eating is what gives him such power over the adult, and that power goes away when he eats.

So far we've listed five ways in which the parents' efforts to get a child to eat can actually interfere with the eating process: they can reward the child with attention for refusing to eat, they can induce rebellious behavior consisting of food refusal, they can give the message that eating is work and no fun, they can create unpleasant experiences that become associated with the process of eating, and they can give the child power over the adult that the child may be loathe to let go of by eating in a regular way.

If you take the above reasoning and apply it in the opposite direction with the overweight child, you conclude that nagging the child about eating too much, nagging about eating the wrong kinds of foods, and so forth, usually makes the child want to eat more.

If nagging the child to eat more or less often induces just the behavior it was meant to reduce, does it follow that parents should nag the underweight child not to eat so much, and nag the overweight child to eat more? Such strategies of trying to induce rebellion have been called reverse psychology or paradoxical instruction. I don't recommend them at all. The major problem is that they are dishonest. If you really want your child to eat less, for example, it is dishonest to urge the child to eat more. Plus paradoxical instructions don't always induce rebellion in the desired direction.

By far the first priority "intervention" with children who present eating problems is to let them do what comes naturally for a while and monitor what happens. If what happens is OK, then the problem is solved, and on you go.

"Trust the Body" Doesn't Work In Certain Respects

Although the body does have a hunger center that has evolved to make sure that the child doesn't starve, the body doesn't automatically guide the child to choose a diet that is well balanced. If there are popsicles, potato chips, candy bars, sodas, and cookies readily available at all times, many children will eat so much of these that they spoil their appetite for foods given at meals that fulfill more of their requirements for proteins and vitamins and minerals and fiber. The ready availability of foods that deliver a rather pure bolus of sugar and fat, sometimes with salt thrown in, is something the "centuries of evolution" alluded to earlier didn't have to grapple with.

Another aspect of modern life that centuries of evolution didn't prepare our bodies for is the degree of inactivity of modern culture. Children spent large numbers of hours sitting at school; then they sit in front of a television, videogame player, or computer. An exercise shortage, combined with an abundance of foods highly laden with "empty calories," forms a recipe for a culture of overweight people.

Third, children's bodies aren't prepared for the situation in some families where adults, reacting against the tendencies toward obesity in modern society, eat extremely low-fat diets and offer these to the child as well. Some fatty acids are essential to the diet. They may be deficient in diets that are extremely low in fat. An extreme low-fat diet may also wind up with inadequate caloric intake for a growing energetic youngster.

And finally, letting the child do what comes naturally, if that means getting the child whatever the child wants whenever the child wants it, may be sufficient to meet the child's nutritional needs but not sufficient to keep the child from practicing spoiled bratty tyrannical behavior toward the parent, which is not in the child's best interest.

Therefore, let's talk about the exceptions and qualifications to "doing what comes naturally" in the food department. How do you exert influence without nagging? The answer lies most fully in the earlier chapter on the methods of influence axis. Let's talk about three of those methods.

Using Stimulus Control, Modeling, and Differential Attention

Three ways of influencing the child's eating are familiar to you if you've read the previous chapters: 1) stimulus situation control, 2) modeling, and 3) differential attention.

Stimulus situation control in this circumstance means setting up the things that the child has around him within sight and within reach so as to encourage what you want to encourage. We can expect eating to increase when the child has food in sight and in reach, tempting him to eat it. There are two situations where the food may tempt the child: at meals, and in between meals.

Let's think for a minute about what sort of situation is the most difficult for someone who is trying to lose weight. Suppose someone is with people he likes, in a festive mood, sitting around a table for a long time having pleasant and interesting conversation, while meanwhile there is always on the table in front of this person abundant amounts of high caloric food. Furthermore, the other people at the table are eating and greatly enjoying their meals. In such circumstances the temptation to ingest a high-calorie meal is quite strong.

For the child who needs to gain weight, then, adults should try to duplicate this situation as much as possible. That is: a "mealtime" exists, where the children and adults sit down together, aiming toward as positive an emotional climate as possible. Food that the child likes is put on the plate in front of him. More food that the child likes is put in bowls on the table. The adults and the child engage in pleasant conversation together. When the child has finished the food that is put in front of him, he can ask for more by saying "Please pass the _______." (Being able to control someone else's action in this way is often pleasant for the child.) If the child does not feel like eating, the child is not urged to eat. However, the child is encouraged to stay at the table and chat with everyone. Thus the child is put into the situation where the natural thing to do is to eat, without any unpleasant pressure on him to eat.

For the child who needs to lose weight, this principle would dictate that either the meal lasts a shorter time, or that the child learns to eat more slowly, and to sit at the table for periods of time without eating.

Modeling, as you know, means showing the child the behavior pattern that you want the child to imitate. In this case, it consists in sitting around the table, talking with other people in a pleasant way, and enjoying eating, perhaps occasionally making a positive remark or two about the food. Modeling for the overweight child might consist in establishing a custom, and modeling it, of sitting and sipping on some water while chatting at the table.

Differential attention means that you pay more attention to the behavior you want to encourage than to the behavior you want to discourage; in doing this you are making use of the fact that nearly all children like adult attention, especially if it is given in an approving way.

An example of how differential attention may be used at a meal with an overly picky child is as follows. The child takes a look at something on his plate and says, "This is yucky!" The adults do not respond to this, and talk among themselves. Later, the child eats some food, and reaches for a bowl for some more of a certain dish. The adults says, in an approving tone of voice, "Want some more of that? Do you want me to put it on your plate? No, you can do it yourself? OK. Hey, you did do it yourself." The approving tone of voice is tending to reward the child for getting more food. Notice that the adults did not use the word eat, and did not directly praise the child for eating the food; if they did that every time the child ate, everyone would get very tired of talking about how much the child ate, and the child might even get the notion of rebelling. The approving tones of voice are sufficient to give the child the message that it's good for him to eat. The ignoring that went on earlier tended not to reward the child for rejecting the food.

What about tones of disapproval when the child does not eat enough, or eats too much? In general, I recommend trying to avoid as much as possible any tones of voice that communicate disapproval when applied to the child's eating behavior. That is, I would recommend not disapproving of the child's eating too much, too little, too fast, too slowly, or too much of one thing and not enough of another thing.

I say avoid "as much as possible" the tones of disapproval. Disapproval and enforcement of limits are appropriate if the child should throw food, spit out chewed-up food onto the table, pour liquids onto the table, grab food off other people's plates, and so forth. A child's needing to gain weight does not give him license to develop bratty habits.

The occurrence of behaviors like those above will likely be rare, however, and the general rule is that eliminating all disapproval connected with eating in any way is the ideal to shoot for.

If the child does do something very inappropriate at the table, like the behaviors listed above, the approach to inappropriate behaviors at the table can be very similar to the approach with undesirable behaviors not involving food (see other chapters). For example, the child can be given a reprimand or a time out and then rejoin his family at the table without further discussion of the misbehavior.

The Composition of the Diet

The currently recommended "food pyramid" conceives of the ideal diet as having its servings distributed as follows, from most to least frequently eaten: 1. grain products and other complex carbohydrates, 2. fruits and vegetables, 3. meats, beans, nuts, and dairy products, and 4. fats and sweets. For both the underweight and the overweight child, a goal is to offer the child a wide variety of foods, with hopes that the child will be able to enjoy all of them, but without getting distressed if the child rejects some particular food for the time being. For the overweight child, the goal is to skew the distribution toward low fat food; for the underweight child, the goal is to skew the distribution toward higher fat and higher protein food.

In influencing the composition of the child's diet, the place to make hard choices first is at the grocery store. If the overweight child shouldn't eat potato chips and peanuts, then don't buy them, or at least not often and not in large amounts. The distribution of foods bought at the grocery store imposes a big influence on the distribution of food eaten in the home.

Many adults are conditioned to think of high-fat and high-sugar foods as being "bad" or "junk". This conditioning is reasonable for people who want to lose weight. However, for children who need to gain weight, it is possible to include more of such "junk" foods in the diet, with one or two major qualifications. The main problem with an underweight child's eating too much "junk" food is that it might crowd out of his diet the other foods that would allow him to get enough protein. That is, if he only eats highly refined sugar and starch and fat, he may not get enough protein. However, if the child gets enough milk products, meat, or nuts or beans or grain products to get enough protein for the day, you don't have to worry if in addition to that he eats foods that provide "empty calories"—calories are good for him. If the snacks that the child likes to eat between meals are also high in protein, then you get the best of both worlds.

If there are certain foods that the child shouldn't eat, such as food that will be given to someone else or used at a party or such, then I would recommend using the principle of stimulus situation control. These can be placed out of reach and out of sight if possible. It's fine not to let the child eat these things if there is something else that he can eat that he also likes.

Influencing the Composition of the Diet

Suppose the child ignores her protein source and fruits and vegetables; then dessert comes and the child wants chocolate pie with whipped cream. The parent knows that if permitted to do so, the child will make her entire meal of chocolate pie with whipped cream. What can the parent do?

One frequently used option is to tell the child that she can't have dessert until she's eaten a certain amount more of her other food. Sometimes this works fine, with no problems. At other times, the child ends up stuffing a certain amount of the other food into the mouth, perhaps hating it and building up an aversion to it. With each bite the child asks if it's enough. The child gets lots of attention over this power struggle, despite the fact that it's often highly unpleasant for child and parent. Adults sometimes disagree with each other on how much should be required for the payoff. Children sometimes gag or throw up while eating the five more bites that they need in order to get the dessert. These side effects lead to a search for other options.

An option at the other side of the spectrum is simply to give the child whatever she wants when she wants it. The child dabbles with the beans and peas and applesauce, and then announces, "I don't want this." The child asks for dessert, and the parent dutifully gets it for her that instant. The dessert is now reinforcing the child's turning down the other food. The child is also getting bad practice with respect to delay of gratification skills and is practicing the entitlement syndrome.

The option I like best is a combination of several features. First, dessert is often skipped, and is often something other than empty calories, for example fruit. Second, when dessert is planned, mealtime has a structure, where the nutritious foods are placed in front of the child, and everyone else eats them. If the child does not eat them, and wants dessert, the child simply has to wait until dessert time comes around. Dessert is not contingent upon eating the meal, although the size of it may be. Now the strategy is somewhat different: you are not using dessert as a reward for eating the nutritious food; you are restricting the total number of empty calories so that the hunger mechanism will increase the amount of nutritious food ultimately eaten. Third, in keeping with this idea, the number of empty calories that the child is permitted to eat in a given day is kept low enough that the child's hunger mechanism will make the child want to eat the nutritious food she is offered. For example, the parent has in mind that the child can have a 100 calorie popsicle, a 100 calorie cookie, a pint of juice for 200 calories, but that all else during the day will be water, grains, fruits, vegetables, dairy products, or protein sources.

Why not simply cut out altogether all empty calorie foods? The reason is that learning to deal responsibly with the availability of fat and sugar-laden foods is one of the tasks that we all have to grapple with sooner or later. Learning to enjoy empty calories in moderation is an important goal. If the child doesn't have any access to junk food, the danger is that the child will tend to overdose on it when he or she comes of age (or comes to the right friend's house) where free access is available.

What happens if the child refuses a meal, eats the quota of empty calorie foods, and later complains of being hungry? You you offer a second chance at the enchilada and and peas and applesauce the child passed up the first time, or some other nutritious food. If she is not hungry enough to want them, but only wants a cookie or ice cream, then she is not hungry enough to worry about.

What about the child who has only certain foods that he or she will eat? If this child is at a level of height and weight that are not worrisome, one option is to continue giving the child what he wants and not worry about it. I think this is usually less satisfactory than the second plan, which is to offer the child whatever the rest of the family is eating, and let the child take it or leave it. If the child refuses to eat anything for a day or two the "hunger is the best sauce" mechanism will usually make it quite reinforcing for the child to eat whatever is offered when he starts back eating. This plan works if the parent can keep straight that the parent's role is to offer nutritious food, and the child's role is to decide how much of it to eat. If the parent vacillates and pleads with the child to eat and gives the child lots of bargaining power based on the child's refusal to eat, the problem is only made worse.

Perhaps the most important thing when dealing with picky eating problems is for the parent to maintain a relaxed, friendly attitude. You should avoid letting the child's eating pattern be seen by the child as more of a problem for you than it is for him. You don't want it possible for the child to use refusal to eat as a bargaining chip. Learning to like a wide variety of foods seems not a good idea to the child, because he would give up a great deal of power over his parent.

In many cases the most difficult part of such a program is the parent's inability to tolerate the child's being hungry. There is something built into most parents that makes this difficult. However, when the child has unlimited access to good, nutritious food, and is still hungry because it's not the food he prefers, or when the child is hungry at a place where food is unavailable, one or two hours after passing up unlimited quantities of nutritious foods, the parent should not let the heartstrings be played upon so easily.

Using Instruction to Influence the Child's Choice of Food

So far I have left out the an important influence method for children, especially those of grade school age or older: teaching the child how to choose a good diet for herself, rather than leaving all the choosing up to the parent. Indeed, once you get out of the preschool years, it becomes impossible for most parents to regulate closely their children's diets, and the self-regulation of the child becomes more and more important.

What do you want to teach a child about diet? Here are some of the high points. You want the child to know what the basic components of food are, and what the purposes of those components are in body functioning. These components are water, fats, proteins, carbohydrates, fiber, vitamins, and minerals. You want to convey the attitude of moderation and avoidance of extremism in diet: that it is OK to enjoy food, that the pleasure of eating is not wrong, that getting all the required nutrients is easy to do in many reasonable ways. You also want to convey that most people in affluent cultures eat too much fat and too much refined sugar. Most people need to use some will power to reduce the fat content of their diets, not to extremely low levels, but to levels lower than what comes naturally by eating what is most pleasurable. Many people find it useful to purposely motivate themselves to enjoy vegetables and fruits and grains, by reminding themselves that these are good for them and actively cultivating the pleasure of eating them. The more calories you burn through exercise, the more calories you will be able to, or need to, take in and still maintain the same weight.

A healthy attitude is that some fat on the body is natural and normal and attractive. Although it is highly desirable to cultivate the self-discipline necessary to keep one's body weight in the normal, desirable, healthy range, it is also important to place in perspective the whole business of weight control, and to realize that making the world a better place is much more important than having a certain weight. It is not our role to blame or demean anyone who is fatter or skinnier than we think best for them.

In addition to these general principles, nutrition education should include teaching about the composition of various specific foods. The child should learn things like the following:

Dairy products have high quality protein, and carbohydrate. Those that don't have the fat removed have fairly saturated fat that you don't want too much of.

In general, those fats that are liquid are better for you than those that are solid, and those from plants are better than those from birds and mammals. Omega-3 fatty acids, which are present particularly in fish oil and flax seed oil, may be useful for mental functioning, and have been found helpful in several studies of bipolar disorder.

Vegetables like spinach and asparagus and broccoli are composed of carbohydrate and protein and lots of water, with little fat. They're a good source of fiber and some vitamins, and you have to eat a lot of them to get many calories.

Meats have lots of protein. Some have lots of saturated fat too, and others don't.

Bread and rice and pasta and cereal are mainly made of starch, with some protein. The amount of fiber in these grain foods depends on how much the bran, or outer portion of the grain, is included or refined out. How much fat there is depends partly on which grain is used, and more on how much fat was added to the recipe.

Beans and peas and lentils are a fairly good source of protein; soy beans are a very good source of protein. When beans and grains are both present in the diet, they make complementary protein that is more available for the body to use. Protein is made of amino acids, and not all proteins have the same amino acids. The body needs amino acids in a certain distribution. Beans have too little of some and grains have too little of others; when you put them together you get a good distribution of amino acids.

Beans and many other fruits and vegetables, as well as the bran layer of grains, are a source of fiber, which is the nondigestible part of what you eat. Fiber is important to prevent constipation and to prevent the ultimate development of hemorrhoids.

Candy, soda pop, and a variety of other foods containing primarily sugar and fat, supply mostly calories without other nutrients. These are called "empty calories." There is nothing sinful or wrong about foods with empty calories. If you have gotten all the protein, vitamins, minerals, and fiber you need, and there is still room in your daily caloric requirement, you can use empty calories to reach your quota, or you can use more "good for you" food, whatever you want.

How do you teach a child these things? As I have mentioned in other places throughout this book, the instruction a child receives from a parent is best received if it is not also a criticism of something the child has done. The parent teaches the child about nutrition in the context of science learning, and not when the child wants some empty calories and the parent is trying to persuade the child not to have them. The parent and child can read together books on nutrition and health, at bedtime for example.

The Role of "Deprivation Fear" and "Fear of Stuffing"

Students of weight gain and loss find that going on extreme weight-losing diets where the person is hungry much of the time tends to result in more weight gain in the long run. One of the several mechanisms whereby this works is that the experience of hunger tends to induce some fear of being deprived of food; then when unlimited food is available, the person tends to eat all he can, to counteract the "deprivation fear." Another mechanism may be that the taste of food is much more reinforcing when someone is very hungry; the more reinforcing eating is, the more it will tend to be repeated. The moral of this is that the child who eats too much should be taught not to try to starve himself, but should be taught to aim toward "moderation in all things."

The opposite of deprivation fear is the fear of stuffing: the fear of that unpleasant feeling when you have eaten all you want and someone makes you eat some more.

The implications of the concepts of fear of stuffing and the fear of deprivation for the child who eats too little or is too picky are less well known than for overweight children. It could be that permitting a child to eat only at meals, and not to eat between meals, will with some children result in more eating overall, because the child is allowed to get hungry. On the other hand, the notion of stimulus situation control would predict that having lots of bowls of potato chips around the house with permission to eat them between meals would result in weight gain. As far as I know, no one has yet done the definitive research on which choice of rules about eating between meals most effectively stimulates the underweight child to gain weight. I think the best a parent can do is to keep in mind the different directions of effect that deprivation fear and stimulus situation control predict, and try to see what works the best with their particular child. That is, when in doubt, do your own experiment.

The Structuring of Mealtime

Some parents, I think, tend to insist on too rigid a structure for mealtimes: that is, we eat only at mealtimes, we must eat everything on our plates, we may not leave the table until the meal is officially over, and so forth, enforced with a rather oppresive tone. Others, however, have too little structure in meals. If everyone in the house simply forages through the refrigerator or the pantry, eating when they want to, with no discrete mealtimes, the parent loses the opportunity to influence the composition of the child's diet by offering him foods in a certain proportion at mealtime.

Because food is regularly eaten by most human beings, meals become an opportunity for making regular certain rituals very important for psychological skill development: the saying of prayers or affirmations, the discussion of moral dilemmas, practicing and using the skills of conversation and listening and disclosure and intimacy and humor. However, for the family who cannot come together at meals, it is possible to reschedule these rituals for other times, and there are many ways to accomplish the same goal.

Definition of Parent's and Child's Role

Some families experience mealtime as a continual struggle. It is helpful for those families to consider the following role division, for young children: it is the parent's role to offer to the child (by putting it in front of him at mealtime) a variety of nourishing food, at least some of which is known to be liked by the child. In the case of overweight children the amount of high fat and high sugar food offered or made available to the child may be limited, but not eliminated entirely. The child's role is to determine how much of each of those offered foods he wants to eat. In other words, the adult provides the choices, and the child chooses. If the child consistently chooses too much or too little of something, then the adult can alter the distribution of what is offered to try to make up for the deficiency, if there is really a deficiency in the first place.

What if a child decides that he doesn't like what he is given for supper, and wants the adult to prepare something else of his choosing, immediately? The fact that the adults are trying to accommodate the child's wishes about what he wants to eat, and give maximum permission to him to eat what he wants, does not mean that the child can become a tyrant and order the adult around to get him anything he wants whenever he wants it. I would recommend not responding to commands from the child to take it away and get something else, except by explaining to the child, once, that he can eat what's for supper now, if he wants, or he can have something else later, but he'll have to wait for the something else.

Some children who have spent time with adults who have deprived them of food will hoard food or binge eat. The hoarding and binging represent a reaction against the deprivation fear they have experienced for some time. My recommendation for these children is to let them experience a free rein in eating. The fastest way to get over deprivation fear is to experience freedom to eat whatever you choose and however much you want, whenever you want, from food that is selected to be nutritious.

As a child grows older and more educated about nutrition, the child takes on more and more of the role of choosing what to eat. Ideally, by the time the child is nine or ten years old, the child has enough education and self-discipline to make informed choices about nutritious food (as well as a major role in preparing it).

Defocussing Eating

Eating can become an obsession. Sometimes one of the major solutions to an eating problem is to start paying lots less attention to it. This is done by paying attention to, and participating, in, mutually gratifying activities between parent and child. Most parent-child relationships where there has been a lot of struggle over eating can use a lot more experiences in which the parent and the child play together, look at books together, sing, do things that lead to laughter, explore the world in a curious way.

Exercise

Exercise is undoubtedly very important and useful for the overweight child. Being able to run or jump or swim or ride a bike or chase other children is a part of childhood that is important in its own right; if a child is not able to do these things, the opportunity should be made available. Most children will exercise (e.g. they will spontaneously run) if they are allowed to be in an open space where they can do so; most of them don't need treadmills or rowing machines or the other equipment adults accumulate in an attempt to make themselves exercise. For the overweight child, increasing the child's opportunity for exercise may be much more effective in the long run than attention to the diet, because it does not induce any deprivation fear. A general recommendation I would make to parents of overweight children is to take a long walk with your child, regularly. In addition to burning calories, you will have a wonderful "stimulus situation" for good conversation. A three or four mile walk every day will burn about a pound's worth of calories every 10 days. That is plenty fast enough for any weight loss program. An overweight child who is remaining overweight by the same amount and not gaining can solve his or her problem without changing diet in the slightest, if about an hour of exercise a day is added to the schedule.

A Program for Obesity

There have been countless books written on the subject of how to lose weight. Here's one possible plan for a child or adolescent who needs to lose weight. First you research what your ideal weight is, and set a realistic goal for achieving this weight, with about a pound a week of weight loss.

The next step is gradually to increase aerobic exercise to about an hour per day. This can burn off 500 calories or more per day. If someone does this and makes no change in food intake whatsoever, he or she will lose a pound a week.

If exercise alone doesn't get the job done, the next step is to eat only at meals, (three or four per day) and eat only "preplanned" meals. This means that you get all the food ready that you are going to eat at that meal, put it in front of you, and then sit down and eat it, without getting any more. This step eliminates "impulse" eating.

If these two steps aren't sufficient, the next step in this weight loss program is to continue the exercise, continue eating only in a preplanned way, but to limit the total caloric intake of sweets and fats to about two to three hundred calories a day, and eat the "good for you" fruits and vegetables and whole grain foods as desired. In addition, you eat what you *guess* will produce a five hundred calorie per day negative caloric balance. This step limits the amounts of high caloric density food you take in and has you work toward a reasonable caloric deficit.

If these three steps are not sufficient, and you are highly motivated to lose weight, the last level of effort involves counting calories. You keep a written record of everything you eat, with amounts, as measured by weighing servings of food on a scale. The more you first guess the weight of the food and then weigh it, the more you can guess the weights of food without weighing them. Learning to guess weights of food is a good mathematics activity for a child or adolescent. Second, you get from tables a good estimate of the break-even number of calories required for maintenance of your weight with neither gain or loss. This number depends on your current weight and exercise level. Third, you set a daily limit of calories somewhere in the region of 500 calories less than that break even point. You use a book or a computer program to calculate your calorie total as often as you need to. When you reach the daily limit, you stop eating for that day. Don't deprive yourself; don't take in any fewer calories than five hundred calories under your daily limit. Choose food so as to get adequate protein and fiber, and skew the diet toward fruits, vegetables, grains, and nonfat milk products. Drink enough water that you won't think you're hungry when you're thirsty.

Following this plan will result in losing a pound every week or so. Slow weight loss is preferable to fast weight loss, because you want the habits that you cultivate to lose weight to generalize to the situation where you are maintaining it. If you're eating nothing but shrimp and grapefruit to lose weight, you are not learning how to maintain weight loss. However if you are losing weight slowly, you are doing almost exactly what you will need to do to maintain your weight loss. When you've reached your desired weight you add 500 calories to the daily calorie limit, and proceed exactly as before. When you are so good at estimating calories that you don't need to keep written records, you stop doing this. If your weight climbs four or five pounds over the ideal weight, you go back to writing down everything you eat.

Using Food as a Reward

Some authorities seem quite sure that using junk food as a reward is a very bad thing to do. The reasoning is that anything that is used as a reward has its value increased. I am not convinced that junk food reinforcers are harmful, and I have seen numerous examples in which they have been helpful. Consider these points:

First, I don't find evidence for the harmful effects of using junk food contingently. I have searched the scientific literature, and perhaps I have missed important research. But I have not been able to find studies documenting that using junk food as a reward has resulted in any higher incidence of obesity or eating disorders than are present in people for whom junk food was not used as a reward.

Second: It appears to me that for most children, junk food is highly desirable no matter what you do. My guess is that the reinforcing value of junk food is primarily biologically determined. Through centuries of evolution, starvation has been much more of a threat to human beings' ability to pass on their genes than obesity has been. Most human beings find concentrated fat and sugar highly pleasurable, no matter whether the food has been used as a reinforcer or not.

Third: In using junk food as a reinforcer, you get tremendous practice in self-control. I have for several years used food as a reinforcer, both for myself and for my children. The key to using food as a contingent reinforcer is that you withhold from yourself that reinforcer at all other times; you also give yourself only a measured quantity when you have done the required work! This is quite difficult. The person who practices such a program gets lots of experience at having junk food available, but waiting until the right moment to consume it. This practice in resisting temptation and delaying gratification is much different from what many people get, who by reflex consume junk food whenever it is put in front of them. Thus: the proper use of food as a contingent reinforcer should give lots of practice at resisting the temptation to consume junk food. It should give practice in rational control over the food intake process, and should reduce the probability of an eating disorder, not increase it.

Fourth: In using junk food as a reinforcer, and withholding it at other times, the total quantity of it that is consumed is probably less than when there is free access to it.

Fifth: Using junk food as a reinforcer harnesses its tremendous reinforcing power for a positive use, namely increasing the secondary reinforcing value of effort. That is: the more the child has been contingently reinforced with a very valuable reinforcer for expending effort, the more effort itself becomes reinforcing. Very important studies by Robert Eisenberger have examined this process.

Controversy over this subject remains. Many parents are more willing to put their children on a potent psychotropic drug for many years than they are to use junk food as contingent reinforcement. If scientists do lots of careful research in this area, the results will be quite helpful.

Chapter 34: Bedwetting

Chapter Overview:

Children who wet the bed have usually inherited a knack of sleeping so soundly that they don't recognize the feelings of a full bladder and the urge to urinate. Children eventually stop wetting the bed as they get older, even if no one does anything. Bedwetting is usually not a sign of psychological immaturity or rebelliousness or emotional disorder of any sort. It is nothing to be ashamed of. For parents, your most important goal in dealing with wetting is to produce in the child memories of kindness and reasonableness and rationality in approaching problems. If a child masters staying dry through the night and then starts to wet again, you should get a urinalysis done, to check for diabetes or a urinary tract infection. One reasonable option you and your child can choose in dealing with bedwetting is to buy absorbent disposable underpants and define the wetting of these as a nonproblem. Another option is using a urine alarm device. This is a gadget that sets off a wake-up buzzer when the child urinates in bed. It has proved very effective. If you plan to monitor your child's performance, focus first on how cooperative the child acts, and only second on whether wetting occurs. Celebration of cooperation and dryness is best done without external rewards and contracts. Asking the child to change the sheets supplies a mildly unpleasant natural consequence of wetting. It helps some children to practice repetitively during the day the pattern of lying in bed, feeling fullness in the bladder, and getting up and going to the bathroom. It helps some children to practice withholding urine in the daytime, and measuring the total quantity when finally urinating. Another option is for the parent to awaken the child a couple of times in the first third of the night to let the child go to the toilet; this technique is based on the fact that wetting usually occurs during the deeper sleep that occurs in the first third of the night. Medications are available that will suppress bedwetting as long as the medications are given; when they are discontinued the problem usually begins again. In an ideal world, there would be no stigma attached to bedwetting, and it would be viewed as a low-stakes issue. Sometimes humiliation of bedwetters by the unenlightened turns it into a more important one.

****

Bedwetting is not necessarily a sign of psychological problems of any sort. People have looked to see what fraction of children wet the bed at any given age. Different surveys reveal different numbers, but it's good to keep in mind that at least ten per cent of five year olds wet the bed, and in some surveys closer to twenty per cent still wet. Among ten year olds five to ten per cent still wet, and even at age seventeen, about one per cent still wet. Heredity has a lot to do with urination in one's sleep. One of the inherited factors is the tendency to sleep so deeply that the urge to urinate or the sensation of starting to urinate does not wake you up.

Doing anything at all to try to end urination in one's sleep is a cost-benefit question. The advances in disposable diaper technology that have occurred in recent years add an option not available before. A child, even at camp or at a sleep-over at another child's house, can wear a disposable diaper at night. It may be necessary to restrict fluids before bedtime so that the urine will not exceed the diaper's capacity. A reasonable approach to the problem is simply for the child to continue to wear these diapers until the nervous system matures on its own to the point where they are not necessary, and not bother with any treatment for bedwetting. As the child gets older, the child can take more and more responsibility for putting on and disposing of the diaper. If people redefine the problem of bedwetting as the non-problem of diaper-wetting at night, and no one attaches any emotional significance to this, then lots of worry and pain can be avoided. This is especially true when the child has no motivation to stop urinating in her sleep, but the main motivation comes from the parent.

If, on the other hand, if the child has motivation to stop wetting, there are methods that are often quite successful in accomplishing this task.

In working on bedwetting, as in working on soiling of pants with feces, the most important goal is that the child, upon looking back at the experience years later, will have memories of you as a loving person, memories that will enhance your relationship, and memories that will make her feel confident in her own abilities. The corollary is: stay cool and be nice.

If a child has gained nighttime bladder control and then loses it, starting to bedwet again, it is useful to raise the question of whether the child has either a urinary tract infection or has recently begun to have diabetes. With infections, there is usually pain on urination, but not always, and a urinalysis is in order. With diabetes, there is increased urination during the day as well as the night, with concomitantly increased thirst. This can also be screened for by a urinalysis. Since a urinalysis is a cheap test, I think it's a good idea to get it for children who begin wetting the bed after a time of dryness. Most of those children will probably not have infections or diabetes, but will have begun wetting again for reasons usually unknown and not necessarily psychological.

If you do want to tackle the bedwetting problem, there are several elements that have been found helpful.

The one method that has received the most research support in the treatment of bedwetting is the appropriate use of a urine alarm device. This is a piece of electronic equipment that senses when the child has begun to wet, and at such time sets off an alarm that wakes the child up. At this time the child gets up and finishes voiding into the toilet, changes the bedclothes and sheets if necessary, and resets the device before going back to sleep. In the literature this device has been called the "bell and pad" because some of the devices use as a sensor a thin pad that placed under the child's sheets; when water comes into contact with the pad, a bell or buzzer rings. A technological advance is a much smaller pad that can be taped right onto the child's underpants, that will detect the presence of urine sooner. Such a device is available by mail from Palco Laboratories, 8030 Soquel Avenue, Santa Cruz, California, 95062, 408-476-3151.

Unfortunately, the studies where this device has been most successful seem to have been those where the parent as well as the child got up with the alarm. Many parents may rightly conclude that "the cure is worse than the disease," if this continues very long. The other option is to let the child do the self-awakening with the alarm, and for the parent to stay out of it. Some children I have known have slept so soundly that the loudest settings of urine alarm systems have totally failed to wake them up.

How does the experience of being waked up as soon as you start to wet help end bedwetting? Various theories have been advanced. The earliest theory was that a child would become conditioned to wake up on his own when the bladder was full, after the bell had helped establish an association between a full bladder and waking up. But lots of children end up not getting up during the night, but holding back the urine. So other people theorized that the alarm was somewhat unpleasant, and children learn to avoid it by not wetting. By whatever mechanism, the urine alarm system seems to be quite effective.

Other techniques are directly connected to our list of nine influence methods. Monitoring is accomplished by keeping a calendar and marking whether the night was a dry night or a wet night. As important is monitoring the child's degree of cooperation with the program. If every night is a cooperative night, then there is much reason for all to feel good and to expect positive results, even if every night is not a dry night.

Reinforcement is accomplished partly by celebration and attention and approval for dry beds. I recommend not bothering with contracts, but simply using spontaneous celebration for the dry night. But just as with monitoring, the approval of the parent should not just be for success in keeping the bed dry, but with appropriate compliance and cooperation with all the elements of the program.

A mildly unpleasant consequence for wetting is used in some successful programs: the child, under the supervision of the parent, provides the labor of changing the sheets. The parent teaches the child how to do this, step by step, by modeling, physically and verbally guiding, and approving, during sessions carried out in the daytime, in preparation for what will take place at night. Then when the child wets, the child changes the sheets, while the adult provides as little guidance as possible and very mild approval. The adult does not want to be terribly reinforcing or excited about the child's changing of the sheets, because that may reinforce the wetting itself.

How is practice carried out? One way is to ask the child to lie on the bed, practice feeling, or imagining, that his bladder feels full, and then get up and walk to the toilet, and position himself to go to the bathroom. Some clinicians have asked the child to do this 20 times, with almost a minute of lying in bed in between each repetition. This procedure has also been used as part of the immediate response to bedwetting, after the sheets and bedclothes are changed. The arduous nature of this practice gives a little more incentive to the child not to wet the bed. But it's best I think to define this not as the child's punishment for wetting, but just as practice that needs to take place if there's wetting, and can be skipped if there's no wetting.

This type of practice can also be carried out in the daytime. In addition, another type of practice can be carried out, namely that of withholding urine. The child who has some urine in his bladder strains a bit until he feels like urinating, but then holds it back and lies down and relaxes for two minutes. If after the two minutes the urge to urinate has gone away, he starts back doing whatever he was doing before. If he still has an urge to urinate, he jumps up from bed and urinates in the toilet.

The practice in withholding urine is aided by some monitoring of how well the child has learned to hold urine back. This is accomplished by letting the child hold back as long as he comfortably can in the daytime, then urinating into a 16 ounce measuring cup. Some studies suggest that learning gradually to hold back more and more will help the child not to wet.

How do we use the principle of hierarchy, setting up a series of small steps that the child can progress along to reach the goal of a dry bed all night long? One way is to have a schedule wherein the parents awaken the child at intervals during the night to allow the child to go to the toilet; the intervals between awakenings are gradually lengthened. Some clinicians have found it useful to have these awakenings start with a schedule of once every hour from the child's bedtime until about 1 or 2 o'clock in the morning—after that, the parent gets some well-earned sleep. Then these awakenings are gradually phased out.

The idea of waking a child periodically until 1 or 2 o'clock in the morning and not thereafter makes sense, because most bedwetting episodes occur in the first third of the child's sleep time. This is thought to be because bedwetting tends to occur during deep sleep rather than dreaming or REM sleep, and the first third of the night is when sleep is deepest.

A more parent-friendly alternative is that the child goes to bed early, and the last awakening of the child occurs just before the parent goes to bed, however early or late that might be.

Another use of hierarchy used in some programs is that once the child has learned to sleep through the night with a dry bed, to challenge the child's capacity to sense a full bladder and get up and void by getting the child to drink much more fluid than usual before bedtime. That way the child gets lots more practice in dealing with a full bladder, and in dealing with a challenge probably more difficult than the usual challenge that would be encountered, say, on a sleep-over with a friend. The goal is to increase the child's confidence. One prominent program, by contrast, has encouraged the drinking of lots of fluids on the very first night of the program, with several nighttime awakenings to help the child through the challenge this presents.

There are medications that have proven effective for bedwetting: imipramine and desmopressin acetate (DDAVP). Usually if one of these drugs works, and then is withdrawn, the bedwetting returns. A decision to use medicine usually means that treatment must be continued for months or years, unless the drug is given only in some social setting such as summer camp. The learning-based techniques listed above have a better chance of accomplishing a permanent change.

One approach to bedwetting is to make available to the child the knowledge of the techniques available, and make available the urine alarm system device and a regular alarm clock for awakening and going to the toilet. If the the child is not motivated enough to use these techniques, the next step is to purchase disposable absorbent underpants and define the wetting of them as a nonproblem. If this doesn't work out, another possible solution is to get a plastic cover for the mattress and teach the child to change sheets. In any case, the proper attitude is that bedwetting is nothing to be ashamed of or terribly concerned about. The problem is worth addressing mainly because of unenlightened children's (and some unenlightened adults') tendencies to humiliate bedwetters, and because of the hassle of changing sheets or using disposable underpants.

Chapter 35: Fecal Soiling

Chapter Overview:

A child's having bowel movements in the pants after the age of 5 or so is called encopresis. As with wetting, your most important goal in dealing with soiling is to produce in the child memories of kindness and reasonableness and rationality in approaching problems. Most people don't realize the connection between soiling and constipation. Usually children who soil are constipated most of the time. Normally we get the urge to defecate when the wall of the rectum stretches, and triggers a reflex that we can override or aid by using voluntary muscles. But when the rectum is filled up with hard stool, and the bowel wall is stretched all the time, that reflex is temporarily lost. Then liquid stool tends to leak out around the hard stool, without the sensation of having an urge to defecate. If the child is putting moderately large formed stools into the toilet approximately daily, you can bet that the child isn't constipated. If the child goes for days without a bowel movement, and occasionally has a very large bowel movement, you can bet that the child is constipated most of the time. When parents and child are upset about the soiling, and the child tries very hard to hold back feces, sometimes he only makes the constipation worse. Thus parent and child should clearly understand that the cure for encopresis is not holding back feces, but having bowel movements into the toilet as often as possible. Mineral oil helps to end constipation and psyllium helps to keep stools soft. It's important for the child to watch carefully for urges to defecate, and act on those urges quickly whenever they come. But even with this knowledge and the new plan, the problem sometimes lingers for a while. In this case it's important that a system be worked out whereby the child and the pants can be cleaned with as little emotional distress to anyone as possible. Using disposable underpants is one approach to this; working out a system for cleaning out and storing dirty underpants is another. I recommend that parents assume that the child is not soiling on purpose.

****

Some children have never been toilet trained successfully and continue soiling; some have been successfully toilet trained for a while but revert to soiling later on. The principles of treatment are similar for both groups.

The most important goal in dealing with soiling is to make sure that until the problem is solved, what goes on between people is still largely positive and happy. Children tend to get over soiling sooner or later no matter what is done; many parts of what I'll tell you about are meant to make it go away sooner. But the most important goal is that whole experience will not damage, and will even help, your child's relation with you and attitude toward himself or herself. How could such a negative experience as soiling actually help a relationship and help the child's attitude toward himself? A soiling problem is an experience of adversity, of hardship, and if people handle a hardship together in a very supportive way and with good coping skills, then this hardship becomes a practice for handling future hardships also with good coping skills.

Here are five major components of a plan to help a child stop soiling.

First, that the parent understand the physiology and the psychology of soiling, and that the child understand as much as he can, depending on how old he his.

Second, that the parent and child reduce as much as possible any hostility, anger, shame, and other negative emotion connected with soiling episodes, and if possible develop a cheerful or at least rational attitude toward facing this hardship.

Third, that the child and parent become motivated toward the goal that the child will have bowel movements more often, and into the toilet, that is as many poops into the toilet as possible. This goal is in contrast to the goal most parents and children naturally adopt, which is that the child will become an expert at holding back stool and resisting the urge to defecate.

Fourth, that the child get unconstipated: that is, that the hard feces be "cleaned out" from the child's bowel.

Fifth, that the child's diet be changed so that the accumulation of hard stools in the future is very unlikely, especially if he stays motivated to defecate into the toilet as often as possible.

The First Goal: Physiology and Psychology of Soiling

Most children over about 4 or 5 years old who soil themselves feel ashamed. If it is embarrassing or uncomfortable for a parent to read about and talk about the details this chapter goes into, those feelings will probably give some insight into what most children feel, down deep, about having a problem with fecal soiling. They often hide those feelings. But soiling one's pants is such a socially unacceptable habit, brings out such rejecting reactions from peers, and has such connotations of being a "baby" that we can assume that almost one hundred per cent of children who soil wish very strongly that they could avoid it. (Children who have very low or disrupted intellectual functioning may be an exception to this rule.)

Soiling sometimes tends to bring out strong emotion in a parent, for obvious reasons. Handling pants with feces in them, or finding feces where they should not be, is an unpleasant experience, to say the least. The notion that the child could be doing this on purpose, just to make the parent angry, is an idea that does usually make the parent angry.

Most children who soil their pants probably do not do it on purpose. Sometimes, however, a child who can't help soiling himself acts as if he's doing it on purpose, just to save himself from some shame. That is, the child sometimes would rather be seen as doing something hostile than doing something that he can't help. Sometimes the child would be less ashamed with someone mad at him than with someone feeling sorry for him or laughing at him. For this reason sometimes children act like the soiling is on purpose when it really isn't. The parent should avoid acting like the child is doing it on purpose, and avoid acting hostile toward the child.

Sometimes "self-fulfilling prophecies" and "vicious circles" can take place if there is enough hostility between the parent and child for long enough over the issue of soiling. If the parent is hostile to the child when the child soils his pants, the child is likely to be hostile back at the parent. The more hostile one gets at the other, the more hostile the other is likely to get. This escalation of hostility is a "vicious circle" that should be nipped in the bud as soon as possible.

Perhaps, sometimes, when the parent and child have been very angry at each other over this issue for a long time, and the child sees that soiling is a way to "get at" the parent, some day a child may actually do it on purpose. If this occurs, then the acting like the soiling is on purpose has become a "self-fulfilling prophecy."

These psychological consequences for what starts out as a physical problem make it important to reduce the negative emotion as low as possible as soon as possible.

Let's talk about the physiology of soiling. Many parents are surprised to learn that constipation is a major cause of soiling. If you can make sure that the child does not become constipated, you have taken a very important step in curing the soiling.

Normally the way the bowel works is that when the walls of the bowel get stretched beyond a certain point by the feces that have accumulated in them, the stretching induces the feeling of having to defecate.

When someone is constipated for a while, however, the wall of the bowel is thought to be stretched so much that it temporarily loses that reflex. The hard feces just remain in the bowel, with more water being absorbed from them, getting harder.

What then happens is that feces start "leaking around" the hard feces that are causing the constipation, and cause the soiling. But because the bowel walls are so stretched to begin with, the person is not sensitive to the buildup of feces and cannot feel the need to defecate. Thus the soiling takes place.

This means that sometimes curing constipation can very much help cure soiling. If the bowel can be emptied of the hard stool, and can have nothing but soft stool in it, the bowel is then thought to regain its ability to have the normal reflexes.

How does a doctor tell whether the bowel has a lot of hard stool in it? One way is by doing a rectal examination, that is by taking a lubricated gloved finger and feeling for very hard stool inside the rectum. Another way sometimes used is to do an x-ray of the abdomen. Sometimes useful information can be obtained simply from feeling the child's abdomen.

Another way of getting an approximation about whether there is a lot of hard stool in the bowel is something the parent can do: look at the child's stools. If the child is having reasonably large "formed stools" (not hard, but solid or semisolid) in the toilet fairly often, that is once a day or more, and the parent can see these stools, then the parent can be fairly sure that the child is not plugged up with a lot of hard stool in the bowel.

There are more "vicious circles" that often occur on a physical basis with constipation and soiling. The child somehow gets constipated—perhaps by the combination of a low-fiber diet and trying to hold back bowel movements when a bathroom is unavailable. When stool is held back, the bowel continues to remove water from it, so that it gets harder and harder. Then when the child has a bowel movement with the hard stool in the rectum, the bowel movement is painful. This can lead the child to hold back more, and try to avoid bowel movements, so as to avoid the pain. But the more the child holds back, the more hard the stool becomes and the more painful the bowel movements are, in a "vicious circle."

Then, when the bowel wall is stretched and the child starts leaking bowel movements around the hard stool, the shame of soiling his pants makes the child want to hold back bowel movements even more. The more he soils, the more he wants to hold back, and the more he holds back, the more constipated he gets; the more constipated he gets, the more he soils, in another "vicious circle."

Second Goal: Reducing the Negative Emotion

The way to reduce negative emotion about soiling is for the parent to get together with the child and figure out a routine that will be done in the same way each time the child soils. When the soiling takes place it will simply be a matter of a little more work to do. The older the child is, the more the child can do that work. The work I'm talking about is to get the underwear cleaned out and stored and eventually cleaned, and the child's body cleaned up, and the child's clothes cleaned. It is not a terribly large amount of work; but the key is getting an automatic sequence that is well rehearsed ahead of time, so that there won't be any hostility between people at the time.

If the child soils very frequently, as a first step in reducing the negative emotion, the child can wear pull-up disposable diapers that make it much easier to get things cleaned up after a soiling. Disposable diapers are available in all sizes.

If the child is a preschooler, perhaps the first goal on the hierarchy, the easiest one to achieve, is simply that the child helps you know when the diapers need to be changed and acts pleasant and cooperative while you change the diaper. If you can get this far, at least you have a pleasant interpersonal situation.

A next stage might be that the child actually takes off the diaper, wipes himself with wipes, and puts a clean diaper back on, with you standing by, helping and mildly reinforcing the child for his or her accomplishments.

A third stage is that the child goes into the bathroom by himself with a dirty diaper and emerges with a clean one.

If the child soils infrequently enough that you want the child to wear regular underpants, I suggest that you go and buy a scrub brush with a long handle, the sort used for cleaning toilet bowls, and a plastic bucket with an air-tight top. Both of these are kept in the bathroom that the child uses the most. You also keep some extra underpants and pants in the bathroom, so that they will be there when needed. You also set aside a certain sponge or washrag for use by the child in cleaning his own body. When the child soils his pants, you go through a series of steps, as follows. First, the child goes into the bathroom as quickly as possible and tries to have a bowel movement into the toilet as well. Then while sitting at the toilet he takes off his pants and underpants and cleans his own body up with toilet paper as much as possible. He flushes the toilet. Then he takes a wet washrag and cleans up his body more, and a towel and dries himself off. Alternatively, he can take a quick shower. Then he puts on the clean underwear and the clean pants. Then he takes the brush and some toilet paper and maybe some scouring powder and cleans off the inside and the rim of the toilet bowl, flushing the toilet once again, so that he will have a reasonably clean area to work in. Then he takes the soiled underwear and the soiled pants and puts them in the toilet bowl, holding onto part of them, and uses the brush to clean the feces out of them as much as possible. Then he flushes the toilet. Then he puts the wet and partially soiled pants and underwear in the plastic bucket and replaces the top. The clothes can then be washed after some of them have accumulated.

Where is the parent while all this is going on? Again, there is a hierarchical progression to more and more independence on the part of the child. At first the parent will need to do the tasks for the child, to show the child how to do the various steps. The only job of the child is to act pleasant and cooperative while the parent is doing the work. Gradually the parent lets the child do them, while the parent functions as a guide, giving mild approval when the child successfully completes one of the steps. If the child really can't remember what to do next, the parent can prompt the child, but remember that it is much more useful to congratulate the child for remembering himself than to preempt his opportunity to remember by telling him what to do too soon. Then, gradually, the parent may stay out of the bathroom while the child does the tasks, and simply inspect and get a verbal report afterwards that they were completed. In other words, the parent gradually trains the child toward more independence in this task. With an older and more cooperative child this movement toward independence may go quickly. With a younger or less cooperative child, the parent may have to stay in the mode of doing the tasks for the child for a longer time.

The most important thing about these tasks is not that the child learn to do them independently. The most important thing is the emotional tone that occurs in the relation between parent and child while the tasks are going on. If the parent can demonstrate a patient, non-excited, just barely on the cheerful side of neutral emotional demeanor, it will help immensely. The sort of verbalizations the parent wants to model are along the lines of, "Here we have some work to do, OK, now we're doing it, now to the next step, now we're done." The adult should be task focussed, not blaming the child, not gushing with sympathy, just acting as if it's no big deal and let's see how quickly we can get the work done. The more the adult participates in the task with this attitude, the more the child will come to show the same attitude.

If there has been a long history of a lot of hostility between parent and child over the soiling episodes, and the parent has been blaming the child for a long time, then it is very important for the parent and child to sit down and have a chat, and for the parent to explain what the "new deal" is. The parent explains that the parent has gained some new knowledge about soiling, and that the parent is optimistic that with this new knowledge they can get somewhere that they haven't been able to get before. The parent explains that from now on the parent will try as hard as possible not to yell at or blame the child, and that they will start working together on the problem as cooperatively as they can. The parent hopes that the child can help out in the cleaning tasks as much as possible, but the parent is willing to help out the child.

Then, they act out or rehearse exactly what will happen each time the child has an episode of soiling. They do this in moments of calm, when both are in a good mood. They list the steps together and mentally rehearse them.

If the parent and child can work together cheerfully and cooperatively when the child soils, and if the parent can approve of the child's gradually taking on more and more of the tasks independently, then they are well on their way toward solving the problem.

It is important that the parent be prepared to "do all the work yourself" for a while, especially with young children. The most important thing is not that the child do the cleaning-up tasks independently, but that the emotional climate is non-negative, matter-of-fact, and unexcited. If you go into the tasks feeling that you have to get the child to do the work, you are likely to get into power struggles that can produce a negative emotional climate. If you are prepared to do as much of the work as is necessary yourself you are in much better position to avoid negative emotion.

I suppose it's possible that if you are too positive and cheerful about the whole clean-up process, the child will be rewarded by this positivity for defecating into his pants, and do it more often. If you're concerned about this, a "slightly on the cheerful side of neutral" or "matter-of-fact" demeanor, one that is not particularly emotional one way or another, will solve this problem. However, if by some chance you are able to achieve a mood of great positivity and cheerfulness, I think that the model you give your child of remaining upbeat in the face of adversity will do you child much more good than harm.

Third Goal: Motivation for Frequent Defecation Into Toilet

Next the parent helps the child to change his thinking in a most important direction. The parent explains to the child the physiology of soiling, and the importance of not getting constipated, and the importance of emptying the bowel as often as possible. If the child understands this, he will be more likely to join in the plan.

Second, the parent gets into a frame of mind to celebrate when the child poops into the toilet. The parent asks the child to go and have a bowel movement whenever he possibly can, and not to flush the toilet, but to come and get the parent's attention and let the parent see the stool in the toilet bowl. Each time the parent sees the stool in the toilet, the parent congratulates the child in a joyous way, and looks happy. If you really want to escalate the motivation for this crucial part of the program, you withhold junk food from the child except as a reinforcer after poop appears in the toilet. This part of the program has made the difference between failure and success for some children I've worked with. You want the child to be highly motivated to get feces into the toilet at every possible opportunity.

I want to emphasize one more time: what you are reinforcing the child for is putting feces into the toilet, and *not* having unsoiled pants. Reinforcing unsoiled pants can make the problem worse, by motivating the child to withhold feces and become constipated. The opposite of encopresis is *not* clean pants; it is bowel movements into the toilet.

Those of you who haven't dealt with soiling problems in a while may not like the idea of going and looking at the feces in the toilet bowl. Those of you who have, know that this is so much less repugnant than actually having to clean them up, that this aspect of the program is no problem.

Sometimes children at school aren't allowed to get up and go to defecate whenever they want to, but can go only at scheduled bathroom breaks. This interferes with the child's following the maxim of "defecate as many times as you possibly can, as soon as you can after getting the urge." A more enlightened policy will allow students to go to the bathroom whenever they need to. The parent may need to have a discrete conversation with teachers or the principal, or perhaps show the teachers and the principal this chapter. The child with a problem with soiling should be allowed to go to the bathroom and defecate whenever he needs to, in as private conditions as possible.

Some children hate to defecate in school bathrooms because the toilets are filthy or because they have no doors on the stalls and peers prevent any privacy. Conditions such as these may contribute to soiling problems. Certainly it is worthwhile to at least ask the child if these conditions present a problem. If toilet seats with urine on them inhibit the child, the child should be taught how to clean them off himself. (First wipe the toilet seat off with dry wads of toilet paper, then with toilet paper wet by water from the sink, then with dry wads of toilet paper again; flush the paper often enough that the toilet isn't clogged up.)

Some parents wonder if their children fail to follow the maxim of "defecate as often as you can, as soon as possible after you get the urge," because they just are too interested in playing and don't feel like interrupting the play by coming inside to defecate. It's surely possible. It's also possible that some children may be more ashamed to leave their peers to defecate, or to ask to use the rest room at someone else's house. Anything that interferes with the child's willingness and ability to defecate into a toilet as soon as he gets the urge is an obstacle to the solution of soiling. For some children it may be very useful to practice thinking that it's ok to ask to use the rest room, that everyone in the world has to defecate, and that having to defecate is nothing to be ashamed of.

I have achieved much better results with the goal of frequent bowel movements into the toilet when I began to advise parents to withhold junk food from the child's diet and to use junk food as a reinforcer for a bowel movement into the toilet. That is: the child's intake of soda, candy, cake, cookies, etc. comes to a screeching halt, but the child gets about one third of the former daily intake of these foods immediately after showing the parent some feces that the child has put in the toilet. For some children this has been the most important and effective portion of the program.

Fourth Goal: Unconstipation

It is not known for sure what fraction of children with soiling also have problems with constipation. For older children some have estimated that it is pretty close to one hundred per cent. If the child is not constipated, it will not hurt to do the major unconstipating intervention that is recommended here, which is to increase the amount of fiber in the diet.

If there is a lot of hard stool in the child's rectum and bowel, how is it gotten out? One way is by giving mineral oil by mouth to the child. Sometimes it may be necessary to give oil or water enemas, or as a last resort to manually remove the impaction with a gloved finger. Your doctor should guide you through the decisions during this phase of treatment. Usually you can use mineral oil taken by mouth. Mineral oil works by going through the bowel without being digested and increasing the bulk as well as increasing the slipperiness of the feces.

If your child has abdominal pain, cramps in the abdomen, nausea, vomiting, or other symptoms that could possibly be caused by appendicitis, then get in touch with your pediatrician and don't give mineral oil or fiber-increasing agents. An inflamed appendix can be ruptured by the increase in movement of the bowel that comes from these agents.

If you overshoot and give too much mineral oil, the child will have more episodes of accidental soiling during this phase. But this is only a temporary problem that should last only a day or two at most. The most important thing is to clean out the hard stool. Try to help the child not to worry about any accidents that happen during this "clean-out" phase.

One way of knowing that the clean-out phase has been successful is by seeing something common in children who soils, which is that the child defecates large quantities of solid stools into the toilet. This gives you some information telling you that the child is not "plugged up" and "leaking around" impacted stool. On the other hand, if you see nothing but liquid stools during the clean-out phase, you are not sure that the child isn't still impacted with stool. The doctor can check with a rectal examination if it is necessary to answer this question.

If the mineral oil only increases the rate of leaking around the hard stool, and doesn't get it out, then it may be necessary to go to enemas or to manual removal of the hard stool. My own tendency is to try to avoid these if it's at all possible to accomplish the same result by a little more patient use of oral agents.

Fifth Goal: Keeping Feces Soft

How do you keep constipation from happening over and over again? There are two main ways of keeping the stool soft. One is the goal we spoke of earlier, that the child has a bowel movement as often as he possibly can. This keeps stools soft by virtue of the fact that the longer feces sit around in the bowel, the more the bowel does its job of absorbing water, and makes them harder. So if the child responds to every urge by getting up and going to defecate, that will help enormously.

The second way of keeping the stool soft is by altering the child's dietary intake so that the child takes in a good deal of fiber. Fiber is the part of foods that goes through the bowel undigested. If the particular type of fiber in a certain food tends to absorb water, then the fiber produces soft stool.

Fruits and vegetables and grains tend to be good sources of fiber. The outer covering of grains, or the bran, is a good source of fiber. Cereals with the word "bran" in them are usually a fairly good source of fiber.

Another source of fiber that you can use to make the child's stool stay soft is a powder from the psyllium seed; the most familiar trade name for this powder is Metamucil. This type of fiber absorbs water and makes a gel-like substance that goes through the bowel undigested; this tends to produce stools that are soft and slippery. It is not "habit forming" any more than any other source of fiber, as far as anyone knows. Children who have had soiling will often benefit from taking a teaspoon of psyllium powder (in a large glass of liquid) every day for a long time.

How do you give this so that a child will like it? It is supposed to be mixed in with some liquid. The orange flavored, finely ground psyllium is not unpleasant to drink mixed with water. It is much better with fruit juice, such as orange, grape, pineapple, or apple juice. It is ok when mixed with pop. It is very good when mixed with a glass of milk with a couple of large spoonfuls of ice cream stirred or blended in with it to form a milk shake. It is important not to give the psyllium powder to the child as a powder, without mixing it with the liquid first, because you don't want it getting stuck in the child's throat. And in addition, you want it to absorb as much water as possible to form a soft mass; you accomplish that by mixing it with liquid in the first place.

As always, the more concrete and visual you can make the explanation to the child, the more likely is the child to understand it. Therefore I recommend acting out for the child with toy people every aspect of this program, as well as explaining it verbally.

Chapter 36: Talking About Traumatic Events

Chapter Overview:

When a tragic or traumatic event has occurred that affects a child, adults naturally wonder how best to help the child. We should remember that the first goal is not to spare the child of all pain. It is natural to feel great grief when one is told of tragic events. The goal is to ensure that the child's memories of the conversations are consistent with the ideas that at least some people are trustworthy and kind, and that it is possible, with help, to handle the event. If an adult lies to a child or witholds facts of major importance in the child's life, the short run avoidance of emotional pain is usually more than made up for by longer term problems. Adults can communicate to children the idea that the event is able to be handled, mainly through tones of voice and facial expressions. It may be necessary to explain very concretely to young children what death means. The best defense against grief is lots of social support: people who are close and loving. For some traumas, the support system must not only deal with the emotional issues of loss, but practical issues such as deciding how the child will be cared for. You can give children permission to talk about their feelings about tragic events by modeling self-disclosure, and by being an empathic, nondirective listener for them when they do feel like talking. When you and the child hear of tragedies more distant from the child's immediate life reported in the news, you can communicate your own value system to the child by the way you talk about the tragedy in the child's presence. Although a specific response to a tragedy is important for a child, what is even more important is the quality of the child's relationship with major caretaker(s) after the event, year in and year out.

****

A child's parent dies, a sibling is paralyzed, both parents are killed, a parent is convicted of a crime, parents decide to divorce, a child loses a limb. Tragedies like these unfortunately are happening somewhere every day. What things are best to keep in mind when helping children deal with them?

Keeping the Goal in Mind

The goal when talking with children about these unpleasant or awful events is not that the child should feel no pain. Relatives and helping professionals feel sorry for the children who have experienced tragedies, and hate the idea of inflicting pain upon them in a conversation about what has happened. Therefore, it often happens that children are given evasive or downright false information about what has happened.

But when we think about it, the most normal, natural, and human way to respond to the death of a loved one or another major tragedy is with a great deal of pain and grief. If a child should hear about the death of a parent, shrug off the news, and ask what is on television next, and never show the slightest pain, we would worry more about that child than we would about the one who looked very sad and cried. (This is not to say that all children show immediate pain and grief. Defending yourself by denying the reality of an unfortunate event is something we do as children as well as when we get to be adults.) The bottom line is that whoever tells the child about a tragedy should not define it as a "failure" if the child is extremely upset at hearing very upsetting news.

So if the goal of the first interactions with the child is not to avoid upsetting the child, what is it?

It's to make it so that the child's memories of the conversation are most consistent with the ideas that (1) people are trustworthy and kind, and (2) it is possible, with help, to handle anything that comes along, including this. ("Handling" it doesn't mean not crying, or not being unhappy, or acting as if nothing happened. "Handling" it means going on, withstanding it, surviving, and having a trace of knowledge somewhere in the back of the mind that some day it will be possible to feel good again.)

The persons speaking to the child after a tragedy may not get any feedback at all from the child regarding whether the conversation has been successful in these goals. The persons must construct the interactions so that if the child does remember them, the child will be able to infer these ideas from what was said and how it was said.

What Harm is Done by Withholding the Truth

Suppose someone decides that the truth about what happened is just too hard for a child to take, and withholds it. How could this do any harm?

First of all it makes it necessary to either lie to the child or evade the truth. If the child is not convinced, but suspects that something is being withheld from him or her, then the child tends to be suspicious that something awful has happened, but he doesn't know what. This can be very scary, at the time, but worse is the fact that in the future, the child can never be sure if something else is being withheld. Suppose just after the tragedy the child is convinced by misleading information that everything is OK, and the child feels optimistic and hopeful. Then, when the child eventually finds out that a tragedy has occurred, the child doesn't forget the misleading reassuring messages that people told him. The child may correctly infer from this experience that reassuring messages he gets from people are not to be trusted.

Children also infer something about their own coping powers from the context of how people act toward them. If information is withheld from them in the belief that it is too awful for them to stand, then when they eventually find out the truth they have less confidence that they can handle it, because even adults, who know much more about the world than they, obviously think that the truth is too awful for them to stand. Thus in addition to undermining the child's trust in other people's truthfulness, withholding the bitter truth tends to undermine the child's trust in his or her own coping powers.

The conclusion from this is that the child should be told the truth. However, it does not mean that the adults involved can't take some time preparing themselves.

Who Should Tell?

The ideal person is a family member whom the child already knows well and trusts, someone with whom the child will have a continuing relationship, preferably the person who will be the child's caretaker.

However, if a family member is not available, or is too injured or distraught to be able to talk with the child about it, and the child is asking for the news of what has happened, my opinion is that it is usually better for a health professional to go ahead and answer the child's question than to evade it for very long. The fact that the child has heard the news from his doctor or nurse in no way obviates the need for the same sort of conversation with a family member when the family member is available.

Communicating the Important Ideas in Tone of Voice

Sometimes it is helpful for whoever is speaking to the child to say directly, "This is something we feel very sad about. But we will help each other out, and we will be able to handle it." However, if the person really believes these things, the general philosophy will come out sooner or later in the tone of voice the person uses. I think that the best preparation for talking with the child about the event is for the caretaker to consider whether those ideas are true, and if they are felt to be true, reminding oneself of them often.

What if the caregiver weeps and looks and sounds very sad while speaking to the child? Then the child is getting a very important truth conveyed, that the tragic event naturally brings forth sad emotions. The child is also getting the chance to learn that it's fine to express those emotions, and that sadness is not incompatible with strength.

Being Concrete About What Death Means

Developmental psychologists differ about the age at which a child is capable of knowing what death means. There is some evidence that children can understand death very early in life, provided that they have had the requisite experiences to know what it means.

It is painful to simultaneously explain to a child what death is, and the fact that a loved one has died, but this must sometimes be done. If the person explaining knows that the child has had previous experience with a grandparent or other relative, or a pet, to know what death means, then the person can assume that knowledge or maybe refer to the experience that taught the child the meaning of death. If the child has had no experience, the person explaining what death is should in my opinion probably explain that a person who will never be alive again, will never be able to do the things that live people do, like walking, thinking, talking, eating, breathing, or feeling anything. It is probably good to explain that we will not see the person around any more.

If there are religious beliefs about life after death and what happens to the person's spirit after death that the caretaker honestly holds, these can be communicated to the child. The child's questions should be answered as honestly as possible. The child may ask very concrete questions about what will happen to the person's body; these too should be answered honestly.

The Best Defense Against Grief

To use abstract phrases, human beings handle stress best when there is lots of social support. In concrete terms, a child will probably handle a tragedy best when he or she is surrounded by family members and loyal friends who are close and loving and who are supporting one another in their pain, as well as the child. It is probably much better for the child to be among people who are weeping and hugging one another than to be removed from them. The child gets the message that this is how you handle bad things: you get help and support from your friends and family, and together you cope with it. All that you can do to bring together the child with his support system will probably be very helpful to the child. In time of tragedy it is important to think in terms of connecting a child with his support system, i.e. helping relatives and friends to be supportive to the child.

Support Systems That Aren't Supportive

If you are lucky enough to have a support system of friends and relatives that is kind and caring, then grief and loss are much easier to deal with. On the other hand, if the people you would naturally look to for support are alcoholic or drug addicted or are embroiled in severe conflict with you, or lack empathy, or are suffering from severe physical or psychiatric illness, or otherwise can't do what is necessary to support the child, then things are much more difficult. You have the task of finding a better support system as well as dealing with grief and loss. You may in this circumstance want to turn to mental health professionals for help.

Tasks of the Support System

If there is a working support system, a family or group of friends, that is dealing with the situation together, they have several tasks. One is for the members to get together and talk with one another, and listen to one another. Another is helping each other through the problem-solving process regarding concrete planning about what will happen next.

The Concrete Planning Process

For many major tragedies, and especially when a child loses a parent, there is not simply a loss of a loved one, but also usually a loss of someone the child vitally depends upon for the necessities of life. It's not as though the child just doesn't get to see and talk to and have fun with the parent. It's also that the child may have unanswered questions about where his food is going to come from, or who's going to protect him from dangerous people in the neighborhood, or whether he'll have clothes to wear, and so forth.

Family members can get together and communicate with each other about what the concrete plans for caretaking of the child are.

As soon as these plans are made satisfactorily, they should be communicated to the child, who may be wondering what is going to happen to him but may be too afraid to ask.

The Long-Term Task of Parenting

Although dealing with the tasks of delivering bad news to children and helping in the immediate reaction to the tragedy are the tasks most on the minds of those responsible for the child, I would guess that these are not as important in determining the long-run prognosis for the child as is the quality of the day in, day out rearing that the child will experience from that time onward.

The Skill of Listening, with Empathic Reflections

In the time following a major tragedy, how often should adults bring up the topic of the tragedy, and explicitly encourage the child to talk about his feelings, and how much should they keep quiet, and risk having the child "hold everything inside"?

I think the best answer is for you to get very skilled at the art of empathic listening: responding to what the child says, in such a way that the child feels understood, does not feel criticized, does not receive premature advice, and feels reinforced for his or her disclosure. Often the reflective statements we've talked about in earlier chapters are most helpful. These are statements of the form, "What I hear you saying is ________," or "If I understand you right, you're feeling _________," spoken in a tone of voice that encourages the child to talk more, is the best way to encourage the child to talk as much as he wants and needs to without having the encouragement backfire.

If it is good for the child to talk about his feelings about the tragedy, the best way to bring that out is to allow the child to hear the adults talking about their own feelings about it. One model of self-disclosure is worth a dozen prying questions.

What should be our attitude toward the child's talking about the tragedy? The idea that the child has to have a catharsis, and get the feelings out, and once they're out, the problem is solved, is an antiquated point of view. It may be most helpful for some children to do a great deal of talking about what happened. Others may have their hands full for the time being just dealing with the present problems of life. Some may do fine without ever doing a lot of talking about it. Guessing when the tendency to repress or forget about painful experiences should be opposed and when it should be allowed to proceed unchecked is an art and not a science. I think the best attitude is to be responsive to the child's wishes to talk, and to reinforce the child's self-disclosures in all spheres, not just with respect to the tragedy, without feeling a need to force anything upon the child.

It's Best Not to Assume Knowledge of How the Child Feels

Many people assume that the child feels nothing but grief and sorrow over the loss when some tragedy happens. Sometimes, however, the child's predominant feeling will be guilt, that he wasn't nice enough to the person who died, or that he wished at some point that the person would die. It could be that the predominant feeling is fear about what the child's future will be and who will take care of him. It could be that the child remembers times when someone who died was harshly punitive, and the child feels a component of relief over the person's death. It could be, as in the case of a peer who has committed suicide, that a child feels admiration and envy. People's feelings can be so unexpected that it is important to listen, and to be able to listen prepared for anything. It is difficult to hear some of these feelings from a child about a tragedy; the listener must be prepared if she wants to avoid punishing the child for disclosing the child's innermost feelings.

One Of the Tasks of Grieving: Habituation

Why is it often a good idea to grapple repeatedly with painful memories, rather than just to shove them out of the mind forever? One theory is that it is not good to carry around memories that, when brought to consciousness, bring you extreme pain. If you are carrying around those memories, it's sometimes a lot of work to keep them out of consciousness. They sometimes pop back into consciousness despite best efforts to keep them out. And sometimes, for example when a loved one has died, the price you pay for shoving thoughts of that person out of consciousness is not being able to reexperience the positive and pleasant memories. People can try to shove out of their brains an enormous part of their experience when the memories of a lost loved one bring great pain. We sometimes use the phrase *unresolved grief* to refer to the situation where someone is trying to keep from thinking about lots of memories because of the painful feelings they bring up.

The word *habituation* refers to the process whereby somehow as you experience something repeatedly, the emotion it evokes gradually gets turned down. This is the same process that allows a person desensitize himself to a fear of heights by gradually exposing himself more and more to high places. So when you have lost a loved one, part of the task of grieving is gradually turning down the painful feelings associated with the memory of the person so that you can, for example, reexperience the positive memories. By repeatedly thinking of the lost person, you gradually become able to do so without extreme pain.

I am talking about reducing pain, not eliminating it. It's natural to continue to feel sadness when remembering the death of a loved one. The task is to reduce the sadness to the point where you can let your mind range over memories without fear of being greatly hurt.

Play Can Have the Same Role as Conversation for Very Young Children

Preschoolers sometimes can't talk about their feelings about a tragedy that happened to them. Sometimes dramatic play is a way for the young child to represent symbolically what has happened and try to master it somehow. If you are good at doing dramatic play with the child, just let the child have fun playing. If the child brings the theme of the dramatic play around to something to do with the tragedy, the adult can be empathic within the context of the dramatic play, or perhaps model dealing with the tragedy within the context of the play. My experience is that with young children, it usually doesn't work too well to interrupt the dramatic play and talk to the child about the real-life event.

When Bad Things Happen In the News

When a national or local tragedy happens, not a family tragedy, people wonder about how to talk with their children about it. Plane crashes, deaths of people the child knew about, war, famines, earthquakes.

In speaking with the child about such events, again I emphasize that the main goal is not that the child feel no pain. To the extent that the child does empathize with the victims, the child will feel pain. To know of horrible things happening to other people, even people far away, without feeling even the slightest twinge of pain is not good. On the other hand, to be immobilized by grief and depression and bereavement over every bad thing that happens represents insufficient defenses. An appropriate balance is called for.

The way in which parents speak with children, and to other people, about tragedies often communicates to the child in powerful ways what the value system of the parent is. For examples: a the child sees a parent responding with outrage, sadness, frustration to the news of deaths from a war the parent regards as immoral and wrongheaded. The child gets powerful messages about nonviolence. These may be much better for the child than a reassuring message that everything will be OK. A good person is assassinated, and the child hears the parent speak with deep regret and moral condemnation of the violent act. The child also hears a recounting of the positive and courageous actions of the fallen leader. The child is learning about what the parent values. The child hears the parent's opinions following the death of someone who was trying to set a record in doing a risky stunt; the child gets messages about the value of self-care for the parent. Children should not be sheltered from the parent's strong feelings about public events, if the parent is sure that such strong feelings are consonant with the value system that is desired to be transmitted to the child.

My impression is that although dealing with specific tragedies is important, it is more important that the child and the caretaker get along well, and that the child is exposed to dependable caretaking and positive models, day in and day out. (Positive models include the skill of honesty.) The needs of children who have suffered tragedy are more similar to the needs of all other children than they are different. Those needs basically include having a stable caretaker or set of caretakers, who are kind to the child, who model reasonable ways of responding to the world, who talk and listen with the child and play with the child, who respond with approval to the child's positive behaviors and with gentle firmness to the child's negative behaviors, and so forth.

Chapter 37: Promoting Language Development

Chapter Overview:

This chapter organizes techniques already described in previous chapters into a plan for stimulating a child's language development. Social relations, psychological skill development, and thinking are mediated to a large extent by the words we learn to say to ourselves and others. Language learning consists in both the addition of words to vocabulary, and the addition of new ways of putting words together to make more complex thoughts. The most useful new words are not exotic animals or cities or other things that can be learned by rote, but basic concepts that describe the relations of things to one another, and words that help in the self-talk associated with psychological skills. Especially crucial is the ability to narrate events of the day. The major engines that drive language development are the wishes to understand and control or influence what is going on. Thus the best language learning lessons take place in real life. Talking to a child a lot and explaining what is going on can occur before the child even learns to speak. The most crucial element of language learning is back and forth interactions in which each person responds to (and is thus influenced by) what the other person just said or did; we can call these reciprocal interactions. The more exchanges, the longer the exchanges, and the more joyous the exchanges, the faster the child will learn language. Tracking and describing means putting into words what the child is doing and paying attention to. Using reflections, or paraphrasing the child's utterance to check out whether one understands it correctly, stimulates positive conversation. Telling the child about your own experience, using facilitations (such as "Yes" or "Oh,") to signal that you are listening, and using follow-up questions and statements also enhance the quality and quantity of conversation. To bring out reciprocal interaction, say something that models how to chat; leave adequate silence for the child to speak; be very responsive when the child does speak. The responsiveness should at the beginning be toward any utterance of the child; later, the shaping process can bring out the utterances that are most intelligible and most prosocial. The child who needs language stimulation will do well to get "hooked" on dramatic play, since this affords countless opportunities for language practice and reciprocal interaction. Reading aloud to the child models use of language; responding very positively to the child's retelling or composing stories encourages the child's expressive language. My book of basic concept illustrations is an adjunct to language learning, meant to show the child the meaning of concepts such as back, front, first, last, top, bottom, and so forth. Any reading activity should be readily interruptable by reciprocal interaction. Don't stop the recreational activity of reading aloud in the family when children are able to read. Reading aloud is a great language activity, especially if the language used in the book is at the "challenge zone," not too

easy and not too difficult for the child. Since language development ideally goes on all day long, use of the techniques in this chapter by all the child's major caretakers is far superior to use only by the parents or only a therapist.
****

This chapter is something of a cross-reference because most of the techniques described here have already been defined in other chapters. Promoting language development is a by-product of many of the procedures I've advocated to improve other psychological skills. For the child who needs a boost in language development, the same techniques can be used systematically toward that end.

When I speak of language development I mean the child's ability to understand and produce spoken language fluently. Articulation, which is the ability to say words clearly, is a different skill referred to as "speech" rather than "language." Language is by far the more important ability of the two. When language is in good shape, speech tends to come around sooner or later.

The Connection Between Language Ability and Psychological Skills

Language is the medium for a great deal of our thinking; the better language users we are, the better are our thinking resources. For example, the child who is able to say to himself, "Hey, wait a second, let me think what is likely to happen if I do this, before I do it," is using a complex sentence with some abstract concepts, including "likely" and "before" and "if." The child who has these concepts in the vocabulary is better equipped to think before acting than the child who does not. In order for a child to think, "I could push him back, or I could tell the teacher, or I could ignore him," the child needs the concept of "or."

This line of reasoning leads us to think about what concepts are most important to get into the vocabulary. Do we consider it langage learning when a child learns the names of progressively more and more species of exotic animals, or when the child can name every instrument in the orchestra? The most crucial words are those that really assist the child in the thinking necessary to be done in the carrying out of the psychological skills. Here are some examples of words and phrases that are useful for various skills or groups of skills:

trusting: trustworthy; some people, all people; knowing someone well vs. not knowing someone well; friendly, unfriendly
social initiations: introduce, invite, interrupt, wait, finish, paying attention to
handling separation: go away, come back, minutes, hours, take care of,

someone we know, someone we don't know
problem solving and decision making: if, want, problem, situation, or, cause, effect, option, different, same, advantage, disadvantage, probable, improbable, likely, unlikely, outcome, desirable, undesirable, should, ought to, utility
fortitude: frustration, tolerate, handle it, take it, put up with, very upset, not very upset, tough, brave, awfulizing, getting down on myself, blaming someone else, learning from the experience
celebrating positive events: hooray, good, celebrate, smart or good, praiseworthy, admirable, compared to what I could do before, proud, accomplishment
delaying gratification: self control, self discipline, work, delay of gratification, concentration, put off, do now, later, practice, repetition-tolerance
relaxing and playing: tense, relaxed, scared, comfortable, secure, peaceful, silly, gleeful, humor, sarcasm
talking about feelings: happy, sad, scared, worried, angry, mad, guilty, ashamed, proud, glad, love, like, dislike, surprised, etc.
awareness of control: in your power to change, something you can control, something you can influence, something you can do something about, partly can, partly can't, make it more likely
imagination: imagine, pretend, fantasy, rehearse, practice, see in your imagination, hear in your imagination
purpose: meaning, goal, worthwhile, purpose, aim, direction, admire, try, want, code of ethics.

These words are of course only a sampling. But it is easy to see how a child with any of these words in his vocabulary would have certain thinking powers unlocked that would be inaccessible to children without such concepts in the vocabulary.

In thinking about the connection between language use and psychological skills, we want to think not only of individual words, but also the ability to connect words into narratives of events. The skill of recounting vignettes from life is extremely important. This book has repeatedly emphasized the central skill-development techniques of recalling one's own positive examples of psychological skills, and celebrating them; and recalling negative examples, redeciding upon more desirable courses of thought, feeling, and behavior, and rehearsing those desirable patterns. Whether one does this formally or informally, all reviewing of past actions, all thinking, "Is there a better way to handle this situation," "What is the best thing to do in this situation," relies upon being able to imagine and recount a situation. Thus a crucial ability is codifying, in words, the situations one runs into; narrating what happened in one's life; telling true stories about the events of the day.

The Engines That Drive Language Development

There are very powerful intrinsic motivations for a child to learn language; in any efforts to stimulate language development we want to harness and strengthen those intrinsic motivations, and not undermine them by turning language learning into a dull and lifeless activity for which the child can't see the point.

Two powerful motivations for learning language include the wish to understand what is going on around you, i.e. to make sense of what people are saying, and to control what is happening in the interpersonal world, i.e. to influence other people's actions by the magic of talking to them. Suppose a toddler hears the parent say, "We're going to go outside." Suppose the toddler gets an image of what "outside" is, and then the outside actually materializes! The child is getting an experience of the magical power of words to foretell the future. When the one year old discovers that by uttering the word "juice" or "pretzel" that the desired object somehow materializes in front of him, he has learned the power of words to influence other people's actions. When the child learns that when he says, "No! I don't want to," that sometimes he doesn't have to, he is learning that these magical incantations have lots to do with getting what he wants. When he sits at the supper table ignored by his parents, and discovers that by saying, "Daddy!" and then uttering some more words, he can get the person of his selection to look at him and listen to him and pay attention, he is getting a very powerful gratification.

How different these motives are from the motive to please someone who holds up a picture of a truck and says, "This is a truck. Can you say truck?... Good! This is a cup. Say cup, please." One motive is that of jumping through hoops for someone, and the others are very vital, self-interested motives, much more powerful and basic.

How can we more powerfully harness the motive of understanding what is going on? First, by talking to the child a lot, explaining what will happen and what is happening, so that if the child can understand it, the understanding will be gratifying. And second, by allowing oneself (within reason, of course) to be influenced by the child's verbalizations: allowing those utterances to have an effect of getting attention, if not getting exactly what is desired.

The main moral of this line of reasoning is that if you want to stimulate a child's language development, you don't just arrange for a couple of language lessons every week. You find ways to increase the natural gratifications of comprehending and using language that occur every hour of the child's waking life.

The Crucialness of Reciprocal Interactions

In an earlier chapter I defined reciprocal interaction as that in which two or more people took turns responding to one another, being influenced by the other person's response. Suppose one person says, "I saw a duck," and the other says, "A duck? Where was it?" and the first says, "It was at the park." The second person by her response gives evidence of having heard the first person—she has been influenced by the first person's utterance. Then the first person, by answering the question "Where?" gives evidence of being influenced by the second person's response.

Each time there is one exchange in reciprocal interaction, the language learner gets the gratification of seeing that her words have an effect on the interpersonal world. By uttering these magic sounds, the things that someone else says are affected. The wider the range of things you can communicate to the other person, the more gratification you can achieve. This is the natural, intrinsic motivation toward language learning that is most important.

Thus: if you want to increase a child's language ability, have as many exchanges of reciprocal interaction as you can—as long a series of volleys back and forth. Keep the ball moving. Taking walks with the child and talking is a good stimulus for reciprocal interaction; the walking provides a way to keep the body busy, while the new scenes encountered on the walk provide stimuli for conversation. Being in the house with the child, and responding when the child comes up to you and speaks is also a great place for reciprocal interaction to take place. Riding in a car can be an opportunity, if you model lots of talk about what you are seeing or thinking. Wherever you have a few minutes to attend to the child is an opportunity for reciprocal interaction and language development. Turn off the radios, cd players, video games, televisions, and other intruders that would lull you and the child into passive silence.

You Can Begin Reciprocal Interactions Before the Child Can Speak

The more practice children get at reciprocal interactions of any sort, the more ready they are for language mediated reciprocal interactions. Suppose an infant pulls a blanket over her face. The adult says, "Where's my baby?" The infant pulls down the blanket. The adult says, "There's my baby!" The infant laughs. The infant pulls the blanket up over the face again, and the game continues. This is turn-taking in interaction, reciprocal interaction, a precursor of what the child will experience in conversation. Or for another example, the child and the adult literally push a ball back and forth between each other. Each is responding to what the other did. Or the infant says "Ba ba ba." And the adult says, "Ba ba ba!" The child says, "Spppp!" and the adult replies, "Spppp!" The adult's imitation of the child's noises is giving the child the notion that her vocalizations have the power to have an effect on what other people do or say, and reciprocal interaction is taking place.

Tracking and Describing

Children learn new words and new ways of putting words together in many ways. One way of accelerating language learning is tracking and describing. We defined tracking and describing in an earlier chapter as watching what the child is doing, and verbally naming what is going on.

For example, an infant has some pots and pans, and is banging them together. The adult says, "Clank clank! You're making a loud noise!" The adult is supplying the verbal representation of a part of what is going on. Or the child sees a rattle, and reaches for it. The adult says, "You can pick it up." When the child picks it up, the adult says, "You did pick it up!"

Tracking and describing doesn't stop when children learn to speak. The adult can show the child more syntactically complex ways of thinking about things, by tracking and describing with just a little more expressive language than the child can currently use. The toddler jumps up and down on the bed, and says, "I jumping." The adult responds, "Yes, you're jumping up and down, up and down on the bed."

Reflections

As the child grows older and makes more complex utterances, tracking and describing of the child's utterances becomes known as what we defined in an earlier chapter as reflections. The adult describes what message he is getting from the child, to see if he understood it right and to confirm receiving it. For example,

Child: That big fish scared me.
Adult: You were scared that fish would bite you?
Child: Yes. He had a big mouth with lots of teeth.
Adult: You wouldn't like to get bitten by all those teeth.
Child: No. But the fish was in the water, and I was on the dock.
Adult: So, you know the fish couldn't bite you, because he was in the water and you were on the dock, huh?

Reflections are conducive to a form of reciprocal interaction that is pleasurable for the speaker, because her utterance brings about a response from the listener, but she has totally free choice in what direction to go next.

Other Conversation-Enhancers

As was mentioned in the chapter on conversation, other ways of getting reciprocal interaction going include telling about your own experience, facilitations, and follow-up questions and follow-up statements.

Telling about your own experience is simply chatting to the child about what is on your mind, what might be interesting to your child. "Guess what happened to me today," and "Want to hear something I did today?" are phrases to use as you prompt yourself to tell your child about your own experience. Telling about your own experience models for the child how to tell about her own experience, whereas asking a new-topic question puts the child on the spot to come up with something.

Facilitations are the words and grunts we use to signal to someone, "I'm hearing you, I'm receiving your message." The tone of voice of those words or grunts conveys how enthusiastic you are to be receiving the message. "I see," "Oh?" "Humh." "Uh huh." "Yes." "Is that right?" are all facilitations, that tend to reinforce the child for talking to you.

Follow up questions and statements are questions or statements that respond to what the child has just told you, as contrasted to those that introduce a new topic of your own choosing. Suppose the child says, "That Mickey is a mean kid." If the parent says "What did he do that was mean?" that's a follow up question; if the parent says "I've seen Mickey do some mean things before," that's a follow-up statement. These are part of reciprocal interaction; they demonstrate that the statement the child has just made has influenced the response that the parent gives.

Modeling, Silence, and Responsiveness

When adults set out consciously to use tracking and describing, or to tell about their own experience, they often forget to leave sufficient space in the conversation for the child to insert her own utterances. This is why the rhythm of modeling, silence, and responsiveness is important to keep in mind. When the adult speaks, the adult is modeling for the child how to make an utterance about what is going on. Then the adult is silent for long enough for the child to compose a reply. If the child does not compose a reply, that's fine, and after a while the adult models another utterance, and offers some more silence. If the child does reply, the adult is quickly and enthusiastically responsive to what the child says, so as to hit the ball back over the net.

Using Shaping

When consciously trying to stimulate a child's language development, it's useful to respond with attention and enthusiasm to as many of the child's utterances as possible. This should help to increase the rate of the child's verbalizations. At the beginning, you don't care whether the verbalizations make sense, are correctly pronounced, are too loud or soft, or what they say: you want to get the child's rate of attempts at communications to as high a level as you can. Once the child is saying lots of things, you will probably naturally start using differential attention, responding more enthusiastically to the ones that make the most sense. At some point, you can then use differential attention further to respond more to the ones that are nicer and smarter utterances. This reinforcement of movements along a hierarchy toward the goal is what we defined earlier as shaping.

Using Dramatic Play to Foster Language Development

Dramatic play fosters language development. This is especially true when the child plays with an older person who can help promote interesting dialogue between the characters. Dramatic play harnesses the power of the imagination to conjure up all sorts of situations to talk about, often more situations than real life is able to present. As the toy characters respond to one another, reciprocal interaction is being practiced. As the child conjures up whatever sorts of situations he prefers, he is choosing the subject that interests him the most at the time. Thus the "engine" of motivation to talk about things that really interest the child tends to gear up readily. For a child where stimulation of language development is a high priority goal, it is a mistake not to spend lots of time in as fun dramatic play as can be mustered.

You can model the process of creating plots with toy characters, as well as modeling prosocial actions, by putting on modeling plays for the child with toy people. Make them very quick if the child has a short attention span. Your goal is to have the child succeed at paying some attention until the resolution of the plot. Even the preverbal child can hear in the tones of voice the inflections of problem discovery and problem resolution. Parents who would like to see models of such homemade productions may look at my low-budget videotape of plays that model psychological skills.

The point where play with toy people really begins to foster language development, however, comes when the child is taking part in reciprocal interaction in large quantity.

As discussed more fully in the chapter on dramatic play, the adult who is playing with the child should play the parts of characters as much as possible and not just speak from his own persona. This of course will model for the child how to do the same, how to pick up characters and have them reply to the utterances of other characters.

A skill very useful for adults who wish to stimulate language development in dramatic play is "advanced" tracking and describing, or tracking and describing from the persona of toy characters. Rather than saying, "Looks like the lady with red hair is starting to drive the train," you take another character and say to a third, "Hey, the red haired lady is driving the train!"

As you do more dramatic play with a child, you focus on several balancing acts: initiating some plots, and waiting for the child to initiate others; having your plots be wild enough to be interesting but tame enough to be prosocial; maintaining adult authority over real life but letting the child's imagination roam rather freely; not encouraging negative patterns enacted by the child but not discouraging them enough so that the whole enterprise ceases to be fun.

A wonderful outcome sometimes occurs when two children have each spent good times in dramatic play with an adult. They each can learn the art of being prosocial and imaginative and generating reciprocal interaction with ever more rich language. The two children can then enrich each other's lives and their language development by doing dramatic play with each other. They leave the parent free to get other things done! A playmate who will model slightly more advanced forms of language than are now present in a child's repertoire can do lots of good for the child's language development.

Reading Aloud as a Stimulus for Language Development

At some stage of development, many children acquire a voracious interest in learning what the names of things are, and will be greatly entertained by doing what I call the picture naming activity. Adult and child look together at a picture dictionary or any other book with lots of pictures in it, and the adult models two acts. First is pointing at pictures and saying what they are, and saying something about them. Second is pointing at pictures and asking, "What's that?" This second activity is done mainly to show the child how to do it, so that the child will come to get pleasure in directing the adult to say what various things are. The adult wants to be very careful to avoid a feeling of drilling and quizzing the child on the meanings of words, especially when the child doesn't already know them. The activities are done with the rhythm of modeling, silence, and responsiveness, so that hopefully there can be lots of reciprocal interaction in the course of the adult's and the child's looking together at the things and naming them. After a period of peak interest in simply naming and exploring passes, the child may go to a stage where the words have to fit together into an interesting story or interesting set of facts and are no longer appealing in and of themselves. The adult should not fight the stage of interest that the child is in, but run with whatever the child has the appetite for, and get maximum mileage from each stage.

Reading modeling stories or any other stories to the child stimulates language development. The less language the child has, the more pictures per word there should be, so that the child at the beginning sees a fairly rapid flipping from one picture to the next. As the child gains language, there can be more verbal input per page. See the chapter on story reading for ways to help a child enjoy hearing stories.

The modeling stories can also be a stimulus to expressive language. You suggest to the child that some day he will be able to tell you the story that you are now reading to him. When the child is capable of it, you want to help the child take great pleasure in flipping the pages and telling you the story from memory or imagination or both. Practice in making coherent narratives that retell modeling stories is invaluable to the child.

In the chapter on tutoring is a description of the technique for eliciting stories from the child, by starting the story yourself and having the child fill in only a word, and gradually letting the child take over more and more of the storytelling. Also described is the technique for eliciting non-fiction essays from the child's dictation to you. You can record the story by typing or writing it or tape recording it. If the child can become proud of her ever-growing "collected works," a major stimulus toward language development is in effect.

The prosocial moral dilemma stories, described in the chapter on moral development, begin to be appropriate as stimuli for discussion with a child when her language level approaches that of a kindergarten child. The more discussion can take place, the more the child's language use gets exercised.

For kindergarten and preschool children certain basic concepts are extremely important: words such as over, under, before, after, right, left, beginning, end, right, left, top, bottom, behid, in front of, first, last, and so forth. A failure to understand some of these concepts can lead the child to act as if oppositional or not paying attention, when in fact the child does not understand the directions she is given. "Please put the star at the top of the page. Please help us put the chairs into rows. Please get in the line, behind Mandy." There are tests, one produced by Boehm, another by Bracken, that measure whether the child has these basic concepts in her vocabulary. If a preschool or kindergarten child appears to have language difficulties, it is useful to measure how many of these concepts are known and unknown, and to consider teaching them directly if many are not known. I say "consider" because the direct teaching of any words should not replace the more vital techniques of language learning driven by reciprocal interaction. However, as an adjunct to those methods, I have produced a book in which these basic concepts are used repeatedly in small vignettes modeling prosocial actions, and then the child is asked to pick out which of two or three pictures illustrates another use of the concept. If the child can enjoy this book, it is possible to cover some fifty basic concepts in a fairly short time.

After the child has learned to read, a major stimulus to langage development is to make a family recreation out of reading aloud to one another. You pick a book that will be at the "challenge zone"—not too hard, not too easy, for the child's abilities to read aloud. You and the child, and other family members, take turns reading the book. This activity can go on for years, into the child's adulthood, and can be a great stimulus for the art of public speaking as well as for language development.

A crucial point to keep in mind is that any time the child wants to stop reading and have a reciprocal interaction with you about anything remotely connected with what you are reading, or even anything off the subject, the reciprocal interaction will be just as good for his language development, if not better, than the reading is. So feel no hesitancy to engage in conversation and return to the reading when the conversation lulls.

The key to all these techniques of stimulating language development is quality multiplied by quantity. That is, you want them done as well as possible, but you also need to think in terms of hours per day rather than minutes per day or per week. Because so many of these techniques are "real life" rather than "instruction," it is possible for a child to experience them many hours a day. If the child is in the care of teachers or babysitters or other caretakers many hours a day, it is crucial to get everyone working together on stimulating the child's language development, in ways that the child will enjoy, for as long a time per day as possible.

Chapter 38: Kindness Between Siblings

Chapter Overview:

Almost all the psychological skills mentioned in this book contribute toward reducing hostility between siblings. There is hardly a chapter that is not relevant to this goal. However, we can think specifically about two goals: prevention of hostility around the time of the birth of a second child, and promotion of positive dramatic play between siblings. When a new sibling is born, make physical changes far ahead of time, don't raise the first child's expectations about having a fun playmate; encourage dramatic play in which the first child takes care of a new arrival; give the older child attention for nurturing a toy character when visitors come; hold the positive traits of the first child up as a paragon for the new arrival to copy someday; respond to kind acts of the older toward the younger with all the techniques mentioned in previous chapters, i.e. enthusiastic attention, the nightly review, making modeling stories and plays, etc. In teaching siblings to do dramatic play with each other, first work with each of them separately till you are sure that prosocial imaginative dramatic play is in the repertoire. Then if possible, get two adults to play with the two children, so that there is plenty of adult attention to go around. The adults use differential attention, by turning attention to the child or character who is acting best. Then a single adult can do the same thing with both children; finally the adult gradually fades from the activity.

In trying to prevent sibling rivalry, avoid giving the impression that you can be totally fair; avoid reinforcing children for complaining that the other one got just a little more of something. You want to give the message that tolerating unfairness is a very desirable skill rather than that the children are entitled to exactly equal treatment. You want to avoid comparing children with one another, favorably or unfavorably. Aim toward the idea that each person is trying to make the world as much better as possible; they are not in competition with each other. Teach problem-solving to siblings, and use differential attention in a direction that helps them solve their own conflicts rather than constantly needing you to referee. Try to model the kindness and rational problem-solving that are the chief antidotes to sibling rivalry. Try to arrange enough individual time with each child; this helps keep siblings from resenting each other for taking away their individual time with parents.

****

The problem of hostility between siblings, like the problem of hostility in general, is addressed in part by almost every chapter in this book. The skills of listening, problem-solving, enjoying doing kind things, fortitude, non-jealousy and magnanimity, and almost all other skills will contribute to better relations between siblings. So the ultimate solution is to promote in each child the greatest possible psychological competence. This chapter provides only a few specific suggestions to supplement the rest of the suggestions made in this book.

Preventing Jealousy at the Birth of a Sibling

The ideas in the following paragraphs were first written by my father, a pediatrician. He gave this advice to parents expecting a second child.

***

To get a sense of how a first child may feel when a new sibling is brought home, it may be useful to imagine that you are living in a time and place where polygamy is common, and your spouse announces (not consults, asks, or arranges, but simply announces) that an auxiliary spouse is coming into the household. From now on you will be one of two wives, or two husbands. The task of your spouse in leading you not to resent or hate your rival is a delicate one indeed. This task will not be easy. It will be impossible if you are neglected and ignored in favor of the new arrival. It will certainly be easier if you are held up as an admirable model, a paragon to be emulated by the new arrival.

Therefore, when you have a second child, hold up the first child as an ideal, a paragon and a model to be copied by the second child. If Jane or Johnny hears mother say over and over to the new baby, "Oh, you've soiled your pants again. I'm sure glad Jane doesn't soil her pants. She's big and uses the bathroom. Maybe you'll be like her when you get big," or "I've got to feed you milk again. I'm glad Johnny is big and can eat from the table. He's my big helper. I couldn't do without him." Such praises won't hurt the baby's feelings, especially if delivered in soft and loving tones, but they will let Jane and Johnny know they are still loved, not forgotten. They will help to prevent the reversion to baby habits or not eating or to rowdy behavior. These are simply a child's way of saying "Look at ME, talk about ME, as you did before this new one came." For while children like to be held, they don't really want to be held all the time. They just like to know their mothers would *like* to hold them all the time.

It's good to make any physical changes made necessary by the arrival of the new baby some months beforehand. Obviously if a child finds a new baby placed in the bed he feels is his, he will howl and want no part of any other bed. Introduce him to the new bed with proper ceremony some time ahead and he will eventually lose interest in the old one. The same thing is true of the room changes and any other physical changes which will be obvious to the child. If a new auxiliary caretaker will come in to help out, it's good to introduce that caretaker a while before the birth, so that the child gets to know the new caretaker when he or she isn't seen as a poor substitute for the mother or father.

Don't raise the expectations of the first child for how much fun it will be to have a new playmate. Having a good playmate is too far in the future for him to understand correctly and usually only adds to his disappointment when he finds that the new arrival can't walk and can't talk and is neither a good plaything nor a playmate.

Try having an entrancing toy to use at the time of arrival from the hospital, that will portray the new arrival for the older child. A toy person or animal that the older child can nurture and take care of, while the parent is nurturing and taking care of the baby, can provide a sense of camaraderie and identification between the older child and the parent.

The strategy of giving the older child attention for imaginary nurturing can be used when visitors come to see the baby. When grandparents or visitors rush in to see the new arrival, if Jane is first detailed to show off *her* new baby, then usually the visitors will take the hint and notice Jane as well.

***

Here are more ideas. Put enjoyment of kind acts toward the younger sibling on the priority list for the older child's psychological skills, and act accordingly. That is, use modeling stories and modeling plays, watch for real-life kind behaviors, reinforce them with lots of enthusiastic interest, talk about them to other people, go over them in the nightly review, and make stories, songs, and plays about them. A kind act of an older child toward a younger child might be: gently patting or stroking the baby, singing a song to comfort the baby, speaking gently to the baby, showing the baby pictures from a picture book, telling stories to the baby, saying prayers for the baby in the baby's presence, saying something complimentary to the baby. These acts should be reinforced also if they are done with the child's fantasy object of nurture, i.e. his toy bear.

The final suggestion applies for many years after the birth of the younger sibling. It is by far the most difficult. It is to engineer enough individual time with each child that the siblings don't resent each other for taking away the individual time with the parent. Many times, I believe, this is a major source of resentment among siblings. Time alone with a parent is precious. It can be quite irritating when a sibling interrupts this time. When this happens over and over many times, much resentment can build up. If, on the other hand, there is a regular time when each child can count on uninterrupted time alone with the parent, wishes that the other sibling would go away forever become less frequent or even absent.

Teaching Two Young Siblings To Do Dramatic Play With Each Other

Let's say you have a 5 year old and a 3 year old who frequently get into conflicts with one another. Whenever you put them together, one of them ends up crying or hitting, before long.

You want to move from this scenario to one devoutly to be wished: where you can put the two children in a room with toy people and houses and barns and so forth, and they will have a great time doing joint dramatic play together, spinning plots of highly prosocial content. This highly desirable goal is not to be reached overnight. We have to use our principle of hierarchy, and approach it through baby steps.

First, both children need lots of prosocial models carried out by the toy people, so they will know how to spin prosocial plots. This may be accomplished by putting on modeling plays for each child separately, or possibly for both of them together.

Second, each child separately needs to become competent at dramatic play with an adult. This means dividing and conquering. If there are two parents who can each do dramatic play well, each can take a child into a separate room and practice. If not, one parent can get a babysitter, and take each child into a room separately to practice dramatic play while the babysitter looks after the other child. All the tips in the chapter on promoting dramatic play are applicable here.

Third, when each child separately is good at dramatic play, the two adults and the two children come together to play together. In this situation there should so many toy people that conflicts over who gets to hold which person are difficult to engineer.

Now in this four-person situation, how do the adults divide up their attention? Does one adult stay focussed on one child? A better plan is that if either child is acting more appropriate and more cooperative and gentle than the other, then both adults turn their attention to that child. Conversely, if one child is getting verbally hostile or boisterous or argumentative, both adults turn attention to the other child. The strategy I have described, of course, is the use of differential attention.

What if both children get into a verbally hostile interchange? And what if both children sit without seeming to know how to do dramatic play? Then the two adults turn their attention to each other, and continue the play. The two adults model extremely kind and considerate behavior to one another, now as well as throughout the entire interaction. If one child leaves the hostile interaction with the other child and resumes appropriate dramatic play, then the adults begin attending to him again as if the hostile interchange did not happen.

Suppose that one of the two children hits or kicks the other? Then one of the adults takes that child for a two minute time out, while the other continues playing. What if both of them hit each other? Then each of the adults takes them to a time out, in a separate room.

Finally, if both children are playing appropriately and cooperatively, the adults make sure that each of them gets enough attention and approval and excitement.

With enough time spent in this four person situation, with parents steadfastly modeling cooperation and using differential attention to reinforce it, while punishing aggression with time out, most pairs of children will come around to being able to play much better with each other than they were able to before.

The next step is to phase out one of the adults. One adult only gets together with both children. Again, the adult uses differential attention, models prosocial actions with the characters and considerate speech toward each child, and punishes aggression with time out.

Next the adult starts taking less and less of a role in the play, but sits back more and more and lets the children carry the ball in determining the plot.

Finally, the adult actually gets up and does something else, while the two players continue playing. The adult comes in and observes them and gives them a pat on the back, without distracting from the drama, periodically while they are playing cooperatively; if they are bickering, the adult stays away; if they hit, they go to time out. Most of the time, if all has gone well, they continue in prosocial fantasy play and prosocial interaction with each other.

It is an arduous path toward this goal, but if the goal can be achieved, its worth is inestimable. Almost all the other techniques mentioned in this book, I again emphasize, will also help in achieving it.

A Few Other Miscellaneous Tips

In attempting to prevent sibling rivalry, a technique that backfires is to try to treat each child exactly equally, in the short run. Avoid the belief that when one child is praised, the other must also be praised; when one gets a gift, the other must also get a gift; when one gets to go on an outing, the other has to have something just as good. In the long run, you want to make sure that one child does not get the short end of the stick consistently. But if you try to balance everything all the time, you are giving the children the message that they are entitled to total fairness at all times. Once they feel they deserve it, they will be unhappy whenever they perceive themselves as not receiving it. And since different children have different needs, those times will be extremely frequent. It's best to let children know that life is not fair. Make no promises that they will be treated equally, but only that each will be treated good enough. Silently try to make things even out over the long run.

Avoid comparing children with other children, favorably or unfavorably. Try to promote the image in the children that each of them is trying to make the world as much of a better place as they can, but that they are not in competition with anyone else. Every contribution helps. The fact that one person made the world 10 units better is not the least diminished by the fact that someone else made it 20 units better.

When children are old enough to speak, start walking them through the problem-solving process as described in the chapter on teaching children problem-solving. Once their skills of verbal problem-solving are up to it, try the following procedure. If the children are having a specific conflict that you want to intervene in, listen to what is going on, state the problem for them, and challenge them to work something out, and to tell you what they were able to work out, if they are able to work something out. Then leave the room. If they are able to work something out peaceably, lionize them both and memorialize their accomplishment in all the ways we have talked about repeatedly.

Avoid the following pattern: You are attending to something else. The children get into a noisy conflict. You yell or speak loudly to them, decreeing a solution to the problem. By this pattern, parents reinforce children's anger with their attention, their excitement. If the squabble is alleviated that too might be reinforcing. The reinforcement leads the children to conjure up another conflict.

Try to present as many real life models of the sorts of thoughts, feelings, and behaviors that you want your children to do more of in their relation to each other: for example giving behavior in response to a conflict, calm discussion and listing options and choosing among them in response to a conflict, complimenting other family members, and offering help. The skills most diametrically opposed to sibling rivalry conflicts are those of tolerating, or even feeling good about, someone else's getting what you would have liked to have. These are the skills of celebrating another's success, talking with positive affect about another's accomplishment, feeling joy over another's joy. The more the adults in the family can model doing this with each other, the more the children will do it with each other also.

Chapter 39: Prevention of Drug Abuse

Chapter Overview:

In a sense, this entire book has been devoted to the prevention of drug abuse, since having the psychological skills conducive to living a happy and productive life reduces the need to find gratification in drugs. Certain specific skills, such as decision making, delay of gratification, independent thinking, and assertion will well equip a youth for making decisions about drug use and resisting peer pressure. However, in addition, it is useful for children to consider the specific ethics of drug use and to know some facts about drug side effects. In many ways drug use is analogous to Russian Roulette, particularly in the respect that all users of drugs are to some extent responsible for the most negative side effects that occur in some users. This is because each user contributes to the social climate that permits and encourages the abuser to harm himself. Perhaps youth can avoid drugs out of a wish to protect their more vulnerable comrades.

The phrase "drug and alcohol abuse" is redundant: alcohol is a drug, the number one drug of abuse. Alcohol abuse is the most frequent psychiatric diagnosis given to males in the United States. About one in six males who drink, and one in sixteen females who drink, become alcoholic. Alcohol use impairs judgment, as is indicated by the fact that its use is significantly associated with being either a murderer or getting murdered, committing other violent crimes, or killing oneself. Alcohol is a large killer of adolescents via car crashes. Use of alcohol over a long time contributes to cirrhosis of the liver, a disease that kills many thousands of Americans each year. Alcohol contributes to Wernicke-Korsakoff syndrome, a brain illness that destroys the ability to form new memories. There is some evidence that in some people, fairly small quantities of alcohol can cause permanent reductions in the power of the brain. Alcohol reduces sex hormone production in men, both in the short run and the long run, such that many chronic alcoholic men get enlarged breasts and female hair patterns. Alcohol, when drunk by pregnant women, harms the brains of fetuses, and constitutes the number one cause of mental retardation in the United States. When alcohol abusers attempt to better their lives, the strategy of totally avoiding alcohol works much better, on the average, than the strategy of trying to learn to use alcohol in moderation.

Tobacco smoke is a highly addictive substance. It is the major cause of lung cancer. It causes several other cancers, chronic bronchitis, emphysema, and heart disease and diseases of the blood vessels. Those who smoke indoors as a group cause cancer, asthma, emphysema, and anginal pain to the nonsmokers whose air they pollute. Women who smoke during pregnancy harm their babies in several ways. There is an unpleasant withdrawal syndrome associated with stopping cigarettes. And in this age of vanity, perhaps those not motivated by health will be motivated by the fact that smokers tend to get wrinkled skin earlier.

With both marijuana and cocaine, it should be kept in mind that drugs obtained illegally have no quality control, and one has to trust an illegal drug dealer with the dose and the identity of the drug. To purchase an illegal drug supports the crime and violence associated with the drug trade.

Marijuana produces a short term disruption of mental functioning, including impairment of driving ability. Marijuana smoke is no more healthy to the lungs than is cigarette smoke. Long-term use of marijuana is reported to be associated with an "amotivational syndrome" where the person has lost all ambition. Adverse effects on sexual functioning have been reported.

Cocaine and amphetamine, when taken in the greater and greater doses required to get high from these drugs, can lead to a syndrome that mimics paranoid schizophrenia. Withdrawal from the high doses can lead one to feel depressed and lethargic. Some researchers feel that cocaine use contributes to manic-depressive illness. Use of high doses of cocaine has been reported to do permanent damage to brain structures. High doses of cocaine or amphetamine can be fatal. In my opinion, the two worst drugs of abuse are inhaled organic solvents (as for example the solvents in certain types of glue) and MDMA, or "ecstacy." These two are the worst because of their capability of producing permanent brain damage.

****

I want to mention several approaches to prevention of drug abuse that a parent can take. The first is to attempt to enhance all sixty-two of the psychological skills on the skills axis, because all of them contribute toward someone's being happy and productive without drugs. The better a person's relationships, the more they feel a purpose in existence, the more they are able to be competent in work and recreational activities, and so forth, the less they will need to find something through drugs that was missing in their lives. Some of the psychological skills, such as independent thinking, assertiveness, and conflict-resolution, are particularly useful in resisting social pressure from peers to take drugs. Self-discipline enables one to resist the short term pleasure that drugs can give, in preference for the longer-term happiness from avoiding them. Carefulness skills lead children not to take unnecessary risks with drugs. Decision-making skills enable them to weigh the pros and cons of using drugs of abuse and see how much the results favor avoiding them. It is difficult to foster any psychological skill without doing prevention of drug abuse.

The second approach to drug abuse prevention is teaching the child the side effects of the drugs of abuse. Can the child list for you the dangers of the various drugs of abuse? If the child does not have knowledge about the risks associated with these drugs, the child is not as equipped to make a rational decision.

This chapter contains perhaps the bare minimum of information that people should know about the most common drugs of abuse: alcohol, tobacco, marijuana, cocaine and amphetamines, organic solvents, and "ecstacy."

The Russian Roulette Analogy

In considering the ethics of drug use, you have to consider not only the effects upon yourself, but also upon those whom you influence by your example. The Russian Roulette Analogy is useful in discussing the ethical implications.

In Russian Roulette, several people agree to take a revolver with one bullet in it, give the chamber a spin, hold the gun up to their head, and pull the trigger. Suppose that someone organizes a Russian Roulette activity, and a few other people agree to participate. They do it, and one person is killed. Who bears moral responsibility for the death of the person killed? Certainly the person himself contributed to it by putting the gun to his head and pulling the trigger. But the organizer of the activity, most would agree, also bears some responsibility, because without his action, the death would not occur. What about the other people who agreed to participate in the activity? I would argue that they too bear an ethical responsibility. If they had all responded to the organizer by saying, "What a crazy idea! You've got to be kidding!" then the notion of modeling suggests that the person who got killed would have also found it easier to reject the crazy idea. By this reasoning, any person who consents to play Russian Roulette plays a causal role in the death of anyone who dies.

Use of drugs is probably an area where social influence occurs much more certainly than in Russian Roulette. People's use of drugs depends greatly upon whom they "hang out with." Each person who uses or refuses a certain drug makes it a little more likely that someone else will do the same.

It turns out that with the use of alcohol among males, the Russian Roulette analogy is particularly apt, in that about one in six users become alcoholics, just as one in six spins of a six-chambered revolver results in a firing of the gun.

The bottom line of this reasoning is that anyone who wishes to prevent drug abuse in other people should avoid even social, nonproblematic drug use in themselves.

Effects of Alcohol

The most damaging drug of abuse is ethyl alcohol. Here are some facts about its effects.

1. Of all the psychiatric diagnoses given to males in the United States, alcohol abuse is by far the most frequent—the number one diagnosis. In females alcohol abuse accounts for a high fraction of psychiatric diagnoses.

2. Of drinkers, and excluding abstainers, about 14% to 16% of male drinkers and 6% of female drinkers report a moderate level of tangible negative consequences associated with alcohol abuse. Thus for males, if the male takes up drinking, the chances are about 1 in 6 or 7 that that male will suffer negative consequences from abuse.

3. A study of criminal offenders convicted of violent crimes revealed that 54% of them had used alcohol just before the offense. Alcohol involvement was particularly prevalent in cases of manslaughter (68%) and assault (62%).

4. A substantial fraction of people who commit homicide had used alcohol shortly before the time of the crime. Among homicide victims, one study found that 33% of them were legally intoxicated at the time of their murder (with a blood alcohol concentration of 0.10% or higher). Another study was very similar, finding that 30% of murder victims were legally intoxicated. The increased risk of being a murder victim, if one is drunk, is partly based on the fact that homicide offenders are more likely to have been drinking if the victim has been drinking and vice versus.

5. Alcohol is also related to suicide. Suicide is one of the three leading causes of death among males 15-34 years old. (The other two are homicides and accidents.) An analysis of 3400 violence-related deaths in which the victim's blood alcohol concentrations were tested found that suicide was the cause of 21% of those deaths. In 35% of those suicides, the victims had been drinking; intoxication was present at the time of death in 23%. Among alcoholics, there is a very high suicide rate. Suicide rates of 8%-21% were found in a review of several follow-up studies of alcoholics. One study of patients who survived unsuccessful suicide attempts found that 50% of male suicide attempters had a drinking problem, with 25% of them classed as alcohol dependent. The proportion of female suicide attempters with drinking problems was about 23% in this study. According to the same study, 74% of the male suicide attempters and 51% of the female suicide attempters had been drinking shortly before the suicide attempt.

6. Alcohol is also related to a very large killer of adolescents, namely motor vehicle crashes. In one large study, more than 44,000 people were killed in traffic accidents on U.S. highways in a year. The blood alcohol concentration was determined for about a third of the drivers in these traffic fatalities. The proportion of fatally injured drivers who were legally drunk at the time of their deaths was about 43%.

7. Liver disease was the ninth leading cause of death in the U.S. in another study, with nearly 28,000 deaths in the study year attributed to cirrhosis of the liver. Probably at least 50% of all cirrhosis deaths are alcohol related; some estimates place this number as high as 95%.

8. Adding together deaths due to suicide, homicide, accidents, cirrhosis of the liver and all other alcohol-related causes, the death toll for 1980 was estimated at approximately 98,000 people. By comparison, approximately 45,000 Americans were killed during the entire Vietnam War.

9. The Wernicke-Korsakoff syndrome is a disorder of the brain resulting from the combination of protracted alcoholism and deficiency of the vitamin thiamine, or vitamin B-1. One of the major symptoms of this disorder is the inability to form new memories. Thus, the person with this syndrome cannot remember recent events and cannot learn new material. But if someone gets adequate amounts of thiamine, that does not necessarily make him immune to the brain damage and memory problems produced by alcohol. There is now impressive evidence that in rodents, chronic alcohol consumption, even with good nutrition, results in permanent learning deficits and significant brain damage.

One study in humans analyzed the frequency of CT-Scan abnormalities and deficiencies in psychological testing results in a group of 39 drinkers who consumed less than 5 ounces of pure alcohol a day. This study also looked at the diet and nutritional status of these people. Thirty-one of these subjects showed some degree of atrophy of the brain on CT-Scan, and 25 of these people also performed poorly on psychological tests of brain functioning. Sixteen of these subjects were nutritionally deficient, and 15 of those had abnormal CT-Scans or psychological tests results. However, there was a lack of correlation between nutritional indexes and the severity of the CT-Scan and psychological test abnormalities. These findings suggest that the abnormalities are probably due to alcohol effects themselves, rather than only to the nutritional deficiencies associated with alcoholism.

10. There are also short-term effects on memory caused by a dose of alcohol. Studies indicate that the tendency of heavy drinkers to forget things that they have done while drunk can be replicated in experiments. Acute doses of alcohol are reported to have disruptive effects on human memory. A blood-alcohol concentration of .04 gr per 100 ml of blood (40% of the way toward being legally drunk) can disrupt memory functions, and memory impairment progresses as the blood-alcohol concentration rises.

11. There is some evidence that alcohol can cause permanent reductions in “cognitive efficiency,” or intellectual functioning, in social drinkers. The investigations of intellectual functioning in nonalcoholic social drinkers have yielded inconsistent results. Some studies do not demonstrate an effect. However, one review cites five studies suggesting that there is an effect on the cognitive efficiency of even moderate social drinkers. Thus, the final answer to this question is not in, but there is

some evidence suggesting that moderate doses of alcohol may be somewhat harmful to the brain, just as high doses of alcohol are definitely harmful to the brain. The summary statement offered by one review is that "It is clear that the cognitive efficiency of moderate social drinkers can be compromised."

12. Alcohol affects sex hormones in men. Chronic alcoholic men sometimes become "feminized," with female hair patterns and enlargement of their breasts. In carefully controlled research ward studies, it has been found that alcohol causes a decrease in the levels of testosterone, the major male sexual hormone, in the bloodstream. It has been suggested that alcohol is a direct toxin to the cells of testes that manufacture testosterone. At some point, after a certain amount of ingestion of alcohol, the changes in the testosterone-producing cells become irreversible.

13. The effects on fetuses of alcohol drunk by pregnant women constitute the number one cause of mental retardation in the United States.

The most obvious cases of the ill effects of alcohol are referred to as "Fetal Alcohol Syndrome." The research on this question started in the early 1970s. In 1973, some investigators described a number of gross physical deformities in 11 very young children of severely alcoholic mothers who drank during pregnancy. These children had small openings of the eyes, drooping eyelids, small eyes, underdeveloped midfaces, skin folds in the corners of the eyes, an underdeveloped philtrum (the depression just above the upper lip), an exaggerated space between the nose and the upper lip, and small head circumference. Ten years later, 8 of these 11 children were re-examined. Four of them had an I.Q. in the range between 70 and 86, which is borderline retarded to low-normal range of intelligence. The other 4 had an I.Q. ranging from 20-57 and were in the severely retarded range. The degree of intellectual impairment that they had was correlated with the severity of physical malformation that they had. Growth deficiency was another prominent problem in these children.

The finding that such severe problems could result large maternal doses of alcohol during pregnancy raised other questions. How prevalent are fetal alcohol effects in the population as a whole? How much of a problem can be caused in fetuses due to relatively milder alcohol intake by their mothers?

The Fetal Alcohol Syndrome, as defined by the deformities, the growth problems and/or the intellectual problems has been estimated to occur in somewhere between 1 and 3 babies per 1,000 live births. If you take the lower figure of 1 in 1,000, this would imply that, of some 250 million Americans, some 250,000 of them are affected by Fetal Alcohol Syndrome.

If a mother drinks heavily during pregnancy, is it not automatic that the child will have Fetal Alcohol Syndrome? For some reason, some fetuses are more susceptible than others. In one study, among the 5% of pregnancies where the mothers drank the most heavily, only 5-10% of the infants scored abnormally low on mental and psychomotor tests when tested at 8 months of age. In another study, only 5 babies among the 204 offspring of a set of heavily drinking women had Fetal Alcohol Syndrome.

However, the lowering of intelligence does not necessarily require the full presence of the fetal alcohol syndrome. In one study, the children of alcoholic mothers scored 15-19 I.Q. points lower than the comparison group of children. The results of this study suggested that, although the children with frank Fetal Alcohol Syndrome, with the physical deformities and the growth problems, showed the lowest I.Q. scores, that children of alcoholic mothers can have their I.Q. scores depressed by their mother's drinking during pregnancy, even without the physical deformities of Fetal Alcohol Syndrome.

The obvious problems of Fetal Alcohol Syndrome represent only the most severe end of a continuum of fetal damage that can be produced by exposure to alcohol in utero. Lower levels of maternal drinking also have some measurable effects upon children. If a lot of alcohol can do a lot of damage, a little alcohol can do milder forms of damage. One large-scale study looked at effects on children as a function of what the average intake of alcohol by the mother was during the pregnancy. The data from this study did not suggest a threshold level of drinking below which there is no effect on the unborn child. This same longitudinal study found that alcohol-related neurological and behavioral effects have persisted in children of heavier-drinking mothers to at least 4 years of age. Furthermore, the more sensitive laboratory tests continue to show reduced attention and slower information processing even in 4-year-old children who were exposed before birth to lower levels of alcohol. The authors advised caution in interpreting these findings. A variety of possible drinking patterns during pregnancy were grouped together in the same average daily consumption categories, and some drinking patterns within each average consumption level could be riskier than others. For example, going on a drinking binge, especially at a critical period of vulnerability of the fetus, may be especially harmful, even though the average level of alcohol per day is not that great. Also, we should note that, although neurological and behavioral deficits in children were found associated with low to moderately heavy alcohol consumption during pregnancy, the deficits were relatively small, and measurements in a large number of such children were required to achieve statistical significance.

Another study looked at eighty-four children of mothers who drank at moderate levels primarily during their pregnancies. Only one woman during this sample consumed more than an average of one and one-half ounces of alcohol a day throughout pregnancy. Binge drinking was very infrequent in these women. Nonetheless, tests performed when the children were thirteen months of age suggested that social drinking during pregnancy was associated with lower scores on tests of spoken language and verbal comprehension in the children.

The evidence that we have at this time is sufficient for a recommendation that a pregnant woman not drink at all during the pregnancy. The same recommendation would hold for a woman who is attempting to get pregnant, or who is fertile, sexually active, and without a fool-proof method of birth control.

14. If someone has alcohol problems, aiming toward "moderate drinking" as contrasted with total abstinence seems to be a bad idea. One very interesting study on this topic looked at sixty-two chronic alcoholics. Thirty of them received training in "nonproblem drinking skills." In other words, this subgroup was taught to drink at moderate levels, rather than to abstain from alcohol. This subgroup, 6 months later, had experienced more abusive drinking days than the 32 people not given this training. In other words, in this study the attempt to teach moderate drinking to problem drinkers was a failure.

Other studies have looked at the results in heavy drinkers who have set the goal of total abstinence versus those who have set the goal of moderate drinking. The relapse into alcoholism was higher in those who had attempted to drink moderately.

Another study looked at 1300 alcoholics and measured how many of them went on to become moderate drinkers. Only 1.6% of them had achieved this status.

In general, the evidence supports the idea that once significant dependence on alcohol has occurred, the alcoholic no longer has the option of returning to social drinking and abstinence is the most appropriate goal.

15. National surveys of drinking practices indicate that approximately 1/3 of the U.S. population ages 18 and over are abstainers from alcohol.

The fact that drinking alcohol is so often a social phenomenon suggests that avoiding social drinking decreases the probability that those who are in your social network, i.e. family members and friends, will become alcoholic. It would also predict that if you want your child not to have an alcohol abuse problem, you will significantly decrease the chances of that happening by being an abstainer yourself.

My own conclusion from reading the literature is that a drug that is the number one cause of mental retardation is by that fact alone too dangerous for our society to play around with, and that in a rational society, the custom of social drinking would go the way that the custom of indoor smoking seems to be going presently.

Effects of Tobacco

Despite the gradual nonacceptance that smoking seems to be encountering, we may continue to speak of tobacco use as the number one preventable cause of death in the United States.

Tobacco is a highly addictive substance; the level of difficulty in withdrawing from cigarettes is comparable to the the difficulty in escaping addiction to heroin. Of smokers who get formal help with their problem, only about 20 to 40 percent are off cigarettes after a year.

There are numerous different substances that make up cigarette smoke. Nicotine is probably what makes tobacco addictive; some of the other components, such as benzopyrene, nitrosamines, and other chemicals are documented to cause cancer; formaldehyde and acetaldehyde inhibit the cilia, or the little hair-like cells that help clean the respiratory system.

Smoking makes it more likely for someone to get coronary artery disease, strokes, and peripheral vascular disease. Smoke accelerates atherosclerosis. A wide variety of cancers, including of course lung cancer, are far more common in cigarette smokers. Smoking dramatically increases the likelihood of getting chronic bronchitis and emphysema. Emphysema is irreversible damage to the sacs that make up lung tissue, reducing the total surface area available for oxygen to get into the blood. In pregnant women, smoking leads to an increase in miscarriages, reduced birth weight of the children, increased perinatal mortality, and increased likelihood of sudden death of infants. Smokers have more sleep difficulties, and tend to have more depression, anxiety, and irritability. Smokers give the people who inhale their second-hand smoke more cancer, asthma, lung dysfunction, and angina. When addicted smokers stop, there is often a withdrawal syndrome consisting of drowsiness, headaches, increased appetite, insomnia, restlessness, irritability, hostility, anxiety, upset stomach, and difficulty concentrating. Smokers get more wrinkling of the skin and tend to look older quicker; thus an appeal to vanity may provide a motive not provided by the wish for health and life itself.

Effects of Marijuana

Two considerations in the use of marijuana, as with any illegal drug, are as follows. First, any drug obtained illegally provides no guarantee of quality control; thus it is not certain what dose of drug is being delivered or whether the drug is actually what the drug dealer represented it to be. To entrust one's brain chemicals to an illegal drug dealer is, arguably, the height of stupidity, and has resulted in death on numerous occasions. Second, to purchase any illegal drug is in a sense voting for the whole set of illegal operations involved in drug distribution, a set of operations responsible for a great number of murders and other crimes.

Marijuana, and its component most responsible for the psychological effects, tetrahydrocannabinol, interferes with short term memory and the capacity to carry out tasks requiring multiple mental steps. There is a tendency to confuse past, present, and future. Balance and stability of stance are hampered even at low doses. Driving impairment lasts 4 to 8 hours, long after the user ceases to perceive the effects of the drug. Higher doses can produce hallucinations, delusions, and paranoid feelings, and confused and disorganized thinking. Exposure of pregnant women to marijuana can result in persistent effects on the learning of the offspring. Chronic use of marijuana is associated with bronchitis and asthma. The "tar" produced by burning of marijuana is even more carcinogenic to animals than that derived from cigarettes. Chronic use of marijuana may lead to an "amotivational syndrome" consisting of apathy, dullness, impairment of judgment, concentration, and memory, and loss of interest in pursuit of goals. Marijuana may have an effect on sexual functioning; in women, anovulatory cycles, and in men, lowered concentrations of testosterone and temporarily lower sperm counts. Inhibition of the hypothalamic-pituitary axis has been reported.

Effects of Cocaine and Amphetamine

Cocaine and amphetamine are similar in their pharmacologic effects. The person who takes them for the purpose of getting high usually finds that a higher and higher dose is required over time for the high to occur. As higher doses are used, toxic effects appear. Grinding of the teeth, picking of the face and hands, suspiciousness, and a feeling of being watched can occur. The user can start having hallucinations: a feeling of bugs on the skin, or visions of lights. Disorganization of thinking occurs. After a period of using these drugs and then stopping, the user will usually sleep for a long time, and wake up feeling hungry, depressed, and lethargic. The lethargy can last for many days, until the use of the drug again interrupts the lethargy and the cycle starts over. Those who get delusions and hallucinations with cocaine or amphetamine may experience a "kindling" process in which a smaller dose, or perhaps only environmental stimuli, may be sufficient in the future to elicit the same response. The paranoia and delusions and hallucinations that occur with these drugs can be indistinguishable from a schizophrenic syndrome.

Cocaine use has been linked by some research to manic-depressive illness. Some researchers feel that an increase in manic-depressive illness may be attributable to the rise in cocaine abuse.

Use of cocaine in high doses has been reported to do damage to blood vessels and to adrenergic neurons in the brain. Long term use has led to exaggerated startle reactions and abnormalities of muscle movement.

Overdoses of these drugs can be fatal.

The Two Worst Drugs In My Estimation

Which drugs of abuse do you think top the list, in the danger category? Which are the ones that people are most ill advised in taking? It would be very interesting to find a rank ordering of the danger of the entire set of drugs of abuse by experts in this field. According to the evidence I read, first place for the worst drug class goes to the inhalants: the chemicals one gets by sniffing glue and other organic solvents. These can cause death or irreversible damage to the brain (as well as to the liver and kidneys). People who use these solvents to get high have been found to have shrinkage of the brain and lowered IQ scores. In other words, they make you permanently stupider if they don't kill you.

My second place designation for the worst illegal drug in prominent use at this time goes to MDMA or "ecstacy." There has accumulated good evidence that "ecstacy" can do permanent damage to memory functions and other brain functions, when the drug is used in the doses people ordinarily use to get high. This drug particularly damages serotonergic neurons, the ones whose functioning the class of Prozac-like drugs seeks to increase. If increasing serotonin levels can help in treating depression, anxiety, and a variety of other disorders, it would appear quite undesirable to kill serotonergic neurons.

Chapter 40: Vision For A Data Bank On Skills

Chapter Overview:

One of the essential features of the competence approach is a large data bank of information about the psychological skills. These include instructional material, directly explaining how to do the skills; modeling material, i.e. fictional or true examples of the positive patterns; and practice material, i.e. hypothetical situations or game procedures that prompt fantasy or role-played practice in the skills. These can be in the form of expository material, stories, plays, songs, games, questions, measuring devices. These sorts of materials can be presented by various media: the written word, words with pictures, videotape, audiotape, interactive computer programs, electronically transmitted text and picture and sound files. For each of these types of presentations, different packages are appropriate for different age levels. This chapter exists partly to list the materials that I have written toward these ends. But it also exists to create a vision of a subculture of people interested in systematically adding to the data bank of all of these materials. In this vision, suppose a child is identified as having certain skill deficiencies. There would then be easy access to instructional, modeling, and practice-stimulating materials for just this child's age level, for the particular skills that are highest priority for the child, and in the particular medium that the child responds to best. If you add the requirement that the material involve characters and situations that the particular child can identify with, there is a need for a very large data bank. But the most important part of this vision is that children would not just be the passive recipients of these materials; they would also be fully involved in creating them. The vision is that every child, before becoming an adult, would have created several contributions to the data bank for each of the 62 psychological skills on the axis. If the education of every child could include exposure to hundreds of positive instructions and models and practice opportunities for each of the skills, our culture would be immeasurably enhanced. Our current culture is busily engaged in presenting instruction, models, and practice opportunities for children with little regard for the how positive the patterns are, but only for whether there is a market for consumption of the information. We can all contribute to creating the positive and adaptive patterns to be preserved in the data bank, and making a market for those that others have created.
****

The competence approach emphasizes that we act, think, and feel according to the information we have available. We are constantly being exposed to information. The higher the fraction of that information is useful and adaptive and good, the better equipped we will be to live our lives happily and productively.

We are now living in an age where information in all forms is accessible as never before, and accessibility is increasing rapidly. Computer networks are rapidly evolving into the central mechanism whereby information of all sorts is stored and disbursed.

And yet with the huge volumes of information that we produce and consume, a fairly small fraction of it seems to meet the test of producing happier and more productive lives. It is produced and consumed according to the demands of the market, which usually translate into the information's ability to produce short term pleasure or arousal rather than long-term benefit.

Let's think about what information we would like available regarding psychological skills, according to several categories.

Ideal Availability of Psychological Skills Information

1. We would like for the information to cover each of the 62 psychological skills, and the subskills of each of them.

2. We would like for the information to be of each of the following sorts: instruction, i.e. directly telling how to do the positive patterns; modeling, i.e. presentation of examples of positive patterns, and practice-stimulating, i.e. presenting open-ended situations that prompt someone to practice a positive pattern. Most of the chapters of this book are examples of instruction. Stories that model psychological skills are an example of models, and situations as presented in the What's Best To Do exercise or the brainstorming game are an example of the third. These roughly correspond to the formats of exposition, narrative with an ending to the plot, and open-ended narrative without an ending but with an implicit or explicit question, what would you do, think, and/or feel? Songs and poems also can present models, particularly of thoughts and feelings. There is also a need for questionnaires, tests, and other instruments that measure and monitor psychological skills of all sorts.

3. We would like to have information in the form of the written word, words with pictures, videotape, audiotape, and interactive computer programs, including videogames. Thus the learner can pick the medium or media that produce maximum learning.

4. We would like for the information to be specifically tailored for the entire range of ages of human beings. This goal entails making the words and pictures appropriate for many levels of vocabulary development. It involves screening out negative models for preschool children who imitate most nonselectively what they see. It involves gradually introducing negative patterns in the form of problems to solve and situations to respond to as the child develops the ability to discriminate what will be imitated and what will not. This task also involves creation of materials appropriate to older people with lower

vocabulary developments, or younger people with higher vocabularies.

5. We would like for the information to permit people of all varieties of social position, ethnicity, and all other life situations to be able to find it relevant. Thus information would have to be tailored to an immense variety of life styles.

6. We would like for the information to be available for those with very short attention spans and very low ability to read, not with the idea that we should be satisfied with only presenting information in this way, but that we should not have to wait for someone to develop patience and reading skills and sustaining attention skills before developing any of the other psychological skills.

When we think of the task in this way, there is a huge amount of work to be done in the cultivation of this data bank. But on the other hand, there is a tremendous amount of energy available for the creation and compilation of such information, and the stakes of the task are enormous.

Some Materials I Have Written

The following are additional materials I have written in partial fulfillment of the above vision.

Illustrated "modeling stories." These are especially for preschool and early grade school children; there are about 150 stories so far.

Stories That Model Psychological Skills. These are unillustrated modeling stories, that overlap somewhat with the illustrated set.

Plays That Model Psychological Skills. These are a set of about 150 printed brief dialogues, each about one page long, meant to be acted out by an adult for a preschool or early grade school child with toy people. These are meant to model the psychological skills on the skills axis. A rough version of some of these is available on videotape; a more professionally produced version is in the planning stages.

Manual for Tutors and Teachers of Reading. On teaching a child to read in a way that enhances psychological skill development at the same time.

Modeling Songs. A CD entitled *Spirit of Nonviolence* contains some modeling songs I wrote and recorded

The Letter Sound Songs. A CD entitled *What the Letters Say*, for preschool or elementary school children, teaches the phonetic sounds of letters of the alphabet.

Prosocial Moral Dilemma Stories. These are some illustrated open-ened stories for young children, ending with a question, what should the protagonist do? The protagonist is put into a situation where he or she must choose between short term pleasure and convenience, versus sacrificing or risk-taking for long term gain or for helping someone else.

The *Basic Concept Illustrations*. This is a set of stories for preschool children meant to teach basic words such as between, forward, row, left, right, etc. while at the same time modeling prosocial actions.

The *Parent Practices Questionnaire*. A questionnaire that asks parents about what they do, with respect to some of the behaviors advocated in this book.

Exercises for Psychological Skills. A book describing some 59 exercises meant to foster the growth of psychological skills.

Programmed Readings for Psychological Skills. A book with over a thousand "frames" consisting of brief stories that give examples of psychological skill concepts, with a comprehension-checking question after each.

Instructions on Psychological Skills. A book of essays on the why and how of each of 62 psychological skills.

****

Of course, I am not the only person who has written materials about psychological skills, or modeling psychological skills. A great deal of fine material is available, interspersed among other materials that I would object to on various grounds.

A Vision of Children and Adults Constantly Enlarging the Data Bank

Let's create a vision where children and parents and teachers and others who work with developing human beings are not just be the passive consumers of materials that instruct and model and provide practice in psychological skills. Instead, people, including children, would also be fully involved in creating such materials. There is no reason why every child, before his or her education is complete, cannot create several contributions to the data bank for each of the 62 psychological skills on the axis. There is surely enough time spent in education for many assignments to be given in which the child is asked to create some expository writing, some story, some song, some play, or something else that adds to the accumulation of positive materials about psychological skills. I have seen children create, and have assisted them to create, stories that I think are just as valuable additions to the data bank as any adult could make.

The existence of electronic networks makes it possible for the creation, collection, storing, and distribution of psychological skill material to be a participatory process much more than formerly possible. I hope that in the near future, an organized system will be in place where children can submit their own contributions to an electronic data bank that is organized by the 62 psychological skills.

In the competence-enhancing culture—or to be more realistic, the competence-enhancing subculture—there would be such widespread availability of positive information on each of the psychological skills that one would have to go out of one's way to avoid being exposed to it. This is in stark contrast to the current culture, where one has to work very hard to avoid huge doses of instruction in the value of limitless consumption, models of violent and otherwise irresponsible behavior, and practice opportunities for "virtual violence." But it is not necessary to destroy the subculture of violent entertainment before building up the organized databank of psychological skills.

Perhaps in the near future, whenever a child has psychological problems, it will be possible to select high priority psychological skills for the child or the family members to work on, and to have immediate access to such a wide range of information on those skills that there is bound to be some portion of it that is attractive to the child and parents in question. A child who has skill deficiencies could be exposed to that are enjoyable but also designed to provide education in the specific skills in question.

Meanwhile, in this vision, children would exposed to huge amounts of this information before any signs of problems arise, hopefully preventing many problems from arising in the first place.

Today we look back upon times and places when inquisitions tortured people for lack of adherence to a particular religious doctrine, when prominent leaders defended slavery, when women suspected of being witches were burned at the stake, and we wonder at how primitive and brutal human life was before the culture improved itself. Perhaps some day future cultures will look back upon our present culture in the same way.

This happy vision competes with dystopian visions of a society that steeps itself in negative models and degenerates toward greater mistrust and hostility. It's impossible to say which direction human culture will go; the only answer for each of us is to insure that our own contribution is toward psychological health and competence and kindness and away from violence, hostility, and despair.

Index

CPSIA information can be obtained at www.ICGtesting.com
Printed in the USA
BVOW06s0748251113

337142BV00002B/6/A